Praise for *While Dragging Our Hearts Behind Us*

While Dragging Our Hearts Behind Us is a great story of hidden Irish history, just crying out to be told. Or, rather, a host of stories, some wildly incredible, some harrowing, some darkly funny - and all (mostly) true.

There are at least three great historical thrillers that might be drawn from Boni Thompson's reconstruction of mysterious exploits, treasonous events, and the creation of an Irish state. There is a dash of fiction, a dash of myth-making, and a solid, satisfying deal of good old Irish story-telling.

A remarkable piece of historical research and recreation, it is the book that Cork and environs deserves in recognition of that area's role in the struggle for independence. How the past becomes personal, and one man's history and stories can become emblematic of the creation of the new nation.

A hugely satisfying, informative, and gripping read.

John McRae

While Dragging Our Hearts Behind Us

Cork, 1916 – 1923

BONI THOMPSON

A Blackwater Press book

First published in the United States of America by
Blackwater Press, LLC

Copyright © Boni Thompson, 2024

All rights reserved. No part of this publication may be reproduced, stored in a retrieval system, or transmitted, in any form or by any means, electronic, mechanical, photocopying, recording or otherwise, without the prior permission of the publishers

Library of Congress Control Number: 2023943154

ISBN: 979-8-9886158-2-8

Cover design by Eilidh Muldoon

Blackwater Press
120 Capitol Street
Charleston, WV 25301
United States

blackwaterpress.com

I am come of the seed of the people, the people that sorrow,
That have no treasure but hope,
No riches laid up but a memory
Of an Ancient glory.

And I say to my people's masters: Beware,
Beware of the thing that is coming, beware of the risen people,
Who shall take what ye would not give.

From *The Rebel*
Pádraig Pearse, 1915

Contents

Introduction	1
1 *Foretell*	7
2 *Join*	23
3 *Ride*	45
4 *Love*	73
5 *Train*	99
6 *Murder*	125
7 *Starve*	169
8 *Grieve*	221
9 *Burn*	275
10 *Spy*	325
11 *Pray*	379
12 *Flee*	439
13 *Live*	531
Short Biographies	557
Abbreviations	569

Introduction

I met my grandfather for the first time when I was sixteen and he was seventy-six. It was my first trip to Ireland; an opportunity for my parents to reconnect with their many relatives and an opportunity for me to meet them.

At the time he just seemed like a rather complacent old man: dressed in a suit each and every day, vest and all done up over his well-fed belly, well-pressed trousers hiked up to reveal his fancy socks pulled up on his skinny, old man legs. He seemed happy just for some peace and quiet, a cigarette and a cup of tea after dinner, both of which he sucked back with gusto while keenly watching the news, which at that time was full of The Troubles. For some unknown reason, he took a shine to me, despite my teenage awkwardness, and I guess that's why I found myself standing behind him one day as he sat in his little parlour chatting with my uncle. I was marvelling over his fashionably long hair, stroking the white locks that reached down over his collar, only to discover a nausea-inducing depression in the back of his head, just behind his left ear. My finger sank into a little pool of soft gelatinous tissue, which indicated that under that little circle of hidden, hairless skin, he was missing a piece of skull about the size of a lucky silver dollar. Totally disturbed, I blurted out my disgust. His response was a chuckle and an "Oh, that's nothing, it's just my old bullet wound."

My uncle, a man who found joy and goodness in everyone, laughed till he slipped off his chair. I suppose it was the horror on my innocent face that did it. "So, you didn't know your grandfather was once a notorious rebel?" After my grandmother stood up,

1

snapped at him about talking nonsense and slammed the door on her way out, I knew I was onto something. As it turned out, I discovered that during the years of the Irish War of Independence my grandfather was a fitting son of Rebel Cork, known for its willingness and ability to out-scheme the British and happily administer a taste of their own bitter, brutal medicine to the outraged oppressors.

I could see that each time I asked him a question, his big blue eyes would soften, and he would do something that he had apparently never done, except, according to my uncle, once or twice when his sons had slyly pickled him with whiskey. He would, with just a cup of tea in hand, travel back to the days of his mind-boggling youth, and pull out for me a story so outrageous it defied fiction. Nothing so unbelievable could be anything but true.

I can see him still, sitting in his chair before the burning peat fire, a rare smile gracing his face, just the two of us in the room. In a low voice, he told me of one adventure after another. He told me of gunrunning, jailbreaks, hunger strikes, ambushes, close calls with disaster, executions, alliances with the likes of local prostitutes, or movers and shakers like Michael Collins, even his own imprisonment and impending execution. He told me of his escape to New York where he spent twelve years, during those truly roaring 1920s and depressing 1930s working for a gangster, and eventually at the posh Heigh Ho Club in Manhattan working for George Putnam and Amelia Earhart.

Long after that first encounter with him, I inherited some pictures of his, and among them was an unusual shot of the four of them standing in an airfield somewhere. What cool customers they are. The women are elegant, dolled up, but even beside Putnam, a giant of New York, it is my grandfather who is The Man. Impeccable, double-breasted suit, fashionable hat of the day, he is casually standing with a hand in a trouser pocket, between the two women. Amelia has her arm through his, but he has his other arm around my grandmother's shoulders. He looks at the camera, oozing confidence and a slight disdain for the photographer. He certainly doesn't look too friendly.

By the time I left Ireland, I was completely smitten with my grandfather. I could not understand why no one else knew his stories, so I assured him that someday I would write a book about him. He just laughed and said, "My, my, that would be quite a story."

I never forgot my promise, and many years later when eyewitness accounts became available, I began researching. It is a funny thing, but as his story got worse, and as details were filled in by the accounts of other men (he never wrote anything down himself), details he never mentioned, I began to feel more and more attached to him. I realised why he had never told his stories. I realised why some would prefer not to know even an outline of what he had seen and done. I realised I had been the recipient of just a few shortened, sanitised anecdotes, totally excluding the harrowing, sometimes bloody details of what had actually transpired during that ruthless fight for freedom. And yet my love for him seemed to swell, no matter the fierce, pitiless details, and each day I would be thinking of what I might discover and write about that evening. He was on my mind continuously.

As I pored through well-known materials, I could not understand why it was so difficult to find information about him, when many of his colleagues were so well known, many of their actions documented in books and articles. He was the only full-time member of the Intelligence Squad of the Cork No. 1 Brigade who was also on the Active Service Unit. He also participated in county-wide activities with the Flying Columns of the area. Why then, is his name, Jim Fitzgerald, or later, Seamus Fitzgerald, very common names in Cork, so difficult to come across? I read many dozens of witness accounts and found only six references to his name. He is included in the list of intelligence squad members found in a couple of period books. I discovered that in fact, many of the accounts of or by members of the Intelligence Squad do not name individuals who are responsible for carrying out specific orders. It is as if they and other members of the IRA shared a collective guilt, shielding each other from outside scrutiny. I do believe that above all he was naturally, and with the support of my grandmother, someone who kept his former life to himself.

However, the actions he took were most certainly recognised by his colleagues and superiors. Some years after the war Florrie O'Donoghue, Officer in charge of the Intelligence Squad, and later a historian of the period wrote a document addressed to the Minister of Defence. Jim Fitzgerald is one of a mere six names listed. Florrie writes: "The work which they were called upon to do was extremely dangerous and in the conditions prevailing in the City at the time could only be performed by men of exceptional courage and resource."

Sometimes, when I would be searching for information on the internet or at the library, and could find no leads, and was second guessing myself as to the wisdom of actually writing his story, a little pearl would appear at my fingertips. Whenever that happened it was as if I could see him again, sitting and looking at me from his parlour, across the decades, a droll smirk on his lips. Perhaps he was anticipating the reaction of my daughter who would read my draft and text me late at night, "… I am on page such and such… are you sure this really happened?"

Once, when I was extremely disheartened, unsure how to write some wretched detail I would rather not have found, I had a thought to check out YouTube. It's been over one hundred years since the bitter days of that war, but perhaps because of the one hundredth anniversary, someone had uploaded a few snippets of ancient, silent-moving-film footage of a large funeral of the day. About mid-way through the one-minute series of short clips, a familiar face stared at me across the computer screen. There he was, my grandfather, tall, handsome, young, and most of all, innocent. For a few short seconds he looked straight at the camera and straight through at me. Then he turned his head and disappeared. I looked at that clip over and over. I marvelled because my grandfather, who is about twenty-one years old in the clip, looked very much like my son, who was that exact age. It made me feel distressed, and for a moment our roles were all confused, and I was the mother, not the granddaughter, and he was the son about to engage in a world of madness and I knew what was to come and I could not alter the path he was about to take, nor even warn him. Somewhat like a nightmare, that instant passed in a flash yet it left a deep impression. I thought how strange that such a short clip should even exist after one hundred years and that I should come across it at that very moment when I was about to shut the project down. I thought also how lucky am I that my own sons will never have to take the road he took.

After scouring every source available to me, and dedicating much thought to filling the many gaps where events took place and nameless Intelligence officers participated, I decided that a creative turn of non-fiction was the best option. This allowed me to remain true to the recorded details, and at the same time insert, when necessary, actions and dialogue which may not have actually occurred, but which project the chilling atmosphere, the bald-faced audacity, and sometimes the sheer terror which most certainly had to be part and parcel of their daily lives.

Though I have no doubt that much is missing from the story, it is as faithful to reality as I could make it. Despite some of the disturbing details of actions and events that occurred by his hand or by his friends and compatriots, in his mind I know that my grandfather considered himself a soldier of Ireland. He was involved in many of the events in the city and throughout the county from 1916 to 1923, but his actions were always taken under orders. I do not believe that he expected to survive that time; nor when he began down that road, did he expect to see Ireland free. Such a thing had been, for centuries, a dream. His friend and fellow officer, Florrie O'Donoghue, once wrote that in their minds they had no idea how Ireland free would rebuild itself into a sovereign nation. It seems the fight came first, and if by some sweet miracle they were successful, and by some benevolent, ensuing miracle they survived it, the details would fall into place.

This story could not have been written without the great foresight of the Irish government who collected, in the 1930s and beyond, the witness statements of men and women all over Ireland, sealed them and opened them only after 2000, making them public and accessible. Many details were also collected from books out of print, culled over years from second-hand bookstores. Now, thanks to the hundredth anniversary of the Easter Rising, many of them have since been reprinted. I also owe a debt of thanks to *An Roinn Cosanta*, Department of Defence, the Irish office that holds the pension documents of those who fought. It took two years to get that document, but when it was delivered to my door, here in Canada, it was a true gift. There was my grandfather's perfect penmanship, letter after letter, page after page, all of which detailed, as he noted, 'a short sample' of the many actions he took part in.

It is inevitable that since the hundredth anniversary of the War of Independence, and the accompanying flurry of books, articles, scholarly works, and deep investigations in the libraries and archives of Ireland and England, that some details in this story may turn out to be imperfect. For this I apologise. I worked with the materials available to me and from my own collection of stories my grandfather told me long ago. I come at this as an outsider. I have never lived in Ireland; I have only travelled there from time to time. However, I hope you will find that the story itself overcomes any minor infractions of fact.

After reading these pages, however you might judge him, know that the extraordinary actions my grandfather and his contemporaries took were a result of over seven hundred years of colonisation. Ireland was, after all, the first colony and the longest held. The Irish were the first slaves in the Caribbean, and victims of literally hundreds of years of cruel, relentless oversight; at times one might argue, intentional genocide. On the other hand, of the colonies, they were the first to achieve freedom and their actions, studied by every rebel leader in foreign lands to come after them, helped to change the course of imperialism and colonialism that restructured the world order. For a tiny island at the edge of Europe, last stronghold of the Celts who in ancient times crossed the continent, that is impressive.

The terrible price of freedom is always counted in lives of at least one generation lost or plundered, their minds or souls altered. The title of this book, *While dragging our hearts behind us*, is meant to be a reflection of that cost. It is a price the Irish were willing to pay not just for themselves but for their children and their nation. My grandfather and his many like-minded contemporaries across the country paid that price in full. It is their story, their lives lived.

And with that, I have kept my promise.
Boni Thompson

May, 2023
100th anniversary of the end of the civil war and the beginning of freedom for the Irish.

FORETELL

CHAPTER 1

1911 – APRIL 1916

James sits and peers out of the window. He is ill today, or at least he has convinced his mother that he is, and so has been given a reprieve from the stupefying repetition of school, which he despises. He is therefore happy—happy to daydream intermittently between chapters of his book. His book, the bestseller that he has secreted from his older siblings' belongings, is *Cuchulainn of Muirthemne* by Lady Gregory. It is a tale of ancient Irish glory more thrilling than anything his thirteen-year-old imagination has ever come across, and a worthy enough reason to tell a white lie and spend the day curled up in the front room.

The rain has kept him and the Celtic warriors of the story company, its soft pitter patter enveloping them all morning long. Outside, there is a thick mist saturating everything in sight, the grey brick of the row houses, the tiny, sparse gardens that preface each home. The impenetrable ten-foot tall, mossy stone wall separating this little street from the park, once an ancient British enclave of power, is completely obscured by the fog. In the distance, the immense bell tower of St Fin Barre's Cathedral, of which this parlour window usually provides a long and scenic view, seems remote, ethereal, its ghostly outline barely discernible. Along the walkway that skirts the homes on this avenue high on the hill, James suddenly spies an old woman as she appears through the mist, trudging along wearily, her long, colourful skirts partially dragging on the ground, but short enough in spots to show her worn, men's work boots, thick and heavy. She clasps her shawl close around her, emphasising her aged, bent shoulders. He recognises instantly that she is a Tinker, a Gypsy woman, probably begging or selling some items of questionable origin. Doubtless she has walked many miles this day, or perhaps her clan has dropped her off at a designated place, riding their sturdy wagons and large workhorses quickly through town, lest they meet with derision from the locals. They would have dropped her off and headed back to their enclave, hidden just out of sight on the outskirts of the city. A group of covered wagons, with young and old, men and women, dressed in their colourful garb, living so close together, it sends shivers up the spine of even the most open-minded Irishman.

To say that James's mother dislikes such people is an understatement, and like many of her neighbours, she will not answer the door when they come calling. Unfortunately for the Tinkers, their reputation precedes them by several centuries. Fortunately for this woman, and interestingly for James, his mother is not home this afternoon. His father is. This is not an unusual turn of events, but it is unusual that James is here, his many siblings are not, and his father is actually in the house, not at his work of baking bread which feeds the City of Cork, or at the kennel, with his racing greyhounds, a hobby that consumes him. James watches as the woman retreats from each home in succession, walking down the short pathways from the front doors, swinging open each gate and stepping back onto the narrow sidewalk, each time seemingly empty handed. As she approaches his own home, James watches. The woman stops in front and observes the house. Has she been here before? James does not know. The woman puts her hand on the gate but hesitates.

James's father, John, is a short stout man, his hair a glistening white mop, his smile a constant companion. He walks now into the room and observes his young son gazing out of the window. He steps closer to the glass to see just what holds his boy in such rapt attention. Well, Jimmy lad, what will we do? Invite her in for tea? James giggles slightly and studies his father. He knows this is unheard of, inviting a Tinker in for tea. His mother would have a fit! He smiles at his daddy, thinking it is a joke. But now – the knock on the door. James watches as his father steps lightly to the hallway, opens the door wide and asks the woman her business. Just looking for a hand sir, she calls out in a rasping voice and quietly coughs into a rag held tightly in the palm of her hand. Could you spare a penny or two, for my own grandchildren is all I ask?

Well now, Ma'am, pence are hard to come by these days. As he replies, James steps out from behind his father's back and looks through the doorway. He sees the woman's wet garments, the bright red scarf wrapped around her head. The few strands of grey frizzy hair that have escaped stick to her face.

Ah, I see you have a child of your own sir, she says. Her eyes are sad and bleary. 'Tis a hard job keeping them fit and healthy, feeding them proper.

Indeed, it is Ma'am, indeed it is. His father looks to James and orders him put the kettle on lad and we'll warm our guest here, and bids the woman step through to the back of the house where the kitchen fire is kept lit. James stares at his father as if he has gone mad. He knows if his mother comes home now there will be hell to pay. His father smiles at him and sends him off to the kitchen to make the tea.

God bless you sir, God bless you! the woman repeats. James's father waves his hand in the air. Sure, 'tis only a cup o' tea. Sit yourself down by the fire. James is in awe. He watches the door nervously, waiting for the fury that is sure to erupt if his mother walks in. Then he turns his mind to concentrate on making the tea. He is not often asked to do this, having several older sisters, and for a few moments must think carefully of the steps involved. He places the kettle, always heavy with water, on the stove and begins to measure out the loose tea from the canister. He takes two everyday mugs, but his father, who is watching and chatting to the woman at the same time, stays his hand and instead reaches high onto a shelf and brings down three cups and saucers of his mother's good dishes. Next, he reaches for the bowl of sugar cubes and to James's amazement, the tin of chocolate biscuits.

He stands waiting for the kettle and watches his father and the old woman. As he does so the air in the tiny kitchen transforms and James knows intuitively that it is the presence of the woman that has somehow changed the atmosphere of the little kitchen. The sun slices through the overcast sky and enters directly through the kitchen window. The fire glows brighter. James feels warmer. The woman, whose clothes were sodden when she stepped through their door, has somehow dried completely and her ruddy cheeks shine, her tiny, recessed eyes sparkle.

James's fingers come to life as he pours water from the big kettle into the teapot and carefully places the kettle back onto the stove. The conversation between his father and the old woman is unremarkable, consisting of the weather and its relentless unpredictability. It is as if neither the woman nor his father notices the sudden transformation of their surroundings. But it is obvious to James that this moment is highly irregular. Tinkers do not get invited into homes. Fathers do not drink tea with old women. Thirteen-year-old boys do not sit on weekday afternoons with strange, wrinkled old tinker women, drinking tea from their mother's best cups. James ponders these things and all the time he watches her. Halfway through her tea, and she does not drink quickly, but seems to linger over each gulp relishing the comfort and warmth, his father presses the small plate of biscuits upon her, smiling. She is reticent but his smile encourages her, and she takes not one, but two biscuits, biting into them with satisfaction, the absence of the odd tooth in her mouth suddenly becoming noticeable.

When at last she is finished she declines a second cup of tea but looks to his father and queries, would you accept a fortune in thanks for your hospitality, sir?

Ah, thank-you indeed ma'am, but 'tis better not to know the future is my feeling altogether. James's father is gracious, but the old woman presses him. Sure, 'twouldn't hurt, but if you are not agin it, I would see the boy.

His father looks at James and winks. James, dredge your cup lad, and hand it to our guest. The old woman takes his cup in her gnarled hands and looks into it. She looks at James's face and again at the leaves that have left a design at the bottom of his cup.

I see here you are a smart lad, she says, but sure you know that already. What you will be wanting to know is your future. Am I right, young sir? James shrugs. He does not know what to say. As a child he was certainly warned against tinkers. He has never been allowed to speak with one. The closest he has ever come is passing them on the street, and at that his mother would always place herself between them as she strode by with her long gait.

His father laughs. Answer our guest Jimmy lad! Yes, ma'am, James replies, wondering what his father and the woman are up to. As if anybody can tell the future! The woman looks into the bottom of the cup intently. She lifts it into the air, twisting it and turning it and James can see light glinting off the gold rim. The green shamrocks seem to jump out from the white background and dance temporarily in the air before alighting again. She lowers the cup and looks at James, her eyes boring into him.

You will live a long life, son. I see a life of equal measures. You will have joy for certain, but there will be many days you walk the earth dragging your heart behind you. You will give joy and sorrow in equal measure. And you will receive joy and sorrow. Yes, in equal measure. James is fascinated. He thinks that perhaps the old woman can see visions of his future life swirling about in a cloud in the cup. As if reading his mind, she puts the cup down carefully on the saucer. Look, she points with a swollen and bent arthritic finger at the dark tea leaves stuck to the white china. I cannot see what will happen to you in your life. But it does not matter. I know the end result. James wonders what a long life is. Far into the future he will look back on this extraordinary afternoon and see it as a portend of his life. Right now, he musters his courage and looks the old woman straight in the eye.

How old, he asks? James's father bursts into laughter. Do you want to know the time and place? He chuckles, the writing on your gravestone? The woman does not smile, but returns James's stare and seeing that he believes, tells him.

Hmmm... If I am no mistaken... you will live ninety-two years. Yes, ninety-two years... now that is a long life. She looks at James's father. You laugh sir, but don't ye know? I have the gift. I'm known for it. Then she turns to James. Her eyes seem to pierce straight through his own and with a wry smile on her face, and without moving her lips at all, James can hear her, clear as day, as she tells him: Life is a mystery, young sir. Don't try to understand it. Sure, it doesn't make any sense at all!

There is much to be learned from a man's name. What it is tells you something. What it is not also tells tales. James is his name. But

Séamus is what it should be, by rights. He is as pure-bred Irish as any of his friends whose names reflect the heritage and history that is the sum of their nation's misery. But right now, he is known as James to his mother and teachers and priest, Jimmy to those who know him best, and Séamus only to those who have a vested interest in all things Irish, an interest that James will soon appropriate as his own.

James has been given his name by a mother who wishes to swathe her children in a blanket of protection. The thinnest of buffers against a hard life of few choices, it is at least a thin veneer of respectability, to be adorned with the genteel names of the Victorian British. Thus, in the midst of the most rebellious of Irish cities, married into a family of known troublemakers, but with the best of intentions, she names her pedigree Irish children Edward and Julia and John and James, nine children in all, with nine very British names, and prays their lives will not be a repetition of her own. She prays that somehow wrongs will be righted. Anticipating that her prayers will go unanswered (as indeed Irish mothers' prayers have through seven hundred and fifty years of history) she insists on education, good manners, proper dress, noble speech and civilised politics of the Daniel O'Connell variety, notably non-violent with change effected through proper channels. She is dumbfounded when her young son Edward blows off his fingertips making a bomb in their back shed.

This happens in 1916, a year that will soon go down in Irish history as the best and the worst of years. James is seventeen years old, and the British have just executed fifteen mostly young, or at least young at heart, Irish idealists who had the unabashed gall to lead their men in a challenge to the British, holed up at the General Post Office on O'Connell Street in Dublin, refusing to give up or give in. They are perceived as a rag-tag, motley group of young dreamers and stubborn old men, desperately trying to turn the heads of their Irish families and friends and neighbours and yes, even their Irish enemies. Taking on the British Empire, where the sun never sets, with a few hundred rifles smuggled in from the Germans and a paltry assortment of antiquated shotguns, farmer's pikes, and dull knives smuggled from around the countryside, commandeered for a surprisingly deadly purpose. The fifteen hundred or so men who gather are laughed at and cajoled and yes, even reviled by their own people. Not right in the head, passers-by think, on this gloriously sunny, spring morning, Easter Monday, April 24, 1916, to be precise, as they march along O'Connell Street, the centre of Dublin City, on their way to certain doom.

Each brigade has a leader with a plan. And their plan entails barricading themselves in a few strategic locations around the downtown core, proclaiming their natural right to self-governance, and wait for the British to come calling. Their leaders know too well their inadequacies, but choose to ignore this, and like children who close their eyes and believe that others cannot see what they themselves cannot see, they pray quietly, just under their breath. They pray that their strengths will somehow outweigh their weaknesses, that they are enough to make a mark, scratch the Irish consciousness, catch someone's attention, somehow change something in this land of complacent, subservient poverty.

Amazement sets in when after a few days they shock themselves and the world at large with their own persistence and surprising effectiveness. The mess of the downtown buildings, pummelled to smithereens by an English army shocked at its own impotence, will become an enduring symbol of Irish determination and fortitude for later generations. In fact, the bullet holes left in the surviving walls of the grand Romanesque General Post Office will be left untouched, to be revered or gawked at, if not appreciated, by the grandchildren and great grandchildren of those who bled quietly to death slumped up against the walls or who got caught in an untimely stream of bullets, crawling across the nearby green. They hold off the Brits through Easter Monday, and all of Easter week and after six days and no other alternative in sight their leaders decide against a suicide mission. The young schoolteacher idealist in command, Pádraig Pearse, accompanied by a fervent volunteer nurse, Elizabeth O'Farrell, hoists the white flag of surrender and meets the very British General Lowe quietly and proudly. They stare him down, eye to eye, refracting his withering, malevolent glare into history.

Those Irish soldiers who are left standing march back down O'Connell Street, this time led by British uniforms, dodging the shattered bits of buildings, the ongoing fires, the stacks of household furniture that had been dragged onto the street and piled high to act as barricades. They listen to the cat calls, the abuse and derision hurled at them by their own ones lining the streets, while the

English soldiers smirk to themselves or shake their heads in wonder while marching them to their certain punishment for such cheek.

The British command does not smirk or shake their heads, however. They know the Irish. They know this minor battle which they, the British, struggled to control, will only work to fire up the relentless, incessant little faction of rebels and troublemakers who are a part of every Irish generation. They will not disappear, no matter what the British do. This nasty lot of overeducated upstarts kept them going for six days – six long days of increasing frustration. They would not have believed it could be done, especially by the Irish. This scruffy, grubby pack has managed to make the entire British Empire look stupid, mean and ineffectual.

The British do not like looking stupid or ineffectual, and in their rage, they make the worst of mistakes. They interrogate and investigate until they can determine the leaders… or at least some of the leaders. They execute those fifteen men, rosy cheeked, poets and farmers and teachers, idealists all, brave and handsome. They shoot them one by one, day by day, against the inner courtyard wall of Kilmainham Gaol in Dublin City. The general makes sure Pearse is among the first. But Pearse, instead of trembling in terror, calmly whistles an Irish rebel tune while the Brits cock their guns. The last in line, angel-faced, much loved, man of the people, Mr Connolly, they shoot after strapping him in a chair, as he can't stand on his feet with his injured ankle, an injury incurred by a British bullet, whilst counselling the men under his direction, behind the post office walls, to fight bravely even in the face of defeat, even in the face of death, even as the average Irish citizen wonders what on earth you might be thinking playing war games with the British who, everyone knows, never lose.

People line up in the streets behind the cold, impenetrable stone wall of the gaol, or crouch in their beds, staring sadly out of the window at the last stars before daylight, or dream fitfully of demons dancing in anticipation. Fingering their beads, mouthing the Hail Marys, they pray quietly, their only balm in times of grating, festering hopelessness. They hear the shots from British rifles rip through the warm spring air, their echo spreading like a cascade of fireworks into the sky and across the dirty cityscape, over the green hills, and fall hard and fast on ears lately grown deaf, waking their owners to a new day. The early morning light is defiled, morning after morning, and the hearts of the people soften and begin to melt, while newly found tears drip quietly off their pale cheeks. Those same countrymen who shook their heads and wondered at the sanity of that crew of stinking, hungry, bedraggled men, marched to imprisonment by the British uniforms, begin to rail over the wickedness of killing their leaders. Men of obvious vision, those lovely, brave men.

Mothers begin to moan as they feel the stirrings of relentless waves of pain, like giving birth, slowly overwhelm. Old women pray their rosaries, silently fingering each bead, each a plea for mercy, all while their old men cry out at injustice and the cruel fates of history. Children stop playing. Young women sob.

And young men? Young men join the IRA.

The city of Cork in this year of 1916 is already an ancient and respected place. The most southerly city in the country, sitting on the River Lee at the mouth of Cork Harbour, it has been a place of trade for hundreds of years. The city is built on two islands set snug between the rippling branches of the River Lee that encircles it, before continuing out to sea further south. The harbour is one of the largest inland harbours in the world, sheltering its citizens from the cold and ferocity of the Atlantic's winds and waves. There are many fine buildings and establishments in the downtown core skirting either side of the wide, picturesque river. Soon these will be burned to ashes by the British, but at this moment, such a thing is unimaginable to the average citizen.

It is a city of hills, a fine hiding place for dragons, as good Fin Barre, revered spiritual protector of Cork, discovered long ago when the islands were just a swamp by the sea. That was back in the year of Our Lord 600 when he had arrived back home from his travels. He had come home by way of a circuitous route, leaving his adoptive family of monks by the western shores and travelling to visit other enthusiastic new Christians, looking, as do we all, for a purpose to his life. In his travels he spends some time chatting with a new friend, the gentle giant and grandnephew of King Arthur, Saint David, who tells him, Go! Speak with our illustrious leader.

He will give you a mission.

Fin Barre is young and impressionable at this point, though he will live to be one hundred – an age James comes close to but doesn't quite reach – and so he takes his friend's advice, and heads for the open sea. Far away in Rome, Pope Gregory the Great is busy dealing with the bands of swarthy, pugnacious Italians, old family Romans, and more recent immigrants, that is, newly settled Barbarians, who are crawling over the seven hills of the Holy City. Yet he is not so busy to stop and take a moment or two to get to know Fin Barre, the strangely luminescent, intensely introspective young man and, recognising the telling humility of a saint, demands to make him an Archbishop on the spot. Fin Barre declines. It is an honour he has no entitlement to, or so he thinks, and with a sigh, the great Gregory recommends to the holy youth Fin Barre's own race of half-pagan, half-new-Christian, tribal, face-painting Celts. He sends him back to monotonously rainy Ireland to quell the various lusts of the irascible Celts from whose loins he had sprung. On his return trip to Ireland, Fin Barre meets an old friend, the pious but adventurous Brendan, off to convert Europe, currently inhabited by the progeny of those same Barbarians who ransacked Rome. Brendan happily raises his arm in greeting to Fin Barre across the water as they meet on the high waves of the Irish Sea. Neither man is aware that they are on the cusp of their separate quests. Quests that will be celebrated for hundreds of years after their own flesh and bones have turned to dust. Fin Barre, on his return, is about to begin the legend that will cement his reputation by taking on the last remaining dragon of the British Isles.

He is without doubt a crafty creature who had obviously chosen to wait it out in that remote southerly shoreline of secret coves and high cliffs, and further inland the green and rocky hills and vales. One may wonder if in fact the dragon instead sheltered itself in a cave not unlike Fin Barre's own low, circular stone cell in the centre of the marsh, waiting for the scholarly saint's influence on the locals to wane. This will surely become a tiresome wait, even for something with the longevity of a dragon. For Fin Barre's teachings will reverberate through the centuries to survive even the mind-numbingly cruel onslaught of the English. Indeed, the locals, the men and women and children of Cork will never give up on their saint. Or perhaps it is better to say that St Fin Barre will never give up on them.

As years pass, the City of Cork grows up the valleys and into the hills in no small part due to Fin Barre himself. The Celts come from far and wide to visit Fin Barre and in due course become lovers of language and learning to augment their already healthy appetite for story. Stories that are so wonderful, we know some of them still. Fin Barre's reputation is helped of course by the fact that once he settles in Cork, the dragon is never seen again. It also helps that he retains his handsome visage the whole of his hundred years, and his gorgeous platinum locks, though shorn and tonsured, continue to rebel by growing thick and lovely despite the saint's horror of vanity. In fact, even Fin Barre's own father and mother are revered by the locals. Living nearby, they watch in awe at their beautiful boy, grown manly and strong. His mother in particular wonders if even an archangel could be so lovely.

But Fin Barre is immune to it all, the litany of stories whispered in ears as he passes by, the attention of the ladies, the lesser Christians of whom believe it quite a waste to have one so handsome, so holy. He focuses instead on building a community of Christians who seek the word of God through learning, as much as faith, and wish to live a life of peace and goodness. He builds for himself a beehive hut in the centre of the marsh, downstream from his birthplace and original home, and his followers continue to flock to see and hear him speak.

After all, he has brought back from his far-flung travels one of the few original copies of St Jerome's vulgate: the ultra-modern translation of the Bible, taken from the Hebrew and the Greek and the Aramaic and whatever else in which it was written, laboriously translated by the linguistic wonder Jerome. Who outside Rome has such a treasure? And yet Fin Barre brought it to them, the people of Cork. The new Christians are compelled to travel to Cork by the stories that arise about the obvious saint, his adventures overseas, his friendships with the mighty of the known world, his complete and utter lack of self-aggrandisement despite stories that tremble with honour and glory, and really lack only one thing: a beautiful woman.

But the new Christians, who are sick to death of the secret ceremonies, the corrupt debasement of Christian values propagated by their old druid leaders who, despite St Pádraig's transformation of the island, continue even in their dwindling numbers to hound the locals with their superstitions, are content to leave the women alone for a change. After all, the druids may be highly educated, speak several languages, know secret cures taken from the plants of the earth, and carry the history of the Celts in their learning. Nevertheless, they are often hoary old men fighting a losing battle with Christianity, bitter, and intent on punishing the people with their terrifying superstitions and insatiable appetites for cruel forms of punishment. In contrast Fin Barre's way acts as a salve to the people's long offended sensibilities, contrasting so compellingly with the rituals the druids constantly promote. The absence of the strong female figure in the stories of Fin Barre, a figure the ancient Irish attend to with rapt devotion, is quelled in part by the story of Fin Barre's own mother.

Still alive and happy, living in the remote and preternatural mists of Gougane Barra, the source of the River Lee that flows south-east to ripple past the city of Cork, can be found Fin Barre's mother and father. It is quite obvious to all who see his mother that she is holder of the looks in the family gene pool. Fin Barre's father, Amergin, artisan to the local king, risked life and limb to secretly marry the much lower-class servant girl. Though no account exists, it is quite probable the lovers, with hearts pounding, stole by the light of the moon to the ancient trysting stone to proclaim to God and nature their intended union. The stone, if it was anything like the trysting stone that stands to this day on Clear Island, far to the west, was a tall phallic stone, thick enough to have the pair stand on either side without seeing each other. At shoulder height through the stone is found a hole, just wide enough to insert one's arm and search for the other's hand, to embrace and squeeze and with quivering voices proclaim their marriage to all who watch, in this case, perhaps only the moon and the local foxes peering out of their den. Shortly after the illicit ceremony, and with the hard luck that starving artists everywhere instantly recognise, Amergin is quickly found, doubtless his hands caressing the love of his life, perhaps stroking the slightly protruding belly of his beloved and whispering sweet nothings as she tries to knead the daily bread. At any rate, the caressing must stop suddenly, for the two are caught and bound.

His anger raging at the rebellious Amergin, the king sputters and spits at the audacity of the artist. Truth be told, the king would hate to lose him because of his unique abilities which translate into the fine handiwork that adorns the king's possessions, ancient Celtic symbols few can fashion. Nevertheless, the king's word cannot be scorned and so, influenced by the gleeful druids, the king proclaims death by that most dreadful and long-lasting of executionary arts, burning at the stake. The two young, illicitly married lovers, bound to the same stake, high on the pyre, and under the scrutiny of the druids, pray in unison to Christ, loudly and surely in terror.

The sun shines down on them, mercilessly it seems, blinding their eyes as they scream for succour. As the flames crawl past the kindling at the base of the pyre and dance and lick their way up towards the trembling toes of the two, a thunderous bolt of lightning shoots down from the heavens, and a deluge of water drenches the crowd, instantly putting out the flames. The confused and terrified druids retreat at the sound of the relieved Christians falling on their knees in song and praise of the goodness of the Lord. The king graciously pardons the two lovers as the rain, the like of which has not been seen since Noah's time, leaves him standing bent and sodden. He notes the obvious Divine intervention that has occurred on their behalf (and possibly his, as he was wondering from where a replacement for such a talented artist might be found) and proclaims amnesty. Thus, Fin Barre's tiny unborn form is saved and indeed blessed. When wandering monks make their way through the mists of Gougane Barra several years later, they cannot but gasp at the beauty and graciousness of one so young and request the great honour of taking him with them to their western monastery, bringing him into their fold for a proper education.

Some thousand years later, good St Fin Barre is remembered by a vast cathedral built on the site of his damp monastery. Alas, he surely turns over in his grave to discover it is none other than the British Protestants who erect this awesome tri-spired structure, replete with stained glass windows, stone naves, and bells that can almost be heard across the sea. Even our saints they take from us, the locals, Catholic as the day is long, can be heard to whisper to each other in their soft sing-song cadence, as their sweat drips and melds with the mortar while erecting the beautiful but awfully heavy stones, one on top of the other.

The stones are new, hewn from the local quarries, despite the fact there are many old stones lying about that once composed the medieval version of St Fin Barre's church, sheltering the grave of the still beloved saint. Those stones had been torn asunder during the Reformation, one hundred-and-fifty years prior, and left by the local English ascendency in a heart-rending mess, as far as the cruelly treated Catholics were concerned.

Nevertheless, it is work that makes the money that buys the bread that feeds the children, and so the Catholic labourers flock to the building site, hoping to be paid for their trouble. They erect the new cathedral and successfully keep the most beloved ancient stone carvings from being incorporated into the blasphemous new structure. One hundred years later, however, they are not so lucky, and with the latest version of the cathedral, completed in 1865, their own great-grandchildren, again acquire much needed pay for labour, first demolishing and then rebuilding.

Eventually the structure is finished as it stands today. The ancient Catholic site, not just stolen from the people, but made so glorious, so striking, it is a marvel to behold. And this time, the ancient carvings from medieval times are taken from the former ruins and incorporated into the new building. The finest and oldest of these they do not recognise. A series of Romanesque voussoirs are to be found still, sitting on a high, deep and dusty window ledge in the Chapter House. These lovely head carvings of folk from about the year 1130 are meant as arch supports and at one time graced the doorways of the ancient Catholic church looking down on whoever entered. Who they are is a mystery, but their faces were carved by the same good artisan who carved many others still to be found across the land in ancient, holy ruins. Are they the faces of Fin Barre and his followers? No matter, sighs the famous English architect, William Burges, and tosses them in the small side room; we will worry about them later. But after he spends £100,000 on the building that was to cost just £15,000, he feels it best to leave the premises without delay, the voussoirs left to sun themselves on the window ledge.

Taking the ancient Catholic ruins and incorporating them into their new very Protestant structure is a minor cruelty, easily borne by the locals. It is after all just a few years since the great famine. The English, by 1865 when the church is completed, are adept at cruelties of all manner, not just the extreme physical cruelties, of which the Irish know only too well, but every degradation they can imagine, just to drive home the unrelenting message of who is in charge. After they collect their pay, the Catholic workers, builders of that fine cathedral, walk down to the river, across the bridge, and attend Mass in the Catholic Cathedral of St Mary and St Anne. Two saints they needn't worry the Protestants will attempt to apprehend.

James grows up in the shadow of the spires of St Fin Barre's Cathedral. He knows the stories of Fin Barre, the great strength of character and virtue he demonstrated amid a humility that was without doubt beyond the reach of your average young man. It is certainly beyond the reach of James, for James becomes focused, not on peace but on war, and humility is not a virtue to be found within the hearts of those bent on death or worse, even if it is in the name of freedom. If Fin Barre terrified the dragon, the dragon has found a friend in James and sets to whispering in his ear, loaning James in his youth a fierceness that the English are unaccustomed to and do not anticipate.

No. James, like the dragon, thinks fiercely, fearlessly, and of his country's enemies. And like the old Tinker woman who foretells James's future, the Irish Volunteers set James and many able-bodied young men his age on a destiny few can imagine. The rest of their lives, if they are lucky enough to survive, will be forever altered. Indeed, those who, like James, begin life loved and tender-hearted, will be transformed. Much like the shapeshifters of Celtic mythology, they will find themselves twisted and turned into something they do not recognise, capable of actions they could never have imagined, and emotions so dark and intense, there are no words to describe them.

JOIN

CHAPTER 2

APRIL 1916 – MAY 1916

And so, James cries out on that fateful day, the day his little brother Edward blows the roof off the back shed along with a handful of his previously-taken-for-granted fingertips. James just happens to be leaning back against the sink, in front of the kitchen window, staring down at the kettle, waiting for it to boil so he can make his own tea, a job he adopted long ago as a boy. He hears what he might describe later in life as a sonic boom and turns to see a plume of smoke escape through the ripped boards of the roof of the shed at the far end of the garden. He ducks and runs through the half-door of the kitchen, across the grass, down the long narrow length of immaculately kept gardens, past his mother's prize roses and stops dead in the doorway of the shed. He arrives just in time to watch his little brother sink to the floor, his back against the far wall, one hand holding the other arm straight out, staring at his hand, specifically, the place where the top portions of his fingers had once been, mere seconds before. The blood spurts out in quick, intense intervals and spirals down his arm in rivulets, spilling onto his rolled-up shirt cuffs as his eyes dilate and he begins to shake and a sound he does not recognise as his own high-pitched scream emanates from his lips. James feels the panic rise in his chest only after he has torn off his shirt and wrapped his brother's hand tightly against the raw red and black flesh. He steps outside the now crooked, partially unhinged door and vomits into the black earth beneath his mother's profuse, scarlet rhododendrons.

Edward is nine years old the day this happens, well almost ten, but still, a young fellow by any stretch thank goodness, because if he had been any older the police that showed up at the door an hour later would surely have taken him to Cork Gaol, a place James will come to know intimately. At the minute, however, he cannot even imagine such knowledge of the already archaic, rat-infested building and he is certainly relieved that Edward will not.

Edward is of the perfect age to be dazzled and dumbfounded by the stories of Rebel Cork—stories that glorify the dissenters, protesters, agitators, and malcontents of the land, both ancient and modern. He is an enthusiastic, if young, member of the local chapter of the Gaelic League, that patriotic, romantic organisation begun by the illustrious Mr Douglas Hyde and the studious Professor Eoin MacNeill a few years back at the turn of the century, and now a thriving stronghold of young and old in every town and village. Twice weekly, young boys and established young men walk or ride or cycle to their local club to inhale their history, ancient culture, dying language, mournful music and energetic dance, and not just a little politics. They practise their new language skills, learn to play hurling, and listen to old Fenians regale them with stories of rebels long gone, as well as more recent, life-threatening escapades, incarcerations and escapes to and from English gaols by the contemporary objectors of the land. Edward cannot get enough.

Up until this moment, James has been an ardent advocate of all of his little brother's revolutionary musings. In fact, it was James who encouraged the entire family, even Edward, though so young still, to join up and come to meetings to learn the hurling game and the Irish tongue so that they might grow into true renditions of Irishmen and Irishwomen. Indeed, he has contributed to the young lad's enthusiasm with his own dreams of valour and hopes of glory, taking on the English oppressors. But until this moment, James has never thought objectively of the sacrifices that such glory demands. Musings of ancient or newer warriors did not include the stink of rotting flesh and the harrowing screams of a young boy. In the wake of this terrible event, after listening to the weeping laments of his mother nursing what is left of her young son's ripped and ravaged hand and feeling the incriminating stare of his father bore into his soul, James reconsiders. He will keep his enthusiasm to himself and hope that his younger siblings will not make the mistake that young Edward did, attempting life-threatening activities on his own. But James will not withdraw his own personal enthusiasm of the cause. Instead, he learns to keep his own counsel and develops a poker face, and dons it all the day, relaxing only in the evening, surrounded by his friends.

James hangs out at the Gaelic League with his buddies, but especially with his best friend (were he to think of it) Seán. If he had to recall how or where they met, he would not be able to tell you because the two boys have played in the field that both their homes back onto for as many summers as he can remember. They look as opposite as two Irish lads can look. James long and lanky; Seán, small, even scrawny, the type of child who always has a runny nose and is badly near-sighted. His father absconded to Australia when Seán was still of a tender age, leaving the family destitute. It was this scarring event that left Seán, the youngest child, the most vulnerable. Seán is two years older than James and so not in the same class at school, but they share a calm disposition and a reticence to say anything more than is necessary. They feel the connection that somehow joins them and stick up for each other. They are at this minute blissfully unaware of their trials to come.

For now, despite all of the activities at the Gaelic League, there is nothing that fires the blood in their veins more than riding their bicycles across hill and vale. For years, their lithe figures have flashed down the hills of the city on their rickety bikes and been seen as far-off specks on the horizon, exploring the county on Sunday afternoons. Watching waves crashing off the cliffs and wandering the secret beaches of the ragged coastline are common activities. More often than not their return home is precipitated by a change in the unpredictable weather. At times they must give way to the lashing of rain and wind that forces them off the road to seek shelter under ancient bridges. The exhilaration of hunger and exhaustion is sometimes mitigated by the kindness of strangers who notice the wiry bodies, slack stomachs, and darting eyes when they stop and ask for a drink from a farmer's well. A slice of bread and butter, and perhaps a rasher of bacon if they are lucky, are dispensed to restore them and enable their journey home. Seán and James are fast friends who know each other well. They know as well each other's families, and some of their secrets.

Though typical Irish pride has kept Seán from sharing his burdens with James, his friend knows that he has suffered from hunger from time to time. His house is poor, his father long gone, his much older brothers and sisters working to keep the family together. James has often had his friend take home the extra bread that his father, a baker, brings back with him each day from work. James's father, God love him, knows the look of hunger only too well and willingly offers what he can. But this is not all that Seán suffers. Seán suffers most from the constant political discourse in his home, the unceasing emotional ranting, the sometimes-hysterical arguing, the hushed planning, the secret meetings, the old stories, the never-ending analysis of political moves from friend and foe.

Yes, Seán suffers most from these and whether James knows it or not, it is the thing that drives Seán to escape every Sunday afternoon with his bicycle, pedalling like the devil to get away out of it all. Seán, having been raised on endless talk of schemes to wrestle their country back from the British, is excited only by the idea of finding a new home, a new country and starting a new life as far away from Ireland as it is humanly possible to go. While they pedal their bikes like madmen, Seán is dreaming of faraway places. James understands that this youngest member of the MacSwiney family is unlike his older brothers and sisters who are known far and wide as the most political family to come out of Rebel Cork in many a year. As for himself, James is happy to enjoy the scenery and dream of his chance, someday, to turn the political tide. But James is about to discover that his chance lies not in some far-off future, but just around the corner.

The Easter Rising had been in the planning for months. It was the brainchild of the Irish Republican Brotherhood. This highly secret fraternity is an off-shoot of the old Fenian movement and its members have all, every one of them, been personally invited to join by an established member of the fraternity, and in turn are expected to invite other like-minded men. The like-mindedness centres around two things: a firm belief that freedom from British tyranny and the resulting self-rule will only occur if and when the Irish take up arms against their foe. The second criterion is an ability to keep secrets, keep quiet, and keep your head down.

The leadership of the Irish Republican Brotherhood is quite different in Cork than in Dublin. As far as James is concerned, the men in Dublin, most of whom at this moment are in the process of going through quasi-court martials, were head-strong and impatient, so impatient that they pressed forward on a rebellion that had been called off in the rest of the country. The great plans of reinforcement from the Irish Volunteers (on the surface a patriotic group of trained men ready to support the British if the unspeakable possibility of invasion during the Great War was to occur, but in truth, the covert military wing of the secret Irish Republican Brotherhood, who had been planning and drilling and marching all over the country for years now) failed to materialise. The Dublin men were left on their own. Brave and handsome they may have been, but seasoned tactical thinkers? Perhaps not. Life goes on, and our mistakes are paid for sooner or later. However much one may have hoped for the opposite, the Dublin men pay for theirs while the world watches.

Seán is horrified. Rebel Cork is consumed with news of the latest British brutality, the suppression of The Rising and the unholy treatment of the men as they are arrested and transported to be incarcerated. It is not only James who is disgusted by the British, disappointed in the leadership of the Dublin men and sick at heart over their flawed attempt at rebellion failing, totally and unreservedly. There are in fact many like-minded young men (though Seán is not one of them) who are at a loss to find a way to ease their frustration and quell the violence of their hearts, simmering just below the surface of their skin. Fortunately, the vast majority manage to keep their fingers. This will be short-lived, however. It won't be long before many of these same young men, given the choice, would gladly sacrifice a finger or two in lieu of what they and their families will suffer.

The missing fingers have a strange effect on James. Where fair Seán, after viewing the mangled hand of Edward, becomes disgusted, thinking of what such locally produced bombs, assembled from innocent household items, might inflict on the body or soul of any man, British or otherwise, James's mind is flooded with thoughts of a much less innocent nature. James looks at the roof of the garden shed and imagines the destruction that a real bomb, not just a fanciful concoction from a young boy, might create. He thinks to himself of the immediate and permanent destruction that might be wrought on a place unwanted. A place the English keep to themselves. A place unwelcome, here in this beautiful city, built by Irish hands, overseen by those who bow to English Lords and Ladies in their fine, unapproachable homes.

James spends the days between the suppression of the rising and the executions, April 29 to May 12, mostly at Seán's home. Seán and James have neglected their beloved ride into the countryside these past two weeks. The tension is so great, they like everyone around them, feel they are being put through a gauntlet of anguish and despair. There is no escape as they wait for news of just how badly the British are treating the doomed leadership of the Easter Week Rebellion. They will not have to wait long.

Outwardly, Seán's home is much like James's own, housing a large family, although Seán's siblings are much older than James'. Perhaps this is why this family is politically active in ways James cannot even imagine, notwithstanding the missing fingers of brother Edward. The brothers and sisters in Seán's house have been at it a lot longer. While James and Seán were busy as young boys, playing marbles in the front gardens of their homes, kicking around a ball in the back field, Seán's older brothers and sisters were reading the latest prohibited publications by Irish activists and anarchists, papers and pamphlets that encouraged a complete rejection of all things British and a return to the culture and language of their Irish forefathers.

But wait just a moment. What was the culture of their forefathers? Who in Cork City has ever heard a word of Irish spoken? Surely the half-starved peasants on the Aran Isles are the only ones who would still understand such garbled talk. And they are a close-mouthed lot, preferring their own way of life and rarely stepping out of it – not least because they are laughed at and cajoled by the mainlanders, their Irish brothers and sisters.

See here, scream the pamphlets: *they are the true Irish and we should all be speaking just like them, and sure you haven't played a true game of sport until you've risked your kneecaps, not to mention your very brains in a game of hurling. A traditional Irish game that will leave the British footballers crying in their mama's aprons, for fear. And naturally if you have a drop of Irish blood in your veins you know that Ireland should be ruled by the Irish, not that pack of bloodsucking aristocratic thieves who have turned our land into a country of vast estates, enjoyed by the British while Irish hands are worked to the bone. Get off your arse, man, and join the Irish Volunteers! Our day will come, and it will come soon and if you don't believe me, believe the best Ireland has to offer, our educated, our intellectuals, our philosophers and teachers. They will give you the same message – in a more civilised essay, if that is what you require to turn your head in this direction.*

And so, Seán's siblings and their contemporaries, a good ten years older than Seán and James, spend their formative years engrossed in learning all things Irish, or at least how they understand Irishness to be; perhaps a tad romantic, but they are young, and full of hope for the future, and honest progeny of 'Rebel Cork.' Their intense desire to become like the good and the strong of ancient Ireland, both the Celts and the saints, is part and parcel of their primeval allegiance to Catholicism. Through St Patrick, St Fin Barre, St Colmcille, St Brigid and dozens more, the Irish have subsumed into their very fibre their Catholicity. Rejecters of the Reformation, the entire nation became a home of rebels, supporting their priests who were outlawed by the English overlords. They fed them, sheltered them, learned from them, hid them under haystacks and in ancient tombs while the English sheriffs hunted them down like foxes, ravenous dogs in tow.

And yes, the vast majority of these men do indeed recite their rosary each night by the fire. They are Catholic as the day is long, particularly appealing because it is something the English will never be, something they rejected three hundred years ago, something they are no longer capable of understanding. In this lies the irresistible appeal to every Irishman, whether he be of a spiritual disposition or not. And for this reason, those who would otherwise be unlikely to lead a life of faith embrace their Catholicity wholeheartedly. They're at Mass every Sunday morning come hell or high water, fingering the rosary in their trouser pockets as they stroll to work, rigorously teaching their children the rituals, the overt manifestations of their internalised beliefs, consciously or unconsciously revelling in what will come to be known in one hundred years as the 'politics of difference.'

But the 'politics of difference' entails another dimension, long part of the Irish persona, and it is this: it is the mission of every good Irishman and Irishwoman to take any and every opportunity to fail to adhere, even if it be in the least observable way, with the English presence that rules over them. It is the mission of every rebel to work towards freedom, whether it be by nurturing each ensuing generation with the hunger for freedom and the quest for self-rule or whether it be to take up arms against the great oppressor given half a chance of hitting your target, never mind surviving the attempt.

This, it must be admitted, is a recurring dream that has afflicted generations of Irishmen since that fateful date, July 1, 1690. Think of it for a moment. King Billy prancing along on his white horse in a show of victory, across the meandering and lovely, but on this day, glistening and dark with blood, River Boyne. He encourages his men to massacre any Irishmen who are left lying in the fields injured, maimed, conscious or unconscious. As each Irishman is murdered by heavy swords wrenched through their guts, hope too is murdered, left bleeding into the soil as it drains from their bodies. This battle, the infamous Battle of the Boyne, was their last chance to mount a reversal of fortunes and put Catholics back in command of their country. Instead, that ultra-Protestant of Dutch descent, Catholic-despising King William of Orange, canters by, plumes in his hat, and as he surveys the carnage, gives neither the lost blood nor the lost hope a thought. He tells his tired soldiers to stack the nearby corpses and use them for seating at their resting fires after the battle. That the spilling of blood will continue through to the end of James's life, another three hundred years thanks to this victory, does not concern King Billy in the least.

The Irish Catholics left lying on the blood-soaked fields are not surprised by their fate. After all, it is a mere forty years since another Englishman, true friend-in-spirit of King Billy (although separated by years, one might assume given their prejudices that they would indeed be friends given half a chance), did the same to their fathers and mothers and grandfathers and grandmothers, and just a stone's throw away in the beautiful port town of Drogheda.

This particular Englishman, Oliver Cromwell by name, favoured a different mode of massacre. He enters the town through the portal of the large barbican, built several hundred years earlier. Cromwell passes underneath with the full intention of leaving no man standing beyond its border. You may go to Drogheda today and pass under it yourself. You might even be able to imagine the sour-faced Oliver on his horse galloping up the hill while his soldiers stand at the top of the two towers that abut the portal, where the slits in the enclosed stone bridge joining the towers, built for shooting arrows at invading Vikings, will not help the locals on this day. In fact, even the four-mile view of the estuary stretching down to the sea will not help much either. Such a view gave the original Irish inhabitants, seeing the fearsome Norsemen rowing like mad up their river, helmets and shields at the ready, due warning to run and hide if nothing else.

On September 11, 1649, however, seeing Oliver arrive does not help them much, and running terrified to their sacred place of sanctuary even less. Oliver understands sanctuary and uses it to his own ends. The civilians he burns alive in St Mary's Church on one side of town, and the soldiers he burns alive in St Peter's church on the other. A man of practicalities, he manages to dispose of all the nearby Catholics in this way, as well as their unnatural and superstitious houses of worship. Yes, kill two birds with one stone, why not? Not wishing to be seen as a man completely devoid of mercy, he takes the thirty men left standing at the end of the day and deports them as slaves to British landholders in the Caribbean, where they can be made useful.

No good deed goes unpunished, as the old saying goes, and sure enough, Cromwell gets his comeuppance in a particularly gruesome way. Years later, three years after he is dead and buried, the English themselves dig up his decomposing body out of his aristocratic tomb in Westminster Abbey and promptly drag it through the streets to the awaiting scaffold, there to be hung, drawn, and quartered. Oliver's poor head ends up on a stake high on the Iron Gate overlooking the abbey, and weathers there for around thirty years until a wind blows it off in a bad storm. Eventually, after residing for the next two hundred years or so in a family estate, the head is received as a gift, macabre to be sure, by Oliver's alma mater, Cambridge University, who, wary of the Irish to this day, bury it in a secret location. Naturally this has nothing to do with Cromwell's treatment of the Irish; nobody cared about that.

Big brother of Seán, Terrence, is thirty-seven years old, and in this year of 1916, unmarried, an accountant by trade and a scholar-poet of some repute. He is also devastatingly handsome. He is an activist, if a romantic one, and has aided in the creation of the Cork Literary Society and the Cork Dramatic Society with his Gaelic revivalist friends, including among others, Daniel Corkery, destined to become a famous author. If you are known to harbour Irish nationalist writings in your home, you may have a copy of his banned newspaper *Fianna Fáil*, Soldiers of Destiny, hidden under a bed and you may pull it out now and again to read the dreamy prose of a man of principle and be renewed in your resolve to fight for your country, should that day ever come.

Terrence quietly crunches numbers by day but come evening, when the fire is lit, he is not to be found reading light prose. No. By night, Terrence is to be found racking his brains with his best friend and colleague, always trying to stay one step ahead of the British, working to find surreptitious ways of training hundreds of local men around the city and the countryside to become disciplined soldiers. Well, perhaps semi-disciplined is a better word: to follow orders, to learn to march, to shoot, to find in their guts the intense desire to fight for freedom. For only this will spur them forward, when the time comes, allowing them to perform acts as yet unimaginable. It is likely that such acts are not closely imagined by Terrence; it is the glory and the final result of Ireland free that he dreams of.

He is closely watched by the British authorities for his growing insolence. This insolence is manifested in the superlative writings that are known to exist, but not always found, as well as certain information that has been extracted from various locals about nefarious goings-on in the form of secret organisations. In fact, our Terrence had founded, three years earlier, in 1913, the 1st Cork Brigade of the Irish Volunteers, which is not yet, in 1916, illegal, but still suspicious and on the British radar. This is the small, tight little group of individuals who form a quasi-military institution which James is about to be invited to join. This institution will give him duties to perform that will make his hair turn white and his blood run cold. The men who run this group will all become famous, most locally, some nationally, some internationally. But that is all far in the future and is in fact dependent upon what our Terrence is about to do now, at this moment in May 1916, just after the Easter Rising, while waiting for news of the Dublin leaders.

Terrence's best friend is Tomás. Tomás MacCurtain, as dashing as Terrence is handsome, as gregarious as Terrence is reserved. He plays the fiddle, recites Irish poetry, teaches Gaelic to any who wish to learn, and is known to be quite the dancer. Ladies everywhere swoon over his charm and charisma, but, alas for them, he is devoted to his beautiful wife, Eilish, a woman with intellect and passion to match his own. She has already borne him five children, whom he adores and imbues with his *joie de vivre*. She will bear him one more before their life together is cut short. At the age of seventeen, Tomás was already holding office in the Gaelic League, elected by his peers of Irish nationalists and insurgents, and so by this time is also well-known to the British authorities. The fact that he is openly seen to be good friends with our Terrence ties the two together in the minds of those suspicious Englishmen and as if to affirm their hunches, where one goes the other will follow, even to St Fin Barre's graveyard, there to rest with the saint after much weary work and sacrifice, battling dragons of their own day, on behalf of their countrymen.

As you might assume, the friends Tomás and Terrence are quite unaware of their personal futures and so are busy. The days after the rebellion are fraught with speculation. The two men ride an emotional roller coaster, hoping against hope that the Dublin leaders will be spared and then as each one is tried, they fall into a despondent slump of mourning. Of the two, Tomás is the least hopeful. In his heart he expects the worst news possible each day. He is tougher, more streetwise, and a better judge of character, although as time will tell not nearly as strong as his friend Terrence, who will, sadly, demonstrate an inner fortitude disturbing in its magnitude.

James and Seán watch in these late days of spring as Terrence grows pale and thin, his normally serene face a tired visage of what will come to be known as 'extreme stress' in years to come. Tomás, on the other hand grows angrier and more defiant with each passing day. They are waiting for news of their comrades and leaders far away in Dublin's Kilmainham Gaol. They are waiting to know their fate, inexorably tied to their own. They know each Dublin man, some better than others, but still, each man. After all, they have been working together, all of the leadership of the Brotherhood from across the country, organising and planning and arguing and searching out arms for years now. Both Terrence and Tomás are part of that leadership, representing the Cork region. They are both stoic in defeat, but nevertheless consumed by fear for their friends and comrades. They know that each man, sitting in God knows what type of conditions, is suffering through untold anguish. For there is one single fact that these Irish friends understand, completely and utterly. There is one single fact that ties them together more tightly than anything else; one single fact, the knowledge of which runs through each man's veins like blood itself nourishing their fear.

The fact is this: the British establishment, army, police, aristocracy, has no conscience where the Irish are concerned. If such a conscience ever existed, it has been long ago smothered by cruelty and self-interest. In short, when dealing with Irishmen anything goes. Anything. Think on this for a while, if you dare.

Despair and hopelessness are suspended in the air like a cold fog. James and Seán watch as everyone around them begins to grieve. Everyone knows what is going to happen next, yet they hope with an irrational, unsupportable conjecture that this rebellion will be treated differently from every other rebellion in Irish history. Back and forth they go, from hope to despair, from despair to hope. Seán and James are unwilling eyewitnesses to this untold grief. They are watching Tomás's young children while Tomás, his wife Eilish, and Terrence stake out their time on watch with other Cork leaders waiting for news of those arrested. They pray one moment and rail with anger, frustration, and bitterness the next. Surely, surely, the British can see they will be making martyrs. Surely they will understand it is better to be lenient with their prisoners.

The British do see, but they do not care. The newspapers in Dublin and Cork and everywhere else do not support the rebels, not at all. In fact, many editorials condemn them. But neither do they wish to see them executed. They are just misguided, victims of the ridiculous Gaelic revival that has been unduly influencing the young to believe that an Irish nation from the murky past might resurrect itself. The British, too, read the editorials. You must be joking, they quip amongst themselves.

It begins with the main culprits, as they are seen to be. Although some might have thought them brave, most undoubtedly deemed them beyond understanding. For heaven's sake, not only did they take on the British Empire with a gaggle of poorly trained dreamers and zealots, they actually signed their names to a so-called 'Declaration of Irish Independence'! They signed their names to the physical evidence that is sure to be produced at their trial for treason in this, the first, smallest, and closest British colonial state at a time when Britain rules the world? How does one classify such an act? An act of selflessness? Hubris? Insanity?

After shocking the postal workers in the General Post Office by storming in and taking control, Pádraig Pearse, the thirty-seven-year-old teacher and leader of the rising, leaves his soldiers to man the building, walks outside and as the newly hoisted, recently homemade flags of the Irish Republic flutter in the spring breeze high on the roof, Pádraig walks down to the bottom step of the great portico and unfurls his lately composed and printed Declaration, a document set at a printer in great secrecy with inadequate letters and hence a hasty, not exactly perfect production. He adjusts his spectacles and proceeds to read aloud with reverence, excitement, and, it might be added, a jubilant sense of satisfaction, these compelling words:

IRISHMEN AND IRISHWOMEN: In the name of God and of the dead generations from which she receives her old tradition of nationhood, Ireland, through us, summons her children to her flag and strikes for her freedom.

The sun beams down. A single greenfinch bird sings its elated song from atop the flagpole and Pádraig's euphoria is palpable. His good friend and comrade in arms, James Connolly, cannot hide his delight as he listens, alternately smiling and shaking his head in approval as the reading continues. It is a long document and as Pádraig reads, people passing by, wondering at the commotion, noticing the strange-looking flags, and therefore feeling a little baffled, move to form a small crowd around him. They are not aware of the dozens of men with rifles inside the building turning over tables, creating barriers and cover for the anticipated British response of voluminous gunfire. Pádraig's emotion fails to move the crowd (although the grandchildren of those few standing there will one day read this document in school and boast that their grandparents were there at the start). They turn their heads from history in the making and carry on doing their mundane errands, muttering to themselves of the cheek of such an otherwise intelligent-looking young man, and who, by the way, were those young fellows about in unfamiliar uniforms?

But it is Thomas Kent, a man of Rebel Cork, member of a family who has a long history of annoying the British, who represents the worst of omens of what is to come.

Thomas does not live in Dublin, nor did he participate in the uprising. He, like all his rebel brothers and friends, had planned and prepared to join their Dublin comrades but at the last minute listened to the counterorder to stand down given by one of the Dublin leaders. He remained in Cork while other Dublin leaders proceeded to their doom. Thomas is well-known to the authorities. In fact, it has been just three months or so since Thomas Kent and his friend and collaborator Terrence shared an intimate moment of being arrested for making a seditious speech to the crowds at a small town just outside the city. After encouraging every available male with two legs to think of freedom, specifically, to think of successfully stealing back Ireland's freedom after seven hundred and fifty years, urging them to come join the Volunteers and train as a military unit, the two were hauled away together. They spent a month getting to know the intricacies of life in Cork Gaol. Released by mid-February, it has been just weeks since their gaolers had them behind bars. And predictably, with the Dublin rebels safely ensconced, their trials for sedition and treason underway, the roundup of known sympathisers around the country begins.

The local unit of the Royal Irish Constabulary, commonly referred to as RIC or 'Peelers' by those who come to feel the brunt of their power, head straight to the Kent home hoping to take in all four brothers, all known troublemakers, all best kept behind bars for the time being, until things settle down. If they thought the brothers would march right up to the truck and put their hands out for the cuffs, those British representatives of law and order must have been remorseful at their own sorry delusion.

The brothers have borne the brunt of British abuse over the years and know exactly what is coming. They have already prepared themselves. Upstairs, looking out of the windows of their beautiful family home, Bawnard House, north of the city, the brothers pull out the hidden rifles from under their floorboards. They distribute themselves at the upstairs windows and call out to the RIC to take a hike back to their barracks and leave decent Irishmen in peace. When the RIC laugh in response, the brothers begin to shoot. First off, they hit the Police Commander, who drops like a stone, to the shock of his troops loosely surrounding the family home. Perhaps Thomas Kent was unduly influenced by his travels to America in his youth and the stories of the gunfights of the Wild West, or perhaps he simply refused to be taken again so lightly to any British prison, especially to the likes of Cork Gaol. But whatever transpired in his mind, he proceeded at the urging of his mother and brothers to carry on fighting and to make that troop of British Law enforcers work for their pay. And so they do, with a four-hour long gun fight and several bullet-induced injuries. The British, however, rise to the challenge, and in the midst of the fighting manage to lodge a bullet into the head of Thomas's brother Richard. Two souls lost, several wounded.

Seán and James watch stricken as Terrence, upon hearing the story of the Kent brothers' battle and incarceration, and the shooting deaths of Richard and the head constable, makes the sign of the cross, while shaking his head in disbelief and sorrow. Terrence has been training men all over the south of Ireland, writing about freedom, proclaiming that Irishmen everywhere rise to fight the enemy. Surely it is a hard job watching the consequences of your own words on the lives of your friends and neighbours. Those consequences have suddenly become deadly. Terrence is shocked. Perhaps by the permanent and radical nature of these consequences to his fine words of freedom. Perhaps because he never really believed the fruit of his labours would be seen in his own lifetime, or indeed result in deadly force upon men he knew and cherished, friend or foe. After all, rebels have inhabited Ireland for generations, their fine words fanning the flames of story and song, only breaking through reality after many centuries.

But break through they have, and James and Seán watch as a shadow crosses Terrence's face, and the last flicker of hope falls from his already pale, gaunt visage. It falls in a slow swish to the ground, and Terrence's body follows, collapses on the green grass, followed by a dreadful moan. The type of moan the likes of which cannot be adequately described, except to say that even a man of the hardest heart can do nothing but turn his head and look away. Terrence moans for the fate of his friend, Kent. There is no doubt what will become of him now that a representative of British law and order has fallen by Kent's hand. He moans too for the fallen constable, a local man, fair and square, known to all. Does Terrence experience a premonition in this moment? A prophetic glance into the future? His own future?

James and Seán are astonished at the intensity of Terrence's response, and it must also be said, embarrassed. They look away, gather up the children and distract them by taking them into the house, leaving poor Eilish to tend to her husband and his incapacitated friend. Later the boys talk among themselves. Seán feels nothing but compassion for his big brother, the sight of whom, lying on the grass, is seared into his mind. God love him he is taking it hard, so he is, he thinks to himself. James, on the other hand, does not say, but is slightly disgusted with Terrence's reaction. For the love of God man, would you not toughen up, he thinks to himself. And all of this for the louts in Dublin who were too stupid to wait for the rest of us. James is but a teenager and we will forgive him his cold-hearted reaction. The Irish, after all, are a people who have learned to stay their hearts and keep their emotions tightly under wraps. Perhaps one day James will weep himself, thinking of this moment, though he will probably not recall his own hardness of heart.

It is May 1, 1916, barely three days since the Dublin men, or what is left of them, were variously stripped, beaten, dragged, cajoled, derided and marched to their places of detention in Kilmainham Gaol, Mountjoy Gaol, and various and sundry others. Hundreds of Dublin men who stood on the side-lines have also been incarcerated by the British and sweeps across the countryside are now expected to be undertaken in every county to pick up any and every Republican lowlife that has ever been on the British radar.

With the arrest of Thomas Kent, Terrence and Tomás know the worst is yet to come. And with the death of the local Police Commander, they understand that the reaction of the British will be swift and severe. The British have been kicked in the gut by this insurrection, from the surprisingly well-worded and passionate Proclamation of Independence to the six days of embarrassing military duress at the hands of a few hundred men, Irishmen at that. They have been humiliated by their own ineptitude, and they are making sure that it will not happen again. Anyone they suspect to be even remotely involved with the Easter Rising, the Gaelic League, any sort of Nationalist organisation, will now be picked up, their premises searched, their friends interrogated, their families harassed, and their hopes dashed.

Expecting the worst, the leaders of Cork No. 1 Brigade begin to mobilise. Meetings are held, but confusion reigns, arguments ensue. Tomás, Officer Commanding, and Terrence, Vice Officer Commanding, begin to plan for any number of untold contingencies. The existing Volunteers of the Cork No. 1 Brigade must not be allowed to slide into despair. First off, dump all incriminating materials. Then lie low. Tomás and Terrence caution the men. We don't want heroes; we want men left whom we can count on. Spread the word, lie low, steer clear of your home, skip town for a while, go visit distant relatives, find a barn to hide in, do whatever you can to evade capture and do it now.

Between themselves they talk in hushed tones, meeting as they do frequently during the day and night. Despite setbacks, they must use what position they have gained and move forward. With the expectation of a significant loss of men to detention, the first thing they must do is find people they can trust to keep the organisations going, both the Brotherhood and the Volunteers. They also expect that the Irish Volunteers, so far permitted by the British, will forever more be completely outlawed. Their relentless work over the last few years must not be lost. The connections, the networks across the country, the secret meeting places, the secret locations of arms, the observation of the British themselves, all these things must continue. They need a small group of men who are beyond reproach, who will not be suspect, who will not be carted away for God knows how many years, if they are lucky enough not to simply disappear. They need a small group of men who can be trusted with this terrible responsibility: to keep the hopes of Irish rebels everywhere alive and simmering. They must look for men who are unattached and not yet responsible for families. They need not look far. Right beneath their noses are two young men, till this moment dreamers, cyclists, and babysitters. That will all change now.

Terrence looks to his baby brother Seán. He will do what he can to protect him, but he is old enough now to join the men. His sidekick, best friend and neighbour, James, can also be trusted. The two are inseparable and will look out for each other. They are young enough to exude innocence around the authorities and smart enough to understand the dire necessity of following orders without question. They have been privy to who is in the inner circle, and so know more than they should. And they are responsible for no one. Terrence and Tomás make a decision. James and Seán are to be held back from the larger group, rendering them unidentifiable by any but them and the next in line of command, O'Hegarty. Were any of the others to be captured and tortured, they will not know Seán or James as members of any rebel group, and so will not spit out their names, gnashing their teeth as their flesh is seared or twisted or torn. They make this decision in the nick of time, just hours before Tomás and a crew of others are taken into custody. The following day Terrence is arrested with many of the men suspected of belonging to the 1st Cork Brigade. Seán and James are not even glanced at during the round up.

And so, on the very day that Terrence is arrested, May 3, 1916, it begins. If before daylight on this morning you were to look closely above the tightly locked door of Kilmainham Gaol in Dublin City, you would see the intricate stone carving of serpents weaving between each other, a warning to all who enter. You might imagine those same stone serpents sway rhythmically, ever so slightly, as if in gleeful anticipation. Whatever your mindset, in the wee hours of the morning, Tomás Clark, Thomas MacDonagh, and Pádraig Pearse, all signatories of that fine, eloquent document which proclaims their names screaming out to the British, become the first example to the Irish nation. They are dragged out to the yard and stood against the wall. Clark and MacDonagh look on in defiance. Pearse whistles a tune. The shots ring out.

On May 4, Pádraig's younger brother Willie, his best friend and confidant, is given the same treatment. A sickly Joseph Plunkett is permitted to marry his fiancée, Grace, a few short hours before his own execution, as fifteen soldiers, bayonets fixed at the ready, line the tiny cell and watch as the lovers murmur their final goodbyes. Edward Daly, brother-in-law of Tomás Clarke, and Michael O'Hanrahan follow. Next morning, John McBride is given this honour alone. It's Friday and things are toning down by the end of the week. The British take the weekend off, but sure enough, early Monday morning, they are back at it with a line-up of four lovely gentlemen, Éamonn Ceannt, another signatory, Michael Mallin, Seán Heuston, and Cornelius Colbert. All pushed against the hard stone of the courtyard, blindfolded, and shot. Their strong youthful bodies slump down, and they fall forward, all hope and vision and yearning for a future worthy of passing on to their children seeming to die in the dust with them. As if this is not enough for the Irish everywhere, the people of Cork are subjected to their own localised display of British cruelty. Thomas Kent is pulled out of the detention cells at the back of Victoria Barracks where he is being held and as the sun rises on the ninth of May he sets his jaw in defiance and passes from the earth, compliments of an accurately displaced British bullet.

But wait. What is that faint melodic hum in the air? Wherever one turns? It is barely audible, yet it is there imbuing the atmosphere with a rich Celtic tone. It is the people, murmuring their regrets and their rosaries, from one end of the Isle to the other, their heads bent in sorrow, as wretchedness and remorse fill their hearts and the slow realisation that these men who are now being shot, are the very ones who tried to save them from this same frightful prospect, this potential fate of strangers, gaolers, warders, and guards sitting in judgement and pronouncing with impunity what Irishman or Irishwoman will live or will die and for what sorry reason.

Not only are the Irish attuned to this sound, a sound that grows incrementally stronger as each day passes. The English too, although their ears are shut to any goodness that may emanate from an Irishman, become aware that something is changing. Ah, but sometimes one's own strength is one's downfall! After wavering for four days, the music of protest can no longer be ignored. Statements are made. Newspapers forward articles about the end being in sight. After all, peasant revolts are the most feared of protests by reigning aristocrats: just ask the French. It is unlikely that more executions will take place, quote the journalists. Of those next in line, some are given commuted sentences. Maybe it was just a bad day for the powers that be, or maybe they just had to assert their supremacy, savouring one last twist of the sword in the collective Irish gut, but in the early morning of May 12 they execute two who will now become the last, Seán MacDiarmada and James Connolly.

The unspeakable news arrives by way of a white-faced courier, not much younger than James himself, just as the teenagers are kicking the football around the yard with Tomás's children. Eilish sits in the yard, staring off into the cloudy sky, wondering where they have taken her husband, what they are doing to him and what will become of him. She is only half-heartedly listening to the buzz of talk around her from the remaining movers and shakers of the Cork Volunteers. The courier tells the story of how the virtuous Mr Connolly who was being held in the infirmary in Dublin Castle, the bones in his leg shattered, and unable to move, is dragged up to a sitting position in his bed, the pain of which makes the tears stream down his ashen face, and put under court martial. Two days later they return at midnight, put him on a stretcher and carry him to Kilmainham Gaol, where the blood of his friends is still wet upon the courtyard's stone. Still unable to support his body weight in a sitting position they strap him to a chair and take careful aim.

This moment is the moment that drives the friends and soon-to-be politicians who are pacing about the premises to make a critical decision. It is the same decision discerned and decided upon simultaneously around the country by men, women, and yes, even children. It penetrates the Irish people at the very moment a British bullet penetrates the heart of that well-loved man of the people, while his fist grasps his rosary, and his lips mouth his quiet, final, secret prayer. This decision will end the already short lives of some and alter others for decades to come. As days pass into months, it will bring about destruction, betrayal, and bitterness. As months pass into years it will carry the seeds of hope and eventually change to all about them. Collectively infused with a mission, in a miraculously short period, the Irish will at last pry freedom from the strangling grip of the English fist, finger by finger.

How can one characterise an almost unconscious yet unanimous decision by a scattering of people, located in every town and village across a country, arrived at in unison? It is a decision prompted by the realisation that there is nothing they can possibly do to the invaders of their land that will ever be worse than what has just been done to their own leaders, their own people, their own country. There is nothing they can do that will ever be as wicked or as weak as sitting by helplessly watching your friends and neighbours suffer at the hands of foreigners. Foreigners, who use and abuse us and our land, take what they will, even our very lives and leave nothing but the ash of bitterness in our mouths.

The soft melody of mutiny diffuses through the air, the faint pounding of its drum reverberating about every man, woman, and child. Fear, indecision, and indifference evaporate in its wake. Overnight, in every village and town and city, men and women trip over themselves, in an effort to join the Volunteers. The decision has been taken. There will be no turning back.

James and Seán watch and learn. They are now the newest members of the 1st Cork Brigade, and most of the Brigade does not even know it. Their first job makes use of their best skills: their ability to cycle like devils, fast and furious and across vast distances in an afternoon; and their natural reticence, their ability to keep what they know hidden dark and deep and as far away from their faces as is possible. Seán wonders how he will ever escape the fate of being born into a rebel family. James, on the other hand, is elated. At last, his chance has come. Someday there will be action, perhaps another rebellion, another rising, and he, James, will be in the thick of it. His heart quickens. His imagination soars.

RIDE

CHAPTER 3

JUNE 1916 – MAY 1917

Like a banshee warning of the impending passing of a soul, the wind soars across the valley with a wail, long and bloodcurdling. James barely notices. It is a dark, moonless night and he is concentrating on navigating the narrow streets. The blood pounding through his veins is obliterating any extraneous noise as the staccato thumping of his heart overwhelms his senses. He pedals uphill with all the strength his sinuous quadriceps can muster. It doesn't help that he was tossed out of bed at an ungodly hour to dispatch this message across town without food or drink. He knows from the frantic way it was whispered in his ear, and the taut, driven look on O'Hegarty's face, a face that is seen only undercover, that the message must come to its intended destination without fail and with the speed of an angel.

Through the dark backstreets of Cork City James pedals, downhill, across the river, uphill until he finds the house whose owner's life, and those of the three Volunteer chaps sleeping in the kitchen, are in peril. Bang, bang, bang on the back door even as the bicycle is still slowing down. James does not even dismount. Through the slightly ajar back window, James half-whispers, half-shouts, Peelers, now! He can see the movement through the dark as the men jump to their feet and scramble for their shoes and trousers. While he wheels away, taking a slightly different route back to O'Hegarty's abode, the men, known to the police as raving nationalists, ones that were missed in the initial round-up, are heading out of the back door and down the back lane with their apparel in hand. They clear off to a different neighbourhood, where the RIC constables, who are at this moment stealthily making their way to the front door, will not find them. The owner of the home will feign outrage and innocence when his door is smashed in by rifle butts and his home tossed about. The RIC commander will march back out in frustration, shaking his head at the lousy intelligence he is expected to work with.

These first duties of James are by his own estimation minor ones. He must take messages to various men around the city. For James nothing is written down, so he must remember. If he is stopped and searched, there is nothing to find, no notes, no secret codes, no instructions. If perchance he is taken in for interrogation, the words he has memorised have no meaning for him and therefore no meaning for the British. They are words that will be understood only by the recipient. This is the way that James's new boss likes to do things. And he must admit it is damn smart.

Terrence and Tomás have been transported out to an internment camp with hundreds of others. The authorities may not have had any evidence about their participation in the Easter Week Rebellion, but they are utterly certain that they are troublemakers and why not get rid of them anyway? When they will be released to return home is anybody's guess, and anybody's guess in Cork City will be given in years, not weeks. It is the new reality of Cork, of Dublin, and of every town where Volunteers are known to the authorities. Everybody knows a family where a young man has been dragged from his home or place of work, thrown in the detention barracks, and packed off to England or Scotland or Wales. There is no one it has not touched. At least, not if you are a member of the Gaelic League or the Gaelic Athletic Association, or more generally speaking a Catholic.

Seán O'Hegarty is not a Catholic. He is an atheist. One might add, with good reason, given what was often the hopeless nature of his young life's circumstances. By some strange stroke of luck, O'Hegarty has been left behind in Cork. Although he is known to the authorities as an old Fenian from an old Fenian family, he is not even questioned. Perhaps at the age of forty he is believed to be past his prime, the British noting the youthful nature of this most recent of rebellions. But it is much more likely that his secretive ways served him well during the roundups. Whatever the reason, he was the last to speak with Tomás and Terrence, and as third in command, now takes over the Cork No. 1 Brigade. He is just the one needed to keep the organisation chugging along the convoluted bumps and dips on the road to freedom. He is fierce, ruthless, and known to possess a pitiless tongue that is employed frequently in slicing down to size anyone who might question him, raise an eyebrow at his methods, or look twice in his direction at the wrong moment.

There are no rosary beads in O'Hegarty's pockets. He does not pray, nor question the fates when unfortunate or tragic events rip through his life. He learned long ago as a child that prayer is pointless and railing at the circumstances of life does not diminish pangs of hunger, or prevent cold rains from paralyzing bare calloused feet, nor does it stop the wind from slicing through undersized and threadbare clothing, inadequately covering a young boy's growing body. As a child he had watched, racked with anxiety, as his mother prayed pitifully for the love of her life, that is, his father, as he lay dying of tuberculosis. Her pleas and promises to the deity seemed not to affect the poor man's disposition an iota, and O'Hegarty watched as first his mother's heart was broken, then, as her frail, hungry body fought poverty so severe the family barely survived it.

O'Hegarty has learned that turning one's direction from supplication of the divine to direct action in the present is the only way to get what you need. It is that or go without. In his mid-age going without is no longer a reasonable choice for O'Hegarty. He will get what he needs one way or another. It is this shrewd, rational cunning that has propelled O'Hegarty through the secret Irish Republican Brotherhood and landed him at the helm of the Cork No. 1 Brigade. O'Hegarty knows his enemy. You might even say he knows the enemy better than anyone in Cork City, perhaps in all of Ireland. He knows that if the enemy is tough, you must be tougher; if the enemy is fast, you must be faster, and if the enemy is cruel, you must take on cruelty with zest. In short you must be a warrior. O'Hegarty is nothing if not a warrior, and James, for some reason, unknown even to himself, feels a loyalty and respect for him that he will never feel for anyone else.

Warriors have been found in Ireland since time immemorial. One might even conclude that the 'warrior gene,' that genetic mutation found in about one-third of populations, is part and parcel of that other genetic mutation of the Irish, the Haplogroup-1 gene, which is undiluted from stone age times in certain remote populations, for instance, in the west and south of the island, where James was born and where his family ancestry lies. We might speculate that the warrior gene and a tendency for red hair are tied in a tight knot in James's history. After all, he is, like his mentor and new boss, Mr O'Hegarty, quick to punish under provocation and a particularly high-risk taker, both of which are defining characteristics of the warrior gene.

Some hundred years after St Patrick and a hundred years before St Fin Barre, Colmcille, grandson of the High King, a majestic man with a booming voice and the stature of a mythical prince, embraced the Christianity of Patrick and set off to study and learn from the best new Christians. He learned Latin and absorbed the Gospels as if through his very skin, so that when he preached, his melodious, hypnotic voice carried on the breeze the words of the Christ like a tonic. He embraced learning with passion and desired to have a beautiful book of prayer. He could not have known that such a desire would lead him to disaster, permanently altering the trajectory of his life.

He travels across the northern portion of the Island from his western home in Donegal, to the tip of Strangford Lough in County Down, where the newly built Movilla Abbey with its soon-to-be-significant library sits at the top of a hill looking out to the world. He talks good Abbot Finnian into allowing him the use of a particularly beautiful psalter to copy. After weeks of tedious, laborious replication from vellum to vellum, and with only a handful of psalms left to complete the work, he proudly shows his creation to the Abbot. Abbot Finnian is astounded by the artistry of intricate Celtic designed letters, and the Gaelic headings explaining each psalm written in Latin below. What a novel idea to explain the Latin verse in people's native language! No one else has ever done such a thing. And all this fine, sophisticated work produced by massive hands with fingers like sausages! Perhaps Finnian is even a tad envious of such a beautiful work? Whatever the reason, he now shocks Colmcille with his announcement.

Why thank you very much for your labours, says Finnian. This will be a nice addition to our collection. At this, Colmcille's magnificent chest puffs out and his fierce eyebrows rise on his face. What, booms Colmcille. Why this is the work of my own hand, and it belongs to me! Abbot Finnian stares up at that magnificent man, and taking refuge in knowing that he is a man of God, looks at him in shock. Hardly, he replies. And then relenting somewhat, but we do appreciate your handiwork. My own monks shall learn this style from you and our library and people will be the better off for it.

This is too much for Colmcille, and despite the implications of two holy men in a tiff, he proclaims a rift between the two. Colmcille is, after all, of royal descent and used to getting what he wants.

Colmcille goes to the High King and demands an army to put Finnian and his damn people in their place. The king agrees that crew has stepped out of line and sends Colmcille off with his best warriors. Clan Neill is a clan of superior physical attributes, and led by Colmcille, a natural strategist, they meet the enemy, that is Finnian and his own troop of warriors (somewhat of a surprise to Colmcille), and proceed to fight what will ever after be known as the Battle of the Book. They trounce the enemy and leave them slaughtered on the ground, not a drop of mercy to be shown, even to the wounded. Lacerated by swords, their bodies weep blood on the field and as the blood flows, Colmcille's anger seeps away only to be replaced by a deep remorse that will never leave him.

What was I thinking? Colmcille asks himself. I am a holy man, known for bringing heathens to Our Lord, who has given me the gifts of the Holy Spirit, able to cure diseases and cast out demons. By the blessing of the Holy Spirit, I can see the future of the Lord's chosen, but clearly, I cannot see my own future! I have slaughtered Our Lord's own creation, loved by him (if despised by me). How will I make this up to my Master in heaven? And suddenly, as he is kneeling on the ground watching the blood of his enemies pool around his knees, he hears the coo of the dove and looks up. In that moment he knows he is forgiven, but at a price.

Colmcille turns and, with a heavy heart, travels to his confessor, St Molaise, far away on the island of Inishmurray. There, he whispers quietly the sin weighing on his soul and bends his ear to hear his penance. St Molaise blesses Colmcille despite his shock and despair at two holy men battling each other. Won't it make his preaching to the pagans even harder to swallow? With a blunt and decisive voice, he orders Colmcille into exile. You will leave your home never to return. You will venture off to the shores of Scotland wherein live the Picts, more depraved and fiercer than any Celt. There you will find souls for the Lord or die trying. Colmcille shudders. He is a man of Ireland, the new Ireland, determined to carry on Pádraig's great work of spreading the good news of Our Lord. He is bereft at the thought of leaving his home; however, Colmcille musters the strength and courage he is known for and rises off his knees. He embraces his confessor and whispers to the Lord, Let thy will be done. Of course, we recognise here that second quality of the warrior, taking risks no sane man would. Colmcille is a victim of his own DNA, but never mind, in the end it serves him well.

He packs his books, including his own personally copied, if incomplete psalter, now only a minor consolation, and takes his group of followers, also monks, only twelve of whom dare make the journey to the home of the feared Picts, in a single leather-bound boat across the sea to the coast of Scotland. Standing on the shore he looks out across the water to the distant hills of his home, and proclaims: No! I do not deserve to even see the outline of my birthplace and the seat of generations of my royal ancestors. And so, he gets back in the boat and heads north. Finally, he lands at the Isle of Iona, there to build a world-famous monastery. After his death, his loyal monks will create a treasure box for the psalter – a brass box two inches deep, and just large enough to hold the small yet oh so precious vellum masterpiece. They will spend hours engraving the box with a vision of Christ and Colmcille together in heaven and decorate it with precious silver, pearls and gems. Of the exquisite, irreplaceable library that will be laboriously established over the next few hundred years, only this will be saved when eventually the Vikings come calling.

Towards the end of Colmcille's life, the story goes, in his travels to convert the Picts, he comes by the River Ness and there on the shoreline finds a group of Picts weeping at the death of their friend whom they have just buried. Colmcille is older now and mellowed somewhat and he feels nothing but compassion for this group of bedraggled heathens who mourn their friend so woefully. As they stand by the shore, a great water dragon rears its head out of the river and pounces on the poor man standing closest to the water. The friends are aghast, terrified, overwhelmed. But not Colmcille. He shouts out at the monster beast, thou shalt go no further. Nor touch the man. Go back with all speed! The soon to be renowned beast drops its prey from its jaws and retreats. Banished for good, it returns to Loch Ness from whence it had come and, according to the locals, can be seen still, if vaguely, on foggy days, coming up for air when it is unlikely to be noticed and incur the wrath of the holy man.

For James's part, he does indeed fear the wrath of O'Hegarty. James has witnessed his withering attacks on incompetent Volunteers and been privy to the vitriol he pours on them when complaining to Terrence or Tomás of the lack of hearty, courageous men in their organisation. Under no circumstance does our seventeen-year-old James wish to be the recipient of such a sentiment. He will ride through the night, loiter for hours around police barracks noting the comings and goings of various and sundry persons, and report back *tout de suite* to his boss. He will carry messages. He will follow his orders without question. Indeed, O'Hegarty will be the only man whom James never questions, even in his own mind. O'Hegarty is not much younger than James's own father, and James is just as open to validation from him as he is from his Da, who smiles at the same rate O'Hegarty scowls and is quietly generous at the same rate that O'Hegarty is bitingly sarcastic. There is something about O'Hegarty that compels James. He cannot say what it is. He respects the man's intelligence but more than that, the quiet aura of power that lingers about his person attracts James. He does not yet realise it is that very quality which has the opposite effect on his friend Seán, repelling him right down to his stomach.

And so, as the spring flows into summer, hope of a return of

Tomás and Terrence recedes with each passing day. They have disappeared with hundreds of others, having been marched the many miles down to the British docks, locked up on board ships and transported to any number of possible locations. The location of each man and who he might be interned with is a mystery. The commuted sentences of those who might have been executed are doled out in decades to be served in British prisons. But the fate of one man still hangs in the balance, and every newspaper carries the spectacular details of the trial. Those who cannot afford the penny for a newspaper crowd around the printing offices reading the paper that is posted daily outside the front doors. Their curiosity is both satisfied and piqued as they learn the finer details of the life of the legendary Irish knight, Sir Roger Casement.

Indeed, the crowds hardly believe that Sir Roger is being tried. He is, after all, one of the most famous Irishmen of his day and lauded by the English as a British treasure. Their emphasis on the British Empire keeps the world from focusing too narrowly on his truly Irish heritage. Sir Roger has, unbeknownst to himself, become a shining beacon to the rest of the world, and will be for generations yet to be born.

In the 1870s after his Protestant father and Catholic mother die within a few years of each other, young Roger is left with his three older siblings to live with an aunt and uncle in County Antrim, at the north-eastern tip of the Emerald Isle. His relatives live in the lovely estate of Magherintemple House, close to the sea where dreamy young Roger will spend many an hour whiling away his youth. Roger loves nothing more than hiking up to Drumnakil Point, looking down on the ancient ruins of Drumnakil Church, a place where our warrior saint, Colmcille, may very well have spent time himself. It is indeed a glorious, if desolate spot at the top of a cliff, looking out across the Irish Sea to the Mull of Kintyre in Scotland. On a good day, with the sun sparkling off the intense blue of the water, Scotland seems so close you might feel like you could swim across in an afternoon. Young Roger watches the waves glitter and the sun glint off the rocks. He climbs over the stones of the ancient ruins finding secret crevices and hiding places, and dreams his own private dreams.

Perhaps it is because he is the baby of the family, and so suffered most the cruel rupture of maternal love, that he develops true compassion for his fellow man. Perhaps it is simply his disposition to be thoughtful, kind, and considerate. Whatever the reason, Roger decides on a life of service to others. When he is barely twenty years old, the tall and stately young gentleman joins the British Foreign Service and is sent to far-off Mozambique. He is to act as envoy representing British interests in that long-colonised chunk of Africa taken over by Portugal in 1500. With experience under his belt, some years later Roger is asked to travel to deepest, darkest Africa, the Congo, to check out some nasty rumours about how King Leopold of Belgium is treating the workers on his rubber plantations. Now this is a bit rich, considering the British record of imperialist indignities in their own colonial nations. However, let's just tell the story of Sir Roger, and bypass the great ironies of which another entire book could well be written!

Roger, yet to be knighted for his efforts, is, in 1903, almost forty years old, strikingly handsome, and so well trained in the correct stance and portrayal of a gentleman that he can do nothing else but exemplify to all who cross his path the true embodiment of Victorian manhood. It is merely the truth to observe that in photos of his younger days, wearing a British uniform, he comes across as a tad cocky. His uniformed chest is puffed out like a red frigate bird announcing his presence to the world and Roger clearly maintains his untarnished male ego. However, in 1903 his chest deflates, his cockiness evaporates in the heat and his tender heart is exposed and shredded by the unimaginable and disturbing awareness of extreme cruelty, brutality, denigration, and otherwise demonic behaviour of those in power towards those powerless and pitiful persons under their control.

Through sweltering humidity in the middle of dense jungle, Roger watches as men, women and children are systematically brutalised with such cavalier nonchalance on the one hand and such intense determination on the other, that he feels he is drowning in his own outraged indignation and anger. His diplomatic status on foreign soil does not permit him to change the terrible circumstances of the enslaved indigenous population, but by God, he will effect change somehow, if for tomorrow. He picks up his weapon of choice – his pen – and writes. In small leather-bound journals, he collects the damning facts – the facts of the indigenous people who are subjugated by the Belgian King, kept in cages, and routinely tortured for minor misdemeanours such as asking for more food for their half-starved children. He writes down names, not only of perpetrators, but of the native innocents. He fights off nausea as he describes the indignities to their person that no human being should have to recount, much less suffer. Yes, Roger spares himself no detail. We will commend him by saying he gave a voice to the voiceless, the powerless, the oppressed. Roger understands that each man, woman, and child must be seen and felt to be just that, a man, a woman, or a child, without regard to colour or race or custom. He writes until he can write no more. Then he takes his journals and uses them to compile an official report. And what a report it is. So startling, so compelling, so compassionate, so indignant, that even the gross imperialists of the European world are shocked and appalled. They work together to eliminate the suffering and give King Leopold the boot out of the Congo.

Roger is rewarded for his efforts by a slathering of praise and honours. He retains his now humble, gentlemanly ways, however, and seeing that his actions had the desired result he feels compelled to travel to Peru when he gets word of similar atrocities in the rubber plantations of that country. This time it is the Putumayo Indians who are treated abominably. Roger repeats the successful steps he followed before, and quickly gets out his journals to take notes. No sooner is he finished writing this report, than he is recalled to England to receive a knighthood for his labours. By this time he is feeling poorly: the hot, humid climates of Africa and South America have wreaked havoc on Sir Roger's health, and he is beginning to suffer chronic pain, breathing problems and his eyes, which have seen atrocities no man should see, are beginning to rebel. Sir Roger realises his health has been permanently compromised and leaves the British Foreign Service, famous, if not rich, and still every bit a distinguished, handsome gentleman, with only the lines on his face telling the story of his suffering. He shocks his very British compatriots when he returns to his homeland to take up the cause of the Irish rebels.

This is itself a great irony. After all, Roger's family hails from the British ascendency in Ireland. Born an Irishman, his teenage years were spent living in Galgorm Castle, an estate of two hundred and fifty acres at a time when your average Irishman thought five acres a massive farm. It is an estate that housed some of William of Orange's army, the very same who trounced the Catholics in 1690 at the Battle of the Boyne. Roger's six years in the castle studying may have been the impetus for him to leave Ireland altogether as soon as his studies were over. The castle, if the locals are to be believed, is haunted by a relative who had sold his soul to the devil for a treasure of gold. Perhaps it was Roger's underdeveloped Catholic sensibilities that compelled him out of that place. Or perhaps it was the atmosphere of the north of Ireland, of Ulster, where Catholics made up the poor and the working-class minority, allowed residency, put up with, only for their labours in industries that the Protestant, British northerners despised. Did Roger know that his mother had secretly, and against her husband's wishes, baptised him a Catholic shortly before her death?

At any rate, Roger comes home. He is a different man from the man who left in his bright red uniform. Sir Roger has become a man of vision, a man far ahead of his time. He is a man who sees people of every race, colour, or custom as worthy of respect, not to mention self-determination. And so, in line with the great ironies of life, Sir Roger, Knight of the British Realm, raised by ultra-Protestant British nationalists, who lived in a castle held at one time by the ultimate conqueror William of Orange, comes home to Ireland a rebel. He begins to use all his formidable diplomatic powers to aid and abet the colonised poor of Ireland in their fight for freedom from British oppression. In other words, he joins the secret Irish Republican Brotherhood.

James and Seán read the papers. They, like everyone around them, are riveted by this, the last trial of the heroes of the Easter Week Rebellion and by any estimation the most puzzling. Everyone else who was tried or deported was if not Catholic, a known Irish nationalist and actually participated in some way in the Rising. Roger, however, is not guilty of this. He was incarcerated at the time of the rebellion and while in jail, told his captors the details that he was aware of, begging his former comrades to put a stop to the rising so that his Irish friends would not put their lives at risk.

Some did not believe him, but those top officials who did, they enjoyed the notion of a little action, trouncing the Irish once again, and let it go ahead just for the military and political satisfaction of putting the screws to those damn rebel Irish who just will not give up on their silly little dreams of independence. It is a little bit of sport to liven up the spring.

It is June 29, 1916, two months since the Rising and weeks since everyone else has been dealt with, sentenced, executed, or imprisoned. The paper details Roger's crime. All spring he was off in Germany, negotiating with the Germans for guns. He is good at this and has done it before. But war is raging, so despite his prestige and diplomatic aura, all he could procure was twenty thousand rifles, a mere tenth of the two hundred thousand he had hoped to transport back to Ireland. Nevertheless, he is escorted home via a German submarine accompanied by a disguised German ship carrying the rifles. Alas, the sensational details of the story reveal that his return was overshadowed by calamity. Three IRA men, sent by O'Hegarty, are killed in a car accident on their way to meet him and pick up the rifles. Without the expected help, the ship is intercepted, the crew taken as prisoners of war and brought to Cork Harbour. But the Germans have thought ahead, and as the ship approaches Cork, they craftily scuttle their own ship rather than have it taken over by the British. It is sunk, all twenty thousand rifles plummeting through the dark blue waters to the depths of the ocean floor. Roger meanwhile has disembarked the German submarine near Banna Strand, a lonely stretch of sandy coastline not far from Tralee on the southwestern coast. His IRA rescuers are nowhere to be found because unknown to Roger, their bodies lie crushed and broken at the bottom of a cliff. Thin, sickly, Sir Roger takes refuge in an ancient Celtic ring fort not far from the beach, where he can rest until such time as the promised IRA men find him. From this moment it will be forever known as Casement's Fort. Sadly, he is quickly discovered and like a true aristocratic British nobleman at odds with the King he is taken straight away across the Irish Sea to the Tower of London.

James and Seán ride their bikes across town to the offices of *The Cork Examiner.* People are clamouring around the front entrance. The young reporter who is charged with posting the latest run of the paper outside can barely push open the door. Seán jumps off his bike, fights through the crowd and calls out to the folks to back off. He pulls open the door and gives the fellow a hand posting the paper behind the glass. As soon as it is up, eyes are riveted by the large picture of the handsome Sir Roger with his piercing eyes and well-groomed beard. A smaller shot of the car that holds him coming out of the gates of the court show the many Londoners also gripped by the story, who gather at the court throughout the trial. A woman at the front of the crowd reads aloud the article for all to hear. The trial has taken a mere three days. Neither James nor Seán is surprised by the verdict. Guilty. They are however, surprised by the sentence. Execution by hanging. Surely, they will not hang their own Knight! Seán and James argue back and forth.

Don't be an eejit, Jimmy, exclaims Seán. Of course they will hang him, and dance while they're doing it! Didn't they just shoot Connolly sitting in a chair, a few weeks ago? He doesn't have a chance. Just think of those rifles sinking to the bottom of the harbour, almost at hands reach! What a bleedin' waste, replies James. And you are wrong, Seán my friend, the whole world is going to screech. He looks like a Brit, he talks like a Brit, and as far as the world is concerned, he is a Brit. So, rich people everywhere will help him out. Sure, the court is just acting tough so they can look merciful later. Bastards!

As it turns out Seán and James are both right. Famous people everywhere call out in protest. Letters are written, notices are posted in the papers by the likes of George Bernard Shaw and Sir Arthur Conan Doyle. Ridicule and outrage at the British establishment are manifested in a searing poem by none other than William Butler Yeats. Sir Roger's lawyers mount an appeal. Sir Roger, however, does not hold out any hope. He knows the British better than they know themselves and anticipates their every move. They will destroy my character and my reputation before they execute me, Roger murmurs to his lawyer. Days fly by. He is ill and very tired. He closes his eyes and sees the Irish Sea sparkling far into the distance from the ancient church at Drumnakil Point. He ponders his life of fifty-one years. Such a long time now since he sat on the cliff and dreamed his dreams. He asks to see a Catholic priest. Roger converts, repents the sins of his life, such as they are, in his final and only confession and receives the sacrament. Quietly he draws the priest close. Bury me by Drumnakil Church on the Murlough Bay, he whispers, if you can.

The clamouring for mercy, leniency, clemency, stops abruptly. The British have tilted the tables in their favour. They release to the rich and famous protestors a copy of a secret diary, purportedly written by Roger. Look! They craw like a murder of crows surrounding a dying deer. Look at the filth your Irish Casement has been at these years. He is a raving homo, and a nasty one at that, with a ravenous appetite for young, defenceless, native boys.

There is a quiet, collective moan from the world. The rich and famous turn their heads and look away, and in the early morning hours of August 3, 1916, Roger, stripped of the Sir, just Roger Casement, Irishman and rebel, is hanged by the neck until he is dead. At that very hour, every Irish Catholic prisoner in every prison on British soil goes down on his knees on whatever cold stone floor he is standing and prays aloud in unison a rosary for the soul of their comrade in arms. The bravest man I ever did execute, the hangman whispers reverentially to himself. Despite heartrending pleas from his family, they strip Roger's body as a final indignity and toss him naked in quicklime in the prison exercise yard. No gravestone required.

O'Hegarty, though he knew Casement and had helped arrange for pickup of the rifles, is more concerned about the three dead IRA men who were wasted on an assignment that O'Hegarty had little confidence in. A long-time home-grown spy himself, he realised that sailing a German submarine and a thinly disguised German boat past that ultimate fighting force, the British Navy, in the middle of the most frightening war they had ever fought, was an unlikely prospect. However, the attraction to guns is O'Hegarty's Achilles's heel, and to his eternal regret he supported the mission. Casement was a bit too much of a Brit for him anyway, and some of the secret Brotherhood did not trust him.

O'Hegarty moves on. He focuses on the present. He wonders how he might find out what they have done with Terrence and Tomás and how he might get word to them. He thinks of where he might find guns that he can steal and stockpile for a future day. He surveys the Volunteers and shakes his head. How on earth will this sorry lot who are left over after the roundups be trained to try again? With the executions and the initial enthusiasm to fight back, the young men everywhere were lining up to join in, but just a few weeks later, with the latest roundups and the disappearance to foreign shores of friends and family across Cork County, the newest Volunteers are losing heart. O'Hegarty rethinks Terrence and Tomás's last directive: lie low. He realises the wisdom and pulls only a certain few, long trusted comrades to him. He uses Seán and James as trustworthy runners and invisible collectors of information.

And so, James is drawn into the secret web of discreet intelligence gathering of which O'Hegarty is a master. James, you might say, becomes his protégé. And this protégé, like all the poor young men of Ireland, gets about long distances through the endurance of his own body, riding a bicycle up and down hills and across lonely country roads in the black of night, through rain and sleet, and on the odd joyous occasion, an afternoon of warm, dazzling sunshine.

It is on just such an afternoon that James comes face to face with the enemy in the form of a jovial police constable whom he discovers watching him closely as he disembarks his bicycle and leans it against the shop window, directly across from the RIC station. James is there to observe, for the third day in a row, to ascertain the number of men coming and going and the number of arms that may be held inside the station. O'Hegarty has been on a bent about guns. The problem being, they have none, not since the RIC scooped the entire cache that had been hidden in Tomás's office, days after the rising. O'Hegarty has not shared with James the rationale for this series of observations, only to observe and report back each night, once the final shift has moved into the station.

It is a glorious August afternoon, possibly the warmest day of the month yet, and James is but a couple of weeks into his eighteenth year. He is dressed like any young man his age, a cap on his mop of auburn hair, a shirt without collar and a pair of roughly spun trousers held up by suspenders. He looks as innocent as the day is long. But the constable looking across the road at him now is himself a man of strong observational skills. He has noticed James these past few days and wonders at his repetitive behaviour, a boy who is not from this part of town. He strolls across the street and calls out to him. Good afternoon young man, I'm Constable Dwyer. And you are?

This is the moment that James has practised for. O'Hegarty warned him it would happen suddenly, out of nowhere, and that he must lie with the tongue of a serpent, while he holds his ground like a well-heeled gentleman, calm but firm. James takes off his cap and nods his head at the constable. Afternoon sir, he says. And while his voice is smooth, his hand crushes his cap behind his back, absorbing the energy produced by the excess adrenalin that is being pumped out at an alarming rate in his body. He is preparing himself to give false information to the constable. This is something he has never done. He has practised several times with O'Hegarty, but this is the real deal. I am John, sir, John Fitzgibbon. James has chosen this name, a combination of his father's first name and the last name of a distant cousin so that he will recall it easily if ever he has the misfortune to come across this particular constable again.

I haven't seen you around this part of town before. Are you new to the area? he asks as his eyes take in the details of James's body, categorising his weight, colouring, clothing, and disposition. Now James must think fast. He needs an excuse that will account for the past three days, in case he has been noticed prior to today. He notes a small bakery called Desmond's Loaves a few doors down this main street of shops and businesses. I am just here to pick up some bread. My mother has taken a liking to the brown loaves from Desmond's. The constable glances over towards the bakery window. Yes indeed, he says. Desmond bakes a fine loaf, and with that he saunters on his way, satisfied that the young man with the rather large blue eyes has obviously been well brought up, taking care of his mama.

But taking care of his mama is pretty much the last thing on James's mind. His mama is still heartbroken about the state of young Edward's mangled hand, and blames James for it. His father has said little to him on the subject, more concerned with consoling and reassuring his wife. And so, James has retreated to life with Seán, who is also under training, so to speak, with O'Hegarty. Seán, like James, is reluctant to stay at home, where his sisters talk of nothing but his big brother Terrence, what he may be enduring at the hands of the British and, worse yet, the possibility of the same fate as Sir Roger. Both young men are therefore more apt than not to be found spending even more time at the call of O'Hegarty.

O'Hegarty is pondering the treatment and whereabouts of his friends when he is delivered of a gift. It is the best information he has had in weeks, and it comes on a warm summer afternoon when James and Seán pedal into the back lane behind his current hideaway in the city. As they stand in the tiny yard enjoying the summer sun, all three of them, they discuss the fate of their, until now, lost leaders. James and Seán have been out biking to a distant source who has confirmed O'Hegarty's information. So, you were right, Sir, 'tis in Wales, a place called Frongoch. That is where they both are. Together with eighteen hundred others. Can you imagine?

Eighteen hundred! Where do they keep them all? Sure, it must be a huge gaol!

It is not a gaol, boys. It is a bloody dilapidated distillery, falling apart so it is. He steps into his hideaway and returns with an atlas of the British Isles as James and Seán look on with curiosity. He searches long and hard before he finds a tiny dot in the mid-section of the north of Wales. A tiny dot in the middle of nowhere, surrounded by forest and hills. The Welsh themselves probably don't even know the place exists. But exist it does.

There is a small brick building for keeping the British soldiers and a series of derelict cabins and decrepit huts for the inmates. Up until the Easter Rebellion, it had been a prisoner of war camp for German POWs. But the lucky Germans are moved elsewhere and in come the Irish. The only blessing they have is to be found in the commander of the camp, who is soft-hearted and not the sharpest tool in the shed. Tomás and many others, some who escaped detection as leaders of the rebellion such as Michael Collins, but who were suspect all the same, will spend their days learning to be defiant and difficult and wrestle from the British every possible concession.

But it is hard going and the British, despite their inept commander, are reticent to give in to these men. They allow them free rein, dispensing food each morning that they can cook themselves and stay clear of their hurling games and discussion groups. The men organise. Of the eighteen hundred incarcerated they determine the skills of everyone present. Who are the teachers? Who the speakers of Gaelic? Who the speakers of other foreign tongues? Who are the well-read, the builders, the farmers, the singers, the storytellers, the athletes? Everyone has a skill they can share. And so, despite the cold and the inadequate food they hold not-so-secret classes in Irish, maths, philosophy, politics and anything else the men wish to learn. They have hurling tournaments and running races. They learn to stick up for each other and work as a team to undermine British control. When one man is harassed for coughing during roll call, all the men cough. When one man stands up in defiance, all the men stand up. The British are quickly sick to death of this crew who refuse to comply or defer and make every minute of the day a trial for the guards.

In response, some of the men are quickly taken elsewhere.

Terrence is one of these and is moved to Reading Gaol, of Oscar Wilde fame, west of London and there he spends his days making demands of his jailors for political prisoner status. He drives them to distraction with his constant carry on about Ireland Free, and refusal to recognise British Law. In truth they would love nothing more than to get rid of him.

As part and parcel of their own training, James and Seán are sent to travel about and vet various households. O'Hegarty is already thinking ahead to a time in the future when the Volunteers might be resurrected, and Part II of the rebellion ensue. To this end he needs as many places of refuge as possible. And so, he sends his two young protégés to get a feel for households where he might lay his trust. O'Hegarty understands the importance of networks, but being the suspicious man that he is, he wishes to be sure that the households who not so long ago pledged their allegiance to Tomás and to Terrence, are in fact, trustworthy. The two young men will find reasons to stop in, spend a night, or join in animated conversations, and all their resulting impressions of the occupants will be relayed to O'Hegarty. They wander from home to home, sometimes together, sometimes alone, and they begin to notice a pattern of who is welcoming and who would rather see their coattails. Talk is of politics, of Sir Roger, of Terrence and Tomás and whatever boys and young men have been dragged from their homes and taken by the Brits. They come to see the pattern of sentiments among their neighbours and friends: who is adamantly against, who is ambivalent, who is wishing to strike back, who is fearful and wishing to hide out of sight.

The variety of feelings and responses surprises them both. Let's face it, when you are young, you believe that your point of view is the only viable one. You are self-righteous. James and Seán are no different. They say nothing to their benefactors but talk between themselves of who said what, who can be trusted, who it is better to stay away from. They check in with their families just enough to keep them from worrying. During the long summer days, they report to O'Hegarty and are sent on excursions far and wide. Often when he is to be found, they camp out in the tiny front room of his flat and talk long into the night, telling him of who and where and what was said. O'Hegarty's eyes flash from time to time, but he wisely keeps his thoughts to himself and guides the boys in how to conduct themselves to keep suspicion from touching them. In their waking hours they mostly keep an eye out for movement of police in the barracks. Where are they going, who are they questioning, and what are they looking for? These are the foundational questions that James and Seán are trained to ask themselves continuously. Not only do they ask themselves, they discover that tossing casual questions out to others – friends, neighbours, acquaintances, even passers-by – results in sometimes unexpected information. They learn that no detail is too small for O'Hegarty's seemingly limitless capacity to hold, categorise, synthesise, and instantly recall information.

Before November rolls around, Seán and James have provided a long list of police constables from around Cork City and even into the outlying towns and villages: names, stations, addresses, family details, known associates and the like. In the process they have cross referenced a different kind of list altogether, one that they did not expect and could never have predicted. They are compiling a list of Irishmen and Irishwomen who spend a little too much time talking to particular constables. However, James and Seán have not yet developed the sixth sense that will serve them so well in the future. That terrible knowledge will dawn on them slowly and painfully as the wind and snow beat down on them, still riding their bicycles up and down the hills of Cork City through the worst winter in fifty years.

The weather demands their attention, barricading the young men inside when they would much rather be out and about. But not only are demands made by the weather. Demands are also being put on James by his family. He must find work. Enough of sailing about up to his eyeballs in Volunteer work, under the auspices of that O'Hegarty man. It is a dangerous job, so it is, with all of the known Volunteers taken away and thrown behind bars. James could be next. Besides, that O'Hegarty is a queer fellow indeed, close-mouthed and cranky, easy to provoke, and shocking to listen to. And never is he to be found at Mass like a decent Irishman. James's family does not appreciate the connection, despite understanding how influential he is.

Seán's family, on the other hand, knows O'Hegarty well. O'Hegarty's wife, Magda, is close friends with Seán's oldest sister, Mary. She is proud that Seán seems to be under O'Hegarty's wing. A trusted IRB man like O'Hegarty will make sure their boy is trained well. But Seán has a day job. Every MacSwiney has to work; the family after all has struggled for years after the desertion by their father and with Terrence out of the picture, every penny is required. Practically a genius, Seán could run numbers in his head faster than anyone in the entire school. He quickly found work due to this obvious mental dexterity. Now it is James's turn. Despite the possibility of a scholarship, James is happy to kiss school goodbye forever. There is no question of proceeding forth to University College Cork. It will be training for a job or a job itself. James agrees mostly because he does not like lacking a few quid in his pockets. His father, who up until this time was generous with James, often sharing his winnings of the greyhound races with his boys, has, following the fiasco of Edward's fingers, become suddenly reticent with his son and more careful with his money.

James decides a junior clerk of accounts is his best bet, just like Seán who already holds a similar position. He heads about the city looking for possibilities. One of his evenings spent out is with a family whose father works at The Cork Distillery. Sure, they are always looking for a smart lad who can work quickly with a pencil. Well, I am just the man they need, replies James with a smile on his face. I will charm them into hiring me!

His first day on the job, as James is disembarking from his bicycle inside the distillery office gates, he is witness to an embarrassing encounter with the Murphy family who owns the distillery. They are the wealthiest Catholic family in all of Cork. And of course, being wealthy, they prefer to stay that way, as would any of us, and so support the status quo, that is, the British political structure. Somehow, through unknown means, the Murphys have come out on top. They managed to grow their whiskey-producing facility over the years and maintain ownership, despite the politics and the Protestant ownership of most of the other major industries in the city. Part of the reason may be that back in 1825, the three Murphy brothers who started the distillery, Daniel, James, and Jeremiah, were smart enough to buy from the British a solid structure, an old military barracks, originally a woollen mill, far outside the confines of the city in a small, unremarkable town. However, the place was built like a fortress, four stories tall with walls of solid stone and floors of thick wooden planks, the size of which are rarely seen today. The British were certainly laughing all the way to the bank because they believed that the old building was worthless, and pointless for any practical purpose. But it was the three brothers who had the last laugh. They had made a pot still for brewing whiskey that remains the largest pot still in the world, holding an amazing thirty-one thousand six hundred and forty-eight gallons! And by God, did they make whiskey! In 1916, the distillery, though the three brothers are long gone, pumps out one million bottles of whiskey a year, aged in oak casks of which there are seven thousand in the still sturdy building. All those years of making money hand over fist hones the Murphy family into a secretive, slightly paranoid group of extreme British nationalists. They send their children to school in London, and the matriarch of the family, a somewhat demented autocrat when it comes to her children, rules their lives with an iron fist. Muriel, the youngest daughter of the family, however, will not be ruled.

As James jumps off his bicycle outside the city office, he hears a shrill laugh, and a haughty, defiant jeer. From around the corner of the building he listens as the voice of a young woman with a very pronounced Oxford accent commands the attention of someone. Bloody hell, James thinks to himself, I thought it was the Irish owned this place. Nicholas, I will not be kept in my room like a criminal in a jail. I do not give a whit what mother says, I will be leaving this week, whether she likes it or not. Muriel, responds a male voice, Mother will not have it, and I do not like it one bit. Those people are thugs and criminals, they are upstarts and troublemakers. Their only prospects are the gallows or the firing squad, just like their friends. Well brother dear, you can tell mother or not tell mother, but I will be travelling to England and Wales to acquire the needed information. I made a promise, and I will keep it. And Nicholas, have heart. I must see that Terrence is in good form. The rumours are that the men are half starved and frozen.

James stands with his bicycle in hand not knowing which way to turn. He should proceed forward and park his bike around the back of the building, but he does not wish to intercept the argument. He stands at the corner and pauses for a second. At that moment, the most beautiful woman he has ever seen steps around the corner and slaps right into him. She is dressed in a thick, luxurious, lambswool coat that covers her body completely. But it does not cover her face. And her face glows. Partly this is because she is annoyed and hence flushed; partly it is just her general state of affairs, to be distractingly gorgeous with a radiant complexion, large, luminous, wide-set eyes and heavy chiselled lips. This goddess confidently nods at James. My apologies, wafts from her mouth and floats in the air, and then she continues on her way as her older brother, Mr Murphy, James's soon-to-be new boss storms after her. Bloody hell says James to the younger worker in the office. What was that? That, he replies, was Miss Muriel, the boss's little sister. Such a princess. But a real looker, don't you think?

Later that evening, when James is having a pint with Seán, he recalls the beautiful woman. You should have seen her Seán. I've never seen the likes of her and aren't likely to again anytime soon. You best get your mind off her Jimmy, sure that is Terrence's girl, Muriel. He has got it bad for her. God knows if he will ever see her again. James looks at Seán as if he has three heads. What the hell are you on about? She is the boss's little sister! Do I need to remind you who my boss is? Besides she talks just like a Brit and is dressed like the bloody queen. Terrence wouldn't be having anything to do with the likes of that, even if she is a goddess. Well, she is a goddess that works with Mary, my sister, and the other women in Cumann na mBan, helping out the Volunteers. So don't judge a book by its cover Jimmy. James learns that he doesn't know as much as he thought he did about the Volunteers. He determines to become more observant of his own organisation, not just the police and other targets that O'Hegarty has him watching closely.

This opportunity is afforded him with the announcement by O'Hegarty that he has a grand idea thanks to James and Seán. James and Seán look at each other and wonder exactly what they might have inspired. O'Hegarty has thought carefully about the quality of work that James and Seán have provided. Despite holding down full-time jobs, the two young men on their bicycles have provided valuable surveillance, messaging, and an all-round mishmash of services that O'Hegarty has decided he would like to increase tenfold or even a hundred-fold. He suffers a stroke of genius when he imagines an entire fleet of James's and Seáns to do his bidding. He decides to create a cycling company within the 1st Cork Brigade.

The idea comes to him on a snowy December afternoon, as the wind blows across dull grey skies and he waits for word from James who must travel to an outlying village with a request for information. O'Hegarty knows that it is a wicked day to be out on a bicycle and that the weather must be slowing his man down. He ponders the idea of a chain of cyclists, who are always fresh and so can ride like the devil for ten miles and pass the message on to another fresh cyclist who can ride just as fast for the next ten miles. No need for breaks, for stops for water, no diminishing times as distances increase, no time needed for rest and recovery. Yes, it is genius, and the Good Lord knows that the Volunteer Hall is packed with young lads who might jump at the chance to be part of an elite squad. The idea is cemented in his mind when James arrives home two hours later than expected, his face half frozen, and his trouser ripped and torn. He has obviously taken a tumble and a bad one at that. The flesh of his knees peeking through the tears is so red and distressed, O'Hegarty fears permanent damage in the form of frostbite. But he says nothing to James except, of course, what took you so long?

Christmas arrives with a blast of cold air, but a warm ray of sunshine in the form of a magnanimous miracle, doubtless a result of the prayers of the people of Ireland that have been banging on Heaven's gate since the executions. It is the release of the prisoners of Frongoch. The British, it seems, have decided that holding on to all of those troublemakers in prison is only making a tense situation worse and they hope that after the example of the executions, and the nasty dose of prison, the whole lot of them will head home with their tails between their legs and shut up about Irish politics. Besides, reports of the terrible conditions the men are living under, with poor food, lacking proper sanitation, no suitable shelter, and no extra clothing, has newspapers around the country badmouthing the British. And even the British resent bad PR.

Tomás arrives home to an ecstatic welcome from his family, their friends, and the men of the 1st Cork Brigade. Then, he picks up just where he left off. Thinner and wiser, he seems to be able to find time where none exists and is in a whirl of activity, organising, scheming, planning, observing the new recruits, and analysing the vast array of O'Hegarty's information, some of which is compliments of James and Seán. He is pleased with the idea of a cyclist company and projects a vast array of services, each more dangerous than the next, that can be derived from the young men on wheels.

The cyclist company is an attractive prospect for many. It means the boys who join will have an edge over their friends, most of whom wish to become active in the cause, doing something worthwhile, instead of just meeting and drilling. Despite the fact that they must supply their own bicycle, train for hours on end on weeknights and weekends, learn to change tires, mend ruptures, dive and roll into hedges, their bikes crashing on top of them, and a select number of other potentially lifesaving moves, the cyclist company attracts a large contingent of young men. After all, riding a bicycle is their main means of transportation and so all of them feel like experts. However, only thirty have the drive to stick it out. They are led by a quiet, polite engineer, who despite his gentlemanly disposition and impressive education is a rebel of the same ilk as O'Hegarty. His name is Donnchadha MacNeilus, usually just called Denis, and his views are rock solid, not speculative. He is for Ireland Free and that is that. Within his like-minded crew of secret Republican Brethren including O'Hegarty, he is respected for his pragmatic approach to problem-solving the eternal dispute with the British, issue by issue, location by location, politics by politics. So enthusiastic is he with the idea of a cyclist squad that he offers to train and direct it himself. In his calm and indirect manner, he manages to steal a British Army training manual for cyclists and follows its precepts faithfully.

James helps MacNeilus out as a pacer, riding ahead of a team of cyclists, teaching them to conserve their energy while moving quickly and steadily. Although O'Hegarty prefers to keep him away from the main crew, James meets a new friend. He is twenty-one years old and has just arrived from County Kerry, a fresh-faced farm boy who is looking to make his fortune, or at least get lucky enough to make a living in the city. His name is Florrie O'Donoghue. His first stop in Cork City was the Volunteer Hall, and O'Hegarty, always on the lookout for new recruits, could scent out this young man, so much older and wiser in spirit than others his age, a soulmate: a tough, fearless type of his own sort. Florrie has joined up with Denis on the cyclist squad. James and Seán sense in Florrie a dedication to the cause and a strong vein of common sense running through his thought. He is not much of a cyclist at the start, but they sense his determination and admire him for it. He trains hard and after a few short weeks can keep pace with his new friends, who only attend intermittently.

March 1917 ends with the faint tease of warmth after the fierce beatings of winter. But it is just a trick of Mother Nature. She is not yet ready to soften her hold on the country. During the opening days of April, coming up to the first anniversary of the Easter Rebellion, the temperature drops, the skies darken, the wind howls and the snow begins to fall. It falls for three days straight. Everyone is locked inside their homes, and woe to them that have used the last of their winter fuel. The sheep are found frozen and buried by thick packing snow in the fields, the elderly and infirm are found dead in their beds, and people mutter to each other, Will we ever see the end of this winter? But incrementally the days grow longer, and the cyclist company training extends in rigour and demands. Each man is required to ride ten miles in the fastest possible time from their home to the home of the next man on the team, all the while avoiding RIC stations or places where the local police constables tend to be found. Each team builds a relay in a particular direction out of the city and to the neighbouring towns. More importantly, each man is required to find on his route, homes of trustworthy friends or acquaintances, families who support the cause and can extend hospitality from time to time if need be, were their man to find himself pursued by the Peelers, or in need of sustenance, rest, or a victim of some unforeseen calamity.

In this way O'Hegarty builds a series of extending circles from the centre of the city to the countryside in all directions. Over time it will become a vast network of safe homes, messengers, rescuers, spies and hiding places. Rebel Cork will come alive, a web of Republican Freedom Fighters, available on occasion, in a pinch, or routinely dedicated to the cause, but there when they are needed. They are not yet aware just how much they will be needed in the months and years to come.

O'Hegarty has a good feeling about his latest recruit. He knows a keeper when he finds one. He brings Florrie into the secret Brotherhood and once MacNeilus has completed the training, he appoints Florrie leader of the Cyclist squad. He is not disappointed with his choice. No sooner has Florrie taken over than he is struck by a brilliant idea. An idea whispered in his ear by the angels themselves. He looks at O'Hegarty and grins. O'Hegarty snaps back at Florrie. What the hell is wrong with you? Florrie, with a sly smile replies, sure, you've been wanting to find out more about that RIC Barracks in the city centre, haven't ye? Well, I noticed the postman making his way up the big hill. I don't see why one of our boys can't borrow his bag of letters before he gets to the RIC station, and return it to him once you have had a look-see! O'Hegarty stares at his newest protégé. Bloody hell, he murmurs to himself. Bloody hell!

There is much work to be done before their scheme can be realised. They have invested time if not money in training the cyclist squad, especially the forerunners, James and Seán. They cannot lose a man through a stupid mistake. The postmen are watched carefully. Their times of arrival and departure from the area of the RIC station in question are clocked and timed. James and Seán are sent on this, their first foray into actual criminality. Should they be caught, they will not get off easy. James and Seán spend a few days getting to know the habits of the postman in question. Once they have the timing of his duties sorted out, they focus on the man himself and follow him to his regular pub, randomly drawing him into conversation. However, the fellow has a head on his shoulders, and he is careful to keep his political opinions to himself. They cannot seem to draw out any Republican sympathies.

James speaks fiercely to Seán. The hell with it, let's just do it. We will pull him into the lane and borrow his bag. I'll run it down to O'Hegarty while you keep him company. It won't take long; he is only interested in the mail to the station. They don't get much. I'll be back with it in fifteen minutes. Seán sighs. He does not mind so much riding around delivering messages or watching stations or people and reporting back. But this is taking things a step too far. What if he will have no part of it? Then what? Do you expect me to tie him up? Gag him and throw him in a shed? And what if the peelers change their route and walk straight by? Then what? James scowls at his friend. For God's sake man, what is wrong with you? Isn't this just what we joined up for? A little action? T'will be alright Seán, all you have to do is chat about the weather to him and remind him of his national duty to his fellow Irishmen! With a sigh Seán replies, no Jimmy, you stay and keep him in place, I will run the mail over. Even better, replies James, it's a deal.

The following afternoon, as the postman begins his trek up the big hill, James is walking down. He strategically bumps into his latest pub friend at the entrance to a side laneway. He gives the fellow a friendly hello with a big smile on his face as he grabs his elbow and half pushes, half drags him into the lane. See here, what the hell? At that moment, from the opposite direction, Seán clips through the lane on his bike with his cap pulled low on his face and his jumper pulled up over his chin. He comes to an abrupt stop just far enough down the laneway to make it hard to distinguish who he is. What's this all about, the postman is nervous and upset. I thought you were okay, he splutters at James. Well, I guess I was wrong there, and I don't have a penny to my name so let me go back to work. It is not your money we want, sure, just a look-see at your mailbag. Well, there is no money in there I can assure ye. Look, we just need to take a look in the mailbag. It's a matter of national importance if you get my meaning!

By this time the smile on James's face is long gone. And the nerves of Seán further down the lane are obvious. The postman sees that these two fellas mean business. He hands over his bag for them to look through, but to his surprise, James carries the bag up to Seán who shoulders it and pedals away as fast as he arrived. James is left with his captive, who tries to run, but finds that James's young wiry body is not as easy to get past as he would like. When he punches James in the face, he realises he has made a big mistake, for the response from James is a ferocious one. The man finds himself on his posterior looking at the sky with James sitting on top of him, his right eye feeling about the way James's left eye looks. Why'd ye have to go and do that? James queries the postman, Are you an Irishman or not? Sure, will you not help your fellow Irishmen on a small matter like looking in the mailbag? T'isn't a lot to ask! When the postman stares back at James, lost for words, James begins his lecture on Irish history with a list of the sixteen executed men of the Easter Rebellion, and a recitation of the Irish Proclamation of Independence.

For God's sake man, get off me! The postman comes alive. I see ye are Volunteers up to some business and I am happy to comply, but I do not want to lose my job. It is the British who pay my wages. I have a family, unlike you young ruffians, without a worry in your head. Never mind, you won't be losing your job, everything will be returned in a few minutes. As the men wait for Seán's return, they resume their previous positions standing inside the laneway. The postman paces back and forth while James leans against the wall and takes out his precious pack of smokes. He offers one to the postman. What's your name lad, the man asks as he pulls a smoke from the pack. Well, now if I told you that I'd have to kill you. James enjoys his joke and laughs heartily at his own wit. The postman stares at him in wonder. I don't know what this is about, but I hope we don't cross paths again! On the contrary mate, I have no doubt we will be crossing paths regularly!

O'Hegarty is so delighted with the outcome of the mailbag adventure that he almost smiles. He foresees a regular inspection on every mail route leading to a police station in the city. James is ecstatic. Seán is morose.

Seán is morose not only about the likelihood of many more mailbag escapades in his near future. He is morose about his brother Terrence. He is morose about his job prospects. He is morose about life in general. The Great War is raging still. There is talk of conscription to the British Army of all young Irish able-bodied men. He has asked for a raise from his boss and been told no. His brother Terrence returned home from Reading Gaol in February and was quickly rearrested. Muriel went to visit him, and they have become engaged without knowing if he will ever get back home. Politics is getting ugly. The new Sinn Féin party is running a man from jail in a by-election. 'Vote him in to get him out' is their slogan. His family home is overwhelmed with talk of Terrence and his engagement to the richest, most beautiful Catholic girl in the land, and the by-election, even though it is far north of Cork, in the heart of the island. Seán wonders what a man languishing in a British prison can do for the country. People have lost their minds. And just recently there have been some mysterious cases of flu popping up. A young lad down the street spent the day in school feeling fine and collapsed that evening, dead the next day. I am leaving this place, thinks Seán to himself, I want out.

James on the other hand is feeling good. People are talking politics all the time. Your man in jail, running in the by-election, McGuinness, wins by one percent of the vote. It is a clear victory for Sinn Féin, the new kid on the political block, and a disaster for the old guard, the Home Rulers who couldn't make Home Rule happen. And now there is talk of a general amnesty. There is an ever so slight possibility that all of the men of Easter 1916 will be coming home from the vast array of gaols in which they have been locked up. Things are looking up. James wonders what the future will bring if the rebels return. Whatever it is, he thinks to himself, I want in.

LOVE
CHAPTER 4
JUNE 1917 – 1919

It is June and the hedgerows of wild roses that line the roads and laneways leading out of the city are in bloom, pink and red and yellow and white and releasing their intoxicating bouquet into the atmosphere. A carpet of purple violets and blue forget-me-nots have temporarily overlaid the green in farmers' fields, and wild honeysuckle vines with their deep orange and red blossoms are twisting and twining their way around fence posts and forgotten gates, wafting their heady scent into the air. The land is lush, the grass thick and soft, the distant hills hazy with warmth and fragrance. The ancient stone circle of Drombeg awaits the summer solstice to define the alignment of the sun and the earth and to assure man that nature has not forgotten its timeless role in the universe.

The druids, before the time of Fin Barre, before the time of Colmcille, even before the time of Patrick, used this stone circle and the great performance of the summer solstice alignment with slight partitions in the encircling rocks, as a place of validation and allegiance to their beliefs. They performed their sacrifices to the gods and their peculiar funerary rites in the hopes of succour in the form of rich harvests, fertile women, and protection from their enemies. James is hardly aware of the existence of Drombeg and the various other ancient stone monuments, though they are only a few miles from the city. However, he is about to discover the thing with which the druids strived to impress their clansmen: magic. James is about to learn that magic exists. If you were to attempt to explain its existence without some form of experience it would be impossible, because magic, much like love, is irrational and unpredictable. It arrives without invitation and performs wantonly. It leaves you startled, discombobulated, slightly unhinged, and if it is true magic, brimming over with wonder, awe, and even love.

In this June of 1917 while the rest of the world prepares for the barbaric slaughter of each other at Passchendaele, Irishmen are only yet dreaming of conquering their enemies. They are distracted by the magic that floats in with the warm air and clear skies in the form of the return of the men of the Easter Rising of 1916. Such a thing they never thought possible. Indeed, they believed that the British would grind their men into the ground before they would ever think of releasing them. But somehow, somewhere, somebody important within the British hierarchy decided to release them. A decision they are probably regretting now, as the Irish go mad, meeting their heroes at the docks of Dún Laoghaire, just south of Dublin, as they disembark from a cargo ship and are cheered, hugged, kissed, squeezed and generally manhandled by a surging crowd of thousands of elated countrymen.

James can feel the change in atmosphere that has permeated Cork. The sun shines. The birds sing. Hope, even happiness, is bubbling out of the earth and infecting everyone around him. As the men and boys return from months and months of incarceration far from home, they are labelled heroes. Given places of honour in the pubs by their mates, they tell their stories of the struggles and triumphs in the internment camps. The Volunteers arrive home to the embraces of mothers and fathers and family, but best of all to the sweet caresses of lovers. And if they did not have a lover before they left, they surely find one quickly. The scent of profuse roses seems to permeate the city. Cork has come alive and for a few short days the magic wafts in the air, in and out of windows, swirling around homes, down laneways and across the green hills of the city.

The magic of this beautiful month of June seems to be everywhere. Just a week earlier, Terrence, Seán's big brother, quietly weds the most beautiful woman in the world, the heiress Muriel Murphy, in a tiny chapel outside the town in England where he had just

While Dragging Our Hearts Behind Us

been released. The Republican friar, Father Augustine, performs the ceremony while the exhausted Terrence, with welts below his eyes, smiles his charming, contagious smile, and beams at his new wife. She has just turned twenty-five and obviously idolises her thirty-eight-year-old husband: poet, intellectual and rebel. Naturally it helps that even at his worst, fatigued and thin, he is handsome beyond words and the epitome of a good man. For the first time in her life, Muriel feels certain that she is truly blessed. Not by riches of which she is heiress, not by looks, of which she is well-aware, but by the love and care of a man who is not the least bit interested in her money, only mildly interested in her beauty, and gravely interested in the goodness of her soul.

For Muriel's goodness shines through her pricey clothes, and her outrageous beauty, which she does nothing to fortify or protect. She is, like Terrence, a confirmed rebel at heart, but with an eye to the women of Ireland, who suffer from poverty, chauvinism, and unfair treatment, especially those poor unfortunates foolish enough to find themselves with child but without husband. She has joined Cumann na mBan and done what little secretive work she can despite her high profile. Today, in June 1917, despite the uproar this marriage will cause between herself and her mother, despite the reservations of Terrence himself, despite the poverty of Terrence and his family, despite the prospects of a life of playing cat and mouse, hide and seek with the British, despite the potential danger of such a life, Muriel is supremely happy. Magic is in the air. They will enjoy it while they can, for it won't last long. Their marriage, their life together, like the lives and loves of so many rebels from the pages of Irish history, is doomed.

If you were to leaf through the heavy book of Irish history and see the lives of the rebels of any generation, you would be hard pressed to find any great romance that survived the British, the wars, or the rebellions. The two most famous rebels of all, Robert Emmet and Wolfe Tone, heroes to Irishmen everywhere, were blessed with true love if not long lives. Their romances are worthy of poems and stories and songs not just because their lives ended in tragedy. The story of their romances is worth retelling because their loves were genuine, reckless, passionate, heart-breaking, hopeless, fated and doomed.

Wolfe Tone was a smart cookie growing up in Dublin, so smart his father struggled to find a school that could challenge him. Wolfe's mind was driven to investigate, analyse, and pronounce judgment on the world around him. His world in the latter half of the eighteenth century was rife with inequality, discrimination, and a palpable revulsion towards the vast majority of Irishmen, Catholics all. So, despite his abhorrence of the rigours imposed by headmasters everywhere, he undertakes to study law if only to redress injustice. Along the way, at the age of twenty-two, he falls head over heels in love with a sixteen-year-old beauty, Matilda, who lives with her ageing grandfather, a Protestant clergyman of some repute. Wolfe is also a Protestant, and from a wealthy family. In 1770, Protestant, power, and wealth go hand in hand in Ireland.

Nevertheless, Grandfather, British to his very core, smells a rat, a man with rebel leanings, and refuses to give his blessing to their engagement. Wolfe, ever the quick thinker, bypasses him completely by convincing Matilda to elope. Off they go and tie the knot in secret, and as Wolfe had predicted to his worried new bride, Grandfather swallows his pride and receives them back with open arms, if only to have his granddaughter back at home. This is good because Wolfe does not have a job or an income. Even as a student, observing the proceedings in the courts, he is disgusted with the treatment of his Catholic neighbours and appalled at the dishonourable conduct of the representatives of British Law who prosecute the poor with undiminished cruelty. Upon being called to the bar, he concludes that no English court of law will ever see fit to extend true justice to the Irish and so turns firmly and forever towards the rebel life. He founds a secret society, The Society of United Irishmen, united referring to the mix of Anglican, Catholic, Presbyterian, and goes off to court the French, who are all fired up about liberty, equality, brotherhood, and executions of the monarchy. He even goes to America, where he looks for support of a rebellion. Sweet Matilda shares his passionate quest for a better world, as well as his belief in the futility of law and order addressing injustice in Ireland. She adores him for it and encourages him in all his wanderings, giving birth to four children whilst accompanying him on his adventures.

But poor Matilda! Like so many wives of Irish rebels across the ages, she is destined to see her husband instigate a failed rebellion, be arrested by the British, tried, and sentenced to death. After his speech from the dock, remembered still, Wolfe requests the death of a true soldier of Ireland, execution by firing squad. O Heartless British! They refuse. He will be hanged like a common criminal. And so, in one last triumphant attempt to undermine their aggressive, heartless, illegitimate authority, Wolfe, unhampered by Catholic notions of mortal sin, steals the spectacle from under the collective British nose and slits his own throat on the eve of his execution. He is thirty-five years old. It is 1798. Brave Matilda quits all things Irish and raises her one surviving son in France. She will outlive the love of her life by many years, dying in New York City having reached the outrageous age of eighty-one.

The lover of the man who picks up the rebel hat from Wolfe and wears it just as provocatively will be just as unfortunate. Sarah Curran is a languorous beauty whose milky white skin and long dark hair are accentuated by the tell-tale signs of a consumptive: bright red lips, glowing cheeks and a frail disposition. She meets Robert Emmett through her brother, who attends Trinity College Dublin with him. Robert knew Wolfe when he was a boy, and is under no illusions as to the fate of a rebel in English hands. Sarah's father, a famous lawyer, also knew Wolfe, and defended some of his companions. Because of this association, naïve Sarah at first believes that their union will be approved. No daughter of mine will be cavorting with that lot, her father tells her in no uncertain terms. Just because I defended them does not mean I actually like the rogues! They are not fit for our family, so keep your distance from this Robert boy!

Things do not improve when Robert is expelled from Trinity College for talking sedition! How dare a British gentleman take the side of the underdog Papists in scholarly debate! But Sarah and Robert are smitten with each other. While father is away defending criminals and vagabonds, Sarah plays the harp for Robert and sings rebel songs. Her brother and friends act as chaperones, but the two young lovers are already entwined in each other's minds. While Robert is planning a great rebellion by day, he writes loves letters by night. After the unsuccessful coup results in the deaths of fifty rebels and twenty soldiers whilst trying to take Dublin Castle, the seat of British authority, Robert escapes and goes into hiding. Come away with me, begs Robert via secret letters, and the two become surreptitiously engaged. Alas, he is caught and thrown in Kilmainham Gaol before they can make their escape to America. From his cell he writes a final letter to Sarah, full of anxiety for her welfare, but he is betrayed by a friend and the letter taken straight to the British. Sarah's house is searched, but not before her sister burns the preserved stack of love letters in the upstairs fireplace while the soldiers question the terrified Sarah downstairs. Can you imagine how furious is her stern father? She is disowned and abandoned, forced to make her way to Cork to find a friend who will shelter her.

Robert is tried on September the nineteenth, and on the twentieth, he is taken to the public square in Dublin City to be hanged, drawn, and quartered. He is twenty-five years old. It is 1803. As an act of mercy, he is hanged first and decapitated after death and the quartering is leniently disallowed. His body is quickly disposed of in the prison yard. But somehow, secretly, his remains are removed and buried elsewhere. To this day, no one knows where he lies. Everyone however knows were Sarah Curran lies. She dies the death of a consumptive with a broken heart five years later, after fleeing to Sicily with a British soldier who doubtless is in love with the destitute but beautiful twenty-one-year-old, despite her pining for a dead rebel. She bears him a son in gratitude and leaves him to join her dead lover. Such is the fate of the wives and lovers of Irish rebels.

And so, what will become of Muriel and Terrence? Their great love? Their great romance? Their story now begins to unfurl. Suddenly Terrence can feel a foreboding creeping under his skin. He can sense it in the cold midnight stars, because late one evening, like the full moon slipping behind dark clouds, the magic that has captivated them all for the month of June, abruptly disappears. Terrence sits down in the dark night, lights a candle, and writes his will.

James's face goes pale when he hears the words slipping so easily from Seán's mouth. Seán is jumping ship. He has bought a ticket to set sail out of Cork Harbour and across the ocean to Canada, that country where the people spend fall, winter, and spring digging out of snow drifts, and all summer fighting bugs while they hack away a little more of the wilderness. James is shocked. Whatever has possessed you to do such a thing? Just when the politics are looking up. The boys are home and the Cork No. 1 Brigade will be back in business, full time, with more men than they know what to do with and plenty of direction from the leaders in Dublin. Tomás and Terrence are home, a little worse for wear, but home, and every bit as determined about changing the country as ever they were.

It is the way things are going, Jimmy, explains Seán. I am done with all the killing, the executions, the prison sentences. You think it is over, but mark my words, it has just begun!

For God's sake Seán, you know as well as I do that 'twill be years and years before we get our country back in our own hands, if it ever happens! We've been living with the British at the top of the food chain for hundreds of years. Did ye think the bastards will just hand it over to us on a silver platter, after last Easter? Not likely!

That's just the point, Jimmy. They won't. 'Twill be years of fighting and murdering and executions and chaos. I am not going to spend my life doing this. You know my family. Politics is all they talk about. It turns my stomach! I am sick of it. I want to go somewhere where I can make a decent living, maybe find a girl and have a family. There are jobs to be had by the fistful in that place, even if it is full of polar bears and Indians. I want a good life, Jimmy. Not this madness of constant subterfuge and the threat of getting caught hanging over your head every day you walk out on the street.

Ah Seán, what will ye do in a place like Canada? Sure, tis run by the British, isn't it?

I don't care Jimmy, I will find something. And it is so bloody far, and so bloody cold, that the British really have nothing to do with it besides swing their flag around from time to time. I am going, full stop. It won't be long before the riots are here in the streets of Cork, and I have no desire to see that!

The newspapers carry the story of the Dublin rally for Sinn Féin, the soon-to-become wildly popular political party whose members are winning by-elections one by one. The party has promised that its members will refuse to take their seats in Westminster and instead will create their own Irish Parliament, Dáil Éireann, or in English, Assembly of Ireland. What an idea! Just flat out refuse to go to Westminster, refuse to participate in the English parliament, and use the English-led election to begin the first-ever Irish home of democracy! The decades of political fighting for home rule, all the political shenanigans, over in one fell swoop. Just say thanks, but no thanks, trade in your ticket to London and head for Dublin. Genius.

So genius the idea attracts thousands of supporters and mystified onlookers alike as the newly revamped Sinn Féin party calls people to the street to hear the brave souls who are asking for support in the general election coming up next year. They are making outrageous, unheard-of promises. Naturally the British are appalled at this in-your-face, insubordinate, rebellious, ungrateful, and yes, even criminal idea. They bring out their RIC constables and not a few special forces blokes and try to keep order while thousands of men and women pulsate like a living being around them. The speakers are hoisted on the tops of men's shoulders and shout out to the crowd. The crowd surges and ebbs, responding in kind with shouts of 'Up Ireland' and 'Ireland Free.' There are the newly emerged national leaders, Michael Collins, Arthur Griffith, Éamon de Valera, and a selection of hopeful candidates for election. They all have their say, projecting their voices across the crowds, lecturing on history, lest anyone forget the hundreds of years of oppression; encouraging the men to get out and vote to make a difference, goading the people into believing that yes, things can be different, if only we can take our own country into our own hands!

If there are any British nationalists in the crowd, they are smart enough to hold their peace until one foolish constable shouts out, God save the King! It is the last thing he ever says. An irate Republican quickly reveals a loosely hidden hurling stick underneath his trenchcoat and whacks him atop the head, splitting his brains wide open. Pandemonium ensues.

James and Seán have read the story and seen the pictures in the newspapers. Bloody brave, that bloke, exclaims James sarcastically. But Seán remarks just under his breath, bloody fools, we all are, more like Jimmy! Sure, what good is that doing the cause? It makes us look like a pack of gorillas, without a single brain between us all! Seán adjusts his round glasses and tosses his hair back with a characteristic flick of his neck. He picks up his pint and drains it, slaps it down on the bar. He looks out of the window at the twilight, where the windows of the shabby storefronts reflect the radiant red and yellow afterglow of the descended sun just below the horizon. Abruptly he walks out of the pub into the late evening, following the setting sun. James runs out after him. Seán where are ye off to? Sure, it's early yet! I'm off to Canada, Jimmy my friend. I wish to God I was already there! He takes a run with his bike, jumps on and pedals hard into the sunset, due west, a direction that will take our Seán straight across the Atlantic Ocean to Toronto, Ontario, Dominion of Canada.

James is confused and disappointed. Walking back from Mass on Sunday morning he decides to ride into the countryside to clear his head and think out his life without his best friend. He pedals hard uphill until he reaches the crest of the valley. From here he can look back east across the cityscape, with St Finn Barre's spire off in the distance. Or he can turn his head to the west and see the undulating hills speckled with cottages and farmer's fields. If he looks south, he can see the coastline and far-off horizon on the ocean. This is where he turns his attention. Screw you Seán! He yells. But his friend is long gone. At the minute, though James does not know it, Seán is violently vomiting into the water, his arms dangling over the rail keeping him in place, his stomach churning uncontrollably. But despite the violence of seasickness, for the first time in his life, Seán's heart feels light and free.

James turns around and rides back into the city, directly over to O'Hegarty. It is Sunday morning and normally O'Hegarty is not the least bit interested in teenage visitors for breakfast. But today he makes an exception. He hears the familiar swing of the back gate, and the almost silent encroachment of the bicycle wheels up the pathway to stop at the wall of the house. Five seconds later there is the tap on the windowpane indicating it is James. O'Hegarty swears under his breath but calls out through the open window, Jimmy, lad, come in. His voice carries the usual crusty tones across the room. I hope ye said a prayer for me, lost soul that I am, boy. More like a prayer for Seán! replies James, failing to keep the sarcasm out of his voice. O'Hegarty watches James's face as he pours tea into two cups sitting on the table. He bites his tongue, swallowing back the insensitive oaths that naturally pour from his mouth. Never mind boy. Your friend is not cut out for our kind of work. Did you not notice that yourself?

I always thought we agreed on things, especially politics, says James. O'Hegarty shakes his head. Yes, indeed Jimmy lad, I know he did agree with us, you are right on there. But sure, did you not notice the trouble it causes him, holding up the mailmen even, or spying on the RIC? He has the politics, but he doesn't have the drive Jimmy, not like you! O'Hegarty says it with a touch of pride in his voice that he instantly regrets. And besides, Terry himself thought it a grand idea for Seán to get out of the country. It takes some worry off Terry's mind to have him out of it. After all, Terry might be Seán's big brother, but he is the only father he has ever really known. Terry promised his mother he would look after Seán. Setting him up to do our kind of work doesn't sit well with him.

Anyway, I have a job for you. And it is a bloody important one so you will have no time for grieving for your exiled friend. We need guns, and your man MacNeilus has an idea where to find some.

But no sooner has O'Hegarty declared his latest intention than the British strike once again. The rally in Dublin has made them wary. The British do not appreciate having one of their own murdered in broad daylight, especially by a hurling-stick-wielding-maniac as thousands watch. They are done with the entire Volunteer movement. They had endured it, given the state of the world, the war to end all wars raging. The Irish had them convinced the Volunteers would defend Ireland if it came to that. We should have known better they say to themselves. They see now they have been totally hoodwinked. The Irish have no intention of using the Volunteers except to fight the British, their own benefactors and rulers. The bloody cheek of it! Their language about defence was all code for fight the British and regain their so-called freedom. We will close every bloody Volunteer Hall in the country, and we will do it now!

The big building on the corner of Sheares Street that houses the Gaelic League, the Volunteer Hall, and various and sundry offices, and meeting places, is raided and searched. Gone is their small collection of arms. Gone is their collection of wooden replica guns for drilling. Gone is their print material for education of the men. Gone is their collection of Irish language materials. The place is sacked, the doors boarded closed, and a notice pinned on the door.

Closed by order of British Government.

O'Hegarty is furious. It was a surprise move on the part of the RIC, and their cache of guns is now history. His hope of adding to his small collection of arms is dashed. But as ever with Mr O'Hegarty, it is replaced with a steely determination to beat the British at their own game. Push me down, you bloody bastards, and I will come up swinging every time. Best look out.

While O'Hegarty ponders the possibility of procuring guns, his friends Terrence and Tomás have thrown themselves back into the fray. They wish to take the people's enthusiasm and direct it into something substantial. One, to vote in the upcoming election and two, to man-up and join the Volunteers, even if they are no longer legal, especially now that they are no longer legal. But by August, predictably, there are more arrests. Éamon de Valera, Thomas Ashe, and Thomas Hunter, all of whom had their sentences of execution commuted to penal servitude for life after the Easter Rising, have been rearrested for sedition, that is, making speeches to massive crowds across the country, encouraging Irishmen everywhere to take note of the upcoming election and vote for Sinn Féin. At the first opportunity, away from the crowds, they are tossed into the paddy wagon and taken to Mountjoy Prison in Dublin City.

Everyone is outraged. Being thrown into prison for trying to take down the British with a rebellion is one thing, but being thrown into prison for speaking your mind? That is a direct hit to the Irish psyche. If there is one thing the Irish are good at, it is speaking their mind. O'Hegarty sees red. He calls a meeting with Tomás and Terrence. We need our bloody guns back before they throw the whole fucking country in jail! MacNeilus has an idea, and it is time to give it a try.

James works alone now. He does not care for it. Seán is gone. Permanently. This forces him to think clearly and double check every detail for each operation. He has no back up and no one to depend on in a pinch. His weekly chats with the postal workers are now given to other two-men teams on the cyclist squad. He continues his observations of several of the RIC stations around the city, but he wants more. He has just turned nineteen years old. Strong as an ox, fit as a fiddle, bursting with energy, and with his friend absconded across the ocean, a bit at loose ends. From time to time, he sees the most beautiful woman in the world, Muriel, and wonders what it must be like to be adored the way she adores Terrence. His eyes linger over her curvaceous form, cinched in at the waist by elaborate fabric belts, her white blouses sporting intricate lace designs. Her feet are clad in the latest fashionable boots with feminine laces and high heels. But what is most striking about her is the complete lack of personal aggrandisement, as if she is not even aware of her beauty, the eyes that shine large and long lashed, the distinct cheek bones and perfect, full, one could even say, voluptuous lips.

James will admit when she opens her mouth to talk, the uppity Oxford accent is a bit of a shock, but it only adds to her allure. Despite James's politics, the accoutrement of classy speech is like icing on the cake. Muriel does not seem to be aware of any of this, which underscores her own belief that she fits in just fine with the other Cumann na mBan girls and women. She believes this but of course it is not true. They with their ill-fitting clothing on mostly scrawny, poorly nourished bodies, and their common, working-class accents. Muriel is a rose surrounded by thorns. But she is a plucked rose, as James reminds himself, and older than him by five years anyway. He drives the thought of her from his mind. He replaces it with thoughts of possibilities. Possibilities of winning a war that has hardly begun. He is itching to do something constructive. O'Hegarty can sense it. He brings James in on a meeting that he will not soon forget.

MacNeilus, Tomás, and a few more of the older IRB men only nod and look away when James walks in with O'Hegarty. James knows his place in this select crowd and says not a word. In fact, given the secretive nature of the Irish Republican Brotherhood, James is almost afraid to look the men around the table in the eye. He can feel their disapproval of his presence. O'Hegarty asks MacNeilus to say his piece. There is a school on the Sydney Place, by St Patrick's Hill across the river, The Cork Grammar School. The older boys there are trained with weapons, just in case they might be needed, for joining up in the army or in the RIC.

Make your meaning clear, says Tomás quietly and politely. He is ever careful of meetings. This one is taking place in a trusted pub in Douglas Street, nevertheless it would be a disaster for all of them to be caught out at once. They must say their peace and disperse in pairs without calling attention to themselves.

It is not RIC; it is not British Army. It is a school for teenagers of the muckity-mucks. But given the war, they train with guns. Real guns. Lots of them. Right under our noses. MacNeilus looks around the table at the eyes staring at him as the information sinks in.

What is the security like? asks Tomás. None, interjects O'Hegarty. None at all!

It is decided James will do a dry run. If he can determine which door or window will be the easiest to run through, there are six of them that will move in, clear out the guns and disappear into the night. James is thunderstruck. Yes sir, I understand. He can barely keep the smile off his face, while his heart pounds with enthusiasm.

Straight out of the pub he goes, turning north, sauntering with a determined gait across the river. Over the bridge and back uphill he marches. Like a lover yearning after his besotted, his excitement grows the closer he gets. He reaches Sydney Place atop a slope, a short, clean, well-kept little road with solid brick and stone buildings of a good size. It is a more Protestant area of the city. The Grammar School abuts the road with only a sidewalk between its sturdy brick exterior and the road. It is three stories with many windows, but the door is a good solid oak. James is careful to note that there is nobody around, and no homes in close range. On the left side of the building there is a narrow lane leading to the back. James skirts the property quickly and quietly. There is no easy way in. The right side of the property is adjoined to another building, in the way a semi-detached house shares a common wall. James studies the front of this building. He moves around the far-right side and notes a back door. It is open.

Like a cat stalking her prey, James works his way through the building. The windows let in some light, but the evening is coming to a close and it is difficult to see. He makes his way to the west wall to see if there are any entrances. He knows from experience that the many connected buildings in Cork sometimes share openings. At the top of the stairs on the third floor he finds a small doorway towards the back of the building that leads straight through to the school next door. It too is unlocked. James takes a deep breath. Somehow this seems too easy. He opens the door and stares straight into the school armoury, a cache of about fifty rifles, neatly placed in cabinets. He quietly shuts the door and stands against it, purposefully relaxing his breathing. He feels absolutely gleeful! Down the stairs, out of the back door and heading down the hill to the river, he can barely force himself to walk at a normal pace. He wishes to run all the way back to O'Hegarty's place. Why didn't he ride his bike? He walks like a man out for a stroll, all the time thinking about this stroke of good luck. He fingers his beads in his pocket. Thank you. Thank you. Thank you.

O'Hegarty cannot believe his story. No locks? No locks! replies James for the third time. The day is chosen, Sunday, the second of September. James's role is to check the unlocked doors, and report back. If all is well, the six men will return later in the night with a car. James will act as lookout. It all runs so smoothly James feels like he is in a dream. He stands hidden in the shadows against the wall of the building nervously looking up and down the street while the six men wordlessly make their way up the side of the building and in through the back door. They light a lantern once inside and soundlessly shuffle up the two flights of stairs and over to the west wall. Opening the door, the lantern light glints off the triggers of the Lee Enfield Rifles. But wait. There is more. A cache of revolvers and a horde of long swords. Take the lot, whispers MacNeilus. Up and down the stairs they shuffle, passing the rifles, then the revolvers, finally the swords, from one to the other across a human chain of salvation, like rescuing a drowning man across the ice.

James is still glued to the side of the building. His hands are in his trousers as he unconsciously fingers the beads hidden deep in his left-hand pocket. His heart pounds, and he discovers he is sweating as he feels a trickle of moisture meet his eye. He watches the cache be loaded in the car, soundlessly and efficiently. He is struck by their ease and confident determination, their complete lack of fear, and their economy of movement. He can see that every detail has been accounted for in advance. How to load the rifles into the back seat of the car quickly, quietly and without incident. How to communicate through eye contact and nods and short quick gestures. How to walk away into the night in different directions without a word. How to be nonchalant in the face of endless possibilities, all of which have unsavoury endings. How to have nerves of steel.

Once the car is gone, James hops on his bicycle in the dark moonless night and pedals home. He realises he is shaking, and his heart is racing. He wonders if their hearts are doing the same, but he thinks not. What is it, he thinks to himself, what is it about these men? So undisturbed by possibilities, extreme possibilities. These men have friends who have been followed and harassed, tossed in gaol, tortured, even executed. But they are like their own special forces branch, smart, tight, quick, and yes it must be said, cold. Cold, hard faces set against the enemy as if to say, come and get me, bastard. But James learns quickly that such men are not quite as stoic and invincible as he first thought. It is only a couple of weeks later when the bad news hits them all like a hurling stick in the gut, despite their nerves of steel. James learns that they may not suffer fear for themselves, but they are sick with anxiety and fear for their friends and comrades when the worst happens. And by the end of September, the worst happens. Again. The British have decided to force-feed the prisoners who are on hunger strike. They begin and end with Thomas Ashe. It is a nasty, barbaric business.

After his arrest for sedition in August, Thomas Ashe is found guilty and sentenced to two years of hard labour. But Ashe has been in British prisons before. He paces the tiny cell with his long lanky legs and thinks hard about the lessons he learned after the Easter Rising. He demands to be treated as a political prisoner. Not likely, snigger the short, brutish, British guards. You are just another stinking Irish lout. And so, Ashe resurrects the ancient Irish form of fighting injustice, the hunger strike. It is psychological warfare against an aggressor, forcing them to feel the pain of the injustice in their actions no matter how long that revelation takes. In ancient times, in the days of druids and kings, a man who had been wronged would, if he was determined enough to find justice, plant himself on the step of his aggressor and refuse to eat from sunrise to sunrise. He will not talk; he will not fight. He simply starves and waits. He waits until the perpetrator of his suffering can no longer bear the incriminating glances of neighbours and friends, can no longer bear to see the slack stomach and grey face of the protestor, and finally gives him an audience and justice.

But it is not the time of druids and kings. More's the pity for Ashe. The British tie him down on a stretcher. They force tubes down his throat and into his gut ripping open his oesophagus on the way, tearing apart his duodenum and emptying putrid slop into his now mutilated insides. The hospital staff are horrified when he arrives in the prison van writhing in agony, blood and congealed slop gurgling out of his mouth as he gasps for breath. There is nothing they can do. Ashe has fought his last battle with the British. Hundreds will line the streets following the funeral cortege of the delightful, eye-catching thirty-two-year-old music teacher. Hundreds more, in defiance and outrage, will bang down the doors of their local Volunteer headquarters all around the country and sign up.

James, like everyone around him can hardly stomach to read the newspaper. It is a new low from the British. Even the top brass at Westminster is shocked and repulsed. The newspapers across the country and into England and Scotland carry the story. Even the Irish don't deserve that, they exclaim in consternation. We are the good guys... Have you forgotten that? What the hell is going on over there? The Prison Authority's wrists are slapped.

James falls asleep with a grimace on his face. He did not personally know Thomas Ashe. But the whole country feels like they know and love him now, for many reasons, not the least of which is his horrid death on their behalf. They feel they know him because of his heroic stance at the Easter Rising, because of his youth and his good looks and his fervour for the Irish race of his ancestors. They feel they know him because he represents everything that is good about the Irish. He is charming and smart and well-read and musical and full of delight. His students adore him. His peers, the men under his direction during the Rising respected him for his bravery, his brains, and his good cheer, despite staring down the barrel of British guns. But most of all the whole country loves him because he has never given in to his enemies. Thomas Ashe is a warrior. James sees Ashe's body lying sideways on a stretcher, pulled into the foetal position, his long legs jutting out over the side. He is in a pool of blood and slop and his curly hair is dripping sweat that trickles across his head and pools in the indentation between his nose and his eye. Suddenly the eye opens, and he stares at James across the room. He stares and tries to speak but the blood and the slop are gurgling, gurgling out of his mouth and James cannot make out the words. He awakes in a terror.

Each morning you wake up the day is like every other day. And each evening you go to sleep and the evening is like every other evening. And then one day you wake up and by the time you go to sleep, everything has changed. Sometimes it is unspeakable disaster. But sometimes, as if the gods sprinkle mercy from on high, it is magic returning, once again blowing in, this time with the cool fall air. O'Hegarty's voice is full of mischief. Your name is Séamus,

Jimmy my lad! Séamus! And Séamus is going to Glasgow.

O'Hegarty has decided, in agreement with Tomás and Terrence, that James is to be trained and sent to the Glasgow docks to steer arms in their direction. The fifty rifles, fifty revolvers, and thirty swords taken from the Grammar School have only whetted O'Hegarty's appetite for firepower. While the hotshots in Dublin's General Headquarters, GHQ, have men in London and Birmingham and other English cities buying up guns from the bad boys, the gangs and the criminals, in Cork O'Hegarty tries a different route. His wide sphere of influence, which extends to America, to Australia and all over the British Isles, has begun to move for him a steady stream of small caches of guns, free donations from a wide array of supporters across the globe. His connections in Glasgow, where many Irish have landed over the years looking for work, form the piece of the chain that intercepts and redirects the arms to Cork. They will use the dock workers and their knowledge of cargo and shipping schedules to send guns his way, but they need a man that can be trusted, someone who knows his way around a world-class docking port for ships. Big ships, little ships, cargo ships. James is told to quit his accountant job and get down to the docks. One of their men will take him under his wing and show him the ropes. Once he is trained, he will make his way to Belfast with a ticket to Glasgow from Belfast harbour. A legitimate ticket and a legitimate job that will be waiting for him. But the work he will undertake will not be legitimate at all.

James trades in his fine work suit and shirt collar for his regular homespun trousers and suspenders. He meets his new mentor on the docks at Cobh, south of Cork. The dock workers have a reputation for being a rough crew. James discovers that indeed they are. The language they use is not his mother's highbrow lovely lilting Irish. Nor is it James's schoolboy proper Irish. It is lowbrow. Very lowbrow with a frequent scattering of English oaths involving the Christ and his mother as well as various bodily functions. These men are not Tomás and Terrence. They are of O'Hegarty's ilk, but without his class. The powerfully built man who takes James under his wing is there for a reason and the reason is to toughen up our boy Séamus and show him the basics of his job. It includes working the hoists to gather the cargo off the ships, stacking the cargo holds appropriately and learning the system whereby things are categorised and accounted for. The accounting part is easy for James. It is a simple system with basic checks and balances that are easily rerouted. It is the physical labour that gives him a run for his money. He is a powerful young man when it comes to cycling, with legs of iron and lungs like a deep-sea diver. But his upper body strength? Let us just note that James is exhausted, his arms and shoulders aching after his first day on the job.

On Saturday night the burly compatriot who is training James takes him out to their usual pub with the rest of the mates from the dock. It is a part of town that James does not frequent, and it is a weekend ritual that he does not share. After several pints and many lurid stories, not all of them political, James decides to take his leave.

Not yet Séamus. His new friend has his arm around James's shoulder and is steering him out of the back entrance. I have a lady I would like you to meet. He winks widely at the scattering of men still left at the bar and steers James out of the back door of the pub. James can hear the laughter of the men behind him. Immediately he knows trouble is on its way.

Down the main drag, around a corner, and through a narrow back lane James's friend, who has not yet let go his arm from around James's shoulder, stops. In front of them is a high, heavy wooden gate, old and weathered, overgrown with a trail of roses reaching from the adjoining stone wall which surrounds the houses on this tiny street. At first it seems like the gate is ancient, stuck in place and unuseable. But his friend reaches down to the left side of the gate and removes a stone from the wall. In doing so he triggers a simple mechanism and the gate swings inward.

Where are we, exactly? asks James in a concerned voice. His friend answers with the address of the house. You'll memorise this address if you are smart. I mean, starts James, but before he can finish, his friend has steered him down the garden flagstone walk, their shoulders brushed along the way by rhododendron, hydrangea, and lilac bushes. It is like walking through a jungle. They reach the back entrance of the house, where the door is opened by a hard-looking, middle-aged woman dressed in skirt and blouse and shawl. Her hair is stringy black with streaks of grey. Her nose is long and hooked like a bird. The only thing about her that does not seem strained or decrepit is her ample bosom which fills out an otherwise thin wiry body. She smiles broadly at his friend and steps back to allow them entrance.

Evening ma'am, smiles his friend at the woman. I would like you to meet someone. His name is Séamus. I hope you won't forget his face. At the words, the woman looks sharply at his friend. Indeed, she replies with a frown. James shudders as her small, black, little eyes look up and then down surveying James from his tip to his toes. The girls are in the parlour. James enters the small parlour room to find three girls lounging about in their corsets and slips, one of them sitting on the lap of a burly lookalike of his friend, pouring stout down his throat. As he enters the room, the other two girls look at James and look back at each other. His friend laughs heartily. At his next meeting with O'Hegarty James notices an unusual twinkle in the irascible man's eye. Remember that place, says O'Hegarty with a grin, although I doubt you will forget it, at your age!

James takes his ticket and walks up the gangplank of the ship. He has assured his mother he is going to a better paying job in Glasgow and she has carefully pressed and packed his good suit. He carries his small bag onto the passenger ship, a regular ferry from Belfast to Glasgow. He will be met by a Volunteer who works the docks, given a room in a local rooming house where many Irish live and the next morning taken to his new place of employment. To get there he must walk through the east end of the city.

The west end of Glasgow is a huge unwieldy place, full of narrow winding streets with tenement houses that open directly onto the road. It is dark and dirty and decrepit and poor. James is slowed down at first by the ungainly accent of the workers, whose working-class tongue, commonly referred to as the 'Glesga patter,' is harder to understand than any tongue James has come across in the past. He feels a little overcome by the sheer size of the place; in 1917 it is, after all, the second largest city in the British Isles after London, holding within its boundaries over one million people. Cork is a mere hamlet compared to this place. The vast number of both Irish immigrant workers and native Scots, and the poverty of the east end make his home of Cork look like a quaint, mostly prosperous village. Where Cork is the home of the poor who live in a large town on the edge of the countryside, Glasgow is the home of the urban poor trapped in a maze, far from the calming impact of green hills and blue shores, and packed like sardines into the vast groupings of tenements. They live their lives desperate to make ends meet without too much hunger until the next pay packet is collected. It is a frightening mix to James who suddenly, if quietly, begins to appreciate his own home with renewed vigour.

The docks lie along the shores of the River Clyde, where the ships from all parts of the world make their way straight in from the Atlantic for import and export, for maintenance and repair and restocking. There are shipbuilding operations here to rival those of Belfast. And because the war is raging still, the shipbuilders and suppliers are working at a frenzied rate.

That frenzy does not seem to help the economics of workers who are expected to work harder and faster and perhaps you can keep your job, thank you very much. There is a long line of unemployed who will be happy to take your place if you cannot keep up. But there is money flowing and flowing quickly straight to the south side of the city where the industrial lords of this age, the hardcore capitalists, are making so much money so fast they do not know what to do with it. They keep their wives amused by adding more luxurious rooms onto their already outrageous mansions. They would sleep well indeed, with their plump bellies in their plump soft beds, if it weren't for the trade unionists stirring up trouble at the docks, making demands of higher wages and something called working conditions. Imagine the cheek of them! And the worst of them are, of course, the Irish.

It is into this mix that James arrives on his first day. He had thought his burly friend who trained him at the Cobh docks was a rough-and-tumble man, but James learns quickly that the world is full of men who are harder, crueller, baser, and more desperate than any other he has before laid his eyes upon. As he lifts boxes and steers rigging, James can feel he is being watched. He has watched enough people himself to know the tell-tale signs. The quick jerk of the eyes, the sudden movement in the opposite direction when noticed. It does not make him nervous; in fact after all of his training with O'Hegarty he feels like a bit of an expert in the art of surveillance. And he knows he is the stranger in new territory. The fellas here are not a trusting bunch and for good reason. James will have to prove himself.

He learns who his friends are and who his enemies are. His friends keep their distance; his enemies come close, looking for information. His friends show him the discreet signs and signals of designated shipments, how and where to steer them and then make themselves scarce. If the truth be known they think him young for this kind of work, but they soon see that young James knows what he is doing. The shipments are small for the most part. A half dozen rifles at a time, perhaps a crate of ammunition. Occasionally he must pick up the odd single hidden revolver and bring it home, there to pass it on to designated travellers heading out to Cork.

If anybody in this Irish Volunteer organisation was starting to feel at ease with their odd bit of treasonous activity, they quickly sit up and take notice in November. The last man to carry an arms shipment across, in this case headed to the Dublin headquarters of the Volunteers, is discovered making way for the Belfast ferry. Two hundred sticks of dynamite and an Irish accent land Joe Robinson, local head of the Glasgow Irish Volunteers and secret member of the Irish Republican Brotherhood, a ten-year prison sentence. Truly he should have known better. His serious well-groomed face is known in Glasgow by every local copper, and the RIC have even sent men over to interrogate him. He is known to have some sort of access to the munitions factories that are spewing out bombs and other supplies for the Western Front across Europe. It appears that Mr Robinson, probably through his Irish Catholic connections, is adept at relaying arms. It is a mystery to the Peelers how exactly he does it, so they have been watching him closely. It is a good thing for James that he has not been seen with Mr Robinson. The man's natural reticence and careful preparation have spared James the suspicion of the local police. Quickly and in the wake of this event James receives a message from O'Hegarty. Lie low until after Christmas.

James has few friends. He makes his peace with the rough crew of co-workers and keeps up with the strenuous manual labour. He knows he must appear steady and trustworthy and at the same time fit in. Off-hours he keeps to himself. He longs for a bicycle to get out of the city and ride downriver to the ocean, away from the stink and the filth and oppressive urban poverty that surrounds the entire district. His contact, who alone knows he has been sent for a reason, keeps his distance as he has been instructed. But Christmas has arrived, and the contact knows James is alone. He bends the rules and welcomes him into his home such as it is, an overcrowded tenement with his ageing mother, several younger brothers and one beautiful sister, Mairéad.

As the dusting of snow falls on their heads, James laughs with Mairéad on their way to midnight Mass. It is Christmas after all and tiny specks of magic seem to fall ever so lightly with the snowflakes. Mairéad despite her Irish name was born into this sorry place. She is a child of Irish parents who fled the rural poverty of Ireland, and like so many others, found only the urban poverty of a huge industrial city so much crueller, in so many ways. But Mairéad finds James to be a pleasant distraction and a bit of a novelty for her life of fourteen-hour days in the sweatshop of a woollen mill. On the eve of 1918 James sings "Auld Lange Syne," that favourite of Scots songs from their revered poet Robert Burns. Mairéad teaches James the words and giggles at his Irish accent singing a Scottish song. She is tender and pretty and has the capacity to wipe James's memory, to realign his thinking and to distract his body.

James spends the early months of 1918 working as hard as ever, regularly rerouting crates, usually sent from New York or Boston. He does this quickly and efficiently but now he is pleasantly distracted, thinking of Mairéad, and living for what few hours they can spend together. He is beginning to look like a dock worker now with arms that have lately grown twice their regular girth. Although he does not split the sleeves of his shirts, like so many of the biggest men, they are tight when rolled up his arms. His hair is longer now. Without his mother to trim and groom him his auburn waves peek out from his ever-present cap. If it is possible to be thinner, tighter, wirier, he is. One fine spring day, Mairéad sources a bicycle. What joy is this! She sits on the handlebars while he pedals them out of the city and along the river road. This will become their Sunday afternoon routine. The best days are long and sun-drenched and Mairéad carries a basket with sandwiches and beer. He feels the magic of June blow in from the Atlantic whilst Mairéad leads him on the quintessential hike of a Scotsman. The ultimate aim to be found prone in the heather, lost to prying eyes, in a world all of their own. James thinks much less now of home.

And then one day the inevitable coded message, plain and simple, arrives from O'Hegarty. Happy Birthday. James reads the telegram. He holds the paper in his hand. It is not his birthday. He was twenty last month. Mairéad baked him a cake. They put it in the picnic basket. And then he recalls, the agreed-upon signal.

Happy Birthday. It means move your arse, get home, now! There is a large shipment just come in. He will escort it himself all the way to Cork on his way home. Obviously, there is something he is needed for. The details of the journey home will already be laid out by Robinson's men.

He has one long lingering moment of doubt. He can feel the magic of summer being sucked from the atmosphere the way a cold north wind steals the warmth from a sunny day. He falls asleep wondering how he might start a new life with Mairéad. Take her away from Glasgow, away from Ireland, perhaps jump ship like Seán, and start over in Canada or New York. He sees them walking up the gangplank of a massive ship. The crowds on the shore are waving and calling and throwing confetti. She is so happy, and he has nothing but prospects for a new life to look forward to. He looks at her pretty face as she smiles up at him, but he sees, just past her, down the deck of the ship a figure lying on a stretcher. It is Tomás Ashe. James freezes. For a single moment he is not sure what to do. Whether to turn back to Mairéad or not. And then he is running, running down the deck to Ashe. Ashe is curled up, pooled in blood, sweat dripping from his head, slop gurgling from his mouth. He is calling James. He is trying to say something. Wait, wait, calls James as he runs hand spread out before him, trying to get to Ashe. But then he is gone and once again James awakes in terror.

The shipment is indeed large. It is a crate with over a hundred rifles. The last package James sent contained just two sticks of gelignite. The deposits are made by the boats at various coastal towns and taken overland to Cork or Dublin. There is no pattern that can be observed and commented on. This is O'Hegarty's way. James is simply responsible for their packaging and send-off. But now James is required home. The election is looming, coming up in December, just a couple of months away and campaigning is in full swing. There is anxiety, disquiet, nervousness in the air. The police are working overtime looking for Sinn Féiners to lock up so as not to sway the people from voting for their usual representatives of British law and order. Despite the increased work from the Cycling Squad, the many mailbags ambushed and read, the surveillance all over the city, the secret drilling of the Volunteers, O'Hegarty needs James, and he wants him back. They will send someone else to pick up James's job, sleep in his bed and parcel up the revolvers that come his way. But what of Mairéad? Will they look after Mairéad?

I will write to you, she says. They will send you back soon. But James knows better. Yes, he replies. I will write you back as soon as I receive your letters. And Mairéad will write, one, two, three letters, and then being a smart girl, if a broken-hearted one, she will give the bicycle back to whom she borrowed it from and toss her picnic basket in the bin.

The British and Americans are on their way to winning the war. The rest of the world sighs with relief. Soon it will be over. But the Irish are just starting to gear up. James lands in Cobh with his crate of rifles and is met on the dock by his old friend, the dock worker, who picks him up out of the sailboat and gives him a bear hug. Séamus, you are a sight for sore eyes! And whispering in his ear, O'Hegarty has been waiting for you. There is work, plenty of work! The man is not speaking of the docks.

It is October. The air is cool. It rains almost every day. James is back on his bike, visiting his old haunts, reacquainting himself with his family and mates. He feels Seán's absence but has little time to dwell on it because O'Hegarty has him learning semaphore, the system of signalling with flags from the lighthouse keeper down the coast. He has him training in Morse code from a newly returned British soldier, an Irish lad who had enlisted and returned with one leg and promptly joined the Volunteers. And just to round out his day, he has two obliging gentlemen of the newly formed Cork telephone company showing James how to tap into the wires and listen in on conversations, police conversations in particular. James is becoming the go-to man for all things surveillance. O'Hegarty is getting sophisticated, thinks James to himself. But he is grateful to use his mind, and not his arms for this new job, training O'Hegarty's handpicked few with these new tools in their surveillance game on the British.

James thinks of Mairéad, especially on sunny days. He fingers her unopened letters, turning them around and around in his hand. But there is no magic now. He senses something else. It is a foreboding, a certain tenseness in the earth as if gravity has increased its hold. Walking and cycling seem to take more energy, as if forcing the air to move aside while you put one foot in front of the other. Nothing is light or free. This new presence does not dance and swirl in the air. It lies stagnant on the ground until you notice it creeping up your leg, wrapping itself around with a tight hold and emanating a strange forbidding sensation.

TRAIN

CHAPTER 5

NOVEMBER 1918 – JANUARY 1919

It is November in Ireland. For the uninitiated this means short, dark, dreary days full of drizzle and biting winds. Mothers everywhere make porridge for breakfast each morning and sometimes every evening if things are tight. It will stick to the ribs until supper when potatoes will restore their families. They put layers of jumpers knitted with unprocessed wool so they are waterproof on their rosy-cheeked children. Often, they knit them themselves in the evenings, sitting by the fire once the family rosary has been said and the children are put to bed. They speak with their husbands and older children about the goings-on. Down the street, in the countryside, across Ireland, is what the conversation is usually about.

But this month is different. This month the papers are full of war. It is not unhappy news. The talk is about the Great War and how it must be coming to an end. The German masses are in revolt. Their navy has mutinied. Their workers are striking. Their people are starving. Their leaders are resigning. Their Kaiser is abdicating. No one feels any mercy or compassion for the Germans. Notwithstanding their once generous contribution to Sir Roger, they are sick to death of them. Cork is full of examples of the treachery and harshness of this war in the form of returned servicemen. They are returned with much less than they left with: limbs, eyes, even intact minds. The British did a great job of campaigning in Ireland, looking for young men to join up in the early years of the war. It is amazing how many young fellas will join up when there is no work, and their still growing male bodies are a burden for their mothers to feed. It is especially amazing that the Irish will join up given the prevailing opinion of all things British. But to be fair, many were conflicted. After all, the whole of the rest the world was off to war, to fight for freedom. And Irish lads are not so different from lads everywhere. When the political parties had a major split over joining the allies to fight the Germans back in 1914, many sided with Mr John Redmond, the eloquent pro-British leader at the time. So many are lost now and won't return.

Take for instance Francis Ledwidge, the famous poet from County Meath. He is a prime example of the conflicting nature of the Great War for so many Irishmen. First, he is against Redmond, then he is for him. He joins up, he fights in Gallipoli and Serbia. He hears of the Easter Rising, gets leave, comes home, and is so proud of his Irish compatriots. He goes back to fight and hears of his friend, Thomas McDonough, one of the first to be executed. Mourning his friend and the disaster of the Easter Rising, he writes for him a stirring lament, while he fights as a British soldier to repel the Hun. He will be killed at Ypres, a cup of tea in his hand, sitting in a trench, no doubt thinking of Ireland when he is blown to bits by a German grenade.

Cork is about to overflow with such stories this November as men return from the front, war weary and sick at heart. They will find a different Ireland, a different Cork from the one they left. The boys who did not join up, the few who refused to fight for the British, it is those few who are now about to begin their own war. Some of the returned servicemen will join them, but many will not, unable to stomach fighting their British friends and mates with whom they managed to survive and defeat their enemy.

James is busy. Earlier in the year, the British had proclaimed the Volunteers, Sinn Féin, Cumann na mBan, and the Gaelic League, anti-British, treasonous, traitorous and highly illegal. All meetings, parades or public shows of organisations were banned. But the Irish are becoming adept at defiance since the example of the Easter Rising. They organise. The work that James has been doing for O'Hegarty is now demanded of every Brigade. All Volunteer brigades must engage in surveillance. Dublin Headquarters of the Volunteers (GHQ) wants a list of every man in every police barracks in the country. They want their ranks, their strength, their armaments, and their likely sympathies. That is, do the men in uniform lean towards the Republicans or are they outright enemies, supporters of the British status quo. To flush out all of this information the Irish get creative. They simultaneously hold illegal hurling matches all over the county on the same day. They publicly advertise meetings of the Volunteers to parade in uniform at a particular location, a grave offence, and then send by word of mouth the true location. The police go and find an empty farmer's field, while the people clap and yell support of the men who parade with their wooden rifle replicas, proudly wearing their privately purchased, haphazard and individually styled uniforms at the other end of town. The women, often members of Cumann na mBan, hold sewing bees to stitch together the Republican tricolour flag. They distribute them and by cover of evening silently leave them flapping in the wind where the following day the police are sure to see them, turning around a corner or high on a rooftop. With twenty battalions of Volunteers in County Cork alone, and nine companies in each battalion, it is impossible to keep up with all of their devious moves and it is making the British look inept. James is not the only one to note that the British have intensified their own scrutiny of the known Irish Volunteers in Cork.

On top of all of this, with the election looming, the talk nothing but Sinn Féin and the possibility of ignoring Westminster and setting up their own independent, if illegal and therefore secret, shop, the British are getting nervous. Very nervous. They concoct a crazy idea and spread the rumour that the Volunteers are in cahoots with the Germans. This is a handy excuse to hunt them down and throw them in detention. They have been watching and taking their own notes these past months and the first man on their hit list is Denis MacNeilus, engineer, speaker of Gaelic, player of hurling, singer of rebel songs, trainer of cyclists, ardent nationalist, and all-round anti-British pain in the arse.

MacNeilus has been keeping out of sight, working nights and using a room in a friend's home to lie low during the day. He is a cautious man, a deep thinker and a thorough planner. But apparently he is not quite as out of sight as he believes. Early in the morning of November 4 he is barely out of bed when five RIC men come calling. MacNeilus is responsible for the weapons of the Irish Republican Brotherhood. He repairs them and keeps them in good working order. He has a detailed list of all the collected arms and where they are hidden for a future day. And today he just happens to have a newly cleaned revolver in his room. This comes in handy when one of the police raises their gun to shoot him. He pulls out his revolver and shoots first. The head constable falls to the floor. But MacNeilus cannot get away. It is a showdown; they are pointing their guns at each other. The police will not leave and MacNeilus is backed in a corner. The head constable seeps blood onto the floor and moans quietly. Finally, backup arrives for the police, five more men, this time with automatics and carbines. MacNeilus has no choice but to give it up. He is tossed into Cork Gaol.

News spreads quickly. O'Hegarty calls a meeting. Things are looking glum. Tomás is deathly ill with the Spanish influenza in Dublin. He is a fighter, but this flu is an aggressive adversary and Tomás has been sick for weeks, not even able to come home to Cork. Terrence is still in gaol, and now it looks like the worst is a definite possibility for MacNeilus. While James was away in Glasgow, Florrie O'Donoghue, the farmer from Kerry, has proved himself so useful to O'Hegarty he has been made company adjutant to the Cork No. 1 Brigade, and unknown to James, a member of the secret Brotherhood. As such he attends all the meetings and takes all the notes. More often than not this very practical young man has a good idea. Today is no different. O'Hegarty points out the obvious. There are two possible outcomes for MacNeilus if the head constable, who is in hospital with critical injuries, dies. They will shoot MacNeilus in the courtyard against the wall or they will hang him from a quickly constructed scaffold in the exercise yard. They will not wait. We don't have much time.

O'Donoghue listens and thinks. Let me go and look about the gaol. I will see if I can come up with a way out. No one is too hopeful about this, but O'Donoghue is determined, and it is obvious no one else has any ideas to contribute. He goes to the gaol to visit another prisoner. While doing so he checks out the guards and the routines. Florrie is a careful young man. He likes to have a plan for every contingency. He sends a mate to go the next day and visit to confirm the routine of the guards. The friend returns with the exact same schedule. Florrie's plan is a go.

O'Hegarty assigns the roles in this very risky caper only to those who volunteer. The stakes are high, and if they are not successful the options are not pleasant. It will be shot on sight or swing from the gallows with MacNeilus. O'Hegarty has no shortage of volunteers. Much of the same group who lifted the rifles at the Grammar School have put themselves forward for this job despite the far greater risk. They are as cool as cucumbers and as eager as young pups to get their friend the hell out of that gaol before another good man is lost. James is desperate to participate but he is not invited. He offers his services. O'Hegarty tells him to go and be on the street when the event is to happen so that he can lend a hand if anything should go wrong. He is backup. This is good enough for James. It is another opportunity to watch and learn.

When the gaol was built in 1818 it was placed on a hill overlooking the city. One wonders at the size of it, given the population of Cork, about seventy-five thousand. After all, the British had just finished the City Gaol, just as big and just as imposing with a similar daunting wall surrounding it and a mere two kilometres away. Victoria Barracks, which the military calls home, is also inside of the city perimeter. But the British had always been wary of Rebel Cork. Even in medieval times they had built a wall around the city, much smaller as it was, to keep the wealthy merchant families in, of whom only two were actually Irish, and the wild natives out. They were terrified of those wild Irish who routinely demanded ransom in return for leaving the place be, letting the people stay behind their silly walls, with their false sense of security. Walls easily scaled and overcome by warring parties of Celts looking for booty. As the British gained foothold, walls up to keep the wild Irish out changed over time to walls up to keep the wild Irish in.

This gaol, the county gaol, was used to house all manner of vicious criminals. Mothers stealing bread for their children, or servants selling trinkets of their English masters in order to generate funds for hard-up family members. Yes, this gaol held many a criminal. In the time of the transport ships to Australia, ending about 1860, the Cork Gaol was the last layover for hardened criminals from all over the British Isles. Most were English, or Welsh, but about one quarter of that population was made up of the Irish. The transport ships routinely cast off from Cork harbour, brimming over with teenagers, sometimes even children, mothers, and men who dared to do the necessary to stay alive, even if it meant infringing on the hospitality of the British overlords by stealing a loaf of bread or worse.

The front entrance to the entire compound of this gaol is a massive Doric entrance portico. It is modelled on the Greek pillars of the Parthenon so that there are four massive pillars holding up a stylised roof. The door is set back into the wall which upholds the back of the portico. It is really a set of iron gates with a grill work above them. They are heavy and guarded and impossible to storm. Once through this gate, the compound holds a multitude of buildings, from the prison quarters to the homes for the prison staff. Up until this time, Florrie and the Volunteers knew very little of its actual composition because the Irish rarely are on the other side of the gate holding the keys. But all they need to know right now is the layout of the visiting quarters and who might try to stop them on their way out.

The plan is simple but requires that the only people in the visiting area of the gaol are Volunteers. The word goes out. Selected Volunteers are stationed along the roadway leading to the gaol entrance, assigned to turn people back who might be heading to the gaol for visitation or even just passing by. No one can imagine what is about to happen because no one has ever escaped from that place, not in the hundred years of its existence.

Today is November 11, 1918. It is being called Armistice Day by the Allied Forces, but it will soon come to be known as Remembrance Day. This is surely a better title for this date, especially for the Irish who will remember for decades what is about to transpire in Cork.

The group must be split into three pairs. In one, a man will masquerade as a priest with a clerical collar, so that they do not arouse suspicion. The three pairs will allow for two men to jump the entrance guard and two men to jump the visitors guard, as well as two men for backup inside the walls. They will get one chance while the sentry on duty is going in the opposite direction. To be successful they will require perfect timing, powerful punches to the heads of the guards, and luck, and lots of it. In case their luck runs out each of the men carries a revolver. Probably revolvers that James has recently smuggled out of Glasgow. There is discussion about the revolvers. No one has actually ever killed anybody. And no one wants to be the first. It is a sure death sentence if they are caught and a clear violation of the Fifth Commandment even if they are not. But O'Hegarty insists. The men need to be able to defend themselves, lest all six of them are taken down in a slaughter if things go south.

James has parked his bike and stands down the street with only a slight view of the entrance. He sees the first two men knock on the iron door. They are big fellas, chosen for their enthusiasm and their ability to knock a man out with one fell swoop. He cannot see it from this angle, but a tiny porthole opens where the guard on duty can view and speak to those wishing access. He hears the clang of the door as it is opened and shut permitting them entrance into the grounds. They cannot go far however, because they quickly come to another entrance for the waiting area. The grounds are constructed so that visitors can never see the layout of the gaol itself, nor the interior grounds. After a few minutes they are taken to the nearby visiting area where MacNeilus sits on one side of the room separated by a half wall, and they sit on the other. The guard stands against the far wall on the side of the prisoner, his keyring hanging off his belt. James sees the second group of men gain entrance and finally the third pair and the giant gate clangs once again. He works his way close enough to hear the iron key turn, locking everyone inside.

Not being privy to the details, James marvels at the backbone of the entire group. Watching as he strolls down the street past the entrance, he wonders how on earth they can get out of there in one piece. They are all locked in. The walls are massive, about ten feet tall. If any of them get out it will be a miracle, never mind with MacNeilus in tow. He knows that there is a man ready and waiting at the back of the gaol with scissors in hand, about to climb the pole and cut the telephone wires. He sees that Father Dominic, the Volunteer's chaplain is down the street, around the corner, pacing, trying to look like he is actually going somewhere. James can feel his stomach churning in anticipation of the likely disaster that is about to happen, the sound of gunfire, and the inability to get inside to help out.

Once everyone is in their positions, the first two men jump the visitor guard, who is alone in the visitor's room. They knock him out, quickly releasing his keys from his belt. MacNeilus hops over the low wall of the visitor area and is given a revolver. Without so much as a word between them, they calmly walk their way back out of the visitor's building and along the path leading to the front gate. Meantime, the men in the wait area, which is positioned very closely to the main entrance gate, jump that guard, and take his keys. They are ready to move, just waiting for MacNeilus. But halfway along the walkway from the visitor building to the waiting building, the men walking with MacNeilus suddenly stop and whisper to each other. They just realised they did not lock the door to the visitor building behind them. One of the men turns and calmly walks back, checks that the guard is still out of commission and locks the door behind him. Just as planned, while the sentry on duty is looking the other way, all of the men walk out of the gaol with both sets of keys and all the doors locked behind them.

James can't believe it. He sees them coming out of the impregnable iron gate. As soon as they are out of the door, the men cannot help but break protocol and congratulate each other heartily. But they quickly realise their mistake, and as if on cue all six separate and walk away, calmly dispersing and heading out in six different directions into the city. But wait a minute. Something is wrong. He can see MacNeilus standing on the street, looking around with a panicked look on his face. What is everyone doing? They have walked away and left him standing. He dares not call out. MacNeilus doesn't know what he is supposed to do. James thinks that maybe there is a pick-up car that is late. But no. MacNeilus begins to walk down the street. James knows that something is wrong. Where are the men who are to pick up MacNeilus and take him to safety? In the intensity of the moment, someone has forgotten something. James turns towards MacNeilus and starts to walk quickly. There is still no movement from the gaol. MacNeilus sees James coming. He knows him of course from his help with the cycling squad and his constant presence around O'Hegarty, but this is no time for pleasantries. He looks at James. Is this for me? he asks, pointing at the bicycle. Before James can say a word, MacNeilus has hopped on his bike and taken off. But where should he go? No instructions, no directions, he heads east out of the city, forty miles away to where he knows of a safe house.

James looks around. The street is eerily quiet. There is still no sound from the gaol. The giant doors remain shut. Even Father Dominic has left the premises. Mystified as to why O'Hegarty did not tell him his bike would be the getaway, he heads straight to O'Hegarty's flat. O'Hegarty looks at him, his eyes as big as saucers. It wasn't, he scowls. Florrie and O'Hegarty have been anxiously awaiting news of the event. Someone has screwed up and they are lucky that MacNeilus is one quick thinker. Trouble is, nobody knows where he is. The plan that was never relayed to him has left those who were to hide him in a panic. But MacNeilus sends word through a bicycle courier and there is a collective sigh of relief. As word goes round, the trusted pub on Douglas Street fills up. There is much laughing and toasting. This is a story for the ages, lads! The first time ever an Irishman has walked out a British gaol and locked the door behind him, trapping the enemy on the inside. A story for the ages. Sláinte!

The British, however, are not celebrating. As the story leaks across the county, across the country, and across the British Isles, it results in two dramatic changes. The first is that there is an upsurge of new men wishing to join the Volunteers. Those who were in doubt now understand that the Volunteer organisation is made of men with the real stuff. They can be a true threat to the British, well-organised and smart. Young men who had never really believed the British could be seriously challenged begin to re-examine their beliefs. When these join up, their brothers do likewise. There is a domino effect in recruitment. The second change is that those Volunteers who are already incarcerated behind British bars become emboldened.

The day that Thomas Ashe had been strapped down and force-fed, the other men who had agreed to be on hunger strike with him were forced to watch. Horrified, terrorised, and despondent, their resolve melts and with their hands shaking, the six in line behind him took the tin of slop and each downed it by mouth, one after the other, before being marched back to their cells. They knew without question that the same fate awaited them if they did not comply. They did so with bitterness and sorrow and no small sense of shame. They became quiet and sickened, the fight seared out of them with the wild look of Thomas's eyes as he flailed against those monsters.

The story of Ashe knocked the wind out of any imprisoned Volunteers. There had been an initial euphoria with the unbelievable outcomes after the Easter Rising. Once the executions had ceased, the internees from Frongnach who were being held without charge were released, and there was a general amnesty for those who had been sentenced. Hope, however, soon dissipated into the wind when the British began collecting the Sinn Féiners like Terrence and Ashe all over again. But this MacNeilus escape lifts their spirits. Once word reaches them, there is hooting and hollering in every gaol in the land. In fact, since the prison authorities were admonished by public opinion and Parliament by imposing forced feedings, they decide it best to keep the peace in gaols. They release hunger strikers and begin to take heed of some of the demands made by the leaders within the prison groups. After MacNeilus's escape the Irish become a little more brazen with every escapade they get away with.

We are not criminals, we are political prisoners, is their mantra, and to keep them quiet the gaolers in some places give them free rein. Most of them are in gaol because they are running for office in the upcoming election or supporting someone who is running for office. So even in the north, in Belfast, where there is no sympathy at all for the Catholics and the Sinn Féiners, the gaols become a training ground for open defiance and for the establishment of political rights. If they weren't criminals when they arrived, they certainly develop the disposition that would allow them to become so. They are a rowdy lot, demanding this and that on pain of tearing the gaol apart. They set up barricades, set fires, create floods, and cause much more work and trouble than they are worth to the British. But the threat of refusing to attend Westminster is a dire one to the British, for it will impede their ability to maintain subordination of Ireland. So they keep them in gaol believing that once out of sight, they will be out of mind as far as the election goes. How wrong they are.

The election is to be held on 14 December and the Sinn Féin party, through their now-illegal meetings, have made it very clear that a vote for them is a vote for an independent Ireland. The people need to hear this message and understand exactly what they are being asked to vote for. The Sinn Fein party members are much more nervous about it than they let on. They are afraid that sensing the overwhelming support of the people, the British will put a stop to the election. But the British do not have a good read on the people. They believe that they can control any situation with the Irish. They always have in the past.

They believe this because it is true. The enemy is very good at controlling the people, especially through terror and unrelenting subjugation. They proved this without doubt when they enacted the series of laws that came to be known as the penal laws, long ago, just before the turn of the seventeenth century. In 1692, mere months after the decisive victory of King William at the Battle of the Boyne, the prevailing opinion of the movers and shakers of the day was that despite the oppression of the people, despite the siege of Ireland by Cromwell in the 1640s and the subsequent elimination of Catholic landowners in the north of the country, despite the native ownership of land right across the country being driven down to eight percent, the damn Irish are just a little too proud, and a little too Catholic. Parliament gets straight to work enacting a series of laws to compel the Irish to convert to the Church of England or forever lose their rights as citizens of Britain.

Henceforth, if you are Catholic, you will be allowed no arms, no education, no inheritance, no books or newspapers, no horse worth more than five pounds, no government office job, no legal or medical professional status, no army job, no navy job, no municipal government job, no voting, no right to demand fair pay from a landlord for fair work, no marrying a Protestant, no teaching in school, all on pain of treason against the British crown and therefore execution. And by the way, if you are any sort of religious figure, for instance a Catholic priest or a friar, you may leave the country now or be hunted down by our very reliable bloodhounds. However, if you change your colours and become a convert to Anglicanism, you may confiscate the property and goods of your own family members or any other Catholic, and all of the rights of a citizen will be bestowed upon you.

There is silence and shock across the land. If you were to be still, and put your ear to the ground to listen, for just a moment, you might hear the resounding FECK OFF that reverberates across the island. Such an attitude will become instilled as part of the national psyche. The Irish begin to organise. Yes sir, no sir, three bags full sir, they sing to their landlords upon pain of torture, starvation, or death. But behind their backs they are hiding their priests, using ancient standing stones of the druids as altars for clandestine community masses, smuggling and sharing books, sheltering teachers and bards who run secret schools for the children in the hedges of the fields, and generally carry on surviving as best they can. Since the time of Fin Barre, they say to themselves, our people, our Celtic, Irish people, have embraced learning, and no Englishman nor English government, no matter how cruel, is going to deprive our children of books and poems and stories and education that are their birthright. Just to drive home the point, the children learn Latin and Greek in lieu of English, sitting in their rags in the hedges, sharing their meagre portions for lunch. Their parents know that someday, somewhere, one of these slight but beautiful children is going to figure out how to fight back and they will be needing their education and the store of Irish history which the enemy wishes to obliterate from memory. Mothers quietly pray their rosaries for just such a day, hiding their beads in secret places lest they be found.

But it will take over one hundred years before the penal laws are slowly dismantled from British policy in Ireland. And when decency and democracy is relentlessly insisted upon by one of these children, Daniel O'Connell, through political astuteness, genius, and years of perseverance, the British will give in to this fine Catholic lawyer, and the entire country will see him as a saviour for generations to come. They will name their children, their streets and bridges and all manner of public spaces after him, lest anyone forget the great good he did his country, after one hundred years of bondage. Of course, the British politicians won't be totally outdone. After repealing the penal laws under great duress through the political wiles of the hated Barrister O'Connell, and after being forced to oversee what will be termed Catholic Emancipation, the British can only be persuaded to give the vote to Irish landowners whose holdings amount to more than ten pounds. They snigger to themselves, that should be enough to keep them in their place. And indeed, it is, since the vast majority of Catholics have never even seen ten pounds. In a population of almost eight million, only fourteen thousand are to be found who are eligible to vote. Naturally this is due not only to the penal laws of the past hundred years, but also to the outright thievery of Irish lands. In 1829, when the laws are finally repealed, there are eight million acres of land owned by six thousand absentee landlords living in London, Paris, or Dublin. They are whooping it up with the average annual income of twenty-five thousand pounds, compliments of indentured slave labour of the Catholics they so detest. Their so-called tenants live with their half-starved families in shacks the owners would not keep their horses in, strategically placed out of sight of the fine, if empty, homes and castles that dot the Irish landscape, rich with crops which will be sold for profit.

James has reconciled with his mother. He pats Edward on the back as he is shown his now mostly healed hand, lacking the tops of two fingers and bits of the others. Sure, you are a brave soldier for Ireland, encourages James. They will be calling you up for full service any day now! Edward beams. Though he is hardly twelve years old, he yearns for the day he can join James as a Volunteer. James's mother is not so hard on James anymore. Especially after watching what other families have had to suffer, with their sons taken away and imprisoned, perhaps tormented, tortured, or shot. Though James says little, keeping in mind O'Hegarty's training, his mother knows that James is deeply involved with the Volunteers. She knows it because she sees James's father handing him money. A job is needed, and James does not wish to work the docks. O'Hegarty does not need him there, having trusted people already in place. James is left to find an accountant position for which he is already trained, or a position as a junior clerk. He takes out his good suit and collar and after making inquiries finds a spot with an insurance agent. It is not full-time, and it is far below James's aptitude for figures and numbers, but it will bring in some cash while allowing him to keep up with the duties that O'Hegarty has seen fit to designate to him.

The election is looming. Terrence, though he is still in gaol, runs for office in the Mid-Cork constituency. Tomás is just now, at the beginning of December, recovering from the virulent flu that has been spreading around the world from the returning armies of the Western Front. The virus that attacks the body, which will come to be named H1N1, causes a perfect storm, a cytokine storm. The healthier you are the more prone you are to its deadly effects. A cytokine storm is the body's own immune system madly trying to attack the invader. But it works so hard that it causes severe side effects and leaves those with the healthiest immune systems with the worst possible diagnosis. Fluid quickly builds up in the lungs; death results in one-fifth of patients. By some miracle Tomás, the workaholic commander of the Cork No. 1 Brigade, business owner, musician, and family man, has managed to pray his way back from the edge of death, but it has been a very slow recovery. Somehow, he senses that he has traded his prayers for only a mere pittance of time on this earth. But who knows what the future holds and what can be achieved in a short space of time? Surely not Tomás.

This leaves James to deal with O'Hegarty and O'Hegarty only. So while James is pushing paper during the day, in the evening he is training very particular Volunteers chosen by O'Hegarty to use morse code and semaphore. O'Hegarty asks him to set up the intricate wiring attached to one of the local RIC stations so that he can listen to phone conversations at will. But there is a problem. They do not have the necessary equipment to climb the poles and splice the wires. James uses his skills to keep watch over the phone company men without their knowledge, learns where they store their materials and one dark night, walks away with exactly what is needed. He does not consider this an act of theft. It is an act of necessity in the service of Ireland.

James takes delight in this new technology, of which he learned the intricacies while being trained by two very sympathetic Republican telephone servicemen. They are acquaintances of Tomás, and Tomás, ever the gentleman, shyly suggested that such skills might someday be useful to him. Acknowledging the men's nervousness about sharing their knowledge, he did not ask them to actually do anything – only to educate – in the service of their country. They could not refuse the kind-hearted, jovial, and highly appreciative Tomás. And so, James and a few hand-picked others are called to an evening lesson in the back of Tomás's shop. James learns that there are only thirty-six telephone exchanges in all of Cork, and many are very small, with one switchboard and operator working only during daytime hours. He learns that the British are impressed with themselves and believe they are on the cutting edge of technological advancement with many calls from their superiors relayed from across the island in Dublin and in Belfast, and sometimes from London. James understands that neither the police nor the military have any idea that the Volunteers are up to anything as fiendish as the possibility of listening in on their private conversations. Aside from the technological wonder of it, this is what sets James to smiling when he is connecting the rigging for listening in on the phone conversations for O'Hegarty: the fact that the enemy doesn't have a clue what they are up to. O'Hegarty as usual does not smile. He is more worried about what he will overhear.

There is talk between the RIC and their commanders about the election. It is talk that sends O'Hegarty's blood boiling. Tomás arrives at their meeting place, just in time to hear the news. They are thinking of shutting down some of the polling stations in the most Republican areas. Tomás is still weak but his mind is immediately absorbed by the problem.

There are times such as this when Tomás wonders at his own decision to leave the secret Brotherhood, 'the Organisation' as it is called by the members. He had quit it with Terrence and a few others after the Easter Rising, believing that it was no longer necessary with the Volunteer structure that had been put in place. But others had disagreed, and disagreed emphatically, especially O'Hegarty. So Tomás, as is his way, shook each man's hand, tipped his cap to them, and left for good, without animosity or rancour. If it had been another man, the Brotherhood would have been worried. It was rare to have a member walk out. It made the Organisation vulnerable. They were more upset to see him leave. He is a man of a tremendous sense of personal responsibility. A man who can be trusted. A man who defines the word integrity: he does what he says he will do and he keeps his own counsel. In all the years he has worked with Tomás as an 'Organisation man' and as OC – Officer Commanding of the Cork No. 1 Brigade – O'Hegarty has never once doubted him. Tomás poured his energy into the Volunteers and never spoke of the Brotherhood to any of the men again.

Today he knows that this election must proceed at any cost. They are on the cusp of a dramatic change in Ireland. He, Tomás, can feel it, and his meetings in Dublin have confirmed the instinct that has stayed with him since first he felt the cold emanate from the cell they shoved him into after the Rising. He had felt fear that day, such as he had never felt before. It was overwhelming, stupefying, and when they had taken his beads from his pocket, he had felt panic, a sense of abandonment. But no sooner had they left him there, a guard, a British guard, had called him to the bars. Tomás had never before seen the inside of a gaol and suddenly the stories of rebels spending years in prison took on a new light. He felt weak in the knees; a cold sweat broke out on his forehead and his hands began to shake. His heart was beating so fast and so hard he thought perhaps the guard would notice the thumping through the worn prison garb he was wearing. The guard leaned close to the bars and in a straight, resolute voice, he whispered, Do not be afraid of any man here. Hold your head high. To this day Tomás cannot decide if the man was an angel in disguise or had been sent by an angel. If he was an angel, he knows he was being looked after. If he was a mere man, he was surely sent by an angel, and so it was a sign of hope. Hope that even inside the enemy's gaol there are decent men, perhaps even Republicans at heart. Whoever or whatever he was, Tomás never saw him again, but from that moment, the fear fled his body, his heart rate returned to normal and he felt an inner strength and a sense of purpose that never left him.

Like Tomás, O'Hegarty knows that the election cannot be impeded in any way. He believes like most of the Volunteers, as well as the Brotherhood men, that the people will speak through this election. If they get half as many Sinn Féin candidates voted in as they think, it will change the political landscape dramatically and give Sinn Féin, party of the Irish, the mandate they believe they have. The British do not seem to understand that Sinn Féin is a political organisation and that the Volunteers are now an underground fighting force. They believe that anyone who is Sinn Féin is also an illegal Volunteer. Hence the roundup of Sinn Féin politicians, thirty-three of whom have been imprisoned without trial since May, including Terrence. But Ireland as part of Great Britain is a democracy, and in a democracy people vote in their representatives. The British are looking for a way to impede the successful election of Sinn Féin candidates without looking like they are obstructing the democratic process.

Tomás calls a meeting. He has received a top priority message from GHQ – the headquarters in Dublin – meaning from Michael Collins himself. Every brigade must choose a Volunteer Officer for the purposes of overseeing the election. That person must be put in touch with the elections officer for their constituency, and on their request perform peacekeeping duties. However, the Volunteer Officer is under the direct supervision of the brigade staff, should direction be warranted. It is a well-thought-out scheme to keep a close eye on the election process under the quite legal and regular practice of an election director, but secretly controlled by the brigade command in each constituency. It will keep the illegal Sinn Féin in the game by allowing them the opportunity to observe through their Volunteer's eyes. Of course, it requires the wink-nod of the elections director, but this seems not to be an issue in the vast number of constituencies since even the elections directors are mostly Irishmen who, despite their British pay cheques, will be voting Sinn Féin.

At the meeting James's presence is requested, as well as an entire gang of Volunteers, most of them, like James, in their early twenties, but also some who are older and more experienced dealing with the British and the RIC. They are broken up into pairs and quads and assigned particular polling stations around the city, and even into the outlying towns like Fermoy and Blarney. Their job: to show their presence, protect the ballot boxes and the polling booths and report to the Volunteer Officer should there be any problems. They are there as a peace patrol, Tomás tells them. Not to start a fight, not to cause concern, just to assure the British that there will be no point in the day when the ballot box is not being closely watched, just in case you were thinking of switching it or emptying it or closing up shop early. And keep yourselves in check. Tomás looks around the room making eye contact with anybody who has a reputation for being a little on the pugnacious side. Have a nice chat with anybody who is hot under the collar for any reason. Perhaps walk them back out of sight of the polling station. We can give the enemy no excuses for changing the routine of the day or discounting any poll. And by the way boys, please do not wear your uniforms. You are a citizen of the United Kingdom, a British national serving your country!

There are in fact quite a number of uncontested seats which will be won by Sinn Féin by acclamation, no matter the vote. It is the contested constituencies that the British are concerned about. They want to make sure the status quo retains their seats. But the

Volunteers are there to see to it that the people are heard. If they vote in the status quo, so be it. It must be a fair vote without interference. Tomás has no interest in dishonest or illegal behaviour. He has high standards and a strong faith in the Irish people. He is not worried at all.

James is assigned to work with an old friend, Mick. On the day of the election, December 14, they are despatched to a ballot station outside the city. It is held in a Church of England vestibule, which James and Mick do not consider a church at all, just a symbol of English imperialism. It is a cold day, and James wears two layers of jumpers under his newly purchased trenchcoat. He knows he will be padding the pavement throughout the day, rain or shine. The coat makes him look older, and with the collar up against the wind and his hat low over his eyes he watches around him without really being recognisable. Both men adopt a friendly attitude to the locals as they come and go, tipping their caps, smiling, while leaving no doubt as to their security-like presence. The people, more people than at any other election, show up to mark their ballot. For the first time in any election in Britain, women over thirty who own property can vote. Men must be twenty-one, or if they are ex-servicemen, nineteen. James is several months too young to vote. But he can certainly stand guard. And an opportunity to exercise some skill at being persuasive is about to show itself.

Along the street come two fellas to vote. Older fellas, well-heeled in drinking whiskey, and seeming to have imbibed more than their fair share for the afternoon. This is exactly the kind of situation that Tomás warned the lads about. They cannot have drunks or disorderly folk giving the British an excuse to shut down shop. Seeing that the men are on their way to the polling station as they stumble and sing their way up the street, James takes some evasive action. He walks down to meet the gentlemen and takes the louder and larger of the two by the elbow to steer him one hundred and eighty degrees back where he came from. Mick takes the smaller of the men and does the same. But James has misjudged his charge. The drunken state of the man does not seem to impede his accuracy when it comes to landing a well-placed fist on James's jaw. James reels back in pain. Get yer hands off me ye git. I am off to vote and ye won't stop me! James is stunned by the sudden violence. He stares at the man with incredulity. Mick starts to talk. Sure, they won't let you in with drink in you. Go back home for an hour and come later. The poll will be open a good while yet.

But James's reaction to the punch, one that nearly dislocated his jaw, is every bit as violent. He looks at the man who is staring at Mick and rubbing his knuckles, and he loses it. Before he can even think to stop himself, he is pounding him in the face, with a quick left – right, left – right, and it is only the sudden spurt of blood from the man's nose onto James's cheek that jolts him back to reality. Mick is shouting at him to lay off. People on the other side of the street have stopped to stare. James's own knuckles are tingling. The men turn now and go their way, both of them trying to stop the profuse bleeding from the larger man's nose. Mick stares at James as if he has three heads. What the hell is wrong with you? We are supposed to stop fights, not start them. If Tomás hears of this, we're dead! James stares at Mick with a face like thunder. He near took my jaw right off, he spits out at Mick. Well, explain that to Tomás when they shut down the poll because of unruly behaviour, thanks to you! Mick walks back up the street shaking his head.

The day after the election, on his way over to O'Hegarty's, James rubs his still-sore jaw. He is worried that O'Hegarty has somehow heard of the incident, and he will be the recipient of a slew of embarrassing vitriol. After all, he does not even have an excuse. He was very lucky the whole episode didn't backfire, resulting in repercussions at the polling station. But today is another day. The whole country has sighed with relief as the stress of the election dissipates with the closing of the polling booths. Now comes the wait for the results, which will not be announced until the twenty-eighth. The city seems quiet this morning and cleansed by an overnight north wind blowing fresh air off the sea and through the streets and laneways of the city. Now the weather has warmed slightly, the snow falls lightly, and the wind is still. Christmas is in the air, only ten days away. The shop windows are full of fresh-cut holly and potential gifts for those who might be able to afford to them.

But James cannot get his mind off yesterday's incident. He thinks of his reaction to the punch in the face and wonders at himself. Well, Seán would certainly have a laugh at this story he thinks. And probably raise me a toast at the pub! As he is thinking of this, he notices across the street a large perambulator, and a woman pushing it dressed in a thick lambswool coat and hat, and walking at a good clip. Tiny sparkles of snow illuminate her dark attire and even though her hat is pulled down to cover her forehead and hair, James can instantly see that it is the most beautiful woman in the world, Muriel. Before he catches himself, he is crossing over and tipping his cap to her. She stops and looks up at his face. He does not know if she recognises him, but Muriel is nothing if not perfectly mannered. Good morning come the words from those perfectly chiselled lips even if they carry that uppity accent. Good morning, Mrs MacSwiney. A lovely wee'un, says James, taking a peek at the little pink face peering out from the plush blankets. I wish Terry every success in the election.

James knows that even if she does not remember him, she will understand that they are players on the same team. Indeed, he does not know if she knows how close he is to her husband Terrence. That he, James, spent his late childhood with Seán, watching Terrence become the man he is today. He does not know if she knows that he was hand-chosen by Terrence, to join up with Seán and work for the Brigade just before Terrence was hauled off to gaol. He does not know if she remembers that James was once, not so long ago, in the employ of her family. James does not know if she is aware of any of this, and he has no opportunity to find out because she nods her head and continues on her way. James stands and watches her go while the snow falls around him. He did not even realise that she had a child. I suppose all that happened while I was in Glasgow, he thinks to himself. Well, lucky Terrence, he has the most beautiful woman in the world and a lovely little girl to boot. Will he ever get out of gaol to enjoy them? James turns and heads for O'Hegarty bracing himself for he knows not what.

When he arrives, he can sense that O'Hegarty knows something, although he does not say anything about the incident. He does, however, take the opportunity to lecture James on the vice of drink. O'Hegarty is a raving tee-totaller. He despises drink and believes it to be the curse of Irishmen everywhere. There is many a mother, watching her husband drink their income, consumed in pints at the pub, who would agree with him. James considers himself lucky he is listening to O'Hegarty vent about somebody else, not him, and takes the lecture in his stride. At one point, O'Hegarty looks twice at the side of his face, but says only, I called you here for a reason. Pull the blinds.

With MacNeilus in hiding across the county, I am forced to look after these damn things. I have no time for this. O'Hegarty pulls out three revolvers from under the kitchen sink. These need to be kept in ready condition. I am delegating. You do it. O'Hegarty hands him a bag with solvent, oil, cloths, and rods. When you are done, wrap them separately, and he tosses James a bag of soft rags. I am going out. I need to find my wife a Christmas gift. Sure, you'll be done before I am back. You know where to put them. And I needn't remind you to lock the door after yourself.

James pulls up the blind a tad so he can see better. He is well-versed in the cleaning and maintenance of revolvers, having been trained well in Glasgow. He shoves the rod, covered in a cloth dabbed with solvent, into the barrel and works his magic. Moisture and miniscule particles are whisked away. There is a rhythm to cleaning a gun that calms the mind. As he works, he thinks of Mairéad and wonders what she is doing this Christmas, if she has found someone else to take to Midnight Mass. He wonders if his replacement, sent by O'Hegarty, has discovered her, if she is sharing her bicycle with the new fella, or even her picnic basket. Screw it, he thinks. He gives the revolvers a fine oiling, wraps each one in a soft, clean rag and hides them back under the sink. He opens O'Hegarty's door and walks into the winter cold. James lifts the collar of his trenchcoat, pulls down his cap and walks sullenly into the street. The snow has stopped, the wind has picked up and the sky has greyed. But James needn't be so morose. He has made a mistake, and he feels it. He does not care for this feeling. It won't happen again.

Christmas Eve arrives, the candles are lit, the church is decorated for Midnight Mass. The children are too excited to sleep, and beg their parents to attend the extended Mass where the children hold a lit candle, and the baby Jesus is put in his crèche watched over by St Joseph and the Blessed Virgin. They will not sleep in despite the late hour of their collapse into bed. In the vast majority of Catholic homes, they will awaken to a meagre stocking stuffed with an orange and an apple, and if they are lucky a small packet of sweets or chocolate. The wealthier Protestant homes will provide a more elaborate stocking and a single gift for each child. But all families will feast as best as they are able. In homes across the land, the fiddlers will fiddle, someone will play the penny flute, and everyone will sing. There will be revelry, wild stories, recitations of ballads and poems and finally exhaustion with a full belly.

By the twenty-eighth, the day of the announcement of the election results, the people are wound back up to their pre-Christmas levels of stress. Everyone is anxious about the election. No matter what happens it will be good for some and bad for others. If Sinn Féin wins it means a new round of challenges to the British. There are no illusions that the British will tip their hats and wave goodbye. If the status quo retains their seats, it will mean more political strife from the Volunteers all over the country. Either way, James is quite sure that Tomás and O'Hegarty will have plenty of work for him.

When the results are finally released there is jubilation across Ireland and astonishment across Britain. The papers all across the United Kingdom and in English-speaking countries everywhere are full of the news.

Sinn Féin gets landslide victory.
Other political parties decimated.

The leadership in Dublin has been expecting victory, although perhaps not to this extent. The men like Terrence and Tomás in Cork, and Collins and Griffith and de Valera in Dublin, who have been working nonstop since the Easter Rising, know that the people are behind them. These gentlemen mean business. They have a plan.

Before they implement their plan, the Supreme Council of the Brotherhood decides they must be prepared and act quickly. Michael Collins, head of the Organisation, takes a few trips to strategic areas of the country making sure the men are ready in spirit if not in equipment or tactical plans. At the beginning of January, he heads to Cork, his home county. He knows they have almost eight thousand Volunteers signed up, with a good number in Cork City. But he also knows there are about fifty-eight thousand British troops and ten thousand armed police from the north to the south of the island. Cork, with its harbour, has more than its fair share of this number, on top of a British Naval presence, as well as the usual intelligence officers, bureaucratic support staff, engineers, medical staff, mounted units, machine gun units, and anything else you could possibly imagine as being part and parcel of an imperialist presence.

Collins takes a look at the sheer breadth of Cork County and the number of men who are signed on, paying their dues, and regularly marching or meeting despite the threat of British intervention. He is impressed. But he knows that eight thousand men is just too unwieldy a lot to keep a tight lid on. They need to be split up and put under a more closely knit command structure. He meets with Tomás and the other leaders of the area and creates Cork No. 2 Brigade for north of the city, and Cork No. 3 Brigade for west of the city. Two new commanders are appointed: Liam Lynch for No. 2 and Tom Hales for No. 3. James will come to know them well. In the meantime, he is astounded by the opportunity to meet Michael Collins.

O'Hegarty has told James to show up for the meeting. He has an inkling that when times get tough, and he is certain they will, the small group of young fellas he keeps within his grasp, including James, will be counted on, perhaps with desperation. O'Hegarty and Collins are both Organisation men and both from Cork. They have long known each other and share a deep knowledge of the scope and willingness of the men of the secret brotherhood to fight in unorthodox ways that others in the Brigade are unaware of. O'Hegarty finds a moment to lead James to Collins during a break in the meeting. Collins gives him a once over and finally grasps his hand, shaking it fiercely. Glad to know ye Séamus, he exclaims loudly in his thick Irish brogue. Collins is a fluent Irish speaker and always uses the Irish name of anyone he meets. But he is also a joker and if there is no Irish translation, he makes one up and swears by it, laughing all the time. James looks at him closely.

He sees that Collins is called 'the big fella' for more than one reason. He is a tall man, about six feet tall, looking James in the eye, but he is also blessed with a thick muscular physique that gives him a strong presence in the room. Since being incarcerated at Frongnach after the Rising, he has managed to avoid detection by being right underneath British noses, trouncing around Dublin like a regular businessman, bowler hat and well-tailored grey suit his uniform. He has many, many friends. This is partly due to his sometimes outrageous quirk of knowing instinctively how to create a good time with drink or without. It is also due to the calculating skills he learned in his ten years in London, working for the post office by day and learning to develop the Organisation by evening, within the London Circle of the Irish Republican Brotherhood. He no longer has a job, despite his lovely suit, but uses the backrooms of various businesses, dairies, and homes of those whose confidence he has secured. In these rooms he works out vast cross-referenced arrays of information about every district in Ireland, every police station, every military barracks, every Irishman who is in their employ, and every secret British intelligence officer he has discovered. Through all of this he is learning to figure out exactly what the British are up to. He has an unholy knack of anticipation, a sixth sense prodding him urgently when things are about to go south. Whenever he feels this distinct, subtle sensation he quickly disappears, usually with a tip of his hat to his benefactor and out of the door, but sometimes through a window, sometimes across a roof. Dublin Castle, the seat of British power, is frequently foaming at the proverbial mouth when they miss him.

Collins is eight years older than James, just old enough to have been part of the Rising, but not old enough to be one of the hunted leaders. James knows he is a man of importance, but somehow Collins rubs James the wrong way. James, despite Collin's already legendary status, is not impressed.

As he stands there, shaking Collins's hand and summing him up, James realises that Collins is checking him out as well. Watching Collins's eyes rove over his good work suit and collar, his closed emotionless face, and tall wiry body, something occurs to James. With the roving eye of the big fella, James has an epiphany. Bloody hell, he thinks to himself. I am not just working for the Volunteers. I am working for the Organisation! This is why Collins is looking me over like a horse he might buy. This is why O'Hegarty keeps me to himself and away from the larger group. This is why I am given so much of the Intelligence and surveillance work. The penny drops, the puzzle pieces fall into place. But one question remains: why has James not been invited to join the IRB?

The IRB is a closed, secret society. It has been around since Fenian times and has maintained its original philosophy. It is a philosophy that every member must be seen to hold before they are invited to join. That philosophy holds that the only way Ireland will regain her freedom is through force of arms. That's it. Politics won't do it. Good will won't do it. Appeasement won't do it. All of those things have been tried over and again. The men of the IRB are convinced by the heavy, sorrowful book of Irish history that Ireland will only be free when the vast majority of the population are ready and willing to fight for it. Not with words, but with their bare hands, hopefully holding a gun.

It is rare that an Organisation man is discovered by the British. And the Organisation is set up so that few people actually know who else is in the larger group. The Supreme Council, the top circle of men, the leader of which is now Michael Collins, is composed of an elected body drawn from the County Circles. The County Circles are drawn from the District Circles, the District Circles drawn from the Local Circles. It is a vast network of men around the country who are forsworn to violence and war when the time comes. James would fit in very well and O'Hegarty knows it. But O'Hegarty has other plans for James.

Later, James tells O'Hegarty that Collins seems well-organised, but that is all he will say. O'Hegarty, who is much older than both men, senses James's wariness and refusal to be pulled under by Collins's magnetic personality. O'Hegarty chuckles to himself. He can see what James cannot. That Collins and James are made of the same stuff—too alike to actually like each other. They are warriors, both of them. What James does not realise, what Collins knows, and what O'Hegarty hopes for is that the time they have all been waiting for has come. Warriors will be needed. Freedom floats on the horizon. It wafts in with the mist off the Irish Sea at sunrise, and glows in the distance of the western sky at sunset. It is there, just outside their grasp. All they need do is reach for it.

MURDER

CHAPTER 6

JANUARY 1919 – MARCH 1920

There is a haunting beauty to the fields of green that make up the area of farmlands called Soloheadbeg. Even for rural Ireland, it is in the middle of nowhere and in January of 1919, unless you are an Irishman of the Tipperary region, you have probably never heard of it. The area lies about one hundred kilometres north of Cork City, east of the town of Tipperary and west of the monstrous castle and ancient seat of power, the Rock of Cashel. The Merlin falcon, a compact, speckled hawk that frequents the area, can often be seen soaring across the sky above, silently gliding through the air until spotting prey to attack and eviscerate. If you saw through the falcon's eyes you would note many ancient castles, estate homes, and picturesque towers that dot the landscape. The soil is rich, the fields are fertile and of an unusually large size for Ireland. Before the land reform of the late nineteenth century, it brought in generous annual rents and crops. These were worth many thousands of pounds per year, and they allowed the many absentee English landlords of the area the means to swagger about in the wealthiest circles of British and European upper classes, even royalty, dripping with money. Though they didn't drip quite enough to their liking. No, these pretty boys, decked out in their finery with their impressive horses, fine carriages and majestic homes, were insatiable.

If you were one of these gentlemen in the first decades of the nineteenth century one way to make surplus cash was to evict a good portion of your tenant farmers. That way you could give larger tracts of fields to one farmer with which he could work himself and his family into the ground and keep the surplus cash from crops for yourself. After all, tenant farmers only made enough to feed their families, no matter the size of the fields. What did it matter if whole families were evicted, burned out of their cottages, and sent packing for no apparent reason? What matter if there was nowhere for them to go, no jobs to be had, no poorhouses to resort to, no human decency or compassion to be found by anyone who might have the means to help?

So dire were the circumstances of the native population of Tipperary, and so terrible were the stories and rumours seeping into England that the English themselves conducted a review of the practices of the landlords to determine just how such unheard-of misery could possibly be happening inside Britain, even if it is just the Irish. No language can sufficiently express the turpitude of their conduct was the resulting pronouncement. But it was just a report to Parliament. Nothing really came of it. People starved in the ditches or were hanged or transported to Australia for stealing bread for their families. The landlords continued to party. Life, such as it was, went on.

Soloheadbeg in 1919 is a quiet rural place where the people are poor, and life is hard. But if the people were permitted an education which included Irish history, which they are not, they would know that Soloheadbeg was once a place of sweet victory. One might even say of uproarious, fantastical victory. It was during a time when England, full of Anglo-Saxons, had yet to be conquered by William of Normandy and so had its own bag of troubles. Those troubles were shared by the native Celts in Ireland and were manifested in the notorious, godless fiends known as Norsemen, or Vikings. After one hundred years of slash-and-burn raids on the coastal areas of Ireland, Scotland, Wales, and England, the British Isles had become, by the year 840, a semi-permanent home for those fierce men. They began to bring their wives and children and liked to set up temporary camps on the coast to plan their raids upstream, by way of the major rivers, to wealthy communities, settlements, churches, and abbeys.

The Irish lived in fear of their surprise attacks, where sword- and axe-wielding men, often of a massive size, roaring an unintelligible language, would appear out of nowhere wearing frightening gear, horned caps, impenetrable shields, and filthy capes of thick fuzzy wool or fur. They looted the churches and whatever else they came across, knocked down walls and burned what they could not carry, killing anyone in their path. They had nothing but contempt for the Celts, who did not seem to be organised well enough to defend themselves and whose men were generally smaller, and nothing but cattle herders, as far as the Vikings could tell. But after so many years of this madness, the Irish are getting tired of the raiding and killing and of the constant thieving of their fine artistry on their treasured and expertly worked belongings, swords, shields, chalices, brooches, and anything else they put their hands to.

The Vikings might be silent masters of stealth on boats, but the Celts are masters on horses. On one fine sunny day in the year of Our Lord 968, the soon-to-be High King of Ireland, Brian Boru, wins a well-planned surprise attack against a recently settled and quite avaricious group of Vikings. His large party of men, composed by way of newly created alliances between clans, steal through the forest and strike the lounging Vikings without a sound. As they work their way through the encampment, silencing the screams with accurately placed blows to the head of every person standing, the quicker individuals run for their lives. But the Irish are not in the mood for mercy, despite the preaching of their now many saints, and they pursue the survivors into the fields of Soloheadbeg. The running, panting Vikings, for once experiencing a taste of their own medicine, that is to say abject terror, do not stop to look back. They cannot see, but they can certainly hear the mounted Celtic warriors behind them, bounding across the fields, fast closing in on them. They can hear the long slow swish of air as the warrior raises his long axe, leans to the side on his wildly galloping horse and lops off the head of the nearest Viking victim with a whoop and a cry of victory. Soloheadbeg becomes a place of wanton slaughter where headless bodies lie still bleeding into the fields and Viking heads roll through the green grass and down the gentle slopes, spewing blood and guts in their path, until finally, their faces frozen in terror, they stare at the sky with glassy eyes. The prouder, more boastful of the Celts collect a few of the nearby heads and tie them by their long hair to a stick. A battle trophy to take home and show off.

On this January day of 1919 such a story is far from the minds of the two police officers who are making their way through Soloheadbeg. They are accompanying a couple of quarry workers with a hundred-and-sixty-pound load of gelignite explosive as they walk from the RIC barracks to a local quarry about an hour away. It is a legal if dangerous transaction for the policemen who have volunteered for this jaunt through the countryside. The old-fashioned cart full of carefully wrapped blocks of gelignite is being pulled at a steady, if slow pace, by a calm, well-seasoned horse. One of the workmen leads the horse while the other walks at the back of the cart with the two RIC. It is raining, but rain is the normal state of affairs in an Irish winter and all four men are just as happy it is not snowing, as it did last week in Scotland and England, practically burying people alive there was so much of it. This day, January 21, is mild in comparison but cold nevertheless, and the workmen are wearing scarves and caps and extra layers of sweaters. The two police officers look comically similar. They are big men, broad-shouldered and tough looking, and both wear the fashionable English accoutrement of a long handlebar moustache, carefully groomed. Their authorised RIC gear keeps them warm and much dryer than the workmen, whose wool sweaters repel the rain but not nearly as effectively as the capes of the police officers.

The cart's wheels turn evenly as the men carry on their conversations. Each officer sports a carbine slung somewhat carelessly over his shoulder. At one point one of the officers stops to plug his pipe with another swatch of tobacco then walks quickly to catch up. As Peelers go, they are not unliked and generally treat the locals with a measure of respect. This is why the two workmen are stupefied when they suddenly hear a shout from the ditch at the side of the road, Hands up. All four men look at each other questioningly, wondering if they heard right. The rain lashes down, the men can barely see as their sodden caps hang heavily down over their brows. The road is narrow and bordered by tall impenetrable laurel hedges. They look in all directions but there does not seem to be a soul in sight. Hands up! This time in a much louder voice, easily carried over the pouring rain. Just to make the point clear, three men step out of the hedge as if from an invisible wall. Two of them have rifles, one a revolver. Soloheadbeg is about to become a place of slaughter once again.

One officer, obviously the quicker thinker, takes cover at the side of the cart. The other, the one with the pipe, begins to fumble with his carbine. He seems to be of the mind that he will shoot, now, if he can just get his gun off his shoulder and into position. One of the men with a rifle shoots, and immediately the other two open fire. Before they can even align their carbines to take aim, both police officers are propelled backwards into the rain and down onto the road, left staring at the clouds that rain down on them. They are gone from the earth long before the paralysed workmen can process what has happened. Several more men, unarmed, appear through the hedge. One takes the horse and cart and immediately mushes the horse forward to carefully dump the gelignite at a drop-off point. Then he takes the horse and cart down a side road to a different location and leaves it before making his escape. The entire crew leave the police where they fell and proceed with their escape plan. They disperse around the country. The workmen, shocked at what they see as cold-blooded murder, will tell the RIC the names of the two men whose faces they are sure they know.

At the very moment that the ambush is being perpetrated at Soloheadbeg, across the country in Dublin City another unheard-of event is transpiring. The first meeting of Dáil Éireann is quietly and semi-secretly taking place in the mayor's residence, the Mansion House. In the famous round room of that estate are to be found twenty-seven newly voted-in Members of Parliament for the constituencies of Ireland, all representing the Sinn Féin Party. All of the men have some connection to the Easter Rising, having been interned on suspicion or sentenced for actual participation in the event. The group stands looking at each other, noticing the absence of so many others and pondering the implications of what they are about to do. They are not celebrating, congratulating themselves. They are sombre and serious and perhaps even nervous. They know the English are not about to take the actions of today lightly. Nevertheless, they muster courage from each other and proceed. First off, the delightful and charming Mr Cathal Brugha is voted in as temporary chairman. Though small of stature he is big in personality, fine manners, and commands the respect of everyone in the room because they know he is absolutely and unequivocally devoted to the cause of freedom.

Mr Brugha accepts the temporary appointment and begins the meeting. All business will be conducted in the native language of Irish. This is not a problem for the men because almost all of them have at least a working understanding of Irish, picked up at their rebel meetings, at their time in Frongnach or other internment camps, or in their youth at the Gaelic League, or even at visits to the Gaeltacht to immerse themselves in all things Irish. Mr Brugha begins with a roll call, and states for the record what everyone in the room already knows: thirty-four members imprisoned by the foreign enemy; three deported by the foreign enemy; five absent; twenty-seven present.

They begin their agenda with a Provisional Constitution. They repeat the Declaration of Independence first written by Padráig Pearse and signed by the executed members of the Easter Rising. They compose a Message to the Free Nations of the World, requesting support for their independence movement and to be seen and treated as a sovereign nation. They create a Democratic Programme as a mission statement and guiding principle. Two hours later when it is all over, exhausted, elated, their heads buzzing with the very insolence, audacity, and ingenuity of what they have just done, they embrace each other like men at a funeral, a squeeze of the shoulders, a firm shake of the hand, a nod towards the historic event they have just participated in. Then they go outside to take a picture for posterity. What they meet as they walk out of the front door shocks them. There are five thousand people packed into the street. Most are Dubliners. Some have come from far away. They wish to be able to tell their grandchildren I was there at the start. They have been as quiet as mice, just standing waiting for a glimpse of these twenty-seven brave men.

Once the people lay eyes on them a roar escapes from the crowd. It changes the atmosphere of the city. The people, tense with expectation, are transformed when they see their leaders. The meeting has been held. It is done. They have done what they said they would, and it is now a matter of historical fact. Another step towards freedom has been taken. There is a groundswell of elation and national pride. The winter wind blows but gently and the tricolour flags so many are carrying are held high to wave in the breeze for all the world to see.

Meanwhile James is again cleaning and conditioning guns for O'Hegarty. His frequent presence by O'Hegarty's side has come to be a given to the men of the Brotherhood. James is not invited to their formal meetings but at casual get-togethers, when there are just two or three of the men, his presence is accepted. Earlier this evening he stopped by on his way home to report on some changes in staff that he observed at one of the RIC stations he routinely keeps tabs on. O'Hegarty pointed at the sink, and James knows what the job is. He doesn't mind as there are others in the front room, and he likes to employ his surveillance skills and listen carefully whilst looking like he is not. Because they are in O'Hegarty's flat there is no drink. As James lightly oils the barrel of a revolver, he listens to the men talk. They are wondering how long Terrence will be kept behind bars and when all thirty-seven elected-but-incarcerated members will be released. Surely the British can't keep them in gaol forever.

Their conversation flips between the happenings at Dáil Éireann and the happenings at remote Soloheadbeg where their IRB brother Seán Tracey shot two RIC point blank, stole one hundred and sixty pounds of explosives and promptly left for Dublin. They know this because his face is all over the country on wanted posters and on the front cover of every newspaper in the land. Beside a picture of him is a picture of one of his accomplices, Dan Breen, who is also believed to have fired a deadly shot. Breen, who is not an IRB man but is most definitely a Volunteer, is a nasty-looking sort with a sneer of arrogance on his face, while Tracey looks the very epitome of a well-groomed, intelligent gentleman. O'Hegarty has conveniently acquired a copy of the poster and it lies on his kitchen table staring up at James while the men are in the front room. They are all keeping their heads down because the RIC are on a tear right across the country. They are spitting mad. The outrage! The murdering bastards! To shoot a representative of the British Crown at point blank range without warning, it is clear unadulterated murder. The reward for turning in the two men is one thousand pounds: more money than the vast majority of the population has ever dreamed about, much less seen.

James ponders the faces on the poster. They just stepped out of the hedge and shot them. Just like that. What the British will do to them when they find them James cannot even imagine. They will bring back hang, draw and quarter most likely. They will put their heads on a spit and parade them around. It will be a public execution, no quiet gaol yard for these boys. The British will create a spectacle. There is no doubt about it.

Tomás walks into the kitchen. He is thinner than James has ever seen him, although he is now fully recovered from the Spanish influenza. He seems a bit worn to James, as if he cannot quite keep up his own demanding pace as he did before his illness. Tomás takes in James's study of the poster and his cleaning of the revolvers. Séamus, how are ye? I hear ye have been working nonstop for our man O'Hegarty while I was vacationing in Dublin. A soft smile overcomes his face. You know that your efforts have not gone unnoticed? They are much appreciated. Trust Tomás to say a few kind words. It is fine work. I have heard that your delivery of training in the Intelligence arts is unparalleled. I especially like how you handled the wiretapping. Tomás gives James a big grin, fine work indeed. 'Tis nothing at all, replies James, but he is pleased nonetheless. All James ever gets from O'Hegarty is an odd grunt of acknowledgement. Tomás pours himself a cup of tea. Do you hear from Seán at all, Séamus? Not a word, sir, not a word! Well, would you like to know why, Séamus? Aye, indeed, sir, and James looks at the now changed face of Tomás. This is going to be bad news; James can feel it and his stomach starts to churn in anticipation. Séamus, our Seán is not allowed to write, explains Tomás, because he is in prison in Canada.

James is shocked. Seán in prison? What on earth happened? Well, Séamus, no need to worry, he is soon to be released and I believe will return to the small town of Berlin, not so far from Toronto. He has been in gaol in a place called Kingston, put there because he refused conscription into the British army. Imagine going all that way only to land in a British prison!

James is quiet. He feels sick for his old friend. But Tomás manages to reassure him. Apparently, it wasn't so bad Séamus. There is a fine Catholic chaplain there who wrote letters to his brother Peter in New York, and we have got the information via him. But he is soon to be released and will be busy back at his new life. Tomás wraps his hands around the mug of tea and inspects the contents, carefully pausing in his conversation. I think it was mentioned he has a girl now. Imagine that, our Seán with a lady friend. I remember him when he was in nappies! Of course, you two were always inseparable, weren't ye Séamus? Seems to me we have crossed paths at the MacSwiney's for many a year!

Yes, and many good times we had. Seán and I used to love to watch you and Terry and your mates and listen in! It was an education for us. Well, I am glad we had some entertainment value at least! Seems to me we spent many an evening singing the Gaelic songs and telling the old stories. Do you remember how Terry would tell folktales he heard from Ballingeary, from the old ones in the Gaeltacht? James cracks a big smile. Aye, Seán and I would look forward to the times he would come back from his travels there. He always had the best of stories to tell. The fairies, the Celts of old, the warriors. Seán and I would be on the edge of our seats. But sometimes it was more the stories of his own adventures that Seán and I liked best.

Well, Séamus, I expect with all of this Soloheadbeg business and the Dáil we will have plenty of work to do in the near future. We will be counting on you. Yes, sir, I am ready whenever you need me. James responds to Tomás not as the older, familiar friend that he is, but with all the respect that his position of Brigade Commander demands. Tomás accepts the deferential tone as is expected, but he warmly pats James on the back as he leaves to join the others, cup of tea in hand.

As January rolls into February the newspapers keep up the story of the Soloheadbeg ambush. The British are influencing the papers to maintain constant references to the outrageous award. They are betting that someone, somewhere, will give up the two identified culprits for such a generous amount of cash. But much to the chagrin and surprise of the British, there are no takers. This makes them even more furious with indignation. Bad enough having this lot to deal with, why are the people not turning them in? They will be sorry they did not take the reward when they had the chance.

The RIC are on a tear for weeks, right around the country, but especially in the outlying areas of Soloheadbeg, in Tipperary, and Cork. The more enthusiastic of the military men and the RIC begin a pattern of midnight visits to homes of known Volunteers.

If the owners, who are usually elderly parents, are lucky, the police or military will knock on the door and search quickly and quietly. If they are not, their door may be hammered to bits by rifle butts and their belongings, furniture and whatever else, trashed. If they are very unlucky, their daughters may be violated, or their sons beaten. Sometimes they will visit the same house again and again. Needless to say, this only serves to build resentment in the population and resolve in the Volunteers. Seán Tracey will continue to plan and execute daring attacks on the British military and the RIC. He will encourage the men under his command to do likewise and they will be successful. In a few months' time both men will be working for Michael Collins, assassinating British special agents, spies, and specific military men who are known to torture incarcerated Volunteers. Tracey and Breen are, after all, from poor farming families in Tipperary. Such families have experience with the worst the British can offer. This will go on until October 1920 when the tables will turn on Tracey and he himself will be shot dead in a surprise ambush by the British. Dan Breen will live to be an old man, and will spend many of his years as a politician. His bombastic ways will be tempered by war and murder and death, but he will never apologise for his actions this winter and indeed he will claim that he was grossly disappointed at finding only two RIC to shoot on that rainy day in January. But all of this is far in the future. In the meantime, the papers quickly have another wild episode to report that will have the men in the pubs of Ireland rolling over with laughter and toasting The Republic.

The thirty-seven newly elected members of parliament remain incarcerated. The British do not know what to do with them. Terry is in gaol. Arthur Griffith, vice-president of Sinn Féin is in gaol. The renowned, aristocratic female Volunteer, Countess Markiewicz is in gaol, the famous Count Plunkett, father of the executed leader of the Easter Rising, Joseph Plunkett, is in gaol, and among many others, Éamonn de Valera, President of Sinn Féin is in gaol. The British know they cannot hold on to them forever. They are coming under fire from the good English citizens of their own country for impeding democracy and bullying the electorate by preventing their representatives from doing their jobs. Their big lie about the so-called German Plot is wearing thin, even with the English, especially since the war has been over for several months now. Nevertheless, the landslide victory of Sinn Féin, the newly elected MPs' refusal to take their seats in Westminster, and now the contemptible so-called Dáil Éireann meeting in Dublin. It is just too much to take from the Irish. And to top it off all those regular Irish citizens waving that illegal flag around like they own the place! No. All of them will stay firmly locked up behind bars in random gaols around Ireland and England. President de Valera, the only leader of the Easter Rising to escape execution, is locked up in the local gaol of the small city of Lincoln about one hundred and fifty miles north of the city of London, in the middle of the country and far from any major centre or port. The British think he is safe there and out of the way, but the British will think again, as the president of Sinn Féin is needed, and he is needed now.

De Valera has been wasting away in gaol for months, reading maths books for pleasure and history books for insight. He sees that the British have nothing but contempt for their efforts at setting up their own parliament and he knows what is sure to come next. They will declare them illegal and shut them down. De Valera is an ardent nationalist and a very shrewd man. In the same way that Michael Collins has a knack for anticipating trouble, de Valera has a knack for anticipating exactly how people will react. In his gaol cell, pacing the tiny floor in two easy strides, he considers all of the possibilities for dealing with the British and their entrenched view of Irish Republicanism. He realises that the British will listen to nobody, not even the Americans whose country is chock full of sentimental Irish nationalist progeny. They certainly will not listen to the Irish themselves. As far as he can see, he needs an international acclamation to exert pressure on the British to cut their strings to Ireland and set them free. The peace conference in Geneva is where he needs to go to petition the newly organised states of the free world to accept Ireland into their fold. There must be a way out of here and fast.

De Valera shares the gaol with, among others, two close friends. Each day they pace the exercise yard together talking under their breath. And each day as they walk around the perimeter of the high, barbed wire-topped wall, they notice a small door built into the wall that seems old and unused. If they could get this far unnoticed, it would be a small matter to somehow break through that door and make a run for it. But the big question is can they get this far?

De Valera, like so many of the Volunteers, is a deeply religious man. Even if he was not, he would still, like all of the Irishmen in this gaol, attend Mass every Sunday when the local priest walks over to the prison chapel early in the morning to attend to the prisoners' spiritual needs. Whether they have spiritual needs or not is no matter for some of them. After all, gaol is above all other things a place of complete and utter boredom and anything to break the monotony is welcome. De Valera, because of his status, has the honour of serving Mass. He wears a black and white vestment which he must don in the tiny sacristy adjoining the chapel.

Lincoln Gaol was built in 1872 to replace the old gaol which was part and parcel of the ancient Lincoln Castle, built in 1068 by William the Conqueror and still standing. It incorporates in its foundation an original Roman wall and gives a fine view of the courtyard, the town, and the vast landscape beyond for many miles. At the juncture of two rivers, Lincoln was once a frequent place of raids by the Vikings, as well as a resting place for travellers making their way from London to the far north of the country at York. It has always been the hallowed home of one of the original four copies of the Magna Carta, a great source of pride for the locals. The oldest part of the gaol has a deteriorating string of cells that is quite separate from the remainder of the gaol. It is decrepit, cold, and possibly haunted. Of course, that is where they put the Irish. But this worn-out, tubercular-inducing section of the gaol has its paybacks. Well, perhaps only one payback: the entire section is secured with many locks – on the cell doors, on the entrance and exit to the courtyard, on the chapel door – but every door is opened by the same old key, a copy of which each guard holds hanging from his belt.

De Valera, devout as he is, decides an angel is by his side when the brilliant idea strikes him. He notices that the prison chaplain has absentmindedly left his prison key lying on the desk in the sacristy. He steps back into the rear room during Mass and impresses the key into a wad of soft warm wax taken from the altar candles. Back in his cell, he sketches the impression of the key on a card as part of a cartoon sketch. It passes the gaol censors, and the card is sent out via the local Volunteer circle to Michael Collins. He knows Collins, his friend, is the man who can get him out of that place if anybody can. Collins understands the message and gets to work. Through a series of ups and downs, keys baked in cakes and taken into the gaol by obliging wives of IRB men, de Valera eventually walks out of the gaol by unlocking the doors and locking them up behind him. Collins is waiting on the outside of the little door that leads from the exercise yard. De Valera returns to Ireland and becomes the toast of pub drinkers everywhere.

When James hears the details of de Valera's escape from the IRB men celebrating with a pint at the Douglas Street pub he is elated. Like everyone around him he thinks that somehow de Valera has been sprinkled with fairy dust. He is luckier than anybody in Ireland. His whole life has been one episode of good fortune after another. Born in America to a young Irish mother and an unlucky Spanish father who dies when Éamon is a toddler, he is taken off to Ireland with an uncle who raises him on the family farm in Limerick. He is beloved by his grandparents and his Aunt Hannie. Smart as a whip, fit as a fiddle, he wins scholarships and hurling matches with almost no effort at all. When he joins the Gaelic League, he learns Irish easily and becomes an ardent nationalist and revivalist of all things Gaelic. He is older and wiser than many of his peers in the Gaelic League and he easily moves up the chain of command, joining the Volunteers at the start in 1913.

With the executions after the Easter Rising, de Valera is left the senior leader. As such he is highly respected by everyone across the country. In 1919 he is thirty-seven years old, married with five children, and determined to see the work of the Easter Rising continue until freedom can be had. But de Valera is a man of practicalities, not just idealism. He cannot do everything himself. He will send a delegation to Geneva who will try their best to wrestle international support, but in the end fail. De Valera, however, is fixated on another important matter. He knows that money must be found for the new republic, or it will be a republic only in their dreams. The best place to get money is America. All of those hard-working emigrant Irishmen living in America have been watching closely the situation in Ireland, and their money works as a substitute for their presence in their never-forgotten homeland. De Valera will return in eighteen months, having crossed the United States and stopped in every city, town, or village in his path, with five-and-a-half-million dollars in his back pocket. It is more money than anybody ever dreamed he could raise. The fairy dust will stick to him until his time is up, far in the future, in 1975 at the ripe old age of ninety-two. This is just one thing he has in common with James.

In the pub the men are toasting de Valera, but the conversation lingers over the Soloheadbeg episode. The possibility of one thousand pounds reward has been routinely discounted by the people everywhere. They know that the man who tries to claim it will be labelled an accomplice and set on by the British. But not before he is set on by the Irish! Though they will not speak of it around the British, the people are worried. Was it cold-blooded murder like the British insist, or was it self-defence, a quick shot before the carbines could be fired but after they had taken aim? And what on earth were Seán Tracey and Dan Breen thinking? Why on earth would they want one hundred and sixty pounds of gelignite?

O'Hegarty is smiling for once. It begins, he thinks to himself. Both Tomás and O'Hegarty know that if the people have to fight their way to freedom, arms is exactly what they need. The best place to get them is from one of the largest stockpiles in the world, right here in Ireland under British ownership. But ownership can change and the Soloheadbeg episode has just embedded in the population the simplest of ideas. Take what is needed right out of the hands of the British, no questions asked. If the enemy prefers to protect the arms with their lives, so be it. After all, the Volunteers consider themselves Ireland's fighting force, its soldiers, there for the purpose of defence of the people. And in order to defend the people, an army needs guns, lots of them.

The newly elected MPs agree. At their next meeting of the Dáil in April, they proclaim the Volunteers the official army of Ireland, whose soldiers have a duty to fight for freedom from the imperialist enemy. And in case you are wondering, be assured that the event at Soloheadbeg was not an act of murder. It was a simple act of acquisition, collecting weapons of destruction from enemy hands. It was a legitimate act performed by soldiers doing their job. Forthwith, all members of local Volunteer Associations may refer to themselves as members of the Irish Republican Army. The IRA is born.

Soloheadbeg becomes an example to like-minded men right across the country. In every town and village, men who are Volunteers, and men who are not, watch as the British military or the RIC go about their business routinely carrying carbines or revolvers or rifles. How might I get my hands on those and get away with it, the watchers think to themselves? And as the collective wheels begin to turn and young men everywhere begin to think of the possibilities, just a few begin to act. First out of the gates after Soloheadbeg are the Volunteers of Araglin, who, after hearing the assurances of the Dáil, muster up their courage, and in April go visiting their local RIC barracks.

Araglin is about thirty-five kilometres north of Cork city. You must pass through the picturesque river town of Fermoy to reach it. When you get there, you will see how rural and small the place is. In fact, it is not even a crossroads, just a tiny group of homes surrounded by rolling fields. Nevertheless, in 1919 it has the usual barracks for the local RIC. The few RICs who inhabit the barracks in this quiet spot are all Catholic. Every Sunday morning one officer stays behind while the other three go off to Mass some distance from the village.

On the morning of April 20, seven Volunteers from the Fermoy Battalion have sourced the permission of their OC, Liam Lynch, to make their move. They wait until the police have left for Mass and then hide out behind the back wall of the barracks. When the one remaining officer leaves the building to get some well water, all seven of them tiptoe into the building behind him. It is a beautiful spring morning, and the officer is happily whistling to himself as he enters the front room. As soon as he sees the seven standing in front of him, he knows trouble has arrived. He throws the bucket at the boys and makes a run for it. But the young bucks in this brigade are up for the chase. They drag him back, and once inside show him their revolvers. He quiets down quickly. Soloheadbeg has been a warning for RIC everywhere. While two keep an eye on their prisoner, the others strip the place bare. They collect six carbines, four hundred rounds of ammunition, another revolver, more ammunition and every file on every local man and every other piece of paper they can find. They tip their hats to their prisoner as they leave and wish him well. He sits dumbfounded, in his mind thanking the good Lord for sparing his life this day. They did not take a single thing other than guns and paper. Even the cake his wife had packed for him was left unmolested. He will enjoy a cup of tea and a slice while he awaits the return of his comrades. He will never reveal the identities of those seven Volunteers, even though he knows every man and where each comes from.

Liam Lynch, Officiating Commander of Cork No. 3 Brigade, is

absolutely delighted with the Araglin event. No one is hurt, guns are acquired with plenty of ammunition for their stores and they have have discovered a police officer who is, if not sympathetic to the cause, sympathetic to the lives of the men in his district. It is a success all round. He is even more elated when a few of the men of his battalion help out the Limerick Volunteers with a successful rescue of the sole man arrested after the Soloheadbeg incident. His name is Hogan, and he is a mere seventeen years old. But he is sure to be executed given the death of the two RIC men at Soloheadbeg and once he is in the rat hole of a British prison, the judgment will be fast and furious. He will be executed with nary a friend in sight.

Seán Tracey, who had fired the first fatal shot at Soloheadbeg, gets word on a cold, windy day in May that his young comrade Hogan has been picked up by the Peelers and will be sent to Cork the following day for court martial. Everybody knows what that means. It means shot up against the prison wall blindfolded or hanged by the neck inside the prison gates while the enemy watches you kick about in the dance of death. It means another good man lost. Tracey won't have it. He gets in touch with his sidekick Breen and together they put together a rescue plan.

It will have to be in broad daylight. There is no time for practice or delay. Tracey knows Hogan will be transported via train under heavy guard to Cork. It is not a long journey from where he has been picked up. A group of the Volunteers meet at the next quiet, countryside train station. They walk on board in their sweaters and caps like any local men. Hogan, though young and naïve, knows trouble when he is in it and is now second guessing his participation at Soloheadbeg, of which he had been, until yesterday, quite proud. He is pondering how they will execute him, and one of the RIC has assured him that he will be hanged like a dog, not to worry, no political status for murderers! He does a double take when he sees Tracey walk right past him staring straight ahead. He can't believe his eyes and looks around the railway car, only to discover five of his Volunteer mates standing around looking as cool as cucumbers while the police escorting him stare out of the windows and yawn.

At the next stop Hogan thinks fast. The doors open and with the speed and agility that only a man about to be executed can muster, he jumps to the platform and runs like a madman while the Volunteers tackle the RIC and then try to escape. The only person who wins in this episode is Hogan, who quickly runs right to his friend, the local butcher who, without a word, cleaves his hand cuffs in two with one hearty swipe. But in all the commotion, while Hogan is running to his butcher friend, two RIC are shot dead and both Tracey and Breen are shot. They make their escape to the local priest's house where the housekeeper is a Cumann na mBan girl. She will nurse them until they can be spirited away by their comrades. It will take months for the rescuers to recover, and they will both suffer greatly. Tracey has a bullet in the belly, Breen a bullet in the lungs. But they fare much better than some others. A year from now two men will suffer the consequences of their Volunteer participation. They will be arrested and put in Mountjoy Prison in Dublin for just this very escape effort. One man was there, helping out, although he did not have a gun, and the other lives nearby but was not anywhere near the train station that fateful day. Who cares? Not the Brits. It is close enough. They will hang, both of them.

The men in the pub are having a heyday, toasting ambushes and rescues. Not only have these things been happening around Cork, but also right across the country. Michael Collins was busy back in March breaking out no less than twenty men from Mountjoy in Dublin. And there have been various ambushes on police constables, acquiring their guns here and there around the country. The pluck of one group of men leads to the audacity of the next. The wildest story is of a large group of Volunteers from Rathclaren near Kilbrittain in West Cork. They are tired of the midnight raids by the local group of thugs who are wearing British military uniforms. Almost every one of them has had their homes raided, their parents terrorised, and their sisters treated disrespectfully. They want guns, and they decide this particular group of nasty soldiers could use a lesson in good manners. One of the boys has his sister, who belongs to the Cumann na mBan, sew up a set of masks from sacks. The men congregate in a short laneway off the road a little way from the barracks. It is one o'clock, dark and quiet. Just as the lorry with four military men and one RIC rumbles down the road, one of the men jumps out to wave them aside. As soon as the truck stops all sixteen masked Volunteers jump them. They wrestle their guns and tie all five of them up together in a single long rope and leave them sitting in their lorry waiting for help. The Volunteers cycle home, jump into bed, and pretend they know nothing when the inevitable crashing down of the door occurs a couple of hours later. They know they must be found at home, or they will be under suspicion and their families will suffer. All of the boys manage to avoid arrest, except one fellow, who in the melée is stabbed in the head with a bayonet and must be ferreted to a local doctor. But once the story gets round, the thought of sixteen masked men tying up a whole truck full of military and stealing their guns has sides splitting with mirth and many a toast proffered to outrageous manoeuvres and good health of the IRA.

The British government is starting to take a lot of heat from Englishmen everywhere. What is going on over there with the Irish? Don't we have the best fighting force in the world? Haven't we set up a police system, the envy of every nation on earth? Why is it things seem to be getting out of control? The British parliament takes a risk. They release the imprisoned members of Sinn Féin hoping that the illegal actions of the Volunteers scattered about Ireland will be brought under control by their lawfully elected leaders. It is May 1919. We will get this nonsense underfoot yet, think the British.

Terrence arrives home to Muriel and his new baby Mhaire. Words cannot describe their elation at being together once again. They have been married for less than two years, and most of that time Terrence has been in prison. He drinks in the sight of his beautiful baby with wonder. The child looks just like her mother with wide-set eyes, an intelligent expression, and a perfect set of chiselled lips. When she falls asleep, he writes poems about her; when she awakens, he takes her on picnics and bicycle rides. June and July are like a gift from heaven. The weather is fine, he regains his strength from the many hearty meals that his wife and her family provides, and he finds he is in love with not just his wife but his baby daughter as well. They ride out to the country whenever a warm sunny day befriends them, and he drinks in the scents and charms of his much-loved Irish countryside. They travel to the Irish Gaeltacht, where he has many, many friends and together they decide to speak only Irish to their daughter.

There seems to be a lull in what the British consider the nefarious activities of the illicit Volunteers, now IRA. The British Command congratulate themselves on a wise decision. The madness of the gaols has been eliminated with their departure and the Volunteers seem to have given up their ambushes and shootings and escapades.

But it is all just a ruse. As Terrence's strength improves, behind the scenes he and Tomás are busier than ever. Terrence has his new job as Member of Dail Éireann with a large urban constituency to deal with. The Dáil cannot disappoint the people. Ministries are formed, committees are struck. They will freeze the British out, ignore their civil courts and create their own, appoint their own judges, work out their own problems. And on top of this work, there is the planning of the next steps to pressure the British, to collect arms for a rainy day and to keep their people who are already on the lists of most-wanted criminals out of enemy hands. As August creeps up on them, Terrence must spend long hours away from his new family.

Muriel is certain that things can only get better. Her husband is home. He is working at a feverish pace, but at some point, soon, he must create a more balanced schedule that includes their family; after all, he is a father now. Terrence, having spent so many months in prison, has had many lonely hours to reflect. He is as certain as he is the sky is blue that things will get worse, much worse, before they get better, and for who knows how long. He tries to break this certainty to his wife without upsetting her. He wants to prepare her. He knows that she is understood within her own family to lapse into histrionics from time to time or, on the other hand, languish in melancholy. That has always been a given. But he is distressed to discover that he had been until now somewhat ignorant of the volatility of her disposition. She becomes emotional, excessively emotional in Terrence's view, and then despondent. Pictures of the two of them taken with their baby show the strain. She is tired already of the rebel life, her husband in gaol for endless months, raising a baby on her own. Muriel is just as certain of her beliefs about Irish freedom as ever she was. But like every mother before her and every mother after her, she learns the hard way that life is very different when you are responsible for a tiny, beautiful, helpless creature. And Muriel learns another harsh lesson. She learns that life is not fair. Despite her wealth and all of the gifts that have been showered on her, Muriel looks at her perfect baby and panics. She thinks of the possibility of her husband gone for months, perhaps years in British gaols, perhaps even worse. He could be tortured or hanged or shot like so many others. The romantic image of the rebel turns to dust, and she is left facing the possibility of an entire life for herself and her child, spent mostly alone.

Terrence is alarmed at her emotional outbursts. He stops talking to try to calm her, but the damage is done. He looks at his wife whom he hardly really knows, and sighs. What was he thinking, marrying at all? Dragging the most beautiful woman in the world into his mad world of rebellion and politics and danger? He blames himself. But what about the child? Terrence waits until everyone is asleep, then he goes to his desk and pulls out his will. He thinks long and hard into the night. Then with a quick and determined strike of the pen he makes a dramatic change.

Tomás has had a request. Liam Lynch wishes to work with Cork No. 1 Brigade. He knows that much of the expertise he needs to deal with the British and to acquire arms is to be found surrounding O'Hegarty, and he wants to make sure that he makes his mark with the least amount of risk to his men. He has an idea. A meeting is called. James is asked to attend. His expertise in intelligence and surveillance is about to come in handy.

Lynch is from Limerick, but he has been working in the Fermoy area for some time. It is a beautiful place with a wide rambling river, and an ancient, long stone bridge across the water supported by many small arches. Postcards of the town routinely keep the sight of the two massive military barracks out of the parameters of their pictures. Why spoil the illusion of a picturesque place by divulging the reality of a police state? Lynch has watched the comings and goings of the two military barracks and the RIC station in Fermoy for some time. He knows there are untold barrels of guns and armaments hidden away in the armoury of each barracks. He knows the place is heavily guarded, unlike the Araglin RIC barracks. No one is wandering behind those gates. Liam has a different idea. One that seems small, but so what he thinks to himself, we must start somewhere.

The British have managed to step up their presence across the country. All of the RIC barracks are reinforced with metal window covers and bars. The military and the police take their steps a little more carefully, with an eye to their backs. They are always fully armed and at the ready whenever they leave their stations. No exceptions. Soloheadbeg and the failure to catch the main culprits keep them on their toes.

There are a group of British soldiers who attend the Wesleyan Church in the town every Sunday morning. About fifteen of them walk down the main street at about ten o'clock every Sunday, rain or shine, singing their British songs and their Protestant marching hymns. They are a rowdy lot, often loud and objectionable. They get some sort of kick from this spectacle, and they bring their loaded rifles with them, not just because it is required while they are in uniform, but just in case any of the locals might wish to challenge them on their behaviour. They are a close group and so feel secure in their arrogant stance. Liam watches the rifles march past one Sunday in August and thinks, yes, we could do with those, and those louts would have a bit of a surprise if we took them from them.

He shares his idea with Tomás, Terrence, O'Hegarty, and James. Tomás is cautious. It must be a tight plan, fast, no shootings unless absolutely necessary and a very savvy escape route. After all, once the alarm is sounded, the military as well as the RIC will be streaming out of there, happy for a little action hunting down Irishmen. James is assigned to check out the possibilities and report back to Tomás and O'Hegarty. He makes arrangements with Liam for a meeting time and place. Later in the day when Liam has left, O'Hegarty does not waste his words on James. Have I taught you nothing lad? His words seethe out of his pursed mouth like a billow of steam. Now listen to me very carefully. The last thing you or I want is for you to waste your life in a British gaol or dance at the end of one of their ropes. If you are going to avoid that you must learn to trust yourself first, keep your head down and always, always, have Plan B, and preferably Plan C in the back of your mind for when things go south. You will cancel your meeting with Liam. You will check this situation out yourself and nobody on this planet will be able to say they have ever seen you in association with any of the lads that will be undertaking this project, assuming it proceeds, especially Liam. There is no doubt whatsoever that he is already being watched by their G men. He is OC of Cork No. 2 for God's sake; do you think the British are not aware of this fact? They probably have his picture up front and centre with Tomás, Terrence and Collins on their most wanted board in Dublin Castle. But they don't have your picture yet and they don't have mine, so let's keep it this way. Go to Fermoy, figure it out, get back to me. He slams the door behind him leaving James blistering inwardly and completely deflated. It was only a meeting James thinks to himself, but as he hops on his bicycle at the back gate, he realises that O'Hegarty is right as usual. The fewer contacts, the fewer people who know your face and associations, the better off you are.

James has been to Fermoy before, and he knows exactly where the Wesleyan Church is located. But he is struck like everyone else by the beauty of the place as he walks out on the main street from the train station, pushing his bicycle ahead of him. It is a Saturday afternoon and luckily a sunny day, so he fits right in with the locals and tourists alike who come to Fermoy to enjoy the lovely scenery, eat ice cream, and walk the river shoreline and famous bridge. James first checks out the church. He rides around the streets checking entrances and exits from the building. He notes that the back of the church leads onto a hill of green grass and into the countryside without fences or gates. He notes the buildings adjoining the church, their entrances and exits, the width of the street, the buildings directly across the wide avenue and exactly where other streets adjoin to create crossroads. Later he pedals down each possible direction from the church for several miles. West then south to Cork, west then north to Mitchelstown, east to Lismore, west then north then a quick right to Ballyduff or a quick left to Mallow. There are many possibilities for escape over the bridge and two possibilities south of the bridge closer to the church. If they can get a head start before the alarm sounds, the British will be forced to check out each possibility and spread themselves thin in an effort to capture them. Many of the roads give a lovely view of the countryside for miles, but there is one road, the east road that is bordered by large leafy trees for a short section just outside the town. James decides they must make their escape to Lismore and those trees are going to help them.

Because of the large military presence, the men know this is a high-risk ambush. But if they are successful, it will be a highly publicised and demoralising one for the British. James reports back to Tomás and O'Hegarty. He learns that there are three others who are to be involved in the plan. They meet at the Douglas Street pub and discuss the possibilities. They will need an escape car, at least one, preferably two or three. They will need a way to slow down the British so that they can get clear away from the area. They do not have enough revolvers for everyone, so the unarmed men must have some type of weapon, a knife or club in order to protect themselves if need be. And they will need a large group of Volunteers to be able to take so many rifles. If the group splits up, they will need viable excuses for the inevitable roadblocks preventing their return home. The other men have two cars lined up to use, but no sense of an escape route. James, however, has thought it out very carefully. He smiles and takes out a piece of paper and a pencil. He draws the town and the escape route and goes over the procedure. As they leave the pub, he tosses the paper in the fire.

O'Hegarty likes the plan. Liam comes again to Cork and the group meets to go over it step by step. They take turns playing devil's advocate. What if this happens? What if that happens? Every contingency they can foresee is discussed. Liam insists on this. As far as he is concerned no man under his watch will be put at risk unduly. He takes his round spectacles off and carefully cleans then with his handkerchief. The men wait. The last thing they need to know is who will participate. They know there have been plenty of Volunteers wanting a piece of action from both Cork No. 1 and Cork No. 2. Some men are willing to travel quite a distance in order to join in. If the men come from Fermoy, they will be recognised and have to leave the area for an indefinite period of time. But Liam, as OC, must make the determination. They decide on two cars from two different places with five men in each. Most of the men will be from the Fermoy battalion. Liam knows them and trusts them best. One of the cars will also carry back all of the guns to a safe dumping spot near Araglin. Several men will be on bicycles and the rest, including James, will be on foot. All of these will have safe houses where they can escape directly. When James hears his name listed as a participant, he is ecstatic.

As the other men leave, O'Hegarty pulls him aside. Remember what I have taught ye Jimmy lad, he says, almost with a touch of concern in his voice. The best place to hide is right under their noses. Tomás, who is also standing in the kitchen, says gently to James, I want you to keep a special eye on our Liam. Aye, pipes up O'Hegarty, he will kneel down and say a prayer to his Guardian Angel before he will think to shoot! Tomás gives O'Hegarty a look as if to say, enough!

O'Hegarty walks to the kitchen sink and pulls out a revolver from the hidden shelf underneath. He hands it to James. Become familiar with your new friend here over the next few days. As he is talking, he is busy pulling a drawer out of the sideboard in the kitchen. He lays it on the ground and digs deep in the recesses of the now empty opening. He pulls out a packet wrapped in paper. O'Hegarty tosses it in the air and James catches it. Try it on for size, it should be perfect, but I can adjust it if necessary. James unwraps the sidearm holster. It has been carefully made from leather and is designed to fit over his shoulder and hold a revolver tucked just underneath his left arm. He has no idea where O'Hegarty has come up with it and he knows it would be pointless to ask. He tries it on and slips the Smith and Wesson into the seat. It glides in easily and stays snug against his rib cage, protected and camouflaged by his arm. Tomás watches with a sad look on his face.

Thanks to his time in Glasgow, James knows his guns. He knows how to clean them, how to dismantle them, how to hide them, how to ship them, how to aim them. But he doesn't know how to kill with them. In fact, there is no one he personally knows who has ever done such a thing. It is true that Seán Tracey and Dan Breen have shot and killed but James does not know them and besides, he believes the shooting was in self-defence, a knee-jerk reaction. After all, Tracey is an IRB man, and has never been on the police wanted list before.

James hops on his bicycle and rides home. The gun is safe against his body, warm against his ribs, but he does not feel safe carrying it. He is more wary than usual, checking his surroundings with extra diligence as he rides home. He turns his head from side to side, looking about as he pedals as if expecting someone to point and gawk.

On the appointed day, Sunday, September 7, the various parties take up their positions in Fermoy. Everyone must be there long before the expected ten o'clock arrival of the party of British soldiers. James had arrived the evening before, and under cover of darkness quietly made his way through the back entrance into Liam's flat. Together with a couple of others from IRA battalions in the area, they painstakingly went over their plans. Early in the morning, before daybreak, James leads a couple of carefully selected men by bicycle to the Lismore Road. They stop at the trees. Halfway through the grove, they choose two trees, one on either side of the road, and begin to saw. It is dark still and one of the fellas holds a lantern. The trees must be sliced in just such a way and to just such a degree that one well-placed shove will topple them when the moment is right. Satisfied with their efforts they disperse, each man taking a different route through side streets to their temporary hiding places in local homes, where they can have breakfast and an extra cup of tea. James does not return to Liam's flat. He could not get anything past his lips if his life depended on it and besides, he can hear O'Hegarty's rasping voice in his ear, the warnings to keep himself clear of suspicion and so he does not want to be seen in the vicinity especially during daylight hours.

James is not nervous. He is not worried. But he has had a premonition about this day. It was just after O'Hegarty had given him the holster. He had ridden home with the gun sitting in its cradle snug underneath his arm and as he rode the leather seemed to become warmer and warmer until he imagined that the friction of the movement of his arm against it was causing it to smoulder and burn. He felt like the gun itself was sucking the warmth from his body and keeping the potential energy inside the barrel. In fact, it was so warm he started to become anxious. He wanted to stop and remove the whole apparatus but of course he could do no such thing in the middle of the street in Cork. As soon as he got home, he wheeled his bicycle down the garden path to the garden shed. With the door closed behind him he tore off his jacket and took off the holster and gun. He was shocked to discover that the gun was as cold as ice and the holster itself was cool and smooth to the touch. The realisation of this was accompanied by an involuntary shudder straight up his spine and across his shoulder blades. As he looked at the gun lying in the palm of his hand he was overwhelmed by the strangest of sensations. He felt in his mind as if someone had just struck him and left his head ringing. He had pondered to himself if something was being called to his attention, the understanding of which was just beyond his grasp.

Right now, the holster and revolver have assumed his body temperature and he has become accustomed to their presence. Actually, he has become quite attached to it over the last couple of weeks. There is a certain power that seems to emanate from it and seep into his blood. The sensation of it makes him stand taller and straighter. He feels a tad cocky, looking people straight in the eye, happy to keep the secret knowledge to himself. In this early morning hour, however, there is no one to look in the eye, and looking in the eye of anyone is something he knows to avoid at all costs. He pulls his black cap down at an angle to provide shade for his face. The sun is coming up and it promises to be a beautiful day. He rides over the bridge and stops in the centre, leaning out over the water, to all appearances enjoying the sound and the sparkle of the rising sun as it glints in the distance. As he stares out over the bucolic scene, he is visualising his various escape routes.

He knows that this is a very brash endeavour. There are twenty-five Volunteers working together to take down fifteen armed soldiers. Between the lot of them they have six revolvers, not including James's gun, which is not part of the count. As one of the men on foot, it is imperative that he get out of sight quickly. To do this James has decided that he must blend in. Plan A is to walk down the street, through a laneway between buildings and out to the back end of the train station. Plan B is to nip in the side entrance of a shop further down the street on the same side as the church, and out of the back door to the fields, where he can follow the line of buildings until they end, and walk across the street and to the train station. Plan C is to use a ladder he has come across at the back of one of the shops to get to the roof. All of the roofs are connected, and he can either hide out there on top, or make his way across until he can get his bike and ride back home. He has made sure that all of the men have a plan. Most of them have a partner or are in a group, especially the men in the cars. But James has been trained well. He will find his own way home; a young man taking the Sunday train to go visit his girl perhaps. James makes his way back to the southern road where the church is located. He pedals past, surveying the area and then leaves his bike leaning on a wall a few yards from the train station. If he gets there on time, he will pick it up and take it on the train with him.

As the time draws nearer to the magic hour of ten, the streets of Fermoy begin to fill. The Catholic church has already had an early Mass and now will be preparing for the mid-morning service. The Church of Ireland has a service as well as the Wesleyan church. The vast majority of people walk to church, even if it is a mile or so from their homes. Sunday morning is a time to worship, but also to socialise. People are dressed in their Sunday best, and it is an opportunity to take time to catch up with friends and relatives, so the various groupings of the Volunteers are not even noticed. A car is pulled over by the side of the road across from the church with the bonnet jacked up and three men checking the engine. A small group of young men stand in a circle smoking cigarettes and having an animated conversation. A pair of men is stopped in front of a shop window commenting on the display. Other small groups are dispersed along the street occupied with conversations. James stands alone at the top of the steps leading to the courthouse with a long view in either direction. He has his hands in his pockets and is fingering his beads. The group of fifteen soldiers march down the street laughing and calling out at each other, their rifles slung over their shoulders. It seems like any other late summer Sunday morning in Fermoy.

Until the moment a second car pulls up behind the soldiers, Liam jumps out and yells Hands-up! At once the twenty-four Volunteers have surrounded the soldiers and are wrestling their guns from them. The six revolvers are out, and the soldiers realise they have been outsmarted. They raise their hands in the air. As the rifles are torn from the soldier's shoulders, they are tossed to a Volunteer who throws them in the back of the car, which now has the hood down and a door ajar and has pulled up close to the melée.

James is not participating but has moved much closer and is standing back watching Liam and taking in the entire episode, so as to report back to Tomás and O'Hegarty. He has let his beads lie and taken his right hand from his trouser pocket. His hand now sits inside his jacket on the revolver. In times of extreme stress, the human mind can display unusual characteristics. James watches as Liam moves towards the corporal in charge, demanding his rifle. It seems to him that time suddenly slows down as he sees Liam place his foot down on the ground while moving his hand towards the soldier's shoulder to take the rifle. But this soldier, the corporal in charge, is no slouch. Just as he is turning towards Liam, somehow Liam trips. His foot slips and he falls down onto his other leg. As he goes down the corporal swings his rifle off his shoulder and moves to strike Liam with the butt end of the rifle down on his head.

It is in this partial second of awareness that James's body reacts in double-time. He removes his gun from the holster inside his trenchcoat and in one fluid movement aims at the corporal's head. He can feel the resistance on his finger muscle, the warmth of the trigger which has absorbed his body heat and the instantaneous push back while the bullet moves towards its target. The soldier crumples to the ground and his rifle butt with him. But Liam cannot get up. Another soldier a few feet away who has struggled free has just fired his rifle at Liam. James is milliseconds too late. However, he aims and fires and this man too falls to the ground. The soldier groans as his rifle is ripped from his hands and his head is given a swift kick by one of the Volunteers. Two more shots from other guns ring out, two more soldiers fall. All the guns are acquired, and Liam is half lying on the ground yelling at the men to go, for God's sake, go!

The escape plans are in motion. Two Volunteers lift Liam and toss him in the car ahead of themselves. The cars fly down the road, the men on bicycles disperse in seconds and the men on foot run like the dickens for their safe houses. James should follow Plan A, through the laneway out of sight and straight to the train station. But he cannot. He needs to see that their trap at the trees is successful, and that Liam and the rifles are safe. He walks down two doors, goes into the side door of the shop, out of the back and runs along the back of the buildings until he finds the ladder that he had lain down in a narrow opening between two sets of buildings. He climbs to the roof, pulling the ladder behind him. There he lies flat on the roof and watches as the two cars now more than a mile away approach the trees. He hears the emergency bugle call of the soldiers and as the military from the barracks stream out in lorries and on foot, James sees the cars move into the grove of trees. There is an agonising moment when nothing happens and then he sees the two cars speeding into the horizon.

The lorries are only five minutes behind them, and he watches as they come to an abrupt halt at the tree line. The trees have been felled successfully, and the lorries must turn around and make a long detour. James takes off his black cap and replaces it with a sandy-coloured one from one of his deep pockets. He leaves the ladder on the roof and hangs down from the eaves trough until he can jump the last few feet to the ground. He makes his way to the end of the line of shops and carefully observes the street. The dead corporal lies on the ground and the three wounded soldiers are waiting for help. All of the others have run in the direction of the barracks. James nonchalantly crosses the street. He makes his way to his bicycle and arrives just in time to hop on the return train to Cork. The next train will be stopped and searched, but James will be home, cycling from Cork station straight to Tomás. He is worried because he does not know how badly Liam is hurt. He believes he was shot in the shoulder, but he has no way to find out until everyone is back where they should be. He does not think of the dead corporal. He thinks only of Tomás's disappointment when he hears that Liam is wounded.

Liam himself is so elated with the success of the ambush that he barely feels the bullet that is lodged in the soft flesh just inside his shoulder. One car goes straight to the safe house to dump the rifles, and the other steers Liam south and east to safety where a sympathetic doctor tends to his wound. He will spend the next few weeks hiding two doors over from an RIC station, from where the police send out patrols looking for him high and low. The people of Fermoy, however, will not be so protected. The day after the ambush the military will go on a rampage, smashing shop windows, looting and terrorising households where any Volunteers are known to live. The families are beaten, their homes trashed, and the windows broken. The second night, however, the people are organised. They gather in one crowd on the main street with pikes, clubs, and knives and dare those soldiers to try to destroy their homes and businesses. The soldiers are sufficiently surprised and intimidated. They head back to their quarters and lock themselves in!

Despite Liam's shot-up shoulder, Tomás, Terrence, and O'Hegarty are ecstatic. They are, after all, all three of them the top commanders of the Volunteers. They have made a major statement with this ambush, and the fact that they suffered no casualties while taking down an armed force of men gives the brigade a cache that cannot be bought. It is the best public relations they could have hoped for and a shrivelling, embarrassing defeat for the British. Heads will roll over this episode in the British hierarchy.

James does not know what he is going to say to Tomás or O'Hegarty. Liam has been shot up under his watch and though it could have been worse if that rifle butt had made contact, the fact is that he has failed his assignment. As he rides down the streets straight to Tomás's home, where he has been ordered to go, he feels sick to his stomach. He can see in his mind the soldier that he shot, almost as a reflex, lying on the sidewalk face down, blood pooled around his head. But the face he does not wish to see is Tomás'. He can barely think of the disappointment that Tomás, he knows, will try not to show. That is, if he is lucky. If he is unlucky, Tomás will be polite but to the point, even harsh, and dismiss him forthwith, never to call on him again. James knows this about Tomás. He is kind-hearted, quick-witted, fun-loving, and he is willing to give anyone the benefit of the doubt. But if you are not up to the job he will not fret, he will just move on.

As he pulls up to the back of Tomás's clothing goods store, above which the MacCurtain family lives, James is still filled with adrenalin and dread. He makes his way through the back door and to the meeting room and finds Tomás sitting staring at paperwork on his desk. James, sit down. You will be needing a cup of tea. James looks him straight in the eye. I am here to report, Sir, as ordered. Yes of course, but sit down and rest, Eilish will bring us a cup of tea. Sir, I am afraid I have bad news. Yes James, I know, but you also have been involved in a difficult episode. I am ordering you to sit down. James takes a seat. He is holding his sandy-coloured cap in his hands and suddenly becomes aware that he is squeezing it mercilessly. James, O'Hegarty has just left, I have been made aware of the circumstances. You should know that Lynch is now in a safe house, being tended by a doctor. So be at peace. Eilish arrives with a cup of tea, but James barely sees her, he is thinking of how on earth O'Hegarty, who was not at Fermoy, has already found out all of the details. He realises that Tomás knows Liam is hurt and he waits for the inevitable consequences.

Tomás sits and sips his tea. He watches James, who does not touch his cup but waits politely for direction from his commanding officer. The steam rises in swirls above Tomás's head. Still, he says nothing. Finally, he puts down his cup and looks James in the eye. You are a soldier of Ireland. You are a valued member of the Irish Republican Army. It is clear to all the world that any soldier has duties to perform which, from time to time, have unpleasant consequences. If in the performance of your duties, contact with the enemy results in their death, this is only an assurance that you have done your job to the best of your ability. I would like to congratulate you James, on a job well done. We have you to thank that Lynch has survived this ambush. Now please drink your tea.

Yes, sir. Thank you, sir. James drops his cap on his lap and puts his icy fingers around the teacup. The image of the pool of blood and the soldier lying face down fades from his mind. He smiles at the thought of Liam relaxed under the care of a doctor. And by the way, James, the tree-cutting was genius. Absolute genius!

As all of the RIC stationed in and around Cork search for the culprits of the Fermoy ambush, everyone keeps their head down. Nevertheless, the police pull out every file on every known Volunteer of the last three years and hunt them down, interrogate them, harass their families if they are not to be found, and generally make themselves as unpleasant as is legally allowed. And just to give them a little more bang for their buck, the British parliament declares Dáil Éireann an illegal assembly. It is now outlawed. They see that the MPs' release has not in fact stopped anything, and those bloody Irish are up to no good all over again. They know now the MPs are only aiding and abetting the local criminal elements. The Fermoy episode was a shocking wakeup call. They know Soloheadbeg could happen all over again, but they will put these bloody Irish in their place.

James, having never been on the police's radar, intends to keep things that way, and so as he rides home after an evening of connecting with his now many collaborators in the shops, the bakeries, and the pubs that are in the vicinity where the police are seen and heard, he decides to duck into a laneway and take a shortcut in order to avoid passing a group of Peelers. This route will have him cut across to Patrick Street, the main shopping thoroughfare of the city, a street he normally avoids because of traffic and steep hills and a strong police presence.

It is a cool October evening. The full moon is out and a breeze blows down the laneway creating a wind tunnel. As he reaches Patrick Street he comes to a halt and peeks out from the laneway to make sure there are no police lurking about. Instead, he notices a familiar figure on a bicycle charging down the hill towards him at top speed, trenchcoat flying in the wind. It is Terrence. Immediately Terrence slows down and both men nip back into the laneway to avoid being seen. They do this without even thinking about it. It is just the way things are now. Stay out of sight. Keep your head down. Jimmy, how are ye? asks Terrence as he straddles his bicycle, takes off his cap, and straightens his wind-blown hair. I am well, sir, very well, replies James as he observes this man, who was a constant sight and influence over his formative years. Terrence makes him smile, the easy way he has and the genuine interest, even affection, that he transmits when in close quarters with others, especially those he knows well. I am sorry I didn't have a chance to meet with you since Fermoy, Jimmy. What a great job you did there. We are all so grateful to you! How is Liam, sir? Ough, sure he is just great Jimmy, just great, no worries there! Terrence peeks out onto the street. Jimmy I am in a hurry to get home. My wife is not happy with me these days, I am late so often. He winks at James, but sure I have time for a fag. He pulls out a soft package of cigarettes and offers one to James. Thank you, sir. Both men huddle over Terrence's match. They walk down the wide sidewalk of Patrick Street, pushing their bikes and blowing smoke into the air. Terrence is speaking of the great need to keep acquiring guns for their collection. He believes that another insurrection is in their future, but they must figure out a way to get their hands on many more guns than they already have.

As far as Terrence is concerned, the fifteen rifles that they acquired are worth much less than the tremendous psychological blow to the British that the Fermoy ambush accomplished. As they talk, their cigarettes burn into the night air, and they eventually stop to put out their butts and hop back on their bikes. As Terrence turns his head to tip his hat to James, he stops and stares at the shop window in front of which they are standing. James turns to see what he is looking at. They turn and look each other in the eye. James knows exactly what Terrence is thinking. He is not one of us surely? No indeed, Jimmy, no indeed! Leave it with me sir, leave it with me. Aye Jimmy, I have every confidence in you. *Slán agus beannacht* Goodbye and blessings until I see you again! He takes off his hat and waves it in the air as he pedals into the distance. James stares at the store's signage: *T.W. Murray's Gunsmiths, Sporting Goods, Fishing Tackle, Guns and Ammunition.*

The next morning James is at O'Hegarty's before the sun rises. He has been up all night, thinking through the details. We had an idea, he tells O'Hegarty. Really Jimmy, we? Well, he didn't say so but I know he was thinking it. Sure, I have spent half my life watching Terry operate! He was thinking the same thing as me! Well, I will have occasion to speak to him at our next meeting. Anyway, what is your plan? That place must be jam-packed with guns. It is a wonder we never thought of it before!

James takes his friend Mick on a shopping expedition. While they enquire about fishing equipment, they surreptitiously scout out the inside of the store, the glass cases full of guns, and the boxes of ammunition on the shelves above. Mick engages Mr Murray in an animated discussion about fishing flies while James strolls about the shop looking at this and that and then nips in the back office of the store. He is looking for keys and it does not take him long to locate them in an overcoat hanging on a hook. Mimicking de Valera's trick, James takes the ball of wax he has kept warm in his hand and makes an impression of the large front door key. They shake the owner's hand and walk out into the street arguing about which flies might be the best to take on their next fishing trip. They wave to the owner and tell him they will be back next week. To avoid suspicion, they do indeed return the next week and choose a couple of fishing flies, talking excitedly about their upcoming fishing holiday on the west coast. The owner wishes them luck as they leave the premises, a smile from ear to ear on both their faces.

During the week of the so-called fishing expedition, they return to the shop, a newly constructed key in hand. They have waited for the darkest night of the month, no moon, and a sky full of dark clouds. The November wind blows but it does not slow them down. James steps out of a nearby lane, quickly walks to the store front, hugging the dark shadows and opens the door with the key. As quietly as possible a car rolls down the hill, no lights, no motor. It stops in front of the shop and a couple of the IRB men from the Grammar School episode quickly disembark the car, leaving the door open. Two walk inside the shop, one man stays at the wheel of the car and two men step into the shadows of the wall. Quickly, efficiently, the guns are passed from one man to the next through the propped open door and thrown into the car. Next come the boxes of ammunition. Finally, without a single word being spoken two men get in the car with the guns. They wait until the other two are away, start the car, and turn onto the next adjoining side street, heading straight to the designated supply depot to make an inventory before meeting Tomás and Terrence to report. Meantime, James jumps on his bicycle and rides to O'Hegarty. By eleven o'clock all of the men are home and sleeping like well-fed babies.

O'Hegarty has left for a few days to visit some of the outlying battalions of Volunteers. He sends word to James to meet him at the newspaper and tobacco shop which he is known to frequent and which James stops at from time to time. As James walks up the laneway to the shop, one of the sisters who run the small establishment and lives upstairs, calls out to James. Séamus, how are ye? Come inside for to get a paper? James is surprised by her invitation and cautiously steps inside the tiny dark shop. The two sisters are ten years older than James, more of an age with Terry and Tomás. They are long past marrying age and have teamed up to carve out a living for themselves by selling newspapers and tobacco and sweets. The shop is in a narrow lane directly across from the St Augustine's Friary church. The rooms they inhabit were once owned by the church next door. Indeed, it has a stained-glass window above the door and unbeknownst to James or anyone else, except perhaps O'Hegarty or Tomás, there is a trap door in the floor that leads directly underground through a tunnel into the basement of the church. There is also a hidden back door that opens onto a tiny causeway leading in a roundabout way out to the main street. O'Hegarty likes the hidden location off the street, the secret exits, and he likes the sisters. They are Cumann na mBan women, highly recommended by his wife for their nationalist fervour and their fearlessness. Why they are not married is a mystery to O'Hegarty, for they are attractive and slim and well-spoken, if slightly taller than most women. But who knows what their stories are? James does not even consider it.

Once in, Nora with her crooked smile and her sister Sheila, both of whom are wrapped in their shawls, smile at James. With a lowered voice, Sheila offers, I believe our dear friend Mr O'Hegarty would like to see you Séamus. Perhaps you could drop by tonight around eight o'clock? What, here? James asks. Indeed, Séamus, says Nora, we are always happy to see our friends! Aye, says James and continues out of the door and down the street, a newspaper in hand, wondering at the likes of those two spinsters whom O'Hegarty obviously has working for him. He shakes his head at the thought and smiles.

James is not surprised to see Mick at the meeting. Tomás and O'Hegarty are in the tiny back kitchen-come-meeting room. Intelligence from one of Tomás's friends has made them aware that a huge order of bicycles for the military has just been delivered to a warehouse. Tomás surmises that the bicycles will be used to trail his intelligence men and other Volunteers through the labyrinth of the cities' back and side lanes that they routinely use to nip out of sight. There will be a large number of men needed to clear out the warehouse. They need to move quickly and retrieve the bicycles before they are delivered to the various barracks. James and Mick are asked to invite a group of men they can trust, doers, not talkers, and meet at the warehouse at night with whatever they can find that will carry bicycles. Carts and ponies, cars, even wheelbarrows will be useful.

James spends the next day making arrangements with the reliable men that he knows from the Brigade. As agreed, they converge in the back lane of the warehouse under cover of darkness. Tomás's man has provided a key, and once the doors are open, they silently get to work. James has the men line up in the shadows on one side of the laneway, and they move towards the giant sliding door, load up, and proceed around the building on the other side. Once each man has as many as he can carry, they leave straight for home or some other hiding place. Some who live nearby return a second and third time. By midnight, all of the bicycles are gone, never to be returned. All of the men have dispersed, that particular group never to be reconvened. In and out, the work spread amongst as many reliable men as possible. Given the eight thousand Volunteers in and around the city, this is not only a sound policy by security standards, it allows every man the chance to contribute. Tomás is concerned that every man in his Brigade be given the opportunity. He believes that someday, maybe far in the future, but someday, these events will be recalled with pride.

Mick pushes the massive warehouse door shut and locks it back up. A good night's work, Séamus! Aye, indeed, replies James, and the friends shake hands and go in their opposite directions through narrow streets until they reach home. Over the next few weeks Tomás will oversee the dispersal of the bicycles to areas outside the city, where they will be slightly altered or painted so as to be unrecognisable. They will be given where the need is greatest, where transportation is often a problem for the locals, who are either too poor to afford bicycles or unable to replace broken ones.

As the November winds chill the air, the citizens of Cork are encouraged to note the first anniversary of Armistice Day on the eleventh. As if to mark the occasion, the heavens open and the north wind blows a terrific snowstorm across the entire British Isles. It is exactly a year since the finish of the Great War. James, however, marks the day with many of his friends at the Douglas Street pub toasting Denis MacNeilus (still in hiding) and reminiscing over the great escape from Cork Gaol. Yet he feels less merry than one might believe. His nightmare of Tomás Ashe has returned. He sees Tomás, whom he never met and only saw through photographs in the newspapers, calling out to him, slop and blood gurgling from his mouth, tears running down his face. He is reaching for James and James is desperate to get to him but cannot. It is as if the faster he runs to his outstretched hand, the faster Ashe recedes into the horizon.

Christmas comes and goes, and the city of Cork is overwhelmed with election fever once again. This time it is the municipal, city-wide elections. The process is to elect representatives for the city council, and once in place the city council members vote in one of their own as mayor. So many of the men running for office are Sinn Féin it seems to be a replication of last December's election. Terrence has convinced Tomás to run for council. At first Tomás is reticent to do so. Terry for heaven's sake, I have six children, a business to run, and a wife who likes to dance, not to mention the brigade. When am I ever going to get a chance to play my fiddle? Terry laughs, what are you talking about man? Sure, everyone knows you do nothing but lie about half the day. I on the other hand have been working as an MP, do all your work for you as your second in command of the Brigade and my wife also likes to dance! Sure, if I can do it so can you! Besides if you run for council and win there will be no doubt that you will be chosen as mayor. Just imagine, officiating commander of the IRA in Cork becomes mayor of the city. We will be able to achieve great things, Tomás. Think of it! They will not be able to hold us down!

Intrigued by the thought of influence, political power, and prestige to be used against the British, Tomás jumps on board. Whether he ends up mayor or not, Terry is right, the position will allow him endless possibilities to pry freedom from British hands. In the meantime, however, there is work to do. Tomás okays a daring raid on three police barracks just outside the city, all planned for the same evening, January the second. There is a strong hope that using the arms so far collected from the enemy and the small number of explosives created in certain households in the city, all three barracks could be attacked simultaneously, and a large number of arms confiscated. Three separate groups of men will be needed. Of the three groups, one battalion leader resigns, too overwhelmed at the responsibility and the possibility of casualties from enemy fire. The second barrack successfully defends itself, the homemade explosives failing to ignite. But the third, at a small village called Carricktohill, is a major success. Explosives breach the walls of the barracks, the police surrender, the guns and ammunition are collected, the police released and everyone hightails it home.

With the rash of recent episodes of theft, the ambushes at Araglin and Fermoy, and now the attack on two barracks, the British have come to the realisation that they are not dealing with fools. They have ordered an influx of their own intelligence officers to move to the city from London and find out how these things are happening right under their noses. They want answers, they want arrests, and they want to make an example. The culprits from Soloheadbeg are still on the loose; not a soul has been found from the Fermoy madness and now guns and bicycles are disappearing in alarming numbers from their traditional holding places. On top of it all, wounding and murders of their own men have come as a great shock.

But a strange turn of events has also occurred. RIC men are beginning to hand in their resignations and their list of new recruits has evaporated into the sun. The once lofty position of Police Constable has lost its shine. In small towns and villages everywhere, the constables, once greeted respectfully by almost everyone, are shunned and isolated. Even the Catholic officers find themselves outcasts in their communities, accused of working for the enemy. The pressure is starting to show. Even the commanding officer in charge of Fermoy has upped and quit after refusing an order to arrest a bevy of men, known to be driving a car the very day of the ambush. He actually filed a report claiming the order to arrest was unlawful! Imagine the cheek. Good riddance to him and his ilk. The decrease in numbers, however, will have to be filled. The British put their heads together and begin to plan. Order will be restored in this country one way or another and if the Irish want to play hard ball, hard ball is what we will play.

On January 30, Tomás is elected in without opposition. The Cork City Council holds their first meeting and within a few moments the vote for mayor is taken. Tomás MacCurtain is the only name on the ballot and wins a unanimous vote from every man on the city council. His easy ways, his kind words, his ability to get the job done, his unrelenting pressure on the British make him the only possible choice for this very first Republican council of Cork City.

Later in the week, his wife Eilish and their six children pose for a photograph for posterity. Eilish seems preoccupied, worried. Her youngest child sits on her knee, her other beautiful children with fresh rosy faces surround her. She is Lady Mayoress of the City of Cork, something she never dreamed of. She has no financial worries, a warm inviting home, and a husband who adores her. She should be smiling. But she is not. From the start of this new year, 1920, she has been having trouble sleeping. Her stomach is in an uproar. She is tired and losing weight. She can barely stand the sight of the RIC or the military as they saunter around the city, rifles in hand, stopping whomever they will, manhandling or harassing as they see fit. Her Tomás is tired also, overworked and under much stress, most of it self-induced, but stress, nonetheless. She cannot see an end in sight.

Tomás, on the other hand, stares at the camera with a smirk and a twinkle in his eye. He is thirty-five years old, and he is flying high on the possibility of moving Ireland towards real sovereignty and the British back to England. He knows in his gut that he is doing exactly what he needs to do. Things are changing, slowly, but changing. Yes, Tomás is happy. He spends countless hours with Terry and O'Hegarty and young Florrie going over intelligence reports from James, Mick, and others, and devising ways of continuing to pressure the British. They know they are having a significant effect because the British are up to something. The conversations via London that O'Hegarty has been privy to thanks to James's wiretapping convinces him that a big change is on the way. They are trying to find ways of reinforcing the police in the barracks to replace the men who are resigning. They are moving civilian spies in, and they are looking to reinforce the military, if that is possible.

The idea of civilian spies is worrisome and requires a concentrated effort by their main intelligence men, such as James, to improve their networks by recruiting people in key positions to pass on information. For instance, railway porters, hotel clerks, postal workers, pub owners and anyone who is in even the slightest contact with British moving in or out of the city. All of this information must be coalesced into reports that help to make sense of what the British are up to. James is a master at this. Whenever there is complicated information, seemingly without connections, James thinks on it, and then with his perfect penmanship he writes a clear crisp report with the possibilities as he sees them laid out for O'Hegarty and Tomás and Terrence to peruse. There is nothing that escapes his eye, and all of his information is included, down to the slightest detail. Once the report has been read and processed by the men in command, it is destroyed. Nobody keeps anything in writing. They do not need to because O'Hegarty has the closest thing to a photographic memory that any of them have ever come across.

James has been made aware of a new man in town. He calls himself Quinn, and there is something patently unpleasant about him. He is a veteran of the war and spent time in a German prisoner of war camp. He knew Roger Casement. This is his claim to fame, but he lets people know that he has a secret message for Michael Collins and needs to meet with him *tout de suite*. James and one of the older IRA men, a commander of one of the city's battalions, check him out in the pub. They are not happy with this sleazy, self-aggrandising man. Something is up. The commander assigns some of his men to keep watch. James talks out the possibilities with the commander and his friend, Mick Murphy, a Cork City athlete who is known as a tough competitor and a dedicated member of the Volunteers.

They consider the possibilities: Spy? Informer? Traitor? If he is on the British payroll, there will be evidence. They want to be sure. O'Hegarty sends out feelers. He hears that he should expect a letter with details about the new man Quinn arriving at a certain RIC barracks, where the coordination of British intelligence is underway. Florrie, Murphy, and James decide to visit the local postman. The British are quick learners, and the RIC mail now comes in a locked bag thanks to the many hold-ups and commandeering of mailbags. The postman is not impressed. Two men in trenchcoats, their hats down against the wind, making demands of the mail? Not likely as far as he is concerned. Get lost, he tells them. James and Murphy shrug their shoulders and laugh. Alright then, sure have it your way, says Murphy and pulls out a revolver from his coat pocket. He points it directly at the postman's chest. James gently pulls the locked bag from his hands. The postman does not give up easily. At least give it back to me when you are done, he pleads. Before James can reply, Murphy, who has no time for this, barks at the man, shut up and get walking or you'll be getting an additional hole in your arse. The postman does as he's told.

Florrie takes the bag while Murphy and James disperse. He takes a knife out of his pocket and cuts around the lock, neatly removing the circle of leather and the lock intact. Indeed, a letter is found. It is in code and must be taken to Terrence, who has a stolen cipher key hidden underneath the bottom of a drawer in his desk. It is exactly as they suspected. The unsavoury man is on the British payroll, sent by Dublin Castle to flush out Michael Collins. He is a Judas, ready to turn over his own for a lousy thirty coins of silver, in this case a hefty hundred pounds.

Now that the men are sure, a heated discussion ensues. This is a dangerous man. A traitor. If he would give away Michael Collins, one of the most respected leaders in the entire country, a survivor of the Easter Rising, and an ardent Republican working tirelessly for the last ten years on behalf of the Irish people, who would he not turn in? Indeed, all of their lives are now in peril. There is no doubt what the British would do to even the least of them if they were turned in and their activities made known. The order is given. He must be executed. The decision weighs heavily on Tomás and Terrence. They know that Michael Collins has been kept safely out of his reach. But they also know that in order to prevent the capture and execution of any one of their own men that he has come to know, it must be done.

But who will do this deed? And how will it be done? Not one of them has intentionally killed anyone, ever. James looks at Tomás. Everyone sitting at the table knows that he shot the soldier at Fermoy. But Tomás is not about to make an executioner of twenty-one-year-old James. He has already done his duty. I will do it myself, he tells the group. Don't be daft, laughs Terry. The mayor of Cork cannot be out executing people. I am Officiating Commander of Cork No. 1. I won't be asking my men to do anything I cannot do. Terry looks at him. Tomás, this is why we have a brigade. You must stay at arm's length. Your job is to give orders. Tomás, head down, thinks for a moment and finally, reluctantly, agrees. Well, if that is true for the officiating commander it is true for the vice officiating commander. He looks Terrence in the eye. Murphy stands up. Consider the job done.

James is relieved that he does not have to participate in this. He cannot explain why. In his mind's eye he sees the soldier that he shot lying face down in the pool of blood on the street in Fermoy. A formerly unknown sensation creeps up his legs and into his chest. He recalls the awareness of this same sensation as he sat in the train on the way back from the ambush, worrying about Liam and about what Tomás's reaction would be. He does not understand it. He is not afraid. He is not squeamish. He knows in his mind that it was the only possible action in the situation. In fact, he would have been remiss if he did not fire, and he would have never forgiven himself if Liam had been killed. Nevertheless, there it is, the barely detectable, yet unavoidable encroachment of a strange physical sensation slinking into his chest, like tendrils twisting around his heart.

The next day, Quinn the spy is contacted and invited to come and check out a cache of guns. Murphy and three other trusted men under his command escort Quinn to the outskirts of the city that evening. They walk in the shadows of a high stone wall that shelters a large graveyard and out to the edge of the city's boundaries to a farmer's field. As they move farther into the field, Quinn becomes nervous. He knows his time is up when Murphy turns on him and empties his pockets. He tells him that he has been found out and as a spy he will be executed. Quinn is at first speechless, but he is a veteran of the Great War. He has seen plenty of death. He scoffs at his executioners. One of the younger men, feeling overcome at the situation, takes his rosary beads out of his pocket and offers them to him. Do you wish to say a prayer? Murphy turns and glares at him. I shouldn't have brought him, he thinks to himself. Quinn takes the beads and rips them in two and tosses them back at his face. Hypocrites, he yells, go on then. Murphy slips his revolver out of his pocket and shoots. Two of the other men do likewise. They turn and leave Quinn the spy doubled over on the frosty earth. Halfway across the field, Murphy thinks twice. He returns to Quinn and gives him a swift kick. The man groans. Murphy kicks him over on his back and shoots him between the eyes. As he puts the revolver back into his trenchcoat pocket, he remembers the scrap of paper that he has prepared. In neatly formed letters it spells out *Spies beware*. He slips the note halfway into Quinn's coat where the congealed blood from his chest will keep it in place.

When James hears the story, told in quiet tones at the back of Nora and Sheila's shop late into the night, he remains cool-headed but fingers his beads in his pocket. God have mercy on his soul. He prays while Murphy talks and Tomás listens with downcast eyes. You have done your duty as a soldier, Terrence remarks. It is unfortunate, but there it is. We must protect our men, and that is what we have done.

As the days pass and the dead body is discovered and written about in the papers, the police become agitated. They know he was a spy. They know from the note found on his chest that the IRA know as well. Somehow, they are organised enough to discover Quinn's intentions and to act on it in a coordinated way. It is time to take off the gloves and put these people in their place. It is obvious to them that the mayor of the city must be fully aware of the murder. The regular patrols in the city are increased in number and strength. An already hostile tone is ratcheted up another notch and the police begin to stop whomsoever they feel like, to randomly search and harass and make their presence known. They redouble their efforts to find the men responsible for Fermoy and Carrigtwohill. They arrest anyone who might be remotely associated with the ambushes.

The IRA, on the other hand, through their growing matrix of citizens who volunteer information, make discoveries about the treatment of some of the men who have been arrested. There are monsters among the RIC and one of them is a local. He is a sadist who is apparently taking delight in driving IRA men to a state where they cry for their mothers. He will be stopped.

The council meeting discusses the information that has come to them. It is appalling. They agree unanimously that Constable Murtagh must be eliminated. He is not one of their own turned spy. He is one of the enemies', and a particularly nasty type. Thinking of the suffering of their men by his hand, they do not second guess their decision. The section of the city where Murtagh is known to reside is made responsible for the operation. Murtagh is followed and shot dead on the street. He did not even see the two trenchcoats slip up behind him in the dark March evening. The alarm sounds, the police pour into the streets, but the streets are empty. The British commander, Lieutenant Smyth, paces his office, his high black boots stamping the wooden floor. They have gone too far these bastards. We will teach them a lesson they won't soon forget. He pulls in a flock of trusted men. Blacken your faces boys. You are going night hunting.

James and Mick are on hand to help with the Murtagh execution if need be. James has his gun in his holster, his trenchcoat on, his hat pulled down. He stands straight against the wall in the shadows of a laneway across the street from the planned area of attack. He watches as Murtagh passes the storefront wherein are hidden the two executioners, men from another battalion. As Murtagh walks past, the two men exit the store without a sound and approach the policeman. He turns but it is too late. The bullets fly, the constable falls, and the men disperse. Just like that, in a flash. In his own head James marvels how quickly life can just disappear. He turns and heads straight for Tomás's place once he knows the two young men are safely away. May God have mercy on his soul, says Tomás, but thank the Lord our men will no longer have to suffer his abuse. It is hard enough being in gaol, never mind with brutes like that making your life a living hell. Though the lights are low James notices Tomás's weariness. The late hour and the shadows accentuate the tired eyes, the creased forehead. Good night, Séamus, and thank you. It is a tough job you are doing for us, but a necessary one. Please understand that it is appreciated. James nods with a straight face, but inside he is smiling at the recognition. Good night, sir.

Tomás heads upstairs to bed. It is after midnight. He is tired. His head is throbbing. He needs to be up early for meetings at the City Council. He needs to meet with O'Hegarty and Terry to decide what to do about the inevitable police response. They won't take this lightly. Eilish is awake nursing the baby. Happy birthday my love! Eilish reminds her husband that it is now officially his thirty-sixth birthday. Tomás come to bed, it will be a busy day tomorrow no doubt. The children are looking forward to baking you a cake! You must be sure to be home for dinner, no matter what comes up. They have a special gift for you. You won't want to disappoint them. Aye, aye, let me just kiss them goodnight, I have hardly seen them at all this week.

Tomás goes to the girls' bedroom and looks at their rosy cheeks poking out of their bedcovers. I am a lucky man, he thinks to himself. He steps to the next room, the boys' room, and looks in on his sons. He is so proud of his eldest son, who is doing well in school and seems to understand how to conduct himself in public, which is much appreciated by Tomás the politician. He goes to his bed and lies down. Just as he falls into a reverie there is a knock on the door. Eilish is annoyed. Stay in bed Tomás, I will answer and whoever it is I will tell them to check in with you in the morning. It is far too late. Tomás doesn't argue.

But as he hears Eilish's voice down the stairwell at the front door, he is suddenly overcome with alarm. What was he thinking allowing her to answer the door this time of night? He jumps out of bed. But it is too late. The thunderous thump-thump-thump of black boots bounding up his steps two at a time sends his adrenalin racing and his young son out of bed and into his room. Eilish is screaming. Tomás, Tomás! Daddy, daddy, his son is reaching for him, terrified. It is the last sound he hears. Men with blackened faces shoot him in the head, leave him lying crumpled on the floor and proceed to ransack his house while his children wail and his wife, crouched over her husband's body, tries piteously to keep him here on the earth beside her. Don't go, don't go, don't leave me. A cold March wind howls through the open front door, slamming it back and forth, back and forth. Tomás leaves the earth while this cacophony of sorrow plays on into the night.

STARVE

CHAPTER 7

MARCH – OCTOBER 1920

James cannot eat. In fact, he cannot get a single morsel of food past his lips. He raises the toast off his plate and dips it into the boiled egg, cooked perfectly to a bright runny mass and carries it all the way to his mouth. But he cannot part his lips. He feels repulsed at the thought of food actually entering his mouth. He lowers the toast to his plate. In the past James has never much thought of food. At least not until Tomás Ashe was murdered. His family has always managed to eat adequately, hence James's tall, fit physique. And so, he wonders at his own reaction to what should be a delicious breakfast, one of his favourites. James understands this revulsion has something to do with the murder, but he does not feel distress, or anguish or even an upset stomach. Indeed, he feels a surreal sense of calm and purpose. His head is clear and attuned to the details of working out the funeral. His mind is serene and so he has difficulty making the connection between his stomach and the murder. However, his thoughts drift continuously to the last time he saw Tomás. He has been trying to recall if he turned to wave as he left the house. Did he see him as he moved into the darkness of the night, or is it just his imagination? Did he actually get his last look at Tomás's face inside the office? He sees him sitting at his desk, his face tired, worn from a long day at his many tasks, but grateful to James for performing his duties, nonetheless. He thinks of him, just moments after he had left, surprised in his own home by those cowardly bastards, shooting him right in front of his family, his own wee'uns for God's sake. But his reverie is disturbed. James's mother has been watching him.

James my darling, you will have to eat sooner or later. Tomás is gone, I know, but it is left to the living to get the work done and you cannot work on an empty belly. Try to eat something my love. But James just looks ahead, pushes himself from the table, grabs his coat and heads out into the darkness of the very early morning. His mother watches him walk out of the door with only the slightest nod in her direction. Her heart glows with pride and pity for her beautiful boy. But she is worried. He has not eaten a thing as far as she can tell since the night of the murder. He looks tired and gaunt. As she watches him push off on his bicycle, she feels with her mother's heart how devastating these recent, terrible events are to him. And yet she thinks to herself, even now, he moves with grace and purpose, looking so much older and wiser than his age.

For his part, James does not feel the least bit graceful or wise. In fact, he feels like he is reeling. He is weak and lightheaded. O'Hegarty opens his back door, takes one look at him, and commands him to sit down. You are as pale as a ghost boy. When was the last time you ate something? O'Hegarty himself is as thin as a reed and has been living off tea and toast for days now. But he understands the warning signs of this neglect of the body. He goes to the kitchen and cuts two thick slices of bread from the loaf and slathers them with butter. He then pours two cups of hot steamy tea, pulls a chair out from the table, and demands that James sit. You and I are needed more than ever today, Jimmy my boy. And a pretty sight we will be if we collapse under the strain. It is men like us who get the job done. The Brits are eating heartily these last days. And rest assured they will be on their toes, taking a sharp look at us. We need to be prepared. Now let us eat this and toast our Tomás. He raises his cup of tea to James and takes a swig, bites off a chunk of bread with determination and watches while James does the same, though with a look of revulsion on his face as he chews slowly and with resolve. That a boy, Jimmy, those bastards will have nothing on us.

Today, the day of the funeral, is dreary and overcast and cold. But the wind is still. Like the people of Cork, it is as if the very heavens are holding their breath, frozen in shock and outrage. The men who were closest to Tomás Terrence, O'Hegarty, Florrie – took it upon themselves to plan the funeral. On the night of the murder, Father Dominic, the Capuchin Friar who is the spiritual director of the Cork No. 1 Brigade, attended to Eilish, who was completely overcome. He was freed from this task only when the most beautiful woman in the world ran to Eilish's side in the early hours of the morning, fighting her way through the crowds swarming out onto the road in front of the MacCurtain home, and beat down the door. Muriel had handed her own child over to her mother at the family estate and spent the next few days looking after Eilish and her children. If the truth be told, Muriel herself feels like she is living in an altered zone of time and space, where people have become reverse versions of themselves. Formerly happy faces are morose and tear-stained; formerly morose faces, such as those of the British military and RIC, are sporting smug, gleeful smirks. Children are listless and apathetic; adults are frenzied and disoriented. The murder has made headlines around the world, and like the astonished deer caught in the headlights, the people of Cork stare out at the world in horror while the world stares back in disbelief.

But the highly aesthetic ritual of the Catholic funeral and burial in all its orderliness, restraint, and discretion, walks everyone through the paces of the death march from church to grave. From dust you came and unto dust you shall return. Harsh words, yet there is a strange comfort in the thought of being relieved of the relentless, inexhaustible demands of life and disappearing without a care from the earth. One moment we are here and the next we are not. It will happen to you and to me, so do not fret, but do not waste a day, you do not know how many have been allotted to you. Such is the thinking of the 1st Cork Brigade Commander. They will waste no time moving forward. They will do it for Tomás in his stead. The foolish British, they have created yet another martyr and hero, and like the world over, the Irish love their heroes. He will be avenged and promptly. Collectively they toss caution to the wind. The British will not be here much longer. We will see to that. Every last man of the Brigade attends the funeral. They will march in unison, a show of strength, determination, and respect for the much-loved Tomás.

You don't have to imagine the streets thronged with people, the thousands who could not fit into the cathedral and spilled out into the funeral route for miles. You don't have to imagine the horse-drawn hearse overladen with wreaths of flowers. You don't have to imagine the hundreds of men marching behind the funeral cortège, dressed similarly in overcoats buttoned up against the cold, and fedoras, tipped at just such an angle as to make the British work a little harder to see their faces. You don't need to imagine any of it. You only need watch the few moments of moving film, taken by someone, who knows who, and preserved. Whoever it is, they are experimenting with the latest invention, newly acquired: a moving picture camera. They are recording a few moments for history, for posterity, perhaps for the police? No matter now, they have all gone from the earth, but the footage remains. It is black and white of course, but crystal clear so that almost everyone can be easily identified.

Watch the film clips. See Tomás lying in his coffin, his face serene, his hands crossed over his chest, his fingers entwined with a rosary. See the Brigade Guard of Honour keeping watch a few feet away, six men in IRA uniform surrounding the coffin, as immovable as the standing stones of Drombeg. See the throngs of people, sullen, crying, yet anxious to get a glimpse of Tomás's last visit to his church. This funeral Mass will be attended by almost every representative of the Church who resides in Cork County, followed by every dignitary, every city councillor, every man, woman or child whom Tomás ever bestowed a kind word upon. And there are so many. See the horse-drawn hearse slowly progressing along the winding streets flanked on either side by hundreds of people. Look at the flowers, a ridiculous number of flowers, so many they smother the hearse, and then more, for which there is no space, that must be carried by the men from the church to the gravesite.

Look carefully at the church steps. See the large group of men just stepped out of the massive cathedral doors and waiting for the people in front of them to proceed further. In the centre of the group there are two men who are each carrying a huge wreath of flowers. It is O'Hegarty and James. O'Hegarty stares at the camera in alarm, then discreetly closes his eyes and points his face up to the heavens. We know what he is thinking. He is thinking *Bloody hell!! Could my timing be worse?* O'Hegarty is a master of secrets and stealth but he has been undone for just a moment. His thick, dirty blonde and greying hair is brushed back off his forehead but won't be controlled and sticks straight up like a bristle brush. His long greying moustache frames the scowl of his lips. He is forty years old but looks fifty.

Now look to his left. You cannot miss the tall, distinguished young man looking directly at you. He is well-built, robust, and handsome. It is James. It is James at twenty-one years old, still innocent, if such a thing is possible, on this day in March of 1920 at the funeral of his murdered friend, mentor, mayor, and brigade commander. James's hair is still dark auburn, barely on the verge of receding. Look at how he is dressed, his lifelong appreciation of good grooming, dressing like a gentleman, obvious to the world. His overcoat is a thick, heavy wool. The collar of his white shirt is neatly tucked into his suit and only his tie is visible. Neither man is wearing a hat. Their hats have been taken off before entering the church and now their hands are full of flowers as they exit. The camera lingers for a moment; James watches it, his eyes following as it pans to his left. He makes the slightest smirk of disdain with his lips and looks away. Now see the grave site, the coffin being positioned. See Eilish sitting nearby, her children surrounding her. The youngest son breaks free of her embrace and his chubby little legs carry him running to the grave. See nine men lower the coffin on ropes into the grave. See James, he is the second man in on the right, bend down as they place the remains of Tomás deep into the earth and rise again. Not one of the men looks at the camera. They seem to intentionally keep their heads turned away. See the British soldiers nearby, rifles out, so outrageously disrespectful, joking around like idiots. Finally, see the temporary cross over the grave which is now filled in with loose earth. See the flowers, so many flowers they seem to cover the entire field of the graveyard. Watch the film clips and feel the pain. But it is just a glimpse, a tiny window through time, open for only a few seconds, and then the blind is pulled taut.

On the last day of March, Terrence MacSwiney is unanimously voted in as mayor of the city of Cork. He is saddened but writes an acceptance speech that focuses on the necessity for sacrifice and endurance. The British will go, he tells his fellow Republican Councillors; we just have to be patient and keep at it until they cannot bear us any longer. In the Brigade, Terrence moves up from Vice-Commandant to Officer Commanding. It is a cruel necessity that the instant one man is fallen, arrested, or otherwise indisposed, another man must immediately assume his position and responsibilities. There is no time to grieve. Tomás is out and Terrence must take over. He knows this and does not hesitate. He will keep the intensity of his sorrow and his loneliness to himself. There is no one who will miss Tomás more, and no one who is more convinced of his reward in heaven. A ripple effect is seen. O'Hegarty is next in line and must move up the chain of command and take Terrence's position. Florrie moves into the job of coordinating the intelligence that O'Hegarty has so carefully been cultivating. The information flows to him along a web of channels spooled all over the city and county. He will now share that web with Florrie and focus on the high-pressure job of command.

First order of business: find the men who did this. Eilish is grilled. We know they were covered head to foot. We know they had their faces blackened. Who pulled the trigger? How tall? Accents? Hair colour? What did they say, exactly? Within days the Brigade has men in every battalion around the city doing surveillance duty on every RIC station looking for one ginger-haired, short man and one tall brute of a man with black hair and a thick English accent. O'Hegarty has put every last man to work on this. It should not take long but for one fact: the British command is in the know, and they have quietly and secretively moved most of the men involved out of Cork and to other parts of the country.

In Dublin, Michael Collins is stewing. He writes to Terrence that he is sick at heart about Tomás and cannot sleep. Collins is not a man to let things go. He finally achieves rest only after he has been delivered of his best idea yet. We will hit them where it hurts, he thinks. And where does it hurt the most? In the pocketbook of course! He sends out orders to all brigade commanders across the country. Easter is in a few days, he tells them, and our people are feeling lowly. They could use a wee gift. Every brigade commander will oversee the burning to cinders of every tax office in your jurisdiction. Do not walk away until every paper record of the taxes owed by every Irish man, woman, or child is but a pile of ash, burned to a crisp, fluttering away in the wind. Oh, and let's make a special celebration of our fourth anniversary of the Easter Rising. Let's put our explosives divisions to work. I know they have been working hard stockpiling homemade bombs whenever possible. Let's test them out. There seem to be quite a few empty police barracks in the countryside these days. Let's make sure they will never be inhabited again. All three hundred and fifty of them need to come down, brick by brick, if necessary, but a little gelignite should do the trick. *Cáisc shona mo chairde*, Happy Easter my friends!

Late in the evening of Holy Saturday, James excuses himself from his family. His mother is not happy about it. She is preparing the traditional leg of lamb with mint sauce for Easter Sunday and has baked an elaborate cake for dessert. His older sisters have come by to help out. His father is in fine form, having won the weekend greyhound races on a five-to-one payout. James would be happy to sit by the fire and talk politics with his family, especially Edward who, James notes, is always the happiest to spend time with him. But the passing of Tomás is still a raw wound. There is work to do. He kisses his mother and as he walks out of the back door, having duly checked the premises from two windows, his father calls him back and slips him a few pounds. Thanks, Da, he says, don't worry, I will stay at a friend's tonight. I do not worry son; I have put you in good St Joseph's hands. He will watch over you. But be careful nonetheless! James smiles to himself. Good St Joseph, I wonder what *he* thinks? He puts his hands in his pockets and fingers his beads. Well St Joseph, I have never done *this* before. Help me to get it right.

James rides his bike over to Pa Murray. Murray, one of the fiercest men James has ever met, is acting as bodyguard for Terrence. He is a good fifteen years older than James. He is big, and burly and fearless. You get the impression, looking at him, that he belongs in the wild west of America, rustling cattle and fighting the bad guys. Murray has taken on the enormous responsibility of keeping Terrence out of the crosshairs of the British. It is clear that Terrence cannot stay in his own home. As the newly elected mayor, and the new Cork No. 1 Brigade Commander, there is a strong possibility that the British may try to pull off the same trick twice. Muriel and the baby have moved to her mother's estate, and Terrence is in hiding at night.

When James arrives, it is dusk, and they are loading their guns. Terrence looks at him but does not smile. James wonders if his face will ever light up again after this latest indecency of the British. His face is drawn with welts under his eyes, and he looks almost as thin as he did the last time he got out of gaol. Terrence glances at James with a reassuring nod. Sure, we won't be needing them, but just in case, Séamus, just in case. Are you loaded up? Aye sir, and James pulls up his loose-fitting, thick woollen jumper to show Terrence his gun in holster. Well, we shouldn't need them. What we do need is fire power of another sort. And he tosses James a small box of wooden matches. We will take the Patrick Street office; O'Hegarty and Florrie will take the northern office. You boys know that all of the offices across the country are being treated the same way, tonight at the same time. The enemy will have a rude awakening Monday morning.

On bikes, the three men cut across town through lanes and side streets. They arrive at the back door of the regional Revenue Office. It is housed in a small building with no signage. Both floors contain offices. There will be much paper. Murray easily gains entrance with one quick, brutal kick to the door. The men enter, quickly close the door, and light a lantern. Outside, the streets are quiet. It is the last day of fasting in Lent and almost everyone in Ireland is sitting by the fire with a drink in hand, looking forward to tomorrow's feast. In Cork, every Irish Republican will pour a drink and toast Tomás. What a terrible Lent it has been.

The three men look around. Desks and full filing cabinets. Terrence pulls out one drawer at random. It lists heads of households, names, addresses, and numbers. The cabinet is a compilation of names of all of southern Cork carefully handwritten and cross-referenced. Upstairs they find the documents that are the key to the cross-reference numbers. Cabinets full of paper with the minutiae of income accrued, taxes paid, taxes owed, collected, in arrears, over the years. Well, we best get this done in bulk. He nods to Murray who goes out of the door to the back of the building and silently returns a few moments later. He is carrying a large metal barrel handily sawed in half, which had been strategically placed outside on Good Friday when no one was around. One half for upstairs, one for downstairs. James pulls the drawers out, hands them to Terrence, who dumps the contents into the barrel and then hands the drawer back to Murray who neatly places it back in the cabinet. Once the fire is lit the cards burn in seconds and they must work quickly to keep the fire going. We are doing this with some class, says Terrence. The lads will be burning down the entire building in some places, but here in Cork we like to send a message! James and Murray smile at Terrence's attempt at humour despite his low spirits. Within a half hour every filing drawer has been emptied and returned to its place in the extensive cabinet, and there is a pile of ash in the barrel sitting on top of the largest desk in the room. They head upstairs. These files are much larger, full-length papers in much larger cabinets. By midnight, the job is complete. They have had to open the upstairs window and dump the ash at one point, but they have not left a single record intact. They do not dump the final burning but leave all the cinders on the desktop. Underneath, the desk is smoking and looks like it may ignite. No one is worried. They extinguish their lantern and make their way to their bicycles. Make sure you head to your safe house, Séamus. Just in case, just in case. They won't be taking this lightly! Aye sir, and James hops on his bicycle and heads out to the home of his sister Dolly. He will sleep in her front room by the fire and join her when she heads to Mass and to the family home for Easter celebrations.

While James is busy burning tax records, the battalions in the rural areas where so many RIC have resigned or deserted are also busy. On the night of Holy Saturday, each of them is razed to the ground. All files are first burned to cinders and the building itself, as a symbol of oppression, completely destroyed. Inside two weeks of the murder of Tomás, the British are paying the price, and it is a debilitating one. But the British are a formidable enemy. They have dealt with the Irish and their rebellions for centuries. Buildings can be rebuilt. Income information for taxes can be recollected. We will get these people under foot, and we will do it now. If they don't care for the Royal Irish Constabulary, men given the privilege to oversee their own people from their own ranks, they can get to know men brought in from England. Good luck to them.

Winston Churchill is a man of foresight. He has been muttering over the Irish situation for some time. Predicting the eventual demise of the RIC months ago, he initiated a recruitment of men to replace the Irish who, under pressure from the IRA, have been deserting their posts and refusing to do their duty. It is a win-win situation for Churchill. So many men in England are out of work after having returned from the Great War, and so are well trained in dealing with enemies and fire power. He will pay them a half pound a day and house and feed them in the barracks that are still standing. All over Britain a certain type of man will line up for a chance at this lucrative position. So what if it means going across to Ireland; we'll show them a thing or two. It's good pay, room and board, back to army life with my mates. There are no jobs here in England, so why not? Mere days after the murder of Tomás, the new police reinforcements begin to arrive across the country. But there is a slight problem. The government does not have enough proper uniforms. They improvise and use a combination of two existing uniforms stockpiled in warehouses, one black, the other tan coloured. The Black and Tans are born.

Meanwhile, Muriel has problems. Her husband is sleeping in the home of a brute of a man at night and working nonstop during the day. She has hardly a moment with him. Though she is busy enough helping Eilish, who is still grieving so hard she can barely look after her children, Muriel nevertheless wants some time with Terrence. He sometimes stops by in the morning around ten o'clock when the RIC are at their tea and unlikely to be on the lookout. But she is lonely and depressed. Tomás's death has affected her as well, but little attention is being paid to her. And the most beautiful woman in the world is used to a tad more devotion than she is currently experiencing. She takes it upon herself to make other arrangements for her Terrence. Her mother suggests old friends of the family, an elderly couple who live in one of the better parts of town, Sunday's Well. They have never met Terrence, but they graciously extend their comfortable home to him every evening. He cannot, however, forgo a bodyguard, and so Florrie, armed to the teeth, begins to spend nights in the home as well. At least her Terrence will be made comfortable and given the opportunity to get some sleep. If he is well-rested, he will be more likely to stop by in the morning to see his wife and child.

The merry month of May descends upon the world, but the people are anything but merry. No one will be paying any taxes for a couple of years but still there is a pall that lies over the city, indeed over the whole country. The murder of Tomás has left in its wake an ominous foreboding that no one can seem to shake. Even the weather seems to be affected. It is as if spring never arrives. As the weeks pass there is nary a hint of warmth. The children continue to be bundled up in sweaters and hats, their cheeks keep the rosy glow of cooler seasons. It will turn out to be the coldest summer on record, and no summer through the remainder of the century will be as bitter, as windy, or as overcast as this summer of 1920.

Word arrives that two of the constables who participated in Tomás's murder have been located. They are to be found at the large King Street Barracks. Pa Murray requests the honour. James also wishes to go. The more he thinks of the last time he saw Tomás, mere minutes before his death, the angrier he becomes. In fact, now that the shock of the entire event has worn off, anger has replaced the initial sense of the surreal. James has joined the legions of the perpetually downcast Volunteers who have not smiled in weeks. They are watching as the Black and Tans get organised in their military barracks. Those are a happy lot. A crew well-suited to army life, camaraderie, a full pay cheque, room and board, something no decent employer in England would extend to this bunch. They are heavily armed and have personalities obviously suited to confrontation, harassment, a bit of illicit fun, and are only too happy to take on the Irish. So many of the lads in the IRA are surviving on so much less, often on the beneficence of their families and friends when there is no work, and no jobs to be had. This is the new face of the enemy, young men, a lot like themselves, but sitting pretty on the other side of the fence. They will be a challenge.

O'Hegarty will not have James participating in the takedown of the two officers. He has invested too much in this lad to have him shot in the street or arrested and hanged in Cork Gaol. No. Murray is the man for this. Brute force will get this job done. O'Hegarty is adamant that James stays behind. We have enough men for this job, Jimmy my boy. No need for you to be taking unnecessary risks.

Murray stakes out the barracks with a group of four other IRA. As the officers leave and prepare to mount the tram to head home, Murray steps out and confronts them. Before they know what has hit them Murray has reminded them of their participation in Tomás's murder and shoots them straight through the heart. They fall on the street, their mouths still forming the rounded O of surprise. There is a third officer who has not been marked as a participant. Murray requests his gun, which he quickly hands over, and then sends him packing. The Volunteers disperse.

But O'Hegarty is not finished yet. Swanzy, the commander who gave the deadly orders, has been moved, smuggled out of Cork and nowhere to be seen. Michael Collins makes it a priority to find this man. All across Ireland the IRA are on the lookout. In the meantime, a new command structure is instituted by the British with the

Black and Tans. Britain looks around at its high-ranking military officers and gives them a new job: fix the Irish situation and do it quickly. You have everything you need: men, guns, authority. Put these people in their place. Eliminate these arrogant IRA. They must be extinguished, sent packing, or crushed. Do not allow the people to harbour them. Punish them if they do so, as necessary. If they wish to be beaten back into submission, so be it.

James is in discussions with Terrence and O'Hegarty. They want some surveillance work done. There is an idea being bandied about that Blarney Barracks should be the next big hit. The Blarney RIC and accompanying Black and Tans are a major interference with communication channels. Too many of the boys have been stopped and searched on their travels in that vicinity. We would like the entire place burnt to the ground. Take a ride up there, Jimmy, and see what you think. Terrence almost smiles at James, his rolling eyes chuckling at O'Hegarty's coded language. Yes sir. Meet us tonight at Wallaces'. The ladies will fix you a cup of tea on your return.

James bikes the seven or so miles to Blarney. It is another cool day with the wind in his face. He is reminded of the many cycling afternoons spent with his old friend Seán. They had been to Blarney years ago, checking out the famous castle. Seán had almost got lost in the adjoining overgrown gardens enclosed in a rock wall perimeter; James had to call to him to help him find his way out. I will go to Canada someday and check up on him, thinks James to himself.

In Blarney, the police barracks is a house that shares a wall with a popular pub on one side. It is in the town square, a picturesque, quaint village with the castle in the distance. But Blarney was once a mill town. Two rivers leading down to the Lee provided plenty of waterpower to turn the mills. Because of this there are many roads from all directions in and out of the village. And in the vicinity of Blarney and Cork there are literally thousands of military men housed in barracks where the main roads lead straight to Blarney.

James sees this problem right away and thinks on it. In order to be successful, the operation has to be quickly executed and just like Fermoy, the escape routes must be fail-safe. In order to do so, on so many roads, many men will be needed to engage the enemy and allow those involved in the takedown to escape the area. Blockages and delays will have to be quickly erected far from the town to allow time for exit. James nonchalantly parks his bicycle and takes a walk around the town square. The barracks, like all barracks across Ireland now, has been reinforced with steel window shutters and doors and waist-high sandbags piled at the edge of the road, creating a perimeter. There will be no surprise attacks from the front or back. He wanders into the pub and has a pint while surveying the wall common with the police barracks. It is a thick, old stone wall but it looks like some gelignite would easily loosen the mortar. Yes, that would do the trick. Once the wall is breached, the men can attack from inside the pub and try to capture as many arms as possible. The blown-out wall will make the barracks unuseable, and they will have killed two birds with one stone. The trick is to get in and out without any casualties, at least no Irish casualties.

While sipping his tea, compliments of the Wallace sisters, James wonders at the ability of these two women to open their doors at seven in the morning and close them well after midnight, selling newspapers and tobacco and all the while catering to O'Hegarty and Terrence and so many others, delivering messages, passing along parcels, guns, or other items of questionable origin, destined for questionable activities. They are surely privy to the equivalent of state secrets, but the two of them just smile confidently, the growing crow's feet around their eyes do nothing to inhibit their highly intelligent visage. Anyone who cares to question them will get a look straight in the eye and a simple, We sell newspapers here, sure I can't imagine what you are talking about. Terrence, knowing how they worship him, is always careful to be professional and business-like, yet he winks at James. Honestly Terry, give it up, he wants to say, but just shakes his head.

O'Hegarty arrives and they go over the details. This will be the biggest operation yet. Terrence thinks out loud. At least twenty men on site, and dozens of others positioned six, five, four, three, and two miles from the site on all roads. We cannot afford a surprise from the military. We will need to choose the road with the best chances for a complete getaway. We'll need several cars. Thank the Lord for the Grey brothers. The other two nod their heads. They are good lads, aye, says O'Hegarty, passing along a rare compliment. I know they started out working for Tomás, but I think they will continue in his name, says Terrence solemnly. James recalls how Tomás passed by the brothers' newly opened mechanics shop a few years back and stopped to meet the brothers and take a look around. They were not Volunteers and were not involved in the Gaelic League or the Athletic Association. But Tomás made a point of looking in on them regularly, sending some business their way and enquiring about their high-tech job of servicing cars. He built a genuine friendship with them, and then offered them an opportunity to help him out from time to time. The brothers were happy to provide a car. That agreement has slowly transformed into providing getaway cars. And the brothers have become eager to do it. They see the way of the future and they want in at the start. They are quick and fearless risk-takers. They use their customers' vehicles and return them to the shop, polished up and ready to be picked up by the owners who are none the wiser. Yes, the Grey brothers will have to provide at least three cars for the Blarney job, continues Terrence. So, Séamus, what are ye thinking?

James asks one of the Wallace sisters for paper and pencil. She hands him a writing pad and a pencil, and he goes to work. Quickly he draws out the route from Cork to Blarney and adds in all of the subsidiary routes with their proximity to military or police. We should go about dusk when the people are winding down for the day. Fermoy was too early in the morning; everybody was ready for a showdown. Dusk will find the Peelers ready for a pint or their beds. There will be no problem bringing three cars up to the side of the pub but furthest from the barracks so that the explosion won't affect them. The wall is old stone with loose masonry. It should fall with a couple of well-placed blocks, or we could make a frame with guncotton, and that may do the trick. Once the opening is breached, we will need to have everybody inside and outside with arms at the ready. Judging by the reaction we got at Fermoy, they will come out shooting, the pack of them. We need a couple of guys across the street, maybe more if we have enough guns and a couple at the back for the big picture, to check if anybody is making any counter manoeuvres. We could use a sniper, hidden on the roof across the street.

Okay Séamus, it sounds good, what about the retreat? Yes, I have thought that through, says James, excited now to tell the best of his plan. We will need to get away out of there like lightning because the first thing they will do after the explosion is shoot off the Varey lights. That will send every military man and RIC in the county storming out to Blarney. O'Hegarty looks at the two men. I know Tomás thought the tree felling was a perfect solution to redirecting the military without casualties. Is it possible this time around? Aye sir, it is, on several of the roads, but not all. The best route to take back home is the Waterloo Road since it is the least likely to be used as an access road from Cork or Ballincollig where most of the military are stationed.

Thorough as usual Séamus, says Terrence, still without a smile on his face. He picks up his pack of cigarettes from the table and offers one to James and O'Hegarty. Smoke swirls about the dimly lit back room and hangs in the air. We want this to go off quickly. I am thinking next week, Tuesday. It will give us time to get everything put in place. It is best if we use the 6th Battalion to help us out with the road obstructions. That part of the city has seen little action and the men are looking to contribute. The 1st Battalion will show them the way. I will have each section be put in charge of one road. Séamus you can work with them to have the tree felling ready and waiting. Also, every man in the cars must be armed and have extra ammunition on him. We don't know just how long this will last. Perhaps you and Mick could spend the day in Blarney and be our eyes until we get there. If there is a problem, you can send a Morse message to my office via the safe house there.

Aye sir, there is something else we should be careful about. Many of us on surveillance duty have noticed the tightened security around the barracks across the city as you know. But I also have noted a strong tendency of the Peelers themselves keeping a look out. They seem to be checking out anybody and everybody in the vicinity of their barracks. Just as a precaution we might want to think about leaving the Grey brothers' shop in intervals, seeing as it is so close to the barracks there at the corner.

I have trained you well Jimmy, O'Hegarty replies. But not to worry, Terry and I will leave in twenty-minute intervals and pick up the lads at different points in the city on the way out of town. You keep a keen eye on the barracks in Blarney and let me know exactly where the trees will be felled. We will create some other roadblocks at these points and wherever else you indicate. O'Hegarty points to the makeshift map. With any luck, says Terry, blowing the last of his cigarette smoke into the fog, we will be long gone and back home tucked in our beds before the military can get into Blarney. And by the way Séamus, Seán sends a hello your way. I received a letter from him a while back. He is thinking about marrying. Imagine that, Seán with a wife! Canadian girls must be something, laughs James. But he is pleased to receive the nod from his old friend.

In the early afternoon of the first of June, James and his friend Mick ride their bicycles into Blarney. It is a beautiful day, and James revels in the warmth and sunshine that has been so fickle in this cool spring. On the way in, he points out to Mick the trees that are ready to be given a last shove onto the road, creating a roadblock. They will depend on the Varey lights that the British themselves will set off as their signal to fell the trees and make a run for it. James has spent the entire week going over the escape plan with the various groups of men from 6th Battalion who will man the roads that the British will attempt to take to get to Blarney once the explosion goes off. Some of the roads will be foiled with downed trees, but others where there are no trees must be delayed with man-made roadblocks of sandbags and gunfire, or surprise attacks from under bridges. These will be the most dangerous. James has made sure that the men will have the cover of ditches, and roadside hedges and a definite route to retreat across the fields and back into Cork. He has not stopped working all week on this and his efforts have been recognised. Before he left this morning, Terry pulled him aside and shook his hand, thanking him for all of his hard work. James's natural reaction is to make light of his own contribution. Nevertheless, it is a great compliment coming from Terrence. And he feels it. He feels that he is part of something bigger than himself, working with men who sooner or later will be recognised as great men for their time. James feels this must be true whether they fail or they succeed. Stories will be told some day, songs will be sung and when Terry is an old man, he will be known as a contemporary of Éamonn de Valera, Michael Collins, and Arthur Griffith, and the rest. And here am I, James, riding a bicycle into Cork on Terry's orders, about to shock the British one more time.

Exactly at the agreed-upon time, the cars begin to arrive. James and Mick are lying low on a roof that affords them a view of the entire countryside. James chuckles to himself to see the vans arrive, five in a row, twenty minutes apart. The Grey brothers must be using a business fleet, he laughs with Mick. The men disembark just outside town and begin to walk into the town square. The drivers take the vans to the back of the barracks and pull over on the

Waterloo Road. All the men will have to do is make it across the back fields and hop into the vans to take off back home.

As the men walk into town, they take up their positions in groups, sitting on the wall, having a smoke, or across the street walking with purpose. The rest wait in the back of the town square with an easy advance between buildings once the charge goes off. At just ten minutes to ten, ten minutes before closing time, a car pulls up to the pub and a group of men jump out. They are walking tightly together, hiding the large frame of guncotton as they enter the premises. Wasting no time, they begin to set up the explosive against the wall, while the man in charge, Sandow, chats with the bartender, advising the surprised but cooperative man to move back and out of the way. He points to the back door of the pub for the few patrons left just before closing to move outside and away from harm. No one is allowed out of the front doors. There is no doubt in anyone's mind of what is about to happen. The men with the guncotton frame set it against the wall, pull handkerchiefs from their pockets and cover their mouths and noses. It is an old stone wall and there will be dust. But although James, who has moved inside the pub, has pulled out his gun in anticipation of the explosion and the Peelers next door responding, he is not prepared for what happens next. The magnitude of the explosion is far greater than anyone anticipated. Everyone in the room is reeling from the impact of the noise and the resulting mushroom cloud of dust and debris which makes breathing almost impossible. The men closest to the wall who were in charge of the guncotton had covered their faces with handkerchiefs, but even they are shocked by the scale of the blast. Furniture is blown up to the ceiling, glasses shatter, and the earth shakes. The sound is deafening and even farmers three and four miles away know something wild is happening. As the dust settles, the men realise that despite the shocking blast, the wall has not been breached. They are looking at the back of a fireplace in the barracks. They had placed the explosive at the worst possible position in front of several feet of thick stone wall and additionally a fireplace behind that. Only two or three of the four layers of wall have been destroyed. James's heart sinks. Immediately he realises a vital error in his estimation of the wall. Suddenly, he sees in his mind's eye what he should have noted last week, the layout of the roof of the barracks and the placement of the chimneys. I should have been more careful. God help us all now.

Just as anticipated, the first thing the police do is run to the roof of the barracks and set off the Varey lights. The flares reach incredibly high into the sky and as they do the Peelers come out shooting. But they are wary and take cover behind their sandbags. Once Sandow and the rest realise they will be getting no guns through this wall they order a retreat. With pistols blaring, the thirty-odd men in and around the pub take off for the vans. The men are in a state of disbelief and disarray. It is hard to believe that an explosion that strong failed to make the mark. And with hundreds of military personnel on their way, there is little time to put up a showdown with the Blarney RIC. The only thing to do is retreat and the men make a beeline for the vans. Further out towards the city, the roadblocks are doing the trick, and the wary military, deceived by the violence of the explosion, believe that a much greater force awaits them and so proceed with such caution they do not arrive at Blarney until midnight.

Meanwhile, just as Terry had hoped, the IRA have put their guns back in safe dumps and tucked themselves in their beds. At the mechanic's garage the Grey brothers have their customer's vans lined up, rinsed off and ready to be picked up in the morning by their owners. James heads straight to the Wallace sisters to report to O'Hegarty and Terrence. He gives them a play by play of the entire event. His one disappointment is that he had to leave his bicycle behind in order to hitch a ride home in a van. Never mind, Séamus, 'twill all be fine in the morning, those RIC boys won't be staying in any building with a wall that has been compromised. They will be packing their bags, and exhausted too, after staying up all night. We on the other hand are home to our beds. Well done Séamus, well done. But sir, I want to make my apologies for erring on the placement of the charge. James feels compelled to admit his culpability. Séamus, don't be daft. We appreciate your reports, always, but you must know we double and triple check everything. Our own Brigade Engineer, Dowling, took a look as well in order to estimate the amount of explosive needed. Even he didn't catch on to the thickness of those walls. And just so you know, Florrie also made a trip up there to check out all of our plans.

O'Hegarty studies James's introspective look. Is there anything you might have done differently, Séamus? Aye sir, there is. I should have paid more attention to the placement of the chimneys on the roof. If I had followed them down, I would have noticed that the wall must have been much thicker than it first appeared. James explains his thinking clearly while Terrence and O'Hegarty listen. Just as O'Hegarty is about to speak, Terrence flashes his eyes at him and pushes himself up from his chair. Séamus, we are all indebted to your keen eye and loyalty to the cause and to us as Commanders. We will all learn from our joint mistakes. Go home, and sleep well. You have done a fine job. As far as I know, and we have had several check-ins via phone already, we have suffered no casualties and not one man of the hundred or so involved in this event has been arrested. That is due in no small part to your significant intelligence skills. Goodnight Séamus and thank you for sharing your insights. Terrence is sincere but still unsmiling. It is as if he has forgotten how to smile. Off with ye now boy, chuckles O'Hegarty, who is happy and relieved that none of his men have been compromised. He waves James out the door. As he walks home, hugging the shadows of the back lanes and side streets, he can't help but remember the fun-filled Terry who he grew up watching and admiring. Terrence is different now that Tomás has gone. Maybe we all are, thinks James to himself.

With the disappearance of Colonel Swanzy, Lieutenant Colonel Brice Smyth is sent to Cork as the newly appointed Divisional Commissioner for the province of Munster. He wants to get his message out right away and hits the road running with a speech to his troops, the local RIC in the small town of Listowel in County Kerry, northwest of Cork City. He enters the police station with his second-in-command and a small group of soldiers. The commander of the RIC and RIC on duty gather to hear what he has to say. Shoot and shoot to effect. The more you shoot the better I will like it… We want your assistance in wiping out Sinn Féin. As the words drop from his mouth, the local men surrounding him stare at each other in disbelief. Are you telling us to shoot unarmed men? asks one of the RIC. Smyth is not a stupid man. He is a veteran of the Great

War who earned medals for bravery and accolades for intelligence, but he is *not* an Irishman. He has been sent here to do a job, and as a man loyal to king and country, do the job he will. The senior RIC officer of the group steps forward. His name is Jeremiah Mee and he will, in a few short months, be working for Michael Collins and Countess Markiewicz. Right now, he is so full of contempt for Smyth that he can barely splutter his reply. He takes off his belt with gun and holster, throws it on the table and tells Smyth, Go to hell, you murderer. Immediately Smyth orders his arrest, but the RIC of this barracks are proud and devoted to their highly respected young commanding officer. They are also, every one of them Irishmen.

Without a word, every man in the barracks under Mee's command moves to surround Smyth, while leaving Jeremiah free to make the next move, and give the order. Mee and Smyth stare at each other with defiance and revulsion. The tension in the room is palpable. As far as Smyth is concerned it is a mutiny. As far as Mee is concerned, it is an outrage of national proportions. It is a shocking moment for both sides. The impasse is contained after a few moments when Smyth's second-in-command leads him to an adjoining room and convinces him to let it go. These may be RIC, but they are Irishmen! Once the politics gets going in their blood, they are fucking impossible. Let's head out. Nothing good can come of this. Smyth and his men leave the building as Mee's group watches menacingly. In the next few days, as the word spreads about Smyth's orders, more than one thousand remaining RIC officers across the country will resign. Keeping the peace as an RIC is one thing. Murdering your own countrymen on the whim of the English is another. It is June 1920, three months since Tomás's murder, and the gloves are off.

When O'Hegarty and Terrence get word of Smyth's orders, they do the maths. Smyth is in charge of all the remaining RIC and the newly-formed Black and Tans. Though many of the rural RIC posts have been abandoned and destroyed, the urban centres are still up and running and working overtime. Add to this the hundreds of new men, English men, brought in, geared up, and living in the military barracks which are far more impregnable than their RIC counterparts with massive grounds, buildings too numerous to count and stockpiles of arms at the ready. Stockpiles which are the envy of the world. It adds up to a devastating number of British on

Irish soil just looking for an excuse to take out the IRA. Something must be done and done quickly. Somehow a message must be sent. A deterrent must be inflicted before the British have a chance to start shooting as per Smyth's orders. Terrence is worried about his men; so many of them from across the entire county of Cork have been identified thanks to the film of the funeral. But O'Hegarty is worried about war. They are not yet ready for a second full-scale rebellion. There are men plenty willing to fight, but nowhere near enough arms, despite their efforts over the last months. Terrence takes a quick trip to Dublin GHQ and meets up with Michael Collins. Get rid of that bloody swaggering big mouth. If it is cold-blooded murder he wants, let him have it. Indeed.

O'Hegarty, through his vast network of intelligence, has every man on the ground keeping tabs on Smyth. In fact, James has spent his twenty-second birthday lying on the roof of a shop with a pair of binoculars checking out the Victoria Barracks, the biggest barracks in the city housing many hundreds of military, and now Black and Tans. But it is not James who discovers the whereabouts of Smyth. It is another of O'Hegarty's men, a waiter at the hoity-toity country club that many of the senior military men frequent. The club serves swanky luncheons, fancy dinners, good scotch and entertains the officers' wives from time to time with music and singers. In addition, there are a limited number of rooms where special guests may stay.

In the early evening of the seventeenth of July, O'Hegarty receives a phone call. He is here, staying at the club. As we speak, he is sitting down to his supper. Immediately O'Hegarty sends out an order to mobilise whatever men from his web who are available. Within minutes a group has been gathered to take care of the commissioner. James is among them. He waits across the street from the club awaiting the signal. When Seán Culhane, a tough, streetwise young man, younger even than James, walks up the steps and brushes his hair back with his hand two times running, it is the signal for James and four others to converge on the steps behind him. Each man is armed. James has his hand on his pistol, resting inside his shoulder holster as always. Culhane steps into the dining room and pokes his gun in the waiter's back to protect him from suspicion, and the waiter leads the group to Smyth. None of the men have even seen his face and they need the waiter to point him out. Smyth is at the back of the room at a round table enjoying his roast beef. It is cooked just as he likes it: runny, red, almost raw. At the moment Smyth raises his eyes towards them it is too late, and he knows it. He bolts for the door, his plate and wine glass crashing about behind him while all five men open fire. He is hit in his head, in his heart, and in his chest. He falls down onto his knees at the door, holding his chest. Blood is running through his fingers and pooling on the floor below his knees when he finally falls face forward onto the floor.

They do not look back and not a man in the club tries to stop them. They step over the body, their shoes dipped in his now freely flowing blood. Once outside, each man runs for the cover of the lanes and side streets. Directly James joins a group, who on O'Hegarty's orders collect Terrence and escort him back to the local mental hospital, wherein he has been offered a room to sleep. It is a brilliant idea. If the military are looking for another high-profile target, they won't be looking in the looney bin. A few stay near Terrence as guards, the rest disperse to their safe houses. As James falls asleep on the floor of his sister's front room, he stares at the flames of the fire. In the moments before sleep overwhelms him, James fancies he sees Tomás Ashe, watching him through the flames, his mouth gurgling slop, his face running with tears.

In the morning, after his sister has coaxed some porridge into him, James heads straight for the Wallace sisters' shop. Sure enough, there is a meeting of men from around the city with Terrence and O'Hegarty. James hangs back and listens. Culhane is there telling the story. James does not care for his boastful tone. He is tough, sure enough. But laying bullets into a man at close range is not something James will describe. Ever. The true story is in the details that are omitted. The look of the man, shock, anger, terror, rolling over his face in split seconds. The desperate fight for life superseding the deadly effect of bullets, if only for a moment. The silent, horrified outrage on the faces of the others in the room. The dried blood on boots, noticed in the morning, just when you thought it was all a bad nightmare. This is the story. But the history books will tell only Culhane's version, sanitised of any niggling details, as if the taking of life, even the enemy's, is simple and straightforward and without consequence to the perpetrator. Terrence catches a glimpse of James's face. Later he pulls him aside. We are at war Séamus, as you know, and it will get worse before it gets better. Had Smyth been allowed to live the consequences would be unconscionable. We would all be running for our lives, and you know as well as I do that Smyth would have no hesitation in taking you and me out given half a chance. You have done the right thing; you followed orders and thereby saved many of our lives. Each man handles these things differently. Some men must talk. It relieves the stress. Then there are men like us, who neither need to talk nor wish to. The important point is the orders were carried out effectively and efficiently. Aye sir, they were. They certainly were.

Winston Churchill is beside himself. On July 19, a curfew is imposed on the City of Cork. Anybody seen on the streets after ten in the evening is taking his life in his hands. The Black and Tans have been given *carte blanche*, and they are about to be let loose on the city.

Terrence and O'Hegarty put their heads together. A message must be sent of equal weight. Take your curfew and shove it. Florrie, James, Mick, and a few select others are sent on a mission. The King Street Barracks. It is where the murderers who took Tomás were stationed. Let us deal with this one first. Dowling has prepared some explosives. Take extra ammunition with you. We aren't leaving until it is naught but a pile of smouldering bricks. I will be joining you tonight boys, O'Hegarty smiles for a change. Once Terrence is safely delivered to the mental hospital, O'Hegarty, James, and the rest, set out to meet at the barracks after ten o'clock. They hide in the shadows until the explosives set against the side wall do their job, suddenly ripping through the silence of the evening and the bricks of the building. Then they open fire. But the RIC have obviously made plans. At the first blast of the explosion, they escape to the top floor and barricade themselves in. Not to worry boys, they will be ripping off that steel to jump from the windows in a few minutes. O'Hegarty nods to Dowling, who sets up several more charges around the base of the building. Alright fellas we best be heading home. We wouldn't want to be caught out during curfew, and he winks at James. As James heads down the back laneway, he can see the flames shooting into the sky and knows the RIC inside will be looking for elsewhere to sleep tonight. The King Street Barracks are now relegated to history.

Days pass. James is working more closely than ever with O'Hegarty. Terrence has ordered the men to be on constant surveillance of the Black and Tans. They are proving to be quite a force of brutes. They routinely scout the city after curfew looking for anybody out and about. They pile onto lorries and tear down the streets shooting here and there, through windows, at barking dogs, or anything else that strikes their fancy. Waiting until people are sure to be in their beds, they seem to love nothing more than barging into the homes of known Republican families, trashing their belongings, roughing up the men and seeing what fun they can get out of the women. Only a few days ago one of the poor girls in the Cumann na mBan, trying to stop the beating of an elderly neighbour, interjected and asked for mercy. The old man was let go, but she herself was dragged into a room in the old man's house. Not a sound did anyone hear from her as the other Black and Tans stood about laughing and waiting, holding the neighbours back at the point of a gun. It wasn't until the big lout came swaggering out and the lot of them took off, shooting at the moon, that the poor girl staggered out of the house to go back home, her clothes in shreds, her face mottled and cut, her eyes on the way to being swollen shut. Similar stories are popping up all over the country.

Terrence is completely and utterly scandalised by the brutality of this new force. They will need all of their wits about them to fight these bastards. They are not the RIC. They are not Irishmen. They are truly the enemy, politically, culturally, and morally. Terrence calls a meeting. They need to put their heads together and come up with a coordinated plan. All of the battalion commanders need to attend. City Hall is closed up by six o'clock: the lawyers, the bureaucrats, even the cleaners, off to their homes for the evening. Meet in my office at seven. Use the back entrance. Take extra precautions.

Just before seven, Terry's private secretary at the mayoral office, Con Harrington, slips across the street for a cup of tea. A little sustenance is in order after a long day at the office. He is required to stay late this evening in order to help the payroll office, his former place of employ. He must do this because his replacement has just been arrested by the Black and Tans and nobody else knows how to do the job quickly so that people can collect their pay packets two days hence. He knows it will be a long night. Back across the street to the huge limestone edifice that is the Cork City Hall, in through the back door, he happens to glance out of a window and see several hundred military and Black and Tans in lorries, advancing down the avenue at top speed. He knows in his heart exactly who their target is. His teacup hits the floor with a smash and a minor explosion of steam as he runs like the wind across the terrazzo floor of the long corridor to warn Terry. But Terry's men have seen them coming through the upper windows and Terry himself is on his way out of the building. Con is worried about sensitive documents that might be found in his office. In particular the cipher key that Michael Collins had sent and that is sitting in the back of Terry's bottom drawer. Is there anything you want me to dispose of? he asks. Terrence doesn't miss a beat. He is cool and composed and his steady gait does not slacken. No, Con, thanks, it has all been taken care of. Make haste now and don't be caught by this crew. You wouldn't know what they would be up to.

When Tomás and his peers were elected as the first Republican City Council in the history of Cork, they had the foresight to know that the day would come when the British would come looking for them. In anticipation of a quick getaway, they had secret doors built into the main floor walls leading directly outside. They are designed to meld into the panelling and are impossible to see. Con and Terry trot quickly down the stairs heading straight for one of these doors. As they reach the bottom of the grand staircase, a soldier who has just entered the building sees them and calls for them to stop. Clearly he does not recognise the mayor, and Terry makes his way around the back of the staircase while Con distracts the soldier and heads for the front door. Alas, everything is against Terry this night. He has forgotten his specially made key for the secret doors at the mental hospital. But Terrence is a resourceful man and not disheartened. He heads straight for the nearest window, quickly heaves it open and throws himself outside onto the grass. He heads for one of the small outbuildings to duck out of sight. Some of his men are already there. It is the only place to wait until the outside patrols give up.

But again, his luck is thwarted. A roving band of soldiers comes around the corner and manage to stick their head in the small building. It is obvious they have orders to look in every nook and cranny, with no going home until the mayor is found. They promptly put him in cuffs. His men who were at the meeting are picked up one by one on their escape routes. The only man in the upper echelons of the Cork No. 1 Brigade not to be arrested is Florrie, who was out of town. O'Hegarty is packed up and thrown in a lorry. Liam Lynch likewise. Joe O'Connor, the Brigade Quartermaster, is tossed in beside them. First Battalion OC Dan 'Sandow' O' Donovan (so-called due to his uncanny resemblance to a high-profile boxer of the day), who had worked on the Blarney event is next, Mick Leahy follows and seven or eight others, including Con. Off to Victoria Barracks they go to await their fate, while the convoy of two or three hundred soldiers follow them. But the British do not leave the area unscathed. Dozens of people have come out to see what this massive group of soldiers is about, and they are scandalised that their Lord Mayor is taken. Given the treatment of the previous Lord Mayor of Cork, the people fear for his safety and yell and boo and hiss at the soldiers. The angrier ones curse them. Some pick up stones and fire them at the trucks. Word of this nefarious deed spreads across the city like wildfire.

Indeed, on what grounds did the British come anyway? The City Hall is locked up every night at six o' clock sharp. Not even a cleaner remains on the premises. Terrence is the only man in the empty, locked building, holed up in his office until ten or eleven most nights desperately trying to keep a handle on his impossible workload. But hardly a man is aware of this. Only Con and O'Hegarty. How is it that the British should come this night of all nights, and at just the time the meeting has begun? No one will ever discover the answer to this question, but it will become painfully obvious to James, in a few short months, what must have happened.

In the meantime, the entire group spends three sorrowful days enduring the hospitality of the Black and Tans at the Victoria Barracks detention cells and worried about the organisation. Collectively they represent the entire command structure of Cork County. The first night in the cold, unpleasant cells, O'Hegarty turns over and over in his mind the possible explanations for how the British came to know of their presence. Liam Lynch prays his rosary quietly to himself. Terrence does likewise. These two, of all the men, are spiritually attuned like no others. Some of the men believe them to be almost mystics in their worldview, connected to the spiritual world in ways men like O'Hegarty simply cannot fathom.

The others pray for a miracle. Nobody is breaking into Victoria Barracks to release them, and the Black and Tans are the least likely of any British force to treat them with decency much less a sense of law and order. This intuitive knowledge works its way to the surface of each man's mind as the night progresses. And so, the men pray. Every like-minded Republican in Cork City prays also. Especially those who are aware of the status of each man in the IRA with their critical knowledge and expertise. James himself is fingering his beads constantly. He is nervous. Very nervous. Florrie, despite his level head, is also beside himself with worry. The two men meet at Wallaces'. They know that of anyone left in the upper echelons of the organisation the two of them are privy to the broadest scope of intelligence and general information. They decide to wait until Monday morning to gauge the British reactions, but at that point James will travel to Dublin to meet with Michael Collins and decide how to proceed in terms of running the organisation in Cork. Florrie will stay put and meet with the remaining men who are in positions of command in the various battalions.

Neither man feels ready to take on any of the jobs now in peril. But James is nothing if not reliable and he sets up the meeting by instructing O'Hegarty's contact to get in touch with Collins. Within minutes he receives a call back. It is the big fella himself. Séamus, aye, good to hear from you. I see we have a wee bit of trouble in Cork. Take the train on Monday morning to Dublin. We will have lunch and chat. And don't be taking any heed of persons on the train who might be nearby. They are friends even though they might be surly-looking! James hangs up the phone and thinks again of his dislike of Collins, his ease and calm, when clearly the sky is falling. Nevertheless, plans must be made. But his greatest worry is for Terrence and O'Hegarty. James thinks of St Joseph and begins a dialogue. Good St Joseph, if I ever needed you, I need you now. If you are with me like my Da believes, please show us the way. But a better thing would be a miracle to somehow let these men walk away. For if they stay in gaol, they are sure to be hanged, and I don't know if even you could stop the British from that.

And on Monday morning a miracle ensues. Not a total miracle, but still a miracle, nonetheless. From the moment they enter the cells, each man refuses to acknowledge the legality of their situation. After all, an Irish Republic was declared months ago, and the British are trespassing on Irish soil. We have our own courts, our own parliament, Dáil Eireann, and our own way of doing things. They decide that a hunger strike is the fastest possible route to release, and they refuse to eat the meagre breakfast they are offered the first morning. Sensing a hunger strike coming on, the British make lunch an appetising hot meal. But despite rumbling stomachs and the smell of sizzling bacon, the men turn their noses up at the food and continue their story-telling and breaking out into song across the gaol's corridors, for even though they have been separated, sound carries like a symphony. They discuss and plan aloud, without fear that their English captors might hear, for they speak in their native Irish tongue. They have become quite accustomed to using it over the last few years and it makes the English guards scoff and rail at them by turns. Not a man can understand the difficult language with its strange guttural sounds, flowing vowels and oddly placed tones of emphasis. After the third day of listening to a foreign tongue banter all the day long, the British become irritated. With nary a morsel consumed by a single man, the British relent and release all concerned on Sunday morning, just in time for Mass. All except Terrence.

James has decided to go to Dublin a day early. He cannot bear the wait-and-see attitude of Michael Collins and he will be happy to tell him so. He is just preparing to leave for the train station when he gets the news. He happily turns around and heads straight for O'Hegarty's. The entire city spends the day toasting their good luck and the multitude of saints who many believe have answered their prayers and intervened on their behalf. But everyone knows it is not a total victory. Yet they are hopeful that Terrence too will soon be released.

But Terrence is not released. He is left to face the charges alone. But what charges? There is only one of any consequence. Possession of a cipher key. Oh, you nasty pack of liars, thinks Terry. I gave that key to my man who escaped with it. My drawer was empty. The British do not know that Terrence actually was in possession of a cipher key. On their initial search of his office, they had found nothing, just as Terrence had assured Con. All they had were some letters in Terry's pockets, among them one from the mayor of Paris requesting information about the ports, and another, a copy of a letter Terry had sent to the Pope in response to the recent beautification of Oliver Plunkett, the first Irish saint to be proclaimed in centuries. But a trial is useless without evidence and so within an hour a party of men are sent back to search once again. Ah yes, lo and behold, a cipher key is found in the very place it had not been just an hour before. It is a coincidence that it is a copy of the very key he has been using to decipher their top-secret messages, picked up on route, and returned to the mailbags. Now a serious charge will be laid. The second Republican Lord Mayor of Cork will be held to account. Terry is not worried. He is however hungry. For while the rest of the men went straight home to a hearty breakfast and a steaming cup of tea, Terry continued his fast. But he is convinced he will follow his men and be released soon, just as every hunger striking prisoner in British custody has been since the grisly, unspeakable death of Tomás Ashe.

Indeed, hunger is a state that the Irish know all too well, thanks to the British. Poverty, often extreme poverty, has meant that malnutrition has been a common enough phenomenon across the island from decade to decade. But relentless hunger, hunger without hope or mercy, that is a thing, the secret knowledge of which is locked in the very genetic code of almost every Irish man, woman, and child born who survived the summer of 1845. That summer the entire country was struck a blow the likes of which is almost indescribable.

Hunger is a terrible thing. Desperate, out of control, wild hunger, is beyond the capacity of our imagination. Emaciated bodies are the result of the unsuccessful quest for the energy that life requires. That energy can come in the form of food, or in the form of stored fat tidily kept in lipid cells here and there within the human form. Those lipid cells give us shape, sometimes exotic shape, or erotic shape, sometimes offensive shape, most times they send out the message of strength and vigour and a robust energetic nature. They send out the signal: life resides here in this matrix of cells and moving parts. But the human body is a marvellous machine. Its many secrets are yet beyond our discovery. However, we have discovered some things. And one of these is that human cells retain a kind of memory of trauma. Passed on from generation to generation in our genetic codes, we carry with us the shock, distress, and anguish of our forebearers' physical misery.

The father experiences physical trauma that induces extreme stress. His genetic code is marked, and when he passes on his genes to his son those chemical markers have an impact on exactly how the genetic code is expressed. It is trans-generational inheritance from father to son to grandson. Perhaps it serves a function, allowing the progeny of those who suffered extreme circumstances to be better prepared themselves for similar events. Perhaps not. Those who study this so-called epigenetics do not yet know with any certainty. But trans-generational inheritance may explain the ability of so many young men of James's generation to undertake hunger as a political tool, and survive its harrowing effects. It is James's grandparents who survived the Great Famine of 1845 to 1847. For if they had not, we would not be telling this story. And it is quite certain that James and Terrence and so many others carried a genetic code that was without a doubt marked indelibly by hunger.

The summer of 1845 was a cool one. Not uncommon for Ireland. But come August the rain began to fall and hardly a day passed that was not cold and damp and windy. The potatoes had been planted in the spring, and previous years had yielded bumper harvests. There was no reason to believe that it would not be the same this year. But Mother Nature turned her back to all of Europe, and especially to Ireland, when a little-known spore, *Phytophthora Infestans*, probably carried aboard ships all the way from South America, made its way into the air, swirled across the rural landscapes of western Europe and finally reached Ireland, where its rampant reproduction was aided and abetted by the unrelenting weather. The spore landed on the leaves of the potato plant and spread a light fibrous mesh into and through the greenery, sucking out the moisture and leaving the plant to turn black and crumble into dust. The rain then carried the spores into the ground where they attacked the roots of the plants and made their way into the flesh of the tuber. There, the least bit of moisture allowed the spores to germinate and attack the potato with white slimy lesions, and with incredible speed reduce it to a black and brown disgusting, putrid pulp.

At this time, thanks to the tremendous nutrition of the potato, the population of Ireland was bursting at the seams. Over eight million people inhabited the island, an increase from two million one hundred years prior. Of course, the English were aghast at such numbers. The large families that could be sustained on a half-acre plot of land, if sown with potatoes, were astounding to them. Potatoes being a complex carbohydrate packed with vitamin C, vitamin B6, potassium, iron, magnesium, and many other trace elements, filled the body with energy, nutrition, antioxidants, and fibre. They are a miracle food first brought over from Peru, land of the Incas, by the Conquistadores of Spain. In a terrific irony, the humble little tuber was planted by the English in Ireland for the first time around 1589, compliments of Sir Walter Raleigh, on forty thousand acres of land just outside Cork.

We need not doubt that Raleigh had no idea how he was about to benefit generations of Irishmen. Sir Walter, handsome, adventurous, well-groomed and with impeccable taste, sporting a clean little pointed beard and oiled back hair, became a favourite of the Queen, Elizabeth I. Some say she was secretly in love with him. But when he started out, he was a typical young Englishman: Protestant, a soldier, an adventurer, an explorer, and charming to boot. Sir Walter was more than happy to make his name on the backs of the Irish, putting down rebellions and making examples of Irish rebels. And in the 1580s rebels in Ireland were coming out of the woodwork. But not everyone was a rebel. The clan system of the Celts has some advantages as a social structure, but it was not a good tool for keeping a country united. Some of the clans had sworn allegiance to the English monarch in a foolhardy attempt to maintain their own personal power at the expense of their native rivals.

To complicate things further, the Protestant Reformation had become problematic for some of the English ascendency who had put down roots in Ireland hundreds of years before. Many of these long-standing family dynasties had intermarried with the surrounding Celtic royalty, and over the years were known to be more Irish than the Irish themselves. They spoke English and Gaelic, and considered themselves the true aristocracy of Ireland, believing the absentee English landlords to be a scourge on the proper administration of the country. Many remained Catholic throughout the reformation and had a hard time reconciling with the Protestant English. They held their own set of grievances against the Crown, usually to do with the insufferable drain that England put on the country in the form of taxes and the outright thievery of natural resources. They held vast estates, and entire generations of Irishmen were born and died on their holdings. They may have been arrogant, self-righteous, and demanding taskmasters, yet they understood the need to treat their people with some semblance of dignity and ensure their welfare, unlike the absentee landlords of the bulk of the nation. A good example of this type of family is the Fitzgeralds of the Cork area. In the 1580s they led rebellions against the British, commonly known as the Desmond Rebellions, the Desmonds being a particular branch of the Fitzgerald dynasty. James Fitzgerald, having had quite enough of his Protestant cousins' demands, travels to Europe to find support in the form of an army. The Pope agrees. Those English must be dealt with, and together with the Spanish, mortal enemies of the British, they make their way to the shores of Ireland on the west coast to aid in driving the British out of the island.

Walter Raleigh, a twenty-six-year-old captain on a British vessel, is in the party that traps the Spaniards and the Papal soldiers on the tip of the Dingle Peninsula at Smerwick. With him is his soon-to-be lifelong friend and famous poet Edmund Spenser. It is a spectacularly beautiful spot, looking out to the ocean and back to the mountains, but perhaps in their case spectacularly disastrous as there was nowhere to run or hide from the superior English fighting force. They retreat to an ancient fort, soon to become known as *Dun an Oir*, Field of Slaughter, but there is little hope of victory. In an apparently compassionate moment, the English offer the trapped men a way out. Surrender in peace and we will let you board your vessels and go back where you came from. It is an offer they cannot refuse because their Irish comrades cannot get through the mountains to come to their aid and are prevented by the British fleet from coming by water. The men acquiesce, put down their arms and send forth their surrender to the British Admiral who promptly reneges on his promise.

All of the men are corralled into one spot. It takes two days to execute them in small groups. This is Walter's job. In typically English fashion he ponders how he can get through this exhausting work with the least effort and the most gain. He decides to behead them, toss the bodies off the cliff into the raging waters below and bury just the heads. After all it is much easier to bury six hundred heads. Think of the graves that would have to be dug for six hundred grown men! Walter is young and full of energy and gets through this work efficiently. However, his superiors have an idea. Let us spare the leaders and have a little fun. We will grant them clemency if they convert to Protestantism. Let's see how loyal they are to their Pope and their Catholic superstitions.

Perhaps after watching the head of every last man under their command roll off shoulders, spurting dark red blood onto the bright green grass, the commanders are feeling a little resentful. Or perhaps they have finally learned their lesson in regard to trusting the British. Either way, not a man relents. They will not face the Christ in judgement, traitors to their faith. These British might have the power to execute, but their power is temporal. Revenge is mine, sayeth the Lord. It is obvious to the Spanish and indeed the Irish that these men will, sooner or later, be rotting in hell. The Papal soldiers and Spanish are as certain of this as the Irish are, once they get a taste of British cruelty. Every one of the thirty high-ranking men has each of his arms and legs broken in three places by the ship's ironsmith. Then they are left to suffer their agony scattered across the field soaking in their own troops' blood for twenty-four hours before finally, mercifully, being hanged to the jeers and catcalls of their captors. The field where the beheading takes place will be named by the Irish, *Gort a Ghearradh*, Field of the Cutting, and the field where the heads are buried will be labelled, *Gort na gCeann*, Field of the Heads. Several centuries later, after the year 2000, archaeologists will finally corroborate the long-told stories of the locals, when the field is slowly eroded by the sea and skulls are found bobbing about after every storm.

Walter returns to England a hero. He is knighted and granted an estate of forty thousand acres east of Cork City at Youghal. After all, he has caught the Queen's attention and she is happy to reward such a charming young man for keeping the Irish under foot. His shipmate, Edmund, is also rewarded with a large estate in the north of Cork City, the ruins of which you may find today. It is under a tree in the yard that he will write his most famous poem for Queen Elizabeth, *The Faerie Queen*.

While Edmund is writing, Sir Walter wanders the massive forests of his estate. The lay of the land undulates with thousands of ancient oak trees. At one time it must have been a sacred place for the druids, who revered the oak. But Walter is not concerned, for his first idea is to cut down those trees and use the wood for wine casks, thereby undercutting the European market and making himself rich. Secondly, he plants his few potato tubers and a little tobacco to see how they might take to their new environment. Edmund will stay for many years in Cork, extend his holdings and get to know the Irish so well that he will write a pamphlet on the impossibility of ever totally subjugating them. Indeed, he will argue, so why not just wipe them off the face of the earth? The island is, after all, such a pretty place for Englishmen to holiday.

Such musings in print must not be allowed, however, and Elizabeth, ever the politician, forbids the distribution of the pamphlets. Eventually Sir Walter will tire of Cork and Ireland altogether. He is not much of a farmer, and those trees are damn hard to saw through. He will return to London. His potatoes will stay. They will thrive, secreted from farmer to farmer across the country. This clandestine, underground crop will save the Irish again and again over the next few hundred years. Indeed, when the British take up the practice from time to time of scorched earth warfare, burning away the crops of oats, barley, corn, and wheat as punishment for some push-back from the Irish, the lowly potato tuber, hidden in the dark earth will become a staple of their diet. It will allow them to survive the ravaging of the land. When under duress, the Irish will harvest their potatoes by night and hide them underground, out of sight of the raging British who are wondering how they survive without grain and vegetables. The Lord knows they are too poor to have cattle or other livestock. We have made sure of that.

But in the summer of 1845, even the potato turns against them. By mid-August, the first of the infected plants are wondered at, as an aberration. But it is no aberration. The rain and the wind spread the spores across the entire island and wherever there once was a potato field, there becomes a sodden mess that disgusts even the pigs.

The British are not too worried about this situation. Their vast estates continue to produce corn and oats and barley and if they happen to come visit their holdings, they find their large vegetable gardens overgrown with cabbage and carrots and turnips. Their cattle and swine and sheep are fat from the lush grass of the hillsides. There is plenty to eat. Who needs potatoes? And if their Irish tenants cannot pay the rent, and have no crops to eat, it is their own damn fault. Be off with them. The landlord will pay fewer taxes to the crown, which is always an advantageous situation. And just to make sure they do not come back, the sherriff is called, the doors and walls of their cottages are broken down with battering rams and the thatch of the roof set on fire. Goodbye and good riddance. Those who have the foresight to sell everything they own before the sheriff comes calling head out to the ports to catch a ship that will take them to a new life in America or Australia or even just in Liverpool. But many will die en route of typhus, their bodies buried at sea. Many more will make it to their new homes only to die of disease before the authorities can even allow them entry. Such is the case in Toronto, where the local Catholic bishop, Michael Power, will set up a field hospital to care for the forty thousand Irish refugees landing at the City Port. They will be tested for typhus before they will be allowed entry and those infected with the tell-tale sign of black sores in their mouths will perish in the tents of the hospital, tended by the nuns, volunteer doctors, and the good bishop, who will eventually himself become a statistic of the deadly disease.

The poor are always with us, says the Lord, but the Irish know he was not referring to the current state of affairs. This is not poverty. This is want. This is neglect and negligence. This is greed. This is stubborn, wilful blindness. This is bigotry gone mad. This is, in the end, genocide. The only explanation: demons have been let loose upon the earth. And those demons, in the form of absentee landlords represented by their agents, make their way through the land, evicting families, burning down homes and turning out hungry men, women and children into the roadside ditches with nothing but the clothes on their back.

Ever ready to take advantage of a good situation, there are some of the British who are willing to sell cornmeal to the wandering hordes at triple the usual price. The few pennies some might have kept close to their bosom are soon gone and desperation and hunger become daily sights for those Irish lucky enough to weather this terror but who have not a crumb extra to give.

While the numbers of starving and homeless create a spectre on the land, the British landlords carry on exporting their bounteous crops out of Cork Harbour, their ships spilling over with grain to be sold for a high profit in the rest of the British Isles. Never mind that Irish lot, look how many of them there are. It is nature's way of controlling that ridiculous population. Next summer whoever is left will eat again. But instead, the summer of 1846 is as bad, if not worse than the summer before. The meagre potato crop salvaged from disaster is planted with great hope, but the spore has not finished its ravaging of the land. The crop fails again. For those who were able to survive 1845 and actually plant in the spring it is a crushing blow. Stories begin to leak out to the good common people of England of the hardship endured by their neighbours. The stories are so terrifying no one believes them. Yet the stories continue to seep into the country and so various newspapers and government committee members are sent to investigate.

Why yes, entire families are starving. Why yes, in some regions, for instance West Cork, there is not so much as a soup kitchen available. The reporters publish drawings of the sights they have been witness to. Whole families, emaciated limbs jutting out of rags, dying together huddled against the cold in the ditches or in abandoned ruinous outbuildings. Finally, when the pictures and the stories continue to bombard the English there is political pressure to help out. The government must do something. This is unconscionable, English citizens call out. But the landlords prefer to wait it out and blatantly ignore the government's directives. It is the Quakers who take it upon themselves to create soup kitchens in the worst areas and distribute sustenance freely. It becomes a common observation that God may have created the potato blight, but the English created the famine. So few landlords actually demonstrate compassion and do something to help out that those who do, the ones who actually took it upon themselves to feed their neighbours or wandering strangers alike, will be remembered for their good works through the generations to come.

Meantime, stories both good and bad infuse themselves into the national psyche. There are the Protestant ladies who are willing to buy the starving children off the starving mothers and raise them as Protestants, if you would kindly just hand them over and be gone. Songs and poems will be written of these terrible encounters. And almost everyone will decline, despite their painful, unrelenting desperation. It is better to enter heaven with my baby, it will soon be over anyway, than to leave my most precious child in the hands of one who would make such a proposal. It is like dealing with Satan himself. No, my child will stay with me, and I will pray I can bury them, before I fall myself.

And in the worst hit areas where help does not arrive at all, there are the stories of tender mercies, subtle, beautiful miracles. Stories of generosity and goodness rewarded by divine intervention. There is the story of the woman who through the good management of her husband has managed to live off cabbage and other vegetables, and who cooks a small extra portion every night lest one of the starving homeless knocks on her door. But over the weeks there are more and more knocks and more and more cabbage is quietly distributed into the shaking hands of the grateful wretches who are momentarily given a measure of hope. At last, the husband, distraught at the realisation that they may starve themselves because of his wife's great generosity, drags her out to the field to see the meagre few plants left. But behold, the field is full, the earth bursting with vegetables, the cabbage thick and green and plentiful.

But despite the goodness of some, most had nothing to offer. The catastrophic nature of this disaster made it impossible to be dealt with locally and those who were barely hanging on to life themselves were forced to watch their neighbours and friends scour the roads searching, searching, for the slightest edible foodstuffs anywhere. Finally, when every possible source, from weeds to insects had been consumed, they are found dead at the side of the road, their mouths often stained green from eating grass.

The streets of Cork City act like a magnet for the rural poor who walk for miles and miles looking for succour. But Cork is run by the merchants, whose idea of charity is to set up workhouses. Their Protestant work ethic will not allow them to entertain the idea of just giving food freely where it is needed. No. Food must be earned through work, even if it is meaningless, undignified work, and even if the calories distributed through the weak, loathsome soup are not enough to support the work of the day. And so, the streets of Cork fill with the rural poor, ejected from their homes, their every possession sold to buy food, their faces beyond human recognition, their starved bodies stinking up the streets where they fall in blissful abandon after months and months of tortuous, desperate acts of survival.

James and Terrence and O'Hegarty know these stories all too well. They were raised on them; their grandparents having suffered through that terrible time. In the Irish language it is known as *An Gorta Mor*, The Great Hunger. Their genetic codes now carry the chemical markers that can turn the expression of genes on and off. But their minds carry the stories of *An Gorta Mor*, the stories of terror and agony and cruelty, and of goodness and mercy and hope. These stories travel the world with the Irish as those fortunate enough to escape look for a new life. Wherever the Irish put down roots, memories of *An Gorta Mor* will put down roots as well, and over the decades, public sculptures and commemorations will dot the places they will come to call home. It will never be forgotten that the British exported food from Ireland while the Irish starved. This single prevailing memory will become the foundation of the mind-set of the new, twentieth-century rebel, the certainty that freedom is the only answer, no matter the cost. Terrence and everyone who knows and loves him is about to discover that the cost of freedom, the price they must pay, is greater even than death itself.

Terrence stands at the trial in Cork City, a tad unsteady on his feet, lightheaded from hunger, and scoffs at the British court. His large and luminous blue eyes seem to be flashing light. You have no business here, he tells them. Ireland has been declared an independent sovereign state. Go home to your own island. We have our own courts here who answer to our own democratic parliament, The Dáil. I am the duly elected mayor of this city and as such the chief magistrate. I declare this court illegal! Any person participating in it is subject to arrest under the laws of the Irish Republic. As for the cipher key, anyone who uses such a device to transmit messages about the Irish Republic is guilty of a crime. It is you who should be tried for possession of a cipher key. And while we are talking about the evidence, let us not forget the copy of the recent report from the inquest of the murder of my friend and predecessor the Lord Mayor, Tomás MacCurtain. Even an English tribunal has found the English government culpable for cold-blooded murder. Yes, don't forget to mention that this was found in my pocket. Write it down in your report! Terrence MacSwiney's blood boils as he watches the sniggering, sneering faces of the British court.

Yes, yes, whatever. The judge calls the witnesses. They have been paid off by the military. It does not take long to find Terrence guilty and to sentence him to two years imprisonment. But do not think he will have the luxury of staying home, in the city where he is the prime leader, his family bringing him tea and crumpets every morning to the gaol door. No, off to Brixton Prison in London if you please, and no time to waste. The ship has been waiting at the docks for a while now. After all, everyone involved has been certain of the outcome of this trial right from the arrest. So, hurry it up. The sea is roiling, and London is far away from this place. Thank God.

If you were to go to the roof of Kensington Palace and look directly south, across the River Thames and beyond the beautiful parks and luxury estates of central London, less than five miles away you might just see the roof of Brixton Prison. It is one of the oldest prisons in England. Built in 1820 to absorb the overflow of inmates from other places, it housed vagabonds and petty thieves, some as young as six years old. Within a year the place had become infamous for the installation of a giant treadmill which turned the millstones to grind the prison flour. The energy source? Inmates. Ten hours a day up the never-ending hill of the turning gear powered by men's legs. It is like a circle of hell in Dante's *Inferno*, a vertical circle. Do not complain or you will be chained to it through the night. The first governor of the gaol, inventor of the diabolical device, develops quite a reputation. People come from near and far to view the inmates trudging up the giant roller that turns the mill stones. The governor will eventually be fired for cruelty. He has a fondness for flogging children almost to death. By 1853, a change is in order and Brixton Prison will become a gaol for females and children only. In contrast to the demon who was the first governor, the governor of the women's gaol is kind and merciful. A nursery will be opened for inmates with children accompanying them as they serve their sentences. But there will be little done to improve the premises, its tiny dark cells will remain and by the 1900s when the gaol becomes a military prison, those same tiny dark cells will house a plethora of unfortunates from the London area. Terrence is about to become Brixton Gaol's most famous inmate.

By the time Terry gets to Brixton Prison he is almost too weak to walk through the gates. It has been six days since he last took food. His eyes swim from time to time and his knees give out from under him. He is beginning to get painful cramps shooting from deep inside his gut. It is a peculiar sensation, difficult to ignore as his body wishes to curl into the pain. He is put straight away in the medical wing. It contains seven empty beds, and Terrence lies down in the one in the far corner. It is the same room in which Sir Roger Casement was housed after being arrested and found to be weak and ailing. Terrence thinks on this and on the feisty, maligned rebel who was Roger. And Terrence knows the worst that can happen is that he follows Roger to heaven. But he is not expecting that. He is expecting to be released at any moment after the reports of his hunger strike reach the public, and pressure is brought to bear on the English government. But Terrence should have known better. Perhaps he did know better and was aware of the latest legal measure of the British to deal with the Irish problem, the Restoration of Order Act which, just three days before his arrest, had passed into law. It now provided for a suspension of other courts and a vast expansion of court martials. The new procedure is to be used not just with military but with civilians. The judges may impose execution by firing squad or internment without trial. It is designed to eliminate the enemy. Yes, the British have just created a new law to circumvent their old laws which are just not quite as effective with the Irish as they would like them to be. Terrence will be their first case. We can easily outlast this pretty boy in a contest of wills, the powers that be quip to each other.

The nurses and doctors admonish him. What are you on about? You are only hurting yourself. Surely you are the most selfish man in the world. What about your wife? What about your child? What about the citizens of your godforsaken Irish city? Are you not the mayor? Terrence looks at them and then turns away to face the wall. I need a little rest, thank you.

James sees the worried look on O'Hegarty's face and knows things have taken a turn for the worse, despite the miracle of the release of him and the other men. O'Hegarty has a sixth sense that is focused on downturns in fortune. He can feel the wind that blows ill far across the water, long before the waves hit shore. Terrence is continuing his fast in London, and here in Cork there are a whole truckload of men in Cork Gaol that have joined him.

Michael Fitzgerald is older than James by a good fifteen years. He is a good friend of Liam Lynch and a devoted Republican, but he is not a lucky man. He has suffered from poverty in his life, especially as a child and he is short, gaunt, and stunted-looking with a crooked face. But Michael is a naturally joyful soul. He loves nothing more than a great story with a great laugh at the end, the best being stories where the uppity British are laid low or seen as fools. Perhaps this is why the British are fixated on shutting him up. Joy borders on insolence. And perhaps sharing a pint in the Fermoy pub he has been overheard by joyless officers. After the Araglin hold up, with no evidence, he was picked up, charged, and given two months in solitary confinement. From his point of view, he was tossed in a gaol and left to rot. But Michael understands hardship and has learned over the course of his life to pace himself. He hears his mother, a tiny bird of a woman, old before her time, doubtless a victim of untold privation, whisper in his ear to offer his trials and tribulations for the release of the poor souls in purgatory. They will help you in return by taking on some of your own suffering. Michael thinks of this, fingers his imaginary beads, and after two months walks from the prison with his mind intact and his Republican sympathies fortified exponentially.

When he is released, he is just in time to participate in the Fermoy adventure. Later, after he is picked up again, he is accused of shooting the fallen officer, but everyone knows he did not do it. Some of the men had seen James in the distance pull out his gun but most had not. It does not matter because the Brigade has developed a tacit policy of collective guilt and no man who pulls a trigger is ever condemned or celebrated. It is war and each man must do what is necessary. The Cork Brigade is a single pliable unit. They will spread the guilt of their actions across the entire organisation, like a piece of hot toast slathered in butter, the guilt and the victories both will melt into the history of the organisation, one action indistinguishable from another, lost in the collective pursuit of freedom. But after being in gaol for over a year with no hope of a trial, Michael yearns for his home territory of Fermoy and to be out and about with his comrades, making a difference. He makes a decision. He convinces the other eleven men, including seventeen-year-old Joseph Murphy, and twenty-four-year-old Connie Neenan, to pressure the British by hunger strike. It is one day before Terrence and the other Cork Brigade officers are arrested. Nobody outside the prison knows anything about it. The British are keeping quiet and focusing on the mayor.

In Dublin, at GHQ, Michael Collins and his men are focused on the British. And it is one man in particular they have not given up the search for: Oswald Swanzy, the perpetrator of Tomás's murder. The man who gave the orders. They have been looking for him and just now, as Terrence sinks into hunger, they have found him. Collins is so happy he does a little jig when he hangs up the phone. Well boys, he calls out to his various and sundry officers, we have got him. We have got that nasty shite, and he is about to have some surprise visitors.

Seán Culhane is determined to do this job. It was him and a contact in the railway who discovered Swanzy's luggage being sent to an address in Lisburn, just outside Belfast. He tells O'Hegarty, I will take Tomás's own gun with me and shoot him with it. O'Hegarty as wry as ever tells him, I don't care what gun you use Seán, just get the job done! And make sure you take heed from the Belfast boys. They know their own territory. Remember in that part of the country you Catholics are persona non grata. Just to be sure the young Culhane does not screw things up, Pa Murray, older, wiser, and calmer, goes with him. On Sunday morning, August the twenty-second, Swanzy walks out of his church dressed in his Sunday best. He is joined by his family. The whole group is happily enjoying the sunshine and camaraderie of their fellow parishioners. Culhane watches the group walk from the church entrance and boldly leaves the car that Pa is driving. He walks towards Swanzy. He wants the best show possible. He stops at a distance that is certain to guarantee success. Culhane raises his gun and shoots. Swanzy drops to the ground. Some of the men who are also leaving church run after the perpetrators, fearless and enraged. Seán and Pa escape after a harrowing chase, as do their Belfast IRA accomplices, but the Catholics of the town of Lisburn do not. That evening there is a rampage on their homes, a raging fire in their squalid part of town and many murders. Some of the orphaned children will be sent down to Cork, to be taken in by Republican families and raised as their own.

With Terrence forcibly absconded to London, and Michael and the others sitting in Cork Gaol trying to distract themselves from their rumbling stomachs, O'Hegarty understands that there has been a shift in British thinking. Too many of their men have been hurt or killed, too much of their property has been damaged, too little public opinion remains in their favour. This does not bode well.

It has been two weeks and Terrence is still fasting. Father Dominic has left Cork with the most beautiful woman in the world to attend to Terrence. O'Hegarty sits in the Wallace sisters' back room stewing about his friends. James knows Michael, his large, happy heart locked inside that tiny misshapen body. He wonders aloud how a body such as that could survive hunger. You'd be surprised Jimmy, the abuse a man can take and still breathe the air. Their focus shifts to Terrence. Seán will be furious if someone does not contact him, says James, thinking aloud. And Terrence will be furious if someone does! But surely it will be over soon. The British can't let it go on, have you seen the papers? Aye Jimmy, aye, says O'Hegarty wearily, and I have no doubt we will be reading about our Terry and Michael and Joseph and the others for a while yet. Do not get your hopes up. I have advised Mary to telegram Seán. She is leaving to be with Muriel and Father Dominic. I have not heard Seán's decision. Why don't you ride over and see if she has had a response yet? James stares at him for a moment and watches as the recent subtle changes to his face come into focus. His scowl deeper, his hair a little more unkempt, his eyes dark and heavy. Fuck, thinks James. This is no fucking political ploy. The British are calling our bluff.

James flies down the hills of Cork City and then rides hard uphill until he comes to the top of Victoria Road. He needs to move quickly if he is to catch Mary before she leaves. He coasts down the road until he comes to the MacSwiney family home. He has to bang on the door several times before Mary, her face stricken, answers the door. She is Terry's oldest sister, the reigning matriarch of the family and a Rebel through and through. She works tirelessly with her best friend, O'Hegarty's wife Magda, to run the Cumann na mBan across the city for which she is equally admired and loathed by the various members of the women's organisation and the IRA. Occasionally she is feared for the potential fierceness of her response when things turn south. She is a formidable woman. And she knows James very well, friend of her wee brother Seán.

Her face softens when she sees him because she cannot help thinking instantly of her beautiful little brother. Oh, Séamus my darling, how are ye? James envelopes her petite body in his arms. I know you are on your way over to London; I am just wondering if there has been any word from Seán? Indeed Séamus, indeed. He is coming home, our Seán. Coming home at last. Pity it is such a terrible occasion. Mary fusses with her coat and her bag, checking that she has everything. She turns to James and looks at him directly. Her eyes are not soft like Terry's, they are cold, steely eyes. Pray for us, Séamus. Pray for Terry. He is suffering. James hears the arrival of the car and escorts Mary outside. He opens the car door for her. She sinks into the seat, heavy with worry and fear. One of the Grey brothers is at the wheel. He raises his hand in recognition and waves at James as the car pulls out onto Victoria Road.

Seán does not come home to Cork. He heads directly for London. He takes a train from Toronto to Quebec and boards a ship for Liverpool. Sitting in the train to London, unable to sleep, Seán's head is swimming. He has had many long days of travel across Canada, across the ocean and now finally on his way to London. He has had plenty of time, too much time, to consider all of the possibilities. He has decided he will convince his brother to give it up. He is not sure why Terrence has even taken this on. Sure, Terry was one of those so affected by the news of Tomás Ashe and what they did to him. But Seán knows that others will already have tried their best to sway Terrence. He knows his big sister Mary is worried. But it is not her telegram that made him drop everything and book his passage. It was O'Hegarty's. O'Hegarty's 'Happy Birthday' telegram. Happy Birthday. No other words, not even his name. But it is the sign. The sign that he is needed, now, not tomorrow, not next week, now. He is not sure what is expected of him and what in fact he can do. But he knows that this decision to come back home has somehow altered the trajectory of his life. His plans of marriage and a life lived through the long cold winters in Canada have been lost in the waves of the open ocean. His brother's large luminous eyes, his sad smile, are all he can see. And now, now that he has arrived in London, he feels nothing but fear. Cold, clammy, and impossible to shake off.

The newspapers are reporting on Terry almost every day now. It has been over a month since he started this madness and Seán wonders at the intransigence of the British who are receiving bad press around the world. The picture of Terry sporting his fedora, his handsome, intelligent face and his bright, blue eyes shining out at the world has been seen as far away as India and it is a daily occurrence in New York and Boston, where so many Irish now live. Reporters are beginning to camp outside the prison gates to get photos and hear comments from anyone leaving the place. The police too wait to see who will show up to visit. While the police watch the IRA, the IRA watch the police. Every day, Muriel and Mary and Father Dominic enter the gates to visit. Some days they are allowed in without fuss. Other days they are not. They are completely at the mercy of the prison officials. The medical staff are cold and practical. They do not understand this Irishman and his insane strike. They do not care for his wife despite her Oxford accent and her uppity manners. They especially do not care for his sister, an Irish schoolteacher, smug and condescending. And the priest! Let us not even mention that strange medieval man with his unsightly brown robes and his ill-kempt beard and his ridiculously long rosary tied to a belt of rope around his waist, swinging back and forth as he paces the room muttering his superstitions under his breath. The staff ignore them all as best they can and do their job, watching over the man who suffers so needlessly.

How he perseveres in his determination is a mystery to them. Daily they bring in food to tempt him. Have a little soup, it is nothing, but you will feel so much better with just a spoonful. They have never seen such resolve. And they do not understand why he is still so clear-headed. His body sends him into agonies of cramps, long jagged stabs of pain attack his gut, the large muscles in the legs, and rear, and back. He is now four weeks without sustenance of any kind, severely anaemic and completely and utterly exhausted. But at some point each day he rallies, he smiles at his wife, he asks for pen and paper and he writes to whomever he has been dreaming of. To old friends from long ago, when he dreams of his days riding his bicycle through the Gaeltacht, learning Irish, listening to stories, eating the simple food of those hospitable, kind people. He writes to his old theatre friends, so eager in those days to produce plays and dramas of the new Gaelic League, the Gaelic Literary Society. To newer friends, soldiers of his brigade, fighters, and planners, and believers in the Republic, he writes when he dreams of their many small, yet victorious battles, their stays in British gaols. In his letters he reminds them of their time together, how precious it all seems now, how wonderful, despite the hardship, the gale force winds knocking them off their bicycles, the aching legs, the hours by candlelight writing pamphlets, the travels to remote places to speak to the people, to talk of the Republic, to gather support, to distribute hope that yes, it can happen, we can make it happen. But he reminds them, sacrifices must be offered. Endurance must be tested. Do not give up.

This is the substance of his letters to friends old and new. He can write for only a short time each day. His wife would prefer that he not write at all, that he conserve his energy. She is still hoping and praying for a miracle. But Terrence knows better. The miracle has already happened. It is the time he has been given each day, free of pain, able to concentrate on writing. But each day when the allotted time is spent, the waves of pain return, crashing in on him. He drops the pen, he groans, his wife grimaces, his sister jumps to his side, his priest bends down on his knees and begins the rosary aloud and in Irish.

When he can bear it, Muriel reads the paper aloud to him. He lies with his eyes closed concentrating on the words, pushing aside the relentless, pounding headache. On the seventh of September, Prime Minister Lloyd George assures the public that Terrence will be released if only he agrees that no more of the Black and Tans will be threatened. Hah! Terrence demands a pen and paper. No, says Muriel, let me write for you. Tell him this condition can only be met if he guarantees the withdrawal of the Black and Tans, that illegal force, those brutes, rapists, murderers, sadists. No response from Lloyd George is forthcoming.

We must prepare for the worst, Jimmy. O'Hegarty is angry. So very angry. Every drop of emotion is instantly converted into raging energy which erupts in the foulest of language for no apparent reason. He kicks gates, throws pens across the room with deadly accuracy, rips buttons off his shirt at the least resistance, smashes his fist into unsuspecting walls. But mostly he plans. He plans long and hard into the night. He meets with every commander of every battalion in the city. Keep up the pressure lads. Do not relent. Every chance you get, shoot them, blow up their trucks, steal their weapons. Determine who are the worst offenders, the rapists and murderers. We will hunt them down like rabbits and make stew with them. And bloody fucking hell, find out where they are getting their information from! They know far too much for the cowardly little skulkers they are, hiding until dark, slithering out of the woodwork with their machine guns and bayonets.

There has been a rash of homes broken into, fires started, windows broken, belongings trashed, mothers and daughters dragged into trucks half-naked, men beaten and dragged to gaol half-dead. Men tortured when they get there, eyeballs sizzled with flames from candles, cigarette butts put out on flesh, backs almost broken from the sharp edge of boots, eyes swollen shut for weeks.

While the war with the Black and Tans rages, there is also a war of words in the newspapers. Official letters and reports are published for the world to see and read. Arthur Griffith's words practically boil off the page: You English are, as Tolstoy said, the most barbarous of all peoples pretending civilisation.

On September 13, Mary, desperate to save her brother, issues a letter to the American ambassador in London. She pleads his case, reminding the ambassador of the murder of Tomás, and noting the British determination to kill heads of the democratically elected government of Ireland despite their pretensions as beacons of democracy. On September 20 Terrence himself issues a statement. God is watching over our country. Her resurrection is at hand.

By now Terrence knows the English will not relent. He is to be made an example. In Cork City, the tiny misshapen man, Michael Fitzgerald finds solace in Terrence's words. No one can believe he is still alive, so emaciated is his crooked frame. Likewise, the other twelve men, including the seventeen-year-old, Joseph, continue to fast. Daily visitors leave the gaol with ashen faces and glazed-over eyes. Occasionally people vomit into the bushes before they get all the way down the stairs.

O'Hegarty has had it. Somehow these creeps are getting information. They know just where to go, what homes to attack in the middle of the night. They have names and addresses. He calls up Collins. You need men on the ground twenty-four hours a day. Sure, you know this, Seán, says Collins. How are they to eat Mick, for God's sake? You Dublin crowd are swimming in money while we here must work our day jobs while we fight the enemy. Fine, I will send you a salary for a small group. Pay them a few quid a week but choose your men wisely. O'Hegarty hangs up the phone thinking, that fucker and his arrogance. Choose your men wisely, as if I don't know every man in the whole bloody county. He calls a meeting with Florrie and James, Tom Crofts, a well-respected, smart, quiet leader, Mick Murphy the hurling player and a few others.

They meet at the Wallace sisters' shop. It is full of smoke, the women pouring them tea, passing out biscuits. We need men on the ground. I want at least one officer from each battalion to join together and create a new unit. An Active Service Unit, ASU. James, who already belongs to the 2nd Battalion, C Company, is told his range of jobs has just expanded. Dump your day job. We will pay you enough to get by. Florrie will continue to coordinate intelligence, and Tom, I want you to look after the ASU. I want you to think hard overnight about who we should include. We need men spread from across the various areas. A dozen is all we can afford. We need men who can get the job done, who are good with the people, dependable, reliable, and no married men. If you all get shot up by those bastards, I don't want any weeping women hanging about. Our first job: find out how these pricks know who to look for.

Towards the end of September Seán arrives in London. The look on Mary's face tells him the worst. She takes his arm and walks him to the prison gate. It is five weeks since Terrence entered through these gates, already hungry and weak. When Seán enters the ward, he blinks and looks around. It is clean, surgically clean, shining walls and gleaming floors, tightly made beds with white bleached sheets, and there in the corner? The slight ridge under a coarse blanket? The skull with taut skin, ridged bones for cheeks, eyes swimming inside huge orbs. It is not possible, but somehow it is true. Terrence lies there, shrunken beyond words, his face almost unrecognisable, his body but bones jutting out at seemingly odd angles. It is only when his eyes open, slowly, and the beautiful blueness of them illuminates the room with colour, does Seán concede that it is his brother. His knees give out from under him. He sinks to the floor and weeps into his brother's pillow.

On September 30, Terrence writes his last letter. He can barely hold the pen in his hands, but he puts his greatest effort to it and manages a long messy sprawl of words. He writes to Cathal Brugha, a gracious man, survivor of the Easter Rising, who has been sending him letters for weeks. Give my best regards to everyone in Dublin. There are so many. He ends it, God give you and yours long years of happiness under the victorious Republic. With a comrade's love, God bless you. He signs his name in Irish, Toirdhealbhach. Then the pen drops. He will never pick it up again.

On October 4, Terrence awakes in the night. The half-moon

is streaming through the window forcing light through his paper-thin eyelids. His bones ache from the weight of the blanket. But he is so cold. His feet and fingers are blue and his body shakes and rattles uncontrollably. His head pounds and with every tremor his muscles send out thin sharp lightning bolts of pain. Deep in his gut his organs search for sustenance, but none is to be had. They punish him with sharp gnawing thuds of pain. He can feel his bedsores, raging against the sheets. Terrence opens his eyes to the light and sees a familiar figure through the window, standing in the shadow of the moon. It is the smiling face of St Francis. He knows it is Francis because of the tonsured hair and brown homespun habit, the rosary hanging down from his side, his feet in plain open-toed leather sandals. A tiny bird sits on his shoulder glowing in the moon's illumination.

Francis steps in through the glass of the window and stands by the bed. He looks at Terrence and smiles. The little bird on his shoulder tweets and hops. Terrence cannot help but smile at the tiny creature. It is a short-toed lark, so common to County Cork, with its plain brown speckled body and its tiny ginger crest on the top of its head. Francis reaches towards the bottom of the bed for a second blanket. It is the thickest, softest blanket Terrence has ever seen and it seems to glow in the moonlight, multicoloured and spectacular, throwing bands of bright blues and reds and greens across the sterile white walls. But he knows he cannot bear the weight. No, Francis, please, the weight is too much to bear on these bones. It is better to be cold. Terrence's teeth chatter as he whispers the words. Francis does not speak, but Terrence hears him, nonetheless. Do not fret my friend. This blanket you will not feel. It will keep you warm for this night. And Francis pulls the cloud of blanket up to Terrence's chin, tucking the unimaginably soft and light warmth around his body. Immediately, Terrence feels something he has not felt in weeks. It is warmth, bubbling up from his toes, across the top of his feet and rippling like a river along his shins, over his knees and straight up through his body until even the top of his head, where his hair is falling out in fistfuls, feels like he is sitting by a roaring fire, the cold evening air just a few feet away, but his face glowing red and warm. For the first and last time in Brixton Prison, on the feast of St Francis of Assisi, Terrence sleeps peacefully, without pain, the gnawing hunger disappeared. He awakens in the morning, warm as toast, tears of gratitude on his cheeks.

The doctors and nurses are mystified by Terrence's perseverance and longevity. It has been eight weeks. Every day, once the visitors have been allowed in, he receives the tiniest portion of the Eucharist, a mere fragment of the host dissolved in a small cup of water given him by Father Dominic. He is alive, and for a short portion of each day, able to speak and listen to the paper being read, respond to the prayers of his priest, and give directions to his wife and sister and brother. And then his eyes will close and all present watch as the agony enfolds him once again. The prison officials decide a guard day and night must observe at his door. Is someone feeding him small amounts in the night? Does the IRA have a spy coming and going from within the prison? Take notes of everything that happens in these walls. Omit nothing. And so, a diary is begun but its entries are the same day after day.

On October 17, Terrence is given word that Michael Fitzgerald has died in Cork Gaol. He sends a message to everyone through his wife. No tears, but joy for our comrade who was ready to meet his God and die for his country. The next day, in his moment of calm, he turns to Father Dominic. I want you to bear witness that I die a soldier of the Irish Republic. A few days later he slips into unconsciousness.

Seán's heart is breaking. He walks the length of the ward back and forth, back and forth, fingering his beads one moment, cursing the next. Muriel is beside herself. She feels like she is in some morbid comedy. Rebels and priests and unanswered prayers. What is it all for? Why is this happening to me? What about our baby? What about my husband? She does not recognise this skeleton under the blanket. She does not recognise this dogged tenacity, even unto death. Who is this man? Why is he doing this? Mary keeps muttering about the republic and sacrifice, but all Muriel wants is her husband. She does not give a fig for the republic. She sees clearly now. The republic can go to hell and take the rebels and the priests with it.

When the visitors leave the building, the doctor sends for the governor of the gaol. The clock is ticking. If you wish to do something now is the time. Every moment counts. Fine, just do it, but be quiet about it. I do not want him dying here under my watch!

The doctor instructs the nurse to prepare a watery cup of nutrition. They begin to slip tiny spoonfuls under Terrence's tongue at regular intervals. On the morning of October 25, Muriel arrives at the hospital at ten in the morning, her usual time. The nurse tells her to wait outside. She sits quietly outside the ward. After an hour or so she politely asks the nurse, Can I see him now? In a while, she is told, curtly. She waits. Can I see him now? No. Muriel stands and walks out of the prison, back to her lodging. She is lost. She does not know what else to do.

A short while later Seán arrives and is allowed in. The doctor tells him they are trying to revive Terry, but it is not working. Try again, says Seán, panic in his voice. The doctor administers a shot of strychnine to stimulate Terry's highly erratic heartbeat in his unconscious body. But it is too late. His body is beyond responding to nutrition or stimulants. Terrence MacSwiney's days have been counted. His time is up. He leaves the earth as his brother Seán, on his knees on the cold British floor, finishes the rosary, aloud, and in Irish.

GRIEVE

CHAPTER 8

OCTOBER – DECEMBER 1920

Seán lights a cigarette just before he walks out the door of Brixton Gaol. He is stoic, and only just glances at the photographers outside the gates who are waiting for word of Terrence. With his new suit and shoes and his round spectacles and Fedora, he looks more like a warden of the gaol than the man from a family of bona fide Irish rebels who just got up from his knees praying the rosary as his brother passed into eternity. The photographers and news hounds do not yet know that Terrence has finally, mercifully, expired, and Seán wishes to escape the prison grounds before it is announced. He wants to find Muriel, who has disappeared. Terrence whispered to him days ago, just before he fell into his final reverie, to watch over her, and Seán is already feeling the weight of his promise. He knows that Mary, and his other sister Annie, and his brother Peter, who have been here at the prison keeping vigil, are strong characters in every sense of the word and will weather Terrence's passing with sorrow and with grief, but they will keep their minds intact. He is not so sure about the most beautiful woman in the world.

And yet Muriel is almost as stoic as Seán when he finds her. She is sitting by the window staring out at the weak English sun, and when Seán enters the room she turns and looks him in the eye. She says nothing but rises and reaches for her coat. He takes her back to the prison to see her husband one last time before the gargantuan machine that will manage the death march to the grave begins to turn. Both Seán and Muriel know that neither of them will have anything to say in what is sure to be a spectacle of unheard of proportions. Terrence's death will make headlines around the world. His radical sister Mary and GHQ in Dublin will be sure to extract maximum attention despite their own desperate grief. For they all loved Terry. Anyone who knew him for longer than a day fell in love with him. It is true he was never as gregarious as his friend and comrade Tomás. But Terry had a quiet way about him that was charming and intelligent and when he listened to anyone speaking, an earthquake could be happening around him, but his attention would not waver. When he spoke to you, you were the most important person in the world, and you felt it.

Muriel and Seán return to the house after a frustrating debate with the officials at Brixton Gaol. The British government does not wish to hand over the body to Muriel. Now they are afraid of these Irish Republicans. The name of the game is damage control. And they do not wish the corpse of this man, mayor of a minor city in the remote south of Ireland, to be paraded across the British Isles with the world watching. They would prefer to bury him in an unmarked plot under the exercise yard, the usual treatment for Irish rebels. However, given the unrelenting presence of the press and the shocking coverage in every corner of the globe, they know this will only inflame the world against them. So they will give Muriel the body. While the cameras are rolling. This is the only solution.

In the evening, word is sent that Joseph Murphy in Cork Gaol has also died. Muriel's face goes ashen. You watch over Terry, Seán. I will go back home and do what I can for his poor mother. God love her, few know what she is going through. I will meet you back in Cork. Seán looks at her in wonder as he escorts her to the train station. The rest of the family will stay and accompany Terrence's body home.

Seán was right. The entire funeral extravaganza has already been planned down to the last detail by GHQ for maximum publicity. A spectacle of unheard of proportions: first London, then Dublin, then across the country to Cork, and finally, after several days, St Fin Barre Cemetery to rest in peace. O'Hegarty is on the phone. Don't worry Seán, it has all been taken care of. All you have to do is follow the casket. Jimmy will be there soon. He will be leading up the Guard of Honour. He will fill you in with all the details. To the untrained ear, O'Hegarty sounds gruff and cold but Seán knows he was one of Terry's closest friends. He loved him like a brother. But O'Hegarty has had his hands full in Cork. The citizens of Cork, at least the Republicans, have been attending prayer vigils for the hunger strikers. The musicians have been sidling up as close to the windows of the gaol as they can get to play traditional Irish music for the suffering men. The talk has been of nothing but hunger strikes and rebels and the cruelty of the British. It does not help that the Black and Tans have ramped up their treatment of the people. O'Hegarty has had his hands full indeed. And now he is preparing two funerals.

Young Joseph Murphy is as light as a feather when they lift his emaciated body into the coffin. The differential in weight from the strapping young hurling player ten weeks ago to this skeleton-like corpse with taut skin, missing hair and a death mask depicting outright agony is completely overwhelming. The turmoil that the family and friends experience over this sight is devastating to witness. It is obvious to the onlookers that this grief is visceral, physically painful, and creates a state of confusion and anguish. The British themselves will recall it as a remarkable display of sorrow. The guards will stand frozen, unwilling, silent onlookers of this terrible mourning.

Muriel arrives back in Cork just in time to attend the funeral. She stays close to Joseph's mother, who is reeling with grief and barely able to stand through the funeral service. She sits in the pew rocking back and forth, her hands crossed tightly across her breast nursing her sorrow. As soon as the priest finishes his blessing and the walk to the graveyard is about to begin, there is a sudden commotion at the back of the church. The Black and Tans have been waiting outside. Now they enter noisily and march up the side aisle to the altar, their boots ringing across the length and breadth of the church, echoing off the high walls. They hop atop the communion rail with guns trained on the crowd. The commanding officer yells out at the startled congregation, Only a hundred people will be allowed to accompany the coffin to the grave. If you are not family, now is the time to return to your homes! The people are so shocked at this craven display of disrespect there is utter silence in the church. All eyes watch the guns held pointed at them. Then, as if they are all of one mind, they slowly, in an orderly fashion, turn their backs to the guns and follow the coffin out of the church. The pallbearers move forward to the street. The family follows, Muriel in front holding the arm of Joseph's mother. As one hundred people pass by the Black and Tans, their commanding officer shouts out to them, That is all. That is all that's allowed. Everyone else return home. But collectively, everyone else keeps their eyes lowered and continues to walk. There are threats shouted out by the uniformed soldiers. Shots are fired into the sky. The crowd continues to walk. Someone begins the rosary, in Irish, and the people respond. *Sé do bheatha, a Mhuire, atá lán de ghrásta, tá an Tiarna leat...* Hail Mary full of grace, the Lord is with thee.

Some of the soldiers move into the crowd and begin to push people with their rifle butts. But the mourners simply huddle closer together and continue to pray and walk. The commanding officer considers the possibilities open to him. He is a wiser man than some, despite his politics, and he decides to do nothing but accompany the crowd. Later, in the stillness of the night, with the full moon illuminating the flower-strewn grave, Joseph's IRA comrades quietly return to his grave and give him a rifle salute, the shots ringing out across the star-filled sky. Their piercing sound is greeted with quiet, sad smiles across the city. It is a final goodbye, and a call to arms. Joseph's body is at rest in the newly apportioned plot at the largest graveyard in Cork. The Republican Plot. He is now the second man buried there. Close by lies the first Republican Mayor of Cork, Tomás. Terrence will be the third occupant.

James takes the ferry across to Wales and the train into London. He is first of a large contingent of men who will be arriving over the next few days to make up the funeral cortège in London and escort Terry's body back to Ireland. As head of the Guard of Honour he has gone over the plans in minute detail with O'Hegarty and then in Dublin, before catching the ferry, with Collins. O'Hegarty will be there to help but Collins will have to meld into the crowd, for he is still at the top of the British hit list. Collins goes over all of the possible disruptions in their plans and reviews the possible responses. He is ever the man for contingencies. Once James is clear about dealing with the funeral, Collins pulls out a bottle of Bushmills from a dresser drawer. They are in the top floor of a large home in one of the better parts of Dublin, one of many where Collins takes refuge around the city. We will toast our Terry, Séamus, *Ar dheis Dé go raibh a anam.* May his soul be on God's right hand. James and Collins talk long into the night, sharing stories of Terry and drinking toasts to his name. By the time James leaves early in the morning to catch the ferry, he has decided that Collins is not so bad as he had thought.

When he disembarks the train in London, James feels, for no apparent reason, quite alright. He has slept well, first on the ferry and then on the train. Of course, the alcohol prompted that, and he is grateful his mother put a packet of sandwiches in his coat pocket, for he is famished when he awakens. Once he eats, he feels clear-headed and hawkeyed, noticing everything around him in sharp clarity as if his eyes and ears have been tuned to perceive a greater depth and range than ever before. He knows Terry is gone. He can feel the gaping hole in the universe that his absence reveals. But James and all of his comrades in Cork have had time enough to prepare, knowing weeks ago that it was just a matter of time, and if the truth be known, James is grateful that Terry's suffering is over. As for himself, he cannot begin to imagine what Terry went through, or how he managed the will power to do it. He is glad that he did not have the opportunity to visit him in prison during his ordeal. But he knows that the mourning and suffering of others are just about to begin. He fingers the beads in his pocket and murmurs a prayer to St Joseph.

As the train pulls into the station, a quick bolt of happiness strikes his heart as he catches sight of his old friend, but it disappears as fast as it came. Seán is outside, leaning against the wall of the station, smoking a cigarette. He blows the smoke down through his nostrils paying little attention to his surroundings. He looks like a bull contemplating his rampage. James notices that his face is thin and drawn taut, his eyes staring down at the dirty floor strewn with butts and refuse. Seán's mind is elsewhere. James alights from the car at the crowded station and makes his way to him. This is the first time he has laid eyes on his friend since he left for a new life. When their eyes meet, James is struck by the deep sadness that seems to emanate from Seán's face and the sense of cool aloofness that greets him. He reaches for his friend and grasps his hand. They shake hands but say nothing. Quickly and awkwardly, they get right to business.

As they walk out of the station James begins to outline the plan for the funeral. Seán listens without comment. After a few moments James notices they are walking past a pub with a Guinness sign, the Irish harp on the window, and he stops. How about a pint, old friend? Sure Jimmy, sure. They enter the premises of the small dark pub and find a seat in the corner. It is early in the day and the lunch crowd has not yet arrived. To Terry, says James, and lifts his glass. Aye, to Terry, agrees Seán, but before he can raise his glass he is doubled over by raw emotion and the tears stream from his face and into his drink. James is about to quote some of the Republican phrases that he has heard over and over about Terry through the last few weeks and days. He is about to say something stupid like, sure, but he died for Ireland. But as the words are about to leave his mouth, he has a vision of Seán on his bike racing away, looking towards the west, to a new life, away from Ireland and its politics and its rebels.

He recalls the previous night with Collins and his easy way with stories and laughter that soothed his mind and soul when thinking of Terrence. And so, he bites his tongue, gets up from his seat and slides in the booth beside his friend. He puts his arm around Seán's shoulders, Collins-style, and begins to recount every story about Terry he can think of. Stories of when they were young boys listening to Terry on his return from the Gaeltacht. Stories of trying to learn Irish from him, such a difficult foreign tongue it seemed in those days. The words would leave their mouths in jagged shards of sound, and they would keel over in laughter at each other as Terry showed them just how to form their lips and their tongues. Stories of their adventures working for Terry and Tomás, their close calls with the authorities, the mishaps riding on their bicycles halfway across Cork County on a Sunday afternoon with secret messages, and Terry's relief on their return. Their tears turn to uproarious laughter and the two men leave the pub with their sorrow assuaged, full of gratitude and a sense of wonder that they should be so closely connected to this wonderful man who was their big brother in truth and in practice. But this little benevolent cloud of peace that hovers over them is quickly swept away. Once the death march begins all ease and nostalgia leave them both without a trace.

O'Hegarty is on the phone again. Jimmy boy, thank God you are there in one piece! I just got word the eight fellas who volunteered to be pallbearers got pinched at the wharf in Liverpool. They have been charged. I don't know when we'll see them again. A new set of pallbearers will have to be chosen. O'Hegarty's voice is clearly on edge. He is anticipating the worst. It's just what Collins warned about, replies James. Seán, who has been standing nearby listening to the conversation, looks James in the eye. Never mind Jimmy, I will do it myself. I can carry my own brother's coffin. He shakes his head at the thought of more men in prison, just for attending a funeral. Peter and I will take the lead. You keep your position in the Guard of Honour and if we need you, I will give you the nod. The first event will be getting him out of that hellhole of a prison. We will see how it goes. I don't trust them for a second.

O'Hegarty arrives in London melting into the crowds as is his way. He is afraid that now they have arrested the pallbearers they will arrest anybody. But the British government's hand has been stayed. The king is annoyed. He had tried to grant clemency and have Terrence released but the government held firm. Now he is adamant that they get their funeral in peace. There are three funerals planned, the first in St George's Cathedral in London, the second in Dublin, the third in Cork City. St George's Cathedral, the Catholic Church that serves the large number of Irish Catholics living in the central district of London, allows the body to lie in state, so to speak, although it is called a wake. Given his office and the attention of the world, they will allow this. They do not want any push-back from the Irish in London and have them join the rest of their country in protests. And so, orders are despatched, the London bobbies will be out in force, keeping the peace, making sure things go smoothly, assuring these people of their day of mourning in London before they get the hell out. They do not expect the English people to be interested. But the British are wrong. Thirty thousand people show up at the cathedral. The bobbies are kept busy holding back the crowds in an orderly fashion so that people can line up and walk past the open casket.

There lies Terrence, so emaciated and diminished he is unrecognisable. There stand his sisters, Mary and Annie, and his brothers,

Seán and Peter. There stands Father Dominic with his long flowing beard, dressed in his plain brown cassock. There are flowers sent from all manner of English and Irish both, living in London, and they create a perimeter around the coffin and adorn the altar. They are beautiful and the scent of them adds to the holy atmosphere in the church. As the people line up to pay their respects, Terry's family and the Guard of Honour maintain a quiet, mournful silence.

James stands at the top of the coffin, a few feet away, just outside the perimeter of flowers. Six other IRA men surround the interior perimeter. They stand at attention for hours. While James stands, he watches. He watches the people, some of whom mourn openly. He watches the police, who are surprised by the crowds. He watches O'Hegarty work his way through the lines of people and the pews where many sit or kneel, saying a prayer for Terrence. It seems he knows every man in the place. He watches his friend Seán who is, without a doubt, thunderstruck at this terrible turn of events. When he had left Ireland, he knew he was escaping trouble, but in his wildest dreams he never thought this would happen to his own beloved brother. He knows that Seán too can sense the void, and it has left him shell-shocked and angry. And as James looks far down the centre aisle of the cathedral to the choir loft above, he watches the famous artist John Lavery paint the entire scene for posterity.

John Lavery was a born artist. An unusually gifted, talented artist. He is so good he has painted various portraits of the Royal Family and earned himself a knighthood for his trouble. Naturally the rich and famous of English society now stand in line to have their own portraits done. His portraits are always beautiful, of beautiful people, dressed in beautiful clothes, surrounded by beautiful things. But if you look closely, you will notice wisps of personality and snippets of character escaping from the subject. Their true self leaks out through the eyes or can be glimpsed dodging the subtle turn of a hand or trying to hide with the impertinent crossing of a leg. Yes, Lavery depicts the obvious physical wealth and accoutrements of whoever is in front of him, but he also shows the intangible, irreducible nature of his subjects, which they may or may not see for themselves. At any rate, it has certainly also benefitted John's career that in his youth he was the epitome of a dashing, passionate artist with the looks and demeanour to match. In photographs his long blonde locks are carelessly tossed over the side of his face and the intensity of his eyes glint out at the audience betraying any manner of emotion. He is an ageing man now, and wealthy, thanks to the British. He owns a mansion off Hyde Park, the poshest address in London. His second wife, Hazel, whom he married sometime after his first wife died of tuberculosis, is a dazzling, elegant beauty from America. Her long slim legs, auburn hair, and large green eyes cannot diminish the aura of intelligence and wit that surrounds her. She is a great asset to him socially and it seems to him he is more in love with her with every passing year. By the time he leaves the earth at age eighty-four he will have painted over four hundred portraits of her. Each one is a masterpiece as far as he is concerned.

What many in English society do not know about John Lavery is that he was born in Belfast City, a little Catholic boy orphaned at a very young age. He is brought to England by relatives and learns to paint in Glasgow. But that was a very long time ago. He is sixty-four years old now and he has long forgotten his Irish heritage. However, as of late he has been interested in the goings-on in Ireland, and the impertinent, outrageous stance of this mayor of Cork has made him think of his own long-forgotten Irish Catholic heritage in the harsh city of Belfast, where Catholics are grateful to be second-class citizens. Today he has cancelled a sitting for the portrait of a wealthy English heiress and come of his own accord to the cathedral to paint Terrence MacSwiney in his coffin, and capture for posterity the solemnity and grief of this event. There is no doubt from looking at this painting that it is a Catholic affair, and as he paints, he does not realise that it is exactly how Terrence would have wanted it. In a few weeks' time he will paint the most beautiful woman in the world dressed in her black mourning clothes, staring out at the world, her wide-set eyes emitting pain and confusion and raw grief, and her chiselled lips barely closed against her desire to shriek and cry and keen.

The following day, October 28, 1920, after the requiem Mass is said in the cathedral, O'Hegarty whispers in James's ear that it is time to pack it in. The funeral cortège must begin the trip to Euston Station, to take the train to Holyhead at the tip of Wales, where they will board the ferry heading directly across the Irish Sea to Dublin. They will walk the route to Euston Station with tens of thousands tripping behind them. It is a final, dramatic farewell for the many Irish immigrants and the many good English citizens who have been shocked and upset by the heartlessness of their own government. As they walk, the preparations are being made for what is expected to be an unheard-of display of national mourning, patriotism, and most anxiously anticipated, unanimous support for Sinn Féin and the IRA. The family are beginning to wonder if they will make it through the next few days. They are, every one of them, emotionally and physically exhausted already. And the death march has barely begun.

The train from London to Holyhead takes a long time in 1920, hours and hours, all night long. When at last the large party of the MacSwiney family, James and the remainder of the Guard of Honour, and a group of accompanying friends and IRA arrive at the docks, there is a long low fog hovering around the entire area. James's sixth sense is ignited as soon as he alights from the train. Walking through the mist that seems to cling to his person he feels wary, as if someone or something is lurking just out of sight. He fingers the beads in his pocket and goes about his business arranging the men to help carry the coffin from the train to the loading portion of the dock. One by one the family joins the coffin and just as they are about to lift it onto the small ferry boat, arranged solely for them, a motorcar can be heard barrelling through the mist. It breaks through in front of the family and an officer quickly alights from the passenger door. He hands Seán, who has stepped forward, an envelope. It is a note written by Hamar Greenwood himself, the Chief Secretary of Ireland, second in the government only to Prime Minister Lloyd George.

> *So sorry for the inconvenience but we cannot allow you to take Mr MacSwiney's remains to Dublin. He will be transported via sloop to Cork Harbour, accompanied by a troop of Black and Tans.*

And just as Seán, with an ashen face, finishes reading the note out loud to the rest of the onlookers, a small, grey, tattered-looking tugboat reveals itself through the mist by pulling up alongside the dock. Everyone stands silent, looking at Seán, who stares at the officer. It is as if he is watching a scene from somewhere far, far away, and in his mind, he is thinking, you smarmy little fuckers. James, in his mind's eye, sees Collins, warning him of all the potential threats, and he slowly lifts his hand and reaches inside his jacket for his gun. He is standing across from Seán and a few feet from the motorcar. With this hand movement, Seán suddenly comes back to life and without moving his eyes from the officer, raises his own hand in the air, signing for James to stop and wait.

He begins to argue with the officer, who is unequivocal. Standing tall, at attention, the officer calmly but firmly announces to Sean, I am under orders sir and am authorised to use whatever force is necessary to ensure the safe transport of the remains. The officer is aware of the delicacy of the situation and is careful to show the utmost respect. It is at this moment that Mary screams, runs the few steps to the coffin and places her hand on one of the handles. Over my dead body. Don't you dare touch my brother's coffin, you heartless bastard. We are taking him to Dublin. You will not stop us. Seán looks at James and sighs. Fuck, he thinks to himself. I am back in my nightmare, and it is worse than I ever imagined it could be. He turns to Mary, but Mary is ready for a fight. No one is too sure what to do and some of the men begin to move forward to shield the family. Seán yells at everyone to stand back. A full troop of twenty Black and Tans appear out of the mist. The officer stands them at attention.

Seán walks over to Mary. It is no use Mary, for God's sake. Will you have us all shot over this? They will take Terry to Cork. It is where he should be anyway. But Mary has a wild look in her eye. NO! They will not take my brother. I will not let them. Seán bends over his sister and whispers in her ear. Mary, for the love of God, we cannot win this fight. I am your brother too. Leave go and come with me. But she will not. The officer has his troop move forward and raise their guns on the small crowd. Everyone, stand back please. I am going to release the coffin from Miss MacSwiney. I am sorry to do this but there is no other option. He moves towards Mary, but she will not let go of the coffin handle. My apologies ma'am, and as Mary screams in his ear and beats him with her fist, he pries each of her fingers off her brother's coffin and lifts her out of the way to her brother Peter, who puts his arms around her while she sobs on his shoulder. The whole crowd watches as Terry's remains are shifted to the small, dirty tugboat and the contingent of Black and Tans jump on board and surround the coffin, their guns at the ready.

The family may accompany the remains, says the officer to Seán. Give me a moment please, and Seán walks over to his brother Peter and motions at James to join them. James reminds them of the eight men who were to be the pallbearers and who are now locked up awaiting trial. Listen Seán, we must be careful. Collins warned me just how bad it might get. And O'Hegarty also knew we can't trust them for a second. I say let them go. We can take another boat and follow them. It is best not to be on that boat, lest they do something and blame us for it. Aye Jimmy, but GHQ will be smoking mad when there is no coffin for their big plans. I don't give a fig for any of it. I just want him buried and in peace. Let me deal with Collins, whispers James under his breath. Mary walks over to the men. We may not have Terry with us, but we are all going to Dublin, as planned, she practically barks it at Seán. Sure, why would we do that Mary? The people don't want to see *us*. Mary spits back at him, We are all they have now, and we will tell our story. We *must* go to Dublin. There is a service planned in the cathedral and we must go.

Seán walks back over to the officer. The family will not be accompanying you. I am entrusting my brother's remains to you. I will hold you personally responsible if anything untowards occurs. And he turns and walks back. The whole group stands and watches as the little tugboat veers into the mist of the open water and disappears carrying the last of Terry with it. James and Seán part ways. Seán and his family take the ferry as scheduled and arrive in Dublin to a shocked public awaiting them at the waterfront. James and a few of the IRA catch a ride on the first boat they can find to leave for Cork. He manages to have the skipper speed up to be in sight of the tugboat. In the early morning hours, he watches from a distance as Terry's body sidles up to shore in Cork Harbour, surrounded by Black and Tans with guns pointed at the crowds pressed along the waterfront.

When the family alights off the ferry in Dublin and the announcement is made of the duplicity of the Prime Minister, the reaction from the crowd is palpable. Now, to add to the grief is outrage, and together they create an outpouring of national mourning. Newspapers around the world carry the story. In Cork, with the remains arriving earlier than expected, the men are rushing to prepare. A central area is roped off in the city hall and the flowers begin to pour in. They are lined up along the interior wall of the building, past the secret door through which Terry had tried to escape. The same floor over which his steps rang day after day since March now holds his coffin, while the people of Cork shuffle past with stricken looks. James takes his position at the top of the coffin. But he avoids the cameras. Whenever he sees a photographer setting up for his shot, he finds a reason to leave the area. He will never be caught again for display as he was at Tomás's funeral. Having been assigned to the Active Service Unit he is being more than careful to watch his step. As head of the Guard of Honour, he is actually putting himself at risk of being targeted and his image appended to those already on the most wanted wall at the Victoria Barracks. O'Hegarty had deemed his participation in the Honour Guard, much less head of the group, unwise, but James felt at least it was something, something tangible that he could do for Terry. And for Seán. Once the decision was made, O'Hegarty was careful to assign responsible young men, all with full-time jobs who are not so involved in the brigade as the remainder of the Guard of Honour. In this way he hoped to deflect interest from James. This is a wise decision, because in James's absence from the city, things have been heating up. The anger over the intransigence of the British has been percolating and as the reality and permanence of Terrence's death has sunk into the national psyche, a deep sense of loss begins to tear at the hearts of the Irish around the country.

The Cork No. 1 Brigade is the hardest hit. They have laboured under Terrence since 1913. The seven years of Terrence's leadership, despite his time in internment and gaol, has allowed him to meet and talk to every single man in the brigade. All eight thousand of them. And there is nary a man who is not impressed with his work ethic and his dedication, even if they may not have approved of his methodology or understood his spirituality or agreed with his philosophy. They all respected the hard-working, handsome, thoughtful gentleman who stood for freedom from British tyranny and was willing to put his life on the line. With the leadership of Tomás and Terry evaporated into the Irish mist, the men who are battalion OCs are left to wonder if their organisation can survive. Morale is the lowest O'Hegarty has ever seen. There is much drinking, to his chagrin, and little camaraderie. Over the last couple of weeks there have been incidents of shootings and take-downs by some of the boys, their frustrations taken out in random violence against the enemy, who they blame for the loss of Terrence. Many of the men are hanging about the city hall, like a pack of lost pups, milling around hoping somebody somewhere will adopt them. But the mourning has just begun and O'Hegarty, Florrie, James and his crew, and Father Dominic all have their work cut out for them. The death march will be long and painful. And the people of Cork are disgusted that they know exactly what to do for the second Republican Mayor of Cork, having been through the paces mere months before for the first.

The night before the funeral, as the remains of Terrence are closed forever in their silk-lined coffin, James and Seán stare at each other with stricken looks. They share the same measure of pain, distributed equally, the grief deep and without relief. The men turn and walk home in separate directions. But a couple of hours later James is to be found sitting on his bicycle outside the MacSwiney family home. He has a light scarf on his neck against the wind and his revolver is cool against his flesh underneath his sweater. Inside, Mary spots him through the window and goes to the door, but James does not respond. He just stays on his bicycle waiting. Eventually Seán steps outside. He looks at James and then turns to the back of the house, finds his old bike, somewhat rusty and abused, and mounts it. The two ride hard, James choosing the toughest route he can think of against the bitter wind and uphill, uphill, uphill. He has some idea in the back of his mind that the exhaustion, the constant beating of the wind will alleviate the heavy mass that he is carrying which seems to reside somewhere just below his diaphragm, the beats of his heart strained by its presence. He can feel the weight of it, pushing against his breath, squeezing his arteries, leaving him feeling choked and tense and on edge with a slow aching throb. But the only relief either man feels after punishing their bodies is a wicked cramp in their legs, and they go to their separate homes to collapse in a heap, their families startled. They awaken in the morning tired and sore but within moments adrenalin kicks in as they prepare for the spectacle of the funeral.

The most beautiful woman in the world feels like she has been cleaved in two. One half of herself sits watching the other half go through the motions of the funeral. She sits with her mother and child and brother in the closed cab hidden from view and follows the hearse through the crowds. She wears a pillbox hat covered in a billow of translucent veil that cascades over her shoulders. The collar of her luxurious coat frames her face. She is gaunt but somehow this serves only to accentuate her beauty. She says nothing. She does not weep. The princess has been cowed. There is no dramatic display that can possibly give relief to the stupefying sense of darkness enveloping her. Even her child she leaves to her mother, looking at her with dead eyes when she cries. Her soul has been tied and gibbeted and she has been made immobilised.

This time James and the rest of the Active Service Unit, all of whom attend the funeral with thousands of others, are sure not to be caught by photographers. Hats are pulled down taut, collars are raised and not just against the cold. Again, there is film taken. Later it will be shown around the world at silent movie houses everywhere an Irish community exists. Look closely, and for a couple of seconds you can see O'Hegarty directing Seán, who leads the pallbearers, to put the coffin in the hearse, overseeing the placement of flowers, turning his head against the camera, dashing quickly out of sight. But unlike Tomás's funeral, there are no other recognisable leaders in this footage. Even Muriel is not to be seen. It is a film of mass hysteria, crowds surging and ebbing, pipers piping, babies crying, a lost dog thin and ragged, running up and down the road between the marching throng of mourners, looking for its owner. There is nothing but forlorn faces everywhere you look. Florrie will write of this time that never did the entire brigade feel so low or so lost. The coffin is lowered into the grave but the identity of the bodies that do so is hidden from view by backs turned to the camera and heads lowered. A man walks by the camera with his hat in his hand intentionally held up at the side of his face so that he is impossible to identify. Is it James? Perhaps. He is tall, after all, and wearing a lush woollen coat. But perhaps not.

The rites and traditions of the death march come easily to the Irish people. It is ingrained into their culture over hundreds, even thousands of years. The evidence of this is to be found scattered across the island in the most barren of places. Since before the time of the pyramids, before the time of Stonehenge, there have been magnificent tombs defined by massive rocks upheld by standing stones. There have been bog bodies lying in wait for hundreds and hundreds of years to share their secrets. Since the time of St Patrick in the fourth century, there have been elaborate crosses reaching up to heaven in graveyards all over the island. There have been reliquaries, small but elaborate little bejewelled boxes holding the relics of saints. All of these point to a culture that has been consistently and indisputably concerned with death and the afterlife.

The tomb known as Newgrange in the Boyne Valley, only a mile away from the River Boyne where William of Orange trounced the Irish and turned the river red with blood, is the most spectacular example of an ancient tomb. It is known by the locals for exactly what it is, but the knowledge of its makers and its original purpose was lost when the local people were decimated. It has been standing there for five thousand years, a silent witness to the history of the Celts, slowly but surely becoming more invisible by overgrowth and neglect across the centuries. It will at last be excavated in the 1960s by a professor from Cork. Professor Kelly will spend ten years of his life searching out its secrets and rebuilding the exterior to its original glory.

It is a circular mound, the base of which is made up of a curb of massive stones lying horizontally on the ground, and the outer wall a circumference made up of thousands of smaller rocks of sparkling quartz embedded into the earthen exterior. They must have been carried for miles from other counties. Restored and newly defined by Professor Kelly, the tomb measures seventy-six metres in diameter and twelve metres high. In 1920 it was quite lacking in grandeur. It looked like an oddly symmetrical flat-topped hill, completely covered in grass and vines. The single entrance to the mound is a simple rectangular opening over which lies a lintel with a very short, shallow, but long window above it. To the untrained eye it is simply a slit in the rocks. But it is through this shallow window that the morning sun of the winter solstice on December the twenty-first pierces through and stretches across the nineteen-metre-long internal passageway into the centre of the mound.

On this solitary day of the year, the chamber, which is in the shape of a cross at the end of a long passageway lined with tall standing stones, is lit up and brilliantly exposed. Leading off from it are three small, recessed areas. In each recessed area, Professor Kelly will discover a basin filled with human bones. The massive kerb stone lying horizontally on the ground that marks the entrance is covered with elaborately carved spirals, the Celtic symbol of life. The spirals hint at what is to be found on the stones within. In fact, most of the stones, standing tall and straight along the passageway, are elaborately carved with a multitude of ancient symbols. Professor Kelly is amazed by the artwork, but what will really make him wonder is the roof. It is six metres high above the central chamber. It is fashioned as a corbel roof, where successive layers of rock stretch farther and farther into the centre to create an impenetrable defence. It is still intact and waterproof after five thousand years.

Across the country in County Clare many more tombs of a different type are to be found. In a desolate area called the Burren, composed of about two hundred and fifty square kilometres of earth laid by Mother Nature with a pavement of limestone rocks, is to be seen from quite a distance, the Hole of Sorrow, the Poulnabrone Tomb. Its massive wedge-shaped rock roof is supported by two standing stones, and the cairn of rocks sheltered beneath hold the bones of the dead. This tomb is almost four thousand years old, and many more like it are to be found in this windswept, lunar landscape characterised by deep fissures between the flat surface rocks, with tufts of grasses and exotic flowers growing straight up towards the sun. Occasionally there are surprises held in the fissures, like the solid gold Celtic necklace hidden two thousand five hundred years ago, picked up by a local farmer one fine sunny day when the glint of the gold caught his eye.

In Cork County, north of Fermoy, off in a farmer's field and partially sheltered by a small row of trees, is to be found the Hag's Bed or *Labbacallee*. This tomb lies closer to the ground and indeed a person could easily skirt on top of the massive stones set just above the line of the earth. Underneath the stones, dug into the earth, is the now-empty cairn where once were found the bones of a woman, all of the bones that is, but for her skull. That was found in the next section of the tomb. It is called the Hag's Bed because it is believed to be the ancient tomb of the Celtic goddess Cailleach Bheara, a formidable woman by all accounts who, having tired of her lacklustre husband, sliced off his head with a scythe and sent it rolling down the hill into the river below.

Other surprises are to be found from time to time in the bogs that dot the western and southern extremes of the island. Bog bodies will be culled from the peat that is cut and stacked to dry as fuel for the fireplace, the only source of heat available to the locals in Irish cottages. The bog bodies are rarely complete, but they are very well preserved. The acid in the peat, the cold temperature and the lack of oxygen deep underground, conspire to preserve even the soft inner organs within leather-like skin. Eyes peer out. Exposed teeth are framed by lips held in a grimace. Raging red hair is still perfectly coiffed with tree resin. Signs of torture are obvious. There are ropes threaded through holes pierced through arms, there are nipples sliced off, there are bodies cut in half, bones hacked with axes. There are the manicured nails of a massive, well-fed, six-foot-six man of royalty, and the harrowing look of a five-foot-two unfortunate. They have been placed as a warning on the border of territories and only slowly sink into oblivion. They call out to the world *see what we do to our enemies.*

In far-off Scandinavia, evidence of Irish belief in the afterlife is found in Viking booty. Small shoebox-size reliquaries are found in hidden hordes of wealth. They are always shaped like a house, made from elaborate woods and precious metals, decorated with jewels. They once held the bones and dust of saints. But according to accounts written by the monks from whom the reliquaries were stolen, the Vikings were sure to dump the real treasure out into the wind before stuffing the boxes under their capes and making off.

So many of the funerary practices of the ancient Celts are lost to the winds of time. Ritual killings and human sacrifice are suspected; druidic excess, appeasement of gods and kings is assumed. A more recent and lasting tradition through medieval times and into the present day is of course the Irish wake. There is nothing quite like a wake. It is civilised now, but in days gone by, in the rural parts of the country, the wake was an excessive celebration of life, a lament of loss, a time of prayer for the soul of the deceased, a social highlight, and an opportunity for food and drink, all rolled into one. Friends and enemies both, even strangers, would walk miles to attend the wake of a member of the community. At every wake the keening of the women was a symbol of distress sometimes imagined, sometimes real. It served as a cathartic release of sorrow and an expression of grief and mourning.

In 1920 the practice of keening is on its way out. But there are still to be found women in the rural parts of Ireland who understand its important role in grieving. This tradition had been handed down from the ancient Celts, but many other parts of the world held similar ritual practices. The ancient Romans and Greeks, the Hebrews, and other cultures around the world had developed traditions of keening. It is a practice that offers some expression of the inner turmoil of the mourner, and so offers some respite from the hair-tearing grief with which those close to the deceased may be afflicted.

In ancient Ireland, the practice of keening began with the bards. In an oral culture, the bard was the repository of history. At the wake he would place himself at the head of the corpse and lead a chant, a poetic rendition of the life, trials, tribulations, joys, victories, accomplishments, and family attachments of the deceased. Surrounding him would be a group of women who would repeat particular lines and sing out the chorus to his verses. With the breakdown of the Celtic clans and culture, the position of the bard was lost, but the tradition of chanting by the corpse mutated somewhat into a tradition of ritual song and grief, cultivated by particular women in the community. The haunting, troubling sounds of the women keening became a communal expression of grief and loss.

October 31 is the Celtic celebration of Samhain. It marked the end of harvest, and preparation for winter. All across Ireland the Celts lit bonfires and left out gifts of food and drink for the souls of their family and friends who would be released from their temporary prisons to travel to the otherworld on this night. Along with them went faeries and demons and gods. The headless horseman Dullahan rides his black horse carrying his own head under his arm. His whip is a human spine, and if it meets its mark your soul will be cast out of your body, and you will be taken with him to your doom. Faeries move from fire to fire looking for victims to torment but during all this chaos in the spirit world, the souls of loved ones find their way across Ireland to a place of rest. Perhaps Terry remembered these beliefs as he grew closer to death. Before he fell into his final reverie, he asked Father Dominic, Will my soul cross Ireland when I die?

There is no keening at Terrence's funeral. The heartache, the grief, the intense sense of loss and overwhelming sorrow, and the searing indignity of injustice is simply absorbed by the participants. The closer they were to Terry, the more colossal is the bitter pill they must swallow. And James and Seán, having been partially reared by Terry, are about as close to him as anyone could have been. And everyone knows that in such a situation, sooner or later something has to give.

There is no respite for the men or for the country once Terry's bones are laid in his grave. The funeral is complete by the afternoon of October 31, but there is no rest for the weary of mind and soul. In Dublin's Mountjoy Prison, the British are putting together gallows for their first execution since 1916.

Kevin Barry is an eighteen-year-old medical student by day, and a Dublin IRA brigade member whenever he is needed. On this particular day he has an exam at two o'clock at the university, but an ambush in which he will participate is planned for eleven o'clock. This is the time when a contingent of soldiers is to stop by a local bakery to pick up bread for their barracks. Kevin is a fine scholar, educated by the Jesuits, and he is not worried about his exam. Nor is he worried about the ambush. It will be an exercise in acquiring a few rifles. He has participated in several ambushes, and no one has ever been hurt. In June he personally let go an entire contingent of twenty-five British soldiers once he had got their guns. Nary a hair on anyone's head was harmed. On this day, September 20, things will be different. As his companions begin to demand the soldiers' guns, their own guns pointing straight ahead, he is surprised when a British soldier opens fire, and he must fire back in order to save his friends. It is a senseless debacle, and it ends in catastrophe. Kevin's gun jams and he dives under a truck for cover. The rest of his mates run for their lives. He is swiftly pulled out from under the truck by the enraged military and charged with the murder of four soldiers, even though they were most definitely killed by friendly fire as panic reigned. While he waits for trial, the British decide they are interested in information and they assume that an eighteen-year-old is just the one to give it to them, with a little pressure.

The pressure consists of beatings, threats of death, and torture. His limbs are practically twisted off his body while soldiers sit on his torso, his head beaten against the stone floor. But Kevin will not tell them what they wish to know. At school he is known as a tough cookie, a rugby player and a man who knows his own mind, despite his young age. After all, he had joined the Volunteers when he was just fifteen years old. Kevin keeps his own counsel, but when he is finally allowed a visit by family and the extent of his injuries is seen, he is ordered by Dublin GHQ to write a statement of what was done to him. GHQ knows that the British are not going to let this boy get off the hook, and they are hoping to publish the statement. The ensuing public outcry will put pressure to bear that will result in his release; or at least stay the execution. But this time it is the Irish who are wrong. The British general replies that the four British soldiers who were killed were also teenagers. Tit for tat. Your boy will hang. The execution is set for the first of November.

Michael Collins is reeling over the death of Terry, whom he knew well, but he has one chance to save Kevin, and that is where he throws his energy. He sets in motion a plan to blast out a wall of Mountjoy prison and allow Kevin to escape. A great irony ensues: it is their own published account that thwarts their efforts. The public is indeed outraged by the treatment of Kevin Barry, and they throng to the front of the gaol in thick crowds to protest both his treatment and the execution. In consequence a large number of military personnel are despatched for crowd control. They are set around the perimeter of the gaol, making it impossible for Collins to set off his charges. At the same time that Terry's funeral is proceeding down the streets of Cork City, Kevin Barry is allowed one final visit with his mother and brother and sister. He is light-hearted in the face of death. I am not the first and I won't be the last, he tells his mother. But pray for me nonetheless, and he smiles his youthful, radiant smile and brushes back his dark hair, his twinkling eyes betraying nothing but serenity and peace. Early the following morning the chaplain accompanies him to the gallows. They pray the rosary together and Kevin slips on the hood and slips off the gallows into eternity.

Grief envelops the country like an invisible net. The cold November winds pick up and their insistent drone and whirl through the air seeps in through every crack and cranny, under every door and into every home. It feels like death is everywhere and the country is hardly a step closer to freedom. But O'Hegarty and Collins know better. They know the worst is yet to come.

O'Hegarty is now in charge. Florrie is nervous. He is now the daily recipient of vast amounts of intelligence pulled from all of the battalions and he begins to understand what O'Hegarty has been doing these years since 1916. He begins to understand the scowl, the pessimism, and the resigned assumption of what will come to be known as Murphy's Law, what can go wrong will. It boggles Florrie's mind, both the amount of information that is coming in from all over the city and county, as well as the type of information. In order to deal with it, he must construe a cross-referenced system of notes. There is no way he can keep all of this information in his head at once. He routinely keeps in touch with Collins. He meets regularly with O'Hegarty. Meetings at the Wallace sisters' are different now. O'Hegarty sports a permanent glower. Any trace of the lightness and goodness of Tomás and Terrence that tempered their movements against the enemy has been eradicated by the cold gusts that fly up and down the hills of Cork. O'Hegarty meets with Mick Murphy now, and Tom Crofts and Pa Murray and Tom Hales and Tom Barry and other battalion commanders, none of whom are the least bit worried about loss of life in enemy ranks.

As a paid member of the Active Service Unit, James is now free to spend his time corroborating important intelligence information, using his own contacts and acting on O'Hegarty's orders. He rarely goes home. He knows that the British have their own intelligence officers, often easily picked out by their comical disguises as tourists or fisherman or businessmen. He knows that these men are looking for information on the likes of men just like him. So he steers clear of his family and goes back to sleeping in areas of the city far from the central core where he conducts most of his daily work. This way he can be sure that no one is following him. He sleeps at his sister's home, or safe houses that O'Hegarty has designated. But James and Florrie are about to find out that O'Hegarty has more friends of an unpredictable nature than either man could ever imagine.

Florrie has been asked by Father Dominic to come and meet someone. Tell no one, he instructs, but meet me at the church after dark. When Florrie arrives, he is introduced to a beautiful young woman. She works at Victoria Barracks, in charge of the female secretarial and clerical staff. She sees everything that crosses the desk of the division sergeant major's desk. This includes intelligence reports, orders to troops, and correspondence with London. This young woman wants to help the IRA. Florrie can barely contain himself. But listen, says Father Dominic, we must help her out as well. She has a problem, a big problem.

Josephine tells her story, the story she originally told Father Dominic, the evening she was feeling suicidal and walked to the church to pray for help. Father Dominic happened to walk into the chapel and see her crying. Josephine is a war widow. She bore two sons before her husband died fighting in France. One son she has with her here in Cork. But her eldest son, who is only eight years old, is in Cardiff with her in-laws. They will not release him to her, and they demand money every month for his upkeep, including their son's war pension. Josephine has taken them to court and lost the case. She will never get legal custody of her eldest son again despite keeping custody of her youngest boy. It has left her despondent.

Florrie listens. We may be able to help. He goes back and tells O'Hegarty the story. Can I go and take the boy? Bring him back to her? O'Hegarty, ever the sceptic, says, yes, it could be arranged, we could use Collins's men in London to help out. But let's wait a while and see what kind of information she passes on.

With the hope of recovering her child Josephine's world regains its colour. She arranges meeting places and times with Florrie throughout the week. He is the only person of the brigade she will talk to. Florrie is adamant about her safety. He is delirious over the sudden availability of high-level intelligence right off the desks of the British command. But the true reason for his concern is the overwhelming allure that Josephine has over him. She is three years older than him, but it matters not. He is smitten. He must be certain that this dark-haired, dark-eyed beauty he cannot stop thinking about never puts herself at risk. You must be so careful, always. Never take any risks. Build trust with the commanders. Never be seen at any time at any Republican function or event or with anybody who might be recognised as IRA.

Josephine types up copies of letters for the commanders. She files their papers. She takes shorthand and writes replies for them. All of the contents she commits to memory or copies for herself, carrying them out every evening to be delivered to Florrie at one of a few local churches during evening Mass. O'Hegarty is ecstatic at receiving the information. Suddenly the bits and pieces of information that come from the surveillance work of IRA and the comments by the people of Cork are corroborated. However, it is his worst fears that are realised when he begins to act on the information that he receives. There are informers among the people. And now it is his job to deal with them.

James knows something is up once he is ordered to check out certain information. He realises that O'Hegarty and Florrie have a new high-level intelligence source, but he is smart enough not to ask. At a meeting of all twelve of the ASU men, they are broken into two teams, each team headed by one of the men. James is in the same group as Florrie. Their leader is Seán Twomey. He is a fearless man, but the day will soon come when he is driven mad by chaos and death and risk. The city is divvied up into sections and each man must get to know the military and the Black and Tans that frequent their assigned area, their schedules for movement, and keep tabs on who they visit. The ASU men must be ready and willing to check out neighbourhoods after curfew when the Black and Tans crawl out of the woodwork and do the most damage. They must be smart enough and stealthy enough not to get caught. The information is needed for two reasons. The first is to be aware of opportunities for ambushes. The Black and Tans must be dealt with, especially the most vicious culprits. The second reason is to find out where they are getting their information.

The Black and Tans are still on their tear. They have not stopped. Not through the trauma of Terry's hunger strike, certainly not through the aftermath of intense grief. There have been notices published in the paper, on the front pages no less, threatening any IRA members, threatening anyone who helps them out. We are watching, the notices claim. We are watching and we will find you.

They are arresting anybody who looks twice at them. They spend their days out on the street, accosting passers-by, interrogating whomsoever they wish, and sometimes hauling unsuspecting citizens off to internment at the Victoria Barracks. They spend their evenings out and about hammering in the doors of known or suspected IRA, setting homes on fire, threatening men, women, and children, and dragging off anybody they think they might get some information out of. They are on a mission to find every IRA member in the city, and it looks like nothing is going to stop them. They are getting information from somewhere and it is the job of the ASU to find out where and to put a plug in that leak.

November's rains are audible. The drops patter on the ground and ricochet off the cobblestone streets with a spiteful intensity. It is dark and overcast. The city is still in mourning. The most beautiful woman in the world cannot seem to shake the darkness that envelopes her. She has left her baby with her mother and is trying to make sense of the days that pass like waves of a flood. Collins contacts her. De Valera, still in America, contacts her. But it is Art O'Brien who finally convinces her to go to America and pick up the lecture circuit so that de Valera can come home without impeding the flow of funds. Muriel feels lost and alone. She refuses to go unless Mary MacSwiney goes with her. O'Brien, a wealthy lawyer in London who is working for Collins on the quiet, is ecstatic. Muriel is the grieving widow of a national hero and Mary MacSwiney could talk about Irish freedom until the cows come home. This will be the best PR possible. Muriel packs her bag. Seán takes them to the train station to make their way to Dublin, then Liverpool to catch the ship to New York.

Talk in the pubs is of Terry and Joseph and the funerals and whosoever in the neighbourhoods are the latest victims of the Black and Tans. James gets called to a meeting with his team. It is to be held in the rooms above the Douglas Street Pub. O'Hegarty is there and so is Mick Murphy. Like all hurlers, Mick is a tough man. But James is about to discover just how ruthless he can be. He addresses the team: Tadg Sullivan was out after curfew the other day, just checking out the area. And who does he find snooping around but a fifteen-year-old. Snooping about my place, nonetheless. The cheek! The boy is scared silly and has spilled the beans. The news is worse than we suspected. It looks like he works for the group who has been putting those fucking notices in the paper, the ones threatening reprisals against the IRA, the ones we assumed were written by the Tans. Well now. You are going to love this. It seems that they are legitimate. There is a group, working out of the Men's YMCA, that are in cahoots with the Black and Tans. Yes boys, it looks like the bloody YMCA has more spies checking us out than we have checking out the Tans. Now isn't that just priceless. Murphy snorts. Also, it looks like the little bastard was working for them the night Tomás was murdered. He had been assigned to watch his comings and goings and report back. Anyway, there may be more information to be had from this little shite. I say we send him out to Corry's farm.

O'Hegarty is standing at the window looking at the street below. He is watching the evening's gas lights cast shadows that dance on the glistening surface of the wet, deserted street. He thinks to himself, if I didn't know better, I would say it looks like demons dancing in the dark. He thinks of his mother and her constant praying on the rosary. Once a Catholic, always a Catholic, she had once said to him when he had dared to renounce his upbringing and laugh at what he called her pathetic superstitions. He turns from the window. James watches him and wonders what this latest secret of O'Hegarty is about. He knows Martin Corry, the Commandant of the 8th Battalion to the east of the city. But Corry's farm? He will talk to Mick or Florrie about it when he gets a chance. O'Hegarty looks at Murphy. Aye, if there is any information to be had Corry is the man to get it. Then he changes the subject and addresses the men at the table. We had best be taking this information seriously. We will get what other information we can from this source. But I need you boys on the street. Cast your net wide. Don't leave any stone unturned. If your sources don't have anything for you, find new sources. We need to know who is letting the cat out of the bag. The men nod in understanding. All of them will be out tomorrow, chatting up their sources, the grocers, the tram conductors, the hotel maids, the ordinary people of the city who are watching and listening and passing on what they discover. O'Hegarty shakes Murphy's hand. Thanks Mick, we'll see what the boy knows and how far it will take us. To everyone in the room, he says, be careful boys, as always. As he makes his way to the stairs, he turns to James and nods. James knows the look; it means follow me.

No one is out on the street. It is past curfew. They will all have to either sleep here or work their way home through the side streets and alleyways as James and O'Hegarty are about to do now. Jimmy, first thing tomorrow, make your way to Murphy's. That boy needs to be moved from his place. One of the Grey brothers will pick you up and take you out to the farm. And as he sees the questioning look on James's face, he explains. It is out in Glouthane, ten miles east. See what Corry wants you to do. You can stay or come back with Grey. Check in with me when you return. O'Hegarty walks away, his hands in his trenchcoat pockets, his collar up and his cap pulled low, and ducks into an alleyway just before reaching the dancing lights.

Dinny is a fifteen-year-old boy who lives with his mother in one of the better areas of the city, not far from the grammar school where, it seems like so long ago, James played lookout for the gun robbery. Dinny's friends and acquaintances belong to the reigning Protestant elite of the city. The YMCA is their organisation. In the same way that the Catholic boys belong to the local hurling clubs and Gaelic leagues, the Protestant boys belong to the YMCA. It is a good organisation, arranging camping trips, fishing expeditions, and football games: activities that interest teenagers and challenge them to learn new skills. But the skills they have recently been charged with learning are somewhat out of the ordinary. They are espionage skills. And the boys have taken to it like ducks to water. Of course, they are given every advantage, allowed free rein after curfew, and directed where to go and who to watch by the men who run the organisation: the shopkeepers, the politicians, and the wealthy loyalists of Cork City. They have been watching the neighbourhood IRA men make their way through the dark to meetings, keeping tabs on known IRA households for movements and identification of who and where, keeping an eye out for guns and arms of any kind. They are a minority in the city, a tiny minority. But the damage they are doing is counted in lives devastated, families wrenched apart, livelihoods disappeared, homes destroyed, and increasingly, murder. Many IRA boys are behind bars, some suffering cruel treatment because of the YMCA spies. If they had a job, they are no longer getting paid, and their families are suffering for it. If they put up any fuss at all, their homes are set on fire or smashed to pieces by rifle butts. Yes, the work of the YMCA has been fruitful indeed.

James arrives at Murphy's home early in the morning. He wears his trenchcoat with his collar pulled up high against the wind and his cap pulled down low on his forehead. He walks with determination past the house without giving it a glance and turns down an alleyway, then works his way back through the connecting lane to the garden entrance. He taps on the door with his usual beat, a signal to those inside of his identity. When he enters the kitchen, he finds the boy sitting at the kitchen table. The boy looks ragged and dishevelled but he is drinking a cup of tea and eating a slice of bread and jam. Standing leaning against the kitchen sink, his gun partially slid into the front of his trousers is Tadg. He also holds a cup of tea and nods at James as he quietly closes the door behind him. The boy looks at James with wide eyes but keeps slurping his tea and chewing his bread. He looks over at Tadg who reassures him. No worries Dinny, just eat up.

James wasn't sure what he was expecting but he certainly wasn't expecting this fresh, freckle-faced boy with a mop of sandy curls and a look of complete innocence. Tadg reads James's face and winks across the tiny kitchen at him. Our friend Dinny here has been most cooperative. Murphy walks into the room and nods at James. No one says anyone's name out loud. The car will be here in a few minutes. Sure, have a cuppa tea afore ye go. But James just nods no thanks. Are ye coming along? he asks Tadg. But Tadg cannot afford any more time away. He still has a job, and he needs to get to it. Tadg is a few years older than James and a dedicated IRA man. He is tall and handsome with a shock of black hair brushed back off his face. He is originally from County Kerry and retains his unique accent and reticent ways. Tadg and James have known each other for years now. Tadg is Captain of C Company of the 2nd Battalion, James's home base before he was assigned to the ASU. But Tadg has remained a point of reference. They sometimes meet at local pubs when James is checking out leads. When standing side by side they make a formidable team, two very handsome, very winsome young men, both with an easy way about them. Tadg, because it comes naturally to him; James because when he is out, he is working intelligence, chatty, open for conversation. Afterwards, as they leave wherever they have spent the evening Tadg will invariably tease him. Too bad they don't know the real you Séamus. Wouldn't they be surprised to know you really are a surly bastard? And both men will laugh.

Tadg walks to the door and James follows. They step outside. I don't know why they are bothering taking this kid to the farm, begins Tadg. Aye, so what is the farm? I haven't been informed about this one, replies James. Never mind Séamus. It's that tough little bulldog, Martin Corry. He's over in Glouthane, but his family has a big wack of land, and it is well camouflaged and hard to find, in behind the village and hidden by trees. It's out of the way and a great hideaway. I just don't know why they don't let the kid go home. He's as innocent as a lamb, just been used by the men to do their bidding. I'd say Murphy scared the bejesus out of him and he won't say a word for the rest of his life. He's told us everything he knows. Aye, well, O'Hegarty agrees with Murphy. I was at the meeting.

Murphy sticks his head out of the door. Car's here. Dinny, says Murphy, we are taking you for a ride in the country. Not to worry, it's just for a day or two and then we'll be bringing you back home. Dinny's eyes grow larger, if that is possible. Sure, can I not just go home now? My mother will be worried sick about me. She will probably call the police. Don't worry about that Dinny, now put your jacket on. You are going to be getting a ride in a motorcar. You'll go with my friend here, so remember to mind your manners. Dinny gives up on negotiating, and searches James's face, but without any satisfaction.

James's face has been well developed these past years. From his gun-running in Glasgow to his current need to be unnoticed, he has trained himself to forego any trace of emotion on his face. He has learned that a flat face is often an invisible face. As the car rolls up to the front of the house, James has Dinny by the arm and quickly leads him out of the front door, through the pitter-patter of another rain shower and to the back seat where he jumps in beside him. Morning, James nods to Jeremiah Grey. He doesn't turn around, but the Grey brothers are a lively pair and Jeremiah especially, the younger of the two, is never happier than when he is engaged in some sort of subterfuge. Another beautiful, sunny morning in Rebel Cork, he proclaims in a sarcastic voice as the rain beats down and wind picks up. Welcome to our visitor. Sit back and enjoy the ride. We will be taking the scenic route for your viewing pleasure, and he laughs heartily at his own attempt to let James know they will be taking the back roads, out of the way of possible run-ins with the Tans. Dinny is put somewhat at ease by the easy tone of the driver and relaxes enough to look out of the window with some interest. Every so often he turns and looks at James but says nothing. They gaze out of the window as they roll out past the neighbourhood and north of the city and the River Lee, to travel through the quiet countryside roads.

Martin Corry's farm is a lovely place. There is the main farmhouse, and several outbuildings as well as a good-sized barn. Tadg was right, it is definitely out of the way. The local geography consists of rolling hills and, in the odd spot, a bog or marshland. From some points the view is spectacular. But despite the location, the RIC have raided this farm several times, especially since Corry is a known IRA man, in gaol at least three times since the Rising. Not only is he with a record, but he is also a belligerent son of a bitch as far as the British are concerned. And if the truth be known, a swaggering brute as far as some of his own colleagues are concerned. But O'Hegarty knows Corry. He has known him for a long time, ever since the days of the beginning of the Volunteers back in 1913. When Corry was growing up, he lived in a small town, down the street from the MacCurtain family, before they moved into Cork City. Tomás knew him well and kept him at arm's length. O'Hegarty knows him well and like every man under his command, O'Hegarty puts his men's most useful qualities to practical use. Corry's most useful qualities are not something O'Hegarty likes to advertise.

It is to the barn that James is directed to take the boy and then told to come back to the kitchen. He walks with Dinny past a shield of tall trees and through the wide-open barn doors. There is a sentry leaning against the horse stall and he opens the gate and tells Dinny to have a seat on the straw. Dinny looks at James with panic written across his face. Until this moment James was planning on going back to the city. Jeremiah is having a cup of tea in Corry's kitchen waiting for him. But the look on the boy's face makes him reconsider. O'Hegarty had given him the choice, so he will stay and bring the boy back himself. We won't be long here, Dinny. Relax.

James notes that there are several men from the Cork No. 1 posted as sentries around the area. They have guns and they are not hiding them. These men are from Corry's battalion, the 8th, and though James is not familiar with them – they are after all country lads, and James's territory is the south side of the downtown core of the city – all four tip their caps to him as he walks, one by one. James is recognised as a leading member of the brigade, one of the ASU, despite O'Hegarty's attempts at keeping their identities as secret as possible. When he arrives back to the kitchen, Corry expects a report. James tells Corry what he knows, that O'Hegarty is looking for a little more information, that Murphy had a go at Dinny, and he spilled the beans about some sort of anti-Sinn Féin Society and the YMCA, that O'Hegarty wants more names. I'll wait around till you are finished with him and escort him back.

Corry looks directly at James with his malevolent face. He is shorter than James, though with the powerful shoulders of someone who has spent years at hard labour. His face seems to have a permanent snarl due to a crooked slant on one side of his head that may or may not be a form of palsy. He is burnt from wind and sun and is wrinkled far more than he should be for his age of thirty years. He stares people down with a haughtiness that James is quite certain puts off all but the most pugnacious of Black and Tans, when they dare to come calling. Well, if this Dinny boy found Murphy intimidating, he is in for a fright with Corry, thinks James. And if it wasn't for the increasing number of showdowns with the Black and Tans, the arrests of IRA men and other innocent citizens, the random shootings, the homes set on fire, that continue to mount every night, James would think twice about letting Corry loose on the boy. After all, the boy is about the same age as his little brother Edward, and James can't imagine Edward in this nasty little bit of trouble. But it must be remembered, the boy was acting as a spy and it is highly likely, at least according to O'Hegarty, that the bits of information he has been collecting and passing on to the Tans have resulted in the dire consequences that the people of Cork have been subject to.

Corry looks at Jeremiah sitting at the table enjoying his tea and asks him what he is planning. Are ye here for the day? This may take a while. Jeremiah senses Corry's antagonism and stands up. I need to head back Jimmy, I can come by tomorrow, early if need be. Aye, that'll work, I'll be ready. James is thinking the farm is as good a place to stay the night as any, but he wonders what will take so long. And come to think of it he does not have orders from O'Hegarty as to what to do with the boy once Corry is done with him. He assumed he would bring him back to town and leave him on the street near his home but in fact O'Hegarty said nothing about the return. Corry looks at James and nods in the direction of the kitchen door. He slips on his rubber wellington boots, his usual attire for about the farm, and then from a series of hooks chooses his dark green IRA military jacket. He does up the buttons, right to his neck, buckles the thick brown leather belt around his waist and walks out, the door slamming back and forth behind him. James follows him out of the house and back to the barn.

When he gets to the barn the sentry, immediately noticing the uniform, realises he means business. He brings over a crate for Corry to sit on. Corry plants himself. Bring the prisoner out, he snarls in a loud voice. Aye sir, and he walks to the stall where Dinny is sitting, and swings open the door. Is it time to go home? Dinny can be heard asking the sentry, but the sentry just shakes his head and directs the boy to stand in front of Corry. You have been brought here to stand trial as a spy working for the enemy. What do you have to say for yourself, boy? Dinny begins to shake. He looks around the barn. It is a barn like any other. It certainly is not a court. Are these men playing a joke on him? The harsh-looking creature sitting in front of him does not seem to be laughing. Dinny knows he is in trouble, but he does not understand what is happening. He scans the room for something, anything, that will guide him in what he should say or do. His eyes alight on James. James is not prepared for this. O'Hegarty said nothing about a trial. Yet Corry is the battalion commander and certainly above James's rank. James holds his tongue, but his face betrays his confusion, and this ever so slight revelation frightens Dinny even more. I told the other man at the house everything I know. He said I could go home.

I don't think you understand just what a serious situation you are in, boy. This is an Irish Republican Army Court of Law. You are on trial. What do you have to say in your defence? Were you or were you not spying for the Black and Tans? Dinny's eyes are as wide as saucers. Aye, aye I was spying, but not for the Tans, 'twas for the men at the YMCA. All we junior boys were helping them out. They would tell us where to go and what houses to watch and we just told them if anybody was coming or going after curfew, 'twas all. So, you admit to being a spy? Yes, if that's what you call it. I am very sorry. I won't do it again. I'll tell my ma I don't want to go to the YMCA anymore. Quiet boy! Corry stares the boy down. He watches him cower. This court finds you guilty. The only sentence for a spy is execution. Now, there are two ways to be executed. You can be hanged, or you can be shot. If you pass on some information that we would like to have, we will treat you like a man and shoot you quickly and efficiently. However, if you choose to be stubborn, you can hang from this beam up here, Corry points above him to the roof of the barn, till the crows come by in the morning and peck out your eyes. Corry stares at the boy with a frightening intensity and nobody doubts him.

James is standing to the side. He watches as Dinny's legs buckle beneath him. He watches as the sentry picks him up under the arms and stands him back up on his feet. He watches as Dinny looks over at him with a wild look. He listens as Dinny first babbles incoherently then musters some self-control and some gumption and stands up to Corry. You can't shoot me. The other man promised I could go home. I told you everything I know. You have to take me home.

Corry ignores the boy's demands. What I want from you, boy, is names of the men in the YMCA who were giving you your orders. Dinny, from somewhere in his gut, finds the strength to rally again. I am not telling you anything. You take me home. My mother will have called the police by now. You better take me home now.

Corry nods to the sentry who walks to another stall and comes out with a long rope tied in a noose at one end. James watches as Dinny's legs give out once again. This time Dinny begins to cry. Please, please, I told the other man everything.

Here is how we will proceed, boy. We are going to put this noose around your neck and throw the rope over the beam here above us. We will pull you up, but if you change your mind, you just raise your hand up in the air and we will let you back down. But don't waste our time. Only raise your hand if you are ready to give us some names. Anybody who directed you or who you know is actively spying on the IRA. Those are the names we want. And Corry nods to the sentry who leads Dinny to the middle of the barn and places the noose over his neck.

James is beginning to feel nauseous. He was not prepared for this, and he is angry at O'Hegarty for not warning him. James knows that if a man is found to be a spy he must be dealt with just as the British deal with the Irish. This is war, even if it is a strange chaotic kind of war. Black and Tans are fair game. Loyalist spies are fair game. But executing a boy of fifteen? Surely there must be another solution. James looks around at the witnesses to this event. They are all men of Corry's battalion, and they do not seem shocked or even surprised. Clearly this is not far off the normal course of events at Corry's farm. James knows he is treading on thin ice, but he walks over to Corry, bends down and whispers in his ear. O'Hegarty didn't say anything about a trial, sir. I wonder should I not be taking the boy back? I wouldn't want to overstep myself by not following O'Hegarty's orders.

Corry turns his head slowly and looks James in the eye. His face takes on a more pronounced scowl. He stands up and walks out of the barn. James can see Dinny from the corner of his eye slide down to his knees in a release of panic.

Outside the sky is dark and menacing. It is early afternoon, but it feels like the onset of evening. The trees are swaying in the wind and off in the distance behind the barn, Corry's kitchen door slaps back and forth in the wind. James can feel the waves of anger rolling off Corry's face.

Now Séamus, I am going to tell you something and you are going to listen. Aye sir. You come highly recommended from our OC. And you should thank your lucky stars that you do, because if you didn't, I would be considering reporting you for negligence of your duties. Corry points his short fat little fingers at James's chest. You might just find *yourself* hanging from that beam. Corry does not stop staring in James's eyes, but James knows a brute when he sees one, and the warrior in him asserts itself. He does not back down but stares at Corry. I hear tell you are in with GHQ, Collins, and the rest. Well, Séamus, GHQ is in Dublin, far, far away. This is Cork and in case you haven't noticed it is Cork that is taking the brunt of this war. Did those British bastards think twice before they hanged Kevin Barry last week? Eighteen years old Jimmy, and dancing at the end of a rope and guilty of much less than this little shite. What's good for the goose is good for the gander. Now I will thank you to keep your suggestions to yourself.

Corry turns and walks back into the barn. He stops at the crate but does not sit down. Up on your feet boy! he barks. Clearly his ire is up. I will repeat my instructions for your benefit. If you change your mind and wish to pass on the information, just raise your hand. And Corry nods at the sentry, who puts the noose over Dinny's head and tightens it and then steps back and begins to pull on the rope. It takes a few seconds before the sentry has pulled enough rope down from over the top of the beam and Dinny can feel the first bit of pressure on his neck. James has never seen such a look on anyone's face. The boy is full of panic, possibly shock, and looking wildly around the room. He settles on James's face and begins to cry for his mother. Mama, Mama, he whines until his voice is stilled by the rope and he is several feet off the ground. His hands grope desperately at the noose, but it is impossible to take off. His feet kick wildly. As his face turns blue his hand suddenly shoots up in the air. The sentry drops him quickly to the ground and Dinny lies crying and slobbering and gasping for air face down on the barn floor amongst the dirt and loose straw. James, in spite of his very conscious need to stay calm, heaves a deep sigh of relief. Another of the sentries who is outside the barn standing guard with a rifle turns and retches into the bushes. Smart boy you are after all, Dinny. Now what do you have to say for yourself? Who were the men at the YMCA that gave you instructions?

Dinny spits out a name at Corry. Not enough, boy. Corry motions to the sentry and says, again! The sentry begins to pull on the rope and Dinny desperately tries to get the noose from around his neck but to no avail. He is lifted up off the ground a second time. The sentry outside makes an audible groan. James does not look at Dinny this time, instead he watches Corry. There is a glint in his eye, and James thinks he is definitely taking some sort of satisfaction in this spectacle. Despite that, he can see that Corry wants those names. It only takes a moment for Dinny to raise his hand this time. Again, he is dropped to the floor. Spit it out boy, you know I mean business. And once Dinny is done coughing and choking and feeling the damage to the now raw skin on his neck, he gives over three more names. They meet every Wednesday at a house. I can tell you where it is. Corry is satisfied. Well, boy, you have earned yourself a soldier's death. We will feed you a bite of dinner and wait till nightfall. Prepare yourself, say your prayers. You won't see tomorrow's sunrise. And Corry nods to the sentry, walks out of the barn and into the wind. Back to his house without so much as a glance at James.

The sentry takes the noose from around Dinny's neck. Settle down boy, you're alright for the time being, and he opens the stall gate again and steers the crying boy onto the straw. James walks into the barn. I can take over for a while. You should go get yourself a cup of tea. The sentry looks twice at James, sensing his disapproval. 'Tis a nasty, bloody business, but Corry isn't a man to mess about. I can see that, replies James. He walks over to the stall, opens the gate and steps in. Dinny is lying on the straw in the corner crying and gingerly palpating his raw, red neck. He looks James in the eye for a moment. I know you. I've seen you around. And this time it is James's turn to be surprised, but he manages to maintain his blank look. Aye, well I am from Cork, just like you. But you live in my neighbourhood. Off the Douglas Road, over by Victoria, where the MacSwiney family lives. James does not agree or disagree, though he is starting to feel a slight tingle of alarm. So, you have seen me around, Dinny. Nobody says anybody's name around here, the boy continues. You IRA guys think you are so secret, but we know about you. Is that right, Dinny? What else do you know about me? I know your name is Séamus. I know you were talking to the mayor the night he was killed.

The tingle of alarm grows exponentially. James realises that this boy was watching him meet with Tomás on that fateful night in March. For a moment he can see Tomás's tired face in the low light of his office, smiling at him. But his vision soon evaporates. He realises the little spy network has been operating for much longer than he thought. Dinny does not know the damage he is doing. He is hoping that James may become his ally and save him if he knows they are neighbours. Why do you think my name is Séamus, Dinny? Sure, I have seen you over at the MacSwiney place and at the funeral. I heard someone call you that. Is that what you told your man, asks James, consciously trying to mask his alarm. Aye, we tell them everything we see or hear. They make a list. And as the words are coming out of Dinny's mouth, he is realising that he has made an error in judgement, but it is too late to pull the words back down into his throat. Desperately he claws at what chances he might have. If you let me go, I will tell them you have helped me. They will take your name off the list. We could leave now, just walk out to the highway and catch a ride back to Cork. They will be very happy to see me. They will give you a reward. My ma will be happy to see me. And Dinny's voice degenerates into gasps and whines. James stands up from his crouched position and walks out of the stall. He calls to the outside sentry to come in and keep watch and makes his way through the overcast, early evening light and the blustery winds to Corry's kitchen.

The boy must be taken care of. We will bury him in the back field. I will send you out with two of my men. They will dig the grave now while there is still light. Make sure it is towards the ditch and deep enough. I don't want to be raking him up in the spring when I turn the field over. Corry glowers at James. You ASU boys get paid for your work. You can do your fair share. You have your gun on you? James nods. He has been given his orders. Now sit down and have a plate of stew. James has eaten almost nothing all day, but he is beyond putting anything past his lips.

Corry leaves the room, and as James sits alone the panic in the back of his mind continues to grow. He is on a list. That means he could be targeted at any time. Dinny's masters will have figured out within hours that he has been picked up by the IRA. They could start working their way through their list in the hopes of finding him. The men will have to be dealt with before they get to anybody. James thinks of the boy. What a fool. But at fifteen who isn't a fool? Nevertheless. My own life is on the line now. Who knows who else is on their list? James rises, washes a plate that sits in the big sink, then refills it with stew for Dinny. He takes a thick slice of bread and butter and a spoon and works his way through the darkness to the barn. The sentry nods to him and looks jealously at the stew. Plenty left in the kitchen. I'll take over for a while.

Dinny has been asleep, curled up in a little ball on the straw. His face is dirty, and tear-streaked. His sandy curls are limp, interspersed with bits of straw. James hands him the plate. He grabs it and greedily begins to eat. He does not talk until he is finished. I have been thinking Dinny, maybe we can trade some more information for your life? You've gotten to know my commander. He may be reasoned with if you can come up with some worthwhile information. For instance, who is on this list you speak of? Dinny looks at James with a slightly elated look on his face. Do you think he will let me go? And then his face falls. But I don't know who else is on the list. I only know what I have already told them. And I don't really know anybody's name. There was one fella, but the Tans already took him to gaol. I don't know anybody else. They keep notes until they can figure out exactly what the men are up to. There are five or six of us junior boys who help them out. James is disappointed. The boy will not be of any further help. It is those men whose names Dinny has divulged, men who are actively collecting information from Dinny and his friend, it is those men who must be dealt with and quickly. If they are holders of a list of IRA suspects being prepared to hand over to the Black and Tans, well they must be stopped. James knows exactly what O'Hegarty will demand. James must get back to O'Hegarty first thing in the morning. Arrangements will have to be made.

The moon is exactly a half-disc, revealed only from time to time as the clouds sail past. The winds have picked up and it feels like a storm is brewing. The night is cool and so very, very dark. Dinny's hands are tied together behind his back. James holds onto his arm and drags him along the edge of the field following the hedge of shrubs. His trenchcoat is tied tightly and blows about him with the gusts of wind. Two of the sentries are leading the way. One holds a lantern and as he walks ahead the light swings back and forth and side to side in an eerie, erratic motion, casting what seems to James threatening, frightening shadows. He puts his free hand in his trousers pocket and fingers his beads. Dinny is moaning and whining and begging incoherently. James can feel the sweat breaking out on his forehead underneath his tightly pulled cap. Fuck, he thinks to himself. God help me. This is not the same as shooting a soldier in a gun battle.

How much farther? he shouts out to the sentries. About a hundred yards. Corry didn't want this too close to the house. James grunts. Dinny's knees give out. The wind howls sending the bushes swaying back and forth. James stops and pulls Dinny up by the arm. Look Dinny, time to man up. Stop whining and say your prayers. You know the Lord's Prayer for God's sake. Pull yourself together and say it. James practically has to yell at Dinny's face to be heard but Dinny only cries louder. Suddenly James is aware of the reeking stench of shit and piss wafting from the boy. Fuck. Dinny is blathering. James thinks to himself it is better to knock him out and carry him than listen to this. The men up ahead finally stop. They turn around and hold the lantern high. It sways unsteadily. You take the lantern and just follow the tree line. We will carry him. And each sentry takes a hold under one of Dinny's underarms and begins to drag him across the ground. Dinny's legs are rubber. His feet and trousers are dragged through the muck, and he cries out for his mama. Good God in heaven, I will fucking kill you now if you don't shut up, hollers one of the sentries. But it is no use, Dinny only rallies… Séamus, Séamus, Séamus, he screams out, don't kill me Séamus, I will help you! I will spy for you. Please Séamus. The two sentries look at each other above Dinny's head. Mother in heaven have mercy on me, thinks James to himself as he stops his trudge through the muck. He glares at Dinny. This is your doing, he snaps and pulls the scarf from his neck that is tucked into his trenchcoat to tie around Dinny's mouth, yanking it so that it sets between his teeth. I told you Dinny, all there is for it is to say your fucking prayers.

After a few more moments pushing Dinny through the muck the sentries call out. Right, here we are. Where do you want him? James holds the lantern high and notes the rough, oblong plunge in the ground, and the nearby shovels leaning into the shrubs. He takes a shovel and measures the depth of the grave. It is a good five feet deep. Better to be six, thinks James, but I cannot take another minute of this. Leave go of him here, replies James, and Dinny's knees sink into the soft, wet, recently harvested earth. There is a sudden stillness to the wind and the half-moon shines down on the four men. The two sentries step back out of the light and against the bushes and wait. The grave is illuminated and Dinny looks over at it and emits a stream of muffled, whimpering noises. Jesus, Mary and Joseph, James says to himself. The sweat is pouring down his face; his heart is racing. Fuck. Fuck. Fuck. Dinny look at me. LOOK AT ME! James takes Dinny's jawbone between his fingers and pulls his face away from the grave to look at him. We will say a prayer now, Dinny. James kneels down beside Dinny and feels the damp earth suck on his trousers. He tears off the scarf and Dinny immediately begins to slobber and cry. The two sentries look at each other and stare back at James. Clearly this is a foreign idea to them. Prayers are not part of the procedure at Corry's farm. James notices their incredulous, sarcastic faces and for just a moment, in the nano-second of time that lies between the scarf ripped off and Dinny beginning his protestations, in that second, the clouds shut out the light of the moon. The wind gusts and blows out the lantern and all is utter and complete darkness. James shudders and looks about him, straining to see. All that is visible is an eerie glow off the faces of the two sentries who stand like two impatient demons, sniggering, while James's heart beats and pounds and almost breaks through his chest.

The moment passes and James quickly begins to pray. Our Father who art in— But Dinny, quiet for a moment, begins to scream even louder if that is possible. Séamus, Séamus, you can't do this. I don't want to go in that hole. I don't want to go in that hole. I didn't know they would kill the mayor. It's not my fault. I didn't know they would kill him. I will work for you, Séamus. I will do whatever you say. But James has given up praying and stands, puts his hand through his coat and retrieves his revolver. He takes it out and points it at Dinny.

Abruptly James realises everything has slowed down to incremental frames of movement. The wind is still, the moon beams down directly onto the grave. The light is reproachful, blazing violently onto the appalling scene. The boy slumped, kneeling in the dirt, hands tied behind his back, screams for mercy. James can see him, but he does not hear the sound. The two sentries on either side of the grave stand waiting. A shudder moves up and then back down James's spine like a man playing a keyboard. The light is so intense it seems to emanate an ethereal, unearthly sound as it glints and sparkles, refracting off the sides of his oily revolver. James feels like the earth has stilled, and all in heaven have gathered together sending forth this outrageous luminosity, stilling the wind, playing the unearthly music. He knows in the depths of his soul that this is an attempt to stay his hand. But James also knows it is a futile attempt.

It is futile because there is something else that James knows. Something he has absorbed into his very bones and that has permeated his psyche. This knowledge now competes with the Fifth Commandment. It is the knowledge that someone, somewhere, must do something to stop the cruel foreign masters of his homeland and send them packing. James feels the weight of this dilemma crushing him until he steels his heart, casts it off and points the gun, holding it steady with two hands. He has made his decision and though he does not wish to, he knows he must, and he fires.

He watches the bullet explode from the barrel in slow motion and quietly he whispers, forgive me. He sees it speed through the night and disappear into Dinny's mound of soft curls as his forehead touches the ground and his tears mix into the earth.

And suddenly the moment is passed. The wind is blowing a gale force. The shrubs are swaying violently. The light of the moon has been eliminated by heavy cloud. The lantern is successfully relit by the sentry and sways back and forth. The other sentry moves forward to take Dinny's body which is immobilised and deafeningly quiet. But James screams out at him. Don't touch him. Go back where you came from. James is still holding the revolver and both young men raise their hands in the air and back off. Put the lantern down. Go back. I will do this myself. They look at each other, shrug their shoulders, and head back to the farmhouse, making their way by following the hedge.

James picks up Dinny by the underarms and drags him the few feet to the grave, lines him up straight against the edge and rolls him over into the abyss. There is a sickening thud as the body hits the earth below. James picks up the shovel and begins the work of filling in the grave. He looks down and sees that Dinny has landed face up. His eyes are open, staring at James with a calmness the boy did not possess in life. A curl relaxes on his forehead. His lips are formed in the slightest of smirks. He is teasing James with a cocky, all-knowing stare. James shudders and throws a full shovel of dirt on the boy's head, but it falls away and the stare continues. James throws down another and another and yet the boy's face will not disappear. The sweat breaks out on James once more. He begins to say his rosary as he tosses the earth back into the grave in wild, frenzied motions. By the time he is finished there is a full-on storm raging against him. The wind howls, the rain lashes at him horizontally and manages to sting his hands and even his face despite his hat. At the last shovel of earth patted down over the mound, the light of the lantern is blown out and Dinny has finally, mercifully, disappeared forever. James throws the shovel into the hedge and walks back through inky blackness in the direction of the barn. He deliberately chooses the stall that Dinny had been in and lies down on the little mound of straw and begins to cry. He takes his rosary out of his pocket, holds it tightly in his hand and curls up, falling asleep instantly.

In a few short hours when the weak beams of sunlight make their way through the old slats of the barn wall, James rises and walks out to the road. He does not enter the farmhouse, and no one comes out to greet him. He waits patiently for the sound of Jeremiah's car. Take me straight to O'Hegarty, he tells Jeremiah and stares out of the window all the way back to Cork.

O'Hegarty notes both James's dishevelled look and his judgemental tone. James is looking at him like he has never seen him before. O'Hegarty thinks carefully before he speaks. You've had a rough night, Jimmy. I spoke to Corry. You don't know the half of it. James is treading on thin ice with this tone, but at this moment he does not care. O'Hegarty stares him down. War is ugly, Jimmy. If it wasn't him, it could've been you next week. You know that. Aye, right now I wish it was. He was only fifteen years old! Could we not have just sent him packing? But O'Hegarty is up for the challenge. Really Jimmy? And how many of our men, their families, their homes, is that fifteen-year-old spy worth? How many should be sacrificed for him so that he can go back to his masters and tell them of everyone he has come across. Do you really believe he didn't know what was going to happen to the men who he informed on? James reluctantly agrees. O'Hegarty continues. For what it's worth, it wasn't supposed to be your job. And I am not sure why Corry has taken such a liking to you, but you may be seeing him again soon, so best to watch your Ps and Qs. We will need to deal with the names of the YMCA men he passed on. James looks down. He feels ill. If that is how we treat fifteen-year-olds, God help the men we get our hands on, he thinks to himself. At least they are grown men, James mutters, not wholly defeated by O'Hegarty's arguments. Go home, get yourself a bath, and a home-cooked meal. Tonight, I want you to join Florrie and Murphy and make a little visit to a house after curfew.

Florrie stands outside the church that Josephine passes every evening on her way home from work. He lights a cigarette and occasionally takes a drag on it, maintaining a straight face, even though he finds it disgusting. It is a good foil for standing about the street. When she sees him smoking, she knows it is her cue to enter the church. The place is empty, and Florrie hurriedly runs over the list of names that O'Hegarty has passed on. Have you seen these names across any of the British correspondence? Josephine looks at Florrie. Yes. In fact, I have been wondering about this name here, Blemens... If it is the same man, he is my next-door neighbour. His name has been mentioned a couple of times in relation to the YMCA. If I remember correctly one of the corporals has correspondence with them. I assumed they were just all on the same side. But there doesn't seem to be anything directly implicating him or the YMCA. Otherwise I would have mentioned it to you. Still, it is suspicious that their names have passed the desk.

At about eight o'clock in the evening three men dressed in dark clothes with black caps on their heads make their way through the alleyways of Cork to the street Josephine lives on. They move around to the back of the little courtyard and each man takes a position where he can sit unnoticed in the dark, behind shrubs or the fence. They wait patiently. Eventually, at about half-past eight, two guests come to the front of the house, make their way quietly down the side to the back entrance and are let in by a teenager. More men follow until there is a group of ten or twelve. Mick Murphy moves to the small kitchen window and risks a peek, but just as he is about to signal to the other two, a lorry can be heard barrelling down the street. It is after curfew and the roads are devoid of traffic so the men can easily recognise the tell-tale sounds of an army truck. A uniformed Black and Tan jumps out and the truck continues its way down the road. He too makes his way to the back of the house, just as Murphy regains his hiding spot. He knocks lightly on the door and gains admittance.

Later, back at the sisters' shop over a late-night cup of tea, Florrie pushes back on O'Hegarty and Murphy's suggestion. We can't shoot them; we don't have proof they are spies! There were almost a dozen men at that meeting. Your list only has four names and two of them are father and son. For God's sake you are talking about an outright massacre! James says nothing. He is thinking of Dinny. It is obvious they are all in cahoots with the Tans, Florrie, says O'Hegarty. Open your eyes. Do you think our people are disappearing into their gaols left right and centre by magic? Of course they are spies. They are giving away every IRA man they can find. Florrie looks at James, who neither agrees nor disagrees. James is thinking O'Hegarty is right if you just think logistically, but who is shooting all these people? Who is the killer amongst them that can do this terrible deed and walk away unscathed? Florrie continues his argument. Look, I agree the four on the list must be dealt with. Their activities have all been corroborated. But the rest will have to wait until we have proper evidence. They could have been meeting about taking the boys on a camping trip for all we know! How do we know they were meeting about us? If we do this, we are no better than the Tans themselves!

Murphy and O'Hegarty grunt. They would both be quite happy to dispose of all of the potential threats at once. But O'Hegarty chooses to give Florrie some leeway. He is after all head of intelligence for the entire brigade. Okay, says Murphy. I will assign some men to pick up these four names. We will take them out to the farm and see what other information we can get out of them. We will leave the others for the time being, but we will keep a close watch. Agreed, says Florrie, without the least bit of satisfaction. Florrie and James leave the meeting together. Have you been to the farm? James wonders if he is the only high-level member of the group who has been excluded. No, I haven't, and I don't want to. I know Martin Corry! Florrie heads home with a nod in James's direction. He does not wish to hear James's story and James does not wish to tell it. Besides, Florrie has other things on his mind.

Florrie is anxious to make Josephine happy and retrieve her child from Wales. O'Hegarty has indicated that he is impressed with the information she is providing (and so he should be, thinks Florrie). It is time for us to keep our end of the bargain. O'Hegarty hears back from Collins, who provides a contact name in London. Florrie will make his move. O'Hegarty tells Florrie to choose a driver who he can trust and make his way to London. He will be picked up at the train station and looked after. Contacts will be made. A car will be supplied. But he will be on his own as far as the operation goes. Florrie leaves Cork with a smile on his face.

On Sunday morning, November 21, as Florrie is sailing across the Irish Sea, Michael Collins has much bigger fish to fry in Dublin. Dublin, like Cork, has been assailed by Black and Tans, and another division of British military, the Auxiliaries, as well as the leftovers of the RIC, all of whom work together to hunt down the local IRA men. Dublin Castle, the seat of British power in Ireland, has its dungeons full, and every night, just like in Cork, IRA men do not sleep at home for fear their homes will be raided and they will be dragged off to prison, beaten, tortured, or summarily executed. There have been outright murders of Irish citizens in the streets and IRA men have been hunted down, their families abused, their homes set on fire, their belongings smashed to pieces. Just as in Cork, the military are getting their information from somewhere, and Michael Collins has expended a lot of time, energy, and men, in finding out just who the culprits are.

He has compiled his own list of most wanted. There are thirty-five men in total. Some of them British citizens living in Dublin, some of them British military intelligence officers, some MI5, and some, unfortunately, Irish informers. The most hated crew they call the Cairo Gang, after their secret meetings in the Cairo Café in downtown Dublin, are regularly watched and listened to by the waitresses and bartenders, who proudly report to Collins. In fact, his original list held fifty names, but Cathal Brugha, ever the thoughtful, just man, refused to sanction fifteen of the names, citing a lack of evidence. Collins spends weeks on the details, using his own intelligence officers to collect the intimate details of the lives of the men on his list. He is prudent, careful, and determined to make a statement. For this reason, even the most trusted IRA men are given their mission only the night before. Early on Sunday morning each man follows his very specific orders, heading to the homes or hotels or rooms of their target, opening the door, firing, and fleeing. By noon, fourteen men are dead: four military intelligence officers, four MI5, one known informer and the rest, British citizens. Collins is disappointed so many of the assassinations did not happen due to faulty information or outright bungling. In the process, one IRA captain is caught but escapes from his holding cell within hours. The military secret service is sent into a tailspin. Suddenly they are on the wrong side of the fence, feeling terror, anticipation of some unknown assailant striking them down. Someone who has been watching them while they were watching the IRA. They fly from the country in droves, shocked into action by the fear that they may be next on Collins hit list. Collins' reputation as a feared arch-rival to the British is cemented in stone.

Unlike the special agents sent from England, the regular military has a different reaction. The Black and Tans in particular do not fly. They think of revenge. One of the latest pieces of intelligence they have received is about a few IRA men who will be attending a semi-final football match at Croke Park Stadium. It is the biggest park in the city. As the game gets underway in the packed stadium, a long line of army lorries encircles the stadium. When the IRA lookouts, who are acting as ticket sellers, see the trucks coming they become alarmed. When soldiers jump down from their trucks with guns in hand, they make a run for it inside the main gates to warn the IRA men watching the game and indeed the crowd. But they are too late. In come the military with their machine guns flying. Panic ensues. The five thousand spectators run for their lives. Some try to scale the stadium wall and jump over. Outside on the road, as the people try to run home or for cover, fifty rounds of machine gun fire are unloaded above the heads of innocent men, women, and children. The dead include a young bride-to-be, two young boys, a well-known football player and ten others. There are seventy wounded spectators. No IRA men are found.

This same evening, with promises of a generous payout, an

informer has given the names of two of Collins's high-level men to Dublin Castle. What the informer does not know is that Collins has a mole, in a British uniform, inside the castle. He will quickly know who turned over his friends and what becomes of them. The informer will not live to see the spring. But he lives substantially longer than the two men he informed on. Those two are arrested immediately and with a friend who has already been wasting away in the dark, filthy cells, they are tortured, beaten, and shot to death. By nightfall the entire city of Dublin is grieving.

On Monday afternoon James sits with Seán in the Wallace sisters' back room. Originally, they were to meet for a pint before Seán begins the long journey back to Canada. But they sit in the newspaper and tobacco shop smoking and reading every paper available. They are reading about what has just been dubbed 'Bloody Sunday'. Ireland has become international news once again. O'Hegarty has already told them about the murders in Dublin Castle, which are not yet public information. He has also told them that Collins is beside himself with rage and grief. Prepare yourselves. We will be busy over the next while. He wants pressure put on every square inch of the country. O'Hegarty has jumped the gun and assumed that Seán will stay and fight, and indeed he is right. Between his two older sisters who are still grieving hard over Terry, and now this Black and Tan massacre, Seán knows in his heart he cannot leave. He longs for the cold, snowy, Canadian winter, and the warmth of his wife-to-be. But instead of buying his ticket back home, he buys a stamp and sends her a letter. Maybe in a few months he tells her. Maybe.

James does not tell Seán the story of Dinny, though Seán would be the only person he might tell. Seán has his own bag of troubles. He does, however, tell him about the list and about watching the secret meeting. He is anxious to get hold of the list of names that Dinny divulged. With the assassination of the military secret service agents and the reaction of the Black and Tans, the men know that the British will pull out all the stops. They may not have much time. They walk across town to meet with Murphy and the other ASU members. It is a cold, sunny afternoon but even the bright sun cannot relieve the gloom of recent events. James considers telling Seán of his recurring dream. It is Thomas Ashe calling to him yet again, Séamus, Séamus, he calls. He is tied into the hospital chair, trying to escape the bonds, flailing with whatever part of his body is not tightly bound. But no matter how fast James runs he cannot get to him. It is as if Ashe's chair recedes into the fog, carrying him with it at the same rate that James can run. The last image he sees is Ashe's face, blue and frantic, gurgling slop, tears dropping languidly on his cheek. James had awoken in a sweat and stared into his sister's grate at the dying glimmer of warmth, wondering what it could possibly mean.

He decides against telling Seán anything. Seán's look has not changed since he saw him at the train station, smoking, leaned back against the wall. He has yet to see Seán smile since the funeral. The pair of them are as morose as two young men can possibly be. Even O'Hegarty has noticed the change in each, though he believes they will come around. Just as he himself did many years ago. He knows that Seán still grieves for his brother, and James recalls the shock and anguish of having to take a man's life. Even in self-defence it is an event that alters your world view, your state of mind. It is profoundly disturbing, and O'Hegarty has learned that each man carries the weight of such actions differently.

While a man stands guard at the front and back of Murphy's house, the meeting inside begins. Murphy lays out the plan. There are two single men on their list and one father and son team. James is given his assignment. He is to watch and learn the habits of a particular man and decide on a good time and place for abduction. He requests that Seán work with him, but Murphy will have none of it. You are too public a figure right now, Seán. Your gob has been on the front page of every paper in the country. We can't risk you being recognised and compromising our plans. Go and see O'Hegarty. He has plenty other work to be done that is not outside tailing people. James shrugs at Seán. It was worth a try.

Over the next two days James finds himself watching an ex-British soldier, Downing, the first name on the list. He happens to be president of an ex-serviceman's club. His full-time job is at Victoria Barracks manning a telegraph station. James is working with Seán Culhane, among others on his team, and they decide to lift the man the following evening on his way to a meeting. James and Culhane agree that they will need to be armed, guns at the ready. He won't be an easy target. As the man walks down the street, James walks up towards him. His cap is pulled down, the collar of his trenchcoat is up, and he is holding his revolver deep in his pocket. As the two cross paths, Jeremiah pulls alongside in a van. Culhane jumps out, gun in hand, and James takes his out of his pocket. The scene is screened from the rest of the street by the van. The back door is kicked open from inside and Downing, with two revolvers pointed at his head, has no option but to clamber inside. James scans up and down the street to ensure there have been no witnesses, puts his gun back in his pocket and keeps walking. The van drives straight out to the farm.

Two days later James and Seán meet again to share a smoke and read the papers in the Wallaces' back room. Before they have even seated themselves, Sheila, the eldest sister of the two, hands James *The Cork Examiner* already open to a specific page. It looks like somebody has got under the skin of the Tans. The notice reads: 'If Mr Downing is not returned to his home within fifty-six hours Cork citizens prepare, especially Sinn Féiners.' It is signed BLACK AND TANS. Seán looks at James. Some poor people are going to pay for this, Jimmy. It's like O'Hegarty says, Seán, we can't go back. We've got to drive them out. And you know as well as I do, we are all hurting right now.

Sunday morning after Mass, Culhane tells the story. Corry got it out of him alright. At first, he wouldn't give, so we put him in Corry's prison for a couple of days. James stops him. Prison? What prison? Culhane is only too happy to explain. They call it Sing-Sing. It's a cave in the Knockraha graveyard, not too far from his place. Once inside there is no escape, you are surrounded by solid rock. It was news to me, but his battalion have been using if for a while now. Trust Corry! Nobody will ever find that place. Anyway, our man knew we meant business after being held in there. He talked pretty quickly. There is a list of men they have been watching. Murphy is on it and so are you James, as well as a few of the Volunteers who live in this area. He was tried and found guilty of spying. We don't need to worry about him anymore. A familiar shiver runs up and down James's spine.

The next names on Dinny's list are the father and son team: James and Frederick Blemens. It is the same house that held the meeting after curfew. O'Hegarty pulls James aside. You saw them. You know the house. Make sure you keep it quiet. We don't want any attention brought to our friend next door. O'Hegarty has told

James they have a secret asset in Victoria Barracks, but he has not indicated who it might be. It will not take James long to discern who it is, and that Florrie is in love with the girl. For now, he understands that O'Hegarty is concerned the entire neighbourhood stay quiet in order to protect even the least shadow of doubt being cast on her. With Murphy, James and his team plan the takedown of the two men.

They will pick up the father and son separately; it is easier to put down one man than two. They know the son's route home from work and on Monday afternoon James can again be found walking up the road, cap pulled down, trenchcoat buttoned and tied against the cold wind. His hands are in his pockets. As he passes the son who is not much older than James himself, the van pulls up, an armed man jumps out and James pulls out his revolver. The son is scooped into the back of the van. But not before a shopkeeper steps out of a doorway, stops dead in his tracks, then turns and goes back in. James is not worried; his back was to the man. He goes back in the direction he came as the van speeds away.

Two hours later James and his mate Peter are inside Josephine's backyard. She is not home so he is not worried about being seen. When they see the light go on in the kitchen, they hop the fence and calmly walk through the back door of the Blemens' house with guns in hand. The father stops and stares. He does not make a move to escape. He knows that he has been found out by the IRA. He knew it was coming after Downing's disappearance. Bring the whiskey lad, will ye, he says to James and points to the cabinet. Without lowering his gun, James opens the cupboard door, takes the bottle of Jameson, and puts it in his pocket. The man is a well-respected teacher, an expert on bee-keeping and horticulture, well-known throughout the county. James can see immediately that he has a quiet, reserved way about him. We will leave through the front door. Put on your coat first. The older Blemens is compliant, but he has a worried look on his face. You can't fool me, thinks James, I know about your list. You probably know my face and name. Maybe even my family. But he says nothing. The three men get into the waiting car that Jeremiah has in front of the house. A moment later another of the ASU, who had been acting lookout, jumps in. It is dusk and Jeremiah moves quickly to get to the main road. They must be at the farm before curfew lest their car be stopped.

Blemens looks at James. How about a swig of that now, son? James passes the bottle, allows him a gulp, and replaces it in his coat pocket. They stop at the farm and Jeremiah, who now knows the routine quite well, bypasses the house and drives straight to the lane that leads to the barn. Blemens follows James across the muddy tracks; he knows a gun is pointed in his back by the man behind him. They walk past the sentries and into the barn. He is shocked to see his son in the horse's stall. James quietly takes the bottle of whiskey out of his pocket and hands it to him as he closes the stall door. He makes his way to the house and goes in through the kitchen. Corry looks up from the table and glares at him. Séamus, lovely to see you again. Corry spits out the sarcasm. I hear you have a couple of guests this time. I suppose you have left them together in the barn. Aye, says Séamus, his back up already, his mind flooded with images of Dinny. Well that just won't do Séamus. I am tired tonight. I will leave it till the morning. You can accompany them to the holding cell. One of the boys will take you on the cart. He nods at one of the Volunteers at the table, who immediately stands up and walks out of the door. Follow me. James leaves the house without so much as a glance at Corry.

The Volunteer takes a few minutes to hitch a huge black mare to an open-aired farm cart and waits for James to bring the prisoners to him. He does not want to get stuck in the muck. Back to the barn go James and Peter and collect the father and son. He puts the bottle of whiskey back in his pocket, takes some rope and ties their hands behind their backs. He takes a lantern from the sentry and with his partner they jump onto the back of the cart, dangling their legs with the prisoners tied up behind them. It is a long, quiet ride. The father begins to talk, but the son tells him to shut up. Clearly, a happy family they do not make. James wants to ask the driver why they are out in the dark after curfew when the barn would have been fine, but he does not.

After several turns into very narrow country roads, the cart eventually stops. James swings his lantern to look around and sees that they are at a graveyard. Follow me, says the Volunteer, and James and Peter walk the prisoners to the centre of the yard, where there is a rounded mound of grass. They are taken around the mound and James is surprised to see a set of ancient stone steps cut down into the ground ending at a thick wooden door attached with iron hinges. There are a few holes randomly drilled into the wood. The Volunteer takes a large brass key out of his pocket and opens the door. James holds up the lantern and can see the shocked faces of the father and son. It is only for the night. You will be questioned tomorrow. Don't worry, says James, though he realises his own voice hardly instils confidence. Once through the door they find themselves in a rock cavern, without windows or seating, just a bucket in the corner. It is sixteen feet long, eight feet wide, and barely six feet tall at the highest point of the ceiling down the centre of the room. James must hunch his shoulders and keep his head down. He holds the lantern high and looks around. He cannot help but shudder. For God's sake, you cannot leave us here! The father moans and James tries to still his nerves. I will be back in the morning, he says, and takes the bottle of whiskey out of his pocket, opens it, gulps down a mouthful, before handing it to the old man.

What if they escape in the night? James asks the cart driver outside. They won't. They could holler for hours, and no one would hear them. Even if they did manage to break down the door, they would probably just get lost in one of the bogs in the area and even we would never find them!

This time James and Peter are offered a warmer spot to sleep in the kitchen of the house by one of Corry's men. The Volunteer takes a couple of padded sleeping rolls out of a cupboard and lays them close to the fire, which is only embers by the time they return. On Tuesday, James hitches a ride back to the city. He tries not to think of the old man and his son in the cold cavern all night. He himself has had some rough nights out and about, rarely in a bed. In fact, he is accustomed to a hard floor for a mattress and a sweater rolled under his head for a pillow. No, it is not the harsh conditions of the little prison that James is worried about. It is Corry and what he will be up to with them. But he fingers his beads in his pocket and remembers his name, Murphy's name, and who knows how many of his friends are on the list that Dinny revealed.

James meets with O'Hegarty and Seán. He is surprised to discover that it is simply a check-in. O'Hegarty grills them on their activities. Then he realises that with Florrie off in England, O'Hegarty is not getting his daily fix of intelligence from around the city and the county. James recognises one of his old techniques. He gets the story from everybody, better to have a clear picture of events and learn a little of how the personalities that make up his crews are getting along. Today, after he is done asking questions, he gives the men a grim statistic. Over four hundred last week. In the city alone. Four hundred arrests. So many the Tans cannot find room for them. They are starting to process them in mere hours and send them out to gaols across the country. Some are even being sent up north. It has to stop and stop soon. Go back up to the farm Jimmy. I want to know every name on that list and every contact that group has.

When James returns to the farm late Wednesday afternoon the interrogation is over. He asks Peter what happened. Well, it was rough watching I can tell you. Corry brought in the son first. He was all decked out in his uniform and told him he was on trial. But the son is a surly bastard. He told them everything he knew, the list of names, nothing we hadn't heard before, and more names of the group that meets. Then he says, maybe the old man has something more for ye. Who needs a son like that? James is listening intently. So, anything from the old man? Well, the old man was so drunk he could barely stand. Corry was pissing mad about that. Good thing you weren't here. But he didn't tell us anything we didn't already know. That must be it for the anti-Sinn Féin society. If Corry has his way, there won't be any of them long for this world. Aye, quips James, and he turns and makes his way to the house.

Just as a matter of course, Séamus, do not in future supply any of my prisoners with whiskey. If I want them drunk, I have plenty of poteen to pour down their throats! James holds his eye contact and lets out a respectful, Aye, sir. You can help out tonight with the sentence. With the two of them we will need an extra hand.

After midnight Corry enters the kitchen. He steps over to the hook, puts on his IRA uniform and slips on his Wellingtons. James and Peter scramble up from the floor by the fire. Then he motions to them to accompany him. Outside on the laneway the horse and cart are waiting. Corry jumps up beside the driver, and James sits in the back dangling his feet. The moon is out, a half-disc once again, though a receding moon instead of a new one. James lights a cigarette and watches. He is waiting for the light to change. He is waiting for the eerie sound and time slowing down. But it does not happen. Once they get to the graveyard Corry jumps down, takes the lantern in one hand and his gun in the other. He walks to the door and motions to the driver to unlock it.

Father and son are on their feet at the first rattle of the key. Their hands are tied behind their backs. When they see Corry and the gun in his hand the father slumps back against the wall. You fucking Sinn-Féiners, you are just a pack of murdering thugs. You have no right to put anybody on trial, least of all me and my Da. We are law-abiding citizens. But nothing more comes out of his mouth because Corry hits him in the face with the butt of his revolver. Instantly blood pours down from his nose. Corry grabs his arm and shoves him towards James, who takes him and walks him up the stairs. Corry does the same with the old man, who says nothing. The driver holds the lantern and leads the small group through the graveyard to a lane. The lane soon turns into a path, but still they walk forward. James feels like it is taking forever to get to wherever they are going, until he realises that they are going absolutely nowhere. Right in the middle of nowhere and right at the edge of the bog.

Corry stops walking and begins. You have been found guilty of spying for the enemy and have been sentenced. You will now pay the ultimate price for your treachery against your neighbours and against the Irish Republic. Both father and son stare out at the men in disbelief. You murdering bastard, shouts the son, but it is no sooner out of his mouth than Corry pulls the trigger and he falls back into the muddy water. Corry turns to James. Your turn. James lifts his revolver and shoots the father straight in the heart. He slumps down to his knees, still looking at James in disbelief. Corry kicks his body over and it lands on top of his son's, pushing him further beneath the surface. Then he asks for the lantern and looks about the path for something. It takes a moment before he finds what he is looking for. James and Peter stand, watching the father and son become saturated with black water. The son is now submerged, but the father is hovering just at the water line. Corry picks up a large rock; his massive shoulders make it seem like light work. He takes a few steps forward and drops the rock on Mr Blemens's chest. James can hear the sickening gurgle of air bubbles as the pair sink deep into the bog pool.

He looks up at the moon but there is no one watching, no sounds, no slow motion. He puts his revolver back in his holster. He feels cold, numb. Resentment gurgles in his chest like the air released from the dead men's bodies. That is five now, he thinks to himself, and turns to make his way back to the cart.

BURN

CHAPTER 9

DECEMBER 1920 – JANUARY 1921

The year is 1166. It is exactly one hundred years since the Norman conquest of England. The old Anglo-Saxon families have successfully married into the families of their Norman conquerors. They spend the days of their lives consolidating their power, making allegiances, and marrying off their daughters into suitable political unions. In Ireland, where Viking raids have resulted in Norse settlements in Dublin and Waterford, the various kings of the Celts continue throughout the rest of the island to steal each other's cattle, attempt to take over more territory than is their right, and generally spend their lives solidifying their power.

In Leinster, the most eastern province of Ireland, King Diarmuid mac Murchadha has got himself into a bit of a bind. He is an ageing man now, sixty years old with one surviving child, a lovely, devoted daughter, Aiofe. Her hair is golden, her face is fair, and she is by all accounts quite a prize. All manner of princes from the surrounding provinces vie for her hand, but Diarmuid will have none of it. As for himself, he is lonely and alone. The true love of his life lives in the next kingdom, married off to his arch-rival Tiernan O'Rourke, a brute even among Celts. She is over forty now but still a beauty. She also is lonely and alone because Tiernan is constantly off fighting useless skirmishes. Diarmuid pays her a visit, and she decides she might as well spend her final years with the love of her life; after all, Tiernan probably won't even notice she is gone. Under Irish law, the Brehon Laws worked out centuries before and agreed to by all the Kings of Ireland, a woman has her due. Her dowry stays with her; it does not become property of her husband, and she does have the right to divorce. So, Lady Dervorgilla gathers up her cattle and her geese, her robes, her furs, and her gold and silver jewellery defined with the fine lines of Celtic artistry. She packs up all the furnishings of her home, her bedding, even her bed. She gathers up her servants and together they escort Diarmuid back to Leinster.

Their happiness is short-lived. Tiernan comes home earlier than expected. It seems he had a change of heart on his last expedition to pillage and terrorise, and instead stopped at Lough Derg, St Patrick's Purgatory, to perform his penance and ask for the saint's succour. He works his way up the rock-strewn mountain in his bare feet, as is the custom, and at the top he prays fervently, asking good St Patrick to help him become a better man. Imagine his outrage when he returns home to find his wife disappeared and her houses abandoned and empty. He is quickly told the story of Diarmuid's visit and Dervorgilla's long walk back to the home of her birth. Tiernan does not take the opportunity to become a better man. Like every woman before and since, Dervorgilla soon learns that her husband's outrage and her lover's protection have little to do with her and much more to do with male dominance, power, and control.

Tiernan is angry beyond words, but alas, he fears Diarmuid, who is a reckless, terrifying fighter. Though he is ageing, his body is like a thick impregnable wall of rock. His hair has remained flaming red as is his long, braided beard. He is a warrior for sure, quick to anger and determined to punish. In his time, he has killed many who would challenge him, and more frightening still, he has let many of his foes live but left them blinded. Diarmuid knows the Brehon Laws inside out and he knows that a king must be without the least blemish, as he himself is. By blinding his enemies, he assures they are relegated to the lowly, their names never to be recounted in the bards' verses, the shame of disfigurement their only entitlement. It is a shocking, barbaric tactic no other Celtic king has ever used.

Instead of galloping straight to Diarmuid to fight it out, Tiernan gallops straight to the high king, Rory O'Connor. Rory is the high king for a reason. He has earned it. Physically perfect and imposing, Rory is also smart. He also has no wish to be blinded. So, he holds a council of all the kings and has Diarmuid banished from Ireland by decree. In this way no one has to fight, but they dispose of this old man whom they all fear. Diarmuid is done with fighting but knowing that the love of his life will be taken back by Tiernan and knowing that his only daughter Aiofe will be married off to one of his nasty sons, Diarmuid is compelled to take on the whole bloody lot of them even should he die doing it.

He knows the Norsemen of Dublin and Waterford do not have the numbers of men that he requires to make a stand. He also knows they are no longer interested in taking on the Celts, many of whom have slowly married into their families. They prefer to maintain the peace in their new homeland, lest they be driven out. So, Diarmuid makes his way over to England and asks King Henry II if he will loan him an army.

Henry is not really interested in Ireland. He has his own mix of politics and intrigue that he must keep under control, and he is very busy making sure the new elite of the country maintain their allegiance to him. It is a hard job keeping everybody happy and powerful, but not too powerful. Henry has far too many distractions to get mixed up with the Celts and their wars. But to humour him, Henry gives Diarmuid permission to ask the noblemen if any would like to take him up on his offer. They can all summon armies from their constituent populations on their estates and in the surrounding towns that they govern. After all, there will be booty and some of those Celtic princesses are a little on the exotic side, with their red locks and fiery tempers. Also, Henry would be happy to have any number of noblemen distracted from pondering possible challenges to his own crown. But alas, there are no noblemen interested in Ireland. Ireland is a difficult country. The Celts have a reputation for being tough and unpredictable.

But all is not lost for Diarmuid. He comes across a nobleman residing in Wales who is down on his luck. He has lost favour with Henry and is worried about losing his title, his land, and his money. His name is Richard de Clare, 1st Earl of Pembroke, but he is known as Strongbow. He has fiddled with the technology of the cutting-edge weapon of the day, the bow and arrow, and has discovered that a bow not much shorter than himself, though unruly to carry, is deadly at long distances. A little roust in Ireland is just what the thirty-eight-year-old earl needs. Henry has refused his blessing for marriage and so Strongbow, even at his age, has not been able to marry. He would like a wife; he would like some property independent of the king and he would like his reputation to be revived. So, Strongbow makes a deal with Diarmuid. I will fight if you give me your legendary daughter as my wife and some property to call my own. Diarmuid agrees, and he heads back to Ireland with boatloads of Welsh archers, a preliminary venture to gauge the ferocity of the fight. They are led not by Strongbow, who is preparing the second wave, but by Raymond Fitzgerald, a fierce warrior, master archer and dependable friend of the earl.

The Norsemen and the intermarried Celts of Dublin, Waterford, and Wexford are shocked by the attack and ill prepared. Fitzgerald takes all three towns. And when Strongbow finally arrives two years later, the Celts are beside themselves. When he easily overtakes their raiding parties from a distance using his superior six-foot-long bows, the Celts turn and go back where they came from. Diarmuid is triumphant and hands over his daughter. When he dies a couple of years later, Strongbow inherits the entire kingdom of Leinster. Aiofe is not unhappy about this turn of events. She gets to stay in her home. Strongbow is a catch as far as she is concerned, a long lanky blonde, old enough to have learned some lessons in life but not so old he is unattractive. Indeed, Strongbow having learned the lesson of humility in his youth, maintains a humble, respectful manner even in victory. However, he knows that victory can be short-lived and so the first order of the day is to graciously appeal to his king.

Strongbow impresses Henry by gifting him all of the lands he has conquered. Henry decides Ireland may not be such a bad investment now that someone else has done all the work of slaying, and absorbed the expense of maintaining an army. So, Henry makes Strongbow Lord of Ireland, gives him back some of the land that he so generously offered, and Henry and Strongbow become the best of friends. Strongbow cannot be happier. He got the girl, he got the prize, and now he has the king. It is time to build a castle. The English are in Ireland to stay.

Two hundred years later, in 1324, Strongbow's castle in the now thriving town of Kilkenny has been rebuilt from wood to stone. It marks an important crossroads and centre of trade. There are frequent visitors and passers-by. Normans come to Ireland in droves. There is land aplenty for Henry's heirs to hand out to their friends, patriots, and kissers of the English arse. The Celts stick to the countryside and the English have free rein of the towns and surrounding lands.

Just outside the castle wall there lives a wealthy Norman lady, Dame Kyteler. She has amassed for herself quite a fortune. She has done it by turning her house into an inn for the many travellers, and also by working her way through four husbands. Just before her last husband died, he adjusted his will to make sure that his wife inherited the entirety of his worth. His grown children are furious at this notorious stepmother who will have inherited at least some of the money and property of her three previous husbands. Now they have been left with nothing, a most unusual set of circumstances, especially for the oldest son. They set out to destroy her. They accuse her of poisoning their father. But surely only a witch would poison someone as lovely as their da. Dame Kyteler and her friends and servants are accused of participating in a witches' coven. Apparently, the dame is in league with a demon called Art who meets her at night and instructs her in spells and curses. Her servants collect the ghoulish bits and pieces she needs, bloody innards and eyes of lowly creatures, secret plants for hidden purposes to burn and stew and smoke. The bishop is called, investigations are undertaken. A relative, a well-placed politician, cries foul. You fools! You are all jealous of her wealth. She is no more a witch than I am. But this only incenses the bishop, who does not care for interfering politicians under his domain. He proceeds with a verdict. Guilty!

But Dame Kyteler is nobody's fool. Before the verdict is even announced she has been spirited away, her pockets and bags full of coins, either by a relative or Art the demon. Nobody ever knows for sure because she is never seen again, although it is rumoured she is happily enjoying her wealth in England. Her servant, however, is not so lucky. Petronella, her maid and supposed collector of the ghoulish bits, will take her place at the stake. Petronella earns the dubious title of becoming the first witch in Europe to be burned at the stake.

The bishop ensures that a massive pyre is built, and a spectacle is prepared for the people. Don't mess with me, is the message from the bishop. It is a message that is quickly understood and absorbed. The Celts, who gallop up on their horses to watch from afar, also hear the message. These Normans are barbarians, they say to themselves. We haven't burned anybody since the days of the druids, since before Patrick, eight hundred years ago. The Normans are really backward thinkers. They lock themselves up in giant stone walls in tiny settlements and then burn each other alive. Stay clear of them! And the Celts go back to their territories with the latest story of Norman nastiness to share with their clans. The bishop, meanwhile, takes note of the effect the harrowing screams and stench of burnt flesh has on the onlookers. Why, this is quite effective, he thinks to himself. When he returns to England, he shares these thoughts with the crown and the church hierarchy. It is a story that is remembered well. Over the next several hundred years, generations of Englishmen will grow up with the traumatic childhood memory of the spectacle of some poor unfortunate, more often than not a victim of jealousy, rage, or political rivalry, accused of witchcraft and their bodies burned to ashes in the town square.

In Ireland burning at the stake will never happen again. Burning of homes and businesses, farms and crops, however, becomes an English pastime perpetrated on the Irish in every subsequent generation. It is a tactic the Irish know only too well.

The men of the YMCA, the loyalists, and the Black and Tans refuse to be intimidated by abductions and ambushes. Downing may have disappeared, the Blemens may have disappeared, but their attitude is simply, Fuck you. We will not be unsettled or overwhelmed by you lot of Pope-loving, lower-class upstarts. We will put you in your place, so don't say we didn't warn you. They revert to the tried-and-true methods of their forefathers.

James is not in the least surprised when the Anti-Sinn Féin League claims responsibility for burning down several homes and small businesses of Catholics in reprisal for the abduction of their missing members. And just to make clear the object of their hatred, they make sure to burn down the local Sinn Féin clubhouse and several buildings where Sinn Féin members thought they were meeting in secret.

All of this happens once the Tans realise that Downing has been kidnapped. Military personnel with blackened faces and dark skull caps seek out the homes and businesses of known or suspected IRA men, burst down doors, douse the premises with petrol and toss in a grenade. The people of Cork can hear explosions and watch the subsequent fires in every neighbourhood in the city. Even the aldermen are not safe. Outspoken Republican aldermen are a special target, and one of them at least suffers the indignity of his home burnt to ashes, his family left with only the clothes on their backs. In the morning, when the sun burns off the early mist, and the nauseating scent and sight of black smouldering buildings dotting neighbourhood after neighbourhood greets the people of Cork, a tremor of fear convulses the city. It is intensified when people begin to notice the posters that are placed near the burnt-out homes. They are referring to the kidnapped man, Downing, and demand his release. *The Cork Examiner* carries the same notice. However, there is an ominous warning included:

Cork citizens prepare, especially Sinn Féiners.

The following night, Downing has still not been seen, and no trace of him alive or dead is to be found. The people of Cork sleep fitfully, only to be awoken at two or three in the morning by the now-familiar sound of petrol explosions, again sprinkled through neighbourhoods but focused more intensely on the central shopping area. This time the Tans are even more emboldened and loot the shoe shops, the jewellery stores, the tobacco shops owned by Catholics or the families of known IRA. As they walk out of the premises, their arms overflowing with goods, they toss the grenades into the petrol-soaked interiors. The people of Cork have quickly learned to expect this and run to the assistance of their friends and neighbours, trying to help the fire brigade, who are completely overwhelmed for the second night in a row.

The entire month of November has gone from bad to worse. The pubs around the country, but especially in Dublin and Cork, reverberate with hushed tones on the terrible grief of losing Terry, Kevin Barry's execution, shootings, abductions, rampages. In Cork it seems like every other day there are notices by the military of officers gone missing. The people do not know what to make of this. But O'Hegarty has outsmarted them all.

From the many arrested IRA men in gaols and barracks around Cork County come the whispered reports of beatings, torture, extended solitary confinement in filthy dark closets, men stripped naked and left in stone cold cells without blankets, food, or drink. Names of the perpetrators leak out with the stories. O'Hegarty collects every sorry detail, and with steam escaping from his very pores, he sends his battalion commanders around the county in every direction with very specific orders. The priority is nine intelligence men, British officers all, spread about the Cork area. Find them. Follow them. Arrest them. Interrogate them. Execute them. Never mention their names again.

The people, if not surreptitiously participating in these events, are watching them in awe and terror. British officers held up at gunpoint on trains, escorted off and never seen again. British officers riding their motorcycles on country roads right into hidden traps, never seen again. But on November 28, all of Ireland gasps at the determination of the men of Cork to take on the British and drive the enemy out of their country.

James knows it is coming, but it is a big question as to how successful this operation will be. Tom Barry is head of the Flying Column, as they call themselves in West Cork. They are a group of men, most of them wanted by the Tans, who come together to lead an ambush or confront the British and then dissipate when the job is over. They are slowly but surely learning the fine machinations of guerrilla warfare. Tom is an ex-British soldier and at first he had a hard time convincing the likes of O'Hegarty and other leaders that he was genuine. But genuine he is. His baby face and innocent look belie the steel-like determination of this young man to face down the enemy. He knows guns, and he knows warfare, but best of all he knows the British military. And Tom Barry is not afraid of any of them.

Tom meets with O'Hegarty to get permission for his latest idea. He wants to hit these British bastards hard. They have been harassing the people of West Cork in the smaller towns and villages with a particular viciousness ever since they arrived. Tom wants to stop them in their tracks. Literally. He knows that they now travel in convoys due to the increasing number of attacks on military who are found in small groups or alone. He knows that they take a particular route once a week from their barracks in McCroom, west of Cork city, through the small village of Kilmichael, and down towards the southern area of the county. He has a large number of men who are willing to join him, and he has been training them regularly to walk for long distances, to handle guns and to follow orders. O'Hegarty is at first worried about taking on a convoy of British trucks full of armed soldiers. But the recent burnings and the existence of the hit list revealed by Dinny has him realising they don't have much to lose. The IRA cannot weather the increase in arrests. Despite the success of the recent abductions of military intelligence officers and their subsequent executions, the drive to pick up IRA men has continued unabated. Over four hundred arrests per week cannot continue. At this rate their ranks will be decimated, their goals made unachievable. He gives Tom Barry the go-ahead.

Tom leaves the meeting with a smile on his face. He is used to daring exploits, hold-ups, shakedowns, confiscating guns, even machine guns. His reputation in West Cork has been growing steadily throughout the year. Each action has just emboldened him to take on something bigger. He has been training his men for the last two weeks. In order to make their final escape from what he has planned they will have to make their way in the night overland, across fields, around bogs, up and down hills, avoiding roads and villages to a distant point far from the area of attack. If not, they will not have a chance of survival. For Tom Barry knows that if he is successful, they will not be able to predict the magnitude of the British response.

The object of Tom's and O'Hegarty's contempt is not only the Black and Tans. It has veered focus to the special force of Auxiliaries that roam around Ireland in convoys, wreaking havoc wherever they step down from their very well-equipped Crossley Tenders, the truck of choice for the British military. The Auxiliaries arrived in Ireland as the second wave of defence behind the Black and Tans who, theoretically, were created to shore up the rapidly diminishing ranks of the RIC. Unlike the Black and Tans, the Auxies, as they are known, are composed solely of ex-officers. They are paid more, dressed differently in dark blue uniforms with heavy leather leggings and holsters, and as Tom Barry will one day attest, as a group they are a heck of a lot smarter. These men leave nothing to chance. Their actions are well thought out and planned ahead of time. They work as a team. They are, as a matter of pride, ruthless, uncompromising, and intent on their objective of rooting out every IRA or Sinn Féin presence in whatever locale they fix their sights on. They are determined to leave a strong message to villagers, farmers, or townspeople alike that those found to be harbouring IRA men will be treated as if they are IRA themselves. As Officers they are derived from the higher classes of British society and, as Tom Barry will also one day attest, they have a particular dislike of Catholic priests.

After observing their technique of skidding into a crossroads or village, jumping down from their lorries *en masse* and lining up every man, woman, or child from every house in the area, without regard for the old, the sick or the young, they selectively beat with rifle butts their victims of choice, those suspected of helping out IRA men. Tom Barry knows that the IRA must send their own message back in their faces. He has in his memory the sight of his friends and comrades, Tom Hales and Pat Harte, members of his West Cork Brigade. In July, both men had been caught by British intelligence officers and left to the vagaries of the Auxies. They were taken to the barracks and set up against the wall to be shot while the entire company encircled them like a pack of hyenas shrieking for their execution. But those in charge had different ideas. They are sent through a gauntlet of men and beaten senseless with canes. They are tortured and finally sent to hospital. A multitude of Tom's teeth had been crushed by pliers in an effort to elicit information about his comrades. He said not a word. Both men are eventually sentenced and sent to British prisons where Pat will be force-fed and within a couple of years go mad, only to die alone and broken in an insane asylum. Yes, Tom Barry is under no illusions about the Auxies.

On Sunday morning, November 28, Tom marches his men to his planned position. It is at a bend in the road south of the main town of McCroom and just outside the village of Kilmichael. It is a lonely section of road where the view is obscured. Scouts are sent out to neighbouring homes down a side road to warn the people to stay away. The sides of the road offer protection in the form of high mounds of earth where his men can lie down in wait, completely out of sight. He assigns all thirty-eight of them their various positions and the entire group settles in to wait. The Auxies travel this road every Sunday, but they vary the time of day that they roar down from the north to the south of the county for the very reason of being unpredictable. Sometimes, the commanding officer, Percival, stands at the back of an open lorry and tries to pick off farmers in the distant fields. It is something that even Collins did not believe until it was confirmed by a trusted source. The convoy could arrive in seconds or in hours. The day is cold, wet, and windy. The men wear sweaters under their trenchcoats, and caps pulled down over their ears. This offers some protection from the rain, but after a while, every man is sodden, no matter what he is wearing. Still, they wait.

Finally, at about four o'clock, just as Tom is considering packing it in, the roar of a truck can be heard approaching the bend. Out steps Tom into the middle of the road and brazenly waves at the truck. He is wearing a British uniform jacket, and his ruse works. The truck slows and as it does, Tom takes out of his pocket a grenade and fires it into the window of the driver's cab. The driver is killed instantly; the truck veers to the side and the Auxies jump out shooting. It is a fire fight of extraordinary proportions. The British go nowhere without a multitude of arms and ammunition, and they now begin to put them to good use. They let fire. But Tom has planned like a genius. With their superior cover, the IRA are able to pick off each British shooter, one by one.

Seeing that this is a losing battle, the British commander raises a white flag. The guns fall silent. Tom from his cover is watching, but he is ever wary of the British. He hollers out to his men to wait. He calls out to the commander. We surrender, is the response. Before Tom can give an order, two of his IRA team jump into the road with victory written on their faces. They instantly fall on the ground, shot several times by the Auxies who have managed to find cover behind the second truck, which arrived within seconds of the first. Tom sees his comrades bleeding on the ground and yells for his men to resume fire. When they are done there are sixteen dead British Auxiliaries lying on the road and one in the field, shot in the back as he ran for his life. There is not a man left to tell the story.

The IRA makes international headlines. There is no doubt anywhere in the world that Ireland is in a state of war.

James hears the story in the evening at the Douglas Street pub where he, Seán, O'Hegarty, Murphy, Tadg, and a few others of the ASU are meeting. They toast their mate Tom Barry and raise their glasses, but O'Hegarty, ever the realist, rains on their parade. Don't think we won't pay for this, boys, he says with a grim face. My guess is somebody may be paying for it now, as we speak. And indeed, as the men down their Guinness in Cork City, the tiny village of Kilmichael is under attack. The Auxies and the Tans, distraught at the treachery played out on their comrades and furious at their loss of stature, pay the village a visit after dark. They have spent the evening searching out the IRA culprits but not one is to be found. Every pub, every suspected safe house, every building from Kilmichael to Cork has been searched and anyone inside terrorised. They return to Kilmichael and light up the night sky by smashing in windows and tossing in petrol bombs. They do not care if the villagers were involved or not. They do not care if innocents are caught in the crosshairs. Whole families stand out in the cold in their bare feet, wrapped in blankets if they managed to grab them, and watch as their homes burn to the ground. The flames sputter and roar, the children cry and the old ones moan. It will be a long hard winter for each one of them.

The most beautiful woman in the world is preparing to set sail for America, where she will dazzle crowds of Irish men and women and the children and grandchildren of so many who survived the coffin ships to America during the Great Hunger. All she will have to do is appear in public wearing her black hat and transparent black billowing veil and her mourning clothes, because her sister-in-law Mary MacSwiney will be doing most of the talking. Mary's enthusiasm for the cause of Irish freedom will be palpable as the sparks fly from her mouth telling the crowd of the by now epic proportions of Ireland's stand against British tyranny. Between the two of them, they will raise funds, raise awareness, and stir the political pot so that the Irish vote will be pandered to, and acceptance of the Irish demand for recognition of Ireland as a sovereign state will become a political necessity for American politicians. Right now, both women require help with their large trunks and they need to be escorted to the ship terminal at Queenstown, now known by its ancient Irish name of Cobh. Seán and James borrow a car from the Grey brothers and take the women in style down to the harbour. James tips his cap to the women, gives Mary a hug, and wishes the most beautiful woman in the world happy sailing. He does not know if this is appropriate given her mourning attire and Terry's recent death, but the entire episode feels like long ago now, though it has only been four weeks. Muriel smiles at him and thanks him, but truly she barely notices him. Both women are more concerned with Seán, who is still as pale as a ghost and as thin as a reed.

Seán is happier these days because he has managed to find a coveted job at The Ford Motor Company just outside of the city. This is, of course, due to connections that O'Hegarty has with the managers of the firm. Seán does not know this, however: worry about money has been subdued for the time being, and though his face will eventually settle into a haunted, despairing visage, Seán is feeling better. Better, meaning less nauseous. His grief has subsided somewhat, and he is focused on learning the intricacies of his new job in a motorcar factory. That is, of course, when he is at work. For almost every other waking hour he is in the tumult of some type of work for O'Hegarty or Florrie. Seán's face is too well-known to be out spying or observing the British at work. He is easily picked out of a crowd as one of those Rebel MacSwineys. But Seán is active in other ways. He helps to plan, he takes time to talk to the men, and he has begun acting as quartermaster, the grand supplier to the troops. All of this takes organisational know-how, an intricate knowledge of secret methods of shipment and storage and supplies, where to get them, and how to distribute them without leaving signs to the British. Just as in the days of cycling around the city and county, Seán has begun to build an elaborate and permanent map in his head of safe houses, arms caches, bomb factories, and supply warehouses, none of it written down, held only in his mind, a mind slowly becoming resigned to guerrilla warfare and Republican politics.

On December 1 Florrie finally arrives in Cardiff. He has spent some days in London meeting with Collins's men and making arrangements. His personal drive to acquire Josephine's son and return the lad to her is fuelled by his now lofty ascent into the clouds of love. Though he is consumed with IRA business, he lives for his meetings with Josephine in the various churches of the city. He knows that the return of her son, given her hopeless situation, will be the high point of her life. Florrie is determined to give her this gift. After a few days with the unparalleled professionals of subterfuge that Collins has working for him, he is set to make his move.

He hails a cab and with his IRA driver they go to a neat, clean little subdivision just outside Cardiff. He asks the cabby to wait for them at the bottom of the hill, and the two men walk up the street to the front door of a very ordinary-looking house, and calmly knock. Florrie is young and handsome in such a wholesome way, and so well-mannered. The ageing woman who opens the door smiles at him. What could this handsome young man with the pleasant look want? But as the door opens wider, Florrie authoritatively steps inside and asks the elderly couple to see Reginald. Out from the kitchen door walks an eight-year-old boy. Put your coat on Reginald, we are going for a ride. Florrie assures the grandparents that Reggie will be well cared for and not to worry. He indicates he has a gun in his trenchcoat pocket, and that he really does not wish to use it. The young boy, pale-faced with a sad, unsmiling countenance, shrugs his shoulders, puts on his jacket, and does not even look back at his grandparents. The three of them walk back to the cab, the driver of which is none the wiser. They sit in the back seat and are delivered outside a safe house. The following evening, they drive through the night to Manchester in a car provided by Collins's men. All three stay with an accommodating family, whose origins are from County Kerry, as are Florrie's. The family feeds them well and puts them up in their beautiful home. The next day, Florrie makes his way back to Cork alone. In a week, the driver's sister is sent out to meet her brother and his young charge, and the three return to Cork as if a young family arriving home just in time for Christmas.

In the Wallace sisters' shop, Seán, James, Murphy, Florrie, and O'Hegarty read the newspaper accounts of the kidnapping of the boy, the aftermath of the Kilmichael Ambush, and the continuing editorial speculations on the abducted men, the Blemens and Downing. Florrie is not smiling. He has been filled in by O'Hegarty and he is nonetheless shocked at the violence that has been perpetrated in his absence. Terry would have none of that! He spits it in O'Hegarty's direction but O'Hegarty spits back. Terry isn't here, is he? Terry didn't have to face the Auxies did he? And don't be so sure what Terry would or would not have done! I spent many a year by his side. He was always committed. He was always thinking ahead. He knew it would come to this sooner or later. As did Tomás! O'Hegarty has thrown the words like short, sharp knives at Florrie, and Florrie withers under his glare. James looks on and wonders if O'Hegarty is right. Would Terry have gone so far in the thirty days he has actually been gone? It is only since his death that the violence has spiked. Seán hangs his head and does not make eye contact with any of them. It still hurts to think of Terry gone from the earth. Disappeared. Absconded to the next life. Seán has had trouble sleeping. He dreams of Terry, but he cannot see his face. He sees him sitting at his desk, working as he always was. He walks around the desk hoping Terry will notice him and raise his head, wishing for the big smiling blue eyes to settle on him. But Terry does not notice Seán. He works on. Just the shape of him sitting at his desk, head bent forward, reading, focused on some difficult issue, how to push the British out, how to win the upper hand, how to help lads in trouble, how to find money, and on and on. His hand smoothing back his hair when it falls on his forehead. He doesn't see Seán. He doesn't even know he is there. He will not look over no matter how desperate Seán becomes. And then it is over and Seán awakens to the cold empty world without his beloved brother. A world quickly going mad. Who knows what will become of them all?

As they skim through the Dublin papers and the London news they speculate on the international point of view. Arthur Griffith has been arrested. Acting President of Dáil Éireann, President of Sinn Féin, the British have seen fit to lock him up, hoping his lack of influence will put an end to what they deem terrorist activities. They have sent him packing to Mountjoy in Dublin, but there is speculation he will be moved to some remote ancient gaol in England or Wales. In Mountjoy, Griffith walks through the dungeon-like corridors each day to enjoy his few moments outside in the yard. On his way out, he passes under one particular stone arch, and it is at this point that he always smiles. The guard can't figure out why. But Griffith is smiling at the verse above the portal that has been hewn into the rock. In the dark corridor, set overtop the arch, it has not been noticed by the guards. Nevertheless, the inmates know it is there, and feel comfort each time they pass beneath. Carved deeply into the stone it will never be obliterated. It is a reminder to Griffith of his old friend, Pádraig Pearse, father of the Irish Proclamation of Independence, martyr of the Easter Rising. Some wily inmate, or perhaps a series of inmates, who knows, at some point since 1916 found the opportunity to hew into the rock high above the archway the final few lines of Pearse's epic poem "The Rebel":

> *Beware of the risen people, Ye that have harried and held, Ye that have bullied and bribed.*

Griffith too derives comfort and courage from the lines, and he thinks to himself, indeed, beware!

The English still seem to believe that Sinn Féin is causing all the trouble. In fact, they have little to do with it. Michael Collins is Minister of Military Intelligence and Minister of Finance for Dáil Éireann but he is also head of the Irish Republican Brotherhood, and it is in this capacity that he designates executions, okays ambushes, and masterminds escapes. Cathal Brugha is Minister of Defence and as such, head of the IRA, but he has little influence beside Collins's towering personality and secret partisan allegiances. With similar-minded men such as O'Hegarty running the IRA locally, Brugha's attempts at civilised rules of war are guffawed at and shouted down in meetings. It is these men who are calling the shots, keeping the pressure on the British, and making sure that for every atrocity the Black and Tans and Auxies visit on the people, there is a reprisal and an attempt to eliminate each and every specific guilty party.

While James and Seán and the others are debating the day's news, a runner greets the Wallace sisters and asks if Mr O'Hegarty is available for a word. He is waved into the back room where he pulls out of his jacket pocket a long handwritten letter sent to him by his counterpart, the officiating commander in Galway. It is a letter of warning, and a request to keep their eyes open for a few particular Black and Tan men. In fact, it is an accounting of the latest Tan atrocity. O'Hegarty reads once, then twice. Everyone at the table continues to read their paper, but all are hoping to discover the latest news. In a moment they wish they had not. O'Hegarty passes the document to Florrie, who reads it and as he does his eyes bulge and his clenched fist smacks the table. He looks at O'Hegarty. O'Hegarty takes the paper out of his hand and begins to read aloud. The Galway Brigade had two brothers picked up by the Tans a few days previous. Their location was believed to have been divulged by an informer. Their bodies have been found dumped in a pond in the countryside. The horrors they endured are deduced by the long list of short notes detailing the observations of the OC. They had been arrested in broad daylight. Once out of sight they were tied to the back of an RIC lorry and ran until they could run no more. Their exhausted bodies were dragged along the road, nobody knows for how long. The older brother, Pat, was found to have wrists, arms, and legs broken, a fractured skull and his body was decorated with brandings and carvings of the diamond shaped badge from the caps of the RIC. The younger brother's arm dangled hideously from his body having been cut away at the shoulder, and two fingers were missing. There was nothing left of his face but his chin and lips. His face had been carved off his skull in pieces. An attempt had been made to burn the bodies.

No one says a word as they digest this horror. After a moment O'Hegarty quietly looks over the letter again as if he does not quite believe his own eyes. These are the representatives of British law and order, he snorts. We aren't finished boys, there's more. They have also murdered a parish priest and a pregnant woman. If they can get away with this, they can get away with anything. Florrie, at your meeting this week make sure you tell the boys to take extra precautions. We don't want to give these monsters any opportunities. And Murphy, redouble your efforts to determine who the civilian spies are. Keep a close watch. They must be dealt with accordingly for our own safety.

Horgan is the last name on Dinny's list. He lives in the same area of the city as James. O'Hegarty has had him watched and there is no doubt in his mind that the man is a spy. His name was given by the boy; he is an ex-British soldier, he belongs to the Royal Army Service Corps, he has been seen quietly conversing with the Tans. He was at the meeting where Murphy and James and Florrie watched outside. Yes, he will have to be dealt with, immediately. Now that Florrie is back, Josephine has passed on some disturbing information and O'Hegarty is seething.

It seems that the boys of the YMCA who are engaged as spies are not just doing so for king and country. What Dinny failed to tell them, perhaps because he had not yet been a recipient of the Tans' largesse, was the generous pay scale that is attached to the successful conclusion of the work of the spies. The boys receive ten pounds per week when they are actively working. If their work results in the arrest of any leading members of the IRA, they receive forty pounds. The grand prize is fifty pounds for information leading to the arrest of Mr Seán O'Hegarty. O'Hegarty laughs at this insult. He knows his head is worth a lot more than fifty pounds, but he is alarmed at this tactic of the British. Large sums of cash have a way of making the desperate, or even just the greedy, rationalise nefarious deeds. A fifty-pound prize on his head takes his already high-risk life that much closer to the edge of catastrophe.

James and Seán are appalled at the money these young men are making. Imagine ten pounds per week! James himself, as a member of the ASU, is given a paltry four pounds to live off. No wonder there are no shortage of takers. But the YMCA spies are beginning to learn that their money is blood money. And not necessarily attached to the arrests of IRA men. In the last couple of weeks, it is becoming a reasonable assumption that working as a spy for the Tans, whether military or not, is a very high-risk behaviour leading to mysterious disappearances of which no information is available. It is left to the imagination as to what becomes of these people.

George Horgan is a spy. Of that there is no doubt. How much damage he has been responsible for is impossible to determine. How much money he has collected on the backs of the IRA is also impossible to determine, without a chat. O'Hegarty wants answers as to what kind of information he and others have been passing on. It is James's job to pick him up and bring him to Peter, who has been put in charge of the operation. Peter has O'Hegarty's ear. He has proved himself to be fearless, calm, and smart: the kind of man that O'Hegarty puts his trust in. James is not sure why O'Hegarty has requested this change of venue, avoiding the farm, but he is happy about it none the less. He has designated the place of interrogation to be at Lakelands, past the eastern edge of the city off the Blackrock Road. Murphy has set up a secure location in an old barn, part of an ancient estate now in ruins. It is a very isolated spot with a long view out towards the estuary of Cork harbour looking east, and a long view of the surrounding countryside looking west. It is a perfect holding location for questioning, and a quiet out of the way spot if the worst must be undertaken and the evidence concealed.

Horgan is twenty-two years old, the exact same age as James. He is tall, fit, handsome, and has a respectable job as a clerk. He dresses well and minds his manners. He lives with his family in a comfortable, if working class home, about a ten minute walk from James. But for the fact he is a Protestant, he is very much like James. But George Horgan has a secret. When he was fighting in the war, he was taken prisoner by the Germans. This event has had a lasting effect on him.

It is the ninth of December, a sunny, if cold, late autumn afternoon. The wind blows lightly against James's face as he walks down High Street with his hands in his pockets and his cap pulled down. He can see Jeremiah Grey in the van up the street ahead pulled over to the side of the road watching. In the back of the van are Peter and Danny, as well as another member of the 2nd Battalion, rope, and a couple of scarves for blindfolds and gags. James comes to the well-maintained home, and before he knocks on the door he glances down each side of the street. He has been watching the house for a couple of days and he knows that at this time of day the only people who should be home are George and his mother. The front door opens directly to the sidewalk, as do all the homes on this stretch of road. There is no one nearby. James reaches inside his coat and pulls out his revolver from his holster. He shoves it in his trenchcoat pocket. He takes a deep breath and knocks on the door. As he does so, Jeremiah moves the van up the street at a snail's pace. The door opens and a small woman wearing an apron with flour dusted in her greying hair looks up at James. The smell of apple tart fresh from the oven wafts across the house to his nostrils. It is a jarring contrast to the cold steel in his pocket and it momentarily puts him off his game. He hasn't had apple tart for weeks. He makes a mental note to go home to his own mother and enjoy a good meal. But all of these thoughts are a mere flash. James smiles at the woman and asks to speak to George. Aye, step in. The woman wipes her hands on her apron and calls up the staircase to her son. Then she makes her way back to the kitchen. She stops, turns her head, and says to James, he'll just be a minute. Always his head is in a book! And she smiles to herself and walks through the kitchen door. She is as innocent as the day is long. From the third floor of the house, steps can be heard making their way down. They are uneven steps. The steps of a man with a slight limp, an uneven gait. As he moves down the stairs and gets sight of James standing by the door he slows, and his nonchalant look quickly turns to one of suspicion. James takes out his gun and points it at George. Careful Mr Horgan, we wouldn't want any accidents. We wouldn't want anyone to get hurt. James nods in the direction of the kitchen. George releases the tiniest of gasps and looks frantically down the hallway towards the kitchen. James puts his finger to his lips as if to say Sshhh, then opens the door and points outside. He picks up a coat off the hook on the wall, tosses it to George and says, let's step outside. Glancing back at his mother, whose foot can just be seen through the doorway into the kitchen, George steps out onto the street. James sees that the van is just ahead. Jeremiah is now ten yards away from the front door. He is waiting. James says to George, who has not spoken a word, put your coat on, let's go for a walk. We need to have a chat. He takes the gun from his pocket and puts it gently against George's side, the barrel leaning against his ribs, easily distinguishable through his coat. As he does so the van doors open, and Peter and Danny jump out. George knows in this instant that he is doomed. He starts to run across the street, but all three men are on him. With two guns now pointed at him, he looks at the back of the van but refuses to get in. Peter cuffs the back of his head with the butt of his gun and George falls forward, blood streaming down his coat. Still, he will not move to get inside the van. Danny kicks him in the back of the knees and his legs give out from under him. All three men grab a limb and throw him face down in the back of the van and clamber in on top of him. James slams the doors shut as Jeremiah pulls into the road proper and begins to drive down the street. Peter takes rope and expertly ties George's hands behind his back while he is still stunned from the slam to his head. From the rear-view mirror Jeremiah can see a woman in an apron come out of the house and look up and down the street. She is calling someone's name.

As the van heads out to the eastern outskirts of the city, the three men sit on the floor and watch George. Peter still has his gun out, but James has put his back in his holster tucked neatly under his arm. He watches as George comes out of his stupor and turns his head side to side to take in his surroundings. Where are you taking me? Clearly George is not incapacitated. He has been rough-handled by much worse than fellow Irishmen and at a fit six feet tall, the only man in the van who is on a par with his size is James. George, a veteran of the Great War, can look after himself. He knows that the longer he is in the van the farther away from the city he is likely to be taken and the less likely to find a friendly face, or even his way back. Despite his hands behind his back, George manoeuvres himself to sit. He seems dazed still, but he is not. The three men watching him discover this when he suddenly lunges for the back door throwing his shoulder against it in an attempt to break through the doors and throw himself onto the road. James sees it all in slow motion: George's shoulder bracing against the door, a latent second before the doors suddenly break outward, the shock of cold air blowing through the van while Peter and Danny grasp at him in panic and pull back. James jumps forward and grabs one of the doors, his hand is slapped by the other door as it moves erratically while Jeremiah hollers and the van sways side to side. James manages to shut the doors but not before a farmer on the road stares at the passing van in disbelief. Once secure he turns around and sees that Peter and Danny have tied George's legs and are about to gag him with the scarf. James doesn't care. He is angry. They all could have could have been killed. They have been seen. He lunges over at George and punches him in the face. Then James tells Jeremiah to take a detour so that the farmer watching will believe they are headed in a different direction. George reassesses his situation as blood pours from his nose.

Near to their destination they pass a sentry who turns and waves a flag in the direction they are moving, uphill. James has moved to the front seat of the van. He looks out towards the water and sees small whitecaps moving out to sea as the tide ebbs and the wind blows. There are tiny flakes of snow that reflect the waning light of day and James thinks to himself, we will see how Murphy conducts himself. Anything has got to be better than Martin Corry.

Once at the barn the men leave George tied up in the back of the van and walk through the dilapidated building. It was once a fine structure with cobblestone floors for the fine British horses that spent their lives there. The stalls and beams are made of thick hand-planked wood and the old-style thatched roof, despite a couple of large missing patches, remains intact. There is even some ancient straw settled into the corners of the stalls.

Further afield, some thirty yards from the barn, is an old outbuilding probably once used for storage of farm implements. There are no windows, and it is composed of field stones, mortared together and roofed with wooden trusses and flat sheets of timber that are now aged and rotting.

It is from the low wide door that an IRA comrade steps out and waves to the four men. They begin to walk to the door, but Jeremiah looks back nervously at his van, or rather his customer's van. I will wait here and keep an eye on our guest. As the men near the tiny building Mick Murphy steps out. How did it go? Peter replies, well, it was fine until he tried to throw himself out of the back of the van. But never mind, Séamus put him in his place. Don't get to see Séamus all riled up much. That was a show, so it was! James grunts. Well men, we have a little camp in the shed. You boys can fix a schedule for lookouts and for watching over our charge. I will have a word with our spy, and we'll let him stew a bit overnight. Peter, you stay and arrange things between everyone. Be sure to keep the sentries, just in case. James, why don't you make our friend comfortable in the barn?

Here we go, thinks James. He makes his way to the van and nods at Jeremiah, who is standing outside the back door smoking a cigarette. Jeremiah opens the door and both men look in to find Horgan sitting up leaning against the wall, desperately working away at trying to get the rope off his hands and feet. His face and chin have a long spittle of dried blood on them. Horgan looks at them without the least bit of fear and with total contempt. He stares at James. You didn't have to take my nose off. Yes well, you didn't have to try and get us all killed. Now I'm going to untie your legs and we are walking out to the barn. I highly recommend that you do not make a run for it. Everybody here has a gun and some of the lads would love a chance for target practice. George sticks out his legs and James unties the rope. He takes Horgan's arm and slides him to the door so that his feet swing out and land on the ground. Jeremiah has already moved to the driver's seat. He does not look at George but stares out of the windshield and waits.

George looks around. James can see that he is quickly trying to assess his situation. From this vantage the only thing that is visible are the tall shrubs that line the overgrown fields. The barn sits looking neglected and lost. James has Horgan by the arm. They walk together towards the door, and as they move James notices the blood on the back of his head and the large welt that has erupted where the gun pounded into his skull. That must hurt, he thinks. Horgan walks towards the barn and then suddenly bolts. He turns and begins to run in the opposite direction and James realises he is running towards the salty smell of the sea that is wafting up the hill from the beach below. But Jeremiah has been watching from the van and he jumps out, intercepts, and tackles him onto the ground before James can get there. Peter and Danny have watched the whole thing and begin to laugh nervously. This man is not so easily intimidated. They will have to watch their step. But everything hinges on Murphy, what he has permission to do and how he will go about extracting whatever information he can get.

James follows Horgan into the barn with the barrel of his gun pointed at the back of his neck. This time Horgan can feel James's frustration and does not wish to feel his fist again, but he walks slowly, making a mental note of his surroundings. James, cognisant of Horgan's strategising, quips, there is no place to run to mate, just settle down and be ready to answer questions. When they get inside the structure James can hear their boots ringing off the cobblestones and he is immediately aware of the gravity of the situation. Though it is a smaller, older, and obviously unused barn, James thinks of Corry's farm and looks up to the centre beam. For a split second he thinks he sees Dinny's frantic kicking legs, his blue face and his hand raised in the air. But it is a passing vision, thank God. Horgan, highly aware of what is going on around him, can sense the change in James's deportment and a shudder runs up and down his back. He has been here before; he thinks to himself. Is this where you took Fred, he barks at James. But James just shoves the gun harder into his neck and pushes him forward.

Murphy stands at the far end of the barn, leaning on a stall watching all. He is preparing himself for what must come. Murphy is a very tough cookie. He does not second-guess himself. Indeed he exudes a supreme confidence. He knows that it is now or never for Ireland's freedom, and he is committed to doing what is necessary to achieve that goal. As an athlete he has pushed himself physically and mentally, and he has learned self-preservation strategies to keep himself in the fight at all costs, and to elicit the kinds of responses from his opponents that allow him to win the game. He applies these skills now and thinks carefully about how to elicit the most from this young man's store of knowledge. He knows he will have to get a sense of him tonight, think on a strategy overnight, and return tomorrow with a game plan. He decides to see how far playing the good cop will take him.

Horgan looks Murphy in the eye. I suppose you're the head of this group of thugs. He spits it at Murphy with a contemptuous, scornful tone. Murphy is not expecting this. He suppresses his instinct to let fly his own vitriol, but his eyes narrow and his body weight shifts. He loses his relaxed pose and instead nods at James, who gives Horgan a shove onto a makeshift stool set up for the purpose. Before Murphy can say another word, Horgan starts firing questions at him. Where's the Blemens? What did you do to them? Who takes a father and son off the street? Two good men like that? Mr Blemens is a beekeeper and a teacher. Are beekeepers and teachers a big threat to you so-called IRA types? Murphy no longer suppresses his urge and takes a step forward and slaps Horgan across the face with the back of his hand. Hard. Murphy is a man with shoulders as wide as he is tall. James gasps and catches Horgan as he falls sideways off the stool from the force of the blow. That will be enough from you. You will talk when I tell you to. Best to think carefully about what you and your friendly group of spies have been up to. I will be expecting answers tomorrow.

Murphy turns and walks out of the barn. He consults with Peter and Danny who come in and escort Horgan into the far stall and tie his legs together. James and Murphy walk out to the van, where Jeremiah waits for them. On the ride back to the city, the three men discuss the likelihood of getting information from Horgan. James and Jeremiah believe he will be difficult to deal with, having already attempted to escape twice. But Murphy knows otherwise. Not to worry boys. He is a soldier, so he seems like a tough nut to crack. But we are all just human, so we are, and everybody likes to tell their story given half a chance. Not me, thinks James. I will never tell this story.

James feels anxious through the night. He sees Dinny's dangling, kicking legs and Horgan's bump oozing blood on the back of his head. He tosses and turns. He returns to the hideout the following day with Murphy looking not unlike Horgan, who has welts under his eyes, straw in his hair and is shivering from the cold. He tried taking off when we let him out for a piss this morning. So says Peter, as he shrugs and points to his own mud-covered trousers. Obviously, there was a bit of a tussle. Has he eaten, asks Murphy? No bloody way, not after that, spits out Peter, not in the least concerned. Feed him, demands Murphy, I want answers from this boyo. And find him a blanket. Horgan, shivering in the corner of the stall enveloped in straw and sporting a swollen eye, shouts out, I don't want your fucking blanket or your shite food. You should be taking me home, because I don't know what the Tans are going to do with you idiots when they get you, but it isn't going to be pretty. At that Murphy steps forward and smashes Horgan in the face once again, this time with a clenched fist. I told you to keep quiet until I tell you to speak. And Horgan falls away into the straw and regrets his loose tongue.

By the time evening has rolled around, Murphy's knuckles are sore, and Horgan's face is barely recognisable. James stands by, occasionally picking Horgan up and putting him back on the stool. He keeps a straight face, but his stomach is mashed up, fluid, swishing in his gut like so much putrid fish in the bottom of a barrel. Murphy, Peter, and Danny leave, but it is his turn to keep watch overnight. There are four sentries from his company manning the upper regions of the hideaway and two at the bottom, keeping an eye on the road in. James sends two off to rest and creates a schedule so that there will be a constant lookout through the night. Then he takes several blankets from the storage hut, a flask of water, and a bowl of cold lamb stew. He moves into the stall beside Horgan and puts the flask to his lips. Horgan drinks greedily. The water runs into the blood in his mouth and tastes metallic, but he doesn't care. He is learning humility. What do you want to know, he asks James? If I tell you what he wants to know, will you let me go? James is stirring the stew in the bowl and is glad his face cannot be seen. Yes. He tells the lie with full knowledge that Horgan will be shot, sooner rather than later. I don't believe you, mumbles Horgan, but with some tiny shred of hope in his voice. James detects this miniscule sliver wafting from Horgan and decides to use it. He shovels a spoonful of stew into Horgan's mouth. Give us all a break, man, and just answer his questions. It is information we will get from someone else if you don't supply it, so you are not saving anybody from anything. And really, I do not care for this decrepit old barn. I prefer my own bed. It is fucking freezing out here! And James gets up to gather straw and sticks and sets a fire under an open section of roofing on the cobble stones. He calls to one of the sentries to retrieve a couple of blocks of peat from storage. Horgan is drawn to the heat and comes as close as he can, lays his head on a blanket, and suddenly sleeps. James sits on the stool and watches Horgan's swollen face in the firelight. At some point in the night, he can hear his name being called as if from a far-off distance, and realises it is Tomás Ashe's face he is looking at and whose voice he's hearing. He jolts awake, wondering if the sentries noticed he had slipped into a reverie, as he sees Ashe's swollen eyes and mouth spluttering slop.

In the wee hours of the morning Horgan awakens and begins to tell James his story. I have been held by worse than you lot, you know. Who is worse than us, quips James? He is feeling quite genuine about the question. The bloody Hun, that's who. Why do you think I have a limp? It's not from a battle wound. Those bastards were professionals at getting information. Not like you bunch of farm boys and school kids. It was just lucky I didn't know anything. I was just a private, bottom of the rung. Our commanding officer complained about my treatment, so they threw me back in the bunkie with the others, but not before my leg was permanently damaged from being tied up and left to rot. A dark little hovel for days. I thought they had forgotten about me. I thought I was going to die there. James says nothing, and Horgan drifts back to sleep. Murphy was right: everybody has a story to tell. He decides to try to sway Murphy's plans of what to do with this young man. Maybe he can convince him to offer Horgan a deal. Or just let him go.

The next morning Murphy is at the barn earlier than expected. He leaves Horgan under the watch of one of the sentries and calls the men to talk to him. James knows by the sound of his voice that there is trouble. He braces himself. The British have declared martial law. It is effective in Cork, Kerry, Limerick, and Tipperary. It is their response to the Kilmichael Ambush. Now, not only do we have curfew to contend with, but it is also no holds barred as far as picking up IRA men is concerned. Anyone found carrying arms or ammunition can be summarily executed. They can search homes without warning and intern suspects without warrants or explanation. This will only empower the Tans. We can look forward to constant raids. They can stop anybody on the street and haul us off to gaol for no reason. It is going to be difficult to get around. We are going to have to be ready for a fight every time we step out of the door.

Murphy looks at James. Did you get anything out of him over night? James is careful to reply with a nonchalant tone. I don't think he knows much. He has been working with a few of their guys trying to get a take on our grand commander. Seems like they still can't get a tail on O'Hegarty, if he is to be believed. Old man Blemens knew what he was doing. They were all working separately and don't have much to tell. James throws out his suggestion: Maybe we should let him go home and keep an eye on him. Maybe we will get more information that way. As an afterthought he adds, he was a POW. The Germans did a number on him. Murphy considers James's idea. I'll think about it. For the time being we will keep him here. We have a meeting with O'Hegarty.

It is Saturday morning. The day is cold, but not brutally so, and the morning sun shines down on the city if but weakly. Jeremiah stops by a flat to pick up Dan, known as Sandow, whose opinion on most matters is highly regarded by O'Hegarty and the rest of the men. Dan, eight years older than James, has been around the block many times with the British and has been with the Volunteers since 1913, working with Terry and Tomás. He is, however, a much fiercer man than his old friends and their deaths have had a profound effect on him. As James will come to know very soon, he is almost reckless in the risks he will take to push Ireland towards freedom.

The men drive into the main shopping section of Cork: the streets are crowded, and the shops are busy. There are men and children on bicycles, and cars mingle with the many horse-drawn carts on the street. The English Market, the central food exchange of the city, is doing a brisk business as women inspect the farmers' winter vegetables and haggle over the price of lamb or bacon. Jeremiah decides it is mayhem to drive any further and he lets Murphy and James and Dan out of his van a few steps from St Augustine's Priory. The men walk separately into the church, kneel down to say a prayer, light a candle, and then when they are sure they are not being followed they go out from the back door and nip into the laneway where the Wallace sisters' tobacco shop is hidden slightly from view. With a nod to the sisters, they enter the back room to find O'Hegarty and Florrie and half the battalion commanders for the entire brigade, as well as a handful of James's colleagues in the ASU. The tiny room can barely hold them all. Some stand against the wall while others sit. Everyone is talking at once. The announcement of martial law has them all spinning.

Throughout November every commander has already had numerous men from their battalion picked up at home or work or right off the street and arrested. The Tans have created an entirely new camp for prisoners in County Down, far to the north of the country. They certainly have no space left to keep them around Cork. O'Hegarty snarls at them all to shut up and listen. There is to be an assault on the Auxies tonight in the city. Everyone who is not involved needs to stay clear. The attack will occur, assuming that everything is as it should be, at Dillon's Cross. There is silence for a moment before the whole room erupts. That is practically on top of Victoria Barracks, points out Murphy. James's old friend Mick, who is in the room, pipes up. Not to worry, we're set for it. There is a clear escape route over the wall and away through Goulding's Glen. We will be long gone before the barracks can mobilise. Besides, the whole point of the exercise is to take out Captain Kelly, our dear friend. Mick speaks with thick sarcasm. O'Hegarty makes it clear: We have reason to believe he will be in a returning convoy sometime in the evening.

Everyone in the room has been keeping an eye out for Captain Kelly. He and his buddy, Captain Hollywood, are the two high-ranking British officers who are on the list for execution but have evaded capture. Both men are notorious sadists when it comes to captured IRA. They have left men broken, their bodies permanently damaged. James himself has been on the lookout for Kelly in particular, who is known to visit Cork Gaol regularly and who is infamous for his treatment of Tom Hales in West Cork. Kelly would be a prize catch. The operation has been well-planned and has been deemed worth the risk.

O'Hegarty raises his voice. With the imposition of martial law everyone needs to be very careful. Be sure you are at your safe houses tonight. If this goes over, the British will be yelping like bloodhounds for our flesh. I don't want to lose any more men. So, all you boys crawl into somebody's bed somewhere safe before eight o'clock tonight and do not show your faces until things are calm. And that may be a while. Now off with ye, before we call attention to our hostesses. The men begin to shuffle out of the room in pairs, but not before O'Hegarty pipes up again. One last thing... expect reprisals ... seems that is the way things are headed lately. The good news is it means we are getting to them. Chins up, soldiers.

Dillon's Cross is an intersection of roads in the northeast quadrant of the city a few hundred feet above and around the corner from Victoria Barracks. This intersection has seen more than its fair share of terror and grief. In the mid-nineteenth century Brian Dillon, a young, sickly boy, lived in a house at the corner of the intersection. He survived a hard fall as a youth and suffered the rest of his life as a bit of a hunchback. Frail and often ill, he nevertheless weathered the wretched famine years. He watched from his sickbed, through the small window at the top of the house, the disturbing vision of emaciated bodies in rags wandering by looking for succour. He watched as military personnel from the nearby barracks shooed the starving masses off the street and to workhouses, amplifying their torment tenfold. Young Dillon is constantly reminded of the occupation of his native land by his close proximity to the largest military barracks in Cork. As he gains strength, he becomes an artist and a rebel. He joins the newly formed Irish Republican Brotherhood, often referred to as the Old Fenians, and with his comrades in Dublin starts planning a rebellion. Alas, before it could even get off the ground, the three leaders, including Dillon, are arrested. With a couple of ambiguous letters and a pair of binoculars as evidence, young Dillon is sentenced to ten years of penal servitude. In gaol in England he is so ill that the British take pity on him and send him home early. He dies at home in the house at the intersection at the age of forty-two. In 1872 his funeral is the largest ever seen in Cork. The crossroad becomes forever known as Dillon's Cross.

On the evening of December 11, 1920, Mick Kenny and five of his men from the 1st Battalion are waiting behind the wall that separates the road from the large expanse of greenery, known as O'Callaghan's Field. The wall is across from Dillon's house. Once in the field it leads to the ravine area known as Goulding's Glen.

This is a wild green space at the outside edge of the northernmost reaches of the city. Through the Glen one can head off into various neighbourhoods of the city or out towards the countryside. At about eight o'clock it is dark and cold, but the men are high on adrenalin and their pockets are full of homemade bombs, their guns at the ready. As two lorries enter the crossroads to turn in the direction of the barracks, Kenny steps out into the road wearing a British officer's jacket. When the first lorry slows down, he reaches into his pocket and takes out a grenade, which he tosses at the truck, aiming for the partially opened window. The second truck speeds up and passes the first, but the men behind the wall are watching and spring forward throwing their bombs and unloading their revolvers at both trucks. There are thirteen Auxies in each lorry. As they are wounded one by one, they go into defensive positions, but by this time Kenny has done the most damage he can, and all six of the men take off in separate directions. They leave behind them one dead British Auxiliary and eleven wounded. All six IRA men escape unhurt. The only trace of them is a cap that one of the men lost in his haste to get back over the wall and away.

James has little to do with the Dillon's Cross ambush. He knows that if any of the men are recognised they will have to go on the run; that is, stay clear of the city, away from home for extended periods of time and move to new territory to help the fight or just keep their heads down and work in another part of the country. Murphy knows they have their own fish to fry in the 2nd Battalion area where there has been much spying activity, and where by now there have been a handful of homes and shops burned to the ground. He needs his own men, especially the crew that he prefers to work with, including James. At the minute there is still the issue at Lakelands to deal with, in the form of the spy George Horgan.

When James arrives back at Lakelands late in the afternoon, Horgan's eyes are still swollen. Murphy has seen to it that he has had a meal and a cup of tea and is no longer shivering. Though he despises the British, Murphy has always been an honourable athlete and just as in a game of football, his basic human decency does not allow him to treat his opponents without some semblance of human dignity; however, trying to elicit answers is a different story. James has been spooked by the idea of being on a hit list by the most innocuous of organisations: the YMCA. He assumes, though

Murphy has said nothing, that he too is worried. Both men feel the pressure of dealing with this potentially deadly situation. And if the truth be told, neither James nor Murphy know what to do about it, but Murphy's orders have been clear. O'Hegarty too is on the list, the highly prized name to be found and reported on. And O'Hegarty wants answers. Who else have they fingered? Who is next for a midnight raid to be beaten and dragged away? How many men have they supplied information on? Who are the contacts within the Tans that receive the reports? Who exactly inside the YMCA has been organising this Spy network? Was it just Blemens? Or are there more men involved?

There is little likelihood that George will be given a reprieve, but James feels like he has made a decent case for letting him go and following up with him later. When he thinks of the execution that must otherwise take place his stomach starts to churn, and he begins to feel the preliminary tension of a bad headache. There is a spot right behind his left eye that begins to compress and burn, leaving him feeling jumpy and irritable. The image of Dinny's head of curls falling forward as the movement of the earth is suspended reasserts itself. Also, there is the undeniable fact that there is something about Horgan that James feels but cannot describe. Maybe it was just the delicious scent of apple tart and the prettiness and pleasant countenance of his mother with flour on her hands and in her hair that has put him off his game. He can see the mother smiling as she commented on her son's love of reading. James too has been a bookworm all his life. If they hadn't gone to different schools as children, James senses that Horgan could well have been a friend. Horgan may have been through the Great War, but he still seems to James like any twenty-two-year-old such as himself. In fact, it has crossed James's mind that if he was sitting on Horgan's side of the fence, he might have done exactly what Horgan is accused of. This thought lets loose a shiver down his spine. Imagine that, he thinks to himself. But James is very firmly on the nationalist Catholic side of the fence. His family history and his own life experience have forged a loyalty to the Republican cause that will remain steadfast. As for Horgan, he may very well be less entrenched in his views. Whatever the case, James has decided that Horgan is smart enough to figure out all of the options and will therefore opt for a chance to go home, even if it means he might have to betray his principles. James has found that a man's principles have a strange way of sliding into oblivion when stone cold reality is finally realised. He will talk to Horgan once more and hope that Murphy has decided in favour of letting him go home.

As James examines Horgan and his swollen eyes, he realises that Horgan is examining him despite his somewhat impaired vision. What's next, Séamus? The tone is familiar. Too familiar. Are you going to put me in the same place you put Blemens and his son, and Downing? What are you going to do, throw me off the cliff into the sea? You might drop the high and mighty tone Horgan. The information you and your lot have passed on means people die. Good, decent people, just trying to change the politics of this country. But the Tans see that as justification for murder and burning people out of their homes. How do you sleep at night, being part of that? James is beginning to feel less sympathetic to his prisoner. I sleep just fine. What keeps me awake is thinking of what would become of this place if your lot actually managed to take over. That's what keeps decent citizens of Cork awake at night! Peter walks into the barn and gives James a quizzical look. What are you talking to this guy for, he seems to be saying, and indeed James wonders that himself. George Horgan is most definitely a spy and not in the least bit remorseful about any harm he may be responsible for. I must be going soft, James thinks. He understands that it is the thought of another execution that is making him revisit his opinions. Dinny's sandy curls falling forward, the suck of cold water as the Blemens father and son sink into the bog juice, the impenetrable wall of cold, damp rock in the middle of the graveyard where Downing may have screamed himself hoarse. All of these thoughts flood James's mind. He fingers the beads in his pocket, stands up and walks away from Horgan. Truly, he does not want anything else to do with him.

Outside Peter and Murphy and James talk. I've been thinking about what you've said, Séamus. Maybe we will give this one a chance to turn over a new leaf. He seems to have spilled what he knows. Everything he has said is in line with the information Corry got from the others. We will keep him on a tether and see what happens. If he talks, we will know who he is talking to and that will help us out. And if he doesn't, well and good. As it is, he knows it is hardly worth his while to keep up his activities. We won't have a car till the morning. I'm going to head back to the city for now. I want to give our man one more night to stew. I will tell him we are thinking of letting him go if he can come clean. He may spill other titbits in the morning so one of you will have to stay back. He is a lucky son of a bitch, though he doesn't know it yet. His friends did not fare so well. James and Peter nod. You go back Séamus, you've been out often enough lately. I will camp here for the night with the sentries, says Peter. Fair enough, Murphy nods in agreement. The boys dropped off some eggs and fresh bread for your tea tonight. I will have one of the Grey brothers bring me back in the morning and we will drop off our guest and head back into the city for a while. I want my own bed. And I want to find out how the ambush fares at Dillon's Cross. Let's hope they get that bastard Kelly! Murphy walks back into the barn. James and Peter can hear the sigh of relief that comes from Horgan after Murphy tells him he may be delivered back to his neighbourhood in the morning. Peter walks James and Murphy to the edge of the property where a young IRA sentry sits in a horse-drawn cart waiting to take Murphy back to his home. He jumps on the end of the cart as Murphy sits atop with the driver. As night draws in, the winds pick up and the air becomes crisp and cold. James breathes in the salty scent and lays back in the straw protected from the wind by the short side walls of the cart. There is a new moon, and the stars sparkle and dance in space. He feels satisfied and relieved that there will be no execution, no grave-digging tonight. For some reason, the cart driver takes the shore road following the river back into the city edge. At the turn in the road sits the ancient round castle, Blackrock Tower. It sits on the beach, long ago a lookout for British masters to keep an eye on both the River Lee and the estuary out to Cork Harbour proper. Commissioned by Queen Elizabeth, it was built to last, with stone walls over two metres thick. James chuckles to himself thinking of the history of the tower, where a hundred years ago the reigning aristocratic family had quite the party and managed to burn the inside of the place to cinders, though the thick walls of stone remained. That must have been quite a welcome sight to the locals on a dark starry night like this, thinks James to himself.

The night is lit only by the interior lights in windows of the houses when James hops off the cart and walks home via back lanes and side streets. His mother jumps from her chair where she is knitting a thick, soft baby's blanket. James's sister is expecting her first child. She drops her knitting and tells James to come and sit by the fire. When he is settled in beside his father, she hurries to the kitchen to warm up a plate of dinner. Again, James feels a sense of relief that they did not execute Horgan. Horgan's mother will be happy to see him as well, he thinks to himself. But just as James is lulled by the fire and a final cup of tea into a quiet, pre-sleep trance there is a sharp, determined knock on the door. His father jumps up in alarm and goes to the window. With a smile and a sigh of relief, he walks quickly to the door and opens it to Seán, who shakes his hand and passes a few words of small talk about the greyhounds and the ups and downs of the racing world. As James comes to the door, Seán looks at him meaningfully and he grabs his trenchcoat and steps outside, closing the door behind him. There's trouble over by Dillon's Cross, Jimmy. The Auxies are out in force burning the houses down. Mick and the boys got away but they killed one and there is a pile of wounded soldiers. Half of Victoria Barracks is out on the streets, and they have gone mad. O'Hegarty wants us in the city centre. James sees that Seán's bicycle is by the road. He looks at Seán and Seán shrugs his shoulders. You know it is the fastest, safest way after curfew, Jimmy. You are getting spoiled being ferried about by those Grey brothers! They ride their bicycles in the most direct route to the Wallace sisters' shop. Because it is after curfew, they would normally work their way across the southern edge of the city and cross the river into an old neighbourhood where there are many back laneways. But tonight, they feel the urgency of O'Hegarty's call, and take the risk of a more direct route straight to St Augustine's. They needn't have worried because any military in the city are fuming in the north-eastern quadrant where Dillon's Cross is bearing the brunt of the Tans' wrath.

When they arrive at the shop the lights are out, and the door is locked and barred. But after Seán knocks his pattern on the door, O'Hegarty himself is heard cursing at the barrier they have constructed on the inside, and the men are given entrance.

At the back of the shop are O'Hegarty, Florrie, Pa Murray, Tom Crofts, and some others. Well, we knew they would be pissed, but the murdering bastards are on a tear like no other. They have started burning the houses at Dillon's Cross. The only thing that stopped them was the Protestant family on the western corner. All the other homes are burnt beyond recognition and several of the family members beaten with rifle butts. I have a bad feeling about this. There were reams of them coming out of their trucks with cans of petrol sloshing it around like buckets of water on a hot day. When the fire brigade showed up, they were turned back! Seán is shocked. Sure, the fire could easily spread on a night like this. 'Tis as windy as can be outside. Séamus and I almost got blown off our bikes on the way over! Aye Seán, it looks like they were happy to watch the fireworks and they are there yet, wreaking havoc. I need you boys to find a location where you can watch and keep tabs. I want to know who ordered this madness and who is participating. We will see to them later; you can be sure of that. Don't take any risks, I don't want you boys pinched, I've spent too much time training ye. A lot of the boys have left town as per my orders the other day, so hopefully not too many of us will be picked up tonight, but we can be sure they will be out looking long into the night. I fear there will be more than one family who pays the price of this ambush.

James and Seán and the other men in attendance work their way out into the city in different directions. Seán and James, on their bicycles, head towards Dillon's Cross. They hope to get as close as possible to the troubled area. Working their way through the side streets to the Bridge Street crossing, they pedal like devils over the bridge and into the laneways of the upper eastern quadrant of the city until they come close to the Dillon's Cross intersection. Already they can see the flames shooting into the sky from a group of homes. More troubling still is the desperate crying and moaning of young and old, as families watch their homes burn to cinders, standing out in the cold not even dressed against the weather. Some men are sitting outside on the kerb, their faces covered in blood, looking dazed and in shock. One man lies on the ground moaning, his leg being nursed by a woman. It looks as though he has been shot in the thigh. James and Seán look at each other and nod. They head in opposite angles to circle the area and get a closer look at the Auxies on guard in the street holding their rifles watching that no one throws so much as a cup of water at the roaring flames. When they meet back, they just miss being spotted by a lorry that rumbles past them, loaded with Auxies. The men are holding petrol cans and bottles of whiskey and firing their rifles into the air.

Something is up, says Seán. Something bad. He is panting hard, feeling panicked and confused. They decide to go to their old lookout points where they can see somewhat into the grounds of Victoria Barracks. They must deposit their bicycles and scramble up a large tree in the dark to get a look. Braced against the branches, the two of them stare quietly at the scene before them. Trucks are being loaded with cans of petrol, men are milling about with rifles in one hand and whiskey in the other. It is obvious that something is underfoot. Seán and James move to follow the convoy of lorries. They can see in the distance that there are several and they are all heading down the Youghal Road to St Patrick's Hill. James's gut wrenches. Seán looks at him in alarm. Both men know exactly what the Auxies have in mind. We need to get word to the boss. I will make my way now and try to get over the bridge. You trail them. I will meet up with you later at the Wallaces'. Let's hope we can get the women out of there before the mad troops arrive. The priory at least should be safe. They can't burn stone. James sails down the side street that will let him get over the bridge before he is seen. It is a risk, but the night is as black as ink, and he has an overwhelming sensation that the convoy will head straight to the city centre. That is exactly where the Wallace sisters' shop lays hidden in a back lane.

Seán trails behind the convoy and watches alarmed, as the first lorry stops dead in the middle of the road three quarters of the way down the hill. There is cheering and revelry as a soldier fires a grenade into a shop window and the resulting explosion blows out of the window completely. The shards of glass are fired into the street and within seconds a fire is blazing. A few Auxies jump down with their petrol cans and begin to slop the fluid carelessly on shop storefronts. A soldier in the truck aims his rifle at a shop window and fires. When the glass collapses the soldier with the petrol pours it through the window and into the shop. The men jump back onto the lorry, and cheer as flames start to leap and lick at the premises. People start to rush onto the road and yell at the soldiers. What are ye doing for God's sake? But one young buck on the back of the truck fires off a volley of shots from his rifle at the protestors. What are we doing? We're only just getting started, he yells back at the small crowd.

Seán watches as the lorries proceed to the bridge. There is a tram that is just starting across from the other side. To Seán's amazement the truck does not slow down but drives right in front of the tram, forcing the driver to stop in the middle of the bridge. The soldiers shoot their guns in the air and the passengers jump off the tram and try to run, but some unlucky few are held back by rifles. They are told to line up at the side of the bridge and are roughly searched. One middle-aged man has his coat ripped open and the Auxies immediately notice his clerical collar and his breviary in hand. Ha, look we've got one of their priests! Shall we shoot him now? No yells another, let him say 'Fuck the pope' three times and we will let him go. The priest refuses. One of the Auxies hits him a few times with his rifle butt. He decides to take his clerical collar, and in the process rips off the man's shirt. Okay, line up, make a firing squad, mates, he hollers. But one young Auxie has had enough. This is going too far. Let him go, we have other things to worry about, he shouts. The priest is told to run, and run he does. He lives to tell the tale, but only by the goodness of one lone man. A can of petrol is produced and sloshed onto the tram. This time they do not throw grenades but cigarette butts, and within seconds the tram is alight. The lorry drives on with the soldiers firing into the air and toasting each other with their bottles of whiskey.

Seán waits until the lorries are gone. He cycles over the bridge, nipping quickly past the smouldering flames of the tram, and pulls over to the side of the street just inside a laneway. The lorries have stopped again. This time they crash in the shop windows, toss open the doors, and make their way inside. Within moments the lot of them are back on the street, their arms full of random items, shoes, blankets, pots, and pans. Some take the time to look around and spotting a small jewellery shop they work together to crash in the fortified door. The shop is ransacked; every broach, ring, and necklace stuffed into pockets. As they leave the premises one of the soldiers tosses a hand grenade behind him and whatever is left of the shop goes up in flames. Seán is becoming more alarmed as every second passes. He turns and works his way through the laneway and to the side streets to get to the Wallaces'. Thankfully nothing has happened in their vicinity yet, but the night is young, it is barely eleven o'clock and the Auxies have shown no signs of letting up. In fact, they are, as the officer told the crowd, just getting started. O'Hegarty and James have moved the ladies to the priory and the safety of the stone church. The priests, who know the women well, allow the sisters in and take them to a comfortable room at the back in their residence. But it won't be long before the chaos erupting across the city can be heard even through the thick walls of the church. No one in the centre of Cork will sleep tonight.

James and Seán look at O'Hegarty with expectant faces. He stares back at them. Not even in his wildest dreams did he think the British would stoop so low. Are they going to burn the entire city? On the one hand he is thankful that he ordered his men to leave. On the other he is thinking that he needs the flying column to take on this pack of murdering arsonists. But there is no flying column available. Do you have your gun, Jimmy? Aye and it is loaded but I have only the six shots. I am not a bad shot, but I doubt I will get six in this chaos. Never mind Jimmy, it is pointless. You could barely make a dent. There must be twenty-five between the two trucks that Seán followed. And there are more heading this way. From what I can gather there are lorries showing up both sides of the river. There have been a couple of families of our boys already burned out in the 5th Battalion area. If we can stop some of the chaos well and good, but this looks to me like a plan. And you boys know the Auxies, they work as a team. All we can do is help out where we can and keep a score card. There will be payback for this sooner or later.

O'Hegarty stops speaking suddenly when a volley of shots is heard nearby. It is a roving band of Black and Tans wandering the streets shooting at anyone they see. Right lads, I think the best thing to do under the circumstances is go home to your families and see they are safe. We are lucky none of us live in the city centre. But it doesn't mean there won't be crews of them out and about other parts of the city. Don't take any risks. These Godless animals are out for blood. They will get a taste of their own medicine soon enough. O'Hegarty turns and walks away swiftly. He will go straight to the safe house where his wife is staying at the outskirts of the city to wait out the madness. But he is worried, very worried. Any men they find tonight won't stand a chance.

Seán and James gather their bikes and plan out their course to get home without calling attention to themselves. They decide to weave their way through the back streets and periodically look out onto St Patrick's to keep an eye as to what is going on. They are amazed to watch trucks full of Auxies deposited on the boulevard and uniformed men with their faces covered in scarves lug jugs of petrol to various shops. The soldiers break through the windows or doors with rifle butts, go inside, spread the petrol, gather up what goods they wish, and then toss in a grenade on their way out. As James and Seán work their way down the street, staying a good block ahead of the soldiers, they start to panic. Sure, they are going to burn down the whole city, the fuckers, says Seán. As he speaks, he sees the fire brigade hurry onto the main drag. The men uncoil their long hose and hook it up to the water wagon. But as they prepare to douse the flames that are shooting out of the broken window, a man with a trenchcoat yells at them in his obvious English accent to back off. When he is ignored, he takes a revolver out of his pocket and shoots warning shots at the firemen. Then he riddles their hose with gunfire.

The fire master is beside himself with rage. He is an older man and having been fire master for decades he has seen much. He has seen homes and buildings set ablaze on purpose for all kinds of reasons: revenge, attempted murder, despair, hopelessness. He has dealt with all kinds of people. He has never seen anything like this, and he has never dealt with people like this. He is hollering at the Auxies, but they just fire closer to his head. Bullets whiz by his ears. He calls his men, and they hop on their truck and leave to work in another area. They are no good to anybody dead. They will find another part of the city that can use their help. God knows the fires are springing up all over the main island. In fact, even with their two trucks and their pumps that allow them to use river water, the fire master knows the city centre's core, that is the entire island is at great risk of being completely eradicated. The winds are strong enough to carry the flames and the Auxies show no sign of letting up. No matter which building the crew tries to save, the Auxies will not allow it. They stop and watch the fire crew for a short while, then casually shoot at the men or shoot at the hose or both. The fire master makes a panicked telephone call to the two largest cities in Ireland, Dublin and Limerick. Within hours, just when the Auxies are starting to meander back to their barracks, tired after a night's work, the Dublin and Limerick crews will arrive via train with their trucks and save Cork from complete destruction.

James and Seán confer with each other. They decide to wait and watch. It is a risk, between the fire and the gunfire, anything could happen, but somebody has got to be a witness. They are not, however, the only ones who are thinking of the future. There are people everywhere risking curfew, watching, and trying to keep out of harm's way at the same time. The brave men who are willing to take on an Auxie or a Tan, shouting at them to stop, live to regret it because they inevitably suffer debilitating blows with rifle butts. Sometimes they are arrested and thrown in a lorry to be taken to Victoria Barracks. Sometimes they are shot in the leg or arm. The trucks continue to come and go, the petrol continues to be spread and the fires grow. The entire night sky is alight with orange and red flames. If it weren't for the wind, the smoke would be unbearable as the interiors of the buildings smoulder, but as it is the smoke is sucked away and out to sea, allowing a clear view of the wild inferno.

The thoroughfare of St Patrick's Street was once, a few hundred years ago, a small channel of the River Lee through the marshland of the centre island. But over decades, beginning in the eighteenth century, the marshland was drained, and buildings replaced the wildlife refuge. Eventually the small channel itself was filled in and became the lovely curving avenue it is today. But the people of Cork never imagined its fine four-storey stone buildings could be treated to such flagrant debauchery. The windows in the higher stories are smashed with flying grenades and the interiors set alight. James and Seán feel the terror of the people as the flames grow, and like a scene from hell overtake and devour everything in their wake. As hours go by roofs begin to collapse and walls implode. The fire grows completely out of control. There is nothing to be done but watch the flames shoot up into the sky in their myriad colours of yellow and orange and red and wonder how and when it will all end. But the night seems endless.

There is more terror to come, however, and on a different scale altogether. Arson is not the only crime, and it is not the worst crime that will be perpetrated this night.

After the Dillon's Cross ambush, the escaping IRA men led by Mick retreat into Goulding's Glen and disperse. But one of the men, in his haste to disappear, loses his cap and does not bother to retrieve it. The military pick it up in their search for the culprits, and realise it is their ticket to finding at least one of the ambushers. They gather up their hound dogs, give them a good whiff of the hat, and make their way in hot pursuit. The capless IRA man and his partner had worked their way down into the valley, across the glen and back up the steep slope of the other side. They have friends there, two brothers, one of whom is known to take care of guns, restore them, hide them, account for them. It was a job he did for Tomás MacCurtain, and any man who was trusted by Tomás is not doubted. Close to the property they meet up with the younger brother Jeremiah and walk to his house with him. The ambush has been over for an hour or two. They talk of the details with Jeremiah and listen as the military start to work their way out of the Victoria Barracks across the glen. The sound carries with the wind and the men realise whatever the military are up to won't be regulated by the purveyors of law and order. Nevertheless, Jeremiah is light-hearted. He tells his friends he has come from confession, something he has not done in years, and he feels like a new man. He tells his friends to go on home and be safe, and as if he has had a premonition, he adds, there is no use in all of us being shot. They drop their guns there, believing them to be safe, and head out. After all, with martial law, getting caught with weapons is the latest excuse for capital punishment. It will be much safer to travel without them.

The two brothers, Jeremiah and Cornelius Delaney, are long-time members of the IRA, having joined up in 1913 at its inception. They are older than a lot of the Volunteers; Cornelius is thirty-four and Jeremiah is twenty-nine. This day, as per O'Hegarty's orders, they have holed up in their parents' home believing that they will be safe there from any fallout from the ambush. They are sound asleep in an upstairs bedroom when a group of Auxies led by dogs surround their home. It is two o'clock. The brothers are known to the police as Sinn Féin supporters. Their names, like so many others, are on a list of IRA men to watch out for. A list probably compiled with the help of informers. The hounds lead the military straight to the back door of the house. On a count of three the door is kicked in, and Special Forces men, those who work intelligence for the enemy, dressed in regular clothing pretending to be visitors to the area, bound up the stairs with their fingers on their triggers. Jeremiah wakes up, jumps out of bed, and begins to make his way across the room. He is shot at close range in the heart and falls to the floor. Cornelius is riddled with bullets as he lies in his bed. It all happens in mere seconds. The Auxies turn and dash back down the stairs looking for more men. Their sister flies from her room and goes to her brothers. Jeremiah, lying on the floor, kisses the crucifix his sister holds to his lips and closes his eyes for the last time. She turns to the bed; Cornelius looks at her and puts his finger to his mouth. Sshhh. He is worried the Auxies will return to the room and finding her, shoot her as well. But their sister sees hope for Cornelius despite the blood pooling in the centre of the bed. She runs from the room to get a doctor. Halfway down the staircase she is met by a Special Forces man waving a revolver and a flashlight. With his thick English accent, he demands to know if there are other men in the house. She hits him in the chest with both hands and pushes past him. Why? Are you going to kill us all? She spits the words at him and runs as fast as her legs will carry her to get a doctor and then a priest. It is all to no avail. Cornelius will follow his brother to the grave in just a week's time.

James and Seán know the Delaney brothers well. Cornelius especially is known to them as one of McCurtain's most trusted men. The brothers were quiet and dependable. They could be counted on at the drop of a hat and there were times that Tomás, and then Terrence, relied on them unerringly. It will be early morning before James and Seán and the rest of the Cork No. 1 are devastated by news of the murders. At this moment, they are watching as walls implode and explosions continue to go off. The sensation of nausea grows in the pit of James stomach. It is not just the fact that the British forces are perpetrating this terrible deed and getting away with it. It is the toll this fire, if it ever ends, will take on the people of the city who are already struggling to get by. So many businesses are being destroyed; even the biggest department store in the city, Cash's, is engulfed in flames. So many people will have no jobs to go to in the morning, or any morning in the foreseeable future. Entire families who are dependent on the income those jobs generate will suffer. James wonders if the bakery where his own father works will be left untouched. He suggests to Seán that they leave the city centre now and move down the island to where James's father spends his early morning hours each day baking the bread to feed the city.

As they bike towards the eastern part of the city's core, James stops dead in his tracks. It is six o'clock now, both men have been up all night and they are exhausted. Standing at Parnell Bridge looking across the river at the City Hall, they see the first flames of fire exploding through the upper windows while the Auxies in their trucks toast each other with their half empty bottles of whiskey and fire their rifles at the sky. In the City Hall, the public records kept for hundreds of years, comprising the written history of the city and the surrounding area, are quickly nothing but ash flying through the windows and into the night sky to be carried away by the wind out to Cork Harbour and lost as specks in the ocean. But this is not what compresses James's heart. What makes hatred boil in his soul is the sight of the beautiful Carnegie Library next door. Free to the citizens of Cork, rich and poor alike, the library is a place where James and Seán spent many an engrossed hour of their boyhood. Full to bursting with books, fine, beautiful editions of the stories of Ireland's glorious past, shelves and shelves of books of history and geography and biography and adventure. James knows where each section lies in the beautiful, rounded building. He knows each volume of legends, especially those authored by Lady Gregory, and the ancient Celtic tales that James and Seán grew up on. It is panic-inducing to watch it disappear. The flames erupt and grow so quickly they are barely across the bridge when it seems like the entire building is engulfed. Hundreds of books, rare, old collections, newer best-sellers, books on anything you can imagine, gone up in smoke and the elegant building with its circular walls and small turrets, on its way to becoming rubble.

James and Seán are too exhausted to watch the destruction of their library. They turn to the road to make their way home. It is not so far, and as they continue east, they are grateful that it is almost dawn and that the Auxies are coming to the end of their orgy of destruction. It means their own neighbourhoods are probably safe. But as they cycle away, behind them they leave the remnants of untold businesses and homes smouldering into history. It has been a nightmare, unheard of in the annals of Cork's history, a new low wrought by the enemy.

James falls into his bed with his head spinning and every bone in his body aching. He feels overcome with frustration, rage, and helplessness. He cannot imagine what O'Hegarty will say or do. James dreams of Thomas Ashe, frantic in his chair tied round and round with tight ropes, unable to move, his face blue, slop and spittle oozing from his tortured mouth, tears dripping down his face. He cannot even call James's name.

Within three hours James is awoken. His mother calls to him. There is a car outside, down the street. Just sitting there. There is a man at the door asking for him. James rolls out of bed, still in his clothes of the day before. He comes to the door to find Peter. Let's go. Mick is waiting for us. Without even a glance at his mother James grabs his trenchcoat and closes the door behind him. The two men walk down the street and as they do so, the car pulls ahead and goes around the first corner. It is Jeremiah Grey and Murphy in the car. They pull over and wait till the men meet up with them. Once inside the car they head straight out to Lakelands. We have unfinished business, says Murphy. And James knows instantly that George Horgan is doomed. Gone is the good will to give him a second chance, to take a risk that he may turn, or see the error in his ways. The Delaney brothers were murdered in their beds last night. Murphy is seething and the words shoot out of his mouth like fireworks. At their parents' home where they thought they were safe! Why would the Tans go there? They had nothing to do with the ambush! Murphy does not yet know the whole story of the visit by the capless ambusher. He does, however, know that the lists of IRA suspects, composed and posted in their barracks by the military, are done almost entirely with the help of informers. O'Hegarty is done with them. From this moment forward all informers will be interrogated, executed, and buried on site. Florrie, as intelligence officer, will compile this information and the location of the burials. No one else will be informed. This scum of the earth will never be spoken of again. It is more than they deserve and better treatment than the Irish get under British watch. George Horgan is the first to fall under the new official policy. He will not be the last.

    The car turns quickly into the old estate and Jeremiah Grey drops off his passengers and saunters over to the storage shed to see if there is any breakfast to be had. He too was up half the night listening to the goings-on, and he is worse for wear. Murphy heads straight to the barn with James and Peter and Danny in tow. James can see that Horgan has been anticipating their return. His face is not as swollen, and he is obviously anxious to prove his worthiness in order to return to his former life. Before Murphy can say a word, he pipes up, I have racked my brains for you and there is only one other thing you might want to know. I think I can recall several of the names on the list they were compiling of men being watched. Spit it out then, says Murphy. Horgan gives over five names, three of which are Brigade Volunteers but not active ones. James memorises the names. Murphy gives the order. Right, then, untie our prisoner, men. Peter and Danny move forward, and Danny takes a knife out of his pocket and slices the rope on Horgan's feet, but leaves his hands tied at his back. He grabs him by the arms and helps him stand. Horgan is smiling in anticipation of going home. He looks over at James, but James quickly drops his eyes to the ground. Immediately Horgan senses a change in circumstances. He looks anxiously at Murphy. You have been found guilty of spying for the enemy. Your sentence is death. Horgan looks at Murphy with confusion written across his face. What the fuck are you talking about? I've told you everything I know!

Murphy says nothing, but turns and walks through the barn doors into the field. Peter and Danny each have Horgan by an arm and James trails behind. He can feel his headache growing behind his eye, pulsing inside his head. His gun rubs against his body with a cold intensity. Horgan is trying to turn around and see James. He is yelling. What are you doing? Where are you taking me? Why are you doing this? James tells Peter and Danny to rest for a moment. He walks around to face Horgan. Your masters set the city on fire last night. And they killed two of our men in their beds while they slept. They found them because of people like you. Are you proud of yourself, giving information to the likes of those animals? James turns and walks on. Horgan is surprised by the news of what went on overnight, but he is more concerned with what is about to become of himself. That had nothing to do with me. Nothing at all. You have to believe me. His voice is taking on tones of panic that James recognises. Don't waste your time, says Murphy. You have a moment to say your prayers. Horgan looks wild-eyed at Murphy. You're going to shoot me here in this godforsaken place? What's wrong with you? And while Horgan protests, Murphy nods to Peter and Danny and they tie Horgan's feet and force him onto his knees. You may have a blindfold if you wish, says Murphy, but Horgan's mind is not processing what Murphy is saying. He looks at James. Don't do this. You don't have to do this. Murphy looks at James. Firing squad is best. Do you have your gun loaded? Aye, and James retrieves his gun from his holster and holds it by his side. Horgan's eyes grow into slits, and he sends sparks flying at his captors. You fucking bastards. Liars! I am glad I told the Tans what I know. I would do it again tomorrow. As Murphy and James raise their revolvers to take aim at Horgan's chest, he looks James in the eye.

God help you… But whatever expletive Horgan was intent on calling James is halted before the sound can reach his lips and dissipates into the air. He gasps quietly with the powerful implosion of bullets inside his heart. In slow motion James sees him slump forward and fall sideways onto the earth. James watches. He waits. He does not know what for. Then he can feel it. Horgan watching him before he slips out of time and into eternity. A shiver goes up his back and, in his mind, he yells at Horgan as he slides away. I had no choice. This is war. Murphy walks over to the body, still in slow motion and aims carefully. He fires a bullet at close range into the side of Horgan's head. James sees it enter the short thick hair just above Horgan's ear. It does not disappear as it did with Dinny. It goes right through his skull and out the other side, causing a ricochet on the ground.

Horgan's upper body jolts up, stays suspended in the air, it seems to James, before falling gently down to meet the earth again. Then the moment is over, and time returns to its regular steady beat. Murphy walks briskly away, back to the storage shed where Jeremiah and a sentry have stepped outside at the sound of the shots. They are surprised that the execution has taken place so quickly after their arrival and they did not even know it. They look at Murphy for an explanation, but there is none given. Get the shovels, is all he says.

It is noon before the grave is finished. The day is cold and the breeze off the sea leaves a dampness in the air that eats through clothing and straight into the men's bones even as they break a sweat shovelling out the hard earth. Eventually Murphy nods, and Peter and James, who happen to be taking their turn digging, throw their shovels to the top and clamber out of the hole. Horgan's body has been set to the side of the barn where his eyes stare up at the sunless sky, and his hands are crossed over his torso. Murphy has sent the sentries down to the lookout points at street level. He does not want this event to be leaked to the rank and file. All four men take a limb, and they carry Horgan to the side of the grave. On the count of three, says Murphy, and they roll the body into the hole It hits the ground with a thud and the earth shakes slightly. Then Danny and Murphy lift the shovels and begin to fill it in. The men take turns until the grave is filled. Then they take the strands of sod that they had initially scraped carefully off the surface and replace them. They are lumpy, though, and need to be jumped on and forced into place.

Alright lads. Let's get out of here. Murphy takes the other shovel from Danny, walks to the storage shed and puts them inside. Grey walks over to get the car and the five men sit in it in silence. The day is dreary, and as they descend to sea level down the long road, they are immersed in a thick fog. Jeremiah curses. He does not care for driving in fog. The chances of hitting something are increased exponentially, necessitating a dramatic decrease in speed as he does not wish to damage his customer's cars. James feels claustrophobic. Murphy sits in the front, James behind Jeremiah with Danny and Peter beside. They pass Blackrock Castle, and James is suddenly reminded of his ride back to the city in the cart looking at the stars and feeling relief that there would be no executions. Not even twenty-four hours ago, he thinks to himself. Fuck. Let me out. James taps Jeremiah on the shoulder. I will meet up with you at Wallaces'. Murphy is immersed in his own thoughts and does not even look over at James as Jeremiah pulls over.

James hops out of the car and is struck by the stench of the smouldering remains of dozens of buildings that wafts across the city. He walks to the top of his neighbourhood, the highest point, and looks north and west. What at first seems like fog, James notes, is not fog at all but smoke trapped in the damp air, blotting out the fresh sea breeze and replacing it with a sickening, cough-inducing char that coats the lungs and leaves a fine black powder on anything or anyone who stands still long enough to collect it. Indeed, there can still be seen the last vestiges of flames shooting out here or there where some explosive material has been touched by the heat. It is Sunday afternoon and there are people out everywhere. Some may be on their way to Mass, but many wander the streets aimlessly, dazed and in shock or agitated and in excitement, exclaiming, crying, trying to comfort neighbours whose lives have been altered suddenly and violently by the loss of everything that ever belonged to them. It is devastating to witness but somehow James cannot help himself. He works his way closer to downtown. Looking across the river he can see just how little remains of St Patrick Street and the streets that intersect it. In some cases, there are only single walls of stone left standing from the formerly beautiful architecture, rubble everywhere.

Later, when an accounting has been made, an inquest held and after an international outcry, the numbers will be shocking. Almost three hundred homes destroyed or damaged. Almost eighty businesses completely destroyed, or damaged, and or looted. And this by the British military. Westminster will try very hard, even with outright lies, to blame the IRA. But the truth is obvious. In the meantime, the people of Cork will suffer through the worst winter since the famine, with hundreds of people out of work or homeless. Within weeks the city will be completely devoid of provisions and unable to meet the demand for basic living supplies. The mayor will make a plea to people across Ireland, across the British Isles and in America to donate whatever they can. Blankets, clothing, food, furnishings; the mayor, on behalf of the people, will gladly accept your generosity! When money and supplies begin to pour in, especially from the Irish in America, the people of Cork are astounded. After witnessing this, the head librarian of the now burned-out Carnegie Library will follow suit. He will send out an international appeal. We have not a single bound volume left. Every book lost. If you have a book you no longer need, we will gladly accept it as a contribution to rebuilding our library. Before he knows it, boxes of books, single volumes, and hefty cheques will begin to arrive from far-off places around the globe. The generosity of the world will leave the British politicians looking like thugs and the British military like criminals.

In the meantime, James does not know what to do with himself. He is anxious and overwhelmed. His head pounds in the spot behind his left eye. Arson, fires like no one has ever seen the like of, shootings, murder, and execution. It is like a vision of hell, a visualisation of a sermon of hellfire and brimstone that he has heard at church from time to time from the older priests. Will it ever end? Is it worth it? Were Terry and Tomás just dreaming all those years? Their whole lives spent talking about freedom. Planning, organising, recruiting, training, scheming, and the weeks and months suffered in gaol. Will he, James, live to see the end result of this chaos? It is quite possible he will not. So many have been shot. There is the list, which he is on, along with Murphy and O'Hegarty and others. He was being watched the night of Tomás's murder. How many other nights has he been in their crosshairs? James fingers the beads in his pocket. He thinks of his count. Six now. He resolves to go to Mass and confession before next week. He is a soldier fighting a war. But it never hurts to hedge your bets. It is the wonderful thing about

Catholicism. There is a loophole for every sinner. James will take advantage and cleanse his soul. I will slip into an evening Mass one night soon, he thinks to himself. After all, Christmas is coming, and I may as well get confession over with sooner than later.

James meets up with Seán at the Wallaces' each morning the following week. Every day that they cycle through the city they are astounded by the destruction. The sensation of feeling completely overwhelmed and helpless in the face of destitution does not diminish. Each day Cork City is in the headlines of papers from around the British Isles. They shake their heads but are not surprised reading Hammar Greenwood's lies to the public. Seán recalls the note sent to him as he stood on the dock with his brother's coffin. James notices his old friend is beginning to wear his heart on his sleeve. James can tell just by looking at him that he is feeling depressed, sick at heart and even, James wonders, lonely. He recalls Seán's thought to get married before he was called home by O'Hegarty. But he dares not mention this to Seán. He wants to ask him if he plans to return to Canada, to the girl of his dreams, but he can sense from Seán that he feels trapped. I will not bring it up now, James thinks to himself. After all, we are all trapped by this fucking war.

It has been quiet all week. The military are hiding inside their barracks toasting each other for a job well done. But James takes advantage of the subdued atmosphere and goes home to his parents. On Sunday morning he attends Mass with his mother and father and younger siblings, something he has not done in weeks. Together, the family takes up a whole pew. When it is time for the homily, the priest enters the lectern and pulls out from a pocket several sheets of paper. Today instead of a homily we have a message from the bishop. He proceeds to read the five-page letter. It is a condemnation of everyone in Cork, on any political side, but especially on the side of the IRA. The bishop does not see their activities as the activities of men fighting a war for freedom. The bishop sees the IRA as murderers, kidnappers, ambushers. Forthwith, anyone who engages in these activities is excommunicated.

James sits listening to the bishop's letter. Anyone who takes part in any of these activities is excommunicated. Imagine that. No more coming to church, no more sacraments. If you die now, you die a lost soul, vulnerable to the possibility of hell. No recourse to be had through intervention of the Divine Will. No prayers will be heard. And if the demons drag you down to hell you can burn there without recourse for all eternity. James's heart freezes just a little, even as he is thinking it must be some wild mistake. The bishop is not well-liked. Though he preaches against the seven deadly sins, he suffers from the first and worst of the list: pride. The bishop insists that he be addressed as Dr. Cohalan, in recognition of his advanced education, instead of simply Your Excellency, or Father, for his humble service to man and God. He is seen as a collaborator with the enemy. Nevertheless, excommunication? Eternal hellfire? This is a sobering thought not only to James but to all the men of the IRA. It is a sobering thought to any man who faces the prospect of capture and execution by the British military. A sobering thought to men who are putting their lives on the line every time they walk out of their front door.

James leaves his family at the church and heads out to the Wallace sisters. He does not wish to feel disturbed by the Bishop's letter, but he is. He knows what O'Hegarty will say in response, and it will hardly bear repeating for the cursing and trashing of priests and their power over the people. He knows even what the so-called saintly Liam Lynch will say. He will accuse the bishop of plotting with the British. But he is interested most in what Father Dominic will say. Father Dominic who ministered to both Tomás and Terry is the man who will have the last say as far as James is concerned.

In the back room with O'Hegarty and Murphy there is also Tadg and Seán and a few others. The men are discussing the bishop's letter, just as James expected. He pulls up a chair, but just as he does a red-faced courier runs through to the back and stops dead in his tracks. O'Hegarty knows instantly it is trouble. What is it lad? Spit it out, he barks with rising intonation. The boy hands him a note. O'Hegarty reads it and stops, looking into some far-off space with a rising flush on his face. The men's talk wanes, and they all look to him. Well men, it seems the Tans have been busier than we thought this week. We should have known better. Someone has led them to the hideout at Lakelands. Some fucking little worm of an informer. They know that Horgan is buried there. The barn and the shed are in flames as we speak.

SPY

CHAPTER 10

DECEMBER 1920 – FEBRUARY 1921

The drops of rain hit James's trenchcoat like pellets propelling him forward with each laboured pedal of the bicycle. He can feel the sting of them battering his back. So heavy do they fall, and at such an angle, that they seem not to be coming from the sky at all but hurled sideways through the air. Seán, who is riding in front of him, has his collar up and his head down and his trenchcoat wrapped around him in the wind like a beleaguered flag. As they move north along the Blarney Road the air becomes colder and the rain begins to transform into complex flakes of snow adhering to their coats and caps, so that when they finally pull their bicycles up to the side of the pub in Blarney, the sentry chuckles at them. The pub is the very one through which they tried to blow out the wall into the RIC Barracks adjoining it back in June. The barracks is boarded up now and deserted, but the pub is still standing, the demolished wall rebuilt somewhat, if not to its original standard.

The barman directs them to head up the narrow stone stairs at the back of the room, and after shaking out their coats and caps they do so to find the upper echelons of the IRA in the room. O'Hegarty is holding court. Some of the men, such as Liam Lynch, Florrie, Jeremiah and Jim Grey, Tom Barry, greet them with a quick nod or salute while others such as Dan O'Donovan, Tom Crofts, Pa

Murray continue to listen. Murphy is reporting the very information that James had supplied to him yesterday about military movement in their area of the southern city core. As James and Seán grab a chair from the back wall, James can feel the heat of eyes on his back and he nonchalantly turns with his chair in hand to find the beady, prying eyes of Martin Corry sending malevolent sparks his way. Although he does not feel cool at the sight of Corry, he plays cool and ignores his presence, continuing to move to the adjacent wall where it is a little more difficult for Corry to stare him down. Just to be sure, James plants his chair slightly behind Seán's, cutting off the line of vision to Corry. But he cannot cut off the sensation of uneasiness that Corry's presence elicits. For a split-second James can see Dinny's legs kicking in the air, his face turning blue, and his pleading, terrified eyes staring at him. But the vision is lost when he hears his own name spoken out loud.

O'Hegarty has informed his officers of his most recent conversation with Collins. He has decided that Collins is right, the Cork area needs a dedicated intelligence squad. If they had heeded this same advice from Collins last year, they would have been aware of the barracks' stockpile of petrol. What they might have done about it is not suggested and indeed unknown. The men of the brigade who act as intelligence gatherers have done a spectacular job thus far. But it is clear since the burning of the city that they all may live or die based on the intelligence they can gather. Who knows what the British have up their sleeve next? A dedicated intelligence squad is the only way to prepare for attacks, and more importantly, to continue to find weaknesses and pressure points in the British military machine which they can exploit. Collins has insisted that they move quickly and decisively to form a coherent squad that will keep Cork No. 1 and GHQ informed of all British movements in the area, and O'Hegarty has agreed. O'Hegarty announces that Collins will fund a squad of six men full time. The squad will report to Florrie. O'Hegarty has already considered the possibilities. He lists six men that are unattached, that is, not responsible for a family, and able to work full time for the brigade on the measly four pounds per week allotment. After this basic requirement, they have been chosen for their trustworthiness, their dedication to the cause, their handiness with a gun, combined with the courage to use it, and finally, their wily ability to run circles around the Tans.

James's head goes up at the sound of his name, and he looks at O'Hegarty. Seán had already told him about a conversation between O'Hegarty and the battalion commanders. The discussion then was an effort to determine who would be suitable as members of this newest squad. Neither James nor Seán expected their names to be put forward. Seán is too well-known, and James is already a member of the ASU as well as part of the most active company in Cork. As if he has read James's mind, Mick raises his hand in protest. Sure, Séamus is already working in the ASU and he's on my team. I am not prepared to let him go. O'Hegarty speaks up. Aye, he's a popular one, that, he says with humour and an undertone of sarcasm. But do you want to argue with Collins? His name was put forward as a direct request from GHQ. The squad stands as we've named it. Séamus will remain available for your team. Sure, your company does half the intelligence of the city anyway Mick. Some of the room chuckles, knowing the statement is true enough, but others resent Murphy's notoriety and thoroughness. Not everyone is happy to see the famous footballer become the famous IRA Captain. Corry continues to scowl. Little acclamation do I get beside the big football boyo, he thinks to himself, even though I am the one taking on the dirty work. O'Hegarty reads his men's faces like a mother bear surveying her rowdy cubs, ready to swat them into place if need be. He does not mind singling out the more successful of the group. Just last week he made a purposeful visit to some of the other battalions, demanding that they muster up some courage and take on the military who pass through their areas daily without so much as an upturned finger much less a grenade to delay them. They might as well be serving those British bastards a cup of tea on their way through. A little heat, a little competition is just what those less courageous types need. O'Hegarty makes his point without even a glance in James's direction. James looks to Florrie, who gives him a nod, as if to say we'll talk later.

Talk later occurs with all six members of the new squad at the Wallaces' after curfew. There is James's old friend Mick, surfaced recently from the Dillon's Cross ambush, none the worse for wear. There is one of the many Aherne brothers, whose grandnephew-to-be will one day, in the far-off future, become President of Ireland, though such a thought is beyond formation at this moment. The other three are from battalions around the city, and of the three

Hegarty, O'Brien, and Mahoney. Mahoney is given the co-ordination role. Florrie is quietly, deadly serious. From this day forward gentlemen, consider yourselves spies. If you have any hesitation about this, now is the time to speak up. You all know how *we* treat spies. Let there be no illusions about the nature of this job. If you are caught, the enemy will be no different and, in fact, your treatment will be worse. You know that is the absolute, unexaggerated truth. James's mind wanders. He sees himself picking up Horgan off the floor and repositioning him on the stool. He sees Mick's powerful arm swinging forward, fist clenched. Then he blinks it away. He is becoming good at redirecting his mind. Practice makes perfect.

Florrie continues. First order of the day: the establishment of a wire-tapping centre. It will be manned twenty-four hours a day. Every telephone call that happens to or from a barracks will be listened to, notes taken, and dispatches delivered to the intelligence officers. Second order of the day: permanently manned observation posts of whatever barracks are left across the county. There will be posts designated around the high points of the county with use of binoculars and telescopes to maintain a constant lookout of the goings-on in the larger barracks, such as Macroom. Every man who works these stations will need to be trained with flags for an early warning system. Thirdly, we will set up a coordinated supply system with the railways. Many of those workers are with us, as you know, and they have found some interesting ways to transport goods under British noses. We will be bringing in more ammunition, if not guns, to maintain our supply. We will work in coordination with GHQ to achieve this. In addition, we will need to be more coordinated with the postal service. While some bags are still being checked, there are others that get by. We will be working on a way to read every last insignificant postcard that is on its way to being delivered to the military, whether at the barracks or elsewhere. Finally, the telegraph service will have to be mined. We have a couple of boys there, but we need a coordinated regular system that keeps them out of danger. As you know all of these activities already exist. Your job is to turn each of them into a reliable system of information gathering, distribution and transport.

Florrie surveys the faces in front of him as O'Hegarty looks on. Just to be clear, none of you will be working these particulars. It is your job to set up the systems, working with whomsoever you can on the ground. Once they are operating, you collect the information that is gathered through your own systems and networks and bring it to me in a succinct concise package daily, weekly, hourly, if necessary. We need your good judgement. We need your ability to influence the men to take risks, to muster up some balls and do it with a smile and a good morning under British noses. One last thing, and this may prove to be the most important: we need you to get to know these military bastards and any little titbits of information they let drop. You will be given an extra stipend of a pound a week. This is for buying drinks at the pubs. Worm your way into their good favour. Tell them whatever you need to. Douse them with drink and see what slips out. Given the braggarts and brutes they are, it may not take much to find out critical information. For instance, as you know, we are still looking for Captains Hollywood and Kelly, the sadists. They are elusive. We need information if we are going to get those two. They are too smart and too cautious to be found on a lark. Also, we are always on the lookout for informers. Who is hanging about them? What is their conversation? If someone is passing information, what is it? They will need to be dealt with, and quickly, before they can do any more damage.

    O'Hegarty walks around the table and thinks before he speaks. The burning of the city, the existence of the YMCA spies and informers, the purse on his own head, the murder of the Delaney brothers, all of these things have shaken him. He knows the next few months will be critical. They must convince the British that the IRA will never let up. That it is hopeless to believe they can be quashed. That they are pervasive across the city. That they, the IRA, are not afraid to take everything they have and use it against them. The British are as predictable as black skies before the rain; they will pull in more men, be as brutal as it takes to get compliance. With martial law, their every firing of a gun, beating with a rifle butt, and burning of a house has been legitimised by the British government. Collins is right: the only way they can keep up the pressure without landing in gaol, or worse, is to know their every move before they make it. O'Hegarty stops his pacing, places his hands on the top of a chair and leans into the men. I am not going to tell you boys that this is an easy job. Sure, we all know it isn't. It isn't for the faint of heart. Each one of you comes recommended from your officiating commander. We need this squad to work like a well-oiled machine.

The British shouldn't be able to take a piss without us knowing. Our key objective once you boys have set up the various systems is to focus on the upper echelons. We have eliminated a good number of their G-men and military intelligence. But they will be replaced. And we want the top brass. They are next on our list. These British bastards don't give a shit about their lowly rank and file. But tap the shoulder of their upper crust la-de-da captains and generals, that's what will get them reconsidering their stay here.

The following day, as James and Seán scout out the possibilities for a wiretapping centre, they are once more to be found on their bicycles working their way across the city through the wintry weather. It is bitterly cold, though still and sunny, and their breath creates tiny clouds in the air that trail behind them as they pedal. James's fingers feel like they are frozen solid in a tight grasp of the handlebars despite the woollen fingerless gloves his mother has knitted specially for him, and as he rides, he alternates placing one hand under his opposite armpit for warmth. They pedal through the city centre on their way out. They are happy to leave this area. A fine powdered ash lingers in the air and the apocalyptic landscape of lone walls blackened with soot and huge piles of stone and rubble stand in the open where a few short days ago the beautiful architecture of Cork City housed the goings-on of commerce and human interaction.

The shops that are still standing have made up their Christmas displays, but the entire city knows it will be a sad, depressed Christmas for most everyone. Good neighbours and good Samaritans have taken in the burned-out families, but there will be little Christmas shopping this year and not just because the biggest shops and department stores in Cork have been burned to cinders. For the IRA members and their families, it is not just the prospect of a poor material showing at Christmas that weighs on their minds. Many have spent their entire lives with barely an orange or a small sweet as a Christmas treat. What is bothering so many of them is the letter from the bishop condemning any of them who are active players against the British to excommunication. The bishop made it clear his excommunication order applies to all men in his jurisdiction of Cork City, British, Irish, or otherwise. But everybody knows there are few British military who are Catholic. In fact, the bulk of the military are already jesting with each other in the pubs, laughing at the bishop's decree. The IRA men, on the other hand, are not jesting at all. They may disregard him as a collaborator, like Liam Lynch; they may despise him as a traitor to the cause of freedom, like O'Hegarty; they may he thunderstruck at the pronouncement, worried for their soul, but whatever the case, no one is laughing. Neither is James.

Everyone is relieved when Father Dominic releases his own statement to Florrie and asks him to share it with the men. The men have a right and a duty to protect Ireland against the occupying army, he tells them. The bishop's decree does not pertain to them insomuch as they are soldiers of the Republic fighting for freedom. Keep up with the ambushes. Keep up with the pressure. Father Dominic sends his letter from Dublin. He has been sent by his order, the Capuchins, to attend some meetings. But no sooner does his letter flutter to the bottom of the post box than he is arrested by the Auxiliaries. Does the military know that Father Dominic's brother is brigade quartermaster in Cork? O'Hegarty fumes and stews. He contacts Collins. Can you do something? Do what? For Christ's sake I am not a fucking magician! O'Hegarty has no love of priests himself, but the gall of these British bastards taking on a man of the cloth. Collins agrees, but what do you expect? Do you think after three hundred years of outlawing priests, chasing them out of the country, executing them, belittling them, terrorising them, they are suddenly going to treat them with kid gloves? The Auxies in particular do not care for Catholic priests and are not afraid to let the world know.

Neither are they afraid to let Father Dominic know. Collins has his mole in Dublin Castle check out the situation. Yes, he is still alive. No, they are not treating him with any respect. Indeed, he is suffering the usual indignities tenfold. What's under that cassock, Father? Are you a man or an angel? Does an angel have a man's parts? Are you ready to fly away to heaven, Father? How does this revolver taste inside your mouth? Would you prefer this noose? See how snugly it fits! Join the Church of England, Father, and maybe we will let you live. Father Dominic experiences some difficulty turning the other cheek and praying for his enemies. He is tried by court martial in Kilmainham Gaol and found guilty of causing disaffection to His Majesty. Good Father Dominic, spiritual support to not one, but two dead mayors, chaplain of the Cork No. 1 Brigade, and a rebel completely and utterly, prays his rosary in Irish as he is sentenced to five years of hard labour. Off with the cassock and the collar and on with the prison stripes. You are just a lousy criminal like so many others of your nation. Enjoy Parkhurst Prison on the Isle of Wight, where penal servitude means hard labour, and hard labour means back-breaking, mindless toil.

Christmas arrives with a full moon beaming down on the city, exposing every last ghostly burned-out wall and pile of rubble. The city is covered in a fine film of light snow that reflects the moonlight, and though the charred remains of the major buildings stand as a hideous reminder to the people of British hatred, the black soot is gently shielded from their eyes as they make their way to midnight Mass. James walks with his family, his young brother Edward at his side, his unsightly shortened fingertips kept warm in his coat pockets. The British do not care about midnight Mass and the curfew is still in effect, so the pastors of the Catholic churches have moved it forward to the early evening. James's mother remarks on the beauty of the moonlight, but James does not comment. The luminosity of the moon will forever more remind him of burying his first body, Dinny, the grimace on his face frozen as he stares at James shovelling earth into his grave.

Reporters have been arriving from all over: the tale of the British government burning down a major city has to be seen to be believed. The City of Cork has become a spectacle. An inquest is called. But the reporting in the major Cork newspaper, *The Cork Examiner*, relied on by the people far and wide since 1841, spins a tale that has the people wondering what the truth is. Were the IRA responsible for some of the burning hoping to blame it on the Tans? Collins calls O'Hegarty. What the fuck is going on down there? The people are on our side, most of them at least, but it won't be for long if they are reading that shite in the papers every day. Aye, says O'Hegarty, well, there is one way to stop that.

A meeting is called for Boxing Day. At the Wallace sisters' shop, the men gather round the back room. We will be needing the biggest and strongest of the boys. And as many sledgehammers as we can get your hands on. Seán looks at James with a raised eyebrow. Sledgehammers? Aye, we will be teaching our newspaper friends a lesson they won't forget.

On the evening of the twenty-eighth, shortly after curfew, James walks carefully from the Wallace sisters' shop. He darts across the main drag and into another laneway, arriving across from his destination of Academy Street within five minutes. The premises of *The Cork Examiner* have been here on this narrow side street for decades when the paper was first started from a printing press of pamphlets in support of Catholic Emancipation, and the great Daniel O'Connell. It seems the current proprietors of the paper are firmly behind the bishop and in bed with the military. They need a little reminder of their original *raison d'être*: freedom from British tyranny. As James makes his way across Washington Street, he sees that many of the younger boys are already in place, leaning quietly inside side streets and laneways, lurking in the dark, keeping a lookout for any Tans sweeping the area. O'Hegarty has made sure they have already worked out a system of decoys to redirect any unexpected military presence by a chase out of the area and away from Academy Street. There are at least fifty lads stationed strategically inside a five hundred metre radius. James smiles to himself. They will give those Tans a run for their money if they come by.

As James walks north into the old narrow street, he sees Murphy, O'Hegarty, and others from his company, whose area it is, converge from the south. A van with its headlights out pulls up onto the walkway right against the stone of the building. Such a dangerous thing to do after curfew, but trust the Grey brothers, they are fearless. The back doors open, and a dozen sledgehammers are to be found neatly arranged along the floor. O'Hegarty goes to the door, opens it with a key (no one dare ask from where it came,) and each man picks up a hammer. Quietly they stream into the building. O'Hegarty lights the lantern and closes the door behind them. Then he leads them through the front office and to the high-ceilinged industrial back room where the two printing presses sit side-by-side. They are complex monsters, giant cubes of connected strips and slabs of iron requiring three steps up to reach their heights, where a series of connecting rollers feed the newly printed papers through to the end of long, back-and-forth conveyor belts, dry and ready to read.

On a table nearby there are several wooden frames full of the letters of the alphabet in a variety of shapes and sizes, carefully placed in small orderly wooden boxes.

Alright boys, get to work. O'Hegarty stands by while the sledgehammers rain down on the machines. The machines are remarkably sturdy, and the men find that it takes many hits to make even a slight dint. The cacophony of noise is deafening, and James takes no joy in this act of destruction. Nevertheless, he uses his upper body strength to wield the hammer like an axe with as much force as he can muster. O'Hegarty gestures and everybody stops. Alright gentlemen, I recommend aiming for the connections. And indeed, O'Hegarty is right. The rollers are knocked out of place, the lighter iron connections more easily transform into beaten and distorted lumps of metal. The typeface also is not as difficult to disfigure and render useless. O'Hegarty calls a halt, and the men step back to survey their handiwork. Much of the core of the machines is still in place but the destruction of some of the lighter parts will prevent publication of the paper until they can be fixed and reconfigured into the larger mechanism. That will do gentlemen; this will send our message, strong and clear. O'Hegarty dims the lantern and pokes his head out of the door. Jeremiah Grey opens the back of the van, the men replace their sledgehammers where they found them neatly in a long line, and then, silently and in complete darkness, they disappear in various directions. The entire enterprise has taken all of fifteen minutes. O'Hegarty is last, watching as Jeremiah leads his customer's van down the road and, following the hand signals of the sentries, makes his way back to a quiet sheltered parking spot. He will walk home through the alleyways and pick up the van in the early morning. O'Hegarty pulls down his fedora and raises the collar of his trenchcoat. But he salutes the sentries as he passes, quietly calling out a well done to the lads without so much as a glance in their direction. You can never be too careful. As for the lads, they cannot see his face, but they glow at his affirmation.

O'Hegarty's push to pressure the British further is realised quickly. The 4th Battalion, which covers the area east of the city, moves into attack mode. As if to prove their worthiness to O'Hegarty and the other battalion commanders, they take on the Tans in broad daylight. They do it vastly outnumbered and on the main street of the town with witnesses everywhere. It is in the small town of Midleton, far east of the city, where the Tans, and the RIC who have joined forces with them, have discovered a foil to any possible ambush and use their new formation regularly. Every day they march the main street, half on one side of the street, half on the other, marching in opposite directions towards each other. They march not close together but far apart with their guns at the ready. Collectively they have a three-hundred-and-sixty-degree view of everything about them. The people keep out of their way, lest they get nervous, or even just trigger happy.

The 4th Battalion knows this formation well, however, and they also know that the only way to hit these men is to take them by surprise. All at once, out of a narrow laneway six men stream into the middle of the street and open fire in all directions. Five Tans fall, the rest scatter, but two manage to get back to their barracks quickly to call for reinforcements. This has been anticipated and two miles out of town an ambush lies in wait for the reinforcements of both Tans and RIC, who barrel down the main road from Cork City at an alarming pace. Not fast enough to bypass the men who lie in wait. The Tender Crossleys are fired on. Two Tans are wounded. The IRA men escape unharmed. For now.

New Year's Day 1921 is a beautiful sunny day. The air is cool, but the wind is still. By mid-afternoon people are out and about on the street, many nursing their headaches and hangovers garnered from the previous night's celebrations. Neither hide nor hair has been seen of the Tans and RIC, who have been locked up in their barracks for the last three days. The people are still talking about the daring exploit of taking them on in broad daylight. The names of the IRA men who participated are pondered on and whispered about. Did you see who it was? Not everyone was from Midleton. Most of the men are from outside the town. Who sheltered them? How did they get away? Who had the balls to plan such an ambush? But all of the chatter stops when a convoy of Tans, standing in the backs of their trucks with guns pointed at onlookers, makes its way from the Cork City Road into the main square across from the courthouse. The colonel stands on the back of the truck and makes his proclamation. His harsh voice crackles through the air. As per order from the British government, the official reprisal against the attack held on December 29 against His Majesty's forces will now commence. He reads out the names of seven families from the Midleton area. Some are in town, others on the outskirts. They have been carefully chosen as families who are under suspicion of harbouring IRA members. Seven homes for seven dead or injured Tans. Tit for tat. With a cold and calculated determination each house is visited, an official proclamation read, and members of the household told they have exactly one hour to remove personal items. No furniture, bedding, or any useful or valuable thing allowed. We will be back in an hour to commence the burning of your home.

The people are shocked. Night raids by the Tans when they are on a drunken tear or just out for a party are regular occurrences, even in Midleton, but an official reprisal sanctioned by the British government? By the time the military has made its round of notices it is time to go back to the first house and begin. By now the entire town has been rallied and the crowds stand outside the first home to be burned. It is the district councillor's home, Edward Carey. He is known to be a Rebel sympathiser, and as political leader he can take the first hit. His wife is in shock and runs about the house picking up random items and putting them down again. Every so often she sends a child outside with utensils or plates or bowls from the kitchen. Not allowed, take it back in, is the inevitable order from the colonel. Eventually she stands with a pile of clothing and looks pleadingly at the colonel. I recommend you place your items back, away from the premises. The colonel is impervious to the tears and lamentations that are beginning to be shouted out by the women and children in the crowd. The men on the other hand are beginning to shout out other things. Step back, the colonel shouts in an authoritative voice, then gives the order to two of his men, who enter through the front door carrying axes. They make their way to the larger pieces of furniture, the kitchen table, the wooden bed frames, and smash them into smaller pieces, all the better to burn faster. As they complete this job, which only takes a few moments, two other Tans carry a bomb into the house, and place it on the floor. All of the Tans exit the house, but before they clamber back into the truck, they pull the plugs off grenades and fire them into the windows and the open door. The gasps from the crowd are audible, drowning out even the children who are crying pitifully. Mr Carey himself does not shout or plead or cry. As his young children hug his legs and his wife moans, he watches the Tans carefully, imprinting their images on his mind. You fucking little demons, he is thinking, don't think this will ever be forgotten. Every last one of you will be thrown out from this country crying or I will die trying. The colonel's truck backs out of the property and moves to the next home on the list. A truckload of Tans remains, shooting randomly into the air to keep the people back. They do not leave until the fire is blazing like hellfire and there is no hope of saving even a single wall of the home. When they are finished with their work for the day, having burned to cinders all seven homes on the list, the Tans return to Cork City, leaving the desperate residents homeless and destitute, dependent on the mercy of their friends and neighbours. It is a terrible omen of the year to come for all of Cork.

O'Hegarty snarls at James. Where is the fucking wiretapping centre? We needed it yesterday! James holds his ground. He has spent several days scouting out the best place to hide a room full of men twenty-four hours a day hooked into the existing telephone wiring that feeds directly to the British military. Not an easy task. But with the help of Seán and Mick, they have found the perfect location. It is north of the city off the Dublin Road where a giant billboard stands close to a convergence of wiring direct from Dublin. He has lads from his company digging a hideout as they speak. It is hard work; the earth is half frozen and they must dig behind cover of overgrown hedges with only shovels. An underground room takes a while, even a small one. Then it must be fortified with a roof of sorts and walls of sorts and some kind of heating. Finally, the wires must be spliced, and the listening equipment set up on desks. The whole thing will be a working operation within a couple of days, thanks to the colossal effort of his company lads, working at the behest of Murphy, and James's own ingenuity at stealing telephone company equipment to get the wiring work done. Only the men who will actually be manning the place are working to create it. Knowledge of its existence must be limited to those as close to the command structure as possible. O'Hegarty snorts. Good, the sooner the better. As soon as we can keep closer tabs on those fuckers the better off we will be. In the meantime, we will give them a taste of their own medicine.

James and Seán are called to the meeting. It is a larger meeting than most. O'Hegarty has hand-picked a crew of men from the various battalions. Murphy and most of the regulars from C Company are there, including Pa Murray, Tom Crofts, and the battalion adjutant, Charley Daly. James is happy to see his friend Tadg O'Sullivan. Florrie and the remainder of the IO Squad are also in attendance. Because these particular men have been called to the meeting, James knows this is going to be important. As usual Florrie begins. He is soft-spoken and behaves somewhat like an elderly gentleman, somewhat like an uptight schoolboy. But James knows that all of the decisions to deal with the likes of informers are vetted through him. He knows under Florrie's fresh, farm boy face, lives a calculating Rebel, honest, fair, but hardly squeamish. Given the situation in Midleton yesterday, it is important for us to make it clear to the enemy that such behaviour will not go unpunished. The Midleton incident involved the RIC to a great extent. Unlike the Tans, the RIC are fellow Irishmen. Those Irishmen should know better, and now they are going to learn their lessons. The RIC command centre on Union Quay is our target. Frank will explain his observations. Mahoney stands and informs the group in intricate detail, the movements of a regular detachment of RIC in and out of the Union Quay Barracks. It is a large four-storey building just away from the southwest corner of Parnell Bridge, down the street from the ruins that was, only three weeks ago, the Cork City Hall. It is a busy section of Cork, even with the City Hall and the library gone. Every day there is a group of twenty-five to thirty RIC, in formation, that move across the bridge on their way back to the Union Quay Barracks, having spent their day patrolling and harassing the citizens of Cork. They seem untouchable because they are a large group in such a busy section of town and it is the end of the workday, the streets full.

O'Hegarty pipes up. But they are not untouchable! All we need is the courage and the smarts to take them out. I do believe we have both in this room, gentlemen. The room erupts with aye and Up the Republic and banging on tables, but O'Hegarty raises his hand for silence. This will be a dangerous operation. There is a greater potential than usual for return fire. Our goal is to isolate the troops on the bridge and administer as many casualties as possible. Rout the fuckers. O'Hegarty's tone is low and menacing.

Florrie continues. We will work in teams. We need men to give us cover and men to fire. Each team must have escape plans A and B, and C if you can manage it. Teams will look out for each other and make sure that all are in retreat when the time comes. This ambush will be a little different due to our acquisition of a Lewis gun, thanks to Mick, who picked it up in Dublin last week. Again, the room erupts in cheers. Mick and a team of his choosing will man this. Obviously they will be arriving by car. They will park in front of the hotel at the corner of the bridge. Assuming the men were to actually cross the bridge, they would still have to get past the Lewis gun to reach the Union Quay Barracks. The range of the Lewis is such that it can hit accurately directly across the fifty yards or so of the bridge span. We will also have a team manning the bombs under the direction of Pa. Once Mick starts to fire, each team will have their direction to aim. There are only so many places they can run. We make our attack. Incapacitate them and get out of sight. In and out boys, that's how we need it to be. In and out, and home for tea.

James can see some of the men looking at each other. It is the question of civilians. A busy time of evening with people returning home at the end of a working day, with a Lewis gun firing so many rounds a minute and teams of men shooting revolvers and throwing bombs. This will be one of two things, thinks James: a massacre, or complete chaos. Either way we do not need civilians thrown into the mix. Florrie seems to read his mind and points out the obvious to the men. There may be civilians involved and I know some of the men are not comfortable with it. We have thought about this very carefully. Unfortunately, this is our best time of day to maximise our efforts. Doubtless any civilians will run from the area. As always, we must be strategic with our ammunition. Aim before you fire, and no one will get hurt. James looks at Florrie and although he has heard the contrary, he wonders if he has ever actually fired a gun in the heat of the moment.

James is quietly relieved that he is not with Murphy and the Lewis gun. Only three can fit in the car, as the gun itself takes up a seat. So, aside from the driver, Murphy has asked Peter to join him. James is to lead a team on the north side covering the exit if the Tans turn back. At a quarter to six he meets his handful of men at a quiet laneway a few blocks from the bridge on the north side of the river. They are due to converge on the bridge at six o'clock.

Twilight is upon them. The teams of men leisurely approach Parnell Bridge from all directions, most of them in trenchcoats and caps or fedoras. In this way their presence is merged with the businessmen and working people returning home at the end of the day. It is Tuesday, and the people have recovered from the New Year's festivities, such as they were in this dark, burnt-out shell of a city. Everyone who has a job to go to is back to their regular routine. It is cold and people are walking quickly, anxious to get home to dinner and a warm fire. The bridge is a swinging bridge that can be moved at a ninety-degree angle through a series of hand-controlled winches, to allow boats to pass through. There is a tiny glassed-in office-like structure at one corner where the lookout man waits and watches for boats needing to pass by the bridge. Today the lookout must be an IRA man, because right now, just before six o'clock, nobody is in the office.

James slows down. Tadg, who is walking beside him, does likewise. They stop and look at each other, two young men on their way home from work having a discussion, maybe about which pub to stop in. His team lingers behind him, spaced at intervals, walking in pairs. They are approaching the north side of the bridge and so are farthest from the actual barracks across the water. Looking across James can see a car slow down in front of the pub, pull over, and come to a stop. He knows it is Murphy and that they are setting up the gun for firing. But there are no signs of RIC anywhere. You do not know what is coming, he thinks to himself. If you are smart you will stay put. But you are not smart. You are only hateful. He stops and leans on the bridge and lights a cigarette. He can see across the water just underneath the bridge, the tell-tale signs of some of the men, probably the bomb unit waiting impatiently. He is happy to see his team are smart enough to keep walking past him, and they do so following the water, but do not cross the bridge.

The plan is to prevent the men from reaching their barracks. James and his men are on either side of the north opening of the bridge when a party of about ten RIC can be heard marching and talking together as they work their way down Parnell Place, the road that leads directly onto the bridge. They walk quickly, probably anxious to get to their barracks and settle in with some hot food. It is a much smaller group than the usual thirty. Lucky bastards, James thinks. He throws his cigarette into the river and puts his hand through his coat to retrieve his gun, but he continues to look across the river, watching Murphy's car. And just as it so often does for him, time slows down. He turns his head slightly and is watching the leader of the RIC pack as he steps onto the bridge. This man is a well-seasoned soldier; he is aware of everything around him, and he has already noticed James and some of the other men lurking about. He turns his head and looks directly at James. James keeps his hand in his coat. He does not wish to release his gun; it is too early to reveal it. He can see the RIC officer marching and turning his head to keep an eye on him as he moves forward, and then he sees him stop, the rounded O of the mouth frozen as he falls to the ground, the first victim of the Lewis gun that even at the long distance across the bridge is making the loud patpatpatpatpat sound that is the signal to everyone to attack.

As the bullets fly and the small homemade bombs sing through the air, James watches as the RIC and pedestrians crossing the bridge fall, and the civilians who are not down run for their lives. Some of the RIC throw themselves on the ground and begin to fire. But others start running back to the street. It is James's job to hit as many as he can as they retreat, and he sees from the corner of his eye that the men on his team are doing their best while trying to dodge bullets. He is not on the bridge and can therefore quickly take cover just behind the first light post abutting the road. He catches sight of a young cadet who has turned and is running straight back up the road from which he came. He aims his gun at the young man's back. He can see the effort he is putting into his sprint, his legs pushing off the ground with tremendous, desperate force, his arms pumping, his head down as if to shield himself. He was a runner at school, James thinks to himself, maybe a rugby player. Maybe he even plays the hurling. He takes aim. He follows the boy in his sights. He imagines closing his finger on the trigger, the bullet straight as an arrow slicing through air, hitting him in the back, shattering his backbone, the boy falling to the ground. But the thought occurs to him, I do not have to do this. I do not have to shoot a boy in the back. Fuck Murphy, he thinks to himself, and lowers his gun. Tadg, who is standing close by, sees James aim and sees him put his gun back in his holster without firing. He looks at him questioningly. And suddenly the patpatpatpatpatpat has stopped and the men are running in all directions and on the bridge lie six RIC and five civilians. James walks calmly across the street as he replaces his gun in his holster, nods to his team members nearby, and pulls down his cap. All of them will have ducked out of sight into laneways and buildings and side streets before reinforcements or ambulances can reach the bodies strewn on the bridge.

We are off to the country, Jimmy lad, for a little training! O'Hegarty is in much better form this week. The wiretapping station is up and running. He has had details of harried phone calls to and from Dublin about the Parnell Bridge ambush. The other members of the intelligence squad have been equally busy. There is a schedule of trains with secret compartments carrying ammunition in from Dublin. There is a regular crew of postal workers handing in mail to be checked before it is even sent to or from the barracks. There are several lookout stations, one with a telescope keeping an eye on the major barracks at Macroom Castle, north of the city. There is information about various military supplies being delivered, which are nipped off the trains before they arrive in Cork and taken to a safe dump at the agricultural grounds. The groundskeepers, the Neville brothers, are in complete control of the place and allow the deliveries in late at night, where they stack and store the merchandise, everything from new uniforms to toilet paper. It will all be lost in a year's time, the brothers given away by an informer, but they will at least escape with their lives. In the meantime, they are now in possession of not one, but two Lewis guns. The senior staff needs to be trained in their use. It is a dangerous machine that eats ammunition, but it is an excellent tool for defence. If the British try another large-scale event like the burning of the city, the IRA now has the means to challenge them. The best place for training is a place the British are never seen nor heard, the Gaeltacht, where there are still many families who do not know a word of English.

It is James's first time in the Gaeltacht. The men, about a dozen of them, are put up by a few Irish speaking families deep in the mists of Gougane Barra, source of the River Lee and ancient home of St Fin Barre. The lake here is surrounded by high rugged hills and St Fin Barre's little chapel sits on a tiny island a mere jump off the shore. The chapel was built in the eighteenth century but the ancient altar stone inside it is believed to have been used by

Fin Barre himself, and by the Celts before him. The entire place is as picturesque as a postcard, even in January when the water is grey and icy cold, and snow hides the crevices atop the protective, brown-grey hills. James quickly realises just how poor his Irish is. It has been a long time since he learned the language from Terry and practised at the Gaelic League. He listens carefully to his hosts, poor farmers living in the hills in a whitewashed cottage with thatched roof, speak to each other in soft lilting voices. The sound combinations and intonations are easy on the ear and make English sounds seem so harsh, stilted, Germanic, and above all, foreign.

The men gather in the tiny village of Ballingeary, a curvature in the road where more small, whitewashed houses join together along the edge of the road and where a few tiny shops are dispersed amongst them. The men who are boarded in the farthest homes are brought via donkey and cart. This is rural Ireland in the extreme, nothing but hills and valleys, green meadows bordered with short rock walls and hedges, and at this time of year, wind and rain. Were a truckload of Tans to come racing into the area they would find men and women and children who would either ignore them or watch them like a spectacle. No one would speak English to them, even those who are fluent English speakers. They represent the enemy, and have done in this poor, quiet, picturesque spot, for as long as anyone can remember.

While James and his mates wait to begin their training in the remote village area of West Cork, far away in New York City, Muriel, the most beautiful woman in the world, continues dark and deep in her abyss of grief over the loss of her husband. On the other hand, her sister-in-law, Mary MacSwiney, is tired of talking. She has spoken at the American Commission on Conditions in Ireland, as well as meeting after meeting in New York, telling the tale of British oppression and the daring fight of the IRA to push them out of the country. Mary is good at talking but it is beginning to annoy her that the most beautiful woman in the world, the widow, Mrs MacSwiney, is getting all of the honours and all of the attention.

She is the first woman ever to be given the keys to the city of New York by the Mayor. She has men of every description tripping over themselves to pay their respects. Fierce, relentless Mary does the work. Beautiful, sad Muriel reaps the rewards. It is time for Mary to go home and get back to her private school that she runs with her sister Annie. Muriel on the other hand has had many invitations to stay and recuperate for a while longer. The constant talk about Terry leaves her in a depressive fog punctuated by bouts of lavish attention from politicians, the media, and various Irish organisations, all of which only temporarily lift her spirits. Also, she does not feel up to looking after her daughter. They will both be expected to live in the oppressive atmosphere of her mother's estate. But that is not what bothers the most beautiful woman in the world so much. She is after all, her own woman now. What bothers her is the child's seemingly cosmic connection with her dead father. Soon after Terry's death she caught her baby whispering into the phone, talking to Terry. It was as if she was answering his questions. Muriel stood and listened, and an eerie sensation that he really was talking to her permeated her very being. And it happened more than once. Muriel does not feel up to dealing with otherworld connections, her mother, or the arrests and shootings. She rationalises to herself that her baby is in good hands and better off with someone who is not grieving. Her mother adores the child and spends hours upon hours with her despite a nanny and several servants at her fingertips. Muriel shakes her head when she thinks of her own childhood where she barely saw her mother and spent the bulk of her young years with cold nannies playing by herself. She has written home to her mother and to Annie, Terrence's sister, that she wants her daughter to get out and be involved with the kindergarten with lots of opportunities to play with other children. She does not wish her to be raised in wealthy isolation like her own lot. Muriel will stay in New York, she tells everyone, because she is a catalyst for donations of cash. The money pours in wherever she shows herself, clothed in black, billows of veils covering her exquisite face. When she does speak, she says little, but she says it with such charm and intelligence and humility that she is irresistible.

O'Hegarty walks down the curving road to meet the men who have gathered by the last house. They are leaning against the short stone wall, some of them smoking, all of them freezing. Collars are up, caps are down, jumpers are layered under their coats, socks are layered in their boots. In a rare showing of good form, he begins to tell a humorous story to lift the men's spirits and take their minds off the cold. Pa Murray looks at him as if he has too heads. He sucks back on his cigarette and James can see that Murray would like to tell him to shut up but thinks better of it. From around a distant bend Murphy appears, travelling from the opposite direction, walking alongside a cart in which sits a local farmer. A donkey is pulling them along the frozen road as slowly as possible. Loaded in the back is a large wooden crate full of various items that might be sold in the local shop: large bags of sugar, flour, dried currants, potatoes. But underneath all this rest two Lewis light machine guns, the prize of the Cork arsenal.

The solid, square man who holds the reins looks much older than he actually is. Like farmers everywhere, his face is lined and prematurely aged from the elements and a lifetime of back-breaking work. Nevertheless, when he speaks in his native language, he smiles and tips his hat to the group of men. *Día dhaoibh ar maidin.* God to you this morning. The men respond likewise with *Día dhuit ar maidin* or *Móra na maidine duit.* God to you this morning, or a more Englishesque alternative, good morning. There are far too many men to ride in the cart, and so they follow on foot, chatting amongst themselves until they come to a cut-off and turn from the valley floor to a narrow uphill path that meanders across the mountain face, avoiding large outcroppings of rock. It is a long way to go, but the exertion of walking up the mountain warms them. As they come to the crest and look into the distance, they are delighted to see a tiny cottage not far off with smoke wafting from the chimney. As far as they can see it is the only house in the little valley that faces them, a lonely vista, strewn with rocks and brambles, and at the base of the valley a narrow creek rushing over large stones racing to meet up with the river Lee a mile or so downstream. The rundown appearance of the cottage tells the men it is a place that is no longer, or rarely, used. Crumbling stone walls surround the tiny property which is overgrown with nettles. Nevertheless, the smoke from the chimney holds promise on this wintry morning. But before they can entertain ideas of a hot cup of tea, the men are called to the wagon and asked to help unload the guns.

James helps heave the box off the cart and carry it to a sheltered position close to the stone wall. When he turns around, he sees a beautiful young girl walk out of the cottage. She is dressed in the traditional style with a thick woollen shawl covering her shoulders, and wide enough to protect the length of her arms. It is crossed over her chest and kept in place by a leather belt tied around her tiny waist. James smiles at her as she walks by, but she averts her gaze and clambers onto the back of the donkey cart. Clearly, she is the farmer's daughter. Her long curly red tresses blow to the side as she slowly disappears over the crest of the mountain. James will think of her often, especially each evening when she arrives to leave fresh bread and a large pot of stew or soup for the men for supper, and eggs and porridge for them to make themselves in the morning for breakfast. By the end of the week, she is speaking to James in her lilting Irish and James responds, he knows not so well, judging by her gentle laugh and quizzical questions. He is teased by the older men, but he does not care. They are better at Irish and can plainly catch his articulation errors. But it is worth the mockery because the girl is a sight for sore eyes and relieves the monotony of long dark nights full of stinking, coarse men.

O'Hegarty means business. He calls on Seán Murray to demonstrate how the gun works. O'Hegarty wants them to be able to shoot, but not just shoot. He wants them to be able to assemble and disassemble this gun so that the various parts can be hidden if necessary. It is a large gun to conceal, and will be more easily out of sight if it can be stored in sections. Seán Murray is O'Hegarty's latest recruit. He likes the man, and he likes that he understands the British point of view and can easily predict their possible moves. He has designated Seán as training officer for Cork No. 1. Seán is a veteran of the Great War and knows the various weapons of the British military well. Indeed, he counts them as his closest friends, having saved his life various times while he fought the Hun in the trenches of France. He is a big solid man, a no-nonsense kind of guy, a few years older than James. Though he worked for the British army, he has no love of the British, and decided early in the conflict to switch teams. He knows the Lewis gun well and he also knows that O'Hegarty will not be impressed at how slow and difficult it will be to set it up. But Seán keeps his thoughts to himself and proceeds to show the men exactly how it works. O'Hegarty calls James to come up first while the men watch. He knows that Jimmy knows his guns, having trained him in large part himself.

James looks at the array of large unwieldy parts laid out on the ground. The rest of the men circle round and watch. Alright Séamus, let's begin with the thin snout here and the large barrel. James rams the pointed snout into the barrel. He looks at the various parts to decide what is next and correctly chooses the pistol grip, sliding it into the other end of the barrel and with just a little difficulty rotates it ninety degrees to snap into place. He sees that this section is done and examines the pieces on the ground. He threads the gas plug, the shroud cover, and the sight together, and attaches them to the barrel. The gun is long and unwieldy. He screws in the foot-high brace just beneath the snout to steady it on the ground. Next comes the magazine. It is a round pan magazine that holds exactly forty-seven large three-inch bullets, each with a sharp point. Each bullet must be snapped into place around the circle one by one. The casing twists onto the top and voilà, James has completed the gun. But it is a machine that needs coaxing. Nothing slides easily. It needs oiling, suggests James to Seán. Aye it does, but even with oiling it is a very tight fit. And not any easier for the weather. Well done Séamus. O'Hegarty does not smile but he claps James on the back and tells him to see to the tea while some of the others get a chance at disassembling and assembling.

James enters the low door of the cottage and must wait for a moment to allow his eyes to adjust to the lightless interior. If it was not for the few sparks left on the fire the room would be as dark as a grave, and indeed these tiny damp cottages are the cause of many fatal cases of tuberculosis across the country. There is the large fireplace carved into the wall with the kettle hanging on a bar directly over the embers. Beside the fireplace are three stools, obviously constructed by hand using local branches. There is a dirty, woven wool rug on the floor, and a table with two rustic chairs and a large teapot sitting atop surrounded by an array of mugs. Against one wall is a bed of straw, above it a tiny window, for now closed off with a shade of linen to offset the cold. James wonders at the ability of anyone to raise a family in this one simple room. And yet he knows that the people in this area did just that and in many cases continue to do so.

He wonders further how all of the crew will sleep in this tiny place tonight. But for now, he builds up the fire and hopes the kettle will boil before O'Hegarty has decided they have suffered enough in the cold.

After a week of assembling the Lewis guns, disassembling the Lewis guns, shooting the Lewis guns, carrying the Lewis guns to different locations, running with the Lewis guns, and recharging the Lewis guns, O'Hegarty finally decides an ambush is in order. We will give it a go, he tells the men. Thanks be to God we can go home to our own beds, snaps Pa Murray. The men laugh, but they are all city men and they have had about as much as they can take of rural cottages in the middle of nowhere. They jump in the cars with the Grey brothers and cheerfully return to their urban lairs sprinkled around the cityscape. On the way they ponder a week lost out of their territory. They do not know that O'Hegarty is thinking far into the future and planning for the day he can get his hands on a Lewis gun for each battalion. For now, the men who do not have his foresight think that a few revolvers in several hands is a better weapon altogether.

The ambush that O'Hegarty is planning is to take on the regiment of Auxiliaries that continue to roar out of Macroom Castle in their Crossley-Tenders, and head straight for the countryside, shooting down anyone in their path. They are known to house the group of murderers, led by British intelligence officers in mufti, who come out at night long after curfew and roam the countryside staking out suspected IRA members. Several have been murdered in their homes over the last few weeks. The Auxies from Macroom are known to have participated in the burning of Cork. The IRA are about to give them a little payback. The ambush will be a message straight to the heart of the British establishment: official reprisals from the British will be met with official reprisals from the IRA. O'Hegarty, James, Florrie, and Murray have travelled to this area to stake out the exact place and time for the attack. They walk along the lonely road from Cork to Macroom. Dripsey, a small village, lies about half way between the two. The men choose a bend in the road bordered by a stone wall and sheltered by thick hedges and tall trees that provide cover and shelter a narrow laneway off the road. It is a perfect location to hide and watch as the enemy advances. This is the area of the 6th Battalion, and Frank Busteed is the vice officiating commander. James does not know him well yet, but the day will come when James will count him as a friend, although whenever he begins to tell the lurid stories of his glory days in the IRA, James will find an excuse to leave the room. But what will happen here at Dripsey will not usually be included in Frank's stories. Not unless he has consumed a significant amount of Bushmills.

Two miles west of Dripsey along the Macroom road is Coachford, so named two hundred years prior because of the tiny bridge that horse-drawn coaches used to cross a small stream, a tributary of the River Lee a mile south. In this area the British ascendancy is represented by Maria Lindsay, occupant of Leemount House, widow of John Lindsay. The owners of Leemount House trace their ancestry all the way back to Cromwell's invasion of Ireland and the Ulster plantation (where Cromwell paid his soldiers in stolen land from the Irish whom he massacred or sent to the barren rocks of Connemara, there to starve, he hoped, as it would be a mercy to the world to be done with papists, especially Irish ones). With this large chunk of free land and the income associated with it, Lindsay's ancestors were able to extend their holdings around the country. In short order, two large chunks of land, two thousand acres and nine hundred acres, were added to their allotment in the south of the country. In 1920, Leemount House is not so grand a house as Irish big houses go; after all it is just one of a number of smaller estates that were built to help manage the land controlled in this area. However, it sits in a beautiful spot on the shores of the River Lee and is more like a farm compound than an estate house, walled around by the traditional rock wall designating the estate demesne and full of small and large outbuildings. In this home Mrs Lindsay lives, catered to by her servants and her butler-come-driver, Mr James Clarke, a staunch Ulster Protestant.

With O'Hegarty's okay, Busteed proceeds to make arrangements. They will lie in wait at the appointed bend in the road until the Auxies descend on them and then open fire with a Lewis gun. They will take out as many as they can, a reprisal for lives lost and homes burnt in Cork and Midleton. Frank sends out word to his battalion and chooses the men who will participate. The story will be told that he did not inform anyone until the day of the ambush itself. James will not say so, but he will think it must have been otherwise. There is no other explanation for the disaster that follows.

A large number of men are involved in the ambush. O'Hegarty does not attend, but James is instructed to make sure enough guns and ammunition are supplied to the men from a dump outside the area. He goes with Frank and Jeremiah Grey to pick up the supplies. Revolvers, ammunition, a dozen rifles, and one precious Lewis gun with ammo. It is a bonanza of firepower. More in one place than James has ever seen. They take the arms to Jackie O'Leary, the commander. He whistles when he sees the lot. James realises that the sight of so many guns makes O'Leary nervous, and watching his face he feels just for a moment a rush of doubt overcome him. It is a long enough moment that he will always remember it as a portend. Once his job is done, unloading the weapons from the secret dump, James and Jeremiah return to the city and leave Busteed and O'Leary to move forward on their ambush plans.

By noon on the day of the ambush, January 28, the entire village of Coachford and most of Dripsey knows what is about to happen. How does this happen? Nobody knows for sure. What is sure is that the parish priest, aware of what is to transpire later in the day, insists the children be sent home from school early lest they be caught in some way in what is to follow. How Mrs Lindsay discovers the intentions of the 6th Battalion is hard to say. There are several differing accounts, and further accounts disputing these; nevertheless, discover it she does. She sees the priest walking down the road and asks him to come into her car to chat. He does so and then leaves. Then, she has her driver James take her into Macroom to speak to the British commander, who happens to be a distant cousin. She tells him everything she knows: the location of the ambush at a crossroads known as Godfrey's Cross, and the fact that there is a large number of weapons rumoured to be on hand. She leaves the commander, content with her conscience, and knowing that as a representative of the British crown he will know exactly what to do with the ungrateful rebels that would wreak havoc in her village.

However a second priest, Father Sheehan, though known to be pro-British, when the going gets tough is an Irishman at heart, and when word of the imminent ambush reaches his ears, he proves his true allegiance by going straight to Jackie O'Leary and telling him that the British know all of their plans right down to the number of weapons. O'Leary and Busteed confer. Sure, Sheehan is nothing but a British tout. He is probably just saying as much so as we will put a halt to our plans and let the British off. They decide to proceed. Reckless? Perhaps. But O'Leary thinks to himself, I do not wish to deal with O'Hegarty's wrath if the information turns out to be false. At about five o'clock with all twenty-five or so of their men in position, with loaded guns on both sides of the road waiting patiently for the trucks to rumble past them, five separate groups of British soldiers leave their trucks behind them and begin to sneak up on the ambushers. Luckily for some, a young scout keen on his job notices British movement and quietly runs back to warn the encampment. But it is not soon enough. A battle between the two forces wages for the next four hours. Two IRA men are injured and eight are captured by the British. O'Hegarty knows, even before O'Leary, that it was Mrs Lindsay of Leemount House who gave it all away. He makes the call to Frank Busteed. Pick her up. Pick her up now! We will use her as collateral against our boys. It is our only hope, God help them, they may be doomed anyway.

James and Seán back in their home base, central Cork, quietly tap their glasses and down their shots of Jameson sitting at the bar on Douglas Street. They are expecting O'Hegarty to drop by for a word. Neither man is smiling. James in particular is feeling morose. His efforts with the wiretapping centre have proved fruitful but not good enough to stem the tide of arrests, shootings and the creeping incidence of informer-related incidents that continue to hamper their efforts at undermining the British. Just last week James's fellow IO, Mick, was picked up in the dead of night at a supposed safe house and is awaiting trial. Denis Hegarty, who worked the northern district, was shot dead in his own home. None of the men could attend the funeral for fear of being targeted by British intelligence, who were sure to be waiting for them.

It is everything O'Hegarty has been barking about these last weeks. The British are getting ahead of them. A couple of weeks earlier, the first of three arms dumps discovered by the military in out of the way farms found young Mary Bowles, a rebel at heart, fifteen years old, carrying guns under her skirt and walking across the fields as the house was being searched. Two other smaller dumps discovered outside the city borders, put there for safekeeping, magically discovered by the Tans in so-called random searches. No other nearby farms searched, no trouble going to exactly the spot where the guns and ammo both are buried in outsheds. Now this old cow

Lindsay walking straight up to the commander's front door and spilling everything she knows like some fucking little queen of the Castle. The upshot is eight men awaiting trial. Because they were involved in a gun battle, they will surely be hanged. Three families devastated, their menfolk dragged to prison, no one left to man the family farms. In Liam Lynch's territory of North Cork several of the boys have been shot and one, Joe Murphy, has been tried and will be executed tomorrow. This month alone at least five innocent citizens shot in their homes or at least on their own property by trigger-happy marauding Tans hunting for IRA and frustrated when they do not find them. Now there is General Strickland on the front page of the papers making appeals to the citizens of Cork to turn on the IRA and report to the military everything they know.

Seán and James drag on their cigarettes and blow smoke into the air. Seán especially is feeling the stress of the latest captures. His eyes are sunken, his hair unkempt. He takes off his round specs and cleans them with a hankie from his pocket, taking time to position them carefully on his face. What do you think Jimmy? Are we going to win this war? Don't know my friend, but I know one thing, we will probably die trying. James, who has trained himself in a constant emotionless face, even to his friend, lets neither hope nor despair shadow his features. The door to the street opens and the wind blows in with O'Hegarty. As usual he has his fedora pulled down over his bristly hair and his trenchcoat collar pulled up against both the wind and undue observation. He signals a hello to Mrs Stenson behind the bar and sits at a table in the far corner of the room near the exit leading to the back door. O'Hegarty never stops thinking ahead. Do you have a nice hot cup of tea at the ready ma'am? And Mrs Stenson brings him a steaming hot mug. Does she know who he is? No. But she knows almost everyone who steps foot in her bar is IRA. She welcomes them wholeheartedly and prays her rosary for them every night. She asks no questions and is told no lies.

As O'Hegarty warms his fingers curled around the mug he looks at Seán and James. What the bloody hell is wrong with you two? You look like you just lost your mothers for God's sake. James pipes up with, Seán was just wondering if we will live or die for Ireland sir. Well, if we die, boys, sure there is no hope for the rest of them. So, you'd better take care of yourselves. This is O'Hegarty's attempt at humour and Seán and James agreeably grunt in accord. Then

O'Hegarty's face gets serious. Seán you should congratulate your friend here. Thanks to his wiretapping centre we have discovered certain information. It has been corroborated by our mole in the Victoria Barracks. We now know that you and I both have been targeted by the Tans. Time to go on the run Seán. Sorry to tell you but you will have to quit your job. In fact, you will have to walk away for an indefinite time. If you choose to stay in the city you will have to be very, very careful. Under no circumstances go home. Your sister Mary is already in their sights and God knows it won't take much for them to arrest a woman. Although I'd be afraid of tackling Mary myself. Another stab at humour, but this time it falls flat. Seán is crestfallen.

James attempts to lighten his friend's load. Never mind Seán, I can let you in on my circle of safe houses. We won't starve, and we'll have a roof over our heads. Under no circumstances Jimmy will you do any such thing! O'Hegarty's twinkly Irish eyes are deadpan, staring James down. You two cannot be together on the streets. Your name has not yet surfaced. Perhaps that list with you on it went to the grave with its author before it was shared. But it won't be long till you are added anew if they see you with Seán. We have lost two of our IOs already; we can't afford to lose any more. Extreme caution on your part, Jimmy. And on yours Seán, if for different reasons. Morning meetings at the Wallace shop from different directions is the only time I would expect to see you both. But just so you know I won't be around much. If either of you boys need me, I will be in touch with Florrie at least once a day. I am moving out of the city and into the Gaeltacht. I would be quite a prize if I were to be picked up. Collins would be spitting angry and kill me himself, before the British could even get organised. In the meantime, I am putting Tom Crofts in my place for anything urgent going on in the city. Seán does not smile. He sits quietly for a few moments then stands and holds out his hand. He shakes O'Hegarty's hand and wishes him luck. *Godte tu slan, Ádh mór ort!* May you go safely, good luck! Sure, talk to my Da at the races if you need me Seán, or Edward at his school. I keep in touch one way or another. Or send out word with the lads. Seán nods as he opens the door to the street. The two men watch him walk past the windows, his head bent against the wind.

With a last gulp of tea O'Hegarty stands. Jimmy, walk with me.

I am on my way to see Florrie. He pulls his cap down over his ears and lifts the collar of his trenchcoat high around his neck. He places his hands deep in his pockets and both men hit the street with a determined if somewhat leisurely pace. O'Hegarty talks. James listens. Your man Tadg O'Sullivan, he has been on the case of finding certain leaks. He has found what we are looking for, and of all places in the post office. Ironic, isn't it Jimmy? We have the entire postal service working for us and with us and who is using the same system? The enemy. There is one man there who was the liaison to the others and to the British. I suppose he was putting his messages in the bags after they had already been searched by us. Was? Asks Jimmy. Aye, he has sent off his last message. His work for the enemy is over. But he has left us his legacy. James wonders at who was responsible for that interrogation, but he knows not to ask. He will talk to Murphy later.

Your friends from November. James immediately realises O'Hegarty is talking about the executions of the YMCA spies. They were just a few of the group, as we all knew. There are more and they are doing us damage Jimmy. He looks James in the eye. They have to be dealt with. It is them or us. James knows that the Dripsey boys weigh heavily on O'Hegarty. Both men understand that all eight of them will be hung or shot, no contest. There is the slightest chance that the kidnapping of the woman Lindsay will have some sway via the British government. But knowing the Auxies as they do, if the men are not hanged, they will be murdered in gaol and their deaths put down to resisting arrest. It will be the same for anybody else who is picked up in the city. It would be the same for them. O'Hegarty's voice is low and menacing. I have thought about it and there is nothing for it but to round up the informers at once. We will use the Auxies' favourite method: swoop in on them when they least expect it and leave everyone around them terrorised. Let's send a little terror *their* way. We will see how that works for them.

Murphy knows how to pick his people. Among them, Willie Barry, captain of D company, Pat Hayes, Frank O'Mahoney coordinator of the intelligence staff, and James. They are meeting at the Seaman's Bar on Albert's Quay, just past the burnt down City Hall, not their usual Douglas Street pub. They are in enemy territory, the very Protestant sector of the city, right on the quay where many Protestant industrial businesses are thriving. James has made it a practice to drop by for a pint and survey the room. He tips his hat to the odd group of Auxies, as is the practice by many of the customers. He listens in on conversations, and sometimes when he is with Tadg or Mick they will join the party. He keeps his story simple. He is in the insurance business, but times are tough, and business is hard. He keeps track of who else in the room tries to speak with them. Murphy, on the other hand, likes to drop in and pump his status as a well-known athlete. His drinks are bought for him, and he melds into the crowd like molten lead working the room, adhering to whomsoever might be dropping information. It is Mick's choice to meet here tonight. He enjoys the irony of it. The men sit at a table in the corner and go over the list that Murphy has memorised. A couple of the names are of prominent businessmen. They are well-to-do, successful men belonging to the chamber of commerce. As such, they often have the ear of the Cork Corporation Municipal Council. A couple are unemployed; a couple are Great War veterans, and one is employed at Victoria Barracks. But according to the latest information they are all part of the Anti-Sinn Féin Society. The same group that have been posting notices in the newspapers with threats and ultimatums; the same group that Dinny spoke of. Clearly Dinny, as a junior member, did not have access to the upper echelons of the organisation. But he knew they existed. He was right. James closes his mind to the image of Dinny on his knees in the rain, begging for his life. He takes a swig of his pint and lights a cigarette.

Murphy goes over the strategy. They will split up the group and watch each target for a few days. Modelling on Collins, Murphy would like to take them out all at once. It is Collins's calling card, and it will show the world that they are one tight team, a national organisation, not just a bunch of boyos from the country. It will require coordination. Each informer is to be left where he falls, somewhere in public, and a sign is to be left by the body. A sign claiming responsibility and warning anybody else who might take it into their heads to make a few pounds on the backs of IRA shot in their beds by the Tans, or tortured in gaol, or dancing at the end of a rope. Their sins will be announced to the world for all to see. Their fate sealed. But wait, perhaps a letter of warning is in order. Let's give them a chance to redeem themselves. Let them know that we are onto them. Maybe they will see the error of their ways. Will they be given a reprieve? Of course not! But at the very least, they will get a taste of their own medicine. A taste of terror. To be followed by a public shaming.

In the year of Our Lord 405, a young teenager hanging out at Bannavem Taburniae, his father's holiday villa on the southwest coast of Britannia, sleeps peacefully in his bed. It is summer and the breeze blows in through the open window looking out onto the rocky beach. He is sixteen years old, a strong boy, athletic, handsome, and a Rebel at heart. He does not care for his father Calpernius's religion, nor his mother Conchessa's exhortations to become a priest like his grandfather. Calpernius, a deacon at the church, frets over his son's casual approach to life. In short, he has attitude, and it is not attractive. I have spoiled him rotten, his father thinks. It is my own fault. Reap what you sow. How now to change the lad's attitude? Conchessa however does not fret. She has been in love with her beautiful boy from the moment she rested his tiny beating heart against her own. She knows his heart is good and once he gets over his youthful rebelliousness, he will become a man of stature. Perhaps he will move to Londinium, the largest city on the island, where the important men hold court and there are many opportunities. Wherever he goes and whatever he does, he is bound to be an impressive figure. This she knows. She cannot in her wildest dreams, however, imagine how that is about to unfold.

The villa is walled on all sides, for protection against the odd band of marauding Picts from the north or wild Welshmen from the west. What passes for centurions in this far-off corner of what was once the farthest reaches of the Roman Empire would certainly not pass in Rome. Nevertheless, they keep watch at night. They look out to the distant hills. They do not look behind them at the sea. Why would they?

The moon glows in the sky, full and round, leaving a shimmering quadrant of light reflecting off the quietly flowing waters. The sea laps onto the rocky shore and the men on the *currachs* do not speak, but gesture quietly to each other, and wait patiently until the tide brings them onto the shore. Each boat is half empty, leaving plenty of room for booty. At once a handful of men work their way up to the villa. It is large and imposing, and therefore likely to contain precious objects. They quietly hoist the youngest among them, agile as a monkey, atop the wall and he scales the top and works the gate from the inside to open it. The men stream in covering the entire house in moments, throwing vases and chalices in their linen bags. The boy upstairs hears something and awakens. He comes down the stairs, thinking someone in the household cannot sleep and has dropped something on the floor. He is faced, not by the cultured, well-groomed man that is his father, nor by the well-dressed quasi-centurions that are the guards, nor by the simple servants. Instead, he faces the wildest-looking group of men he has ever seen. Some are tall, some short. They wear animal skins and coarsely-woven woollen shifts that do not even reach their knees. Their feet are bare, and their flaming red hair is long and coiffed with resin into outrageous designs. But their bodies are chiselled, hard knots of muscle protruding from their impressive shoulders supporting wraps of fur to the length of their legs.

At the sight of the boy, the largest of the men turns his head to his group and smiles at them. At once the boy is rushed, picked up by a dozen hands, one of them across his mouth. They begin to retrace their steps and carry him out of the door, and it takes the boy a few moments to overcome his shock and allow the dread to flow through his body and out of his mouth. He wriggles in their grasp like a worm on a hook and manages to scream as he is carried down to the beach and thrown into a boat. His last look at his parents is in the moonlight, rapidly disappearing in the distance, his mother wailing, his father more helpless than he has ever seen him.

It is not a long trip across the water to Hibernia. By dawn they have reached the coast, then allow the current to carry them home to the north of the island. It is from here that the boy Patricius is taken as a slave inland to Slieve Mish, their lone mountain home, to toil in loneliness and obscurity for the pagan Celts.

Slieve Mish rises above the plains like a sphinx. The flat top of the mountain is covered in sharp rocks, but the slopes are fertile and green. It is here on these slopes that Patricius spends all of six long years tending to the sheep of the Celts. He is but a slave, and most of the time they ignore him, unless a sheep goes missing.

Patricius is left to fend for himself, watch over the sheep, and protect himself from the terrifying buzzards and huge ravens that nest on the mountain. When the Celts have plenty, he has enough. When the Celts have little, he has nothing. Because of this there are times he almost starves to death. But there is a kind elderly man, a Celt, who watches over him. He is a tough old bird, and he begins to teach the teenager everything he needs to survive, after he changes his name to Pádraig. The Celts successfully resisted the influence of the Romans for a couple of hundred years; they will not have any part of their language, even a man's name, corrupted. Over the course of the seasons, Pádraig learns their ways: the festivals, the marriages, the skirmishes and battles between tribes, and the undying influence of the druids. He sees the power and prestige of warriors, the admiration and respect of artists, the exceptional poetic abilities of the bards and the skills of rhetoric and politics of the chieftain. Pádraig thinks of his friends back home whose education is just becoming serious, focused on careers, and rues the days he spent skipping school and making fun of his teachers. He challenges his mind by learning the language and analysing the power relationships of the clan. And when he watches the cruelty of the druids and the suffering they are responsible for inside their own clan, he feels hopelessness so extreme he begins to pray. He thinks of the prayers his mother and father taught him and the rituals of the Christians that he laughed at; the focus on goodness, and virtue, and peace, and he sees what all good men see eventually. He sees we are doomed, full of pettiness and greed, and jealousy and lust, and he sees that our only hope is exactly what his father and grandfather tried to teach him. Too bad he has had to learn the hard way.

Pádraig turns to prayer and like a hermit, his spiritual life becomes so intense his physical life becomes almost meaningless to him. But one fine morning he awakens out of a dream hearing a voice. The voice tells him it is time. Time to go home. Pádraig waits and watches until the moment is right and then makes his escape. He heads for the coast where he can find a boat to take him across the water. Because he knows the language, he seems like a Celt himself and a happy group of wayfarers invite him to join them crossing the sea. They are a rowdy bunch, and Pádraig decides they will become his first effort at conversion. The men laugh and cajole him about his one true God. That's a joke they say, do you really believe some poor bastard who was hung on a cross by the Romans three hundred years ago is God? The only God? Have another drink! But Pádraig is given an opportunity to prove his thesis.

He sticks with the men once they land, but it is a wild place where they disembark and begin their trek inland. They quickly run out of food and need to hunt. Nary a rabbit nor squirrel crosses their path. After days the men become weak with hunger. They decide to give Pádraig's God a shot. In front of the now chastened, hungry group, Pádraig gets down on his knees and, raising his hands to heaven, prays for succour from the one true God. Before he finishes his prayer a herd of wild pigs reveal themselves out of the bush. The men set on them and their food-related worries are over. As the juice from the succulent pork runs down their chins, they decide that this strange boy Pádraig might be on to something. Once they reach a village, Pádraig goes his own way. He knows exactly how to get home. His mother falls down on her knees when her beautiful boy, now twenty-two years old, walks through her door.

Pádraig now knows his life's path. It is to become a Christian priest like his grandfather. He soaks up his learning like a sponge and thanks God every day for his re-found abundance in all things. But Pádraig cannot stop thinking about the Celts he left behind. Several years later he awakens to another voice. This time it is a voice he recognises. It is the voice of Victoricus, the Bishop of Rouen deep in the land of Gaul. Gaul is the Roman name for a region of France. They are Romanised and Christianised and inter-married with other groups now, but Victoricus knows that the island of Hibernia is bursting with Celts, pagan every last one, and controlled by those wicked, demonic druids. It is a scandal that his own people should still, in this day and age, live this way. They must be saved. He sends a local bishop, Palladius, to begin evangelising the country. But Palladius finds these Celts to be barbaric, violent, unpredictable, and unruly. He has difficulty with the language, not to mention their coarse customs. The Celts, for their part, can sense his Roman superiority complex and send Palladius and his retinue packing. The druids cackle amongst themselves as they watch his servants paddle back across the water, double time. They do not cackle for long. however. The chief druid has a nightmare, a prophetic dream, and shares it with the high king. Another will follow. It won't be long until this new one has the whole island on their knees in stone houses calling out Amen, Amen!

In his dream, Victoricus smiles knowingly at Pádraig. He hands him a letter. It is from the Celts of Ireland. As Patrick opens it, he can read the words, though he need not, because the voices call out to him. Holy boy, we beg you come back and walk among us once more! When Pádraig.'s mother hears that he will return to the Celts she falls on her knees once more and weeps in sorrow.

Many years later, when Pádraig is old and seasoned, and seen everything there is to see, he counts not hundreds but tens of thousands among his converts. In fact, he is well on his way to Christianising the entire country. But not every Christian is a good and honourable man. Patrick has to worry not only about the pagan Celts and their druids who constantly work against him: he must also worry about Christians from Britannia. There are many so-called Christians who wander the world performing the work of demons. One of them is Coroticus of Alt Clut, a king on the River Clyde in Alba, who likes to augment the coins in the counting room of his castle by selling the Celts of Hibernia as slaves. Coroticus is a Romanised Pict. He combines the swaggering superiority of the Romans with the ruthless barbarism of the Picts. Few will challenge him. He has trained his men to travel to far-off places, swoop in on horseback and round up entire villages. Anyone who fights back is killed instantly. It is a well thought-out strategy of using terror to subdue. He gathers up what men are left, takes them back across the water, and sells them as slaves. The women, at least the good-looking women, he keeps for his men. They get passed around from soldier to soldier and, if they survive, eventually end up in the kitchen with their much luckier less attractive friends and neighbours.

Pádraig has just left a village where he has baptised scores of new converts, when a scout chases after him and reports. He had no sooner left than the entire village was attacked by Coroticus's soldiers. The women stolen, many of the men murdered, the entire place looted. Pádraig is used to dealing with unruly Celts, but having to deal with evil Christians makes his blood boil. He sends a messenger after Coroticus demanding return of what he has stolen. He makes this demand in light of Coroticus's Christian beliefs. The messenger is laughed out of the camp. So, Pádraig makes a decision. He will write a letter. Not to Coroticus, but to the people. A magnificent letter in the style of the Gospels. A letter with a particular rhythm that Christians everywhere will recognise as emulated from the Holy Book. He will demand that this letter be read at every hamlet and village and church and monastery and every king's court, here in Ireland, and everywhere in Britannia. He will publicly name Coroticus as a traitor to Christianity, a man who cannot be trusted, a man whom every good Christian should steer clear of in the name of their own safety and in the name of the Christian community.

It does not take long for Coroticus himself to receive a copy of the letter in his castle at Alt Clut. He smirks at it, until he hears from the messenger that the letter is being read aloud to the people in every parish across the land. His homeland, where he maintains a certain reputation as a leader, and as a good Christian, where stories of his exploits in neighbouring lands are subdued and hidden. But the news is out now: Coroticus is a traitor, a hack, a tyrant, selling his own people, albeit spiritual kindred souls, that is Christians, for cash. Any good he might have done in his life is forgotten. His reputation is destroyed. He will never recover his lost status. He realises he's taken on the wrong man.

James is assigned several names from the list to put under observation. Murphy knows that James cleans up nicely, so he has him on the case of Beale, the wine merchant. With O'Reilly, the justice of the peace, Beale is one of the two who are well-to-do and well-respected. He is to watch and learn the man's habits, and in consultation with Murphy and the rest of the group, decide how best to flush him out and execute him. Where and when, without being seen, is the big question. They have not yet decided on a date, but it will be soon. Yet it is difficult. February is starting out mercilessly cold. People do not muck about outside; they rush to work and at the end of the day they rush home to the warmth of their dinner by the fire. There is little tarrying on the street. There is also the matter of the recent surprises by the British. Many of the men are on the run. Even Tadg has left the city for a few weeks. He was spooked, sure he was being tagged by British intelligence. O'Hegarty sent him to

England on business, just in case. Murphy has already given the squad a list of where these people work. The squad starts at their places of employment and follows them home. They work as a team of two or four in order to eliminate suspicion, taking turns passing by and keeping watch from a distance. They are looking for routines: pubs they frequent, stops they make, people they talk to. The days of meeting Tans or Auxies directly are over. Nobody in their right mind will do that anymore. The atmosphere is too tense, the episodes of violence too frequent, the politics too strained. James works with his team, watching, before and after curfew, during the day and at night. They meet with Murphy over the next few days to determine the facts. Routines, times, and places where the targets can be found alone and in an isolated area. Murphy is thinking in another few days he will have a plan. And then the worst thing happens.

Seán has left the city. He knows he is under observation by British intelligence. Since O'Hegarty's warning he has been very careful. James has done his own investigating and it is clear that British intelligence is keeping a close eye on both Seán's work and home. James knows that being on the run will be hard on his friend, so James will let him know when they let up. Seán moves out to the Cork No. 2 Brigade area, Liam Lynch's old haunting grounds north of the city, and picks up with a crew of men there who move around constantly, never sleeping in the same house two nights in a row. Thus far Cork No. 2 has been much luckier than Cork No. 1. Now that Liam Lynch is off working in Dublin for Collins, Seán Moylan has taken over its command. Moylan is not a man to take unnecessary risks. The responsibility of the men's welfare weighs on him. They have a series of safe houses where they know they are welcome. Any time of night or day they can find a warm fire, a simple meal and a barn or a mat on the floor in front of the fire.

After a week of managing being on the run Seán is exhausted. He is used to a clean, orderly home run by his sisters. He never has to lift a finger. They see to his laundry, his meals, and anything else he might need. They remain unmarried. Not even their good looks and comely figures can overcome the intensity of their personalities, their fiery approach to politics even in Republican circles of men who might otherwise be attracted to them. Seán, since he has returned from Canada, has become the man of their house, and their hope is that if the day ever comes when this war will be won, he will stay.

Seán has made an error in judgment. He has hooked up with Con Conroy. He should know better. Conroy was, until very recently, a mole inside Victoria Barracks. A tall, handsome, athletic twenty-six-year-old, Con is an ex-British army soldier who survived the Great War. He can play the British to a tee. But now some papers that he smuggled out were found in one of the weapons raids. The paperwork leads right to him. It is only because of Josephine, Florrie's lover, that he is still breathing the cold February air and not dancing at the end of a rope. Josephine caught the message and delayed it getting across to the colonel's desk until she could contact Florrie. Now Conroy is planning his escape to America to join his brother, because he knows what they do inside Victoria Barracks. He knows that chances are slim he will outlast this war. While Conroy waits for his ship, he is on the run, north of the city, out of the prying eyes of the British intelligence officers who are searching for him.

Seán knows Conroy supplied a steady stream of information to Florrie and O'Hegarty. Furthermore, he knows Conroy suffers from good spirits he cannot shake even in the worst of times. Partly, this is his natural disposition, and partly it is because Conroy survived the horrors of the trenches, and so is quite certain he has seen the worst. This makes Conroy the perfect mate for Seán. After a few days, Conroy sees that Seán's depression is going nowhere. He decides Seán could use a bit of a racket, that is a bit of a party, a singsong and a few drinks. He takes him to a home in the countryside where a farmer who has a piano in his house entertains any boys on the run with a pot of stew, a cup of tea, and a whole lot of craic. Seán looks around at the boys singing and carrying on like they have not a care in the world and wonders which of them will be alive a year from now. Who will be caught and shot against a gaol wall? Who will be hanged? Who will be tortured and left for dead? Despite Con's best efforts, Seán cannot lose the sense of doom that hangs over him. Once the party is over the question becomes where to spend the night. The farmer will entertain and feed, but he will not endanger his family by having the boys stay overnight.

A few miles away is the home of a prosperous businesswoman, Bridie MacKay. Con does not care for Bridie despite her somewhat obvious advances towards him. Bridie is used to getting what she wants. She is an attractive woman, but older than Con by fourteen years and though Con can flirt with the best of them, he's guarded around Bridie. Bridie is on her second husband, the first having died and left her a business she folded into her new husband's business of metal reclamation. The British made them rich during the Great War, though she does not advertise this fact. They have a huge warehouse on the docks of the quay where she has patiently bought up adjoining properties over the years. Her current husband usually stays in their home in the city, but Bridie likes to come home to the country a few miles north. Here she entertains various IRA types and slips what information she can glean to the British. After all, some of those IRA boys are handsome and exciting but do you really want them running the country? No. Bridie is quite happy with the status quo. Business is good, so let it stay that way.

Lately the British are putting pressure on her for a little more than minor details from conversations. They are looking for Con Conroy, the spy who slipped away, and they are willing to pay to get their hands on him. Bridie, when last she saw him, invited him to stay at her house if ever he found himself caught out after curfew. Conroy, despite his reticence about Bridie, decides it is just the place for Seán. Another cold night in a barn without hot water or a cup of tea might just send him over the edge. Con tells a few of the other boys to join him, and six of them walk the few miles to Rahinsky House, Bridie's second home. They are not disappointed when they get there. Bridie is surprised that Con has decided to take her up on her offer of hospitality. She has her servants see to a roaring fire and a late meal of bacon and eggs and strong tea. She has beds made up on the floor of the sitting room for a good night's sleep. Then Bridie turns her attentions to Con. Seán, despite the good meal, the warmth and the camaraderie, cannot shake his gloom. He watches the evening unfurl with a careful eye. Each man is armed and Seán is used now to sleeping with his gun. It has become his best friend of late; his only defence in the open country moving from barn to barn.

As the evening wanes, Bridie announces to the men that they should hide their arms. You are perfectly safe here she claims, but you never know what, with those wicked Tans racing about at night. 'Twould be better altogether if the guns are hidden under my mattress. Seán's eyes narrow. Yet, she is right. If they are caught with guns there is no escape. It will be execution for sure. If they are caught, but without guns, the British will have to make a case for convicting them in court. But what are the chances that the Tans should target this house tonight? Still, Seán has been trained by the best and he can see O'Hegarty in his mind's eye nodding at him. Reluctantly Seán and the men unload their guns and holsters and ammunition and toss them under the mattress that Con holds up. Seán counts everything meticulously. When four more men show up at the door, they too unload their guns and ammunition. Eventually the men fall asleep, one by one, but still Seán watches. He is the senior officer in this troupe of outcasts, most of whom are wanted by the British by name or by sight or both. All of the men have been involved in ambushes or take-downs or simply self-defence. Seán makes sure that some semblance of military routine is kept to. He makes a schedule and posts a sentry for lookout. He observes as Con retains his good manners while rebuffing the lady of the house, who is quietly and subtly trying to draw Con away for a tryst. Seán watches long after Con has made his way to the sitting room and found a place to lie down among the others. He sees Bridie sitting at her kitchen table with a dram of whiskey. He sees her leave her kitchen and go outside the back door. She does not return for an hour. Seán lays back on his mat and closes his eyes. The men around him snore and grunt and pass gas. In his mind he leaves the room and makes his way back to cold Canada. He wonders what his girl is doing now without him. Sitting by a roaring wood fire no doubt. Perhaps thinking of him. He is jolted out of his reverie at five o'clock and curses himself as he is awoken by shots being fired outside, as the sentry runs for his life and the front door of the house is rammed in by the Auxies. It is Tuesday morning. Seán has lasted but a week on the run.

On Tuesday afternoon, Murphy looks up as James enters the Douglas Street Pub. Florrie sits on the bar stool beside him. He is as dejected as a man can look. Have a drink, Séamus. Murphy nods to the bartender for another Jameson. This is unusual, and James is immediately suspicious. What's up? he quips, without touching the glass. Seán has been picked up. With eleven others just north of the city. Eleven. That's a hard blow to take, and Seán of all people. Everybody knows Seán. He is a quiet, intelligent man. He has his wits about him as well and the men respect him. The people respect him. Murphy hates to think of Seán in prison. He is not as tough as some. Murphy lists all of the men who have been taken with him. James knows most of them. They are being held at Victoria Barracks. James picks up the glass of whiskey and downs it in one gulp. Jesus, Mary, and Joseph. What happened? Murphy tells him what he knows. It is an inside job for sure. Somebody let them know the boys were there. No other homes in the area were touched. These fucking informers will be the end of us. Florrie nods and takes a long quaff of his Guinness. All three men are quiet. It slowly dawns on James that he is here alone with Murphy and Florrie, and that no one else is going to walk through the door. This meeting was just for him. So that he won't hear it elsewhere. James knows this means it is a bad business altogether. Chances are Seán will be executed. All of them will be executed. He fingers his beads in his trouser pocket. He sees the boy on Parnell Bridge, running, running so expertly, like a natural athlete trained for competition. He sees himself ease off on the trigger. Why? James doesn't really know why. But he says in his mind. I let one go. It's a fair trade. And then he asks for another whiskey despite the slow twist of his gut.

I got a message from O'Hegarty this morning. Florrie has set down his pint and is obviously relieved the news has been shared and he can move on. Florrie is deeply entwined in Josephine. He has difficulty focusing on work. He worries like an old woman about the dangerous things she is doing. More dangerous than any man in the county. He must distract himself from thinking of it too much, because they need her there doing just what she is doing. They need her desperately. O'Hegarty's message was sent by one of the Cumann na mBan girls. There are three names he wants dealt with immediately. He has new intelligence that the men listed are delivering information to the enemy almost daily. One of the names is on the original list. The others are not. We know the wine merchant Beale is guilty, no question. The other names I will have checked out before we proceed. Ah for God's sake Florrie, just give me the names and we will look after them with the others. Murphy looks at Florrie as if he is a schoolboy. But Florrie stands his ground. There is enough blood being spilled, I won't be having any of it without assurances that it is deserved. Murphy doesn't roll his eyes, but he does give a quick glance at James, as if to say, farm boys, church goers, have no business in intelligence. As of now the plan to deal with all of the names on the same day is aborted. Each team will deal with their names as quickly as possible. This handing over of the men has got to stop. And Séamus, Murphy looks him in the eye, don't forget to leave a calling card. This time round we want these bastards to know what they can expect when they hand over their fellow citizens to the enemy in Cork. Let the world know they have turned on their own people.

On Wednesday morning James awakens with a sense of determination. He lies in his makeshift bed and goes through the plan in his mind before he rises to kick his team into consciousness. James has already scoped out the two most affluent of the men on the list. The first is the justice of the peace, Alfred O'Reilly. He is an older man, in his late fifties, and well-liked. But what the people do not know, and will soon discover, is that he has been feeding the Tans information on any and all IRA boys he comes across. O'Reilly quietly considers the IRA an organisation of social misfits led by inept dreamers and criminals. It will be a terrible shame to turn the country over to that lot, he thinks. But the day after Seán is taken, Alfred will become the first reprisal.

He is riding his trap and pony home for his dinner. He lives in the same section of the city as James, and indeed over the years James has seen his familiar figure many times. James listens for the clap-clap of the pony and then steps out from a side street with three other members of his team. Once O'Reilly has reined in his pony, he nervously hollers over the evening wind. Aye gentleman, can I help ye? James sighs and pulls out his gun. Off the cart! Stand up against the wall. O'Reilly is alarmed at the sight of the gun. A feeling of dread rises up from the earth and entwines itself in his legs. He cannot move. James's partner grabs him by the arms and walks him over to the wall. Look here boys, what are ye up to? What is this all about? James looks at him. He sees the placid, friendly face and it only enrages him. It is because of the likes of you that good men are executed. Seán may be executed. He keeps the rancour from his voice and his face remains blank. The IRA has collected evidence that proves you are a spy. You are the worst kind of traitor. You have blood on your hands, old man. We will give you a moment to make peace with your maker.

The old man begins to panic. He has been a justice of the peace for years and he is well-versed in pleads of innocence that are false.

Suddenly, brutally, he sees years' worth of faces pleading for mercy. He sees them in a different light as he studies the determined faces of the young men in front of him. His voice rises and he begins to call out into the street for help. For fuck's sake, says one of the team, and lifts his gun, carelessly shooting O'Reilly in the face not once but twice. The first time in the mouth, the second in the forehead. Shut the fuck up you lousy spy! He spits it at the old man as he sinks down against the wall and crumbles onto the ground leaving a stream of blood working its way down the incline of the road. At any other time, James would be disgusted with his team member for such a callous display. Not today. What tiny bit of pity, mercy, or understanding he might have had for the men deemed to be guilty has dissipated into the cold February air like so much warmth escaping from an open door, leaving the room empty and frigid.

James reaches into his pocket and takes out his previously written sign. It reads, *Spy, by order of IRA. Take warning.* James leans over the dead man's coat and pins the sign onto his chest. It sits propped there like a corsage for a dance. All four men turn and disperse. There have been no witnesses. But Mr O'Reilly's body will soon be found, and tomorrow a full article in the paper will announce the mystery of his death to all of Cork. Though the article will claim he is an upstanding citizen, the sign left on his body assures the people otherwise.

On Wednesday evening, James goes to Mass. He slips into the church and quietly kneels in the shadows at the back. His head throbs just above his left eye and his gut is twisted. The candles on the altar flicker and James fingers his beads. He wishes that Father Dominic were still here in Cork. Father Dominic is a man first, a priest second. He understands the necessity of what they are doing. The one priest who has vision enough to see that change must come, or they must die trying. The one priest who understands that it is a soldier's work they are undertaking, no matter how it may look. But Father Dominic is nowhere near Cork. He is sitting in his cell far away, exhausted from a day of useless, back-breaking labour. It is like an endless circle of hell, and the only thing that gives him hope is the thought that he is doing his purgatory now, on earth. This secret thought sustains him through the worst. James's secret thought, however, is the opposite, his fear being a long, long list of atonement that will catch up with him, in this life or the next.

As James sits in the shadows trying to pray, he notices an attractive woman enter the church and sit quietly on the other side of the pews. Her long dark hair is carefully pinned up and she is bundled in her winter coat with the thick collar upturned against the weather. She is sitting for less than a few minutes when James sees Florrie enter the church. He looks around carefully and then sits beside her. James takes the risk of bending forward out of the shadows to watch them. They are in love. There is no doubt. She takes off her gloves and caresses his cheek, as they whisper *tête-à-tête*. This is the mystery woman. The woman for whom Florrie risked himself, to pick up her son and return him to his mother. The mole inside the barracks. James turns and makes his way out from the side door of the church. He feels cold, tired, and alone.

On Thursday morning, James sits down and writes a letter. It is to George Tilson, the next name on his list and a well-off businessman. He is sending terror his way, it is true. But he tells only the truth to Mr Tilson. You are being watched. The IRA knows you are a spy. Your days are numbered. James believes he is giving the man a running start. An opportunity to change his ways. If he is smart, he will leave town like so many other families who have connections to the British. He does not need to be found dead on the street with a sign pinned to his coat. Get out while you can, James thinks, and he hands the letter to the clerk who is his main contact in the post office. Deliver it with the regular mail he tells him. Today.

James spends the weekend casing some of the other men on the list. He is hoping that Tilson will save him the trouble, but he knows Beale must be dealt with. O'Hegarty's orders. He has been watching Beale, spoken to him even in a pub one evening, and he feels confident he knows exactly where he will be on Monday afternoon. In the meantime, he helps his teammates, Mahoney and Aherne, check out the less affluent names on the list. There is John O'Leary, a veteran with a false leg. Wounded he may be, but he is selling the Cork IRA boys to the enemy and it is going to stop. Saturday night they escort him out of the pub, put three bullets into him before they are interrupted by curious patrons also leaving the bar. They must disperse before they are finished, but it doesn't matter. O'Leary will die three days later in hospital.

Monday is St Valentine's Day. The team decides they can get rid of two in one night. They have been trailing an unemployed Great

War veteran by the name of O'Sullivan. He lives in a sorry little room on the wrong side of the tracks. For him, informing on the IRA is clearly a case of economics. James puts forward a suggestion to Murphy. Why don't we send him a letter? This man is doing it for the money. He could leave town. What's got into you? quips Murphy. Where the hell is he going? If he had anywhere to go, he'd be there already. Just shoot him like the rest. Sullivan is found on a roadside at the outskirts of town, hidden in the shadows outside the enclosing wall of St Joseph's Cemetery. *Spy. Penalty: Death. All spies and traitors beware.* Blood from his wound has coloured the sign pinned on his chest red.

James's mates offer to help him out with Beale. Don't worry about it, boys. I've got it. He has already enlisted the help of the Grey brothers. At five o'clock, James, dressed in his Sunday best, is cruising the southern end of the city in a fancy touring car with Jim Grey. Jim is as handsome as a film star and as debonair as English royalty when he wishes to be. The two young men look like they just swung out of Hyde Park. Just the kind of man Beale likes to do business with. As Beale gets out of his own Ford in front of his comfortable home, James pulls up behind him and calls out the window. Beale recognises him, and remembers their conversation about fine wines in the pub the previous week. James invites him in for a spin to discuss a large order of wine. Beale hesitates at first. There is something not quite right about this. But the opportunity to do business supersedes his own good sense, and his fate is sealed once the car door is closed. Tomorrow his body will be found on the outskirts of the city between the road and a farmer's field. His hands are tied behind his back. He has fallen back on his knees, a small round hole in the exact centre of his high forehead. *Spy: Traitors Beware* is found flapping in the wind, pinned to his luxurious winter coat.

James sits in the Wallace sisters' shop and reads the papers. They are full of the latest spree of killings, the notes on the bodies making big news. O'Hegarty was right. A little terror goes a long way. James cannot help but think of Seán, and the group that will shortly be going on trial. O'Hegarty is not here. Seán is not here. Tadg is not here. There are only the intelligence boys left, and only four of them at that. Florrie walks into the back room and sits down. He picks up a newspaper and quickly skims it looking over the headlines. Florrie has been working regularly in his cousin's drapery manufacturers.

Does he know his cousin is a spy for the British selling out any information he might garner for a few shillings? Years from now some will speculate that he did know. Perhaps this is why he tells James now that he will be joining O'Hegarty in the Gaeltacht.

O'Hegarty wants to launch a major ambush on the Macroom Castle lot. He is thinking Coolavokig is the place. There is a tremendous view from the top of the ridge as well as a good local battalion, but we will need experienced gunmen. James is not excited about this pronouncement. Sure, we are only halfway through the list as far as I know. Florrie shrugs. You will have to finish up in the next few days. O'Hegarty wants us at Coolavokig inside the week. James does not show any signs of pleasure at returning to the countryside. The only pleasant thing about his January visit were the country girls. Florrie knows this feeling. It is the same with most of the city men. At least we will be travelling in style, Séamus. The Grey brothers will be our chauffeurs. Murphy, Pa Murray, Tom Crofts, Peter, and Sandow will be joining us. We will take two touring cars. Once the ambush is done with, we will race back here. But Séamus, I will be staying, and I need you to do something for me while I am gone. James raises his eyebrow. Sure Florrie, what do you need? I need you to keep an eye out for Josephine. If for any reason you believe she may be in danger, put her in a car and bring her out to Ballingeary. Her boys will be fine with her sister. Florrie looks him in the eye and James realises he knew that he, James, was watching him in the church the other night. Probably Florrie was trailing him on his way to Mass. There is a reason that O'Hegarty wanted this one as head of intelligence. James nods. Right Florrie, no problem. I will keep an eye out.

Murphy downs his Guinness. It is Friday night, and the pubs are full. Right, men, let's get this over with. There are six of them altogether, and they have met specifically to do a job. The next man on the list has been hiding out in the Cork workhouse. Normally he works at the Ford plant, but he has figured out that somebody is tailing him and has stopped showing up at work. Information about his whereabouts is delivered to intelligence via the IRA men who work there. The Cork Workhouse is the establishment's answer to extreme poverty, untenable circumstances, personal disaster. It has not changed much since the time of the famine. The philosophy remains that we will feed you in exchange for work, no matter how meaningless. But the workhouse also has an infirmary. The man Walsh has been feeling distinctly ill since he realised he is being tailed. Who would take a sick man out of the hospital? Clearly, he does not know who he is dealing with.

Murphy goes into the reception area while the others wait outside on the street. I am looking for Michael Walsh, he tells the porter. Walsh is in the hospital wing. The porter expects Murphy to leave, and he is astounded when instead Murphy sticks his head out of the door and within seconds five more men dressed in trench-coats march past him and down the hallway. They push open the swinging doors at the end of the corridor and find themselves in a common room. The people, who are in various stages of illness, look up meekly. A nurse and doctor approach. You gentlemen are not allowed in here. Murphy takes the revolver out of his pocket and points it at the pair. We are looking to visit our friend Michael Walsh, and we would like some privacy if you don't mind. The nurse and doctor look at each other in alarm, but wisely follow Murphy's lead. He puts them in a small office and closes the door, but not before giving them a wink and a nod. The men walk down to the room to gather up Walsh. He is frozen in terror when he sees them. Two of the men pick him up off the bed by each arm and drag him down the corridor, past the office, past the porter, through the front door, past the gates, and onto the street. Walsh knows his time is up. He is blubbering like a baby. I am innocent. I am innocent. You are making a mistake. We don't make mistakes, quips Murphy. Three of the men take out their revolvers and fire. James pulls the hand-written sign out of his inside pocket. *Caught at last. Spies and Informers beware.* He pins it to Walsh's hospital pyjamas as his blood pools and his empty eyes watch accusingly.

On Saturday night James is sitting in the Douglas Street Pub. The wind is howling outside, which, thinks James to himself, just about matches the howling inside my head. Lately the throbbing behind his left eye won't let up. He can hear the hot swish and thud of constricted blood as it pulses past his eye over towards his ear. It is a terrible racket, and it makes him squint and involuntarily push with his fingertips the pressure points of his upper sinus at the top of his nose. His old friend Thomas Ashe has been visiting him again in the night. Crying and spluttering slobber. Calling his name, receding from view, even while James's legs will not move fast enough to get to him. He awakens with the sensation of trying to run upstream in a fast-moving river, his arms outstretched reaching towards the ghost. It leaves him in a cold sweat every time and he must pray to the Virgin to calm his racing heart and dispel the sensation of doom.

Murphy is trying to work through the list as quickly as possible. He has pulled in a few trusted friends from other battalions to help with the work. There are three more names, proven spies all, selling out the boys. Every time James thinks of Seán locked up in Victoria Barracks, he feels a renewed sense of determination to eliminate these bastards. He strolls by George Tilson's place and stands outside his house watching him. Tilson stares back at him for a moment and then runs inside. Well, he has got his mail, thinks James. On Sunday morning Tilson's time is up. James and Jim Grey cruise over to his house. From a distance they see someone pull into Tilson's property. Tilson leaves his house with a suitcase in hand. He gets in the car and James and Jim Grey trail them all the way to the Cork ferry terminal. They watch as he gets out of the car and buys a ticket. They see him excitedly talking to his friend, perhaps a brother. It's just as well, James says to Jim. He is spooked. I was wondering how I might convince him to get in the car. Some hours later, just outside London, Mr Tilson is found in the train washroom, his neck sliced by his own hand, blood squirting from his jugular. He is holding the knife in one hand and a suicide note in the other. Just before he leaves the earth he manages to whisper to the porter, the IRA is after me.

On Sunday evening James is thinking he is done with this nasty business. He settles down to a pint of Guinness at the Seaman's Club, intent on gleaning whatever information he can from the conversations going on around him between off-duty Tans. He is hoping for conversation about the recent arrests, especially Seán. But within minutes cold air blows through the door and accosts him as Murphy walks in, head down, collar up. Unfinished business. Drink up! As they walk down the waterfront quays, Murphy explains. We need to run by and pick up another couple of lads to help out with this. Our man tried to take out Mohally but was interrupted. The word from the boys at the hospital is that the doctors retrieved the one bullet he managed to get into him, and he will survive. Not on my watch he won't! Mohally is one of the last names on the list. A Great War veteran, the only job he can find is as a night watchman. Spying for the Tans brings in much-needed extra cash. William Mohally has just discovered the extra cash is meaningless beside his life.

Jim Grey picks up Murphy, James, and two accomplices and together they drive out to the South Infirmary Hospital. Wait here in the car, Jim. We may need to exit quickly. The four others make their way into the hospital. Murphy stops the first doctor he sees and asks where Mohally might be found. Murphy senses the doctor's reticence, looks him in the eye and points his gun at him. Sure doc, we are in a bit of a hurry. He points at a couple of nurses that have entered the hallway and marches all three to the nurses' station. He corrals them inside and asks again. The doctor assesses just how serious this man might be and decides two nurses and a doctor are worth one seemingly shady patient. He relents and tells him in what room Mohally can be found. Murphy, James, and the other two walk into the room and wheel the crying Mohally outside on his stretcher. James helps pick him up off the stretcher and place him on the ground. Before a word can be said, the accomplice that James does not care for bends over Mohally, inserts his gun into his mouth, and shoots. There is a moment of silence and then a slight moan can be heard through the darkness. Murphy says, give him another. Another shot is fired through Mohally's cheek. There is no sign prepared and so they leave Mohally on the cold ground, the blood on his now shattered face slowly erasing his identity. The group quickly walks to the car. All four are as quiet as mice, looking out of the windows as they drive away. Jim Grey steers the car and whistles a lonely Irish lament.

On Monday morning James risks a visit to his family home. He takes every precaution, watching carefully to be sure he has not been followed. Then he jumps the back wall of the property, not into his own yard but into a neighbour's. From there he makes his way into another neighbour's yard, before hopping the fence towards the back of the property to his own mother's home. He makes his way past the garden shed where Edward blew off his fingers, and into the back door of the kitchen. His mother is shocked when she sees him. James my darling, sit down and I will put on the kettle. Although it makes her stomach churn, she feels compelled to inspect him like a man buying a horse. His cheeks are sunken. He is thinner than ever. The colour is drained from his face. He looks like he has not had a hot bath in days. When he takes his coat off his body odour would knock you over. She has never seen her son in this condition. I am going out to the Gaeltacht for a few days, Mama. I thought I would just get a bit of a rest here before I go. I won't stay the night, but an afternoon nap in my own bed would be wonderful. Julia hugs her boy to hide the welling tears. We will feed you up first my boy, and when your stomach is full you will sleep well. I will fill the tub with hot water and Epsom salts. You will soak while I get dinner together.

The hot water and sweet wholesome soap that was once a mainstay of daily life now feels luxurious. Nevertheless, James's mind is not at rest. Late last night he was given word that another group of men had been given away to the Tans. The Flying Column of East Cork, who had been training in the countryside outside the little village of Clonmult just north of Midleton, were surprised by a large group of Tans, Auxies, and RIC in the lonely barn they used as headquarters. Seven of the boys are dead. Nine were captured and are now keeping company with Seán and his crew and the Dripsey men at Victoria Barracks. They have executed every informer they could find and still the boys are being sold to the enemy. James pushes the pressure points on his forehead. He sinks down in the soapy water now topped with the flotsam of his body's sweat and dirt, and falls asleep. He is awoken by his mother, who suds his hair for him, sets him down in front of a huge plate of steaming potatoes, cabbage, and ham, and then pulls the drapes in the tiny room he shared with his brothers and quietly closes the door.

On Tuesday morning Jim Grey is in fine form. The touring car that he has commandeered from some unsuspecting patron is packed to the gills with officers and gunmen from Cork No. 1. Grey is in his element. He sings bawdy songs that no one would expect to hear coming from such a handsome, cultured face. The men cannot help but laugh. All but Pa Murray, who hollers at him to shut his gob from time to time. It only makes Jim sing louder, and the boys echo his verses. By late afternoon they are deep in the Gaeltacht, meeting O'Hegarty at a tiny pub in Ballingeary, warming themselves by the fire, and drinking Guinness. O'Hegarty is happy to see his crew of regular officers, the trustworthy group who can be depended on to get the job done come hell or high water. He takes time out to speak to each one, asking about their family, their latest assignments, close calls, and successes, and passing out validation like so many hard-earned medals of valour and courage. The day will come, many years in the future when these men will be formally presented with a medal designating them soldiers of Ireland in the fight for independence. But at the moment not a man can imagine such a thing.

O'Hegarty focuses on the job at hand. He knows the city men are not excited about being in the country, but he lets them know just how necessary they are. He gives them a rundown of the local men: who are reliable, who are proven leaders, who can be trusted. Already O'Hegarty has chosen the exact location to launch what should be a successful assault on the Auxies that barrel through the area at random times. For the last few days, he has the entire 4th Battalion on alert. About fifty men start off hiking just after daybreak, across from their various billets in the area, to find their pre-determined teams and careful hiding places where they sit in wait, overlooking the long road from Macroom to Ballyvourney. With the addition of the city gunmen, they are now about sixty men. In the morning they will take up their positions again. There are two Lewis machine guns placed at strategic heights looking over the road, and groups of men located on both sides of the road, completely under cover by large outcroppings of rock. If the enemy ever arrives, they will have one hell of a welcome.

After three days of hiking across half-frozen landscapes, to sit in frost all the day long, only to turn around before sunset and head back, the city men have just about had it. But they watch their country counterparts, speaking to each other in Irish, dressed practically and warmly in layers of wool, their permanently rosy cheeks maintaining a steady smile. They are proud, tough, committed to their battalions, and they know their own minds. They do not suffer fools lightly. My job is tough, thinks James, but in a different way these country men have it just as bad. If they are chased out of their homes by the Tans there are no laneways to duck into, only open countryside, which they know like the back of their hands. Often, they head straight for the bogs, able to pluck their way across from stone to stone and hope that the enemy tries to follow them. Rarely does it happen. The Tans have had to abandon their beloved Crossly-tenders more than once, sunk down past the axles in black bog water. They have learned the hard way to wait for another day.

On Friday morning James is anxious. He knows that Seán and

the lads have begun their trial in the library of Victoria Barracks. There is no word yet as to their fate. He wishes to be back in Cork City so that he can at least keep on top of whatever is going on. Everyone already knows that five of the Dripsey men have been found guilty and are awaiting sentencing. James is hoping this ambush will come off soon, because as soon as it is over, the plan is to head straight back to the city. He does not have long to wait.

Having just taken up his position with his team, including Seán Murray, the weapons training officer, and Peter and Sandow, they hear a low whisper from across the road. The official signal has not been given, but nevertheless a long slow-moving convoy of Auxie trucks preceded by a touring car has just appeared in the valley. It is moving so slowly the men will later speculate that the Auxies knew their position and that they must have been given up by an informer. In front of the touring car four men are walking. They are local farmers and shopkeepers, picked up and used as human shields by the Tans. The convoy crawls along and still the lookout does not give the signal. The men must call out to each other quietly without giving themselves away. Look east. Look east. As the touring car approaches their well-hidden positions, the first Lewis gun prepares.

The men hidden behind the rock faces can clearly hear the major bark at the human shields to stand on the road in front of him. One of the Macroom Volunteers whispers to his mate. Let's make an example of him. He fires his rifle and the Auxie falls to the ground. The human shields run for the low rock wall along the road and jump over. Another Auxie barks at them to get back and stand where they are told. They are the last words he speaks on earth. A third Auxie can be heard yelling. They only have revolvers; we will soon flush them out. It is at this moment that the one Lewis gun high on the hill begins to fire. The man on the second Lewis gun jumps and runs from his position across the fields, deserting his post. Later it will be discovered that he was working for the Tans; a spy, if under duress. He had been tortured in prison and finally caved. But you are not in prison now, O'Hegarty will reason, and makes a mental note. To cover, other men must crawl army style to take over the Lewis gun position.

James sits with his team behind a rock face and carefully picks out Auxies and Tans as they stream from their trucks. There are two lonely cottages on the side of the road and the men try to leave their lorries for the much better cover of the cottages, where they set up their own powerful weapons and fight back. After four hours of fighting and over thirty dead or wounded enemy lying on the road, O'Hegarty gives the signal to retreat. From his position high on the hill, he can see far in the distance and barrelling along the road is another convoy of thirty trucks full of Auxies and Tans on their way to rescue their mates. Someone got through to the castle for reinforcements. It is time to pack it in. Hallelujah, thinks James. He has not given a thought to the men he has shot lying on the road. His thoughts are consumed by what is happening to Seán and the others in the cells of Victoria Barracks.

PRAY

CHAPTER 11

FEBRUARY 1921 – JUNE 1921

James fingers his beads as his feet negotiate the steep hill of St Patrick's Street on his way to the Wallace sisters' shop. It is dark yet, but he does not dare impose on the good people who offer him a safe house to sleep. O'Hegarty's training has kept him in good stead. He spreads himself around and is sure never to go to the same house two nights in a row, and to leave before the rest of the house rises. The house that he has just left was very close to the Victoria Barracks. Since Seán has landed there, it is as if he subconsciously finds his way to that part of the city. It is as O'Hegarty always told him: stay close to the enemy, the place they will never find you is right under their noses, and it holds true, for this part of the city seems to take much fewer hits of midnight raids than other sectors.

James is hungry, and his head aches behind his left eye. He feels exhausted. He either sleeps like the dead or spends half the night awake, thinking of the dead. He cannot decide if it is the dead that are making him feel so depressed or if it is the living. This morning he is looking forward to the cup of tea and boiled egg that he will get at the Wallace sisters', to enjoy over the newspapers, though the news will without doubt be hard to take. There is a pallor that sits heavily on the city. It is reflected in the news, but this morning it is not just the news. This morning the Dripsey men are due to be executed. Every Republican in the country, but especially in Cork County, is seething with rage, begging for mercy from providence, or simply feeling weary and full of despair. As James fingers his beads and thinks murderous thoughts, he becomes aware of an uncommon scene playing out around him. He notices a hurried movement on the streets which are usually empty at this hour. The movement is all in the same direction.

It is women. They are filling the street, pouring in from every intersection. It is a slow trickle that quickly becomes a rippling river. He understands immediately where they are headed. He turns and retraces his steps. Once in sight of Victoria Barracks he finds a quiet alley through which to watch. Women from all over the city are fearlessly making their way to the bastion of British power in Cork. Women young and old, wealthy women in their fine coats, and poor women in their black woollen shawls. They walk, they ride together in carts. Some take the first trolley of the day. Some arrive by car. Within half an hour or so at the entrance of the massive compound is a vast crowd of women of every description. They stand, straight-faced and immovable, ignoring the menacing looks of the guards at the gate. James watches as without so much as a nod to each other they kneel as one on the cold, wet ground and begin to recite the rosary.

There are so many women, their voices carry past the tank that is aimed right at them. The soft, resonant lilt of their prayer is propelled past the armed guards. It cuts through the enormous, impassable gates and gently swirls and seeps through the barred windows of the prison cells, to reach the men inside. What do the condemned men of the 6th Battalion feel inside those prison walls? Panic? Peace? Gratitude? Hopelessness? No one will ever know. They are alone now, and will be to the end. Once the prayers have been said, many of the women make their way to home or work, some continuing to pray, others weeping, others nursing a bitter hatred. It is shortly after this event that all five accused are taken out, one by one, to the wall of the exercise yard, and shot. The one man left inside, the one who was wounded and so put on trial at a later date, listens as every fifteen minutes there is a volley of shots. Outside the prison walls, still tucked in his dark alley, is James, hunched down against the wall out of sight. He fingers his beads and tries to pray as he listens to the shots ring out in the distance. But his heart is squeezed with hatred and despair, and later in the morning, as he makes his way to the Wallace sisters' shop, he realises he has somehow, inadvertently, torn his beads asunder. They lie like so many cold tiny pebbles in the bottom of his pocket.

The executions are a debilitating event for the entire city, though there is not a soul in Cork who expected anything different. The families of the accused had petitioned the government for mercy and when that was not forthcoming, for a Christian burial. General Strickland called up the barracks. Throw those bodies in an ambulance and take them over to Cork Gaol before the families figure things out. Bury them in the exercise yard with the rest of their ilk. And do it quickly. We do not want a spectacle. And so, the families are shocked when they receive a note after the fact.

> *Regret exceptional treatment cannot be accorded in this case. Body has been disposed of in accordance with usual custom. General Strickland.*

It might have said their bodies will be buried as per any criminal, in the exercise yard, without a marker of any kind. The quicklime we will shovel on top of them will dissolve their bones so that no trace of them will be left on earth. Irish prisoners in shackles will trudge over the top of their burial place as long as England rules this country. Have a nice day.

The lonely, wounded prisoner, friend to them all, left inside to await his own fate at a later date, is taken out to the exercise yard for his short breath of fresh air, only to find the spattered and pooled blood of his friends against the stone wall, glistening in the weak morning sun. His heart pounds, his hands shake, his eyes weep, and his mouth quietly forms the words of the rosary in Irish.

O'Hegarty however, is not praying. He is planning reprisals. O'Hegarty knows that the Dripsey boys are just the first of four lots. Next to come will be Seán and his group, who were caught at Rahinsky House. Then there are the Clonmult boys, that is, those of the group who were not murdered. And there is another small group waiting with the other two, caught thanks to the unspeakable deed of yet another informer at Mourne Abbey. O'Hegarty knows the British are gaining on them. In the last few weeks they have been able to flush out some of the top men, many of them on the run. O'Hegarty has thought long and hard. He does not consult Collins, or anyone else. He does not wish to hear the many logical reasons why what he is about to demand may be a bad idea. He feels the weight of the executions, the weight of the nightly tears by Auxies through the city, now not so random, but focused on finding specific men, officers, flying column men, and others who are the most dependable of the lot. There has been a shift. The IRA is in trouble, and something must be done to turn the tide back in its favour. O'Hegarty has slipped back into the city and is holding court at the Wallace sisters' shop, despite the danger. He does not want Tom Crofts, who has taken over for him, to be responsible for these orders. He will tell the men himself. He will hold himself solely responsible for the outcome. He has called all of his available officers to this meeting. He will tell them exactly what he has already told the men of the outlying battalions. However, he knows these men, the city men, have a greater opportunity and more experience with guns, with shooting men down in cold blood and escaping without a trace. And that is exactly what he orders them to do tonight. The British want executions? They will get them. There are no jokes or snippets of song at this meeting. The atmosphere is grim, sorrowful, and angry. Any man in a British uniform is fair game, he tells them. Let them know that for every Irishman they execute at least one British military officer will be treated likewise. In particular, we want to target the highest commanding officers we can find. The higher up the chain of command, the harder it will hit the entire organisation. Armed or not, on duty or not. Anywhere in the county. You find them. You shoot them. But we know where they will be. In the pubs, toasting themselves on a job well done. With the whores, celebrating Irish executions with a party.

James feels the desperation in O'Hegarty's voice. He has known him so long now and witnessed his responses to God knows how many difficult and stressful events. When he was younger James believed that O'Hegarty was a marvel, some kind of superhuman genius. Nothing seemed to get under his skin. He was always quick as lightning to respond with a clear, concise answer to whatever desperate situation any of the boys found themselves in. But today is different. O'Hegarty is on his own. He feels the loneliness of his position. The best friends he ever had, MacSwiney and MacCurtain, are no longer on the earth. There have been murders and executions. There have been hunger strikes. There have been burnings and beatings and torture. O'Hegarty alone knows the sum total of morbid details and the catastrophic statistics better than anyone, and until today he has kept all of that under his hat, tucked away in a recessed part of his brain where he can shut the door and continue to function, to plan, to drive the cause forward. But today James can see the welts under O'Hegarty's eyes. He can hear the miniscule crack in his voice, the infinitesimal shift to a higher pitch, the more frequent use of profanity. He can see the hand comb through the thick bristles of hair quickly, and with a jerk. He can feel the anticipation of more executions to come, and he can see that O'Hegarty is willing to try anything to avoid this.

It was only three days ago, while James and the other city men were in the Gaeltacht shooting up the Auxies, that Seán and Con Conroy and the nine other Rahinsky House men had their initial hearing in the library of Victoria Barracks. The only hope they have is that guns were not found on any of them. If they had been, they would all have been shot on sight or as soon as they were taken to the barracks. The IRA had already decided to have the men represented by the best of O'Hegarty's lawyers, and construct alibis. Let the British prove the men are indeed Rebels. At least some of the men might then have a chance. But Seán had other ideas. While all of the other men refused to testify to anything other than being an invited guest at the house of Mrs MacKay, Seán knows that the packed room, full of citizens of Cork and reporters from across the country, all know otherwise. He tells his men to stick to their stories, but he himself will make sure that the world gets a chance to read about the murder gangs of Auxies, particularly the Manchester Regiment, as well as Tans and the British intelligence officers who are roaming Cork seeking out men in the IRA to kill in their beds. The judge bellows. Seán stands. He tells his story. Yes, I carry a gun. I do it for self-defence. There are Black and Tans and Auxiliaries wandering about Cork looking for me. They have asked for me by name. If they find me, I am quite certain they will try to kill me. And I will use a gun to defend myself if need be.

The next day this sensational story, told by the highly respectable brother of the dead mayor, is reported word for word on the front page of *The Cork Examiner*. It will soon be read all over England

and America and wherever the Irish have a voice. James reads and rereads the article over his morning tea. He understands Seán's altruistic motives, but he shakes his head. He wants to take Seán by the shoulders and shake him. He wants to slap him across the face. He wants to shout at him. How are we going to get you out of this now? Sentencing will be in another couple of days. O'Hegarty's plan is their only hope.

O'Hegarty knows it is a cruel plan, but he knows also just how callous and uncompromising British command can be. After several days of watching her IRA captors and their lack of appropriate respect for her obviously superior British status, Mrs Lindsay, who with her chauffeur was spirited away to a remote location by Frank Busteed, had been convinced that the suggested letter to the major at Macroom was her only hope of escape. She was given a pen and some paper, and with a scowl on her face and embarrassment deep in her heart she wrote a short terse note to her distant relative, the major. If I am to be saved you must rescind the execution orders of the Dripsey men. I believe they will release me if this is done. A young boy on a bicycle whizzed past the watchman of the castle and dropped the letter at his feet before disappearing.

Frank Busteed is beside himself. He sits at the meeting and quietly squirms on his chair, shifting his weight, crossing and uncrossing his legs, periodically surveying the room and the faces of the other men. He does not finger his beads as so many of the men do under stress. Frank is from a long line of Protestants, raised as a Catholic, but his own personal opinion is that the whole idea of religion is bullshit. He has left Mrs Lindsay and her chauffeur in the bog-surrounded cottage of a poor turf cutter and his elderly mother. They are under twenty-four-hour guard while he returns to the city to take on a variety of tasks. When O'Hegarty tells him that the British have flat-out ignored Mrs Lindsay's letter, and without so much as a nod in her direction, shot those boys and buried them in quicklime in the exercise yard, he feels a rage that he will never be able to describe or explain. He knew each man, his family, his home, his commitment to the cause. The Dripsey ambush was his doing. He knows that O'Leary, the official commander of the battalion, is too gentle a man to bear the tragedy, despite his commitment to the cause. Indeed, O'Leary will suffer a nervous breakdown in the coming days. Frank feels the weight of the executions on his own heart, and if the only thing he can do to relieve the pressure is to exact revenge it is precisely what he will do.

James looks around the tiny room and nods to Tadg and Charley and to his frequent partner Peter. Tadg and Charley are two men James knows well. He knows them well enough to notice their transformation in the last few weeks. Tadg returned from England and at first seemed his usual self, but nights on the run have worn him down and his normally tall, dark, and handsome visage has lately been reduced to a thin, haggard aura. Charley, who is now the battalion adjutant, has lost his chubby cheeks and twinkly eyes and also looks thin and tired. Both men are nervous. Very nervous. Their families, friends, and neighbours have had their homes targeted in the night, Auxies bursting in at two, three, four in the morning, asking for them by name. Enraged when they do not find them, they beat the men of the house, abuse the women, and trash the place or set beds on fire before they leave. Sometimes all of these. The only mercy is that they do not spend much time doing it, unlike a year ago. They are hunting for particular trophies: big names, officers, organisers, gunmen. They know just who they are looking for and they do not waste time.

James's group of four men wait until nightfall. They have decided to use their tried-and-true strategy for executing whatever officers they come across. One pair will walk in front, the other pair twenty feet behind. As they come across an officer, the first team will shoot. If there is any problem the pair behind will finish the job. It is a strategy that James knows well.

There are two areas in Cork City that house ladies of the evening. One on the central island, a stone's throw from the Wallace sisters' shop on Coal's Quay, and one on the south side of the River Lee, overlooked by St Fin Barre's cathedral. Busteed will wait until dark and make his way to Coal's Quay, the street where one of the brothels is run by a good-hearted Republican prostitute called Katy. Katy keeps what is known as a *shebeen*, a house where liquor is sold on the sly but also a place of refuge for IRA on the run, where they can get a hot meal and rest for a few hours. It is a place that is needed, a place where James will never be seen. Next door, the ladies of the evening do business with the Tans by night, and by day report whatever titbits of information they glean to the IRA. Busteed knows he will be sure to meet up with unsuspecting targets here and indeed he does, killing one and wounding another. After this success he will attend to the unfinished business of Mrs Lindsay.

James will head to Barracks Streets with St Fin Barre's towers looming over lanes of small row houses. It is here that the men know they are probably to find several high-ranking targets. Once they claim it as their territory, the remaining IRA stake their own areas across the city in other haunts of the Tans.

The night is dark, full of unrelenting swarms of cloud that make it difficult to see. But James has seen darker nights. They lie in wait across the street from the door of one of the small brothels. When their target makes his way into the street, James breaks off from his team. He has been standing quietly, thinking about shooting a man in the back. No. Instead of falling in behind his victim, the tall officer who is with a certain smug grin of satisfaction sauntering down the street, James boldly walks out under the light of the gas lamp. He cuts off his target. Peter, his partner, stops mid-step and freezes, sensing the worst kind of danger, that of losing his life, and bites his tongue from calling out to James. James reaches for his gun from inside his trenchcoat pocket and points it at the uniform. It does not matter who is wearing it or what he may or may not be guilty of. He is British military. James keeps his gun steady, and the officer keeps his hands up in the air. You are being executed as an official reprisal for the illegal executions of Irish citizens undertaken at Victoria Barracks this morning. The 'O' of surprise is barely formed when James fires, followed up by two more shots in the back from his team.

The morning papers report that six British military are dead, eleven wounded, and there are probably many more who are not accounted for after this night of terror. Shootings occurred all over the area, the newspapers report. James and Peter, Tadg and Charley sip their tea. Once finished with their work, the four had spent the remainder of the night in the brothel, the girls generously giving up their beds for the exhausted men. Now they look each other in the eye. Let's hope a little terror will go aways to help out Seán and the boys. All three nod at James in agreement.

Busteed is determined to make sure that the informer Mrs Lindsay is executed. However, in their efforts to find her, the British are out roaming every road and byway in the Gaeltacht and beyond. Busteed does not risk getting caught himself or being followed to her hiding place. He stays in Cork City, waiting with James to hear the sentencing of Seán and the court martial of the last two men of the Dripsey Ambush. Seán's sentencing comes first. Seán and Conroy, and every man accompanying them, are given a life sentence. The court does not believe their stories. They know there were guns on the premises, though not proven to be owned by the men. If the court did not believe the story they should have been executed. O'Hegarty's bet has saved Seán's life. A life sentence is only a death sentence commuted. Their tactic has worked. James does not think twice about the night of terror. The random executions undertaken by the IRA were worth the price. The British do not wish to unleash another wave of indiscriminate murders of their officers. Seán and Conroy and some of the others are sent to Spike Island, the Alcatraz of prisons in Ireland, found at the very entrance to the city in Cork Harbour. Not to worry, thinks James to himself. Collins is not the only one who can break men out of prison. We in Cork started that tradition back in 1918. We can do it again.

Charley Daly feels the upsurge of bile rise into his throat. He pushes himself from the pub table, walks outside to the street and vomits in the grass. Florrie wipes the sweat off his forehead and calls for another drink. James stares out of the window. Mahoney picks up his glass and downs the contents. Tadg follows Charley outside and leads him back into the pub, out of the pouring rain. Florrie has just read out the coroner's report from the latest murder by the Tans. The murder is of a low-level Volunteer in Cork No. 1; a member of the 2nd Battalion, and so his face is known to all sitting at the table. He is a young man with a steady job at the railway station. His name just happens to be Charley Daly. He is younger and much more innocent than Charley Daly the officer. His body was found inside a railway tunnel just a few days ago. Witnesses saw him led away from his work by a group of Tans. The report lists the agonising injuries he incurred: six bullet wounds, five bayonet wounds, broken eye socket, crushed skull, fractured ribs, fractured fingers, broken arm, broken leg. Everyone sitting at the table knows he was tortured and killed because of his name. His murder was due to a simple case of mistaken identity.

It takes Busteed several days to find his way out to the isolated cottage where Mrs Lindsay and her chauffeur, informant on the

Dripsey boys, is being held. He has managed to convince five of his column officers to accompany him. None of them have any desire to be part of this assignment. No one wants to execute an old lady; no matter that she is an uppity, long-despised British lady. The weather does not make it any more inviting. It is early March, with rain and mist and occasionally frost still in the air. When he gets there, he finds both her and her chauffeur, Clarke, in deplorable condition. They have both been fed well at the expense of the poor turf-cutter, subsidised by the IRA. In fact, as far as the turf cutter is concerned Mrs Lindsay has had a Sunday dinner every night she has been there. Nevertheless, she has lost so much weight her dress hangs off of her. Clarke too is emaciated-looking, his hair long and dishevelled and filthy. He is obviously suffering a mental breakdown; wailing and whimpering over his innocence from morning till night, and even after he has been thoroughly soused with poteen. His moaning is driving the guards back and forth from mercy to madness. The owner of the cottage is relieved that Busteed has returned. He and his IRA guards tell the story of the recent happenings in the area. The military searches were closing in on them. They were beginning to panic but were given a reprieve when Seán Moylan of Cork No. 2 flying column took on a convoy of Auxies out towards County Kerry. In the melée Moylan managed to shoot down the captain of the convoy, Major Seafield Grant. It seems Major Seafield was a good friend of General Strickland, and Strickland is seeing red about it. He completely discarded the search for Mrs. Lindsay in an effort to find the killers of his friend. Every Tan and Auxie in the county have been moved north and west in the vicinity of the ambush to try to flush out Moylan. Mrs Lindsay has been forgotten.

Busteed doesn't waste any time. With the images of his executed men and their heart-broken families in his mind, he and his men walk out to the bog. It is getting dark and so he hangs a couple of lanterns on the branch of an ancient, barren, gnarled tree that stands lonely and forgotten a way into the bog. The light illuminates the men as they dig a single grave into the soggy ground. They dig only three feet deep because everyone knows nothing returns from the bog but is only sucked down deeper into the earth. When the digging is done, Frank and his men head back to the cottage. He dismisses the local men. Go home. Tell your battalion leaders they needn't worry about this any longer. The men are only too happy to exit that lonely place and begin to make their way by the quickly dimming light across the path of stones laid on the only safe route through the bog. As they go, they can hear the screams of hysterical pleading by the chauffeur echo and reverberate through the encroaching darkness.

Frank ducks his head and enters the cottage. The two are brought before him, and he announces that their execution is imminent. You may have five minutes to say your prayers, he tells them. Mrs Lindsay stares him down and snaps that she wishes no special favours from the likes of him. Frank notes she has not lost her infuriating attitude. She snaps at Frank in the same manner she has been snapping at her Irish servants for years. She is contemptuous and dismissive of any native Irish Catholic, and Frank sees her as a prime example of the worst of the British national character. There is not a soul on this earth who will mourn her, he thinks to himself. Mrs Lindsay puts on her hat and coat, while the officers hold down Clarke and pour poteen down his throat in an effort to shut him up. It is pointless, for the man continues to scream. For God's sake, stuff somebody's sock down that, Busteed orders. As Mrs Lindsay gingerly picks her way across the bog to her own gravesite, the chauffeur Clarke must be carried by two men. Once in front of the grave they tie the chauffeur to a shovel struck into the earth in order to keep him upright. The stench of excrement that has run down the hysterical Clarke's trousers wafts through the air and sits on the mist as it forms around them. Mrs Lindsay uses a blindfold and stands straight, staring at her executioners with a calm, cold, hateful eye. Her expression never wavers. Clarke moans through the gag in his mouth, and with what strength he has tosses back and forth against the shovel. On the count of three, shots are fired by all six men. The sudden silence only emphasises the thud of the bodies as they topple into the grave on top of one another. The shovel is untied and used to mound the soggy earth on top of the bodies. The men work as quickly as they can. No one says a word.

The following night, Frank and his men make their way to Leemount House. They have brought barrels of petrol with them. It is late, and as they quietly and slowly drive the pony and trap up the driveway they are nevertheless heard by the young girls, Mrs Lindsay's servants, who live in the top floor of her home. The girls are nervous, having been in the house for weeks now without a word from their mistress. They have kept the place spotless and prepared food each day, anticipating Mrs Lindsay's return. One of the girls opens the window and looks down at Frank and his men alighting from their cart. He calls up to them and tells them that they have minutes to get dressed, get their belongings, and get out. The house and everything in it will be burned. The girls are in shock. What do you mean? You will burn Mrs Lindsay's house? Yes, yes, get out now! But Frank's officers, local men who understand the dire need the girls will be thrust into without employment, convince Frank to let them take what they can carry with them. Frank relents and gives them thirty minutes to accrue whatever might be of value to them. Eventually out they come, three young women lugging luxurious wool blankets filled with silver, and velvet curtains filled with clothing and linens. Keep it well hidden for now, Frank warns them, and they struggle off into the night with their bounty, payback for years of pitiful wages and endless days of work from before sunrise to well into the night. They do not give a thought to the old woman who ordered them about, never satisfied with a single thing they ever did for her.

Frank and his men walk through the house splashing petrol on every last item of big house luxury. The fine furniture brought from London, the magnificent beds, and carved dressers; the kitchen full of every type of Victorian dish, serving trays, and silver to accommodate fine dinner parties; the plush settees and chairs and lamps; all of the accoutrements of a wealthy British family living in Ireland. Busteed does not think twice about the wealth, or the waste. He is interested only in the message. The flames quickly lick up into the night sky. Get the fuck out of my country and take your informers with you. It might as well be spelled out in the sky by the thick orangecurls of flame, sparking and shooting out of the conflagration. Frank's message is sent loud and clear, reaching far beyond Cork County, wafting across the smoky sky and over the Irish sea. The owners and occupants of every big house in Ireland sleep fitfully from this day forward. They hire guards to watch in the night. But who can they trust? For all they know the guards may be secret IRA. What is to be done? The British parliament begins to feel the pressure, not just from the English citizens, but from the very MPs who are sitting in the House, as well as the wealthiest of English society. So many of them have estates in Ireland or have family or friends who have estates in Ireland. Will they be the next target? Something must be done.

In only two days' time Frank will realise that his message was sent at an unbearable cost. The following evening four Auxies break into Frank's mother's home in Blarney. They ransack the place, destroying her furniture and belongings as they search for traces of Frank or clues as to where he might be hiding. She is bedridden, in her room at the top of the stairs, unable to move, but nevertheless crawls out of her bed and across the floor on her hands, dragging her legs behind her to the top of the stairs. The intelligence officer bounds up the stairs, jumps over her, kicking her to the side, and ransacks her room, smashing her belongings around her on the floor. Do you want help getting downstairs? he sneers at her. Then all four men pick her up and toss her down the stairs. Her back breaks and she lies paralysed until she is found by Frank's brother. Her dying words are a warning to Frank. Tell him that one of the officers was missing an arm, she whispers. Frank will find them.

As the month of March progresses, it seems like everyone on both sides of the war slows down and takes a breath of air. There are no ambushes in the vicinity of the city. There are no street executions of informers or military by the IRA. The number of midnight raids on homes in Cork drops dramatically. There are still four of the intelligence squad, including James, working the streets, keeping tabs on contacts, looking into reports, remaining on the lookout for opportunities to take out British military, acquire badly needed guns and ammunition, and equally as important, maintain a constant vigilance regarding possible informers. They roam the streets on the lookout for wanted British, the dreaded officer Captain Kelly, who can never be found but is known to spend his Saturday mornings at Cork Gaol or the barracks, torturing IRA men. Lieutenant Keogh, who works as a liaison between the RIC and the British military machine, maintaining a constant thread of intelligence between the two, is also a prize target. The third, an officer by the name of Hollywood, is known to be trigger-happy and prefers to shoot men in the back, why waste time asking questions? These men are wanted badly by the intelligence squad because every week their men inside the gaol and their men inside the barracks give them depressing reports on the treatment of the boys held within.

O'Hegarty returns to the Gaeltacht. Tom Crofts is managing

the ASU and the intelligence squad, but he too seems somehow quiet and reserved. Even Murphy has taken off for a stretch in the Gaeltacht, having been spooked by the proximity of British intelligence agents, dressed as tourists and looking for famous footballers. But all is not as it seems. The quiet period that lasts only a couple of weeks is in truth anything but. The British are desperately working on flushing out the leadership of the IRA. British intelligence is culling through anonymous letters from loyalist citizens too afraid to give their names but also afraid of what will happen to the status quo if the IRA ever gains the upper hand. They divulge what details they know of IRA activity and membership by letter, encouraged by the frequent requests from General Strickland to do so, printed in the papers, conveniently including an address.

O'Hegarty, Crofts, and Murphy are planning their next moves, and James, though he continues to work collecting intelligence, has his mind focused on something else entirely. He takes a daytrip down to the lower harbour off the small coastal town of Queenstown, locally known by the ancient Irish name of Cobh. It is where just a couple of years ago he was helped out by a faithful dock worker, one of O'Hegarty's trustworthy friends. Standing on the shore he can see clearly across the water, past the first small island of Hauwboline on the west side of the harbour, to the second island smack in the middle, Spike Island. It is a clear day. The sun shines, salty sprays of water crash against the rocks and jump up from time to time to hit him in the face. The seabirds squawk and call out at him. Black cormorants with their long necks beat their wings and cackle. The smaller waders, the redshanks, tweet tweet tweet relentlessly. They call out to him. James hears them as clear as day. It can be done. It can be done. Seán and whomever he can bring with him can be rescued from Spike Island. It can be done, and soon.

O'Hegarty is deep in the Gaeltacht but a steady flow of information reaches him each day. He too is thinking of Seán, but more urgent matters keep him up at night. There is the matter of the trial of the boys from Clonmult, as well as from the Mourne Abbey ambush, both outside Cork City but still inside Cork County and the Cork No. 1 area, so under his purview. He again assigns lawyers to develop a defence, and hopes that somehow executions can be avoided, and not only for the IRA boys. O'Hegarty is well aware that shooting unsuspecting men in the back is considered murder by some, and though he himself considers it an act of war, part of a larger strategy to save as many of his own men as possible, in this, his generation's fight for freedom, he knows the religious men, of whom there are many, now have a weight bearing on their souls. The bishop's decree of excommunication is still in effect. He does not reject the responsibility, but he puts these facts in the closet of his mind and gets back to work.

By the third week of March, the quiet period that had settled so uneasily on the people of Cork explodes into fireworks of shock and revulsion. In the tiny village of Ballycannon, west of the city, six IRA men taking shelter in a local farmer's barn are surrounded by Black and Tans. They sweep in on the men in the middle of the night, tie them up, and one after another torture them, seeking information. The men's screams can be heard clear across the fields in the surrounding farms. So can the shots, shooting them in the back after they are done with them. Some brave local farmers who can hear exactly what is going on leave their homes and make their way to the barn with trepidation, only to be stalled and prevented from proceeding by the local RIC men. As they argue with the men who were once legitimate police officers of their area, the Tans, impervious to criticism by the Irish, and in full view, drag the bodies out of the field in sheets, toss them in the back of a truck and carry them off.

Florrie learns from Josephine that the boys in the barn were given away by an informer. An IRA man no less. The same man who left his Lewis gun and took off across the field, deserting his position when the Auxies came to visit in Coolavokig. He is known to the men as Cruxy, a benevolent tag appointed to him because he earned the French Croix de Guerre in the Great War for bravery. He was a machine gunner then. But it seems his streak of bravery has run dry. In hiding since Coolavokig, once Cruxy learns what the Tans have done with his information he runs straight to the docks and catches the first ship out of the country. O'Hegarty makes a vow to himself and his officers. We will track that traitor down if it is the last thing we do.

James and Peter are on the hunt for the officers who are on the IRA's own most wanted list. They spend hours wandering the streets in locations around barracks, clubs, brothels, and the homes of known supporters. With the help of witnesses, moles inside Cork

Gaol, Josephine, and citizens who dutifully contribute their tiny tit-bits of information, they have learned that the despised and fearless Captain Kelly, Saturday morning torturer and hateful sadist, has lately been visiting a small brothel in Barrack Street. It seems he has found a girl to his liking and has been visiting her at odd hours. On a rainy afternoon, James makes his way to the brothel to question the girl and try to determine when she might next be expecting Captain Kelly. As he gets closer to the area, with St Fin Barre's spires glinting occasionally through the foggy day, he realises there are patrols of Tans in the area. He ducks into a laneway and considers the possibilities. If he is randomly stopped and searched and found to be carrying a gun, it will be the end of him. He thinks for a moment and decides to carry on without the gun. He slips off his holster and gun and puts each above a door jamb. They do not fit exactly, but the alleyway is dark, and he won't be long. He comes to the tiny brothel, a regular little row house towards the end of the street. The bird of a madam who runs the place assesses James's high-quality clothing and his well-groomed presentation. This is her usual routine, pegging a man's worth through his appearance. But the madam is also Irish. Her girls slip information to the IRA regularly about the British who come to access their services. The madam tells James to say hello to Mr O'Hegarty. James chuckles to himself as he walks up the stairs. Is there anyone O'Hegarty does not know? He knocks on the girl's door. The room is small and the single mattress on the iron bed pushed into a corner takes up most of the available space. There is a window, however, that gives a perfect view of the rooftops of the rest of the street leading the onlooker's eye to the massive twin spires of the cathedral.

The irony is not lost on James, and looking out of the window he jokingly asks the girl if she is inspired to say her prayers during her working hours. Immediately he regrets it, as to his surprise, she answers, yes, indeed. I keep my rosary under my pillow. She is new to this trade, obviously a country girl and probably with no one in the city to take her in. Naturally Kelly would sniff out one like this, thinks James to himself. The girl has no idea when Captain Kelly may next arrive. His visits are irregular and spontaneous. But they are always memorable and not in a good way. She will not give the details, but she assures James that the captain is a rough man, with little to recommend him. As they speak the girl suddenly freezes.

She walks to the door and locks it, listening intently with her ear up against the tired peeling paint. James looks quickly around the room. There is no closet or cupboard in which to hide. He will have to crawl out of the window and onto the roof if need be. And he will have to do it without attracting the attention of the military men lounging across the street smoking cigarettes, waiting to whisk their superior officer back to the barracks. But James has no time to make his escape.

There is a banging on the door and the girl looks at James in horror. She dares say nothing but stares at him with a pleading, overwhelmed visage, as if to say, we are dead now. James looks at her and winks and then lies down on the floor and scrambles underneath her bed as far into the corner as he can manage. There is a bed skirt that mercifully drags on the floor and so covers his hiding spot. He knows his lanky legs on his six-foot frame will poke out the bottom edge and so he contorts himself into as flat a shape as he can manage. As he listens to Captain Kelly's voice, he spontaneously reaches for his gun. Fuck, he thinks to himself, I am in trouble now. What was I thinking? The anxiety that he feels without his weapon makes the sweat break out on his forehead. But he controls his breathing and he looks for his beads in his trousers pocket. Good St Joseph, if ever I needed you, I need you now.

Captain Kelly wastes no time. James can see only his feet through the gauzy fabric but in his mind's eye he watches every move the man makes. First, he carefully lays his gun and holster on the tiny side table. Then he sits on the only chair in the room and quietly regards the girl. He does not bother with his uniform, his jacket, or shirt. Nor does he fuss with his boots, leaving them tied up tightly, his socks in place. He only undoes his jacket and the thick leather belt that holds the trousers on his athletic body. As he does, he quietly but purposefully orders the girl. Remove this, remove that. Turn around. Kneel down. Bend over. Lay down. Wider, wider.

As Captain Kelly grunts and groans James can feel his cheek burning a hole in the floor. The fucking pig, treating this waif of a girl so roughly. He is like a wild boar, rutting to kingdom come. James tries to close his mind to the sound and actions going on inches above him and concentrate on contingency plans. He curses himself for leaving his gun behind, for coming alone, for not waiting for Peter. He could do so much more if he had a gun and back up.

They could have taken out Kelly and his men guarding the place while he ruts like a pig. None of these thoughts help stem the flow of sweat off of his body. And so, he concentrates on his prayer. Good St Joseph, protector, family man, a saint James has called on before. And look, he James, is still up and moving, working for the cause, while others lay in their graves or rot in prison. No one will ever tell James that Joseph is anything but dependable.

Kelly is obviously feeling quite satisfied and lies on the bed directly above James and tells the girl to stop whimpering. He will leave her an extra coin, their secret, she need not tell the madam. James waits until he hears the door close, the girl locking it behind him. Then he slides himself out from under the bed and looks quickly out of the window. As he does the girl signals him to be quiet and points towards the door. They can hear other British accents speaking as they move down the stairs. James sticks his head out of the window to give himself a view of the street below and sees that there are military guards stationed strategically at intervals down the street. He quickly moves back into the room and decides to wait out their departure. After all, he is alone and by the sounds of the voices, there are three officers here and now, all three are moving outside. James knows a military vehicle will be waiting just around the corner and within seconds the entire crew will disappear. Again, he curses his bad luck in being outgunned and outnumbered. If only he had known that the man coming in the room was the very man they have all been searching for, for weeks. He has lost his chance, and if the girl is any judge, Kelly is unlikely to return for about a week. James is annoyed, but then chuckles to himself, thinking of the laughs his story is sure to generate at the pub tonight. Any opportunity for some merriment is welcome, even if it is via Captain Kelly.

After his story has garnered the expected glee, the men get down to business. Peter, Tadg, and some of the intelligence men are at the trusted Douglas Street pub to work out some ideas. The intelligence squad is feeling alone and lonely. Despite the leadership of Tom Crofts, a gentleman through and through, there is not a man who does not miss the presence of O'Hegarty. The risk of incurring his wrath and a vicious dressing down now seems like a small price to pay for the assurance of a visionary leader who looks out for each man. In fact, they are missing many of their city comrades. Murphy,

Pa Murray, and others have had to leave town after discovering the British are looking for them by name. Some of the other men like Tadg and Charley should leave as well, but they have jobs and are supporting other family members and do not have the luxury of taking off for weeks at a time. Instead, they move around constantly looking over their shoulders, but delivering their pay packets to their families every week, even if they rarely see them. The intelligence squad and a few lonely members of the once fulsome ASU are the only men left in the 2nd Battalion area that are still actively working, gathering intelligence to be forwarded to Florrie, looking for the bad guys, sniffing out military operations, patterns, and personnel.

Mahoney looks at the faces around the table and tells a tale of more mistreatment at Cork Gaol. As leader of the intelligence squad, he has been keeping tabs on the goings-on at the gaol through his moles. The boys are not in good shape. Some of them are being punished for failing to give up information during interrogation by being stripped naked and kept in cold cells without blankets. Others are being beaten and then locked up without medical attention. Seán Forde, sometimes known as Tom Mallone, aide to Collins and temporarily working out of Cork No. 3, has been picked up also and word has leaked out that he has been tortured mercilessly. The irony is he was being questioned about himself. He gave an alias when he was picked up and the Brits have no idea that he is the very man they are looking for! He has lost many of his teeth, his mouth having been used as target practice for Auxies' boots, and his back has been permanently branded with hot pokers. This treatment was allotted to him more than once, and it was only his impending death lying naked on a freezing cell floor that saved him. The visiting chaplain discovered him quite by accident and demanded medical attention. By some miracle he survived.

Something has to be done. The incarcerated men's spirits are low. They do not see light at the end of the tunnel. Many of them believe they will die in custody, their deaths rendered useless by this punishing regime. They believe that history will repeat itself yet again. Another Irish Rebellion trounced totally and utterly by the ruthless, merciless British hierarchy. Mahoney asserts himself. It's time we got our boys out of there. If Collins can rescue men from Mountjoy in Dublin, surely we can get a few of our men out of that rat-infested hellhole here in Cork.

Mahoney carries on with a simple inchoate plan. He has been talking to the chaplain who visits the men whenever there is a sympathetic British soldier who allows him in. There is a man in gaol who the British believe to be IRA. His name is Murphy, and they believe him to be Mick Murphy, who is now on the British most-wanted list. The poor fellow was picked up on a raid but was in fact an innocent bystander. He has been interrogated and tried and sentenced to death. The British believe him to be a notorious killer of military men and useful Irish spies. He is nothing but a good citizen, keeping his head down, all through the conflict trying to sit on the fence. Alas, he has fallen off and he is, as far as the good Padre can see, losing his mind to despair.

The men hatch a plan. The chaplain is willing to carry in a gun in an effort to save the innocent man and however many IRA can escape with him. Mr Murphy is due to be executed early on Saturday morning. The chaplain will carry a gun and deposit it with Seán Forde. Their mole inside the prison will see to it that he is not searched, and will also make sure his cell door is left unlocked. When they come in the early morning hours to take Murphy out to be shot, Seán will be lying on the floor above watching through the iron grid and waiting with the gun. The shots will be the signal for all of the men sitting now at the table and as many others as they can find to scale the outer wall of the gaol and storm the place. Seán will grab the key, and in the ensuing chaos, they should be able to release a large number of men. A group will be assigned to take the main entrance and hold it until as many have escaped as possible. The Grey brothers will see that cars will be waiting nearby to pick up men and take them out of the area quickly.

On Friday night, James, Peter, Tadg, Charley, Mahoney and a few others are due to meet on the quiet laneway outside the gaol's massive stone wall. They have hooks with ropes and homemade rope ladders. They will wait to welcome the twenty or so who will come at different times during the night, from all directions, and converge with them, lined up against the wall, black toques over their heads, black sweaters or jackets on their bodies. As James makes his way in the dark, darting from laneway to laneway, a keen eye open for the many patrols out after curfew, he stops by the imposing tower of the Church of Saints Peter and Paul. It is not James's regular parish and though the imposing building is in the vicinity of the Wallace sisters' shop he has rarely had reason to enter. But tonight, as he passes by, he sees the crucifix atop the tower glinting in the moonlight. It is a cold night for March and James thinks he is early enough to stop by. He knows the Padre at this church is a friend of O'Hegarty and has been known to harbour the boys when necessary.

James does not even try the heavy front doors. They do not have handles, and he knows they will be bolted tight against marauding Tans or Auxies. Instead, he works his way through the gardens at the side of the church and to a small dark doorway cleverly concealed around a tight corner at the back of the sacristy. Sure enough, it is unlocked. James walks by the tall chests of long drawers carefully crafted and designed specifically to hold vestments, a drawer for each one, each one a different colour and design for the various feast days of the year. On top of the dresser he spies a plate covered with a tea towel and an urn of tea. The tea is still warm, and underneath the towel are a couple of sandwiches, thickly sliced bread spread with butter and holding some leftover ham from supper. James knows the good father has himself gone to his rooms in the rectory and left this small portion of sustenance for any of the boys on the run who might find their way to the church. It would not be the first time the church has been used as a night-time shelter.

James smiles and takes one of the sandwiches, walking quietly through a side door into the church proper. He automatically genuflects in front of the tabernacle, the tiny glowing flame in the red candle holder shedding the only light in the cavernous church. He does not feel at ease so close to the altar sporting an irreverent sandwich and so makes his way to the front pew, sits down and chews. I should pray, he thinks to himself. I should pray for a successful storming of the gaol. I should pray for the release of the men. I should pray this fucking war might be done with one day. I should pray I might live to see that day. I should pray for Seán, that we can get him out of Spike Island. He thinks he should pray for all of these things but somehow, he cannot bear to ask for favours. Instead, he takes out his latest set of beads, his mother's replacement after finding the remnants of beads lost in his trouser pocket, and begins to pray the rosary. He prays in English because it is what comes to his mind effortlessly. He fingers the beads and recites the Hail Marys, but as his fingers work along the string his mind reverts to his plans for the evening, all of the possible outcomes, good, bad, and ugly, and suddenly he realises he is fingering his beads to thoughts of shooting guns, killing guards, and freeing prisoners. He puts the beads back in his pocket and makes his way out of the church.

By three in the morning all of the men are assembled. The British are unpredictable in their execution times. Often it is about five o'clock, but not always. Sometimes if they want to move the bodies before anyone knows any better, they will execute earlier. The men do not want to miss their chance. They assemble at the university, a stone's throw from the gaol wall. At about three o'clock the long line of men quietly makes their way to hide in the dark shadows against the twelve-foot walls at the side of the gaol. They are excited, and some of the less experienced men are talking until a patrol of Tans speeds by them. It is just a tiny reminder of the precarious nature of their situation, of the utter disaster that could befall them at the drop of a hat. It has every man reacting instantly. At any minute things could turn on their head. They wait patiently or impatiently, those who have watches checking the time until finally a runner makes his way down the laneway quietly seeking out Tom Crofts. It is a message. The execution has been temporarily postponed. Disperse. Quickly and quietly. We will reassemble when we know the new date.

A few days later word reaches the intelligence squad that the execution has been reset for the following Saturday morning. Again, on Friday night and into the early hours of the morning, the men assemble. They wait in their dark clothing, tight against the stone wall, their rope ladders ready to be put to good use, lookouts posted at either end of the laneway. It is a long, cold, damp night. The drizzle is light but steady. After an hour the men are drenched. Inside, Tomás Mallone, also known as Seán Forde, lies on his cot with the revolver reassuringly pushing into the base of his neck underneath a thin bit of rolled-up blanket used as a pillow. With his tongue he traces the line of broken and missing teeth in his mouth over and over again waiting, wondering, if he will get out alive, in his mind counting out the number of men he may be able to release after shooting the guards and before the place is overrun by British military. But it is all in vain. Just before five o'clock, firing squad time, Forde can hear the guard's footsteps ring across the gaol. He listens as Murphy is told his sentence has been commuted to a life sentence. Too bad Murphy, he thinks to himself. We all could have got out of here this morning, and he rolls over and tries to get some sleep. Life sentences are becoming the norm inside Cork gaols. Outside, James and his crew shake their heads in disbelief. The rope ladders are collected, rolled up and tied and the men make their way out of the laneway, dispersing in all directions.

Each day James makes it his business to take a walk past the Cage. The Cage is the set-up contrived courtesy of the British military to show off the men in custody and hope that the good citizens of Cork will recognise their faces and tell the British their real names. It has become apparent to them that just about every man they pick up gives a false name and address. James makes it his business to observe the observers, people checking out the men inside. He watches from a distance as men and women walk past and take a peek through the observation holes in the tarp that covers the twelve-foot-high walls of barbed wire. Through the peepholes they can see the guards patrolling around another ring of wire. Within are two small huts and a variety of men lately picked up, but whose identity is uncertain, at least to the British. There is a hand-written sign posted in front of the cage: *Rebels. Can you identify these men?*

There are spies working for the British. Some are to be found looking through the peepholes. Some are to be found inside the gaol. One such man, known as Monkey MacDonell, routinely joins patrols with the Tans and Auxies picking out IRA men as they cruise down the street. How does he know them? He used to be one. A traitor through and through. He joined up with the IRA when he returned from the war, but some say he was a spy from the beginning. Others say he is full of sour grapes, no one appreciating his expertise in the groups of thugs and cowhands that make up the Republicans. MacDonnell was an RAF pilot during the final days of the Great War. He knows the massive machine that is the British military. He has placed his bets on the very favourable odds that the British will win this war. He knows that if he is caught by the IRA he won't be long for this world, and so he beds down with the Tans and the Auxies inside Victoria Barracks and joins them on their midnight tears through the city, terrorising the families of known IRA men. But if MacDonnell hasn't learned yet that the IRA are a resourceful crew, cowhands and thugs notwithstanding, he will soon.

As March comes to a close, the winds begin to blow less fiercely.

The weather is warmer, and the days are longer, but the curfew continues. The British are beginning to change their tactics. So many men are on the run, never spending a night at home, that they have decided they have a better chance of finding the men on their list if they wander the city streets during daylight hours. Monkey MacDonnell helps out with this. He points his finger at a group of men walking down the street. That one there in the middle, in the tweed cap. He is so and so, such and such battalion. The men are pulled over, the identified man thrown into the back of the truck, not to see the light of day for years to come. But it is not just Monkey MacDonnell who is handing over his fellow Irishmen to the enemy. The British have called in their favours, and they have a number of ex-servicemen, most down on their luck, who have been drawn into the informer game. Both Josephine and O'Hegarty's other mole inside the barracks have passed on the names of some that are being paid cold hard cash for their treachery.

It is Holy Saturday. Easter weekend. Tom Crofts calls a meeting. The holidays are hard on the men. He knows it only too well. Easter is a big event for the Irish. The end of Lent, a feast for Sunday dinner and a few treats for the children. The churches are full, the choirs singing, the whole country praying. Praying for an end to madness is top of the list for many. Praying for an end to the British is the top of any Republican's list. Florrie, James, and the rest of the intelligence squad meet up at the Douglas Street Pub. Crofts has a sentry with him, a young lad to keep watch. Crofts is jumpy. He is a gentleman, but not afraid to use a gun; something he has proven several times in the past few months. Nevertheless, it has got under his skin that the British are switching tactics. They have far too much information. Many of the officers are now in the Gaeltacht hiding out in thatched cottages and helping the local farmers and turf-cutters when they should be in the city continuing the fight. It is solely the informers who are preventing this. The intelligence squad is still intact, less Mick, still languishing in prison. As they sit at the back of the tiny pub, close to the exit door at the back with a sentry in front, Crofts starts down his latest list. The list of known informers, all paid by the military, all ex-servicemen.

This flow of information has to stop. Crofts smacks his whiskey just a little too hard onto the table. He wants O'Hegarty back in the city. He wants his former life back. He wants the swelling ranks of

IRA men arrested for no apparent reason to be released and return home. He wants these swaggering British military off the streets of Cork and out of his country. But the thing that bothers him the most is the sure knowledge that he too is on a list, a British list. He spends his days dashing from one location to another, ducking in and out of laneways like a Charles Dickens character, meeting up with messengers of every possible description sent by O'Hegarty from his multitude of safe houses, pubs, and cottages tucked away in the bogs. There are young girls from Cumann na mBan, old women from God knows where, and odd characters, tough old men with connections to O'Hegarty that Crofts can only guess at. He is sure of one thing though: each messenger can be trusted. And with each messenger a name is divulged, a name and an urgent message to deal with them. Crofts does not have to guess at the meaning. Neither does any man in the room. The names and all of the known information about each man is discussed. The men decide on partners. If they don't have a sanctioned friend they can rely on, they will pair up. Crofts prefers to spread the team out, lest they are picked up and with one fell swoop, all his men transported to The Cage. James knows Peter will back him, or Tadg.

On Sunday morning James makes his way to Mass. He does not go home to his family. It is exactly what the British are hoping for, to find men at home. James has no reason to believe he is a target but always he acts as if he is. As he approaches the church, he sees that the British have their intelligence men smoking outside, hoping to blend into the congregation. To James it seems like they are screaming out at him, they are so obviously not of the local population. He sees a target outlined on their foreheads. He thinks of pulling out his gun and shooting. So what if it is Easter Sunday, in front of the church? Dead is dead. But he does not. Instead, he avoids the front door, walking past and around the corner of the church property and makes his way from the back, through the garden to the hidden door at the back of the sacristy. He slips inside and waits up against a wall. The father and his entourage of altar boys in formation for the beginning of Mass walk right past him on their way out to the church proper. Even the young boys know not to call attention to the fact of this young man in the sacristy where he should not be. As the priest walks by, he turns to James and quickly blesses him. God be with ye. James waits for a few moments, listens as Mass begins, the comforting Latin phrases that he has heard week after week for as long as he can remember. He fingers his beads in his pocket. But within moments he turns and retraces his steps. James knows he has no business at Mass until he goes to confession. And confession will have to wait. There is more work to be done.

James meets up with Tadg and Peter. The three men will wait patiently for their intended target, the name given to James specifically, Thomas Goulding. Like all of the names, Goulding is an ex-soldier, hard up for cash and willing to sell out his countrymen to keep himself supplied with pints at his local pub. James has been watching Goulding and knows that he takes a short cut through Fitzgerald Park on his way home in the evening. It is here that the three men wait, sheltered in the shadows of tall trees that are just starting to sprout new leaves.

The park lays on the edge of the River Lee, at the most western corner of the island that is the city centre. Though it is only a few minutes' walk for James from the Wallace sisters' shop, it is a quiet, natural oasis from the centre. It is April 1, and spring is on the way. The large groupings of shrubs and flowers are in bloom and the pond has come alive with birds. A family of ducks wades quietly at the edge of the water. There is a single-storey building at one end of the park, sheltered by trees. The whitewashed building sits empty except on the days when an IRA circuit judge uses the upstairs room as his courthouse. It is for this reason that the men know the park so well. They are often assigned duty here when court is in session. Since the burning of the city in December, this building has been used for various municipal functions as well.

While they wait, James sitting on a bench feeding breadcrumbs to the birds, the two others leaning against the trunks of the newly green, giant oaks, they can hear the leisurely footsteps of their man. He is smoking a cigarette and as he walks, he slowly takes notice of James. I've got you now boyo, thinks James to himself, and does not break his gaze. As Goulding nears, he coolly calls out to him. Good evening, Mr Goulding. Did you know there is a special place in hell for informers? Best to take a minute and say your prayers. He reaches into his trenchcoat and takes his gun in hand. Goulding stops mid-step. He turns and runs like the devil, off the path and through the trees at breakneck speed. James fires but misses. He curses to himself. Ammunition is in short supply, and he does not like to waste it. Peter and Tadg take off after Goulding, but James moves in the other direction in an attempt to head him off. As Goulding runs, he can see James coming around on his left and doubtless he can hear Peter and Tadg behind him. James stops and fires, and this time he hits Goulding in the neck, and though his head jerks it does not slow him down. Goulding takes a flying leap into the river and swims for his life. He is saved by the current that quickly carries him out and downstream. Goulding will survive this attempt on his life and be nursed back to health in Victoria Barracks. In June he will be found once more and survive another attack. Goulding perhaps has said his prayers.

James and Mahoney report to Crofts. Crofts in particular is disappointed. Another name on the list, Flynn, shot by other members of the team, also escaped. He will have to tell O'Hegarty that they have missed not one but two. It is the lousy ammunition they are expected to work with. Crofts shakes his head. If it is not one thing it is another. He assigns James another name. Don't let this one get away, damn it.

His name is Donovan, and he too is an ex-soldier, down on his luck, willing to sell out his countrymen. James follows him carefully for two days, then he walks over to visit the Grey brothers at their garage. This time there will be no chases. Jim Grey is more than happy to lend a hand. Grey chooses a regular van; it has always served well in other jobs. In the late afternoon as Donovan is making his way home from work James walks towards him, his hands in his trenchcoat pockets, his cap pulled down against the light drizzle. He is sure to keep his gaze averted. But just as both men approach the van from opposite directions, and as they are sheltered from street view, James pulls his gun out of his pocket. Fancy a lift? he asks, while Peter has his own gun pointed straight at Donovan's heart. Donovan knows by the cold steely stare that he may get in the van or be shot now on the street. He clambers inside the van, and as James holds his gun steady Jim Grey ties up Donovan's hands. A feeling of doom overcomes Donovan as he watches his captors. Two handsome young faces. They can't be older than twenty-five or twenty-six. But those handsome faces show no signs of mercy or empathy or anything else for that matter. They are flat and emotionless.

Quietly he begins the rosary in his head. But his prayers are spontaneously interspersed with pleading, promises, and possible pacts with divine providence. Pleading for life. Pleading for salvation from these two young men whose indifference towards him is palpable. But Donovan feels only the emptiness of a void across the cosmos. He focuses all of his energy on garnering what drop of divine mercy might, pitifully, fall upon him. He murmurs his prayers under his breath as the sweat gathers at the back of his neck and slowly slides down the centre of his back. Jim drives to the city outskirts. Once he finds a clearing of fields with no line of site towards homes or barns, he stops. Jim goes round to the back of the van and opens the door. Both men help Donovan clamber out of the van. James takes him by the arm and leads him a few feet into the field. Donovan can hear his own voice pleading for mercy while his eyes search the faces for a glimmer of hope. It is futile. Grey tells him to kneel down, and Donovan does so. Give me a moment to say my prayers. I need to say my prayers. Yes, take a moment and say your prayers. You are going to need them where you are going. Do you know how many men have been locked up, tortured, killed because of you? Donovan begins to whimper. I have no beads. I have no beads. James takes his own beads out of his pocket and tosses them. Donovan scrambles with his tied hands to capture the beads. He brings the crucifix to his lips and kisses it. James fires straight into his heart and Donovan's body first slumps and then slowly falls back, the rosary pressed tightly between his fists. Without a second glance both men calmly get back into the still running van and drive back into the city.

Florrie cannot stop himself from pining for Josephine. The two have come to a decision. Given the desperate situation so many of the IRA men find themselves in, and given that it is only a matter of time before Florrie may be actively hunted down by the Tans, and given that Josephine lives a precarious existence at the best of times, they shall marry. They have known each other for only a few months, but why wait? Either of them could be dragged off to stand in front of British justice and executed at the drop of a hat. It is too bad that Father Dominic is still in prison; both of them would have preferred that he perform their marriage ceremony, but it is no matter. They will make use of the good Padre at Saints Peter and Paul. It is to remain a secret. Josephine's very life depends on it. Florrie will take no risks. In his worst nightmares, those who know the secret are picked up, tortured, spill the beans and Josephine is discovered. Florrie's heart rate rises every time he considers the possibility. It is for this reason he does not even tell O'Hegarty. Only the good Padre knows, and he does not even make a written record of the event. Instead, he takes the form, fills it out, but leaves the names blank and puts it away in a drawer. If they live through this war, he can worry about it then. But Florrie's domestic bliss is short-lived. O'Hegarty sends an urgent message. Somebody is writing in to the general with information on the top officers. What bothers him the most? He has no idea who the perpetrator might be. Not a fucking clue. The mail must be intercepted, and anything sent to the military retrieved. Florrie kisses his new bride goodnight and gets to work.

The following day forty postmen are held up simultaneously around the city of Cork, their bags intercepted, the contents carefully rifled through. O'Hegarty's information proves true as usual. Several damaging letters are found. The writers will soon find themselves banished from the city, given twenty-four hours to get out, escorted to the docks and told never to return. As James pours through mailbags, he smiles thinking of his first hold-up of a mailman, his accomplice a very nervous Seán.

April is proving to be a rainy month. The flowers drink and bloom, the grass begins its annual evolution into tints of sparkling emerald and shades of deep moss. On the farms in the outskirts of the city the lambs stay close to their ewes, the calves to their cows. James roams the streets of Cork keeping an eye out for British intelligence men and the wanted military officers. His trenchcoat flaps in the breeze and he wears his preferred newsboy cap, his hair slicked back with the drizzle. He has been wearing his cap more regularly lately. The last time he was home his mother looked at his hair and remarked on the change in colour. His dark auburn hair is streaked with tiny specks of white. How peculiar, his mother remarked aloud, but to herself she wonders how one so young, at merely twenty-two years old, could go grey. She cannot recall such a thing happening to anyone else in her family. It must be an aberration from her husband's line.

The intelligence squad moves more carefully around the city. The Cage is full of IRA men, all of whom have given aliases.

With the execution of informers, the numbers of those who

peep through the looking holes has diminished. This does not seem to affect the steady onslaught of Tan and Auxie raids seeking out IRA officers by name. Florrie, Charley, and Tadg are all becoming worried. All three have had the eerie experience of being watched or followed, and all have had at least one close call ducking out of sight of intelligence men or military and losing them quickly. James himself has had the unsettling feeling of being watched. But he has rationalised to himself that everyone is being watched by everyone else. Regular Republican citizens are watching, looking for informers on the IRA; informers are watching the IRA for the British, the British are watching regular Republican citizens. It is a mad circle of spies everywhere, thinks James to himself, and many do not realise just what a dangerous game they are playing. But James knows. Even the British command has been overheard warning the new intelligence men that Cork is a city of spies. It is no surprise to James when Florrie tells of his own close call. One of his younger lads to whom he assigns regular lookout details came and asked him if he could shoot a man he believed to be a spy, a man he had observed slipping over a fence and into a yard on several occasions long after dark. When given the address, with a roiling of his gut Florrie instantly recognises it as Josephine's address, and just as quickly realises he, himself sneaking in to be with his new wife, was being watched by his own men. This young lad did not have the training yet to move forward and discern faces in the dark. Nor does he carry a gun. Thank God! Without giving them the address, nor sharing the reason for his whereabouts, Florrie shares the story with James and the squad. This is why we ask for permission to shoot he tells them, emphasising permission. James thinks to himself, what are you doing Florrie, sneaking around after curfew, what risks are you taking? But I know whose house you are visiting. Don't worry Florrie, your secret is safe with me. But Florrie cannot read James's thoughts. Florrie does not care for the way some of the men in the ASU and intelligence squad have been taking initiative. There have been rancorous phone calls from GHQ in Dublin, not from Collins, but from Richard Mulcahy. What the hell is going on in Cork? Get your men under control. You are making the IRA look like swarms of thugs instead of a proper disciplined army. Florrie does not care for Mulcahy at the best of times. Any meetings he has had with him leave a bad taste in his mouth and it is only Mulcahy's once close friendship with Terrence that prevents Florrie from dismissing him out of hand. Nevertheless, he tells Mulcahy, Cork is not Dublin. Our men are doers, not talkers. Mulcahy lets fly the expletives for which he is famous, and Florrie thinks to himself, my mother would wash your mouth out with soap.

James spends the first week of April awake at nights thinking of possibilities for breaking Seán out of prison. The weather is good, and he makes another trip down to Hauwboline. He brings field glasses this time and lays himself behind rocks on the seashore and watches Spike Island across the water. It is easy to see the walls of the prison proper, and on the shore he can make out men working outside. He can just discern faces that are barely recogniseable. There are British officers standing about smoking, the prisoners working on the ground, creating a small road or wide path. Prisoners are dotted around the shoreline. James adjusts his glasses and waits patiently as the men work their way in his direction. There are men here from all over the south of Ireland. Of the dozen or so men outside, he does not recognise anyone until he sees not by the face, which is too far away to bring up clearly, but by the specs and the stance that it is Seán. As he looks around, he also sees Con Conroy; a bigger, more athletic man by far, and he sees one of his own battalion officers, Seán Twomey. The Cork men stick together, even in prison. James's mind starts racing. He observes the mainland shorelines all around. He knows there are small towns right along the coastline here that are easy places to get lost in if you can just get there. Easy places to hide and disperse from. But as he watches across the harbour, he also notes many British Coast Guard boats, their flags flapping in the breeze, and he thinks of the British guns in every soldier's hands. Nevertheless, he begins to make notes on the types of vessels, their location, and the direction they are moving. He draws himself a sketch. A homemade map with the coast guard routes and times. After a few hours he notes that there are periods of time that would allow for a boat to cross to shore and not be caught. He resolves that something can be done, a fisherman's boat at the right part of the island shore at exactly the right time. It could be done. With mounting excitement James makes his way into a Cobh pub and calls up Jim Grey. Fancy a ride to the country? He will visit O'Hegarty and make his case.

Word is sent to O'Hegarty to meet in Ballingeary in the tiny pub on the main street. James and Jim arrive in the late afternoon and note the presence of battalion men long before they come to the main drag of the village. The battalion men are openly carrying weapons in this part of the country now. Since Coolavokig and the kidnapping of Mrs Lindsay, and the burning of Leemount house, the British have closed up shop and let the entire territory go to the dogs. Or so they think. In reality the IRA battalions have turned into local police forces, with battalion commanders holding court and acting as judge. Most of the people are happy about this, except of course the reigning economic interests, who no longer have sway with the powers that were. Fairness rules now when disputes occur, not wealth.

James can tell by the way the faces of these men look at himself and Jim Grey as they drive past that the battalion boys are on the lookout. They are watching over O'Hegarty like he is king of the Celts and they are his Fianna, his fellowship of youthful guards and warriors. They know both James and Jim from the Coolavokig ambush, yet still they regard them coolly if politely. City lads and country lads. O'Hegarty, on the other hand, is delighted to see his men. He is so happy he does not even protest when they ask for a pint. He claps them on the back and says, why not? With that, the barman brings two tall glasses of Guinness and a cup of steaming tea. O'Hegarty warms his hands around the cup and sips his tea.

He looks his men over and is happy with what he sees. Both men, but especially James, look so much older to him. In his mind's eye James is but a lad of seventeen riding his bicycle like the devil. Somehow, he has become a tall, handsome man. Slim, but wiry with muscle. O'Hegarty notes with mild alarm the traces of grey and white in James's hair, though he says nothing. The twinkle in his blue eyes is gone; the smile that was once so ready to be flashed around the room has disappeared and only a straight sensuous mouth graces his face. A mouth and eyes that divulge no secrets, though O'Hegarty knows there are a multitude of secrets stored up in the recesses of James's mind. God help us all if those ever come tumbling out, he thinks. Jim is older by a few years and is truly in his prime as a young man. He looks like he just walked out of a Hollywood film with large handsome features and thick dark hair pushed back across his forehead. Like James, he carries himself as if he has not a care in the world. He too is full of secrets, as O'Hegarty knows only too well. Someday, God willing, he will grow to be an old man who reminisces over a pint with his comrades, telling stories that will need no embellishment and that most will find unbelievable. James, on the other hand, is another cup of tea, and O'Hegarty senses his secrets will be safe there. In fact, James is just the type to find a reason to leave the room when others are reliving their glory days. But that day may or may not be in their futures. They could all be hanging by a rope before they know what hit them.

O'Hegarty listens while James puts forth his ideas for rescuing Seán. All we need is a fast boat in the exact place at the exact time. I have timed the coast guard patrols. It can be done. Jim is stretched out with his long legs pointed into the room, his arm resting over a chair. Jim is happy to participate. He knows Seán well, but he is here as a driver and will follow orders. O'Hegarty notes the difference in the body language of the two. James is sitting on the chair with his feet crossed beneath him, his hands holding his pint, face inclined, voice lowered. He is intent on his description of the island, and his idea of setting a boat across in such a way that coast guards and prison guards both might be evaded.

O'Hegarty nods to James. Aye Jimmy, it is a fine idea. They have the boys building a golf course for the officers so they do and I am not surprised that they have volunteered to be outside working instead of inside those dungeons. But surely you know Seán is not our primary issue at the minute. We have executions coming up, two of the Mourne Abbey boys are due to hang at the end of the month. If anybody is going to escape it should be them. Also, Jimmy you must know how risky a boat escape would be. One turn of a British seaman's head and we would be run down by several boats and probably sunk at sea. Do you fancy drowning? You know they won't be throwing us life rafts after they shoot us down. O'Hegarty can feel James's disappointment, though his face is as deadpan and cool as ever. O'Hegarty knows what it is to lose friends who are in trouble. Listen Jimmy, I will put a word out to our man in Cobh. Seán Hyde is there now. He had to leave Collins's team in Dublin because the G-men were almost on him. He is sharing command there. He will have the local boys with the better knowledge of the water. We will see what we can do with this plan of yours. But to himself O'Hegarty thinks that Seán is safer where he is. If he escapes and is caught, he will be executed for sure. Nevertheless, an escape from Spike Island will drive the British mad and O'Hegarty has his contacts who can smooth out the process. There is a prison officer who feeds him information, and the good Father Fitzgerald who visits the men there is a reliable messenger. O'Hegarty will make some calls.

When James returns to the city the following day, he meets the team at the Douglas Street pub. He has come to expect that either terrible news will be divulged, or new plans announced. This seems to be the way things work out at the pub. As he walks, James takes off his cap and lets the spring breeze wash over his face and through his hair. He runs his hands across his scalp and thinks of the grey and white that is speckled through his once deep auburn hair. I will be twenty-three in July, but I am beginning to look like an old man, he thinks. At the pub, a change in tactics is discussed, just as James expected. James's ears perk up significantly when he hears Martin Corry's name and that he is expected to make a trip to the farm. He pipes up and suggests otherwise to Pa Murray, the current head of the ASU. Sure, 'tis better somebody that bastard gets on with goes in my stead, James says. We all know that one and I do not get on. Peter volunteers to go with a driver to pick up the bombs Pa Murray wants. Martin Corry's farm is not just a place of execution and burial; it has also become a bomb factory. We will be putting those bombs to good use lads, says Sandow. We have to up the ante, those bastards are looking for us by name. We will try to chase them out of the city altogether. That's the plan for the next few weeks. Drive them out of the city the same way we did in the Gaeltacht. After Coolavokig, the locals started up in full force, cutting communication lines, trenching the roads to disable their lorries, demolishing bridges, and pulling up sections of the railway lines. That's what we have to work on, boys. Making life so miserable for them here they'll be crying for their mamas, if indeed they have any, the fucking monsters.

On Tuesday morning James finds himself hovering about in Washington Street. He stands looking in a shop window. What he is looking at he cannot tell you because he is thinking of the bombs that his hands tenderly hold steady, deep in his pockets. Peter is across the street tucked into a laneway and Pa Murray stands inside a shop door, a bomb in one hand, while innocently chatting up the pretty salesclerk behind the counter. Two other members of the

ASU are nervously nursing their guns in their pockets as they stroll down the street. The lorry of Tans they are expecting can be heard in the distance. It passes quickly around the bend in the road and whizzes past them, well above speed. But the three men are waiting, and in one go they step onto the sidewalk and let fire straight into the back of the lorry. Of the five bombs, two explode on top of the Tans, injuring some of the men. One misses the mark and bounces down the street, rolling to a quiet stop. Two more are also duds. The men with guns let fire before they duck into laneways as the machine guns are activated by the men still standing in the back of the lorry. As James runs down laneways and through the back doors of shops, he curses Martin Corry and his inferior bombs. *I should have known better. We could all be killed compliments of that eejit.*

North of the city in the village of Blarney, Frank Busteed has come to his family home to visit his brother and his mother's grave. He is exhausted and sore from spending so much time on the run, sleeping in barns, dependent on good families to prepare him a hot meal. He keeps seeing his mother's face, her hand waving goodbye to him, her rosary woven through her fingers. His brother fries him bacon and eggs and for the first time in weeks Frank eats his fill and then sleeps peacefully for an entire blessed afternoon, while a couple of the local IRA lads keep watch outside. Late afternoon he awakens and decides to walk down to the village shop and get himself a packet of cigarettes. As he nears the shop, a man walks out carrying a newspaper and a box of cigarettes. Though he is dressed in civilian clothes, his get-up could not scream British military any louder if he tried. He is wearing a tweed golfing suit, complete with knickerbockers and green stockings. *For fuck's sake,* thinks Frank to himself, *you have got to be kidding me.* He whispers to the local lads to head across the street and cover him. Frank walks up to the major, pulls his gun and tells him he is now in the hands of the IRA. Your name and rank, sir? asks Frank, with all the British politeness he can muster. Major Geoffrey Lee Compton Smith, DSO 2nd Battalion Royal Welsh Fusiliers. And who exactly might you be? This Frank chooses to ignore. *Well, well, well,* he is thinking to himself. *This is just what we need.* He nods to his sentries who walk over to join him. Do not imagine that I will not attempt to escape, says the major. He is a gentleman through and through, the manners taught and expected of him from a young age by his wealthy father, a well-known lawyer in London. He has medals from the Great War and is known for his valiant actions protecting his men at his own risk. He is not your average Black and Tan ruffian. Indeed, it is a mystery why he is even here, given the crew that he must work with. As Frank regards his prize catch, a neighbour, a woman and her young son, walk by and stop to chat. She does not question why Frank is holding a gun on the gentleman, but instead says hello to Frank and tells him that her son is off to Cobh to catch a ship that will take him to New York. Good luck to you, says Frank, and the major, ever the gentleman, tips his hat to the lady. It is the last time the major will tip his hat. Frank gets in touch with O'Hegarty. I have a little surprise for you sir, perhaps a bit of leverage against the upcoming executions.

As the British search for their missing major, he is quietly moved from house to barn outbuilding across County Cork, until at last he is walked across the stones of the primordial bog towards the turf cutters' cottage, the same turf cutter who sheltered Mrs Lindsay. The turf cutter and his ancient mother make the sign of the cross when they see them coming. God give us strength, she prays, and immediately gets down on her cracked, arthritic knees, and prays the rosary in Irish, though the pain in her joints is unbearable. We are doing our purgatory here on earth, son. God help us all, especially the poor sinner they are bringing us now.

O'Hegarty smiles to himself. Indeed, Major Smith is a bit of leverage. Perhaps they will put a bit more value on his head than they did on the Lindsay woman. He writes General Strickland a letter. Your major is a guest of the nation. We will happily hand him over in trade for the four young men you are about to hang. Your call. Then O'Hegarty calls up Connie Neenan. Connie has just made his way home from England after spending the last two years behind bars. He is a braggart, but he has balls. He will have to do. We are running out of men. You will have to take charge of the city, Connie. We have a prize British officer we are holding as leverage against the executions due for the Clonmult boys and the Mourne Abbey pair. We need to keep up the pressure. Keep your men busy. Every informer, every military man you can take out, do it. I need a little back up for my message, a little incentive for the general.

Yes, it's a problem Séamus, the poor quality of the bombs, we know it. We are working on it. James is sharing a pint with his friend

Tadg. They are alone in the Douglas Street Pub and so James is more relaxed. He is recounting some of his adventures to Tadg, who has spent a good part of the winter in England. James notices that Tadg does a second take when he takes off his cap and his hair is revealed. He can see the change in James that James sees in Tadg. Both men look older, thinner, tired, strained. But unlike James, Tadg's hair is still thick black, despite him being a few years older than James. As they sit confiding in each other, a runner, an IRA lad, one of Florrie's boys, hurriedly makes his way into the bar. He stops in front of the men and takes off his hat. Excuse me sir, I have a message for you. I'm to tell you that Mr Crofts has been picked up a short while ago. We believe he has been taken to the Victoria Barracks. Both men stand, nod at each other, and head out of the door in opposite directions. Séamus, be careful, Tadg calls back as he walks away, his trenchcoat blustering about him in the early evening air. He can feel caution taking over his mind and body. He walks warily down the street, gathering his coat around him, pulling his cap down, walking quickly down Douglas Street towards his digs.

It is the unknowns that drive James immediately into his self-protective training. They do not know under what circumstances Crofts has been picked up. He could have been given up by an informer, caught in an operation, or randomly picked up off the street. It is unlikely that he was in an operation, or I would have at least heard about it, thinks James. Therefore, it is an informer, or bad, bad luck. Indeed, he will discover that Crofts was picked up in a random street check. He turned a corner into a waiting posse of Tans who did not like the look of him and took him in for questioning. Do they know they have the leader of the city IRA in their hands? Probably not. Doubtless Crofts will give an alias and be thrown in the cage. But as James walks down the street towards a meal and a safe house for the evening, gathering distance from Tadg with each step, he misses the action going on behind him in the opposite direction. Tadg's sixth sense has been dead on and as he walks past a short intersection, two British undercover Intelligence agents walk right into him. Tadg knows instantly that one of them is the dreaded and elusive Sergeant Hollywood. They look at each other's faces, and Tadg knows he has but one short, and unlikely chance. He runs like the devil down the street calculating as he goes the amount of time before their guns are drawn and cocked, a mere five seconds.

One thousand, two thousand, three thousand, four thousand, then he smashes through a house door, straight up the stairs into a back bedroom. He will jump down to the backyard and take off through the laneways. But Tadg has difficulty opening the window. His body is only halfway out of the opening when the bullets of Hollywood, followed by those of a group of Tans, explode through the back of his lungs, shatter his spine, and burst his heart. The last thing Tadg O'Sullivan feels is the smashing of a boot into his backside and then the swirl of cool spring air whirling around him as he falls into eternity. The British crowd to the window and look down. They do not so much as bother to gather up his blood-spattered body lying sprawled on the grass below. One more Fenian fuck off the list. Let's go out for a drink to celebrate.

James patrols the streets alone. In his mind he is calm. It is his own body that betrays him. His hand reaches to his gun frequently during the day. He will then realise that he is thinking of Tadg's twisted and torn body. He feels a cold sweat break out on the back of his neck and he suddenly realises he is thinking of a much-desired confrontation with Hollywood. Or, as he walks, he suddenly realies his feet are taking him straight to the closest Tan barracks and his hand is caressing his gun. And yet some part of him knows that he must be smart. He must stick to his training. But he keeps his gun out of his holster and in his coat pocket, and as he strides quickly down the streets of Cork he keeps the cold metal of the barrel in his hand. He will be ready when Hollywood bumps into him and he will take down as many as he can manage. He does not care if there is an entire company with him. His anger bubbles just below the surface of his skin. He can feel it; the rage and grief pushing him from the inside out. But there is nothing to alleviate the pressure. There are no Tans to shoot, no Hollywood or Kelly. They have all gone into hiding. He thinks about just walking up to a barracks and knocking on the door. How many could he take out before he is shot himself? Peter is worried. He feels the self-imposed isolation into which his friend Séamus has retreated since the murder of Tadg. It is a bad sign. And Séamus is not the only one to be cut down when a friend is killed, or to show signs of stress during active operations. It seems to Peter there are cracks and fissures all around him. No one is as they were. Men on the run have the look of hunted men. Thin, tired, worn. It has not been unusual for men to get sick this past winter. Some with pneumonia from being out in the elements. The men in the city are constantly on their guard. Should I carry a gun or not? Shoot or be shot at? Every day is a gamble. When a man like Tadg is hunted down and shot in the back, the others know that the likelihood of their own demise is high. The pressure is ratcheted up one more notch.

But suddenly there is something else to think about. A phone call from O'Hegarty. Jimmy lad, your plan may just work out. Liam Lynch has wind of trouble. We need to pick someone up quickly. Your man might come along for the ride. A tiny ray of light pierces the dark horizon. James smiles. He sets about gathering up the men who are still in town. Sandow, Peter, Mahoney, a few others. The operations commander from Cobh is coming in for a chat. Let's go out for a meal and talk gaol breaks. The men meet in the little café run by O'Hegarty's wife, Magdalen. Sentries are posted. James presents his plan. The men talk into the evening.

In 1904, Lady Augusta Gregory, the elderly widow of the Governor of Ceylon and an Irish country girl at heart, publishes a collection of Irish myths and legends. This is the same year that she works with the great Irish poet William Butler Yeats to create the Abbey Theatre in Dublin, which will play a central role in the Gaelic revival. She learned many of the Celtic legends as a child at the feet of her nanny in her nursery on the family's thousand-acre estate in County Galway. This estate is a mere fraction of the total lands owned by various branches of her English family who, serving the English crown in the seventeenth century, were awarded land for their loyalty. Though Lady Gregory marries young and spends many years travelling the world with her husband, she never forgets the stories and legends told to her as a child, nor the hardworking native Irish that man her father's estate. Lady Gregory observes the colonial legacy of England in her travels around the world. She develops a revulsion for imperialism, and a latent, but fierce, Irish Republican fervour. When her husband dies, she returns to Ireland and spends years researching the old Celtic stories handed down through generations.

Back at her home in Galway, living in the grand estate, Coole Park, she seeks out the elderly of the area and writes down their versions of the legends she remembers, as well as others she does not. She travels to the Aran Islands and does likewise. Finally, when she moves to Dublin to work with the theatre group, she spends days that stretch into weeks and months in the National Library of Ireland, researching. At last, she puts pen to paper, and the grand result is several volumes of stories. Lady Gregory gives the Irish a great gift. She returns to them the long-lost memories of their ancestors. She passes to them the quickly disappearing recollections and reminiscences of times of glory and accomplishment, and with that, their culture and heritage. It is as if she reaches into the fog and captures what has been quickly receding. Her books are runaway best sellers.

When at the age of eighty, Lady Gregory leaves the earth, she leaves behind a massive estate that becomes a national treasure. Go there now and walk the paths; see the ancient, entwined trees, hundreds of years old, with initials of the famous people of the land, visitors to that fine estate, who stopped to leave their mark. Marvel at the landscape; a tiny window into what Ireland looked like before the devastation of occupation. Feed the swans that live on the lake and read Yeats's famous poems of the place. And after you do these things, say a little prayer of gratitude for the gift of one single woman to an entire country of people. A woman with passion and foresight, determination and kindness, generosity and intellect. A woman who helped forge a nation. Did James ever say a prayer of gratitude? Perhaps. Because it is from her books that James, as a young boy, first learns of those who will become his favourite literary characters. Evening after evening, with his family surrounding him, he sits by the fire and reads the outrageous stories of the heroes of Ireland. But one story in particular he will dwell on. It is the story of Fionn mac Cumhaill and his brotherhood of warriors, the Fianna.

The young boy Fionn is the product of an illicit relationship. His father, Cumhaill, leader of the Fianna, pays for his existence with his life. Fionn's mother Muirne Muincháem does not have the blessing of her father, Tadg the high druid, to marry Cumhaill, because the families are enemies. He forbids Muirne to marry him and makes war on Cumhaill. When Cumhaill is killed, Muirne marries a lesser king elsewhere. She cannot keep the child, who she names Demne, with her because all know he is son of Cumhaill and therefore outlawed. His mother, fearing for his life, takes him to two women she trusts, the good druidess Bodhmall, and her sister, the famous woman warrior Liath Luachra. Muirne leaves her beautiful boy with them deep in the forest. The women dedicate the next few years to his education. He learns to run like a deer and hit targets at a great distance with bow and arrow. He learns of the plants and herbs of the forest and their healing properties. Through their constant challenges, he learns bravery and confidence. These two women fear nothing. They depend on their own self-sufficiency and teach the child through example and challenges to do likewise. In short, Demne soaks up all the learning he can, an accumulation of all the knowledge of the learned druid and all of the knowledge of peace and war from the warrior.

At last, it is time for the boy to leave the women and make his way into the world. They change his name to Fionn, which means bright, or light, not because he is the light of their lives, which he is, but because his hair mysteriously turns white: quickly and prematurely before he leaves them. Fionn wishes to find his father's people, but the women know his life would be at risk. When a troop of poets stops nearby, the women allow Fionn to go with them for a time to learn the stories and ballads of the people. But danger lurks. The women hear that Fionn's existence has been discovered by the enemies of his father, and they have set out to put an end to him. When Fionn does not return, the women search, and sure enough he has been entrapped and held in a cave by lackeys and informers. The druidess works her magic, and brings Fionn home, back to their secret forest enclave.

As the women grow older, they realise they cannot keep Fionn forever. They give him their blessing and let him go to meet his fate, whatever that may be. In his travels he meets the dwarf druid, Finnegas, with whom he stays for some time studying and learning. One day Finnegas has the great good fortune of catching the salmon of all knowledge. He tells Fionn to prepare it for him, but not to eat it. After touching the salmon, Fionn burns his finger in the fire and puts it to his mouth to sooth it. From this small, innocent action, Fionn is imbued with wisdom.

Eventually, and with a long list of adventures, Fionn makes his way to the high king. There is no hiding his parentage. Fionn is as big, handsome, fearless, and skilled, as his father, but a different man altogether. Where the Fianna were once a fellowship of warriors, bent on fighting at the drop of a hat, Fionn, thanks to his upbringing, is not only a highly skilled warrior, but a man who can bring people together. His wisdom and goodness are evident. The king ponders making Fionn a member of his Fianna, his own brood of warriors. Doubt flees from his mind the night Fionn resists the magic of Aillen, an ancient enemy, a giant who every year at the feast of Samhain makes his way to the king's territory and burns down the people's homes. Fionn stays awake, challenges the giant, and manages to cut off his head and bring it to the king skewered on a spear. In the king's mind, this feat has won for Fionn the exalted position of head of the Fianna, just as his father was once head of the Fianna of another King. With Fionn's leadership, the Fianna is transformed. Gone are the pointless, costly, dangerous physical challenges of a posse of proud boastful warriors. The men of the Fianna pledge their allegiance to Fionn. His closest Fianna friends, Caoilte, Conan, and Goll, will stay by his side for the rest of his life. Fionn and his Fianna become the saviours of the people. They fight off enemies, work together to bring peace and plenty, and become revered as wise warriors, fearless in the face of challenge, even the evil magic of foreigners and their dark wizards.

While James is enjoying a meal out with his battalion, Frank Busteed sits at the tiny kitchen table in the cottage of the turf cutter in the middle of the remote bog, having a cup of tea with Major Compton-Smith. The major is a true gentleman. He has had many a conversation over the last couple of weeks with the poor turf cutter and with the IRA guards that are posted day and night around the property. It is apparent to everyone who has encountered the major that he is at heart a good man in the wrong place. True, he is an Englishman through and through, but a better representative of the English people would be hard to find. He should not be working with the Tans, and the fact that he is alone on his days off corroborates that fact. Busteed has developed a grudging respect for him despite his ridiculous green socks and knickerbockers. Though he espouses different politics, the man is intelligent, and a talented artist. He demonstrates uncommonly good manners and asks for almost nothing. But Busteed knows that despite all this, he is still an enemy soldier and would not think twice about cutting him down in an instant, given half a chance. Busteed pours tea into the rustic mug. Tomorrow, April 28, is execution day for our lads. We have had nary a word from your general. Prepare for the worst. If we do not hear by dawn, I would suggest you write yourself a letter. We will be sure to deliver it. Indeed, the major responds, indeed. When Frank leaves, he picks up a pen and begins a letter to his wife.

Seán Forde sucks in the smoke from his illicit cigarette with satisfaction. The day is fine. The work is light, and though the prison of Spike Island is old and decrepit and the men endure debilitating conditions, he knows he is one of the lucky ones. Though he is cruelly scarred with welts on his back and missing or broken teeth in his mouth, he is alive and strong enough to fight another day, should he ever make it back to the mainland, unlike some of his friends. But Seán freezes in horror when an inmate, adept at the black market of the prison, spies him from another section, and thinking he is doing him a great favour, asks the guard to deliver a package of cigarettes to Seán Forde. The guard is intrigued. Seán Forde? That man there? That is not Seán Forde. But to himself he thinks, bloody hell, maybe it is the infamous Seán Forde, the man whose name is on every most wanted list in the country, the incalcitrant Rebel who has been tormenting the RIC and Tans in the Limerick area for years now and somehow eluded capture.

The guard informs his superior officer, who sends a dispatch to the city of Limerick where the infamous Seán Forde is known for being a bad influence on the locals, and worse, a known operative in several violent actions taken against the Tans. The unlucky courier, however, is stopped by members of Cork No. 3 Brigade, in whose territory he is found. The dispatch is read, and the imminent danger reported to Liam Lynch. Liam is back in the picture now, having spent months working in Dublin for GHQ: he moved back to be with his brigade in the new year, once hostilities had heightened. Lynch does not hesitate. He sends a two-man team to Listowel to take down the RIC inspector, who is just leaving to go and identify Forde. The man does not even make it out of the town. But the British, as always, are resourceful, and even though the district inspector is not yet even in his grave, they seek out another who knows the face of Seán Forde.

The following morning, the British proceed with two executions of the original eight prisoners of the betrayed Mourne Abbey ambush that occurred back in February. They shoot the men in Victoria Barracks as per their usual custom, and then transport the bodies to Cork Gaol to be buried in the exercise yard. One of the men is just eighteen years old, the other twenty-four.

The men in Spike Island are far removed from the happenings, and no news is shared with them of the goings-on outside. But the good father whispers in Forde's ear the story of the interception of the mail and the execution of the RIC inspector. Forde knows that another will be found to replace the first. Sure enough, that same day O'Hegarty's mole, one of the prison guards, makes his way to Forde and quietly gives him the news. You are to be sent back to the city tomorrow. They must have new information on you. Prepare for the worst. As Father Fitzgerald leaves the island after his early morning visit, Forde whispers in his ear. It must be today. Tell them it must be today.

Father Fitzgerald steps off the boat on the mainland and heads straight to the nearest phone. He calls O'Hegarty. Well, if it must be today, today it will be, Father. Never worry. Within an hour or so Seán Forde, Seán MacSwiney and Seán Twomey have returned to their afternoon work of helping to build a path around the newly laid golf course. They have been at this for a while now and no one seems to mind that they are taking their time, not even the prison guards. It is a beautiful day, and everyone is happy to be outside with the sea breeze washing over them and the sun pouring down. There is a guard, a golf course supervisor, and a military man. When they stop for a smoke they offer the men a cigarette. The three men take their cigarettes and clamber down a short gorge to the rocky shoreline below where the water laps at their feet. It is a quiet spot where they are slightly out of view. This is their usual practice for enjoying the odd smoke that comes their way.

The two guards that usually supervise this detail are not bad fellas. They always give the men time to enjoy their cigarette before they call them back to work. But as Forde inhales on his cigarette, looking out on the water, he sees a fishing boat heading straight for them. There is a small Union Jack hoisted on it, but Forde knows that is exactly what he would do, were he to be trying to hide his true identity. He watches as the fishing boat slows down and meanders its way closer to the shoreline, the skipper controlling the engine and the four men inside looking like they are out enjoying the sunshine, hoping to catch some dinner. When the boat is close enough Forde sees that it is none other than Seán Hyde himself, come to make sure the job gets done. He whispers to MacSwiney and Twomey to take care of the two guards and he will look after the military man. Forde turns suddenly, grabs a hammer from the nearby tools, and races up to the sentry. Before the soldier can load his rifle, the hammer swings through the air like a tomahawk, and with a sickening thump is driven into his temple. He quietly keels over onto the ground. Forde, ever a man with an eye for a gun, picks up the rifle, scoops up the ammo and throws it across the water and into the boat. Meanwhile MacSwiney and Twomey have worked up behind the other two and swung rope around their necks, tackling them down, gagging them and tying them up. Back down the slope they clamber into the boat. But just as they are making their way into open water, another sentry sees the downed officers and shoots in the air, giving the alarm. The men have mere moments before they will be intercepted by a coast guard vessel.

Mick Burke, the officiating commander of Cobh, and Seán Hyde had, at the dinner meeting with James, worked out a clean plan to get Forde and MacSwiney off the island. They had organised the boat, convincing the local skipper to make this small contribution to his country despite the fact he is not in the IRA. *If you get caught just tell them we put a gun to your head!* They had people lined up to bring in the boat at a certain hidden section of coastline and help the men escape in various directions without a trace. They had a plan for hiding the skipper's boat and then getting it back to Cobh. They arranged with the Grey brothers to have cars ready to take the men in opposite directions. They had thought of every detail. That was yesterday. James planned to return later in the week to help make it happen. But with the call from Father Fitzgerald, Seán Hyde, trained by Michael Collins himself to make good on every opportunity, never to wait for tomorrow if the job can be done today, charged ahead. Sean Forde, the escapee will live to be an old man and will tell his story always acknowledging the bravery of those five men in a fishing boat. James will regret missing out on the opportunity to save his friend, but he knows it was his idea that got both his best friend MacSwiney and the fugitive Sean Forde out of harm's way. James will never be one for stories anyway.

The three escapees and their rescuers smash the boat into the shore and run, bullets whizzing just past their ears. Forde dives for cover and then shoots out with his stolen rifle at the coast guard patrol that are firing on them from the observation tower high on the hill. The coast guard wisely decides to back off. Out onto the road, the first vehicle they run into is a small cart with a donkey taking its time, enjoying the sunshine. The men jump on board and drive that cart so fast that after a few miles the axle falls off. The men scatter like foxes chased by hounds until at last Forde makes his way along a hedge and up a long gradual hill. He looks back to see the British cordoning off the area around the coastline. What a beautiful day, he thinks to himself as he walks across the heather towards home.

James and Jim Grey drive out to the countryside, avoiding the area cordoned off by the British, to find Seán and bring him to a safe house. They dare not bring him back to the city. Even Jim is feeling the heat and has decided, with the number of street patrols and roundups, he had better take a scenic route out in the country and stay off the main road. The men find Seán in the back room of a pub, harboured by a very nervous local IRA pub owner. His prison stripes have been thrown in the fire and he is dressed in borrowed clothing, so ill-fitting on the usually perfectly groomed Seán that all three men laugh with relief. It is the first time they have laughed in a long time.

With a picnic basket of ham sandwiches and lemonade and pound cake compliments of James's mother, Seán eats ravenously in the back seat of the car. He sits beside a large woollen shawl at the ready to pull over himself and cover the seat if he must dive to the floor and hide, which he does whenever they pass anyone on the quiet country roads. Seán knows both men have guns, James in his holster and Jim Grey probably in a hidden section of the car. He knows they will not be stopping for military or anybody else, and he says a quiet prayer that they arrive at Ballingeary to meet O'Hegarty without incident. As the evening wears on and darkness slides over them, Jim Grey finally quiets down from his singing and stories. In his mind's eye, Seán sees the military man lying on the grass with a hammer hole in his forehead. He sees him mere minutes before, handing the fellas cigarettes and nodding at them to take their time and enjoy. He feels slightly nauseous now. He is sure the man is dead and says a prayer for his soul. I hate this fucking war, he thinks as he sinks into the seat, covers himself over with the shawl and falls asleep dreaming of his-never-to-be-seen-again fiancée.

Frank Busteed, on realising that a last-minute change in sentence is not in the destiny of the two Mourne Abbey men, suddenly feels all appreciation of the major fall away from him like water off a duck's back. These British hit new lows every day. They could have had their major back; a fair price for those two young bucks who never did anything their whole lives but work hard for their families. They have commuted sentences before, but whoever is in charge of the decision just will not give in to an Irish demand. Well then, thinks Frank, this is on your head, you uppity British fucks. Your major can sink into the bog, joining your Mrs Lindsay, and good riddance. But Frank does not go back to the cottage in the bog quite yet. He cannot. He is distraught. He will not let anyone see him like this. It is about this time that Frank's face develops the despairing look that he will carry for the rest of his life. His lips sink down at the edges, dark circles leave an indentation under his eyes, he loses all expression on his face. He has difficulty sleeping, and whenever at last sleep does come, he sees nothing but his mother lying at the bottom of the stairs with her back broken and her little house trashed about her.

After two days, Frank finally makes his way back to the cottage. Did ye write your letters? Yes. Give them here. Out to the bog. And the IRA guards walk the major across the stones and to a lonely spot. The major looks at Frank and thinks that Frank is upset because he must follow through on this, his execution, because of the recalcitrance of the British government. He feels that Frank, too, is a gentleman following orders, just as he, the major, would do in like circumstances. He moves to shake Frank's hand, a gentleman's gesture, soldier to soldier. Does Frank appreciate the gesture? He will speak of many things in the future, but Frank will never speak of this. Say your prayers. Ready. Aim. Fire. The major collapses into the previously dug grave, a quiet prayer for his beautiful little daughter Anne the last words to fall from his lips.

As April turns to May, the spring rains recede and the sun beams down on the City of Cork, indeed all of Ireland. The refuse of early spring flowers wilts into the ground and recedes to allow the lavish blooms of early summer to take over. Though it is only May the weather is such that the sun seems to pull the plants from the earth, drawing them up, up from the ground to blossom out in tall, profuse clusters. The vines twist and turn, the young foliage of trees grows thick and unrestrained. The farmer's fields seen from every hill on the outskirts of the city glow in varied tints of green. They are sprouting forth a short thick carpet of seedlings. In the autumn of 1921 they will become a bumper crop of every vegetable and grain that is grown in Ireland.

In Dublin, the colossal Sinn Féin election machine gears up for the election of 1921, envisioned by the British to be the answer to all of their problems with the Irish. The British do not seem to understand that they are only providing an opportunity to strengthen the politics of Irishmen and sympathetic English, Scottish, and Welsh citizens everywhere in the empire, indeed even of citizens in far reaches of the globe, where the colonised peoples watch the goings-on in Ireland with surreptitious smiles and darting glances from one to another. Truly the British should know better. They are holding an election as a result of a new law pushed through parliament. It is a response to the wealthy of the land, who have holdings and estates and who fear for their property in Ireland. It is a response to thoughtful, decent Englishmen who, reading of the chaos occurring a stone's throw across the Irish Sea, insist that the Irish Situation must be dealt with. The law is also a bow to the wild men of Ulster, Orangemen, who are more British than the British themselves, radical, defiant, and itching for a war.

In truth, Churchill and many other English politicians see the north of Ireland brimming over with violent anti-Catholic, anti-Irish Orangemen as a monkey on the collective English back. Even in an age of imperialism and colonialism they are seen to be a clinging, worrisome headache, some of them quite insane, even to Englishmen. Pity the poor Catholics having to live under their purview, Churchill thinks to himself. But politics is politics, and they must be appeased before they start their own war with the south of Ireland, and Churchill is put in a position of having to support them. So, 'better government' is defined as Home Rule. One parliament for the North of Ireland, the six counties of Ulster that are populated by the progeny of Cromwell's soldiers. They are hateful to the native Irish and their religion, and their politicians are seen as pompous British social climbers. Simultaneously, there is to be another parliament for the south of Ireland, in Dublin. The expectation is that this will appease the Irish citizens who will then rid themselves of the troublesome Sinn Féin and see sense. In their conceit, the British parliament names the new law An Act to Provide for a Better Government of Ireland. The Sinn Féin party, the IRA, and indeed every Republican in Ireland laugh till their sides split.

Just as they did in the general election of 1918, the IRA and Sinn Féin use the electoral infrastructure of the election to run their own spectacle of democracy at British expense. The entire south of Ireland prepares to vote. A plethora of Sinn Féin candidates announce their intention to run. Among the many young men and some few women who throw their hat in the ring is a young man from Cork, brother of a martyred mayor, Seán MacSwiney.

James decides to stay put in the Gaeltacht for a few weeks with Seán. After all, Seán needs a hand. He is running for the constituency of mid-Cork. The IRA's deep connections with Sinn Féin translates into IRA men helping out the candidates wherever they are needed. James bunks up in a tiny cottage with Seán, compliments of a poor yet generous Republican family, and helps work out the details. He acts as messenger, travelling into neighbouring villages to pass on dispatches and pick up information. He helps Seán write letters to various organisations in the city of Cork, election promises to help out the area and its people. He helps Seán write speeches he will need if elected. The two men work continuously. They meet with Florrie, O'Hegarty, and many of the other men who have sought refuge there. If the weather is fine, they join with the local battalion and march to the heights of the mountains, marvelling at the spectacular view all the way to the sea. At night they lay their blankets on the floor and instantly fall asleep by the dying embers of the turf fire.

It is just as well that James spends the initial couple of weeks of May in the Gaeltacht. All around him a determined, systematic military machine is cutting through IRA territory and IRA men. West of the Gaeltacht, in County Kerry, in the small town of Rathmore, after a well-planned ambush of the Tans by the local IRA boys, the military hits back. A few days later, on a rainy afternoon, they arrive *en masse* and force four families out of their homes with only the shirts on their backs. Surrounded by guns pointing at them, they stand shivering in the pouring rain and watch while everything they ever owned goes up in flames. One of the homes belongs to Florrie's elderly parents. It is a message to the local IRA, but it is also a message to Florrie. You are now a known commodity. If we can't find you, we will find what you hold near and dear. I will never be able to leave here, Florrie thinks to himself. Even my poor parents are a target for British cruelty. They know everything about me. Everything but the most important thing: Josephine.

East of the Gaeltacht, back in the City of Cork, James's friends are dropping like flies. On a sunny morning Peter and Seán Twomey turn the corner of Brunswick Street on their way to the Wallace sisters' shop and walk straight into a line of Auxies. The Auxies do not like the look of them and carry them off to Victoria Barracks to be thrown in the cage. But Seán Twomey, once inside the barracks, just turns around and makes his way to the exit. The military men look at him and laugh. Where are you off to mate? Seán keeps walking. He is shot eight times but will live to tell the tale. While Peter is in the cage a few days later, he finds himself making room for his commanding officer Sandow and none other than Seán Culhane. They look glumly at each other and share their alias names. They have been picked up off the street in a military roundup. Lorries of Auxies and Tans just sailing down the city streets, stopping whenever they see a face they don't like, and throwing the men in their paddy wagons. Finally, on May 14, O'Hegarty meets Seán and James and Jim for what has become their regular foray into the tiny pub on the main street. He turns his steaming cup of tea around in the saucer. Bad news boys. Bad news. The general has shut down the Wallace sisters' shop. It is sealed up tight as a drum and they have been evicted with barely the clothes on their backs.

James and Seán are shocked. How many hours have they spent in the tiny back kitchen, reading the papers, joining in meetings? O'Hegarty looks despondent. That's a low blow, so it is, says Seán. How are the sisters? Last I saw Nora she had a terrible cough, so she did. The doctor told her to rest, she has ruined her lungs, probably catching pneumonia while on business for us! I suppose she will get some rest now. They are the two of them moving in with some family for the time being. Seán nods his head. He has a soft heart for the sisters, as they all do, but Seán more than most. He knows how they idealised his brother, and also Tomás. They went out of their way for those two on many an occasion. James thinks the two sisters were probably in love with Terry. After all, who wasn't? I don't suppose it matters now, he thinks to himself, but his thoughts are interrupted by his newest orders. Jimmy, you'd best head back to the city. We are low on men. You boys will have to organise to meet at the café, or the Douglas Street pub. Connie's hands will be tied with so many men picked up. He will need as many hands on deck as possible. If the British want to continue with their official reprisals, we have to fight back. If they want burnings, they shall have them. We need to find a way to take down the remainder of the barracks in the city. We need to cut the Tans off at the knees. There is still much work to be done.

Aye, there is indeed. James and Seán look at each other. They both know what that means. Connie has been behind bars these past two years. This is why he is a good choice to take over from Crofts. His face is not known to the local Tans. It is Murphy and Mahoney that will be needing you. And Jimmy, O'Hegarty looks James in the eye, I want those officers. Hollywood, Kelly, and the rest of them. When we get them that will be a turning point for us. Don't let up until they are sent straight to hell, where they belong.

James spends his first night in the city at home. His mother makes up a hot bath, cooks a thick, fragrant lamb stew, mends and cleans his clothes, giving him clean replacements of everything he is wearing. She shines his shoes and wipes down his trenchcoat and brushes off his newsboy cap. As he eats his stew with his family, he would smile in a rare moment of domestic happiness, but he cannot. The latest news is out. Éamonn de Valera, surreptitious President of Ireland, Prime Minister of the Dáil, survivor of the Easter Rising, has been found in one of his hiding places, arrested and thrown in Portobello Barracks in Dublin. It is a bad turn of events for sure, and a sign that the British are learning that their handy plan of home rule and two parliaments in Ireland is seen as a sham. It seems to be slowly trickling into the collective British political machine that all of their tardy political machinations to do something about the Irish situation will be bulldozed over by a Sinn Féin landslide. Another election that they, the British, have set up and fostered only to be taken advantage of. The talk at his mother's kitchen table is of this and only this. It is a nerve-wracking event for the people of Ireland. Will the last hero of the Easter Rising be executed? De Valera is the visionary leader who has taken them all this far. Before he leaves, James's father thrusts a small roll of bills into his pocket. He hugs his mother, and despite her protests takes off for a safe house. He refuses to bring attention to his family's home. He never enters or exits by their front door but hops the high wall at the last house on the street, just two doors over, and makes his way through the field into a different set of streets.

As James heads through the back lanes of the city in the still bright evening, across the River Lee in the north part of town, Liam di Rioste, Teachta Dála, or in English, Member of Parliament, representing the City of Cork in the outlawed Dáil Éireann, is feeling nervous. Liam is also the president of the Gaelic League in Cork. He knows everyone in the city, rich and poor, IRA, wealthy Protestant business owners, folk in the lunatic asylum and in the workhouse. And everything Liam hears seems to be bad news. Bad news from every quarter. The election rhetoric is in full swing, and he expects to be returned for the second Dáil. There is nothing but support for him around the city.

Liam is a more spiritual man than many. He supports the fight for freedom, but privately he is troubled by the violence, the reprisal followed by reprisal followed by reprisal. For this reason, he is not as enthusiastic about the IRA as some. Nevertheless, the British anti-Sinn Féin machine is oblivious to such minor distinctions. With all of the night-time raids looking for IRA, and the number of men being shot in the back or in their beds, Liam decides it may be prudent to learn a lesson from his IRA counterparts and make sure he is out of his own house by curfew to spend the night elsewhere. However, Liam has a boarder at his own home. The boarder is a priest, Father O'Callaghan. Surely the priest is not in danger, even if the Tans come calling. Everyone knows what Liam looks like; there would be no mistaking the two of them. As Liam learns later in the night, his nervousness was indeed warranted. Late at night his home is suddenly battered in by Tans looking to shoot him in his bed. When Father O'Callaghan explains that Liam is not home, the

Tans decide to shoot him instead. After all, the country is overrun with these Catholic priests anyway.

The following day, a group of Tans walking down the street in the southeast district of the city are surprised by a group of James's colleagues. This is the new tactic they are using in Cork City. The Tans and Auxies group together, six or more to a team, and patrol the streets looking for IRA. Any face that scowls at them or even looks them in the eye are fodder for their abuse. Into the wagon they are thrown. Destination? The cage. Recourse for those arrested? None. They can rot in the cage for as long as it takes for somebody to turn them over as IRA. And if they are not IRA? That is the cost of supporting Rebels in your midst. But this day they will get a taste of their own terror thrown back at them. Mahoney has been given advance warning of their route. He quickly gathers what men he can find, and they lie in wait for the patrol. Out of a laneway they come firing, and five Tans drop. Four dead, one wounded, one left alive and uninjured, intentionally. The man left alive is Mahoney's mole.

The following day the Tans go on a tear. What difference does it make, Murphy quips? They are on a tear day and night now anyway. But this time it is an official reprisal. Everyone knows what that means. It means more families will be thrown in the street and their homes burned to cinders. This is exactly what happens. The four families are known to be IRA sympathisers. They stand outside and watch their belongings smoulder and sputter into thin air and wonder whatever will become of them.

Enough! hollers O'Hegarty into the phone. Gather up your crews. Find the biggest, most luxurious homes in the south side. Four of them. Get to work. I want it done today.

James finds himself in front of Lady Kate Dobbin's mansion. Her husband is High Sheriff of the city and owner of a tobacco company. The Dobbins are as wealthy as they come in Cork. Lady Dobbin is a watercolour artist of some repute. She creates beautiful romantic paintings of the many scenic hills and vales, the ancient towers, and beautiful coastlines around the country. But Lady Kate, though she has lived much of her fifty years in Ireland, is English. As English as the day is long. Mahoney leads the team. Bang-bang-bang on the door of Frankfort House, her luxurious home overlooking an inlet of the sea. Inside the butler has looked out of the window and seen the five men with torches and barrels of petrol, just taken from Lady Kate's own garage. He knows what's coming.

He frantically tries to explain to Lady Dobbin. Yes, yes, I understand she says, and opens the door. This is a reprisal for the official British policy of burning the homes of Irish citizens. Lady Dobbin looks at the men's faces. Only two look back at her. The other three turn their gaze. They may be IRA, but centuries of kowtowing to the British cannot be changed in mere months. James looks at her coolly. She was once a beauty, he thinks to himself, and what a shame to burn down a house the likes of this. It stands in the centre of beautiful gardens, tall and dignified. But Lady Dobbin is not concerned about the house, so much as she is about her vast collection of paintings. She asks for time to remove them. Mahoney stares at her. The gall of these fucking people. The four families whose homes were burned down yesterday weren't allowed so much as a pair of shoes for their children's feet. I understand, but Lady Dobbin is not about to give up, it is shameful, so it is. However, burning to cinders my life's work won't change that. No indeed, says Mahoney. But that is not my concern.

Lady Dobbin's face becomes frantic, despite her efforts at keeping a stiff upper lip. James watches her. There is something about her that reminds him of his own mother. Both women are of the same age, tall and slim with impeccable manners. James calls out. We will give you an hour. Better get to work. Lady Dobbin stares at James and then turns and runs inside her home, calling her servants. Mahoney looks at James with a quizzical look. What's got into you? he says. Who knows? She reminds me of my mother. The other men all laugh and relax. They watch as an army of servants carry out painting after painting and stack them far from the main house on the driveway. With a few minutes to spare, Lady Dobbin gets cheeky. She has her butler help her carry out an ancient elaborately carved table. It has been in her husband's family for centuries. I suppose we are done now, says Mahoney, and begins to douse the torches in petrol while James and another of the crew walk through the home sloshing the stinking gasoline on furniture, floors, and curtains. Once done, the men walk around the outside and toss the torches in through the open windows.

The flames lick up high into the attic of the home and it seems like only seconds before the entire house is exploding. James and his crew walk down the driveway to their waiting car as Lady Dobbin wipes the tears from her eyes. Murphy has just come from another mansion. He is waiting for the men at the end of the driveway. Follow me, he calls out to them, and both cars race along the manicured streets and out into the country. James sees the sign for the Douglas Country Club and knows exactly what Murphy is up to. A den of imperialists, Murphy has been known to call the golf club. Both cars roar up the driveway and pull alongside the empty club house. Out come the barrels of petrol from the back of Murphy's car. The door is kicked in, the petrol sloshed around the room, the match lit. The cars race down the driveway and out of sight.

In all, four wealthy influential families are put out of their homes, and their lavish mansions torched. The exclusive golf and country club is burned to cinders. The people of Cork are shocked. But secretly they smile. What's good for the goose is good for the gander they are heard to whisper to one another.

With the Wallace sisters' shop out of commission, the meeting place for James and his regular intelligence colleagues must be changed. His group has been decimated. He misses Tadg, whose massacred body is now buried in St Fin Barre's cemetery not far from Terry and Tomás. He misses Peter and Dan, locked up in the cage. He misses the odd visit of Seán Culhane, who tells a grand if embellished story. He misses Seán, who is still in hiding in the Gaeltacht, and who will now probably stay there, given de Valera's arrest and the attempted murder of di Rioste. He even misses his friend Busteed, who has vanished completely since the execution of the major, hiding out somewhere in his battalion's territory. Tom Barry, head of the West Cork Flying Column, and many of the others who used to come into the city for regular meetings, are keeping their distance from the city, and instead report to O'Hegarty in God only knows what lonely bog-filled places.

Murphy feels the strain of the recent arrests, the roundups, the night raid murders. Now the most recent atrocity is weighing on his shoulders: one of O'Hegarty's relatives of the same name has been raided. Murphy is not sure if the Tans were looking for Denis Hegarty the intelligence officer, or if it is just a coincidence, but they broke into the house of Dan Healy, fine citizen of Cork, and tried to arrest him. His beautiful young wife, seven months pregnant with their first child, argues, begs, and pleads that her husband has nothing to do with the IRA, which, outside of full tacit support, is absolutely the truth. One of the four Tans tells her fine, if we don't get your husband, we get you. He drags her into her own kitchen, and while her husband is held down by the other three, she is violently raped. His wife loses the child and indeed will never bear another. Healy is so devastated he can barely spit the words into Murphy's ear. He will never mention it again. But Murphy will never forget it. The information only works to foment his resolve and sees him devising new plans for taking out the local barracks from which the demons were let loose.

Pa Murray at last gets the tiny tidbit of information he has been waiting for. It is Saturday morning and Captain Kelly is to be heading out of the gaol and back through the city within the hour. He is in a hurry and will probably take the main drag of Washington Street. Pa calls his men into action, ASU, intelligence officers, anybody with two legs to stand and one arm to throw grenades. That is who is needed and that is who shows up. The men are stationed along the road. Only a few of the men familiar with the homemade grenades are actually given the bombs to work with. The others keep their guns in their pockets.

James has a grenade. He holds it gingerly in his coat pocket. Just when he thinks his information was faulty, Pa, who is at the top end of the street with the best view, sees the car speeding through traffic, zigzagging by the other cars, practically running them down. Kelly is indeed in a hurry. Pa signals to James. James does not look in the direction of the car. He waits and counts. Then he turns as the car whizzes by and throws his bomb with the precision of a seasoned baseball pitcher. The bomb sails through the air and lands exactly where he wants it to land: right on Kelly's lap. Kelly picks it up and tosses it back out of the window. It rolls down the street and comes to a quiet stop at the curb. Another bomb has been thrown by someone else on the other side of the street. It misses the mark and explodes in a tiny puff of smoke on the road, not enough to harm a fly. Guns are pulled out; shots are fired. Captain Kelly laughs as he sails away down the road. He has nothing but contempt and hatred for these Irish fools and this incident only confirms his low opinion. Does he give James the finger as he disappears into the horizon? Perhaps. James is so angry he could spit. That fucking asshole Corry. My wee brother Edward could make a better bomb in his sleep. Corry couldn't make a bomb if his sad little life depended on it.

May flows into June and the weather begins to turn. Gone are the drizzly afternoons, the cool evenings, and occasional rain-soaked days. The sun awakens the city every morning raging forth in colours of pink and orange and beams all day long. Trenchcoats are peeled off and men and women everywhere are seen around the city in just their shirt sleeves. It is unheard of. But it is welcomed. The people drink in the sun, dry out their homes, open their windows to the fresh sea breezes and head down to the beaches in droves. The IRA men find this turn of events disconcerting. Their trenchcoats and sweaters and other layers of clothing have always acted as camouflage for their guns. Now, if they carry a gun, they must be creative. James, however, cannot bear to lose his holster. It sits beside his skin underneath his shirt. He dons a suit vest, compliments of his father. It is a tad short but loose enough to hide his bulked up left side. James carries his jacket with him, sometimes laying it over his arm or hanging around his shoulders, the sleeves flapping in the wind. He is now working with a crew of men who have always been part of the larger ASU or C Company groups, but nevertheless were one step removed from him. Peter and Dan and Tadg have been replaced by Mahoney, O'Brien, and Hegarty; all of whom James has worked with before, but somehow nothing feels the same. His tight group of men have evaporated. They sit in the cage and wonder what will become of themselves, where they will be sent, and how they might escape.

The election has come and gone. Seán has been voted in, as has every other Sinn Féin candidate. No one knows, however, when the Dáil will meet. Arthur Griffith, the acting president while de Valera was in America, remains behind bars. He has been there for almost six months now, although he, too, has been re-elected for his home constituency in Tyrone. Everyone is nervous about de Valera's arrest. Anything can happen inside a British gaol. Every Irishman on the planet knows that. His fate is made even more precarious by the rage of the British over the failure of a home rule parliament in Dublin. It has been boycotted utterly. The British attempt at appeasement in order to control the Irish situation is a wash-out. But not so in Ulster. The king himself has given a speech proclaimed over the airwaves at the opening of Stormont, the Northern Ireland parliament. Even the Irish found it hard not to believe the sincerity of King George when he stated his hopes for a new peaceful era. James had sat at the radio and listened, and thought to himself, good luck with that.

Murphy has already had one meeting with the men to get the plan up and running for taking out the local barracks. There are three he wants to hit and hit hard: Tuckey Street, Shandon Street, and Douglas Street Barracks. All three are stuffed to the gills with Tans and Auxies who only leave the premises in large heavily armoured groups. Murphy has arranged with Martin Corry for homemade grenades to be delivered; he has stockpiled ammunition from the company's quickly evaporating dump, and he is ready to roll. Today, they will make up the groups, assign drivers and work out the overall coordination. Murphy wants to be sure that all three are hit at the same time so that they cannot reinforce one another. It will happen tomorrow with any luck.

James makes his way to the Douglas Street Pub. He has left earlier than need be and chosen to walk across town. Somehow, he finds himself walking in the direction of the Wallace sisters' shop purely out of habit. The sun bears down on this glorious day, but for some reason James feels uneasy. He decides to take a slight detour and makes his way to the church of Saints Peter and Paul. As usual the massive handleless doors are locked from the inside, and James does not even try them, but skips through the back garden to find the hidden sacristy door.

Inside, the church is cool and smells faintly of incense. He kneels at the communion rail and wonders why he is here. As far as the bishop is concerned, he is excommunicated from the church entirely. He has not gone to confession in months because he cannot even begin to list the many offences of which he knows he is guilty. In the last few months James's one tiny prayer has been only to St Joseph, and only when he feels in imminent danger. Other than that, he realises he has forgotten to pray, or perhaps he wonders to himself, I am losing my faith altogether. James closes his eyes and begins the rosary. Within seconds, his mind has wandered, and he realises like the last time he was here, his lips might be saying the words, but his mind is going over the details of death. Deaths that will be at his own hand. He rises from his knees, and as he walks towards the door, he dips his finger into the dish of holy water.

James blesses himself and, in his mind, calls out to St Joseph. Don't leave me Joseph. Do not abandon me. He pushes open the door, the sun streams in and blinds him for a second.

At the pub the men arrive, pick up a drink at the bar, and then move to a table at the back. Usually, Murphy will use the small back room, but today he decides to stay out in the open. He does not like that the back room has no windows and no exit. Normally he would have a sentry posted outside and inside the pub, but he is running short of men, and this is to be a short meeting. One drink, in and out. James opens the door and sees that most of the men have arrived. The door closes behind him, and the light in the room dims to what seems to James to be a dark, murky smear. Murphy is holding court surrounded by seven or eight men. James goes to the bar and orders a pint. He is blinking, trying to adjust to the sudden lack of light. As he walks across the room, Denis Hegarty, who is facing the front door and window looking out onto the street, suddenly jumps to his feet, knocking over his pint.

It is at this moment that everything slows down for James. He knows with full certainty, without so much as turning his head, that the front door of the pub is about to be opened and Tans are about to swarm the place. He watches in slow motion as Denis lunges for the back door and makes it out, his voice trailing in the air behind him, giant isolated segments of sound exploding in everyone's ears. G E T O U T! But James can also see the splattering beer has distracted them, for just a fraction of a second. But it is long enough. The Tans are in the room, their guns pointed at heads, their faces showing their delight at the complete and utter shock of this crew of IRA troublemakers. All are standing staring, the O of surprise on their lips, their hands lingering in the area where their guns might have been hiding, had they been carrying them.

All of this is occurring as James continues to move, oh so slowly, towards the door. But he knows, as certainly as he has ever known anything, that he will not breach it. He knows because in his altered state he can hear the bullet spinning through the air, coming from behind, slicing through time and space like a boot through thick mud, slowed but not stopped. In one last desperate effort to outrun the bullet and escape, he lunges through the air. His intent is to crash through the door, roll onto the grass, and make cover at the side of the building. His outreached arms push the door, and the brilliant sunlight instantly blinds him as the back of his head explodes and time regains its regular, furious pace, and his body collapses. His legs lie on the dirty pub floor, his arms and head projected through the partially opened door on the sparkling green grass outside. His last thought is a carefree, floating epiphany, wafting through his mind as his own warm blood pours from the back of his head and spills from behind his left ear and is sopped up by his clean, pressed white shirt.

So, this is what it feels like, he thinks, as his eyes close.

FLEE

CHAPTER 12

JUNE 1921 – JUNE 1922

Hugh O'Neill is handsome and broad. His hair hangs in long, wavy, auburn locks, and his wide chest and perfect proportions denote an athletic, aristocratic young man with a natural predisposition of health and vigour. To your average Celt, his demeanour screams: I am from a long line of Kings. To your average Englishman, it screams, I am an uppity native. Pander to me or watch your back. Even as a teenager surrounded by the enlightened, highly educated minds of England and Europe that frequent Queen Elizabeth's court, Hugh is a proud Celt.

In the Year of Our Lord 1569, Ireland has become a complex patchwork of territories. Some areas are ruled by the old Celtic families, especially in the north and the west coast of the country. Some are ruled by the now intermarried early English settlers and the native Celts of Strongbow's era. The major port cities along the east coast such as Dublin and Waterford are populated by the progeny of intermingled Celts and Norsemen, and the large castles such as Kilkenny and their surrounding territories dotted around the country are controlled by the English. Elizabeth would like to push forward on her father's goal of complete ownership of Ireland. She has many powerful families who have been fighting the Spanish on her behalf and who need to be rewarded, and the island to the southwest is a bounty of natural resources and beautiful tracts of land as yet uncultivated or organised by the natives, at least by English standards. Over the years there have been battles between the Irish and the English. The Irish have won some and lost some. The net effect is that the reigning Celtic kings have made some political truces in an effort to avoid war. One of these truces involved the illustrious, ancient Celtic family of O'Neill, rulers of Ulster. Conn O'Neill was the first high king to formally submit to Henry VIII, part of a political and economic game of subterfuge the English invented called surrender and re-grant. As a sign of good faith on the Celts' part, and on the English part, in an effort to anglicise and influence the royal line of Celts, Conn's grandson Hugh is sent to England to be raised at court. He will learn English ways and be given an English title in Ireland.

Hugh O'Neill does not suffer from jealousy or feelings of inferiority at the English court. Hugh has been immersed in learning of every kind from a young age. His mind is quick and as a newly introduced teenager he drinks in foreign learning from the scholars that inhabit the periphery of Elizabeth's court. Like all royal warrior Celts, he is an outstanding horseman, at one with his animal, the two of them working together to outrun and outmanoeuvre any opponent. He is fearless learning the English arts of war, and adept at quickly picking up their customs of civility and graciousness. As a young child Hugh learned the importance of hospitality and welcoming, the mark of a truly aristocratic Celtic family. The result is an Irish teenager at an English court who charms his hosts, is at ease socially, and quickly builds a wide network of influential friends.

Elizabeth watches the young Hugh work his way around the wide variety of personalities at court. Ever the calculating, pragmatic mind, she thinks to herself just how she could put his obvious charm and social acuity to her best use. A young man such as Hugh could give a strong rallying cry to the Irish on her behalf. She is a practical woman, Elizabeth, and constantly on her guard with her own power-hungry nobility. She is ever aware of the need to satisfy their relentless quests for power and prestige in order to maintain her support, and lately the acquisition of Irish land has been on her mind. It makes good political sense. Having a young aristocratic man like Hugh, who is held in high esteem by his own people, work on her behalf, would be a master stroke of political manoeuvring and his presence and influence may lead the natives to be less difficult. All of this comes down to money for Elizabeth. Wars are expensive and she would much rather pay off the Irish Chieftains and kings with English titles and political pandering than have to rout them off the island. After all, the Celts are fierce warriors and winning another war is not necessarily a given.

Elizabeth speaks to Hugh. She wonders aloud if he might show his gratitude for her largesse at court by accompanying her man Sir Gilbert Humphreys to Cork to acquire some property. Of course, replies Hugh. I should be honoured to represent your majesty in negotiations with my people. Yes! thinks Elizabeth. This should be a quick and easy changing of title and I shall have thousands of hectares to bestow upon those who will serve me best. But Elizabeth will soon regret her decision about sending Hugh, as well as her choice of envoy in Humphreys.

Sir Gilbert is quite the pretty boy. In 1569 he is thirty years old with coiffed, chestnut-coloured hair, and a carefully contoured and groomed goatee. He likes his fancy dress, wild shades of yellow silk with magnificent puffy sleeves that give him the look of a much bigger man. In his dealings with fellow Englishmen, Gilbert is charming, displaying his keen intellect and well-considered manners. But Gilbert's narrow, sly eyes betray his self-interest, and to those who should know better, they hover over the person, taking in their net worth and calculating a quotient of dispensability according to Gilbert's whims of the moment. But despite all of this, Gilbert is a man out for an adventure, and he has plans to make a name for himself. He knows one sure way to make that happen is to become useful to the queen, and so to Ireland he will go and thousands of hectares he will acquire, come hell or high water. As a helping hand to Gilbert, and to achieve her objective all the faster, Elizabeth summons the reigning nobleman of the Cork area, the Earl of Desmond, to court. The earl, James Fitzmaurice FitzGerald, is the descendant of Strongbow's right-hand man, and his family has ruled the area for generations. He is mystified as to why he is being called to London but goes all the same.

Once Gilbert lands in Cork, it does not take the old English families, nor the Celts, long to see what he is up to. On the pretext of setting up trading centres at the various ports of call along the southern coast, Gilbert soon moves inland and begins his march through the province, clearing the land of the indigenous population by slaughtering their cattle and scorching their fields. It is an efficient move on his part because by the time the intended recipients arrive from England, the fields will be fertilised and regrown, and the place empty. Despite the absence of the earl, the reigning families band together and prepare to fight. But Gilbert is determined and is more than happy to take on the challenge. With Hugh by his side, and a well-equipped English army behind him, he begins his campaign of attacking the local castles, in which every well-placed Celtic family has their seat. In fact, Gilbert develops some ingenious ways to burn out the inhabitants and partially destroy the structure, just enough to leave it uninhabitable. But it is what he does to the innocent families attached to the local chieftains that leaves Hugh in a state of shock.

Gilbert pronounces to the inhabitants their single opportunity to swear allegiance to him, knowing full well they will tell him in no uncertain terms to go back where he came from. After this moment he is determined to show no mercy. His soldiers appear from the shadows and gather up entire families. He likes to make them watch while all of the men, young and old, are lined up, forced to their knees, each one in front of a soldier. Gilbert likes a show of coordinated strength and at his count the axes swing, and the heads roll *en masse*. But Gilbert does not stop with just the men. Women and children, too, are put to the axe, the faster to clear the area, the better to spread terror in the surrounding communities and gain possession all the quicker. As a final *coup de grâce* Gilbert instructs his men to put the heads on spikes, especially the children's, and thrust them into the ground so as to line the walkway to the entrance of his tent. This way the surrounding community leaders, indeed any family members who happened to miss the destruction of their villages, can easily find the visages of their children and relatives. Terror is what will put the rebellion down and hasten the expropriation of land and the flight of the people.

No one knows for certain how many castles Hugh witnessed being destroyed, and the people tortured in this way. But we know it didn't take long for Hugh to realise he was standing beside a monster of mythical proportions. Indeed, the whispering behind Gilbert's back that seemed to follow him wherever he went is now credited with a stroke of veracity. Gilbert is a secret pederast, though if the queen too heard the whispers, she did not act on it. The whole sickening picture comes together for Hugh, and he leaves his own pretty Tudor outfit on the grass leading his horse north, homeward bound. Hugh is nineteen years old and for the rest of his days he will fight the English and their steady, violent, encroachment into his country. The lasting image that will drive him is that of Gilbert smiling with glee at the sight of young Irish children's faces on pikes, frozen in terror, their red locks blowing in the wind.

Ten years later, when Hugh is twenty-nine, he champions his ancient Gaelic title of 'The O'Neill' denoting his station of High King in Ulster, though to the English such a title is now illegal, and he is nothing more than the lowly Earl of Tyrone. Hugh becomes a horrified, if not surprised, witness to Gilbert's half-brother, Walter Raleigh, beheading hundreds of Spaniards at Smerwick. But Hugh will also have his successes. His men will lay waste in Armagh to a thousand English soldiers and their commander, and cause Elizabeth to wring her hands in consternation. The very thing that Elizabeth had hoped to prevent, the constant drain on her treasury through war, keeps her up at night. But to give her her due, Elizabeth is not pleased with Gilbert and his contemporaries. The queen likes to be loved, and even she knows that beheading children crosses several lines. But wait, is there a line when it comes to the Irish? Perhaps not. The Tudor conquest of Ireland continues. Induced famine and extreme methods will forever cast the English as a brutal, inhumane race in the eyes of the Irish. Does the average English citizen know what is afoot in Ireland? Indeed not. Elizabeth is sure to keep the barbarity under wraps. She would not like her own people to think poorly of her. Instead, Ireland is portrayed as a land for the taking; the natives there as an illiterate lot, speaking some garbled tongue and available to keep the vast estates of the English lords in tidy working order. The south of the island, much of the area of Cork, at least the area with rich, arable land, is overcome and distributed to Elizabeth's lackeys who build their big houses, some on the sites of the very castles of the old Celtic families that Gilbert has decimated.

In the north of the island, in Ulster, battles continue. Hugh gains for himself quite a reputation among his people. Despite his Irish title, he is often referred to now as the Earl of Tyrone, an assuredly English title, but this is just a testament to the confusion and chaos of the lives of the Irish who must endure the madness of continuous political machinations between their leaders and the English. Yes, we want our Celtic heritage. Yes, we want our ancient Brehon Law to be supreme. But sometimes, the wily Celts believe it is no dishonour to acquiesce now for political reasons, and worry about reinstituting their ancient ways later, when it is more convenient, and they have at last routed the English.

Hugh plots and schemes in conjunction with his cousins, Rory O'Donnell, king of the Donegal area, the north-western corner of the country, and also Red Hugh O'Donnell, a Celtic prince who hates the sight of the British with a passion. They are joined by a nobleman from Fermanagh, known as the McGuire. Together these men work to bring an end to the English and their relentless acquisition of land and imposition of foreign ways. They successfully build alliances with the Spanish who come to their aid, to the great frustration of a now ageing Elizabeth.

Elizabeth has forsworn every penny in her coffers, every spy in her service and every proud Englishman at her fingertips to be rid of the foreign Catholic interference of the Spanish in her grand scheme for crushing Ireland. After all, if they are successful in Ireland, England will be their next goal and God help us all if the good English citizens are forced to bend their knee to a foreign monarch. Such a thought is anathema to Elizabeth. She will not have her legacy destroyed. The Spanish are routed at the battle of Kinsale, and the Irish, unfortunate enough to be caught, along with them. Later, Red Hugh O'Donnell, on a trip to gather more support from Spain, is poisoned by one of Elizabeth's spies. The O'Neill is devastated but not undone. The memory of Gilbert and the spiked heads of Irish children will never leave him.

At last, a glimmer of hope shoots into the sky. Elizabeth dies and her closest relative, James VI of Scotland, becomes James I of England. James is a wily politician, as needs be, dealing with the many clans of Scotland. He calls a truce and sends out an amnesty for the native leaders of the north of Ireland. Come back to the table and we will re-negotiate. You will remain kings of your lands; they will just be smaller, tighter packages of land so that you might share with your dear friends the English. The Celtic leaders play politics and go to the table. But it isn't long before they realise that their very heads are being pursued on the quiet by James and his ilk; the greedy, insatiable landowners who already have stakes in the north. There are English spies and Irish traitors afoot. It is safer altogether to leave this place, go to Spain, and return triumphant with an armada of Spanish ships to take on the English when they least expect it.

The O'Donnell and the McGuire make plans. They secretly have a French ship come to their rescue. Hugh, the O'Neill, is hesitant. The people will be helpless without us and who knows if another Gilbert will arise to decimate the population. But does it matter? That will be the end result if something is not done to conquer these English bastards once and for all. Hugh makes a decision. He gathers up his best men and the remainder of his own family, lest they are murdered in his absence, and together they head out to Lough Swilly, a north-western port in Donegal, to meet with his countrymen and board the French ship that will take them to Spain. However, just before he goes he makes a stop at the ancient abbey of the Holy Cross, to obtain from the good friar a tiny relic of the True Cross, which has been held there in reverence and pride since the abbey's foundation several centuries earlier. Hugh carefully packages this holiest of relics in Ireland, along with several other lesser relics from saints across the land. They are his insurance for safe passage and his guarantee of returning in the name of his native people who claim the relics as their birth right.

Once aboard ship, the families and their entourage, almost one hundred people altogether, sail out of the lough to the mournful cries of the locals who feel a melancholy descend on them in their abandonment that will indeed afflict the people for centuries. This scene of the ship sailing into the distance with the last of the powerful Celtic families aboard will become known to subsequent generations as the Flight of the Earls. Even this name tells tales of the end result. It is not known as the Flight of the Kings, as it would have been had history unfurled in a different way. Some of the men, who have left their wives and families behind, are incredulous. Sure, we will be back in no time, with the Spanish and their war machine beside us, and it will be the best thing that has happened to Ireland since before the time of Strongbow, five hundred years ago.

But Hugh wonders. When they are but halfway to their destination a hurricane alights on them seemingly from nowhere and they are certain the fury of Hell has been unleashed. A thick unworldly fog envelopes them and the boat is tossed from side to side, waves the size of which have never been seen toss the ship like a cork along a river of white caps. The sails look like they are about to be lost in the wind and the women and children cry out to the heavens for deliverance. Hugh takes the relics from around his neck and ties them to a rope tossing them into the sea at the stern of the ship, and immediately the demons depart with the ungodly fog, taking the wind with them and leaving just the heavy waves to find their equilibrium behind them. It is September 14, 1607, the Feast of the Exaltation of the Holy Cross. It is the last miracle that Hugh will encounter. Indeed, he will come to believe that the remainder of his life is a punishment for deserting his people – a people he will never stop thinking of or pining over for the rest of his days.

The ship does not make it to Spain. The French sailors head home after this terrible fright and the Irish disembark and make their way by land across France and into Italy. Hugh is treated like the royalty he is by the families of Rome, and spends the remainder of his days in the Holy City constantly making plans for a comeback; however, anyone who is sent to Spain ends up dead in mysterious circumstances. Elizabeth's spies have become James's spies. Even Rory O'Donnell will die of a mysterious fever in Rome within weeks of his arrival. Within a few years, Hugh dies, and his dream of freeing Ireland from a succession of Gilberts dies with him.

When you are in Rome next, go to the Church of San Pietro in Montorio on the Via Garibaldi, and you will find his tomb in front of the high altar. You will know it by the inscription, *Prince of Ulster*. Hugh, it seems, left a lasting impression on the Italians.

Of his seven sons, not one will live to father a family. They will, each one, be murdered by English spies and agents, in Spain, in Italy, in the Tower of London. Even Hugh's youngest, thirteen-year-old Brian, sent to Brussels for protection, will be murdered in the street. Over the next hundred years, Ulster, the last, lovely, coveted province of Ireland, will be ravaged by Cromwell and finally William of Orange, until every rebellious or indeed pandering, begging native is displaced, massacred, burnt alive or sent as a slave to the Caribbean. The cruel antics of Gilbert will become a footnote in history.

By 1610, when it is evident to the people that there is no rescue in sight from the Spanish, and that their own leaders are not returning home, it is as if the Irish people know what is to come. They are lonely and forlorn. An observer will write:

> *There is no laughter at children's doings, music is prohibited, the Irish language is in chains. Irish Princes, unusually for them, speak not of wine-feasts nor Mass. There is no playing, feasting, nor any pastime. There is no trading or riding horses or turning to face danger. No praise poem is recited, no bedtime story told, no desire to see a book, no giving ear to the family pedigrees... How shall the oppression be lifted from the bright fair-haired race of Conn?*

James looms in and out of consciousness. The back of his head, just behind his left ear, is shattered. The thick, smooth skull is now missing a piece of bone the size of an American quarter, perhaps two. The army surgeon has been able to pluck out the shards of bone that remained floating on his flesh and is able to keep the membranes around his brain intact. There is a large, jagged flap of skin, thick with salty auburn hair, that is stretched over the wound and sewn in place with crude black stitches. At first James is given morphine to quell the pain, but as he becomes conscious for longer periods the morphine is kept back. Why waste it on a rebel? For a few days James lingers between life and death. He has lost a lot of blood. He will learn later that none of the British soldiers were too concerned about taking him to the infirmary. Naturally he is not surprised. It was his friends who were processed first. Perhaps the British hoped he would save them the trouble of using up good medical resources on an Irishman.

James watches his body from above. He feels like a bird perched on the high window casing, towards the ceiling, looking down on his surroundings with an aerial view not normally allowed to mere mortals such as himself. He looks around the room, noting the various beds, the white walls, the filthy windows, light fighting the rivulets of dirt, desperate to enter. As his head slowly turns, he notices his body lying face down in the sterile hospital bed, the shattered and patched up skull towards the base of his neck like a bubble about to burst, swollen and gelatinous. He looks over, and, in the bed next to him lies his old ghostly friend, Thomas Ashe, watching over his body with wide, alert eyes, bound onto the bed tightly with wraps of sterile sheets, his mouth gently bubbling with gruel and blood and slobber. James watches Ashe watches him on the bed, and he smiles. I am not alone, he thinks to himself. Right there on the bed next to him is his frequent visitor. And as James smiles down on him, Ashe turns his gaze upwards and looks at him sternly. James can hear his voice, though his lips do not emit sound, only the continuous gurgle of slop. The voice is clear in James's head, though. *Come back. Come back. There is work yet to be done.* And with that James is no longer enjoying the view but is acutely aware of the rough sheet against his cheek and the throb of pain at the base of his skull. At other times James finds he is not in the bed at all, not even in the barracks hospital, but standing on the street holding his gun, the bodies of everyone he has ever shot piled before him in a bloody mess. Dinny lies on the ground beneath them all, his arm and head instantly recognisable, emerged from beneath the pile of chests and heads and limbs bleeding rivulets of blood. He is staring up at James with his large, luminous, accusing eyes.

When the morphine is withdrawn, the ability to see himself and transport outside his own body dissipates. In fact, the pain at the back of his head burns like a red-hot poker and he feels his very being contracting into one single condensed ball of agony, radiating out from the sides of his wound and impossible to escape. When the doctor hears the moaning that begins to emerge from James's mouth, and his action of hitting his head over and over again against his bed, he takes pity and administers another shot.

After two weeks in the infirmary, James is sitting up, able to feed himself and move about, if slowly. He has lost weight; mostly muscle mass, given his wiry frame carried no fat to lose. His face is gaunt and wan. When he looks in the tiny mirror, he sees not himself but an older, ashen face with heavy black welts under the eyes and a mess of thick hair that is now white and grey with thick streaks of auburn. It is July 1921. James will be twenty-three in a couple of weeks. Who is that haggard old man in the mirror? When he touches the back of his head, still wrapped in bandages, his fingers are keenly aware of the circular ridge of bone, and he cannot stop himself from applying a slight pressure, even though it is painful, and feel his two fingers sink into a place where no fingers should ever be able to go. He is amazed that the rest of his skull is still intact and that all his faculties are about him: surely it is some kind of miracle. He lays back in his sterile bed and daydreams. He sees an ancient face with a red scarf tied tight over soft tufts of frizzy grey hair. He is propelled back to his youth, the day the old gypsy had tea with him and his father and read his tea leaves. With a smile he remembers the prediction of a life ninety-two years long. Then his smile leaves him when he recalls the qualifier, the part about joy and suffering in equal measure, both giving and receiving. He hears the old woman with her raspy voice and his father chuckling.

But James is suddenly catapulted out of his daydreaming when he hears the doctor saying his name. Not his alias, John, but his name. He experiences a terrible moment of panic as it dawns on him through his pain that the doctor, and therefore anyone who cares to find out in Victoria Barracks, knows his real name, and therefore probably his address. He sits up in his bed and stares at the doctor in alarm. He does not wish to answer and therefore acknowledge his true name. He looks at the doctor and gives it his best shot. I don't know who you're talking about; my name is John.

But the doctor has been well-informed. He is used to these IRA types showing up in his ward with a variety of injuries, incurred as far as he is concerned escaping arrest. And not one of them ever gives his actual name. The brazen ones make up wild Irish names no one has ever heard of, Aloysius or Colmcille and the like. For those with no imagination there is always Seán, or Séamus, more of them than you can shake a stick at. Nice try. The doctor raises his eyebrows and looks at James. Listen, save your breath. When your friends thought you wouldn't make it, they gave over your name. I guess they think it's the right thing to do, to let your family know you are on death's doorstep. He says it with a kind of sneer, as if the doctor does not expect James to understand common decency. He is an army doctor after all, and charged with fixing up his own men after they have been shot up by the likes of James. Then it occurs to James that the doctor has used the present tense to describe his condition, not the past, and James pauses for a moment, taking in the implications.

James says nothing, but he can feel the anger rising in him. He knows the doctor is a liar at worst, misinformed at best. Not one of the men in the pub would have given over his name. Even if he were to be executed, the IRA knows better than to allow the British access to their people. Once a name is known, whole families come under surveillance, perhaps even dragged in and interrogated, and by what means is anybody's guess. If I find the little fucker who turned me over, God help him, thinks James. In the meantime, I must get warning to my parents. Who knows what they will do to my parents's home, or to them? And now, as if to match the throbbing pain at the back of his head, James develops a sharp headache over his left eye, and he closes his eyes, and sinks into his bed.

He feels overcome with a wave of weakness. Tiny sparkling lights dance in front of him and he wonders why a miracle such as surviving that bullet is being wasted on him. Tomás should have been the recipient of this miracle. Over a year ago now, though it feels like a thousand years. Not James. Not James the spy. Not James the kidnapper. Certainly not James the executioner. But in his confusion and anxiety, James masters his thoughts. Focus, he thinks, and while his eyes are closed and he is as still as a corpse, his mind is whirling in every direction.

What happened? He goes over the details again and again. He sees Denis flying across the room, and himself lunging for the door. He can hear the British intelligence men bursting into the room behind him. As he pushes the back door open, the streak of brilliant sunlight blinds him. And that is it. James does not remember another thing. Who have they arrested? Who escaped? Who else is wounded or worse? James forces his memory back inside the pub, standing with his pint in hand, looking at the table in front of him. Who is there? Denis Hegarty got out, but did he get away? Murphy certainly was there. James can see him nursing his pint, a cigarette in hand. Mahoney was there. He can see him, his head turned talking to Paddy Murphy, one of the ASU boys. Con Cogan is there too, another of the ASU. He is facing away from James, and James in his mind's eye can see his back, a light short-sleeved shirt tucked into his trousers, a thick leather belt around the back of his waist. After concentrating for some time, James suddenly sees Jerry O'Brien standing behind Mahoney. James can see these men clear as day. But there are others, who? James is not sure; their forms and faces are shadows in his memory. But surely anybody behind him as he went for the door would have been caught. What are they doing to whomsoever of his friends and colleagues that they got

While Dragging Our Hearts Behind Us

their hands on?

And then everything comes into crystal clear focus. James sees again Charlie Cogan's back, his light, short-sleeved shirt. And his head explodes with certain uncompromised knowledge. My gun. I had my gun on me. But who else? Who else was stupid enough to come to the meeting armed? James focuses on the faces around the table and tries to see their clothing. Cogan surely was unarmed, as most of the ASU boys would be. They keep their guns in dumps and use them only when involved in an operation. Even Murphy may not have been armed. He had just got back from the Gaeltacht. Denis, Denis would have been armed. But perhaps, just perhaps he managed to give them the slip. But if Mahoney has been taken as well as Jerry O'Brien, and James is here in Victoria Barracks and Mick Kenny is still rotting, probably on Spike Island, that leaves the squad with only two men: Denis and Bob Aherne. They will be the only men left in the field. Florrie and O'Hegarty will be beside themselves. But the question is, if they know my name, thinks James, do they know the names of everyone at the meeting, everyone they managed to corner? Will I be executed alone or in company? Or have they already executed the rest?

It will be a quick sentencing, whenever I get there. Unless there is another miracle to bolster the first and they dispense with martial law, my days are up. James closes his eyes and sees his own self standing up, bandaged head and all, against the wall of an exercise yard he is yet to visit, blindfolded, hands tied behind his back, waiting for the shots. But in his mind the rope holding his wrists together feathers to the ground and he pulls out his gun from his holster, just underneath his left arm and fires. He fires in slow motion and watches as the bullets fly one after another, emptying his gun, twirling in six neat bow lines straight for six British military foreheads.

Once he is showing signs of recovery James is relegated back to the regular cells. This is exactly where he needs to be in order to discover the fate of the rest of his party. In the medical wing there is no one but quiet, cold-faced orderlies, none of whom will divulge information. He is lucky if they even give him his food, such as it is, intact. Whoever O'Hegarty's mole is, and he knows there is at least one, they have not come to visit. After staggering through corridors accompanied by four guards, James enters a cold, dark holding cell. The metal bars close with a ringing clang that penetrates his perpetual headache and intensifies it. But as his eyes adjust to the dim, shadowy lighting, he quickly realises that his headache may become the least of his worries. After the sterility of the hospital wing, the cell appears utterly filthy. The floors may never have been washed. They are black with extended patches of filth. An ancient, corroding tin bucket sits in the corner, the stench of urine and faeces floats above it in a fetid, malodorous cloud. There is one small bench and one ragged woollen blanket, streaked with dirt and probably crawling with vermin. At first James was happy to be out of the sterile whiteness of the hospital, but now he wonders. Men have died in these cells. But surely someone will contact him here. O'Hegarty will see to it.

But James must wait. After some days, he again begins to panic. James's cool face, though haggard and hollow, is starting to take on well-known characteristics found on prisoners in this place. Even the toughest men can fall prey to terror; this is something James knows very well. Now he is beginning to feel the effects of incarceration; that is lonely, one man to a cell incarceration. James is not in solitary confinement; he has just been left alone. His body jumps at the sound of clanging doors. His head winces at the harsh yells of guards, of military in some distant corridor. Again, James disciplines himself. Listen you timid little shite, many have been here before ye, and many will be here after ye. 'Tis nothing you have had to endure at all, but a bullet you dodged by some miracle, God knows why. Patience man. Patience. You are one of the Squad for God's sake. Everybody in the brigade will know you are here.

But despite his self-talk, James is certain that he has been forgotten, it seems by both the British and O'Hegarty. He talks himself through his doubt. On the one hand being forgotten in itself bodes well. He is not considered high-profile, or they would have been on him instantly. That means his friends have not been considered high-profile either. Perhaps my miracle was extended and shared around the room. James thinks. His hand instinctively looks to his trousers pocket to finger his beads. No trousers, no beads, worst of all no gun, only stripes. James knows better than to put his still healing head on the filth of the bench. But he feels exhausted, and so he takes off his prison shirt and rolls it up making a thin pillow. Better to be cool than infected. Then he lies face down, as he has done for weeks now, careful that his stitches are to the open air and his face as far from the bucket as is possible to breathe.

He waits for the few rays of sun to infiltrate, fight through the blackened glass of the tiny barred window and shine, if only for a short while, directly into his now condensed, compact world. The sun only illuminates the dirt in the air, but the particles dance for James, twirling like tiny ballerinas, from time to time sparkling and exploding around him. As the day unfolds, minutes feel like hours and James forgets his caution and turns on his bench, sometimes taking his fingers and playing with the bubble at the back of his head. He shows it to his mother, who tells him she will be back quickly with the doctor and some proper bandages. He shows it to his brother Edward, who is in awe. He sees Tomás Ashe sitting in the corner of the cell, across from the bucket. He is tied up in a straitjacket but sits on his haunches leaning back into the corner, his eyes watching James, never leaving his face, his mouth slightly open, blood and gruel and spittle dripping ever so slowly from his lips.

James tells Ashe he is glad to share the cell with him. He is happy not to be alone. Don't worry, he tells Ashe, my mother will be back soon, and we will be home. She is an awesome force, my mother. You wouldn't want to cross her, and he laughs to himself. But after a while James decides it has become cold in the room. He shivers and reaches for the blanket, vermin and all, but it is so hard to reach. His head pounds as if he is being beaten with a sledgehammer. The light in the room seems to recede, but through the gloom he can see Ashe, still watching in the corner. Sure, Ashe will be freezing, leaning against those cold stones. He should come and sit beside me on the bench. James tries to move, to get up off his prone position and make room, but his body objects. His limbs lie like felled trees on the road, trees felled to keep the British at bay, that is what his legs and arms remind him of. And he is sorry they are too heavy to move.

He calls out to Ashe. I am sorry, I am sorry. I cannot seem to move. And as he is calling out to Ashe, his cell door clangs open and there is Father Fitzgerald and he is calling, calling out for a guard, and demanding a stretcher, a return to the hospital wing. This man is on fire, you bloody heathens, he snaps. He needs a doctor. What eejit brought him to this filthy hellhole with a gash in his head a mile wide? Father Fitzgerald does not mince words. But he is careful enough to keep himself from being kicked out. And then James is floating down hallways and Ashe is sitting on the edge of the stretcher for the ride, still in the straitjacket, and his lips are turned up in the smallest of grins and his eyes twinkle at James. His voice carries across to James's ear, though his lips do not move. Never mind, Jimmy boy, says Ashe, 'twill be alright now, 'twill be alright.

In the Gaeltacht, O'Hegarty is reeling. With most of the intelligence squad behind bars and practically everyone in the 2nd Battalion picked up by British intelligence or plucked off the street in a round up or shot in the back, there are few men to replace them. He had to scramble the day that Murphy and the IO boys were picked up. What a terrible blow. He shouted at Neenan on the phone. Quickly! Gather up what men are left and have them attack the three barracks; continue with the operation they were planning. He, O'Hegarty, was not thinking now of taking out the Tans. He was thinking of saving his men. The operations must be completed despite the arrests in case the British have information. Do not let the bastards know what a prize they have in their grimy fists. And so the few that were left collected the bombs and did drive-by bombings of the barracks. It was not as successful as it would have been had Murphy and the boys carried it out. But still, it was enough to let the British believe that they had not got anyone of importance.

James learns later that all but him were put in the cage, in the hope someone would give over their names and other information. This means their visit by the Tans was sheer bad luck. They have not been trailing the men or they would have a file on them. So, most of them are safe. But not Jimmy. His hard head meant the shot they took at him ricocheted right off his skull. And though he was taken to the hospital wing, he is not even on their radar. But the gun is what they will pin on him. O'Hegarty makes a call to the lawyer.

O'Hegarty knows that there are limited men available who can do what the Intelligence Squad or Murphy have done. In fact, he is keenly aware that the cumulative numbers of the Volunteers have dropped dramatically since 1918, the conscription crisis during the war, when the British were thinking to force young Irishmen to join up. This was when the numbers of Volunteers hit their peak. Mulcahy at GHQ has told him so in his own biting, disappointed, frustrated words. Where once, a short time ago, there were eight thousand men in Cork alone, the numbers have steadily declined to a grand total of three thousand all across the country. The IRA are a shadow of what they were just a couple of years ago. It seems that war is not to everyone's taste. O'Hegarty believes if it wasn't for his own dependable crew of men, sparse though their numbers may be, the Irish people as a whole would simply throw their hands up in defeat. It is as if the country is being dragged into fighting for freedom. And it seems to O'Hegarty that it does not matter what he does to stop the steady flow of his men into the enemy camp. It does not seem to matter who they, the IRA, execute. Every time they get rid of one spy, ten more take their place. Florrie just looks at him. Are you kidding me, he says. Florrie has developed more of a domestic attitude since becoming a married man. He now feels the pressures of a man responsible for a wife and children. Men without work, with families to feed, they are desperate. But O'Hegarty will hear no excuses. Are we not every one of us suffering? Are our boys not out sleeping under the stars, going hungry, being hunted like dogs? Being shot in the back? Tortured for fun? Don't tell me families are desperate. Steal a fucking loaf of bread if you're hungry. Don't sell your soul to Satan, for Christ's sake. Don't sell out your neighbours, fellow Irishmen, to the enemy. And he walks outside, slamming the door behind him.

O'Hegarty does a lot of walking these days. It is a way to work out the tension that he feels squeezing his brains continuously. Those secret compartments in the back of his head full of the sum total of suffering, death, risk, madness, that his men, now a mere quarter of the original eight thousand, have endured, the doors on those secret compartments are bursting. He sleeps but a couple of hours a night. As a young man he was in love with the Gaeltacht. But in those days, he was with his wife, his Magdalena, and every hill and vale and haystack was an opportunity to show his love. These days Magdalena is in hiding in Cork, running her café, working with Cumann na mBan. He is terrified to be seen anywhere near her, lest he inadvertently leads the enemy in her direction. Now he spends his days with rage and futility roiling in his gut. He walks up and down barren hills for hours, sorting out in his mind what needs to be done and where and how it fits into the bigger picture. What can be done next to drive the enemy out? He eats little and lives off a cup of tea every hour or so, maybe a bit of toast and butter, a boiled egg from time to time. He is thin and haggard like so many of his men. And to top it all off, the whole crew he had with him in the spring picked up the itch. As if they don't have it hard enough. He had to send for the doctor and each man had to be treated. And now the worst disaster. The thing that grinds him down. Another execution. This time it will be young Jimmy. Young Jimmy, who has been with him from the start. Some days he feels like there is indeed a God and he is working directly against him.

And then one day out of nowhere, just when most of his best men are behind enemy bars, when even the leadership at GHQ and at the Dáil are being hunted down, Éamonn de Valera is mysteriously released from prison. Two days later Arthur Griffith is also released, along with a few others. That same morning, de Valera is delivered a letter from a Lord Midleton, representing the British government, Lloyd George specifically, and asking him to very quietly, oh so quietly, get together and talk about a truce. De Valera's heart thumps in his chest. He puts his hand over it, to calm himself. He breathes deeply. He thinks of the terrible sacrifices that have been made. He sees Tomás's smiling face, Terry's piercing blue eyes. And then he lets the whispering of his angel settle on his soul. This is your chance. This is your chance.

He gathers up a couple of calm, deep thinkers, Sinn Féin men, and quietly makes his way to London. As he is walking down the street on his way to meet Lloyd George, he walks right into the most beautiful woman in the world. Muriel is with her girlfriend, and both women have stopped in London on their way to Germany. She has left her young daughter with her mother and is going to see a doctor. She is hoping that the doctors in Germany will be able to relieve her of her melancholia. Terry has been gone now for months, but the most beautiful woman in the world cannot get herself together. De Valera hugs her tenderly. He too loved Terry. When he embraces her, he feels for a moment the tremendous void that Terry's loss has created. Even so, he thinks to himself, imagine going all the way to Germany to see a doctor! He wishes her luck and waves goodbye. As he takes his long strides away from her, he cannot help but wonder at the coincidence of seeing her here in London at this critical moment, a moment that Terry believed he sacrificed his own life for.

While de Valera quietly negotiates in London, in Cork, Charley Daly is picked up in a sweep with twenty-three other IRA men in Waterfall, just west of the city. The Tans have been looking for Charley. There were, up until a couple of months ago, four Charley

Dalys living in the city. Now the other three have all been murdered, and Charley Daly, Adjutant, Cork No. 1, is about to be the fourth. He is taken to Victoria Barracks where he gives a false name and is duly thrown in the cage. Within hours he is identified by a spy and taken to the library for a hearing, where a long list of evidence against him is read out. They know his name, they know his rank, they know the role of adjutant and just how necessary it is. Charley is returned to his cell only to be taken out the following day by three military men. He is shot while trying to escape, or that is their story, and his body is given over to his family. Before they bury him in St Fin Barre's cemetery, a doctor does an autopsy. The list of injuries makes his mother and father weep and his seven siblings rage. Black eye; extensive bruising on the back from the shoulder blades to the thighs; two fingers broken; left arm broken above and below the elbow; skull driven in at the back of the head; broken ribs, both sides; left eye broken; bayonet under the right cheek, five bayonets in the back; one bullet at the top of the head; one bullet at the side of the head; one bullet straight to the heart; all bullets at extremely close range.

Does James hear what is happening to his friend Charley in some far corner of the barracks? Does he know Charley is even on the grounds? Probably not. James, after all, is in the hospital wing, in his own delirium, teetering between life and death. But later, weeks from now, James will hear what happened to Charley. James's soul will wither just a little more.

O'Hegarty is shocked when a messenger arrives right at the very door of the secret little house he is currently staying at in the Gaeltacht, with a special delivery from Dublin. Why are the eejits leading people to me? What in hell is so important they can't just call and go through the regular channels? But when he opens the envelope and sees it has been sent directly from Collins, he sits upright in his chair. The orders are short and sweet. Rein in your men. Get them off the street. We have a truce coming into effect in two days, July 11, at noon. O'Hegarty sits back in his chair and breathes deeply while all the bursting doors in his head slam shut. Bloody hell! We are getting to them after all. Bloody hell! They are running scared. Who would have thought? And then after a moment, an irrepressible smile dons O'Hegarty's face. I will be reining in my men alright Michael. I won't be wasting any time. Regroup, train, guns. We will stay out of your way, off the streets. But I will tell you where we will be. We will be here in the hills. We will be training our men and stockpiling our guns. The tension flows out of him, and he laughs. Then he calls to the young girl who keeps house. What's for dinner lass? I'm famished, so I am!

James, however, is not laughing. He stands before a military tribunal in the library of Victoria Barracks, the back of his head bandaged still, and faces three impressive-looking officers commissioned with determining his destiny. James is alone. He has discovered via O'Hegarty's mole, who stopped by his cell one day, a nasty-looking sergeant, the type of man you would least expect as a secret Irish Republican, that all of his crew have already been sentenced to six months hard labour for evading arrest. Not one had their real name divulged. And though they had been sent to the cage to be gawked at by any Tom, Dick, or Harry, anybody in Cork City would know better than to identify the likes of Mick Murphy, famous footballer, not-so-secret Captain of C Company, hunter of Tans, destroyer of barracks, perpetrator of violence. He has gone through the court using his alias, John O'Brien, and if anybody knew any different, they remained silent.

For James it is different. Somehow the Brits know his name, but they do not have a single file on him, nor do they have a clue that he is an IO responsible for any number of executions, operations, and mayhem perpetrated upon the military and police. They do, however, know that he was carrying a gun at the time of his arrest. And for this offence he will be shot. Correctly this time, through the front of his head, not ricocheted off the back of his skull. The trial takes mere minutes. James stares at his accusers with a palpable hatred. In his mind he is thinking what he would like to say: Get the hell out of my country. But he bites his tongue. O'Hegarty has sent a lawyer to put forward a defence. It is pointless, and the lawyer knows it. It is simply a message of hope and gratitude from O'Hegarty. The message is not lost on James. He knows that O'Hegarty cannot possibly provide a lawyer for every trial. There have been hundreds of them. He keeps the lawyer for the highest profile cases. The lawyer gives it his best shot and everyone in the room, which amounts to James and his lawyer, a couple of guards, and the tribunal, is not in the least bit interested. Yes, fine, thank you for your statement. You are hereby sentenced to death by firing squad. Sentence will be carried out tomorrow morning. And James stares at the tribunal as the words rip into him in a staccato eruption like machine gun fire. Fast, efficient, straight to the heart. But James knows it cannot possibly be true. He calmly, and with his best blank face, shakes the lawyer's hand, thanks him for his efforts, and is then escorted back to his cell by the guards. It is the morning of July 9, 1921.

James sits in a different cell, but it is just as filthy as the last. He feels numb. The back of his head continues to throb, although the pain has dulled over the last week. He brings his left hand up and feels the ridge of bone surrounding the soft, gelatinous hollow, and his stomach reels. *How ironic, to survive this bullet only to have another waiting for me with my name on it.* But as the day wears on, his flat, unaffected response to the announcement of his impending execution begins to peel away and expose a raw, ill-prepared young psyche. James thinks of his parents. They will be devastated. And his little brother, Edward. The boy will be inconsolable. *Funny to think like this. That in a few hours I will no longer exist. This body, these hands and feet and face will lie on the earth immune to the world. Where will I, James, be? They will bury my body under the exercise yard at Cork Gaol. That's what they do with us. Bastards.* He knows what will happen. His parents will try to claim his body. They will want a funeral Mass, burial in consecrated ground. But it will never be allowed. If the British wouldn't hand over Sir Roger Casement, they surely will not be handing over James, a nobody as far as they are concerned, another Fenian, stupid enough to be caught with a gun. Good riddance.

James paces in his cell. Back and forth. Back and forth. *Perhaps they are planning a rescue? Think again,* he tells himself. *This is Victoria Barracks. No one in the entire history of the place has been rescued or escaped from this monstrosity of a compound. No. I might have had a slim chance of rescue in the gaol. Here in the barracks, it is not in the cards. And besides, who exactly would be rescuing me? There is hardly a man left standing.*

Maybe a last-minute appeal by the lawyer? No. There has never been such a thing in the British court martial system. At least James has never heard of one. The British would just tell the lawyer to go blow it out his ear.

In truth, James understands there is no alternative. Many men have been shot in this place before him. Many will be shot in the weeks and months and possibly years to come. This is the English way. And as the reality of his situation sinks in, James can feel his perpetual headache over his left eye flare up. He watches the light fade, the dancing particles of filth imbued with magic by the sun, disappear. Time seems to evaporate. James feels like slow motion has taken over altogether and he will sit here on the bench, in the dark, for all eternity. It is pitch dark now. He has only a few hours. He will stand in front of the firing squad at five o'clock.

James lies down on his back and cradles his head with his hands. He watches the dark shadows dance on the wall. I should pray, he thinks, and he begins the rosary in Irish. But no sooner has he started than his mind wanders off, and a warm sense of peace descends on him. He feels a calm; a tranquillity that he has not felt in years, indeed he cannot remember such a feeling. His heart rate slows, his body relaxes. So, this is what you get James, he thinks to himself. This is it. Not quite twenty-three years. The old tinker woman was wrong. Of course she was wrong. But really, I am luckier than some. Look at some of the boys executed at eighteen. I guess I have done pretty well, considering. But this is all just blather. Say your prayers, you eejit. That's what you need to do. And James focuses his mind on prayer, but it will not come to him. And slowly, oh so slowly, panic begins to trickle in. He gets up from the bench and begins to pace. This time tomorrow where will I be? He stops pacing and the panic creeps in a little more. I will be with Tomás and Terry, with Tadg. Wherever they are I will join them. I won't be alone, that's for damn sure. But instead of seeing the faces of Tomás and Terry in his mind, James sees other faces. The faces of those he himself has sent into the next life. He sees their cold faces frozen on the ground, their prayers, just released from their lips, wafting in the air above them as their bodies drain of life and love and hatred and all things of this Earth.

James bangs on his cell and calls the guard. He keeps on banging until at last a guard appears. I need to write a letter. I need to write a letter now. The guard looks at him and takes pity. Right mate, just a moment. He returns with a pad of paper and a pen. Write your letter. I will see it gets delivered. James's hand can hardly hold the pen, he is shaking so badly. He knows he needs to write a letter to his parents. He knows he must not break his father's heart or tinker with his mother's sanity by leaving the earth without a word. He knows this, but it is not his main motivation.

James breathes deeply and calms himself. He squats on the floor with the paper on the bench, and begins to write. Dear Mama and Da. He stops writing. A thousand things he wishes to say. His heart swells, his eyes weep. In the end he can say nothing. James wipes the moisture off his cheeks. He picks up the pen again. He writes. Pray for me. Your loving son, James. He thinks, but does not write: because I cannot pray for myself, and I am full of terror for what is to become of me. Then he pushes his back into the corner, just the spot that Ashe had squatted watching him, and James watches his life pass before his eyes.

When he awakes in the morning, the letter still on the bench, himself collapsed into the corner, cold and shivering, he sees that the sun is up. It might be seven or eight o'clock. Certainly five o'clock has come and gone. Those fucking bastards, what are they doing? Then his tray arrives with the dirty mug of weak tea and slice of bread. Wait, wait, what's going on? The guard passes by without a word. James rises up and shakes off the night. He combs his fingers through his unruly hair. Fucking British. What game are they playing now? Apparently executing a man is just a footnote on their to-do list for the day. James paces back and forth, back and forth. He stops and picks up his letter off the bench and reads it.

Dear Mama and Da, Pray for me. Your loving son, James.

There is nothing else to say.

He carefully folds the piece of paper and is about to write the address on the back, but something stops him. It goes against all his training, to freely give away information. He puts the paper back down on the bench. Surely there will be a priest he can have a word with before they take him. He will give the letter to him and whisper the address in his ear. After a couple more hours, James picks up the cold, weak tea and drinks it. After another hour he picks up the stale bread and eats. What the fuck is going on? What kind of new torture is this? These fucking bastards. He bangs on the cell door. Nothing. He bangs again. Nothing. His head begins to pound. Alright. Calm down. What are you doing? Maybe you get another day. It must be past noon. The British don't execute in the middle of the day, or at night. Maybe they have forgotten about me altogether. Finally, at about four o'clock, a guard appears with another mug of tea and bowl of food. James looks at him. It is O'Hegarty's mole, the sergeant. He leans in and winks at James. Looks like it's your lucky day, mate. There's a truce on, as of tomorrow morning. The brass have been having a discussion about what to do with you. They want to shoot you, make no mistake, but they don't want to piss off Lloyd George. My best guess is you will get a reprieve. And the irascible looking sergeant winks again. Good luck mate, and he disappears down the hallway.

James stands still and tries to process what he just heard. A truce? Since when was anybody working on a truce? Then he sits down on the bench and smiles for the first time in months. That wily de Valera. The man disappears for months, and everybody thinks he is missing in action, and doesn't he just pull off the very thing we need at exactly the time we need it. The next morning, James is brought before the commander. Your sentence has been commuted to six months hard labour for evading arrest. You will be sent to Cork Gaol in due course and from there moved to Spike Island. You are one lucky son of a bitch. And with that the commander turns and walks away leaving James standing. He looks up towards the heavens and closes his eyes. The roof is rent asunder and the sun shines down on him, not a cloud in the sky. The birds fly overhead, and he can feel the salty breeze of Cork harbour caress his face. Thank you, St Joseph, thank you. James knows better than to thank the good Lord. As far as he is concerned, Joseph has been pulling strings for him. Only God knows why.

James wiles away his days in Cork Gaol, waiting impatiently for his transfer to Spike Island. He has nothing but escape on his mind. After all, if he can get Seán off the island, Seán should be able to return the favour. James feels this is absolutely possible because it is where most of his friends, at least the ones who still walk the earth, are now bunkering down. Men like Tom Crofts, Mick Murphy, men who know how to take the British for a ride and aren't afraid to do it.

Meanwhile, the people of Ireland come to believe that they have been granted a great gift. Not only are the British taking a pause from their incessant belligerence and unprovoked attacks, but the weather, the unusual, warm, wonderful weather is smiling down on them. In years to come, men will look back on this summer with great nostalgia. They will call it The Glorious Summer of the Truce, and describe it as the only period in living memory when the sun shone continuously for months, the temperature hovered in the twenties and thirties, and most wonderful of all, when it rained, it did so just enough to water the crops, and never during daylight hours. In fact, it would become the driest, sunniest summer since 1788. The people of Cork head to the coastal beaches in droves. Gone is martial law, gone are the roving bands of Tans arbitrarily stopping and arresting people on the street, gone are the nightly raids, the smashing in of doors, the houses set on fire as reprisal for God knows what. Gone too are the frequent newspaper reports of citizens stolen off the streets or from their homes, never to be seen again. The people heave a collective sigh of relief and begin to relax. They sleep a little better at night, they get a little sun during the day. But they resist the urge to hope that it might just last. Everyone knows that the truce is temporary. The people of Cork are fully expecting that one day soon it will all blow up and the British will surprise them all with some terror. And what will become of their civilian army then? What nasty solution are they working on to deal with the bane of their existence, the IRA?

The IRA is not in the least bit worried. It too, fully expects the British to jump out of the truce any day. They are not wasting any time. O'Hegarty makes sure the regular rank and file report for a couple of weeks of training as quickly as possible. If the men who are now in prison have to be replaced, as well as the men who have been taken from them through murder and execution, time is a luxury. New men must be found, and the remaining membership must step up to the plate with courage and skill. Fortunately, this is not an issue. Talk everywhere is of the battles and shakedowns, and IRA men who should know better are filling the pubs with tall tales, testimonials and drunken re-enactments of their bravery. The drinking will become so outrageous in some areas that Seán Moylan of Cork No. 3 will write to Mulcahy at GHQ that something must be done, and quick.

With the talk in the pubs transformed from worries and speculation to stories of glory, burning down barracks, shooting up Tans, stealing guns and throwing bombs, young men who were not about to join the IRA when the fight was on are now only too happy to gather up a few rays of glory by joining. Oh, how disappointed they are when they discover that the OC of Cork No. 1 is a mean-mouthed tyrant who expects them to move to the Gaeltacht and train. Train out in the bogs, march for hours without food, learn to dismantle a gun and put it back together blindfolded. Become adept at handling one of the many Thompson machine guns that the IRA have managed to accrue. Learn how to throw the little hand bombs that can be kept hidden in a pocket quickly and accurately. The things they are learning would boggle the mind. The only saving grace is the glorious weather. O'Hegarty knows that a lot of the new recruits are as green as grass. But he doesn't care. It is men they need, and he will make sure that they are transformed from mealy-mouthed little show-offs to the tough crew of doers and risk-takers that he needs in order to win this war when the British return. While James focuses on getting onto Spike Island so that he can escape, O'Hegarty, Florrie and the rest of the command focus on training and knitting together the units of the newly formed 1st Southern Division encompassing Cork and Kerry into a tight little web, while Frank Busteed continues to focus on revenge.

Frank's brother has re-joined the British Army with the sole purpose of finding the killers of his mother. He is a veteran of the Great War and an experienced armourer. The British took him back, no questions asked. Naturally they had no idea that he was related to the notorious IRA Officer, Frank Busteed of Blarney. Days pass, and Frank's brother does his job and waits. Sure enough, one fine evening there is talk in the mess, by drunken military, of the killing of that Sinn Féin prick Frank Busteed's mother. The names of the killers are learned, and sent to Frank. Frank knows where they are stationed now and sends word to all of the pub owners in that area to keep an eye out and let him know if they ever show up. He, Frank, will be ready for them.

Once James arrives at Spike Island, he immediately begins to wonder what he was thinking. Checking out Spike from the shoreline of the mainland is a lot different from actually being on the island itself. The island is about one hundred acres. The main prison area was closed in 1883 but reopened after the Rising in 1916. It was here that the doomed ship *The Aud*, Roger Casement's disastrous German ally, was scuttled. To say the buildings are dilapidated and in poor condition is an understatement. The facility is surrounded by a high stone wall in the shape of a flattened six-pointed star, a typical design for a military fort. The front gated entrance leads into a massive square surrounded by buildings on three sides. There are two blocks, A and B, with cells on the first and second floors and also in the basement of the buildings. There are a few huts outside the main blocks for prisoners, but in the evening, the wind whistles through them with the shrill call of the banshee.

All of the cells are for groups of men; as many as fourteen to a cell. There is no privacy, ever, and lacking in even basic amenities, such as blankets. During this beautiful, hot summer of 1921, all of the men long for the allotted time outside where the sun is pouring out its warmth on the earth. Because of the fine weather, and because the guards also prefer to stay outside, the men are allowed out for hours at a time. But by six o'clock they are again locked up. Back inside their cells, the cold, moist, stone immediately robs them of the heat and sends damp chills through their bodies. The food arrives to them cold and watery and some men find it is so disgusting that only severe hunger will allow them to get it past their lips. The leadership of the IRA men make a deal with the governor: Let us cook our own food, at least the potatoes will be hot and what little else we are given will be prepared as best as can be made under the circumstances.

The governor accedes to their request. If the truth be known, he is in awe of these men. He has mentioned it to more than one of his friends and colleagues. Look at them, he will say, have you ever seen such a strange assortment of characters working together? Only the odd one seems like an actual criminal, although they are all in here, he knows very well, for belonging to the IRA, and many are definitely responsible for acts of war, acts that to outside eyes are crimes of the worst kind. Many have the look of poor men, yet they are for the most part highly educated and well spoken. They are not afraid of looking you in the eye and challenging you. This is a new breed of Irishmen indeed. And not one to the governor's liking.

James is immediately pulled into the circle of friends and colleagues who had disappeared off the streets of Cork, one by one, over the last few months. Sandow, his frequent officer commanding, and Peter, his frequent partner, are both here. Tom Crofts, Seán Culhane, the men who were captured with him, are all here under assumed names: Mick Murphy, Frank O'Mahoney, head of the Intelligence squad and his other team member, Jerry O'Brien, is here and many of the ASU such as Charlie Cogan. Seán Moylan from Cork No. 3 is here as is his compatriot Seán Hales. In fact, there are in total over five hundred men from Cork and Kerry alone. And of all the men, the men of Cork City are considered the toughest, the most battle-seasoned. Together, the men have elected an officer commanding, a vice officer commanding, and an adjutant of the camp. Their first priority is escape.

James is greeted with a mix of disappointment and elation. The last bit of information known at Spike was that Séamus had been readmitted to the hospital and was on the point of death for the second time. They look at the back of his head in awe and wonder. How on earth did you survive that? It is either a miracle or you have horseshoes up your arse. The crude stitches and lumpy flesh are still swollen over the overflowing pool that pushes out trying to burst its borders. His hair is growing back in a white patch over the skin, and it brings to their attention the transformation of his hair from a solid, thick, dark auburn to the mix of salty streaks that it has become. But these physical markers of stress can be seen everywhere around him. Men who are far too thin, men whose lungs are worn down by constant exposure to the elements and who cough and hack far too much, even in the warmth, men whose faces are weather-beaten and who look ten years older than they should.

He sees and learns to recognise men who are on the edge. They have been tortured, or their families have been killed or their homes burned down, or perhaps they have just had as much uncertainty and anticipation of certain doom as they can take. These men are nervous. Their eyes flit from place to place. They are afraid of the guards and jump at loud noises. Sometimes James can hear them crying softly at night. But these men are few and far between. By far the prevailing attitude at Spike is one of defiance, rebelliousness, and insubordination. Although they must be careful not to push the wrong guards. There are those guards who are decent to the men, and there are those who would not think twice about shooting first and asking questions later. Back in the spring, one of the guards shot a man dead, only because while trying to catch a football he overstepped his tacit boundary. The guard is still at Spike, glowering at anybody who looks at him the wrong way. There is no doubt in anyone's mind that he would happily have a repeat performance.

Into this mix of men James finds himself welcomed and treated with respect. His own crew from the 2nd Battalion, the flying column, from the ASU and the IO squad, treat him as an equal. These men know each other's sins. Around Spike itself, word is out that another of O'Hegarty's men has found his way in. This instantly affords James status. But James is still not well. His head throbs. He is as thin as a reed. And he is tired. Oh so tired. Too tired to care about status. He heads outside with the rest of his crew and longs to lie down on the grass and sleep in the sun. It is only the existence of the truce that has stopped the hard labour. But lying in the sun for a nap is asking too much. Instead, James sits and acts as scorekeeper for games of football. He takes slow walks around the perimeter and gathers up what information he can from the other prisoners. Most of all he spends his time assessing the possibilities for escape.

The officer commanding of the camp, Buckley, from the 9th Battalion, learns from Tom Crofts that James was the main architect of the MacSwiney/Forde escape. He pulls in his Vice OC, Quirke, and together they grill James. With the truce on, and the abundance of men on the inside, they all know the likelihood of an escape plan hatched from outside the island is near nil. So, they focus on working backwards, and devising a way out on their own. No one could swim the mile and a half of exceptionally strong current, certainly not in their present physical condition: they need a boat. Indeed, there are boats, says James, along the side of the small pier, on the shoreline facing towards open sea and so outside of view from the mainland and outside of view from the high walls of the fort. But the pier is there, and chances are, boats are still there as well. They are small fishing boats, probably used by guards from time to time, but James made note of them when he was thinking out Seán's escape. So, assume a boat at the far pier. How do we get to it? The prison is surrounded by a forty-foot moat, both sides of which are circumnavigated by eighteen-foot-high walls with ramparts. The inside wall, closest to the camp, is lined at the top with barbed wire and is patrolled day and night by guards. At night, lights are shone at regular intervals. So once past the moat to get to the boat in the absence of the spotlights, we need the cooperation of the moon and intimate knowledge of the guards's schedules. There is no way to climb over the inside wall. Can we go under it, or through it? During their outside time, the men find every reason to patrol the remote areas of the wall behind the prison blocks. They can find nothing.

But there is a spot where an old passage across the moat is joined up to the back of A Block. The entrance to this passageway was bricked up decades ago. It is in a remote spot on the ground floor of the A Block and when they are inside, the men examine it carefully. Sure enough, the brick is loose and can be removed with some work. A small hole through the brick could be made bigger. With lookouts keeping an eye on the guards, James and Crofts and Buckley and Quirke clean out the small area. They succeed in creating a large enough hole to crawl through. Then they replace the bricks. Now, the next step, how to get across the forty feet of moat and over the outer wall? James explains the ladders the men used when they were planning the storming of Cork Gaol, however that was a much shorter wall. This wall will require a cat ladder. No rope is available, but they can make a rope from electric lighting wire and use chair rungs as foot pieces. The difficulty will be finding long planks to attach the chair rails to. Around the prison in every cell a rung is taken from every chair that can be found. Slowly, and as time permits, the men create the rope, taking it in and out of a reliable hiding place in the ceiling of their cells. They study the phases of the moon and predict exactly when the darkest night, at exactly the right time, will lead them to success. The next question is who will join in. Tom Crofts insists on going; he wants out to help O'Hegarty organise the men in the city and prepare for the resumption of war. Quirke and Buckley are determined to go. Richard Barrett, a comrade of Tom Barry's in West Cork, is willing to make any sacrifice to get out and adds his name to the list. James too wishes to go. Altogether there are eight men. Any more, and they risk getting caught. As commanders they also want to make sure that no other men suffer for their determination if the worst happens, and they are spotted and shot on sight.

It takes the men over two months to come up with the plan and find all of the various pieces that they need. But still, they lack the long planks which are the only way they can see to create a ladder. After much discussion and exploration of the camp, it is decided that a couple of floor joists are needed. However, ripping up floor joists and finding a place to hide them until the ladder can be built, then finding a place to hide the completed ladder, are the minor details that will make or break their plan.

In the meantime, the sun continues to shine, and each day James grows a little stronger. His mind is active now and he does not always notice the progressively weakening throb at the base of his skull. As the men walk around the area, the vastly outnumbered guards give them wide berth. Some of the men, emboldened by the sunshine in a yard chock full of prisoners, send menacing looks or make stinging comments as they walk by. On the other hand, the smarter inmates, men like Seán Moylan, have made friends with a select few of the guards. You catch more flies with honey than with vinegar, and Moylan proves it is true. One day, while he is sitting outside in the sun on a tiny porch off the medical wing, Moylan watches as some poor guard, as punishment for an ill-advised transgression to his superior officer, melts in the sun. He marches with a full kit along the top of the inner wall. Moylan and his mate, Con Conroy (of the Rahinsky House raid) take pity on the poor devil marching in record-breaking heat, sweating so that the water drips into his eyes and pours off his chin in rivulets. They toss him some oranges to quench his thirst. For the remainder of Moylan's time at Spike this young sergeant supplies him with cigarettes. So many cigarettes that Moylan, who is not a smoker, is able to pass them out generously to the men. James pulls on his gift of a cigarette like a thirsty man guzzling water and smiles at Moylan's smarts. He's wasted as a commander. He should be an intelligence officer.

While James and the others prepare for escape, de Valera paces back and forth in Dublin, preparing for talks with the British. No one really believes that the war is over. Collins is quite certain that at any moment the British will hit them broadside with a surprise attack and try to take over the island by extreme force. Most of Collins's men believe likewise. They are desperately trying to get as many men trained across the country as is possible, and while the training is happening, they are even more desperately trying to find guns. One of the five Hales brothers has been living in Genoa for some time. He is acting as a European ambassador for de Valera by day, but by night he is working a deal with the Italians to transport thousands and thousands of guns to Ireland. Collins also has men in England and Scotland and even in America searching out gun dealers, looking for ways of getting large numbers of them into the country in time to head off what is sure to be an English invasion. But despite de Valera's precautionary measures, he has in his mind the tiniest flicker of hope.

It is a hope placed not in the English high-level politicians, nor in the English aristocracy or parliamentarians. It is a hope placed in the pressure put to bear on the British movers and shakers. It is a hope that teeters on that thin line in the British class hierarchy of influential policy makers, politicians, and wealthy landowners whose popularity with their own people is either necessary for the continuance of their positions of power or desired as a result of their vanity and pride. De Valera learned much during his months in America. The vast Irish diaspora in America is almost unanimously behind him. They speak with their wallets. The voice of Irish Americans is being heard across the water, not only in Dublin, but in London, slammed in capital letters across the front pages of newspapers everywhere. De Valera is also cognisant of the goodness of the average English citizen. The people themselves, those who are horrified when they hear through the press what the Black and Tans and Auxies are doing to their neighbours. The English press is loud and clear in their condemnation of official reprisals, torture, and burning down innocent families's homes. De Valera senses another type of pressure, hidden just below the skin of the proud faces he must deal with. It is the fear that the English people might find out the worst of their sins that weighs heavily on the likes of Lloyd George and others. Finally, there is the pressure that de Valera and Collins are putting on the aristocracy, the owners of vast estates in Ireland, whose yearly income is dependent on Irish workers, the owners of the hundreds of Big Houses with their farms and businesses who are being burned out and boycotted. All of this pressure, internal and external, is weighing on Lloyd George. Even the king, it has been rumoured, is coming down hard on the government to end this madness and treat the Irish with a little respect.

De Valera is not saying much, but he is holding tight onto this kernel of hope. He has one hand behind his back, preparing the IRA, fine-tuning his own government departments and hierarchy, getting ready for the worst, and with the other hand pointing towards the future to a tiny light through the dark tunnel of war, a tiny, bright, hot light, on the other side of which lies freedom. Total and complete freedom. Something the Irish have been massacred, starved, decimated, worn down and punished for striving toward. Something that has been over seven hundred years in the making. No one else seems able to see that light. But de Valera is focused on it and he will not allow himself to blink, not even once.

De Valera's government, however, is another story. The members of the Dáil meet for the first time since the election in August. The truce is still on and so they meet openly in the Mansion House in Dublin without fear of British reprisal or disturbance. They are one and all members of the Sinn Féin party. But that doesn't mean they agree on everything. In fact the cabinet, at least some of them, can barely stand the sight of each other. Partly this state of affairs is de Valera's own doing. Collins is minister of finance. Cathal Brugha, minister of defence. Richard Mulcahy is chief of staff. One might forgive Brugha the illusion that he actually controls anything about the IRA. Yet everybody knows Collins is the mastermind behind the war. As far as Mulcahy is concerned, he himself is Collins's right-hand man, and Brugha is not in the know. So, when Brugha starts sending him orders and directives and ultimatums, Mulcahy sends back his own cutting responses. Brugha appoints a deputy chief of staff, Austin Stack, and Mulcahy ignores him, excludes him from every meeting and decision. Mulcahy appoints his own assistant chief of staff and does not inform Brugha. There is a war going on in the war office. When Brugha and Mulcahy confront de Valera, each looking for validation, de Valera bellows at them to get out of his sight. He will do all their jobs himself if necessary and they can all go to hell if they don't grow up.

There are only so many hours in the day, and de Valera spends most of them thinking through the process of wrestling freedom from the British. To all of Ireland's continuing amazement the truce holds. The glorious summer sun continues to shine. Behind closed doors, de Valera's team and Lloyd George's team are negotiating the next step forward. Formal talks, gentlemen. Formal talks! Imagine! The British sitting down with the Irish! To talk! A delegation from each side will get together and hash it out. We will come up with an agreement. It will be a win-win situation for each of us. De Valera looks down the tunnel and sees the little light grow. Infinitesimally perhaps, but it is brighter none the less.

At Spike, Seán Moylan is released. James is sorry to see him go. He is a good man, dedicated to the cause, devoted to his men. He holds high standards for all of them and is not averse to letting them know it. The men adore him and stand taller when he is around. When he goes things might change, James thinks to himself. As days go by Crofts, Buckley, Barrett, and Quirke become desperate to figure out some way of getting a ladder together. They have searched the grounds, the dormitories, every cell everywhere. Morning and evening a guard patrols each cell and accounts for each man. There is no way that they can tear up floorboards without being noticed. The reaction to this may be a lockdown, and no one will ever escape. So they must tread carefully.

September arrives and brings with it the first hint of autumn. Still the sun pours down on them. The men have the phases of the moon predicted through September, October, and November, all the way to Christmas. The darkest nights of the moon cycle are necessary to escape and so the men know that they have only a few days to choose from, and a ladder must be had. They meet to discuss it under the guise of a camp council meeting. How on earth to get the floor joists, long enough to make a ladder that will allow them to scale an eighteen-foot wall? Think lads, think!

There are men here at Spike who have been around gaols, holding cells, internment camps, everything the British could throw at them since the Rising. They know how to get what they need in prison. A suggestion is made. A riot. A riot in one or two of the cells to smash them up, break the beds, smash the windows, rip the blankets and by the way, tear up the floor joists. Leave the whole place a smashed-up pile of trash and nobody will notice a couple of missing joists. There will be a price to pay for sure. They may be moved out of Spike to another gaol, perhaps even in England. This would actually be something many of the men would prefer. It is much easier to plan an escape from the smaller gaols in the city. And even those who may not be brash enough to attempt escape would at least be able to receive packages and perhaps visits from relatives. Another possible consequence is that they may be put in lockdown and their beloved exercise time eliminated. This, however, would be temporary. The worst possibility is they may be put in the punishment cells, but that also is usually temporary. So, why not? It is worth it. After all, autumn is rolling in quickly. The breeze off the water is starting to bite. The sun is still shining, but it is losing its heat and it won't be long before the drizzle and wind will combine to make their unheated cells as cold as an icebox.

So, it is decided. A riot it will be. Crofts thinks carefully. They will need perhaps a day or two to get the ladders made and hidden properly once they have the joists. The men decide which cells will riot. They are far from the cells of the men who are planning the escape. They will dig up a cover of grass that can be raised up slightly, just enough to hide a long ladder, and then replaced overtop until the time comes. It will be at the back of the building, a place where no one walks, infrequently patrolled. They put together a schedule for working on the ladders. They will need a hammer and nails and the chair rungs and the electric wire to use as rope. They need to give themselves some time in case of unexpected delays, but not so much time that they risk the ladder being found. The men decide, working backwards on the moon's schedules, that the date of the riot must be the end of September and the escape will be attempted on the first moonless night a few days later. It is to be limited to two large cells in the top floor of B Block. The joist can be ripped off and tossed out of the window to men waiting below and quickly buried. Later, during exercise, they know that a couple of them will be able to make their way behind the building and quickly nail the chair rungs onto the joist, creating a cat ladder that can be scurried up quickly and then pulled up and over to the other side. The men of the cells are willing to take whatever punishment is meted out for the little bit of fun they will get with this meticulously planned madness.

It is only a few days before the selected date of the riot. James is making his rounds. He works the exercise yard like the old pro at intelligence gathering that he has become. He elicits tidbits of information about the guards, screens the men, keeping an eye out for anything suspicious that might indicate men are colluding with the authorities. After all, James knows very well that informers are everywhere in Ireland, especially the gaols. It is one of the favourite tricks of the British to plant them in amongst the men and wait for the inevitable talk with which they incriminate themselves. But James is up to their tricks.

Men can't just riot with their bare hands. It is best if tools are at their disposal. Certainly, tools will be needed to cut out the floor joist. Hammers, crowbars, a saw, anything with some weight to it will be welcomed if they are to push a full-scale riot. James talks quietly with Crofts. We need men who are on various work details around the island to bring in tools. We need a place to keep them, says James just below his breath as he walks the perimeter with Crofts. Aye, I will call a meeting, responds Crofts, but James stops him in his tracks. That's not how it should be done, too risky. Let me call a meeting. The men who are to escape should not be anywhere near it. In fact, the rank and file should not even know that we are planning this escape. If word gets out, you don't know what they will do, truce or no truce. Crofts nods his head slowly. You are right Séamus. Alright then, call a meeting. Make it on the other side of the square. We will play by your rules. You know your game better than anybody. James sends out word that just before roll call at six o'clock, a group of men from B Block, the designated leaders of the cells, trusted, dedicated men, should meet with him.

It is a gorgeous day with a cool breeze off the water. As he makes his way across the yard stopping from time to time to talk, he has caught the eye of one of the guards. It is just bad luck and bad timing, but it is going to cost him. The men gather together and stand about looking disinterested, but they are all ears. James lays out the problem. They need a joist. A good long one, two if possible. They need hammers, nails, electrical wire. Hammers and nails need to be collected from the various work sites, hidden under clothes, and brought back. But the best way to get their hands on the joists and wire without anyone noticing is a riot. A contained riot. No injuries. Only property damage. Only specific cells. Cells where the joists can be hoisted out of the window and quickly buried under the grass, a slit in the ground that will be cut and waiting. Just as James is finishing up the details, he hears the warning whistle from the lookouts. And just like that it is all over. The guard has been watching him from the time he started his walk across the square. To this seasoned British soldier, James's behaviour is suspicious. As the men disperse from around James, the guard maintains his ground, looks James in the eye, turns and walks away. By seven o'clock, after roll call, James is escorted to the governor's office.

I hear tell you are having meetings in the exercise yard. You should know that is expressly forbidden. Exactly what was your intention? The governor asks the question without expecting an answer. He is wary of these IRA men. They are smart and savvy. and though they look like a pack of farmers they are far from it. James looks at the governor. He already has put together an elaborate story of innocence. But something about the man annoys him. Maybe it is his thick eyebrows knit together in a grimace, or maybe his ridiculous moustache. Instead of playing it safe and protesting his innocence, James stares at him and says nothing. He is thinking that this is just the kind of man who gives orders that brutes in uniform will follow while he turns his head and looks the other way. It is just the kind of man that would stand by while men are force-fed or tortured. A man who has the power to make it right but chooses not to. James thinks of Ashe and his horrifying ordeal. He stares down at the governor.

From behind him, the guard at the door, sarcastically, threateningly, pipes up. At Spike, we answer the governor when he asks us a question. James just continues to stare. Fuck you, he is thinking. The governor gets his message loud and clear. He is done with these young bucks who do not know their place. He will teach this one a lesson he won't forget. Maybe his friends will perk up and pay heed as well.

Why don't you make room for our friend across the way, in the other block? Perhaps he will have changed his mind by tomorrow. And the governor turns his chair around to look out of the window.

James is taken on a long walk across the grounds to another building. He enters it to find a cheerful fire blazing in a small room with a couple of chairs. He is under no illusions who the fire is for: not for him. He knows he is about to be deposited in the punishment cells. He has heard rumours of them, but since his arrival in July he has not known of anyone who has been left here. They seem to have been reserved so far for the other half of the prison that contains the regular criminals. He is about to find out that the punishment factor of the punishment cells is mother nature herself, cold crisp breezes through the open windows at ground level that swirl down into the cells and suck away any warmth in a man's body, leaving only a frightful chill.

James is walked down to the third cell. It is far from the wall behind which the fireplace disperses its heat. The door is opened. He is told to step inside and strip. Yes, everything mate, even your skivvies. James knows better than to take on the two large men staring at him. His prison stripes are kicked out into the hallway, the door is pulled shut and locked and James looks around him in the dying glow of evening that illuminates the plank floor and the stone walls. There is no bench, no mattress, nothing but a bucket in the corner. It is the third week of September, and James is lucky that the summer has lasted so long. But even the hot summer heat has not reached the depths of this unit. James feels their wrath through the night. By morning he is exhausted, his lips and fingernails blue, his teeth chattering. He has tried exercising in the night to raise some body heat. Push ups, marching, lying on his back and cycling like the devil, his eyes closed, his legs taking him up and down the hills of Cork City. But he has been provided no food, no water, and his body soon revolts. There is no energy left, except for shivering. And yet, when the door is opened and he is asked if he is ready to talk to the governor, James turns his back. He is left a dirty, cold mug of tea and the door clangs behind him.

On the second day, walking around the short perimeter of his cell, James sings every song his mother ever taught him and every rebel song he can think of. He sings loudly. He sings softly. He sings of Kevin Barry, hanged just last year. He sings of the Fenians and of Wolfe Tone and of Robert Emmett. His head is light. He is starving, pangs of hunger like knives reaching down into his gut, but eventually the hunger leaves him. After a short time, he is too tired to sing. The evening breeze begins to carry in through the window and he tries to find the least exposed portion of the cell. I cannot imagine the horror of this place in the dead of winter, he thinks. He tries the corners, but the cold coming off them would freeze his back in minutes. So, the centre of the room seems best, away from the stone walls. He sits and curls into a ball, his arms around his legs, breathing down onto his chest, trying to generate some warmth. It is futile. His fingers and toes, his nose and lips are completely blue, his arms and legs shake uncontrollably. In fact, his entire body has resorted to shivering. He can feel even his neck jolting awkwardly from side to side. He feels like an old drunk with the shakes.

On the third day, he is asked again if he would like to answer the governor's questions. But James does not care to answer. He is feeling quite warm. In fact, he is feeling hot all over. His face glows and the hollows of his eyes stare at the guard with a questioning look. He looks over at Ashe hunched in the corner against the stone. Don't worry, he tells him. I won't leave you here. Then James's eyes roll up into the back of his head and he collapses on the ground. Oh, for fuck's sake, the guard yells for his companion. Best get a stretcher, this Fenian shite is out of it.

The next thing James knows he is being fed soup in the medical wing. You can thank your truce for this, the orderly snarls at him.

Otherwise, you'd a been there till you learned yer lesson! Two days later James is on a boat on his way back to Cork Gaol. The governor, annoyed that his orders are questioned by his superiors, has disposed of James in the best way he can without losing face.

Through the months that James has been padding the pavement around the military fortress on Spike Island, de Valera has been padding the pavements of Dublin and London. He knows this is their chance. He can feel it in his bones. De Valera knows his Irish history. He knows this is the closest anyone has come to prying freedom from the British in over seven hundred years. This is no mean accomplishment. And as if to convince himself of this fact, he has a continuous gnawing in his gut and a small but sharp voice in his head. This is it. This is it. And yet, there are so many obstacles. So many people to be won over. So many political and ideological walls to jump, climb or crawl over or under. When he goes to London, the Irish residents there and yes, even the English, clamber and cheer and wave. Barricades must be set up so that he is not mobbed. His tall, determined figure inspires awe and hope. After all, he was a Rebel leader in the Easter Rising. He was almost executed. He lost his friends and allies and yet he pushed forward. He spent months in America, toasted and admired by politicians across the land. Money he collected from Irish Americans has funded much of the war. He has been in and out of gaol so many times, the people have lost count.

Yes, de Valera is the face of Irish Republicanism, the calm, classy, determined face, that is. The bespectacled, well-dressed, American-born, intellectual face. A face that is quite different from the ambushers and murderers of RIC and British troops. Here is a man you can trust. The better side of the Irish. Nevertheless, he is the warrior who faces down the enemy. Even his enemies feel he is a worthy opponent. De Valera feels it all coming to him in waves across the crowd, waves of anticipation, expectation. And at night, when he can no longer keep his eyelids from slipping down over his eyes in exhaustion, it is the anxiety of failure, the terrors of defeat, the blood yet to be spilled from a war yet to be fought if he does not succeed, that invades his dreams, twisting them into unspeakable nightmares.

All summer long de Valera has been sparring with Lloyd George. They throw out words at each other and bluster and heave over the effect such words will have on their respective political partners and foes. Words like 'Crown', 'allegiance', 'Dominion', 'oath', and 'Empire', all of which have particular positive or negative connotations depending on one's point of view. They must find a way forward before their respective teams even meet on the field, lest they shoot each other down before the game begins. Finally, Lloyd George tosses his hands in the air. De Valera, sensing the danger, sends a message of hope, of confidence. Fine, forget this back and forth between us, it is pointless. Let's put the teams together and maybe we can work something out. De Valera accepts the invitation. On October 11 they will meet in London.

It has taken weeks to determine who exactly will represent the Irish. He must have a balanced force. Men who can negotiate, but men who keep the Republic as the end goal. Men who are strong and respected. They will after all be facing Lloyd George, Winston Churchill, Lord Birkenhead, Hamar Greenwood, and Austen Chamberlain. A more formidable force is hard to imagine. Collectively these men run the entire British Empire, countries of which could swallow Ireland whole without even noticing.

De Valera decides at the outset he will not attend. He wants to be one step removed. He knows the pressure on the chosen men will be difficult to withstand. He wants them to be able to say we have to check with the boss, were any deal actually to be contrived. He has been enduring frenzied, passionate discussions with his cabinet. He needs at least a five-man team, and Cathal Brugha is his first choice. Brugha flatly refuses. You aren't putting me in that trap, he tells de Valera in no uncertain terms. I've spent my whole life fighting for this country, I will not be the scapegoat when the English sabotage us. De Valera moves on.

Arthur Griffith is the natural choice. He was acting president while de Valera was in America, and Griffith is a gentleman. This is something that cannot be underestimated when dealing with Englishmen. De Valera believes that he also needs a nut that is impossible to crack, someone who can see through British subterfuge and stay focused, his eye on the prize, without wavering. In de Valera's mind there is only one person who fits the bill. It is Michael Collins.

Collins is outraged. He visits de Valera privately. What the hell are you doing putting my name forward? I want no part of this. I have no patience for these men and their political games. But de Valera insists. You are the toughest, smartest man we've got. You will give over nothing. Who else could be as strong an opponent to the political pandering that they will put forth? You know as well as I do how this will go. Collins looks at him. Exactly! And when this charade is over, we are back at war, and I will have nowhere to hide. My intelligence gathering will be completely destroyed. De Valera pours them both a whiskey. Don't you see, Michael? This is it. This is our chance. We can make this work. Yes, we will be ready to start up war once again if it all implodes. But it won't, not with you at the helm. You will be the one who will pressure them. You will be the one to put a spin on the wording to make it palatable to them. If you can't do it no one can. History is calling, Michael. Will you turn her down? Will you walk away from everything you have spent your life working toward? Collins stomps from the room. De Valera has somehow twisted him into a politician for the time being, and he does not care for it one bit.

Once Griffith and Collins have been brought into the fold, choosing the other men is hardly a problem. De Valera will send his converts. He will let Lloyd George know that the Irish too have their intellectual, highly educated, Protestant lawyers, rebels all, duly elected members of the Irish parliament, all members of Sinn Féin. He will send the two educated English lawyers, Robert Barton and George Gavan Duffy. One, a lawyer from Oxford; the other, a lawyer from Cambridge. That should send a message, and besides they are both men he can trust and, better still, they know the British from the inside out.

Barton, who fought in the Great War, was raised on an idyllic ancient Anglo-Irish estate a stone's throw from Glendalough, magical valley with the round tower and ruins where St Kevin in the sixth century built a thriving monastic community. Barton is proud of his heritage, both Irish and British, and it is not until, as a soldier sent to Dublin in the aftermath of the Rising, he witnessed the treatment of the Rebels, that he signed off on British dominance forever and join up with the rebels. He even ran for the 1918 general election under Sinn Féin and was voted in hands down. For all his trouble he was arrested for sedition and thrown in Mountjoy Prison in Dublin. Barton knows prisons from the outside in, and after convincing the authorities that he must be housed in the medical wing to be saved from the flu epidemic running rampant through the gaol, he was given his wish. As a political prisoner he was allowed to wear his own clothes, and when his lawyer friends brought him a saw, he hid it down the inside of his boot.

Barton knew what he was doing. The medical building is not attached to the main gaol: it is separate, small, and quiet at the back of the gaol property. Three days later he had sawn through the bars of his window. He created a stuffed version of himself under the blanket, and before jumping through the window, crossing the grass, and climbing up a rope ladder thrown to him compliments of Michael Collins on the other side, he sat down and wrote the governor a cheeky letter asking him to look after his belongings until he has a chance to come back and collect them. He left the letter sitting just so on his pillow. That was St Patrick's Day, 1919, an auspicious day for the newly-patriotic Irishman. But his good luck didn't last, and he found himself once more in prison, caught in the roundup of Sinn Féin members of parliament who, despite their best efforts at meeting in secret, got caught. He would not be released until a few days after de Valera himself in June 1921, completely missing any opportunity to engage in so-called illegal activities. In the end, this was the best thing that could have happened, because the British know for certain he is simply a misguided Irishman, innocent of any real wrongdoing.

George Gavan Duffy is another Englishman who turned colours due to the dramatic circumstances of the Rising. Duffy was born and bred in England, from a long line of illustrious lawyers and judges. He attended Cambridge, resigned to be an English lawyer the rest of his days. But then something happened which changed the trajectory of his life: he was assigned to defend Sir Roger Casement at his trial. The trial scars Duffy, and turns his head in the direction of the Rebels. In fact, his sister had already lived in Dublin for years, and herself participated in Patrick Pearse's column during the Rising. So, though Duffy spent his own youth in Europe becoming fluent in French and Italian, he moved to Dublin, became a Sinn Féin member of parliament and when de Valera asks him, he is only too willing to play his own role in the fight for Ireland's freedom.

Éamonn Duggan is the final lawyer de Valera picks. He is an Irishman through and through, and a smart one at that, often to be found at de Valera's side, giving him advice. As a young man, handsome and wily, he could charm the bark off a tree but now at forty-seven years old he has seen much more than a lifetime's worth of death, destruction, and chaos, and his face shows it. He has a cold stare that no longer charms but inspires fear and he is not afraid to use it.

In attendance with these three lawyers is a fourth, Erskine Childers, who will act as secretary. Erskine is Robert Barton's cousin and when Erskine's parents died one after the other at a young age, Erskine and his four siblings moved to Glendalough to be raised by his aunt. He too became a highly educated lawyer, and Cambridge graduate. While he was there, he was editor of the university newspaper, a member of the debating team, a rower and a sailor. Erskine was nothing less than a fine example of imperial Britain's educated class of gentlemen. During the Boer War, Erskine began to see a different perspective on the Empire. But it was in 1908, after Erskine and Barton returned from a tour of the agricultural enterprises of southern and western Ireland, that their views on Irish politics took a radical leap. By 1914, Erskine was sufficiently transformed in his political leanings that he made a gun-running expedition in his yacht, *The Asgard,* landing in Howth Harbour with a partial load of fifteen hundred German Mauser rifles and ammunition to much fanfare and a waiting regiment of Volunteers led by none other than Cathal Brugha. Erskine becomes famous for this act of defiance towards his own government, although suspicions about his background will forever follow him, until at last, he proves his mettle.

De Valera believes that these four lawyers, educated at the best schools in the world, devoted to the cause of freedom, will act as a powerful force against the British Empire. But de Valera is mistaken.

The delegation arrives in London, each member hosted by family of the upper echelons of British society, but all with Irish roots or connections. Each of the men is nervous, though they do not show it, and face the cameras with stoic, brave faces. Each day they meet for an hour or two and hash out their points of view about how Ireland should or should not maintain an allegiance to the British Empire. It is only hours before everyone in the room realises that the illustrious lawyers, Barton and Duffy and Duggan, will be tossed to the side while Lloyd George, Winston Churchill and the rest focus a sharp-edged sword at Collins and Griffith. Within a couple of days Griffith begins to crack. His health is affected. Day after day he must leave the talks, lie down, and nurse his pounding head. Just as de Valera predicted, it is Collins who must stand resolute and make the British believe they have given away nothing, when in fact they have given away everything.

In the evenings, Collins retreats to the sumptuous London home of Sir John and Hazel Lavery, the artist who painted Terry's funeral and the portrait of the most beautiful woman in the world. There is no doubt that Collins found some refuge from the heavy weight on his shoulders in her home; and for her part, she worked her magic on the men she knew so well, Churchill and the rest, to ease their minds' journey to the idea of Irish freedom.

By December 5, almost two months since the Irish delegation landed in London, Lloyd George is done with negotiating. He has gone further than he ever believed he would. He has pushed and pulled and prodded the rest of the British political establishment, finally dragging it with him to agree on a treaty. He has had it with John Craig, head of the Ulster Unionists, who is trying to prevent the treaty through political machinations and barely veiled threats. He has constructed a document that, once agreed to, will allow the northern counties to back away and independently maintain their allegiance with Britain, thereby washing his hands of the north. There is not one iota more he can do without committing political suicide. He pulls Collins aside. This is it, Collins, this is all you are getting. You and your men sign it tonight. You do it or so help me God, your country will suffer an invasion the like of which you can't even imagine. So, here's a dram of whiskey. Go talk to your mates and do the right thing.

James is firmly ensconced in Cork Gaol when the treaty negotiations begin. Amongst the men there is hardly a soul who actually believes that the British will agree on terms. It is only the dreamers and fools who have any faith in it at all. Everybody else is in preparation for the war that is sure to come once the talks break down. O'Hegarty has been on his commanding officers to stamp out the drinking, the talking, the cavorting with the enemy, and to send every pair of walking legs under their command to training, especially the new recruits. If they want the glory, it doesn't come cheap. O'Hegarty himself has been focused on acquiring guns. Guns from Italy. Guns from Germany. Guns from America. He will take guns from anywhere he can find them. O'Hegarty has no doubt that they will be absolutely necessary if the fight for freedom is to be won. The trouble lies in the fact that every time they come to a deal to buy a shipment some damn thing happens, and it all falls through. The American shipment is intercepted. The Italians change their minds. The Germans cannot find their promised loot. O`Hegarty is fit to be tied, but the lack of guns is not his only problem.

On Spike Island, plans for the escape move forward. At the end of October, the men can wait no longer. It will be war and soon and they need to get out. The riot in B Block is carefully planned. The men spend the night sawing through a couple of floor joists, leaving just enough cohesion to keep them together. The next day, in the morning when the coast is clear, they finish the job and carefully hoist them through the window to men waiting below, ready to bury them under the grass. Then they get straight to work trashing the place. Instead of going outside onto the grounds at the usual time, they get to work barricading themselves in their cells. They use the bed frames, the paillasses, the straw-stuffed mattresses, and everything they break and drag is piled up against the door and the windows. Finally, they get to work pulling up the floorboards and using them as firewood in the grates.

It takes the British an hour to smash in the door, by which time they are well and good done with Irishmen. They take the clubs to those men and herd them out into the main square, all six hundred of them who have taken part. The officers of each cell are removed down to the punishment cells and the regulars are sent back to their trashed cells to enjoy a night on the floor of what is left of their areas. The next morning, they start at it all over again. They will do a remarkable job of this, so much so that the governor will remark to his superiors that he is not dealing with men at all, but animals. Every item that can be burned is burned. Every item that can be shattered is shattered. Every item that can be rent asunder is so. B Block is left with only enough floorboards to keep from falling through the ceiling. For their trouble they are herded out onto the square a second time.

The governor is beside himself. Go get their officers and return them, for God's sake, or who knows what they will do next. The guards can hear the men laughing and sniggering and they tell the governor that despite some broken bones and bruised faces the lot of them look like they are up for another day of destruction. The governor paces back and forth. Put them out in the moat and keep them there until I decide what to do. All day long all six hundred are left in the moat, guarded from above. All night they are left there. No food is given them, and the governor can only smile when it starts to rain buckets. In the morning the men are drenched, shivering, starving, and willing to agree to be nice. The governor is so happy he will not have to deal with their madness, he has the kitchen cook them up the best meal they ever had. Over in A Block, which has kept quiet through the entire affair, Tom Crofts and his crew are happy to enjoy the spoils of the event. The good meal will help bolster them in preparation for their escape in a few days.

Once things have settled down and the moon works through its course, Crofts and his men make way. It is a stormy night, and much darker than they had anticipated. Being seen will not be a problem. They head to the old entrance at the back of their cells and move the debris from in front of the ancient iron door. The hinges have been sawn through, and they lift the old monster out of the way, go through the opening, and then replace it after themselves. Out to the moat, pull the ladder out from under the grass, hug the inner wall and time each dash across the moat to match the turn of the sentry, eighteen feet above them. Up goes the ladder in the darkest turn of the wall and each man scurries up to the top, and lies flat. The last man pulls up the ladder placing it outside the wall and they scurry down, pulling the ladder with them and hiding it in amongst the tall grass. Finally, they make their way around the shoreline to the dock.

Then panic sets in. The wind is howling, the rain driving down on them and lo and behold, there is not a boat in sight. It is the sailor amongst them, Jack Eddy, who, when the clouds miraculously part for a moment, sees the glint of a tiny rowboat swaying back and forth off the pier, obviously anchored with a rope. He takes the one knife they have between them, puts it between his teeth and swims out to the boat and begins to cut the anchor rope. He is so cold his teeth chatter and his fingers begin to freeze up and the knife slowly drops to the bottom of the sea, eluding him as he dives in a panic trying to catch it. Jack knows he can give up now, go back and be shot by a British firing squad, his name forgotten, or worse, held in contempt, or he can get his act together and bring this boat over to his friends on the pier. He puts that rope between his teeth and chews through as if his very life depends on it, which it does. Almost dead of exposure by the time his mates throw themselves into the boat, he rallies and asks for the paddles. The men look at each other when only one paddle is produced. Back onto the pier they tumble, searching for a paddle. No doubt the Catholics are praying to the mother of God by this time, and their efforts are rewarded, for one lonely broken paddle is found under the pier. Jack navigates as the others row, and they are all safely in Cobh tucked into warm beds with full bellies, smiling in their sleep, by the time the British discover they are gone, the following day.

Word of the escape reaches James in Cork Gaol, and he cannot but smile and sing an old rebel tune. The escape is hardly the big news in November of 1921. Inside the gaol and all over the country speculation is rife. Will de Valera's team of plenipotentiaries be able to do a deal with the devil? Will Ireland be able to walk away from British occupation without firing another shot? Collins begins to sneak home when he can. Often it is to Cork, his own county, though not always to his family farm in Clonakilty. He keeps up with his men, making contingency plans for every eventuality. If there is war, his face will now be known by every Tom, Dick, and Harry across Britain and America thanks to the press coverage of the treaty negotiations. It will be the men under him who will have to carry on surreptitiously, while he goes into hiding. If a miracle actually occurs and they reach some kind of a working document, there will be a whole country to build: a bureaucracy, a political forum, an army, the list goes on; so many details it boggles the mind. And if a country is to be built, Collins is determined that his boys in Cork will be a big part of that. At home, despite the hours it takes, it is worth it to go back to his roots, to talk to the people he has been fighting for all this time, people like his own family, farmers, and teachers. He finds the stuffiness of the upper crust of British society stifling, despite his good treatment. They live with their heads in the clouds, those people. They are educated to beat the band and he is weary of constantly being reminded, if only by his own acrimonious mind, that he is but a post office boy.

Collins has other reasons for returning home. He is feeling wary of his old friend de Valera. He resents de Valera's insistence on placing him in the spotlight. They fought most of the war, surely the nastiest parts of it, while he was safe in America being touted about by the *nouveau riche* and the idealistic Irish diaspora. Now de Valera is calling all of the shots. He resents de Valera's pressure on him. The idea that the whole damn house of cards rests on his shoulders, he resents it, but he knows it is true. He sees Lloyd George, polite, but dismissive of everyone but him. He sees the little wheels turning in Lloyd George's head, trying to move him, trying to see how he sees, think how he thinks and, in the end, outmanoeuvre him. And yet, while Collins sees inside his head, he learns also how Lloyd George must play his own house of cards, his own political opponents, and his own set of madmen, ready to go to war, their heads in the sand. He senses how Lloyd George, Churchill, and the rest are fed up to kingdom come with the Irish altogether. Collins senses all of this, and he knows de Valera is right. This is their chance. And he, Collins, has to make it happen.

On the night that Lloyd George presents Collins with the final document, the Irishmen retreat to discuss it. It is far from what they had originally hoped. The deal is that Ireland will retain a status somewhat like the Dominion of Canada, though it will be referred to as the Irish Free State. The new Irish parliament will swear allegiance to the king. But they will rule themselves, continue with the Dáil, institute their own fiscal policy, collect their own taxes, run themselves for themselves. The British military superstructure will be turned over to them and except for a few ports, the British will go home. But Ireland will remain a key component of the British Empire. There is no doubt in Collins's mind that he cannot squeeze another drop of freedom from Lloyd George and Churchill. He also has no doubt that the moment the Irish walk away from this deal will be the moment Churchill picks up the phone and quietly announces to his generals: invade.

The deadline for returning with the signed document is midnight. It is December 5, 1921. They have been at it straight for two long headache-filled, high blood pressure-inducing months. The last few hours are no better. Collins, Griffith, and Duffy are all for signing. Barton and Duggan are not. The arguing starts even in the taxi to their meeting place and each man is surprised at somebody else. Collins is all for signing. Nobody but Griffith expected that. Griffith had had secret talks with Lloyd George about the north of Ireland, and no one knew until now. Barton and Duffy and Duggan agree on little. The squabbling, the what ifs, the doom and gloom, and the endless list of contingencies is gone over for the thousandth time. In the end Collins calls a halt. We are going around in circles, boys. Don't you see the English are done with us? It is this or back to full-fledged war. Get the British the hell out of our country and we will sort the rest out ourselves. Let's sign the damn thing and go home. We will convince the people that it is just the first step. As years go by, we will eradicate the British completely. Patience, men. Patience. Tonight is the first step of many.

Erskine Childers is beside himself and lets his cousin know in no uncertain terms. Everyone knows that with signing the document, the battle has just begun. The real fight will be in Dublin, and the first obstacle will be de Valera himself when he discovers they have signed the document without consulting him. We are done with this. Let's just sign it and get the hell out of here and go home. And so, two hours after the deadline, and several hours after arguing, shouting, almost coming to blows amongst themselves, the Irish delegation returns to 10 Downing Street and hands over the signed document. History is made. For the first time during the entire two-month stretch of talks, the Englishmen at the table shake hands with the Irish. They are delighted to see the end of them.

James's six-month sentence is almost up anyway, but he is ecstatic nonetheless when he is released with all of the other political prisoners in Cork Gaol, and indeed across Ireland. He is as surprised as anyone that the negotiations have ended, and a treaty has been signed. The stress that was weighing on him, the idea that he might not be out in time before war starts up again, that he might be stuck inside the gaol indefinitely, that stress melts away in the rain as he practically skips across the streets of Cork. Immediately upon his release he goes home to his mother, who cries at the sight of him. She is not used to seeing her beautiful boy in such an unkempt state. Nor is she happy with the gaunt face and leaner than ever frame. She examines the still slightly protruding bubble at the back of his head and says a quiet prayer of gratitude. It is obviously a miracle that her son survived. She feels validated in her prayers, so many rosaries, especially for James, who has been on the frontlines of this mad war. She puts on a leg of lamb and gets to work making rice puddings, custard tarts, and sweet bread pudding. Once bathed, shaved, fed, and dressed in his now loose clean clothes, James feels like a new man. He struts over to Seán's place, expecting a night out at the pub and to meet up with other officers of the brigade. He expects jubilation, victory toasts, and rebel songs. Instead, Seán is dour-faced and chain-smoking.

Have you not read the papers, Jimmy? Seán looks at him with incredulity. All of Cork has been reading the papers, morning and night. All of Cork has an opinion on the treaty terms. All of Cork agrees that the treaty terms are worth the price of a few MPs swearing allegiance to a king nobody cares about. All of Cork is ecstatic that life as it once was, before the madness, can resume. All of Cork, that is, except the men who did the fighting. My brother didn't die for this. This isn't freedom. Swearing allegiance to the king? How is that freedom? Look at everything we've been through… was it for this? What was Collins thinking? Where is our Republic, Jimmy? Answer me that! He didn't have any right to sign off on that treaty. It should have been brought home to the cabinet to decide if it was to be signed. He overstepped himself, so he did. He's thrown everything we've fought for to the dogs.

The bubbles of elation bouncing around inside James's head since he walked out of Cork Gaol begin to pop. The two men are walking towards the Douglas Street Pub. Seán gives James a warning. If O'Hegarty is there, don't be a bit surprised at the mood he is in. I don't think I have ever seen him so foul. He is mumbling about treason, Jimmy. Treason! None of us like the treaty, but I don't know if I would go that far.

At the door, James hesitates. The last time he was here he had to be carried out on a stretcher. But he sucks in a lung full of air, braces himself, and opens the door. The pub is crowded with just about every officer from Cork No. 1. Immediately he can see why. There in the centre of the room sits O'Hegarty, holding court with his cup of tea at hand. He is surrounded by his most reliable men. There are so many they can hardly fit in the small room. It is obviously a homecoming party for many, but there is a strange atmosphere in the room. The men are torn between excitement at being together, out of gaol, free from threats, openly meeting, and at the same time arguing excitedly about the ramifications of the treaty terms. There is anxiety in the air. Not everybody knows what to think of this historic development. Some have a deep trust in Collins. Yet if O'Hegarty is openly contemptuous of his efforts, what does that say? Should they keep on fighting until they drive the British out, or should they embrace the new agreement and ignore them? Cork No. 1 has always been an organisation where the men have felt free to voice their opinions and they do so now. But some of the men who might think otherwise are keeping mum today. They can feel the seething anger of O'Hegarty across the room. Our men who fell, our men who have been executed, they have died fighting for a republic. Not a sham agreement allowing us our own parliament. We bloody well already have our own parliament. It's called Dáil Éireann for a reason. We created it. We don't need the bloody British to sell it back to us.

Seán is right, thinks James, and just as he is about to tiptoe his way to the back of the room and give O'Hegarty a wide berth he hears his name and turns to find O'Hegarty standing up, waving him over to his table. Jimmy lad, come here with ye. Let me get a gander at this hole in your head I've been hearing about. And James makes his way through the parting of men that allows him through. O'Hegarty is genuinely pleased to see him. James shows off his wound, and the men toast him and crack jokes. And while all of this goes on, O'Hegarty whispers in James's ear. Don't get too comfortable Jimmy. There is work to be done yet. Meet me at the sisters' shop in the morning, and at James's questioning look, he says, aye, they are back up and running, another little gift, thanks to the truce.

And so, one day after James has left gaol, he begins again his work as intelligence officer for the Cork No. 1 Brigade. The details of the job at hand give James an insight into just how upset O'Hegarty is about the treaty. There is an American journalist in Cork who is writing in the papers. What he is writing is not truthful, and is bound to give people the impression that the IRA supports the treaty terms. O'Hegarty has contacted him and let him know he would be better off if he were to represent the voice of the people a little more accurately, especially when it comes to the voice of the IRA. Foolish man. He thinks he can just pack up and move to Dublin to avoid O'Hegarty. Naive man. He will soon learn how far O'Hegarty's arms reach.

The Wallace sisters' shop has been restored to them and the two women are delighted to be in their own home once again. Despite being only in their early thirties, they appear even more frail than they did in the past, especially Sheila, who was appointed some time back as a communication officer for the brigade. It is obvious that she was worn to the bone for the months that she did that job. The layers of jumpers and shawls cannot hide her emaciated shoulders and the occasional deep, disturbing cough appears to James to be an ominous sign of poor health. Nevertheless, the sisters are ecstatic that things have returned to normal, and the steady stream of officers has returned. There is a pot of tea on the table and a tin of biscuits, a rarely seen luxury that the sisters have offered in their celebratory mood. As James enters the dark little back room he can sense, before he can actually see, that O'Hegarty is sitting at the small table, several newspapers in hand, steam coming out of his ears, eyes narrowed down to slits, a snarl on his face. Would you look at this shite they are publishing Jimmy? This just won't do. Off to Dublin and find our man here writing this nonsense. See Seán for some funds, stay as long as it takes. As soon as you know where he is, give us a call. We will send a team to pick him up and convince him of the error of his ways. As far as O'Hegarty is concerned, it is as if James has never left. Back to business as usual.

James takes a walk over to the MacSwiney home. Seán has been appointed brigade adjutant, replacing poor Charley Daly. He has been organising the ins and outs of the brigade, the training, the search for guns, the development of a new safe house network, a new network, about which the British or Collins have any inkling. Given the amount of information that the English managed to get their hands on by the time of the truce, O'Hegarty's orders had been clear. He has been preparing nonstop for another onslaught of war and Seán's job is to make sure that preparation is cemented in stone. He has been living at home with his sisters and while they have been working with Cumann na mBan, he has been O'Hegarty's right hand man. His sister Mary cannot be happier. She opens the door to James and reaches up to give him a hug. In truth she is delighted every time she sees a Cork IRA man who has survived, but James is special. When he was shot and arrested, Mary felt a panic overwhelm her, almost as if it was Seán. She looks at James and though she says nothing but how good it is to see him, the gaunt, pale face and remarkable white streaks in his hair assure her that he is doing his bit and then some for Ireland.

Armed with some cash and his best clothes that his mother carefully preserved while he was behind bars, James takes the train to Dublin. It doesn't take long to ascertain where most of the journalists are staying; in fact, within a couple of hours he has made contact with the Dublin IRA and discovered the location of the hotel without so much as a step out of time. He calls down to Cork. Keep an eye on him, Jimmy. We don't want him slipping away. I will send Jim Grey with a car. 'Twill probably be Dan and Mick and that will join you. Jim will have a destination for you. We are borrowing a wee cottage on the seaside. You can have a bit of a holiday if you keep him within arm's reach!

The following day, about mid-afternoon, James is sitting in Bewley's café, just a stone's throw across the River Liffey from the General Post Office where a few short years ago Pádraig Pearse and James Connolly and the rest started it all. Just like Cork, Dublin still carries the scars of British domination in the form of destroyed or damaged buildings and debris. James watches, sitting at a table in the back of the sprawling room, and listens as patrons order their tea and discuss the treaty. Just like in Cork it seems to be the only topic of conversation. He is sitting with one of Collins's men. James knows that O'Hegarty would not like it, but he also knows how to do his job quickly and efficiently, and look now, here is the proof in the pudding as Mr Kay, the *Times* journalist, walks in with a crowd of other journalists and takes over a large table. James's compatriot, that is, one of Collins's own intelligence officers, does not know of course what he, James, is up to, and he will pay later for his negligence when Collins erupts. But in the meantime, James is his own cool self, not giving away a thing. The names of all of the journalists are given to James by his IRA companion, and James duly notes all of them. He tells him also that they are all staying at the same hotel and once he is alone, he follows the journalist back to his hotel, gets himself a room, and makes his call.

The following morning, if a stranger happened to be looking, they would note a beautiful silver Rolls Royce glide up the street and pull over in front of the café where a large group of international and domestic journalists have established a routine of morning tea. The driver, who they would not be able to ignore, is as handsome as a film star, and just as well dressed. The car doors open and out step two famous footballers from Cork: Mick Murphy and Sandow. The stranger might not realise who they are because they are wearing fedoras pulled down strategically to hide their faces and well-tailored suits. They blend in perfectly with the upscale crowd that frequents the café. The stranger would also note that the Rolls Royce pulls over to the side of the street, and the driver waits patiently. Were the stranger to watch for just a few minutes longer they would see the two famous footballers half-carry and half-drag an English journalist through the door and bundle him quickly into the back seat, sitting on either side of him. A few seconds later they would see another well-dressed young man, tall and slim, in an expensive overcoat, serenely exit by the front door, immediately open the front passenger door of the car, look from side to side down the street, and slip inside. No one, stranger or not, will see anyone in that car for another week, despite Collins sending his own intelligence men after them once he has heard what has happened.

James and Murphy and Sandow roar with laughter as Jim Grey sings one of his uproarious songs, his own bawdy lyrics to well-known tunes. The journalist Kay is terrified for some time, and occasionally as they drive through the odd village, lurches across one of the men, attempting to gain some attention from someone who might help. Each time his shoulder, even his head, is grasped in a pair of thick sturdy hands and put back in place in the comfortable leather seat of the Rolls. Now, now, Mr Kay, not to worry, is all the men will say, at which point, all four of his attendants burst into laughter. Once they are in the countryside well and true, and on their way to Cork, they enlighten their hostage. Sure, we are just off for a wee holiday by the seashore, so we are. Our commander is hoping that during your stay you might come to understand another point of view in regard to the treaty.

James spends several days with Peter and Mahoney keeping watch while Mr Kay is fed and seated by the fire to listen to various points of view about the treaty. The IRA position, as far as O'Hegarty is concerned, is explained several times, though O'Hegarty himself does not come near the place. After five days, Mr Kay is driven back to his Dublin hotel. Jim Grey and James drop him off and tip their hats to him. A grand gaggle of chaps altogether, he is heard to exclaim to his journalist friends who wondered what had become of him. They have some interesting ideas, from the Irish perspective of course. It would appear that the IRA is not in agreement with the treaty terms after all. Mr Kay writes a new article for the *London Times*, this time pointing out his obvious omission from the last.

The new point of view published in the papers does not, however, quell the seeming tide in pro-treaty views. Rebel Cork my arse, O'Hegarty hollers. James says little. Even if he wanted to, he could hardly have expected to get a word in. Sandow considers aloud the possibility of executions. Seán looks at him coldly; after all he is a member of the Dáil and believes in democracy. But even Seán is dumbfounded at the creeping popularity of the idea of selling out to the king of England. While O'Hegarty is furious, Seán is deeply disappointed. Each man has confided in James. After all we've been through, Jimmy! Imagine, to give in like this? Day after day the papers are full of it. O'Hegarty has finally had enough when Liam de Róiste and Liam Deasy, two Cork members of the Dáil, publicly proclaim their agreement with the terms of the treaty. Traitors! They are traitors to the Republic! All the men Jimmy, you know all the men who have died for the republic. We are so close. We cannot abandon it now. Write us up a note Jimmy, and we'll send a special message to these politicians. And so, James in his impeccable penmanship crafts a letter to be sent to all of the Cork Members of the Dáil.

> *From Cork 1 Headquarters:*
> *To all TDs [Teachta Dála's] in Cork 1 Area:*
> *On December 10th the Staff of the First Southern Division and all Brigade Commandants sent forward to G. H. Q. unanimously a demand for the rejection of the Treaty proposals. You are reminded that it is your duty to support this demand. To act otherwise would be treason to the Republic to which we have all sworn allegiance.*

James and Peter set about delivering copies to the four TDs. Liam de Róiste will write in his diary that he believes the note is a warning of execution to whomsoever the Cork No. 1 sees as a traitor. Perhaps that is a bit dramatic. Or perhaps he just knows the authors. In any event it is blatant intimidation as far as he is concerned, yet dissension continues.

Seán prepares to go to Dublin for the debate on the treaty. It will be held over several weeks at University College Dublin in a lecture hall deemed large enough to contain the unruly and enflamed members and their audience. Indeed, James has heard the finer points of the anti-treaty argument from Seán long into the night before he leaves. Sure, there will be peace, but at what cost?

There is the issue with Ulster. How can we have Ireland without the north? It is madness to let them walk away from the country. There is the issue of a governor general, as in Canada. A representative of the king in our Dáil Éireann? No. No. No. There is the issue of the British maintaining military bases, though they be few in number, and the issue of the British maintaining control over telegraphs and wireless stations. But the most gnawing issue of all, the one that crawls under the surface of every Republican's skin, is the issue of their democratically elected members of Dáil Éireann, their own sweet, ingenious creation, swearing allegiance to the English King. That is just too much to take. Where is your dignity, Irishmen? Where is your national pride?

Three weeks of hot-headed accusations tossed back and forth across the cavernous lecture hall between those for and those against the treaty are interspersed with weekends home for Seán. He reports to O'Hegarty. It doesn't look good, so it doesn't. De Valera is working hard, but he is routinely overrun by Collins and Griffith. They have an entire faction of pro-treaty supporters. Some of the southern TDs are with him. O'Rahilly is one of them. He has written a pamphlet supporting the treaty, and since he is a professor from University College Cork, he seems to have a lot of sway. When Seán walks out of the door, O'Hegarty leans into James. Get a few of the boys together, Jimmy, O'Rahilly wants to publish pamphlets? He had best be finding himself a new printing press.

James finds himself, for the second time in his life, late at night, with a sledgehammer in hand and a printing press bearing the brunt of his assault. Within a couple of days the pamphlets are sent to another printer on the other side of the city, and he finds himself there, doing the same job. When the Cork Chamber of Commerce, run by the pro-British element of the city, decide to begin a campaign urging the public to sign a petition supporting the treaty, James and his crew stroll over to the offices, politely hold out their guns, and with a nod and a smile, make off with the petition books.

Finally, on January 7, the members of the Dáil have said everything that can be said about the treaty. It is time to vote. The motion to accept the treaty passes by a mere seven votes. De Valera and his entourage of anti-treaty supporters rise up and prepare to storm from the room. Mary MacSwiney yells across the hall: This is a betrayal! De Valera begins to call out as well but is overcome by emotion. Collins, perhaps momentarily stupefied by a vision of what is to come, calls out after his friends. His voice is desperate, pleading. De Valera and his entourage walk across the floor. Collins is left standing, staring after them, his eyes brimming with tears. It is later on this day that he famously remarks: I have signed my own death warrant. He is under no illusions about the stalwart determination of Irish warriors.

It does not take Collins long to wipe his eyes and get to work. Once the treaty is ratified, the British start packing. Across the country the barracks that are still left standing are emptied. The British leave behind everything but the guns. Churchill has agreed to supply the new National Army with everything it needs, from major artillery to handcuffs. Within days, the Union Quay Barracks at the bottom of Parnell Bridge, the same barracks whose men came under fire on the bridge exactly a year ago, is handed over to O'Hegarty. As the quartermaster, Seán is stationed there to organise and inventory what has been left. It is a massive job and so with a little encouragement, O'Hegarty is convinced to create a new position for James. Assistant quartermaster becomes his new title, although there is no question that he is still working intelligence for O'Hegarty.

Taking over the barracks is a moment of sweet, palpable victory for the two young men. They watch as the last of the British soldiers march over the bridge in formation, their rifles hoisted across their shoulders, never to return. Never to shoot another Irishman in the back. Never to drag another man into the barracks for God knows what kind of treatment. The two men take a look at each other and then head in through the fortified entrance. On the top floor they find the officers' quarters, and each claim one for themselves. This will be their home for several months. Seán is happy to be out of his family home, which has once again become a place of hysterical arguing and emotional chaos. His sister Mary is violently against the treaty, seeing it as a betrayal of everything Terry had worked for, and has great difficulty calming her frenetic mind. James also is happy to have his own space in a place away from his family home. His new rank leaves him in intelligence, but in the eye of the storm as far as operations of the entire brigade go. Between Seán and James there is nothing that transpires within their brigade that does not pass over their desks.

In the evenings, once O'Hegarty and some of the other locals have headed home to their wives and families, in the top floor of the barracks in their quarters, they light a candle and take out the bottle of Jameson Irish Whiskey. They sit and look out over the River Lee and go over the events of the day. Inevitably they end up talking about Tomás or Terry and others they have lost, Tadg, Charley, like two old men looking back on their lives. Indeed, they feel like they have lived through a dream in the past few years, and they often remark to each other that it is a miracle they are sitting where they are, in a former bastion of British power. It should be a time they will remember with great fondness. But that is not how it will play out for them, or for anyone. Over the next few weeks, Seán and James watch as the city and country around them begins to break into brewing, gurgling pockets of chaos.

The two young men are amazed at the political bitterness that is manifesting itself in various quarters, and not just from duelling pro- and anti-treaty IRA. The railwaymen go on strike for weeks. The dock workers shut down much of the harbour, and the city is cut off from receiving regular shipments to business. The Labour Party throws out nasty news about the Sinn Féin Party. An election is due as part of the treaty agreements, and for the first time since 1919 Sinn Féin will have opposition. It is a socialist, rebellious opposition, full of people without jobs and no hopes of better prospects. They have bought into the Bolshevik creeds of Russia and wish to create a worker's paradise.

Much of the city is appalled. In Dublin, the anti-treaty IRA, Irish Republican Army, a title they continue to use despite the forces being renamed in Dublin as the National Army, have been robbing banks to get the funds for their full-time members since Mulcahy and Collins have cut off funding for anybody who is against the treaty. Indeed, James and Seán are working for free: O'Hegarty too has been cut off. Many of the IRA men who are on the anti-treaty side have been roaming the shops, commandeering goods. Regular mercenary criminals have caught on to this trick and are doing the same, leaving bogus chits for the materials they take, claiming they are doing so for the Cork No. 1. Tom Hales, commander of the Cork No. 3, publicly vows to shoot anybody who is caught doing this. De Valera, president of Dáil Éireann, is working against Collins, against the treaty. The newspapers are full of his proclamations of doom and gloom. The country itself is beginning to take sides, and just as these two national leaders begin to butt heads, so too do friends around the country, but especially in counties Cork and Kerry.

Collins knows that his old friend de Valera is the most respected politician in the country, and he sets out to undercut his message of fractious disregard for the peace process and misunderstanding of the long-term goals of the treaty negotiators. Collins, backed by Griffith and his team of supporters, plans to go straight to the people and make sure every single man, woman, and child shares his vision for moving Ireland forward without suffering more war. He arrives in Cork on a cold, blustery March day. He visits his sisters on the family farm and walks along the country roads chatting with the old ones. The grandmothers, worn beyond their years in black shawls; the grandfathers in tweed jackets and caps pulled down on aged faces expressing a lifetime of poverty and want. He breathes in the salty air, the scent and taste of home, and knows in his heart that he has done the best he could do. He knows too that it is enough for now. That it is just opening the door to freedom and that in a few short years to come they will step right through and shut that door closed behind them. He will connect with his former circles in Cork, the IRB boys, the Sinn Féin boys, and most importantly Cork No. 1.

Later that evening Collins arranges to meet with O'Hegarty and his Officers. They choose O'Hegarty's wife's café in the centre of the city. Magda is ambivalent. She knows her husband is against the treaty. She herself is against the treaty. Collins led them to the brink of victory. It is the honest truth that his leadership, his ingenuity, his brash, aggressive fearlessness was the decisive factor against the enemy. Yet now he has pushed for a treaty that recognises the very king we were working to rid ourselves of. And now the people of Cork look like they are abandoning Cork No. 1 and supporting Collins. Magda is not sure what to say to the man. Nevertheless, she has the Cumann na mBan women prepare a small feast of sandwiches and cakes and pots of tea. And knowing that Collins will want a drink, she second guesses herself and has crates of beer and whiskey brought in for the occasion. A crew of young lads, new to the IRA, are found to stand guard outside, while O'Hegarty and Pa Murray, Sandow and Seán Culhane and Peter, Florrie, and James and Seán, and a whole gaggle of others fill the café and break out the drink. The men might be happy to see him and flattered that he wishes to spend an evening with them, but like Magda they are discombobulated, unsure what to say or do in front of the great man who led them so far and then threw them under the bus, just when total victory was near.

Collins takes a deep breath when he arrives at the café. *Off to fight another battle, this time with my own people.* And he steps from the car with his head down, his fedora shielding his face. Old habits die hard. He has to remind himself that those days are over. That he is now the Chairman of the Provisional Government of the Free State of Ireland. He has to recall that his face has been splashed all over the newspapers of the world, not just Ireland and England and America. He can never hide in plain sight again. He stops and raises himself up to his full height and takes off his hat, and after shaking the hands of the young bucks on guard duty, he barges through the door and into the sea of faces that he does not necessarily know, and for a mere second he is lost for words. The faces of Cork No. 1, the movers and shakers, the risk takers, the men who were able to perform the deeds that needed to be done, the deeds that screamed out at the British, *You have met your match!* These men, these faces stare out at him and not a sound is heard in the room, not a movement is made.

Even O'Hegarty hesitates. Is it in this moment that Collins fully understands the calibre of his opposition? The uphill battle he must face to win over these faces, the faces of men who have made sacrifices, compromises with their own better judgement, spent weeks in filthy gaols, endured abuse, watched their friends being murdered, executed, even tortured, stood mute and boiling with rage while their friends' and families' homes burned to the ground as the British cheered. Is it in this moment that he knows it is Cork where he, Collins, will meet *his* match?

James looks across the room. He is one of the taller men, and he sees Collins's face dead on. His eyes taking them all in. The wheels in his head turning. What is he thinking? James wonders to himself.

The whole country knows that Cork No. 1, or most of it, is against the treaty. O'Hegarty has made sure of that. What is Collins going to do about it? O'Hegarty breaks the silence by striding over and shaking Collins's hand and the room erupts. Politics can wait for the morning, tonight they will toast their shared successes.

But as the night wears on and the drink slowly disappears, inevitably the talk begins to flow freely and it is as it has been for weeks now, about politics. Late in the night, Collins, looking around the room, spies James's face and strides over to see him. Séamus! Good to see you. I hear you took one for the team, says Collins as he raises his glass to James. Aye, says James, and he raises his and slugs it back. He does not care to elaborate on his wound, and Collins, sensing this, realises that James is not the type to blather on with war stories. This indeed was the quality he noticed first about James, and why he made sure that he would be designated intelligence officer.

He changes the subject abruptly. Séamus, you realise since the last of the British have shoved off, there will be positions to fill. You need to consider your future. Collins calls out for another draft, Sure another for my man here. Collins slides it over to him and James handles it for a moment, pushing it side to side on the surface of the table. He is feeling like he has had enough to drink for one night. He is wondering why he is talking to this man. This traitor to the country. Traitor to Terrence and Tomás, both of whom are probably rolling in their graves at the thought of pledging allegiance to the king.

Séamus, says Collins, leaning into him, I know just who won this war for the country and I know how they did it. And now we need those same men to take their rightful place in the new Ireland. You, Séamus, we need you. James looks at Collins and wonders what he is getting at. Need me? Need me for what, thinks James to himself. And then the words flow out of Collins's mouth, but James can't quite put them together coherently. They are floating in the smoke that pervades the room and James has to raise his voice and say, what was that? And Collins claps him on the shoulder. Yes, Séamus. Officer Commanding of Cork City, Commander of Victoria Barracks. There's a place you know well! Sweet victory that is, Séamus! That is the job for you. Commander of the barracks. With you at the helm 'twill be run like a well-oiled machine.

James looks at him again and his head spins, and he thinks to himself, he is trying to buy me now. He knows I stand with Cork No. 1, with O'Hegarty. He is trying to buy my vote and hope that others will follow. Suddenly, James feels enraged. He looks at Collins. He picks up the draft and holds it in front of him. He stands for a moment and looks Collins in the eye. Then he turns the draft over slowly and with a look of disdain pours it on the floor. The beer splashes up and wets the trouser legs of both of them. Collins instinctively jumps back from the frothy liquid. Then James turns around and walks away, leaving Collins staring back at him. You think you can buy me? I don't care who you are. I also know who won this war and how and I know we are not finished yet. Take your cushy little job and shove it.

The following morning, on St Patrick's Day, Collins looks in the mirror. He is tired. Tired of talking endlessly about why this treaty is the way to go. Tired of listening to the madness that is coming out of the mouths of the Cork IRA men. Do they really believe they can win a war if Britain chooses to invade? We've won this war by hook and by crook, by shooting people in the night, by blowing up barracks, by stealing guns, by terror and intimidation. That's how we've won this war, and if the truth be known, not one of us expected to make it through alive. We all expected to be added to the long, long list of Irish rebels and martyrs. We expected, all of us, to dance at the end of a rope or be shot in the back, and if lucky, buried beside Tomás and Terry. Yet by some miracle here we stand, those of us who are left, and we have driven the enemy back across the water and it can all be over now but for the signing of a piece of paper. And yet they want to keep on risking lives, their own, their families', their neighbours'. But we will see what the people think, what the regular Irishman thinks, sick to death of war, destruction, harassment, and terror. We will see what those people think.

Collins makes his way to a rally in the centre of Cork City. A rally to reach out to the people. His own people. After all he, Collins, is a product of Rebel Cork. He understands the pull of the old rebel stories, of the collective pages of Cork history, a book thick with suffering and rebellion. He is ready to sell his success story. Like the ancient Celtic kings, he is ready to sell the people on political machinations to outwit the English enemies. We have done it, he will tell them. It is our generation. Our generation, after seven hundred years of occupation, who have finally succeeded in pushing the enemy back to their own shores. It is us, the men and women of Cork, who have sent them packing. And if we don't like the words written on the paper that has been signed by all parties, then in a few years' time when their backs are turned, and we have back everything that belongs to us, we will toss those words into the wind and write our own words on our own papers. And by the way, building a country means running a country, and running a country means jobs. Lots of jobs, and not only in Dublin, but here in Cork, just where they are needed desperately.

By noon there are fifty thousand cheering, waving Cork men and women screaming themselves hoarse at the sight of him. If you wish, look at the moving picture, taken of this mad crowd, Collins on a podium in the centre, thousands and thousands of hats of every description being waved in the air. Talking movies have yet to be invented, so we cannot hear the odd explosion of a gunshot rising into the sky, doubtless the gun of a Cork No. 1 man, furious at this scene of uproarious affection and support. Who is shooting their gun? Not James. A friend of his? Perhaps. A colleague? Certainly. But despite the shots, the cheers continue. We cannot hear the adulation, the gratitude, the excitement at being in the presence of The Big Fella. The image, however, says everything.

Despite the spectacle of love for Collins the traitor, Cork No. 1 believes they own the moral high ground. Sure, he was a great man getting us this far, but to sell out to the English king? Who are you? We thought we knew you, but we don't. You are a stranger amongst us, perhaps even a monster. Later, when the rally is over and Collins leads his troop of men on a walk to St Fin Barre's cemetery to pay homage to his old friends, Tomás and Terry, Cork No. 1 will have none of it. These are our saints. They are turning in their graves at the thought of you claiming their allegiance when they have no voice to mouth the obvious. A squad of men is waiting at the cemetery gate with guns drawn. General Seán MacEoin, one of Collins's right-hand men, draws his own gun, but Collins turns away and the party follows him. Later in the evening there is a concert at the opera house in honour of Collins. The place is packed and just as the show begins, another of James's colleagues standing on the balcony gently blows on a large container of red pepper spray. The fine mist floats down onto the heads of the people below, and within minutes the entire audience is coughing and spluttering, their eyes running, their voices crying out. The Cork No. 1 men shoot their guns in the air and make a run for it. James, on hearing of these antics, wants to shake them to their core. You are making us look like a pack of eejits, he wants to scream at them.

The IRA has been torn in half. Most of the men of the south are anti-treaty but there are a good number who are pro-treaty right from the start. When Collins advertises for positions in the new National Army, derisively referred to by the anti-treaty crowd as 'staters' and decides to pay the new recruits no less than what their British counterparts were making, there is a minor stampede to sign up. As far as O'Hegarty is concerned, this is a disaster. The seasoned officers, Sandow, Pa Murray, Tom Hales, Seán Culhane, Florrie O'Donoghue, all stand with O'Hegarty. It is the less involved Volunteers who are now jumping ship, the lure of a decent, well-paying job suddenly softening their judgement on Collins. O'Hegarty knows it is his officers who should be awarded the plum jobs in the new army. They have been the army for years now. Who else did the fighting? Yet these newcomers are being awarded uniforms and guns and barracks and big paycheques.

De Valera and Collins both know that this is just the kind of disaster that allows political opponents to worm their way through the cracks. Who knows what political aspirations or oppositions might arise within such a powerful group of men? With no agreement about the acceptance of the treaty in sight, the IRA decides they will hold a convention open to all brigades across the country to discuss their continued differences over the treaty. The Dáil cabinet gives their approval hoping that some consensus can be achieved and the IRA, especially in the south, will shut up and put up. But Mulcahy gets nervous. Why are we giving them a forum to plot against us, he asks Brugha and Stack, two men whose judgement and intellect he has no high regard for. He doesn't wait for them to answer but announces a ban on the convention. Collectively the IRA roll their eyes. You, sitting nice and cosy in GHQ, are going to tell *us* that we can't meet? You dishonour your uniform, Richard. Now get lost.

O'Hegarty decides there is nothing for it but to make a personal appearance. If a spectacle of himself and his boys is required to turn heads and pay attention to the dire mistake this treaty is, then a fine spectacle it will be indeed. After all, it is because of the work he and his boys did, that freedom was won at all. Without Cork No. 1, Collins would not be where he is today. Ireland would not be here at the brink of political sovereignty. Here in the south it is Cork No. 1 that has always been supported by the people. O'Hegarty won't be letting anybody forget it.

Before they walk out of the door, O'Hegarty does an inspection. All ten men, including James, are dressed in trenchcoats buttoned up and belted around the waist, high-collared shirts and silk ties, leggings burnished to a fine sheen, boots likewise. Their hair is combed, their hats sit just so. They pull up in front of the Mansion House in Dublin in the armoured car of Cork No. 1, a stolen, refitted Rolls Royce that is described by some as a cottage on wheels, but affectionately named The River Lee. They parade into the already packed hall, and as they enter a silence descends on the room. It is exactly what O'Hegarty hoped for. Look at us! He wants to shout out at them. Look at us! We are the men who have won this war. We are the men who took the risks, who pushed the envelope, who did the deeds which no one in this room wishes to think about or remember. And now you are selling us out? Well, take a good hard look, boys. Do we look like we'll be putting up with that?

But O'Hegarty does a double take. As he looks around the room, he realises he is putting on a show for the converted. Most of the pro-treaty IRA men obeyed Mulcahy's orders and did not show up. James sees O'Hegarty's face, and realises the grand ploy is for naught. He will be hell on the ride home, he thinks to himself. Nevertheless, as the men find their seats with Liam Lynch and Florrie O'Donoghue and Liam Deasy and the other 1st Southern Division officers, James gazes around the Mansion House Round Room in wonder. It remains the forum for the Dáil, as it has been since January 1919, that first day the brave new Sinn Féin members of parliament double-crossed the British. Here in this room. This is where history was made. This is what Tomás and Terry were fighting for. This is what they trained me for, everything working towards this, our own government in our own country. A room full of people, Irish people, who represent us all, rich and poor. Irish people making law for Irish people. Too bloody bad we can't agree on a damn thing.

On their return to Cork, two things happen that James will never forget. The first is set in motion by an item of information that makes its way across the sea from New York City and into James's hands. It is a letter from an Irishman in New York to his family in Cork. In the letter he writes that he has seen Cruxy Connors. James reads the letter and his eyes narrow. Cruxy Connors, the turncoat who gave away the small unit of men in the barn. All of them tortured and then shot in the back, their bodies dragged across the fields and dumped in a British truck, never to be seen again. O'Hegarty does not even blink an eye. He sends for the fierce, fearless Pa Murray. Find a crew, Pa, and get yourself a ticket to New York. You've always wanted to see America? Here's your chance. And don't forget your gun.

After dropping Pa and his two-man crew at Cork Harbour to catch the next ship to New York, James, Sandow, and Mick Murphy head over to meet with some of the Cobh Volunteers. Another piece of information has reached O'Hegarty and he has decided to act on it now, while they have the chance. It is insurance against a future of uncertainty.

O'Hegarty has learned a snippet of intelligence that makes his heart go pitter-patter. Guns. More guns than you can shake a stick at. He learns about this from his contacts at the Harbour Commission, which continues to be run by the British. In fact, all of Cork Harbour remains under the British flag, as part of the treaty terms. He learns that as the British have been clearing out the barracks across the country, they have been stockpiling the arms at the Hauwboline docks and are about to send a shipload of every imaginable gun, explosive device, and barrels of ammunition to match, off to Portsmouth to warehouse. Ireland has been, after all, the location of the greatest stockpiling of weapons in the western world. When the pile is to capacity, the *Upnor*, a British tug, will haul the whole massive lot of it out of Cork Harbour, across the Irish Sea to find a new home in Portsmouth, another massive British artillery stockpile.

O'Hegarty thinks of the days when James was in Glasgow, sending him a few measly pistols, a handful of bullets every week or so, and he O'Hegarty was so excited to gather them up, his men cleaning them, oiling them, hiding them with such reverence. He thinks of the choices he had to make, going over in his mind who to give them to, when and for what, rationing them out like crumbs to starving men. They were a precious resource. And now a stockpile of thousands of guns, machine guns, rifles, ammunition, just sitting on the dock. How did we win this war with those few handfuls of guns against those stockpiles? It is a wonder! But now, O'Hegarty thinks, those guns don't want to leave home. Let's find a new storage facility for them. Somewhere in Cork, distributed around the county, just in case the anti-treaty side wins their internal fight, and the war starts up again. O'Hegarty is delirious with glee.

James sits in the meeting with the captain, who has volunteered to steer a large boat, a steam launch, owned by IRA sympathisers from Cobh. The captain is a seasoned mariner who is also against the treaty, and a man who knows the water. Nevertheless, James and Peter will keep an eye on him in the days before the operation proceeds. The Cobh men organise the commandeering of the boat and the plan to apprehend the British ship and the city team of cars, vans and traps, under Jim Grey and Seán, to meet at a tiny inlet in Ballycotton, a small fishing village on the coast. The plan is to overtake the *Upnor* in the open sea, guide it into Ballycotton, unload it onto the waiting vehicles, and run for the hills. In anticipation of a good haul, certain trustworthy men in each brigade are given the object of devising an impregnable location to dump a share of the booty. Seán thinks to himself, 'twill be a sad day if we ever need these, but he makes up his list of dump locations as is his duty as quartermaster of the brigade. O'Hegarty sips his tea and smiles. This plan ranks with the best of the brazen strategies he has ever imagined, and he can hardly wait. I'll be joining you on this one, boys!

The men wait for the call from the Harbour Commission informant as to when the *Upnor* will set sail. At eight o'clock on the morning of March 29, O'Hegarty gets the call. By ten o'clock he, Murphy, Sandow, James and Peter, Tom Crofts, Mick Leahy, and seven or eight others are sitting at the docks in Cobh. Murphy holds the admiralty ensign in his inside coat pocket. It is the flag that when hoisted tells British ships there is an important communication from the admiral, and they must set out a boat to receive it. It was stolen from the admiral's residence in Cobh. They are looking for the *Upnor*, but it is nowhere to be found. What the devil is going on? There is no boat. It has disappeared. Later they will discover that its owner, the weather being fine, decided to go for a little fishing expedition, having no idea that O'Hegarty would need the boat that day.

The men look round at each other. The captain, feeling the

steely gaze of O'Hegarty boring through him, makes a suggestion. There is a newly berthed boat in the Deepwater Quay, *The Warrior*. It is a British boat, but it is big enough to do the job. The Cobh Volunteers are sent down to arrest the captain of *The Warrior* and keep him in hiding while the job is done. Once he is off the premises, the Cobh captain boards, followed by a crew of mariners from the Cobh Volunteers followed by O'Hegarty, Sandow, Murphy, James, Peter and the rest. All of the men are armed; James has his pistol in his trenchcoat pocket. Murphy holds his favourite, a Thompson machine gun, at his side. The men are sent below deck, out of sight while in the harbour; all but Sandow, who acts as ship's mate while the captain gets the boat up to speed and out of the harbour.

Meanwhile, the *Upnor* has already made its ways out of the Hauwboline Military Marina, past Spike Island, and is far in the distance on its way around Roches Point and out to the open sea. The only blessing is that it is towing the barge and so is slowed down considerably. As the day progresses into afternoon, in Ballycotton over a hundred men are assembling, some from long distances, with cars and vans, even carts and donkeys. They wait patiently into the night, everyone anxious, saying little, waiting for two sets of lights on the open water to make their way towards them.

After a couple of hours, the captain is working the *Warrior* at its maximum and there is still no sight of the *Upnor*. O'Donovan consults with O'Hegarty and the captain. No one of Cork No. 1 likes being out on the open sea. They are city boys not sailors. He wants this job done and over. The captain suggests resetting a course for Portsmouth. O'Hegarty nods in agreement. His enthusiasm is also waning thin. The captain's sailor instincts prove correct. Within an hour they see in the distance the slow-moving *Upnor* dragging its barge behind it. It is accompanied by two impatient, well-armed trawlers, but these are far ahead and with any luck won't bother looking back.

It is about six o'clock in the evening now and the sun is descending on the sea. The *Warrior* speeds up to overtake the *Upnor* and once it is within one hundred metres, raises the admiralty ensign. O'Donovan holds up an envelope and waves it at the crew. He is wearing the British captain's hat. Completely duped by the admiralty ensign, the cap, and the envelope, the navy immediately set out a small boat with four sailors and make their way over to the

Warrior. Once alongside, one man holds out his arm, reaching for the envelope, Murphy reaches over and with his short but massively muscled arms, grabs a hold and pulls one of the crew onto the *Warrior*, while Sandow and Crofts train pistols on each of the remaining men. On seeing the guns aimed at close range upon their heads, no argument is fielded. The men clamber aboard ship. They begin to argue, make threats, but a glance over to the side and there sits James staring them down with a raised eyebrow and a Lewis gun trained on them.

One look at James's cold, calm stare has them tied up without so much as a word, and put below deck. Murphy, Sandow, Crofts, Peter and a mariner from the Cobh brigade board the small boat and make their way the short distance across the water to the *Upnor*. James stays on board with the others, keeps his head down and watches through an opening under the railing. He is just as happy to be on the larger ship, not in the small rowboat on the open sea. Murphy is carrying the more compact Thompson machine gun under his trenchcoat, and the other men each have two pistols in their pockets. Sandow boards the ship and holds out his pistols, one aimed at the captain, the other at a crew member. The captain is furious at this treachery but if the truth be known more so at his own stupidity. He shouts and points his finger, jabbing it in the air like a knife. This is piracy on the high seas. I hope you know what this means! Murphy doesn't say a word but pulls out his machine gun, points it at him, and the captain quickly goes mum. The crew is tied up and put below deck. The Cobh Volunteer then hustles to the control room and begins to set a new course. The *Upnor* is then aligned with the *Warrior* and both ships make their way to Ballycotton, side by side at top speed.

Seán has made sure the town has been sealed off ever since the commandeered transport arrived. There have been crews set out to cut telephone and telegraph wires. There have been crews sent to Roches Point to intercept navy correspondence. O'Hegarty and his team have thought of everything. After hours of sitting about playing cards, the men begin to catch a nap. It is late and the night is dark, and they have been there much longer than they anticipated. Finally, at about two o'clock, two sets of lights can be discerned on the horizon. Jim Grey and Seán mobilise the men by lining them up at the docks. This will be as quick and as orderly as Seán can make it. He has been getting nervous out here in the open for so long. And no one really knows the political temperament of the small fishing village.

Seán knows only too well that one smart rebel can change everything, even now when the British have packed up for the most part. He is relieved when the *Upnor* is brought alongside the dock and the long process of unloading proceeds. As each man fills his commandeered vehicle with guns, machine guns, ammunition, or explosives, Seán and James take careful note and send them on their way. O'Hegarty, Sandow, Crofts and the rest, wobbly after hours at sea, find their rides home. Seán and James stay to oversee the disbursement of all of the materials.

Finally, a few hours after sunrise, the last load is sent packing and Seán and Jim Grey look into the distance to see a large British ship heading straight for them. They yell at James to move it. The British crew had been taken off board with the captain to a small pub and fed and plied with whiskey, which they eventually accepted with gratitude. They are put singing and waving a bottle of whiskey back on board, and James and Seán tumble into Jim Grey's latest Rolls Royce and take off. They leave skid marks on the ground as the navy ship steers alongside the *Upnor*. All three men are exhausted, starving and giddy. Well boys, Jim Grey chuckles, we can be adding 'piracy on the high seas' to our long list of accomplishments these past years. Don't you just feel like Captain Cook after burying his treasure? Aye, indeed, I doubt he was as bone weary as us, complains Seán, and James prods his friend in laughter as Jim starts up one of his infamous uproarious ballads.

By April the weather has changed definitively. The sun shines between light showers, the grass sparkles, the flowers bloom. It has been six years since the Easter Rebellion, six years since James and Seán joined the IRA, four years since the end of the Great War, three years since James became an intelligence officer, two years since Tomás was shot in his bed, one and a half years since Terry starved to death. The British are almost out, almost but not quite, they are due to hand over Victoria Barracks in May.

Out in the Bandon Valley, west and south of the city, there is trouble. Local farmers have been killed in the night, a dozen of them. They are all Protestant, and they are said to have been murdered by the local IRA. Nobody seems to know who the killers are and if they are or are not IRA, but many of the locals are not waiting to find out. Over a hundred people from the area pack their bags and run.

There are a suite of robberies and assaults in the city and around the countryside. It seems like some elements are taking advantage of the lack of police and organisation of the IRA police to settle old scores or stock up on supplies, either because they are out of work or for the black market. Either way, shopkeepers are furious that nothing is being done to stop it.

In the city the Labour Party is actively canvassing against antitreaty Sinn Féin and the IRA. An election is due in June, and they want their fair share of seats. Enough of a one-party Dáil Éireann. They will capitalise on the lack of cohesiveness of the IRA and so in the first week of April hold a mass meeting. Much of the city shows up in the streets and they are treated to a dressing down of the local IRA, who are against the treaty and yet cannot seem to control their own members, and certainly do not seem to be able to serve all of the municipal functions, like police that seem to be so needed at the minute. The Bishop of Cork, Daniel Cohalan, the very one who excommunicated the IRA after the burning of the city by the British, jumps on board and uses the platform to denounce them again, this time as traitors to the cause of a peaceful Ireland. There is no mention of the treaty terms, the partitioning of the north, the loss of the republic, the allegiance to the enemy king; only fire and brimstone for the IRA, who continue to keep the city tied up in a tight little Republican knot against the people's wishes, were you to believe the speakers.

Suddenly there is a disturbance in Macroom, a confrontation, a showdown with the British, some of whom are still hanging about. But not just hanging about, collecting intelligence on IRA, antitreaty or pro-treaty, they don't seem to care. Churchill has all the bases covered, just in case. The British intelligence officers, all in mufti, are sitting enjoying another drink in their long afternoon in the pub of the small hotel across from the imposing gates of

Macroom Castle. This is a place they once knew quite well but has since been handed over to the local IRA, the 6th Battalion, Frank Busteed's own unit. James has been to Macroom Castle on and off with Seán, taking stock of their new holdings as part of the quartermaster duties of the brigade. But neither James nor Seán is there today. On this day however, Frank Busteed is. And it is on this day that Frank discovers the men who murdered his own sweet mother are within arm's reach. The three sorely wanted British intelligence officers, that is, torturers and murderers, make a very poor error in judgement. They seem to believe that the treaty terms will protect them. Indeed, the treaty terms should, but that will not hold back Frank Busteed from dealing with men who threw his mother down the stairs in her own house, just about a year ago now, and left her to die in agony with a broken back.

The IRA have lookouts all about the castle, the town, and the surrounding countryside. The three officers and their driver have no sooner left their jeep than a lookout, who cannot believe his eyes, goes into the pub and orders a drink, just to be sure. After quickly downing a pint, he casually strolls across to the castle, gains entrance and goes straight to the second in command, Charlie Browne. Charlie cannot believe it is indeed the men in question, so he himself strolls across the street to check it out. Eejits! Charlie and Frank know each other well, and Charlie knows that Frank has been waiting to find these particular gentlemen. One of whom has obviously lost his arm in the Great War and wears his jacket sleeve pinned to his coat. Charlie also knows that these men, two of them at least, are on the IRA most wanted list. Charlie introduces himself to the men and invites them over to the castle. Fools! In their inebriated state they comply, and thinking they are going for a look about, are shocked to find themselves disarmed, pushed into holding cells, behind bars, and no longer holders of the keys.

When Frank gets the call from Charlie Browne, he immediately goes into action. He calls up O'Hegarty and tells him the news. O'Hegarty has been deep in thought and when these men are mentioned the fat inventory of atrocities that they have committed begins to turn in his brain. There are many cards. He is quiet. Frank waits. Aye, deal with them, Frank. You know the protocol. Frank knows the protocol exactly. He calls up Jim Grey. We'll be needing a car and a few of the boys.

When the three officers, their driver, and indeed the giant Newfoundland dog in the back seat go missing from their jeep, last seen escorted into Macroom Castle, the British get worried. The treaty terms prevent any misdeeds, but who knows with the Irish? Maybe we have taught them one too many tricks? The local British commander heads straight to GHQ, the former Union Quay Barracks and asks O'Hegarty point blank: What have you done with them? Release them now. Seán watches O'Hegarty savour the moment before he looks the officer in the eye. Do I know you? Sure, never bother, doesn't matter at all. Off-duty officers, you say? Going fishing? Brought to Macroom Castle? No idea what you are talking about. And O'Hegarty sniffs the air and turns to re-enter his office. This is a bit much to take. Nevertheless, the military jeep full of uniforms makes its way back out to Macroom. The following day, the same officer bangs on the front gate of the castle grounds. The IRA men standing guard do a once over and let him wait while they get Charlie. Charlie invites them in to search for themselves. They do, but they smell a rat, and speed off from the castle empty-handed and seeing red.

Two days later, Field Marshall Montgomery arrives in the centre square of Macroom sending an envoy to bring the OC of the castle to him. Charlie obliges Montgomery but remains silent about the missing officers. In return Montgomery asserts that this is a violation of the treaty, and that the evacuation of the British from Ireland will be stalled until such time as his men reappear. Montgomery is not leaving Ireland without them. Charlie shrugs his shoulders and makes his way back to the castle, the convoy of British rifles trained on his back.

Finally, after two more days, Montgomery returns. He speeds through the narrow streets of Macroom and arrives before the castle with sixty men, four armoured cars, and lorries full of military. Unbeknownst to him, however, he has just parked his car over a landmine, and lurking in the hills and under cover are over one hundred IRA men watching his every move, two battalions of reinforcements. Still feeling intensely his English superiority, like the master of the house watching his servants run amok, Montgomery has just about had it. He demands to see the OC, and as Charlie saunters out of the front gates a sniper sitting in the turret above covers him aiming directing at Montgomery. Montgomery has had guns aimed at him before and he is not about to let an Irishman intimidate him. He doesn't hold back. He barks at Charlie like a schoolmaster scolding a recalcitrant child. But Charlie is not a child. He looks at Montgomery, tells him he has ten minutes to get lost or he can pay the piper. Then Charlie walks back through the gates as Montgomery loses his temper and continues to scream at his back. It is a loud whistle that gets his attention from a nearby doorway, and Montgomery looks over at the 8th Battalion Commander who says nothing but points out various places where his men are stationed, above and around the British convoy. Montgomery may not like the Irish, but he respects a worthy opponent, and he realises he has just been outsmarted and outmanoeuvred. He turns from Macroom and never comes back.

By this time of course Montgomery's missing officers have been gone from the earth for days. Their bodies lie in a bog north of the town, even the dog, and Frank and his team of executioners long dispersed. After being fielded by questions in parliament, Churchill throws out some ambiguous answers, but finally, several weeks later, Prime Minister Chamberlain admits in parliament that the missing men were indeed intelligence officers. The fathers of the lost officers begin a campaign to find the bodies of their sons. It will not be until the end of 1923 that a gruesome, detailed account of the exhumation in a lonely bog is published in the London papers. The remains are brought back to England and buried.

All of the commotion, the publicity about the missing officers only fuels the growing sense of chaos in the city. Where large tracts of the country continue to celebrate the treaty and are impatient for government jobs, rebuilding, organisation, order, and a life free of marauding English, not to mention marauding IRA, the diehards of Rebel Cork are still hoping to alter the terms of the treaty. They do not want a Free State. They want The Republic of Ireland. The Republic is what they fought for, and they are not about to give up on it.

At about the same time that Frank is dealing with his long sought-after English officers, O'Hegarty has other things on his plate. He has been watching the mood of the people. It was the reception of Collins, the wild, adoring masses made up of his own people that have turned O'Hegarty's head. He has been at meetings also, too many to count, and he has watched as his own organisation breaks off into cliques of moderates and diehards. The diehards have no give in them and want nothing more than to force the hand of their former comrades, whom they now are freely talking of as traitors to the Republic.

Liam Mellows is one, a tough little hardass if ever there was one, but there are plenty more, Liam Deasy, commander of the 1st Southern Division, and the men right here in Cork: Murphy, Sandow, Seán Culhane, Connie Neenan and in the west, Tom Barry, a raving Republican ready to fight anyone who is against him, if such a thing is even imaginable. Florrie, on the other hand, wavers from side to side, as usual seeing all possible points of view. But it is O'Hegarty's wife Magda who opens his eyes to how the people are thinking. Unbelievably, the Cumann na mBan, so vital to the day-to-day survival of the IRA, they, the mothers and daughters and sisters of his men, they are on the verge of abandoning Mary MacSwiney and embracing the treaty. Indeed, many are speaking against her outright and each day that passes finds more and more support for the treaty amongst the women who fed and clothed and nursed his men. O'Hegarty is as chauvinist as anyone else of his generation, but he knows that women hold sway inside many of the homes of the country and if so many of the Cumann na mBan, all Republicans mere months ago, are leaning towards the other side, there is trouble indeed in paradise.

O'Hegarty knows if he is losing the women, he is losing the people. His sixth sense is telling him something else. Something he does not necessarily wish to hear. But O'Hegarty learned long ago to listen to the tiny voices whispering in his ear. He listens now. He makes a decision. He will hold a parade of the Cork No. 1 and declare themselves non-political, no longer taking sides, open to brokering between pro- and anti-treaty, democratic supporters of the upcoming June election process, willing to fall in with the will of the people, but most of all wishing to keep the IRA and the new National Army together, despite differences of opinion, working under one roof. He will show the city of Cork that Cork No. 1 is with them the people. Indeed, he will remind them that it is the people's support of Cork No. 1 that brought the country thus far. Cork No. 1 will not abandon them now.

When the parade is called, the officers are wondering what O'Hegarty is up to, but James and Seán have seen it coming. They have been watching O'Hegarty at the barracks, day after day, and his transformation has not gone unnoticed. Between the two of them they speak of his unusual silence and ruminations, his locking himself in his office for hours at a time, his unusual walks around the city, stopping people and talking to them. They speak of this unusual behaviour at night, with a dram of whiskey, and wonder where it will lead. But even Seán and James are shocked when O'Hegarty proclaims to the men that he will organise a neutral position, and the men are invited to join him.

This happens after the parade. All of the battalions have shown up, not all of their men, but each battalion has a decent showing of twenty or so. They walk through the streets, their rifles on their shoulders, fallen in, their trademark trenchcoats blowing in the spring breeze, their boots reflecting the sun. But if O'Hegarty was expecting the adulating crowds that welcomed Collins, he is sorely disappointed. People step out of the shops, take a gander and go back to their errands. There is no waving of hats, no shouts of admiration, only the odd whistle and 'Up the Republic' from one or two brave souls.

Mick Murphy stares at him as if he is mad. Sandow looks over at Murphy. James watches the faces in the room turn as Florrie announces he will stand with O'Hegarty. All of the officers are invited to do so as well. Nobody moves. Neutral? Since when are we neutral about anything? We have, all of us in the room, been working for the Republic. We are not politicians. We are the Republic. Without us there is no Republic. Are we going to let that lot of politicians in the Dáil, Collins included, walk over us, and tell the people there is no Republic? If it weren't for us, there would be no Dáil. We started this war, and we will end it, exactly when we see fit.

O'Hegarty sighs. He is years older than the oldest man in the room. He knows this group of men inside out. He knows they think of themselves as the men of the south. Not politicians but soldiers, risking their lives for an idea, an ideal. After all they have been through, not willing to settle for anything less. But O'Hegarty is a man of the people, and he has slowly come to the realisation that the people have had as much as they can take. These men are tough cookies. They can take what they need, live out of barns, endure torture and murder and give back the same.

But the average citizen in Cork cannot. So many people are out of work, poverty is rampant. The city centre is still piles of rubble from two years ago. The City Hall likewise. There are burned out homes and businesses dotted around the city. The many, many children with worn shoes or boots too big for them, or indeed the many with bare feet. How are they even being fed? Fully one third of the male population are out of work with no prospects in sight. There are rumours of families actually facing starvation in the city. There are homeless numbers never seen since the Great Hunger who sleep together in groups under bridges and in the local parks. The treaty promises work, better days, a land of plenty and freedom from British oppression. Who gives a damn about the king? We never cared before, and we still don't. Freedom written into your precious constitution in due time, but let's eat first.

O'Hegarty is worried. There is almost no one who sees the calamity that is about to befall them if the army and politicians can't get it together. He does not like the treaty, but the thought of civil war is much worse. Something has to be done. The country is being run by hot-headed blockheads. He calls up Collins. I am coming to Dublin. Aye, get up here old friend as quick as you can, the house needs to hear from somebody on the ground, someone with vision, someone who sees, as do I, a future we can yet avoid. O'Hegarty listens in despair to the debates going on in the Dáil. It is philosophy and fine words and proud personalities, and nobody is talking about the children of Cork going to bed hungry. On May 3 O'Hegarty addresses the Dáil. The army is a mess, there is talk of civil war, it is your responsibility as political leaders to work together. He gives them an idea, a starting point. O'Hegarty feels like an old, tired schoolmaster berating the teachers into controlling their charges.

Back in Cork, his face looks haggard and exhausted. James and Seán exchange glances. Disaster has been averted. The committee formed at his bequest has agreed to a division of power in the army, half for, half against the treaty. They will work together. For now, he quietly adds, as he strokes back his bristly hair and puts on the kettle. His sixth sense niggles at him still, but he suppresses it when he goes on May 18 to accept the handover of Victoria Barracks from the British.

James listens to O'Hegarty going over the formal plans for the exchange of power. Does he know that Collins offered me Commandant General, overseer of the barracks? James never spoke of it except to Seán. But O'Hegarty knows everything. He turns to James. Never mind, Jimmy boy. Nothing is written in stone yet. The men are exultant, lined up in a show of force, watching their former enemies march out, taking their hated British flag, and yes, even the flagpole with them. You would never know that they are arguing amongst themselves for or against the treaty. Today is a day of triumph.

There are thousands of people in the street, a marching band, hats waving in the air. The vast barracks is open for exploration, for the first time in Irish history they are looking at this bastion of power from the outside in. Some of the men break down in tears when they see their former cells, and the execution yard where once their friends stood against the wall, their blood soaked into the earth below their feet. James walks around the medical unit and rubs the back of his head. He looks up at the ceiling and sees himself looking down at Tomás Ashe. He can hear Tomás's scolding voice. Come back Séamus, there is work to be done yet. Seán sees the emotion on his friend's face and claps him on the back. Never again, Jimmy. Never again. By the end of the day the barracks is occupied with a compendium of men from the various battalions. Some are pro-treaty, some are not, but Collins has taken a chance and is hoping that they will all see eye to eye once they feel the power of their position.

On election day in June, warmth invades the city. The wild roses wrap around the fence posts, the water sparkles at the seaside, the people of Cork quietly vote for those representing a practical position of working through the treaty. Gone are the political hardliners. Mary MacSwiney barely holds onto her seat. The people will vote for whoever seems sensible enough to move forward, not those stuck in an ideological war of words. Some Sinn Féin candidates lose to the Labour Party. Seán, considered anti-treaty, is not re-elected. He does not seem to care. He shrugs his shoulders at James. I'm not much of a politician anyway, Jimmy. I cannot stand all the blather.

The two men light a smoke and clink their drams. They still believe that somehow things will work out. How can they not, after coming so far?

With the news that there has been further drama at the Dáil, Seán and James head out to the Wallace sisters' shop. Both women are there but neither are looking so great. Nora in particular seems as frail as a leaf and is evidently suppressing a cough. But they are, both of them, Republicans to the heart, and so they happily put on the kettle. Since the treaty, the shop is no longer a dispatch hideaway of rebels. More's the pity, they say to themselves.

James and Seán read the papers over tea. The hardliners, Rory O'Connor, Liam Mellows, Joe McKelvey and others have been occupying the Four Courts in Dublin since April. Now they have barricaded the place, making sure no one but themselves can get in or out. They have locked out Liam Lynch for God's sake! Are they mad? And Florrie, once on the IRA executive, has been voted out. If he really believed he was to be made a general, and James and Seán know that he ordered himself a uniform, the idea is put to bed for good! And Tom Barry has gone absolutely nutters. He wants to attack the remaining British, still evacuating, starting a new war. He actually thinks the rest of the country will back him. Seán and James look at each other. Nobody likes the treaty terms, but this is madness.

So now Jimmy, here we sit with not just two but three splits in the IRA. We've got the pro-treaty boys who are all clamouring for the jobs sure to be divided up, many of them never having so much as fired a shot in the last few years. We have the hardasses who won't be happy till they start another war with the British to drive them out of the north. Have they not realised they will have to decimate four-fifths of the population of Ulster, since the four-fifths don't actually want to be Irish? And now we have the only cool heads in the entire organisation hated by both of the opposing sides. Seán is despondent. I should have gone back to Canada when I had the chance. James seethes. Sure, the English will be having a fine laugh at us now, occupiers of the Victoria Barracks or not. But never mind Seán. De Valera and Collins will get it together. Everybody can see this is going downhill. One way or another, the men will calm down and get to work. Seán looks at his friend, and wonders.

And then disaster strikes. The IRA men in London, the ones

who had worked so closely with Collins over the years, the ones who helped James on his way to Glasgow, those same ones, take it upon themselves to assassinate Field Marshall Wilson, right on his London doorstep. Collins holds his head and rails at the gods. The gods rail back at him. *You* created this monster, they laugh in his face.

The men are caught, and will hang for their trouble, but in the meantime Chamberlain, Churchill and the entire British Parliament turn and howl in unison at Collins. Shut down your factions now or we will shut them down for you. And Collins must choose between watching the British war machine march into Dublin and shoot up his former comrades, or he, Collins, must shoot them up himself. He chooses the latter. Does he think he can control the damage, convince them to give up and stop this ridiculous show of defiance? Whether he thinks so or not, he is determined to try. The last thing he will do is hand his country back to the British. He orders a planned assault on the Four Courts. He is hoping against hope that the men inside will see sense before he has to fire. Alas, it is not to be. In the melée that follows, two of Collins's closest friends will perish because of his orders; his personal best friend Harry Boland, and his colleague in the Dáil, ardent Republican, Cathal Brugha. Collins is devastated.

As soon as word comes down that the first shots have been fired, O'Hegarty calls a meeting. His most trusted officers meet at the Union Quay Barracks Headquarters. There are OCs, officers commanding from the various battalions and his own city men. Murphy and Sandow are there, Peter Donovan, Pa Murray, Tom Crofts, Connie Neenan, Mick Leahy from Cobh, Seán Culhane, Sullivan, the brigade adjutant, Seán and James, twenty-four in all sit and listen to what he has to say. It will only grow from here now, boys. The first shots have been fired; they won't be the last. Nobody in Ireland wants this. The people of Cork do not want this. We need to take a stand on the side of peace and let our differences lie for the time being. Heads around the room look down at the floor. O'Hegarty senses the resistance but he tries again. I know I was one of the first to cry foul at this treaty. But take a look around boys. If the fighting starts up, we have no hope without the people behind us. The people are not behind us. At the very least we must stay neutral and let the dice fall where they may. Taking on the British was one thing, taking on our fellow Irishmen is something else entirely. No good can come of it.

Who is the first to speak against the great chief? No one will ever say. Maybe in the arrogance of their youth they are thinking that he no longer has the guts to do what is necessary. Maybe they smell his common sense as weakness infiltrating the cracks of a man of a previous generation. No one will ever say, because when they call for a vote, twenty of the twenty-four men vote against their master. They vote for war. Dominic Sullivan, his adjutant, will forever have peace in his heart, knowing he was one of the only men to stand behind him. When the vote is read out O'Hegarty rises from his seat, bids the men good luck, walks upstairs to his office, picks up the extra shirt that his wife insists he keep there. and walks out, never to return. Sullivan quickly gathers up the latest paper off his desk, sticks it inside his shirt, and trails behind him. James and Seán sit in shock. Were they the other two votes against war? Perhaps. Do they consider resigning themselves? Perhaps. Doubtless whoever cast those two remaining dissenting votes will come to wish they had walked out with him.

Mick Leahy, vice OC is shocked to find himself the new commanding officer. He is a capable man, an engineer, an accomplished mariner from Cobh, a man proven unafraid to use a gun when the need arises. But he isn't Seán O'Hegarty. Nevertheless, the men rally around him, and they begin to make plans. Sandow moves into vice officer commanding. Seán and James soon discover that their vaulted status as 'one of O'Hegarty's boys' is no longer a vaulted status. They are the brigade quartermasters, yes, but they are now given jobs hither and thither. Go check out this, go pick up these guns, go take a crew and trench some roads into the city. Do this, do that.

And while all this planning is going on O'Hegarty thinks to himself, there is one more person I can get to, maybe. He drives out to Mallow with Florrie, who is now also out of a job, unwilling to fight as part of the 1st Southern Division, unwilling to hand over his intelligence network, the one in his head, to men who just may consider the possibility of killing other Irishmen should the need arise. They drive out to find Liam Lynch who, though kicked out of the Four Courts by his erstwhile friends, is just as happy now and has hightailed it back to Cork to arrange fighting against the Free State.

Florrie and O'Hegarty say nothing on their return trip after being rebuffed by Lynch. We are doomed, O'Hegarty thinks, and turns his attention to finding a safe house for his wife while the war that is sure to come begins to gather up steam.

In the city, Murphy and Sandow and Pa Murray have taken over the planning. Everyone has a job if Cork is to be saved for the Republic. Scouts are set on duty overlooking key points around the city, an eye out for the Free Staters that have pledged to gain control of every corner of the country, yes, even Rebel Cork. In the future, this time will become known as The Republic of Cork. Units are sent to Limerick and Waterford to help hold these southern cities against the Free Staters and while they are off, Seán and James take control of the policing and try to quell the marauding of the shops and pubs and everything else that is going on in the name of the IRA.

They find themselves almost alone in the barracks; it seems like everyone they ever knew is off to Limerick or Waterford and there are only teenagers left to defend the city should anything happen. Seán makes a proclamation that only chits signed by him, quartermaster of Cork No. 1 should be honoured. The newspapers are taken control of, and Erskine Childers, who has escaped Dublin, assumes editing powers. He moves from house to house in the country and the city, and works quietly on his anti-treaty propaganda, making sure that the people of Cork get the right political message. All of the officers are making predictions about how and when the Free Staters will arrive. They know it will be by boat. The question is what village or port will they quietly sail up to and when?

As it turns out the Republic of Cork lasts barely six weeks. They are long weeks for the citizenry who carry on as best they can. They become accustomed to lorries of IRA roaming the streets. It is nothing new to them, after all: for years now they have been used to watching lorries of British soldiers. At least there are no atrocities, no houses being burned. But Free State sympathisers are being picked up from time to time and thrown in Cork Gaol. Their families come around and demand visiting rights and holler at those who would incarcerate their own neighbours, those who were all on the same side just a few months ago. Cork No. 1 begins to collect their hidden booty from the *Upnor*, and though they now have guns they have no money. Never fear, say the boys at the Port Authority, we are still collecting taxes from what trade is coming in, and so Cork No. 1 makes a trip to the bank and has them defer the funds into their own coffers.

But after all of this effort, the day finally arrives when harsh reality hits home. Sandow has predicted the town of Passage West as the landing spot for a Free State offensive and indeed he is right. The people of the city have barely got home from the seaside, enjoying the long weekend bank holiday in August, when Generals Tom Ennis and Emmet Dalton and their entourage of ships and arms creeps into Passage West and begin to unload their cannons. The men on their way back from trying unsuccessfully to hold Limerick and Waterford for the Republic struggle into the city, most sleep deprived and hungry, defeated completely in both places. Nevertheless, they rally under the command of their officers to hold the city. It is all for naught. After just three days of the Free Staters launching the odd artillery shell, the harsh truth settles in and the men who had voted out O'Hegarty, the men who thought they could hold the south with a few stolen guns against the likes of Collins and his new British-supported army, those same men turn around and tell everybody to run for the hills.

Seán and James are at the barracks when word gets to them to abandon ship. They know what they have to do. With the sound of the crowds of citizens cheering the Free State army as it marches into the city, they slosh barrels of petrol around the barracks, starting up stairs and working their way down. Well Jimmy, it was good while it lasted, and the two men throw their matches into the glistening pool of petrol. Standing outside, they watch as the upper floors shoot billows of smoke and flames through the exploding glass of the windows. Then they make their way across Parnell Bridge, doing up their trenchcoats, hiking their rifles over their shoulders, and once on the South Mall, as the noise of the cheering, singing, exuberant crowds just behind them increases, they pick up speed and begin to run.

The following day, August 12, James and Seán are in Macroom Castle where headquarters has been amalgamated for the First Southern Division. Many of the men have been taken by Free State forces during the evacuation of the city, or in the lost, pathetic fight for Waterford, or the disastrous battle for Limerick. Tom Barry has been captured and brought to Kilmainham Gaol, mere months ago a hated symbol of British power, now being put to good use by the Free State to maintain their own hold on power. Luckily Seán and James are senior enough, and Seán at least well known enough to be able to commandeer a vehicle to get outside the mayhem quickly.

In the castle, they are given priority status by the men who hold it. This is a good thing because many of the Republican anti-treaty-ites have been turned away and told to slip back into the city and go home. Macroom Castle is full. Full of the glitterati of the anti-treaty faction of the IRA and the Irish government. Erskine Childers is here. So is Michael O'Donovan, in years to come to be known as Frank O'Connor, a man who will write stories of his life and times like no other. Liam Deasy is here, and Liam Lynch comes and goes keeping in close touch with his officers.

It is known to the two strategically placed men that de Valera has been quietly talking to Liam Lynch, telling him enough is enough. Our chances are done. We have lost Cork City, time to back off, bow to the will of the people, and find our way forward without guns. Seán is ecstatic. Almost time to go home, Jimmy, thank God, this sharing a room with ye is too much for me. Who knows, maybe Collins will have a change of heart and you will end up a general after all. No hope there my friend, replies James. He is keenly aware that his hot head has changed his fortunes and not for the better. No worries, Jimmy, Collins knows how we were all feeling about the treaty. He will come round. Wait and see. And James begins to feel hopeful for the first time in weeks, when the latest bomb of bad news hits them with a jolt.

The Free Staters are making their way to Macroom. The men must evacuate. Sandow is outside yelling at the top of his lungs, Every man for himself. He occasionally shoots his rifle in the air to get everyone's attention. Make your way home where your mother or your wife will shower you with tender loving care if you are lucky. Or, if you are a diehard Republican right to your very core, make your way into the hills of St Fin Barre, to Gougane Barra and Ballingeary, and the tiny Irish places where there are still people who will hide you and feed you, though they will speak Irish doing it. And do it all oh so quietly. If you sneak past the Free Staters, they may look the other way and leave you in peace. They will probably not come in the night, banging down doors. James and Seán, like all of the officers, head for the hills. They head to Ballyvourney, the next stop on the road from Macroom, where they set up temporary shop. Once there their hopes for a change in fortune are shattered.

Liam Lynch has told de Valera he is dreaming. He will not go down in history as the man who gave up the Republic. Seán's heart sinks. What is he thinking, Jimmy? Is he out of his mind? The Free Staters have the country. The only place left is here to Kerry. And who cares about West Cork or Kerry? Sure, they have given up the north, but they may leave us here to rot with Lynch as dictator. Won't that be fine? But there is more bad news, and it is dropping fast.

The two men who took out Field Marshall Wilson on his doorstep have been hanged in London. Joe O'Sullivan and Reggie Dunn, both members of the IRA in London, were two men who could not stand by and watch their Catholic friends and countrymen being slaughtered, tortured and burned out of their homes in the north. Field Marshall Wilson was well known to publicly support the antics of the insane Orangemen of the region. No one knows for sure if the men acted alone, but many friends of Collins had heard him ruminating on getting rid of Wilson, especially when the news coming out of the north was particularly devastating. Both men, the dour Joe and the smiling Reggie, gone from the earth. Two more to add to the long list in James's head. And yet, the bad news does not stop.

Arthur Griffith has bent down to do up his shoelaces and never risen again. He is dead of a cerebral haemorrhage. This terrible single line of information sent on a telegram from Dublin cuts right through James and Seán. Arthur Griffith, a mere working-class printer, founder of Sinn Féin, President of the Dáil, founder of the Republican newspaper *The United Irishman*, humble, principled, an Irish gentleman through and through. To the average Irishman, the man is a wonder. To the average Republican, that man is a god. The work he did during his life was dedicated, every moment of it, towards building an independent Ireland. The fact he negotiated the hated treaty is a minor point for Republicans on this day. It seems like the whole world stops while Ireland focuses on the funeral of its national hero. 'Tis this bloody civil war bullshit is what did it. That is the talk on the street and indeed, a thought ruminated by everyone in the country. The man was only fifty-one years old. The entire idea of civil war made his blood boil. He was furious beyond words with the likes of de Valera and his ilk who would tear down everything they had all achieved with so much sacrifice.

James and Seán are wistful for the newspapers at the sisters' shop. They must wait here in the hills for several days to catch up on the news. The funeral is plastered across the front pages of every newspaper in Ireland and Britain, even in America. The entourage is a massive horse-drawn carriage carrying the coffin with the IRA generals walking alongside. There are two long lines of them on either side of the coffin. Emmet Dalton and Tom Ennis, who took the City of Cork, are both there. All of the IRA are there, or it looks like it from where Seán sits. And I would be there too, he thinks to himself, were it not for this madness we are engaged in. The two men study the photographs in detail. The people of Dublin are lined up along O'Connell Street for miles. Collins heads the group of politicians and dignitaries following the coffin. I am sick to death of funerals, James murmurs in a low voice to his friend. Seán, thinking of his brother says only, Aye.

Collins too is sick to death of funerals. There is speculation he cares not for his comrade Griffith. Griffith, after all, was pushing a hard, hard line against the Republicans. Collins understands better the intense ideological position his old friends of Rebel Cork have taken. But it is an unfair judgement on Collins, whose heart is rent by the death of his friend, no matter the difference in their opinions. He also knows that Griffith's hard line was a result of intense frustration. Placed between a rock and a hard place by the British, nevertheless, he was a man of vision and he above all others could see the path to freedom, a much shorter path with the treaty than without it.

Collins makes a decision. This is the last funeral I will be attending; he thinks to himself. I am off to my home, and I shall make a deal with the Republicans that they cannot refuse. I don't care what it takes. If it means war again with the British, so be it. 'Tis better than war against my own people. Besides, the British bastards are not following their own agreement. There is mayhem in the north. The Catholics are being burned out of their homes, shot in the streets, captured and tortured just for fun, and this while Churchill's police stand by and cheer. Why, just last week a young girl was burned alive. Fucking maniacs, the Orangemen are and this even after they get their northern counties as part of the treaty. But

Churchill has reneged on the boundary commission and is letting that slide. If I have to fire on my own detractors from the treaty, you do not get to ignore yours, Churchill. Your day is coming, and it is coming soon, when you will have to make your own decision about your own people. Meantime, the Catholics are streaming into the south in droves looking for help and you are not lifting a finger, not even to wag it at your nasty lot of English aspirants.

The following morning, so early the sun has not risen, he telephones O'Hegarty. Haven't ye heard man, I'm retired, O'Hegarty exclaims with bitterness in his voice. A lot of bollocks, so that is. I am coming to Cork, and we are going to fix this damn mess and be done with it. And then I am going to make you an offer you can't refuse. And we will never speak of this madness again.

Collins makes his way south. Emmet Dalton goes with him. He has been pushing the Free State apprehension of Cork towns and villages since they took the city. They will be entering the city quietly. Neither man is in any mood for fanfare. Collins leaves Emmet to his work and walks over to Magda's café. Inside O'Hegarty is waiting, sipping his tea. The two men, in the dark silence of the closed café, let their hair down. Nothing but the truth flows from their mouths. They have known each other too long. They understand each other too well. They lament over lost friends and determine to make a plan. These are the men you can turn to your way of thinking. Lynch has gone mad and will not bend. There are a handful who will stick it out with him. You must override them, put them in a small minority, appeal to the men with a pick of sense left in their brains. Lynch will have no choice if the majority walks out on him. I do not like it but the alternative of sticking with this fight is unconscionable. I have thrown in the towel and have no say. I am retired. O'Hegarty grunts.

Retired my arse, says Collins. You are being commandeered by the government of Ireland to reach out to the lot of Republicans you yourself trained, and bring them in line. I wish, says O'Hegarty. I have made some mistakes. I realise it, but the boys do not. They have been carrying on behind Lynch and Deasy, but many are wondering themselves why they are doing it. Especially now, when the men, the officers at least, are well aware that even de Valera is appealing to Lynch to give it up. Even the 2nd Battalion, C company, my own group of dependables, have all turned on me. Sandow,

Mick Murphy, the whole lot of them have gone mad. Sure, Dan was talking about putting poison in the River Lee to get rid of the Free Staters. I don't recognise my own men anymore. You will have to talk to them yourself and you will see what I mean. They themselves voted me out, all of them, but a couple of dedicated boyos.

You and I both have created monsters we can no longer control, thinks Collins to himself. But out loud he appeals to O'Hegarty. Arrange a meeting, Seán, and I will go to them.

And as Collins leaves, he thinks to himself, but just in case, I will help them along in their decision to give up and give in. Collins heads straight to the bank in Cork City and has the accounts that Mick Leahy and Sandow set up to filter the Harbour Commission taxes rerouted into his own government accounts. You are going nowhere without your cash boys. This will help you come to the right decision, and quickly.

There is only one phone in Ballyvourney. James gets the call from O'Hegarty to quietly arrange the key players. And Jimmy, the Long Fella, de Valera will be there. Lynch is not to hear even a whisper of this. Aye. This phone call comes the day after a meeting with de Valera, Lynch, Tom Hales, Erskine Childers, Liam Deasy, Seán Culhane, Seán and James and the rest of the officers who have escaped the castle and the sweep by the Free Staters who are now sitting pretty in Macroom.

In Ballyvourney, at the most western edge of the village in the two-hundred-year-old Stagecoach Inn, the men had sat and argued. Sentries outside made sure there were no uninvited guests. Seán and James had looked over at each other as the arguments about next steps led to the worst disagreements between officers they had ever witnessed. De Valera had risked driving through the territory now held by the Free State to come expressly for this meeting. He was determined to have the army executive change their policy and stop the fighting. Limerick and Waterford were a disaster, the City of Cork is lost, the towns are being taken one day at a time as the Free State works its way across the land. The people themselves are welcoming them as they come and saying good riddance to your men, Liam. But Lynch, Chief of the IRA anti-treaty army faction, will have none of it. I will not give over the Republic so easily. He glares at de Valera as if he is a traitor.

De Valera stands up and paces across the small room, stopping many of them speaking Irish to the locals, who very well may be welcoming them just as the Irish are welcoming the Free Staters everywhere they go. Just last week they landed by sea in the tiny port of Courtmacsherry, James's own birthplace, and are working their way across the coast to Kerry, the last bastion of Republicanism in the country. When he is not thinking of Collins or Seán, James is wondering at the wisdom of O'Hegarty and Florrie. Both of them threw in the towel and walked away from the fight. O'Hegarty was right. I should have walked out of the barracks with him the day of the vote. What was I thinking? He is right, he was always right, no good can come of this. And now that Collins has been killed there will be no negotiating. The Free Staters will make the men of Cork pay for this terrible deed.

As the days turn into weeks and James languishes behind the doors of his cell all of his worst fears come true. With Collins and Brugha and Griffiths all gone, Mulcahy has taken over the army. He will never get over Collins's death and the people who did this to Ireland, and to him personally. They will feel the terror of their own deeds come back to them. Mulcahy will see to that. As fast as he can recruit and train new troops, he orders them to be sent to the south to flush out every last Irregular. This is the new title that he has demanded the papers use to refer to this, the new enemy to replace the British. He cannot abide that they refer to themselves as Republicans. They are not soldiers, but fanatics, murderers. They do not get to call themselves Republicans. No. They are the opposite of the new regular troops, the soldiers of the Free State. They are Irregulars.

All of the newspapers fall in line with Mulcahy's wishes. In the end, it will matter naught, thinks Mulcahy. I will flush out every last one of them from their hiding places, especially those traitorous self-serving monsters, Lynch and de Valera. He has total support from every one of his generals, except, ironically, Emmet Dalton, the man who was with Collins when he died.

Dalton will be forever horrified at the entire situation and will refuse to fire on Irishmen. He will soon give up his general's cap rather than follow the shocking orders he will receive regarding how to deal with Irregulars. Mulcahy has less support from the members of the Dáil who keep asking inconvenient questions. He wishes to deal with this smear of Irregulars, the die-hards, the ideologues, the self-righteous. They are fascists and they don't even know it. He will never feel the least bit of sympathy or common ground with these men. As far as he is concerned, they have destroyed the dream and trampled on the nascent state, responsible for the deaths of the best of their leaders. Though they all fought the British together; it will not matter in the least. The bitterness that is spawned from this great divide will last for generations. Emmet Dalton will be heard to call de Valera, even decades later, 'that sanctimonious, hypocritical megalomaniac.' These will be among the kinder words that will be spoken of him by the Free State men.

O'Hegarty cashes in a favour when he makes his way into the gaol to visit James. The men have not been allowed visitors. He does not say I told you so, but it hangs in the air like an invisible punching bag, asking to be beaten. O'Hegarty looks at James and though he does not show it, he feels a slight panic rise in his chest. James's hair is full of white and grey streaks. The auburn is lost, and he looks twenty years older. With lack of exercise his muscular frame has diminished. He looks like a bag of bones. A haggard bag of bones. Keep your chin up, Jimmy. O'Hegarty's harsh rasping voice is momentarily calmed, nervously, and perhaps unconsciously, trying to soothe the obviously stressed prisoner. Let's see if we can get some packages in here for you. I'm sure your family will send you some home cooking if they are let in. Good luck with that, sir, says James. No Republicans anywhere in the country in any of the dozens of gaols and internment camps are allowed visitors or packages. Never worry, I will see to it, says O'Hegarty, and he shakes James's hand as he leaves. Don't worry about the men, Jimmy, they are off in the hills, they haven't been found yet. Seán and some of the others are trying to get Lynch to turn, but it is a hard go. He will meet a bad end. Aye, says James. We will all meet a bad end one way or another. There is no doubt about it.

After a few days, James receives a package from his mother. But only one is ever allowed in. He sips at the cold stew and wonders how it can be so much work to chew food and swallow it. Outside the gaol in Cork City the people are beginning to gather up some hope. Government relief funds have been made available to the destitute. Parts of the city are beginning to be rebuilt. Roads, bridges, buildings are being repaired. That means jobs. And just like Collins had promised, there are jobs to be had. Government jobs. Well-paying jobs. And guess what? Known Irregulars need not apply. The jobs are going to the same former Great War vets who were once despised. Now they are becoming the new army, the new police. Men who never joined the Volunteers, who sat and watched while others were risking their lives for freedom from British tyranny, those men are benefitting with well-paid positions that have never been open to the average Irishman. What bitter irony, thinks James, when news of the various economic initiatives reaches the men in the gaol. Justice has taken a turn and everything he hears is backwards, upside down, incomprehensible, it is so foreign to the vision of a new Ireland that once was shared by the men of Cork No. 1, all of the men in the IRA.

After several weeks, James begins to discern the presence of Ashe once again. Ashe sits with him on the side of the road, and they watch the showdown between Collins's entourage and the rebels hidden in the hedges. James watches transfixed as Collins jumps out and takes position lying on the ground just beside the car. Bullets stream across the road from the bushes in slow motion. Perhaps the men behind the bushes do not really wish to be there, shooting at their much-loved former leader. Collins, Dalton, and the others fire back against the lousy shots, and so it goes for ages it seems until it stops. They watch as Dalton looks down over the top of the car and they see his face contort as he realises Collins is not moving. There is a hole in the back of his head. Not a neat little hole like James's own. No, this has been caused by a bullet ricocheting off the car and directly into Collins. His face rests on the road, his eyes straining out. The blood from the back of Collins's head gurgles into a puddle. Ashe watches and looks over at Jimmy. He is in the straitjacket still and there is slop on his chin, but James can hear his words, though he does not speak. *Look at that Séamus, if I didn't see it with mine own two eyes, I would nary ha' believed it.* James cannot speak nor move his head, all he can do is stare at the lifeless body. He awakens with his heart pounding hard and fast as if he is running, running, running, and he gasps for air.

One bleary, wretched day in November, James wakes with a start with an anxious, overwrought mind. He suddenly feels the jolt as the world grinds to a halt. Ashe is sitting on his haunches in the corner of the cell, his straitjacket pulled tight around him. He is watching James, who lies on his cot at intervals pulling up the blanket over his shivering shoulders and then kicking it off as his body heats up and steam seems to waft off his head. But all of this stops when James notes the tears dripping from Ashe's face. James freezes because he knows something terrible is about to happen. He can sense it in his bones. He can almost see into the mind of Ashe, the panic, the helplessness, the frustration. What is it? He calls out at him. What is it? But instead of Ashe answering, the guard walking by the cell turns and looks through the tiny window. He gives James a puzzled look. It's the executions this morning, he calmly says to James. The Dubliners are playing hard ball now, so they are. And James looks over at Ashe and he too feels overwhelmed with helplessness and despair.

It is November 17, and four quiet, innocuous would-be-rebels picked up in a round-up, guilty of nothing but being of an adventurous age, carrying a gun like the rest of the country, are walked down the corridor from their cells, tied by the wrist, blindfolded and put against the killing wall of Kilmainham Gaol, where a mere six years ago their heroes and predecessors left the earth. Those men, Pearse and the rest, their names will live down through history. Try to find the names of these four poor unfortunates if you can. It is a hard slog through witness accounts and old books. Their names have been forgotten, found only in a minor footnote in the older version of a thick history of the period. Peter Cassidy, John Gaffney, James Fisher, and Richard Twohig, rank and file men, involved in little, but their time is up, nonetheless. Their presence, standing there in that place, and the outrage against them, is merely a setting of the devil's stage.

James is right to cry. He does not know it at this minute, but these four are the first of over seventy executions that the Free State will perpetrate in the coming months against their former friends and neighbours. Many will claim these four young men are being used as stooges to prop up this stage. Their trial and execution are carried out swiftly, their families unaware of their deaths until they receive a telegram: Remains of your son have been coffined and buried in consecrated ground. The smugness of it is cruel. It might as well say, unlike the British who would have thrown the body in quicklime in the exercise yard. We didn't do that at least. Clearly the telegram was a hasty incidental, because, who the Free Staters really wish to execute, and with total impunity, and the very reason they have executed the innocent four men just now in order to set the stage, is that bloody Englishman Erskine Childers.

Childers has been caught at his childhood home, Annamoe, the estate of his cousin, Robert Barton. There is no doubt he was given away by someone. Who knows who is responsible for this travesty? Surely another informer, this time not for the British, but for the Free State. Childers is a prime target for the Free State. The Free State government, composed of every friend he ever had, men he spent a lifetime with, talking and wishing and planning and scheming to free the Irish of the terrible injustice of English occupation. His Oxford accent and eccentric English ways make him easy to hate now that he has taken an opposing side. The fact that he is using his formidable brain for the Irregulars burns those Free State arses. They have been looking for revenge for Collins's assassination and though they will never admit to it, they are about to quell it on the life of their former colleague. After all, he is a perfect answer to their bloodlust. He objected to the treaty, almost from the beginning, and was nothing but a thorn in the side of Collins as he tried to move forward.

A secret trial is held, and he is found guilty of possession of a firearm. The firearm in question is a tiny, old-fashioned pistol about four inches long, a joke really that Collins had tossed to him one day when he disparaged the idea of carrying a gun. Once Collins was himself shot, Childers took that pistol and stuck it in his coat pocket, close to him, not as a weapon but as a reminder of Collins himself, and it stayed there right until the day he was arrested. How ironic that it is the perfect excuse for his execution. He is persuaded to appeal his sentence because after him are eight men lined up, with trials to follow. He is persuaded his own appeal may be a basis for saving those unnamed fellows whose fate will surely mimic his own if he does not appeal. He knows in his heart it is quite useless. He has seen the monster that lurks about his former friends. It will be satisfied one way or another. Indeed, he is right, as the execution proceeds without the least worry about waiting for a response to the appeal.

Childers is fifty-two years old when he is taken out of the Beggar's Bush Barracks in Dublin and put against the killing wall. He is tired and thin, but he has calmly written to his wife and expressed his hope that somehow this sacrifice of his life will come to some good end soon. He looks cheerfully at the lads in the firing squad and politely refuses the blindfold. Then he tells them, Take a step closer, lads, it's easier that way.

When James hears of Childers's execution, he does not know what to think. The executions boggle the mind. James himself crossed paths with Childers here and there as they moved about West Cork, always evading the Free Staters. Nothing he ever heard that had come from the Free State camp was remotely true about Childers, who was a pleasant enough man though reeking an aura of high-class English everywhere he went despite his own best efforts. He talks over the execution with Ashe. Sure O'Higgins, the Minister of Defence who was ultimately responsible for the execution, knew Childers well. It doesn't matter, Séamus, look about us. The men on both sides have gone mad. He leans across the cot and whispers in James's ear. Séamus, in a few days O'Higgins will sign the death warrant of his own best friend, Rory O'Connor, best man at his wedding. James looks up at Ashe, who is leaning over him. Ashe's eyes are fearful. He bends towards James's ear and whispers, We are all in danger yet, Séamus. We are all in danger yet. And James closes his eyes and his mind swirls, and he does not know what to think about anything anymore.

The next time O'Hegarty visits he is alarmed. James is shivering, sitting with the ancient, filthy, threadbare blanket around his shoulders. It is just past noon and indeed the cells are cold. The British preferred them this way and it seems the Free State has seen the logic now that they are on the other side. O'Hegarty pushes his luck and asks for another blanket. The guard on duty just shakes his head. No sir, we have already made that request and it has been denied. O'Hegarty looks down at the ground. He takes off his jacket and puts it around James's shoulders, though if the truth be known, he is thinking that if ever it is returned to him, his wife will soak it in steaming water, lest the vermin sure to be on the blanket find a new home.

Despite his condition, James's mind seems sound and O'Hegarty answers his questions about the men. They are all off in the Gaeltacht, probably in the mountains in Kerry at the minute, he tells James. Lynch saw red when they executed Childers and has issued new orders that have been sent around the country to every anti-treaty man still standing. The men are to execute any members of Dáil Éireann they can get their hands on and anybody else who has anything to do with them. The vast majority of men are loath to do it, Jimmy. They are calling them 'the Orders of Frightfulness.' Now isn't that just the right name for them? But the Dubliners have a right crew of hardliners. They have followed orders and shot Seán Hales in the street. James sits up straighter. What, Tom's brother? Aye, indeed, Jimmy. 'Tis madness so it is. Shooting British bastards is one thing, but shooting your own brothers? And that's not the worst of it. Mulcahy and O'Higgins are near out of their minds over it and they have executed four men in reprisal.

James looks at him and feels like a child wanting to cover his ears. But O'Hegarty, like a doctor doling out bitter medicine, spills it out into the air. Do you remember Dick Barrett from Spike? What a brave lad he was. Gone now thanks to a Free State firing squad. Along with him went Mellows, Joe McKelvey, and Rory O'Connor, shot up against the wall by their own men. It is unspeakable so it is. And to make matters worse they did it on December 8, the Feast of the Immaculate Conception. The churchgoers are outraged.

James is stunned. Has the devil himself taken control? To O'Hegarty he says, Aye, my own mother will be upset over that. As if the executions themselves are not insult enough to the good Lord. Surely that will be it now, it will all stop? Indeed not. Indeed not. They have murdered O'Higgins's elderly father when they couldn't get O'Higgins himself and burned down his house. A few Dublin men tried to get James McGarry the TD. James's head perks up. The McGarry who escaped from Lincoln Gaol with de Valera back in 1919? Aye, the very same, and when they couldn't, they burned down his house instead. Jimmy? O'Hegarty has been pacing the tiny cell but stops and looks down at James. James knows something terrible is coming. He looks over in the corner at Ashe who is hunched down gurgling slop, quietly crying, refusing to look him in the eye. O'Hegarty continues. His seven-year-old son was hiding from them upstairs in a bedroom. He was burned alive.

The air in the tiny cell seems to compress into unbreathable crystals. The room seems to shrink, walls folding in, claustrophobia and fear invade the space. James looks over at Ashe. You were right. You were right, they have all gone mad. And O'Hegarty suddenly notices that James is not talking to him but to a figment of his imagination, and he looks closely at James and sees that his eyes have glassed over. He puts a hand on his forehead and realises that he is burning up and calls for the guard. Jimmy, I will go now. We will see what we can do about your situation. But James does not notice O'Hegarty now; he is busy trying to console Ashe who refuses to look at him and is crying shuddering gasps of tears.

Outside the cell, O'Hegarty demands the medical unit for James, but he is told in no uncertain terms, no sir, it has already been requested and denied. And you had best take your jacket sir, for it will be taken from him when the shift changes. But O'Hegarty heads straight for the exit muttering language under his breath that shocks even the guards he passes.

O'Hegarty heads straight for Victoria Barracks. He does not bother with the OC of the gaol. It is a man who was never a Volunteer, and is a vindictive little prick as well, thinks O'Hegarty to himself. Seán Murray, the former Cork No. 1 Brigade training officer, has been appointed OC of Victoria Barracks. It is a good choice, though Jimmy deserved it more, thinks O'Hegarty. Although Seán is a pro-treaty man, he is a man with a head on his shoulders, experienced in the Great War and understands how an army works. He looks at his former anti-treaty colleagues as misled rather than enemies, no matter what the madman Lynch proclaims. It is for this reason that O'Hegarty thinks he may get a reasonable response for his request.

O'Hegarty had received the keys to this, the biggest barracks in Ireland in the spring, and at that time had been full of wonder and glory that the British were out of this massive garrison and the Irish were in control. He salutes the Free State officers at the gate and makes his way towards Murray's office. It is not the tight ship it was under the British. Murray has walked out to meet O'Hegarty and the two men stroll the grounds as they talk. Does Murray know that he was second choice to James as OC here? Probably not. But he does know James, and remembers him from their time in the Gaeltacht, near Gougane Barra, where he trained the men in the Lewis gun. O'Hegarty explains James's condition. Sure, he is an intelligence man, is he not? asks Murray. There is no Cork No. 1 as you know, Seán. There is no longer an intelligence squad. There is no worry here, I give you my word. Murray looks at O'Hegarty and considers his request. He has never requested a favour before and Seán Murray, as a former subordinate of O'Hegarty, owes him a lot. Aye, I will make a call. We will have him released. But it must be done very quietly. Who are his people? And O'Hegarty opens the inventory in his mind and rhymes off the address of James's family home.

Inside the gaol, the duty officer writes James's name in the appropriate logbook and beside it, released in ill health. He will cover his arse just in case he is called to task by the OC. But if he knows O'Hegarty at all, he knows that is not likely to happen. There is a man with friends in high places.

When the cell door opens and James is asked to come out, he cannot stand on his own two feet. In fact, he cannot rise up from the cot. The guard must call for assistance and between the two of them, James is lifted under the arms and supported to the exit. As he is being half-carried, half-dragged across the floor, he turns back to look for Ashe. Come with me. Come with me, he calls out louder and louder. But Ashe remains where he is. James's last glimpse of him is inside the cell against the wall, hunched down, staring at him, shaking his head. He can hear his voice calling out to him, No Séamus. I will see you again, but not for a while. Be strong Séamus. Be strong for all of us. James feels a panic surge inside him and begins to holler back at Ashe. But the guards tell him to shut up and quick, or he will go back where he came from and then James is temporarily blinded by the light that rushes in to meet him when the door opens. He can hear the voices of his father and his brothers, but he can barely distinguish the words from the gasps, and he finds himself floating and gently propelled into a waiting car.

Oisín, the last great warrior of the Fianna, is the son of Fionn mac Cumhaill, and keeper of volumes of history of the Fianna, carefully set in long curled garlands of story encased in his fine mind. The Fianna has separated, each going his own way for a time, and Oisín has an idea to go hunting. He wanders to the western sea. There is a deer that likes to tease him on the western shores, and he feels up for a challenge. In the past, each time he has come across the deer, it runs like the wind, impossible to catch. Through the dark forest, across the fine meadows of grass and wildflowers and far across the strand, until finally leaping over ribbons of waves onto a stone that reaches above the waterline where the waves crash into it.

After a long hard chase, she settles herself on the rock, turns to face Oisín, and stands, staring at him as if to say, you can't get me now. It seems to Oisín that the deer lies in wait for him, just for the glory of winning the race, overcoming her adversary, and poking fun at the wild warrior. Oisín, proud and accomplished warrior and bard, well, Oisín does not care for the deer's flagrant display of attitude and so he decides he will outsmart it. He gathers his friends, the young Fianna aspirants, and spells out his plan. Then, alone, he returns to the shore where he can see ahead of him the distant rock. The waves crashing into it send out sparkling sprays of salt water high in the air. He looks at the surging water coming right at him, and thinks to himself, whatever, I can do this, and boldly crosses, breaking through the waves, to alight on the stone. He sits quietly, drenched, it is true, but so what? Some things must be endured if life is to go your way. He sits and shivers and enjoys the sunshine while he waits for his comrades to chase the deer along the usual path and right into his trap.

After a time he can hear, even across the waves, the thundering of hooves, and looks to see his mounted devotees leaned into their horses, riding the wind as the deer sails ahead of them. In her usual move, she turns to the water's edge and at just the right moment, propels herself into the air and across the waves, and lands, to her shock and surprise, right on the lap of Oisín. But it is Oisín who is the more shocked, the more surprised, when the deer begins to talk to him.

The deer turns into a beautiful young woman who leads Oisín across the western sea and into the land of Tír na nÓg. This is the land of eternal youth, where all is good, delightful, and lovely. Oisín marries the young girl, whose name is Niamh, has several children, all of whom will generate life stories of their own someday, but while they are young, Oisin entertains the inhabitants of Tír na nÓg with stories of the Fianna. Every night he finds within himself a different strand of story and unfurls it for his audience, to their utter delight. He tells of his famous father, Fionn, his sidekicks, Caoilte and Conan and Gol. He tells of their defence of the nation from enemies without and within. And as he tells his stories, he is left thinking of the great life he left behind him when he came across the western sea. He begins to feel nostalgia for all that has passed, and a deep loneliness for his homeland of Ireland comes upon him. No matter how he counts his blessings his beautiful wife whom he adores, his delightful children, his life of plenty devoid of cares, the great esteem he is held in by the people of Tír na nÓg despite all of these blessings he cannot shake the longing that grips him. And so, he determines that despite all that he has here in Tír na nÓg he must journey back to Ireland to see his homeland and his beloved gang of warriors, young and old, the great Fianna.

Naturally, Niamh tries to talk sense into him. It will not be as you think, she tells him. Time has passed; your friends will not be as you left them. It is she who knows the secret of Tír na nÓg, where time slows down and every year that passes is worth a hundred years of regular, relentless time in the outside world. She is full of dread for what might become of her glorious, warrior husband if he leaves. She has seen the outside world and knows how men must battle the ravages of regular time, their youth behind them, their great deeds lost, sucked into the cracks and crevices of the quagmire that is history. And just as is always the case with warriors, it is a pointless endeavour. Don't be ridiculous, Oisín tells her, all will be well. I will see my friends, my father, we will go on adventures, and then I will return feeling much better. No Oisín, you will not; in fact, I fear you will never return. Oisín just laughs at his beautiful wife. Women! Finally, she accedes to his longing and gives him a magnificent white horse that will take him across the sea and back to Ireland. Before he goes, she warns him: Do not step foot on the land of your former home. Stay on the horse, do what you will, but do not get off it. Do not let go of your new life. If you do, I tell you now, all will be lost.

Oisín gallops across the water full tilt. He fairly bristles with excitement. He thinks of how wonderful it will be to see his old crew of death-defying, dazzling warriors, courageous, gutsy, spirited, daring, lovers of song and dance, food, and wine. When he spies land, he calls out to the horse to fly faster, and so he does. He makes dry land and looks about. Not a soul does he see. The horse is as rested as if he just woke up from a most delicious sleep. Something is off. Nevertheless, he scolds himself, and decides to visit his father's castle. When he arrives, expecting to find guards along the route, he finds no one, and looks up to the high ridge where he sees it lying in ruins, the main tower standing but the walls broken, the large stones scattered on the steep hillside, brambles and weeds overtaking the lot. Oisín feels a panic rise in him. What has become of his father, the great Fionn? He determines to find his friends and gallops off to other secret places he knows, where they may be. At each home or castle he finds the same situation. Not a man to be seen, great stones lying overgrown with vines and brambles. Nary a fire, nor a creature nearby.

His great leader, Fionn, his own father, has disappeared. He has looked high and low across the land, but not a trace of him can he find. Fionn's best friends, Cailte, swiftest of runners, great Goll of the one eye, even Conan, the man who never turned from a fight, they have all left their homes, one way or another. Their legendary pack of warriors tasked with protecting Ireland from tyrants, tyrants from away and tyrants from home, has dissipated. Oisín thinks of his wife's warning, and he fears that their blood has seeped into the earth, along with the stories of their great feats and legendary deeds.

Still on his horse, he walks the old paths in search of the secret places of the Fianna. There is no one to ask, where is my father, the wondrous Fionn mac Cumhaill? Where is the Fianna? What has become of them? And then, suddenly, deep in the forest he spies an elderly couple. They stand before a meagre cottage, their home, and they are struggling to move a large, heavy stone, a trough for water. Oisín instantly forgets his wife's warning, and with a chivalrous heart jumps down to the ground to help the couple move the stone. He does so, easily placing it to their liking, and then slowly he feels a great weariness overcome him.

Oisín has just spent what he thought was three years living a life that none could imagine in Tír na nÓg, only to discover that in truth it is three hundred years that have passed in Ireland. Oisín is sick at heart, for in all of his wildest dreams he could not have imagined that such a thing would or could ever happen. How could men so great fall so low, even their memory lost to the people?

Once Oisín had alighted from his horse, with a whinny and a nuzzle the great white beast turned and galloped away home, leaving the three-hundred-year-old Oisín lost and alone. What a terrible sight to see him shrunken, wisened, a beard as long as a horse's tail. And this is just what the great St Pádraig sees as he stumbles across the lump of an old man lying on the road. Pádraig is travelling across the land converting the people from their pagan ways, encouraging them to love and serve the one true Lord. Pádraig stoops over and takes a gander at the weak and diminished old man. Realising this is a man more aged than he has ever seen, he exclaims to his retinue of priests and monks and bishops and star-struck followers, look at this poor old man! The Lord has surely put him on our path for a reason, let us see to him. And Oisín feels himself lifted and carried to a warm shelter and fire, and fed a hearty, nutritious meal.

After some rest and nourishment, Pádraig begins to ask questions to the stranger. Tell me your story, says Pádraig, and Oisín stretches back into the furthest reaches of his mind and begins to unfurl the stories that he realises now are from so very long ago. He has hardly got started when Pádraig laughs at the old man… are you jesting? he says. What tales are these? Fionn mac Cumhaill as tall and as strong and as feared as all that? His crew of wild men and their unbelievable feats and deeds? And you one of them? That's a joke if ever I heard one. Oisín is outraged. Why you, you ridiculous man with your silly hat and your retinue of chanters and hangers-on, your lousy cooks and your sackcloth. What right have you to mock me? Fionn was my own dear father, a better man has never walked the earth, generous to a fault, fearless provider to the people, especially when they were being stricken by a foe, from near or far. If what you say of your God is true, he knows my father and loves him as much as he loves you, despite your obvious foibles. Pádraig grunts and wanders away, thinking to himself, what on earth did the Lord have in mind, sending me this pugnacious old codger to torment me with his nonsense?

But later that evening, Pádraig, on his knees in prayer, after all others have collapsed into their beds, hears a familiar swoosh behind him. It is his guardian angel, Victoricus, friend and confidant, whose presence is a great gift from the Lord, sent to him to guide his thoughts as he travels across Ireland, taming the wild Celts. Victoricus admonishes his charge. This old man, Oisín, is hard to take, I know, and his stories are tall tales indeed. They are from a time long ago, before the people knew the Lord. But you should know this, good Pádraig: The Lord loves the unruly Celts with a special love, a love for the strong, the courageous, the chivalrous, for men and women too, who will fight for the downtrodden, give away their last crumb to the hungry, offer shelter and hospitality to every lonely stranger, and persevere against unrelenting evil, even in the face of disaster, without regard for their own demise. Yes, our magnanimous Lord loves this people indeed. And for this reason, Pádraig, you, Bishop of Ireland, servant of the Lord, you will listen to this old man's tales with humility, and you will have your scribes write them down for the ages. For the time will come in far-off days, long after you and I have gone back home, when these very stories will comfort and sustain the good Celts of times to come, and give them much needed hope, and courage to face their enemies.

Pádraig sighs. Yes Victoricus, this I will do. But God help the poor Celts of future times who will need such stories. It will be a terrible enemy they face indeed, if these outrageous tales of strength, resilience in the face of dreadful monsters, and stoic courage in the face of wretched suffering are to be their solace. And Pádraig turns to see that Victoricus has left, and he calls out in the night for his scribes. Bring your quills and your vellum, and perhaps a drink. We are going to need it, that's for sure.

A few weeks before Christmas, Pa Murray checks in on James. O'Hegarty, though he is a committed neutral and has built up his Neutral IRA organisation to a reputed twenty thousand members, continues to watch out for his men and help out those who need it, if he can. He has convinced Pa that James is the best man for the job he is about to undertake. Pa is heading back to London, where Lynch has made him OC of the entire anti-treaty British contingent of the IRA. But wait, who are the anti-treaty IRA in Britain? The vast majority openly sided with Collins and the treaty. It is Pa's job to find out what the situation is with the IRA men in England. Collins had a strong contingent there, as James well knows, men who found jobs for his men, shipped guns, raised cash, and kept an eye on the reigning British government. Who is pro-treaty, who is anti-treaty? Who will reach out to Lynch if he needs some dire action taken?

Lynch is thinking ahead. He believes that the best solution to the current impasse is to piss off the British as mightily as possible, driving them to turn around and come back to Ireland. The common enemy will unite the two Irish factions, they will fight off the British together just as they did before and proclaim the Republic in the end. Win-win for both sides. Lynch wants to know who he can count on if he needs some support from the IRA in England. Perhaps a bombing campaign in London itself? That might do it. Before Pa accepted his new commission, he had asked Lynch, what exactly do you want me to do? You have very few on your side. What do you propose? Shoot a few people? Burn down a few houses? Pa is asking tongue in cheek, but the sarcasm is lost on Lynch, who believes Pa is going to London for him, to help the cause.

Lynch is so out of touch with his men he cannot fathom for a moment that a man like Pa is actually taking on the job with total self-interest in mind. Yes, he will organise, find out who is backing Lynch, but he knows nothing will come of it, and so far, his few weeks in London have confirmed this gut feeling. Sure, will he not just pack it in? asks James. No, he won't Séamus. No, he won't. James knows that Seán is still in the Gaeltacht with the bulk of the men and has been working overtime trying to find men who will work with him to change Lynch's mind. He has a group of good dependable men who are trying to make Lynch see the light. Sooner or later he must realise the country is against him. I, for one, am just as happy to get out of here, says Pa. We have a target on our backs, so we do, Séamus. You and I know Lynch is a madman, our friends, well, some of them haven't come to that realisation yet. Sandow, Murphy, Crofts, the Grey brothers, he has quite a few still on his side. Come to London with me and we will get out of this mix. I can use a good IO to keep us on top of the coppers there. No harm in giving Lynch some information about the English crew. If we are seen by the wrong man, walking down the street here in the city, we will be sent to join our brothers behind bars. And you for one, Séamus, can't risk that.

James feels slightly insulted, but nevertheless, he knows that Pa Murray is right on the mark. His own mother is relieved that this opportunity has come up, though she herself has no idea why he is going. That he is getting out of danger is all she is concerned about. It is a fine Christmas gift for her. James has recovered quickly once out of the gaol and tenderly nursed and fed by his mother. She says nothing about his alarming transformation from a young, fit, handsome man to a gaunt, ill one. Instead, she focuses her mind on the positive. He is leaving the country, and with a smile on her face she packs him a suitcase full to bursting with warm clothes and food. At least in London she will not have to worry that he will be thrown in a Free State internment camp, or that her boy will die of pneumonia in an Irish prison. The two men will leave straight from Cobh avoiding any interactions with Free Staters, and quietly board a ferry for Liverpool. Before James leaves, his father slips him a thick roll of bills. James balks at the handout, but his father assures him it is simply the fruit of a lucky day at the races.

James stands on deck and watches as the boat makes its way through Cork harbour and out to open sea. It is a cold day, almost the new year. He will miss the festivities in Cork, but if the truth be known, few of his own friends will be celebrating. The civil war hangs over their heads, no matter what side they have taken, and James is happy to leave it behind. He is, after all, taking O'Hegarty's lead, turning his head and mind away from fighting his own brothers. This is the better way. O'Hegarty knew it from the start.

A light snow falls, and the backdrop of Cobh with the cathedral spires reaching up to heaven reminds him of St Finn Barre in the city. As the boat travels south and the shoreline fades into mist, James thinks how beautiful it is on the surface. He also thinks that he does not need to scratch too deeply to see just how unimaginable it all is, the way things are playing out, one Irishman against another, so many of the leaders of just a few short years ago dead and gone, and the country a mess. Does James know he will not see this shoreline again for many years? Does he feel nostalgia, or simply relief at leaving it all behind? Like most everything about this time in his life, he will never mention it.

In London, Pa has already staked out the lay of the land. Indeed, there are few who support Lynch. Everybody else is appalled at his behaviour and mystified as to why the men are following him in the first place. The English IRA were behind Collins from the start. After all, Collins started out here in London, joining his first IRB cell in that city. Because of Collins, the two men are fêted by the anti-treaty English IRA. It takes James several weeks of work to determine who is really with them and against them. He warns Pa of the possibility of the infernal, dangerous traitors, informers, that

James can now smell a mile away. Pa Murray in particular is well-known to the team there. He had been sent by Collins to be ready to assassinate a British MP. That was over two years ago now, back when Terry was on hunger strike. Collins had abruptly cancelled the operation, but Pa Murray is not a man anybody forgets. They settle down for the winter and spend mornings drinking tea and reading the newspapers, of which London has many. They read in quiet desperation about the cat and mouse game that is being played out in pockets of the country, in particular their own pockets of the country, Cork and into Kerry. They say nothing, but James quietly moans to himself each time he reads of his former comrades-in-arms killing each other.

The winter is long and cold and dull. England's IRA does not know what to make of these two fierce men, neither of whom ever seem to smile or give away any sign as to their internal dynamic. They are professionals however, of that there is no doubt. Pa Murray is quick to build a network of groups who, philosophically at least, support Lynch. He reports back to Lynch telling him there are men here who hope for his success, but don't expect it, and are unwilling to take action on English soil. In short, no one believes Lynch's plan of dragging the British back into the fray will have any result other than dragging unwilling men to gaol for pointless, regrettable violence. Despite this, James puts his own set of skills to work. Within weeks he has a list of police and intelligence operatives who are keeping an eye on specific anti-treaty men. Their targets are the same men who were considered dangerous IRA elements when the War of Independence was raging. It is easy to see that the British police have kept a pace with them, and it is only a matter of time, as far as James is concerned, until the police act. After all, people everywhere are outraged at the civil war, and the English especially find that their opinion of Irishmen has sunk lower than even they believed possible. James is certain that someday soon an informer will loosen his tongue and some of them will be brought in for questioning or worse. This will be a shorter wait than he originally expected.

The general public of the English nation all seem to share the same opinion. We are better out of there, is the sentiment culled from the dwindling number of editorials and articles that James reads. But it is the upper echelons of British society who begin to demand that something be done to end the civil war. They are lamenting the loss of their big houses that dot the Irish countryside. The Irregulars are burning down big houses faster than you can shake a stick at them. By the end of the spring, two hundred across Ireland will be torched or blown up by Lynch's men. It is a futile effort to have the British re-engage in Ireland. Lynch's dream of uniting back with his recalcitrant brothers on the Free State side, in order to recreate the Republic without British terms is dissolved in the smoke of the fires and carried into oblivion, though Lynch won't admit it. Perhaps he is too deranged to see it.

As the relentless reports of arrests, executions, assassinations, and yes, even atrocities perpetrated by the Free State forces, reach James and Pa, they keep their heads down and look for work. There is little available to them. Billeted in homes of Irish Republican families, the men have roofs over their heads, but they need work. It is clear to James that Pa has no intention of returning to Ireland while the civil war continues.

Pa is an experienced carpenter and the IRA connections supply one job. James reverts to his skills on a bicycle. He acts as courier for the many central London firms on Fleet Street and the Square Mile, the financial section of the city. With a few well-placed recommendations, he quickly builds a dependable reputation. He is a no-nonsense worker, a hard rider, who delivers sensitive materials across the street or across town with no fanfare. It is easy work for James, though the pay is slight at first. He learns after a while that he can trade larger fares for faster work and builds up a clientèle that routinely call on him. He wears his newsboy cap, and ties his trouser legs with string so that he can pedal like a madman. It is a release for him and a game to see just how fast he can get to where he needs to go. He learns to negotiate the London traffic, and quickly memorises the tiny laneways that are safe to take and those that are not. It is not the best job in the world, but James is happy to have work. The regularity of it lends a forgotten stability to his life and the intensity of riding his bicycle is a welcome exchange for thinking about home.

Occasionally word reaches them from Seán or contacts of Pa about the inner circle around Liam Lynch. Liam spends his days moving from hiding place to hiding place, always in the Gaeltacht where his beautiful Irish is appreciated by the locals, if not always his politics; or in the area of Fermoy, his home base where he can count on protection from his people. He prays his rosary as ever he did, often found on his knees if any of his men were to walk in on him in the evening. But prayers or no prayers, he will not give an inch, not to any of his men who have been trying to persuade him of the futility of his plans, not even to O'Hegarty or Florrie, who find their way to him, neutral though they may have proclaimed themselves. No, not even to O'Hegarty will he concede a single point. He is convinced that sooner or later the Free State will bend to negotiate with him, and though he is told the opposite, day after day, dispatch rider after dispatch rider, trusted man after trusted man, he believes his prayers will be answered. It is hubris hiding under a cloak of piety, but as the Good Book reminds all of us: Pride goeth before destruction, and an haughty spirit before a fall.

James thinks of Seán and the other men, most from Rebel Cork, rebels to the bitter end. James knows he too would be with them had he not been called back to the city by O'Hegarty. He knows that like Seán, he too would not, perhaps could not, have walked away. But it is all just speculation now. As word of the roundups reach Pa and James, they know they cannot return home. They will be thrown in internment camps like the thirteen thousand who are there now, spread across the country. Who knows when they will be released? It won't be anytime soon!

At the end of March there is more bad news, this time on English soil. All three of the IRA cells that Pa has so laboriously organised in London, Manchester, and Liverpool are raided within days of each other and their members thrown in the clink. Pa is safe, James is safe, but for how long? Obviously an informer is at work, and neither man wants to wait around to see who is next. James has to make a decision. Do I stay in London, working as a delivery boy for high powered lawyers, or do I go elsewhere and start a new life, or at least wait out the internment camps until it is safe to return? America is the place to go. New York City. But without papers, nobody is getting through Ellis Island. Australia? Canada?

James thinks of Seán's brother Peter, who lives in New York City and at the time of Terry's funeral encouraged James and Seán both to come out and join him. He shakes hands with Pa and wishes him good luck. I am off to Canada, he tells him. It is a long border; I will find a place to get across and make my way to New York. Sure, that can all be arranged, Pa tells him. Pa, after all, spent last spring in New York hunting down an informer. I will get in touch with the Clan na Gael. They will have a way to get you in. And I have an address for you. It will give you a roof over your head until you get on your feet. James, through O'Hegarty, gets in touch with Seán.

Come with me Seán, we will go to your brother Peter. But Seán is still working day and night to arrange meetings with people who might convince Liam to stand down. Meetings with de Valera, meetings with O'Hegarty, meetings with those of the Irregular command who are themselves wondering why they are still fighting. At any rate, he tells James, I cannot leave and even when I can, I must go to my sisters. Both of them are still recovering from a hunger strike that they undertook outside the gaol walls in Dublin, to protest the treatment of the Republican men inside. You go ahead, I will join you once my sisters are back on their feet. In the meantime, you should take our old friend Mick with you. He is on the run from the Free State and running out of hiding spots. Indeed, I will. A travelling friend would be just fine. Send him over here to Liverpool. Seán is quiet for a moment. And Jimmy, when you get to New York, forget Ireland. Become an American. You will see how quickly this place and all its madness will fade from you. Get yourself a good life. You deserve it, my friend.

And with that James makes his way by train to Manchester, to spend a few days with his sister and her young family. On April 4 he buys a third-class ticket for the *SS Marloch*, departing Liverpool for St John, New Brunswick, Canada, on April 13. He fills out the form for the Canadian authority. He lists his trade as 'draper' borrowing Florrie's line of work. He writes the name and address in Toronto that Pa has given him as his destination. He writes that this is his uncle whom he plans on joining. This is, of course, untrue. The name and address are of a Clan na Gael member who will take him to Niagara Falls, and hand him over to another member who happens to be an American border guard. He will find yet another member to take him to New York City once he has made his way to the American side. Meanwhile, his old friend Mick, himself a veteran of Cork Gaol and intelligence work, quietly makes his way to Liverpool and buys himself a ticket under an assumed name with a different set of addresses. There is no way of connecting the two friends on paper, though they will travel together over the next few weeks and indeed spend the next ten years re-designing their lives.

On April 11, two days before James's departure for New York, he picks up the *Manchester Guardian* and momentarily the old truism comes to mind, 'the more things change, the more they stay the same.' He wonders how the Wallace sisters are. Are there any Republicans left who steal down that little alleyway, who knock on their door any hour of the day or night with the hope of a cup of tea and a read of the morning papers? James looks at the paper in front of him. *The Guardian* is one he read himself, many a morning, trying to stretch out the cup of tea before his wanderings. Today there is nothing about Ireland. Not a thing. The English are done with us at long last. It is just as Terry said, they will go when they cannot bear us any longer. After seven hundred and fifty years, that day is here. And suddenly, buried on page nine, the headline hits him:

LIAM LYNCH DEAD
WOUNDED IN FIGHT AND CAPTURED

Liam had made for a new hiding place early in the morning of April 10. In order to avoid the Free State soldiers who are known to be combing the area, he works his way on foot across the Knockmealdown Mountains on the border between Tipperary and Waterford. He has barely started out when at about nine o'clock in the morning a bullet from an unseen solider singes through the air and rips sideways clean through both of Lynch's hip bones. As he lies immobilised on the mountainside, he insists his men run for their lives and take all of the sensitive papers he has been carrying with them. He rests his head and prays, or perhaps weeps and wails, while he waits alone for the troops. Two young soldiers arrive after a while. At first, they do not know who he is. He has to explain to them that they have stumbled upon a great prize for their commander, Mulcahy. They carry him down to the bottom of the hills using a greatcoat tied to two rifles as a stretcher. An unfortunate farmer is relieved of his donkey and cart, and they move him along the dirt road jostling side to side until a house can be found. Liam is in agony. A doctor is called. Eventually he arrives and examines

Lynch. Say your prayers. There is nothing to be done. Finally, in the evening, Liam leaves the intolerable pain of his wounds and the handwringing, gut-wrenching worry of the civil war behind him. His last words? It never should have happened. Poor Ireland, poor Ireland. Though his friends and comrades loved him, surely there was a sigh of relief all over Ireland at his passing. When this news diffuses out into the open air, the civil war is done.

The rank-and-file pool their rifles together and dump them under the hay in barns, inside trunks in high attics, in deep root cellars with the winter carrots, in secret caves and burial places, someday to be found by their grandchildren and great-grandchildren. They head to the pubs, have a long-awaited pint, wish each other good luck, and make their way back home, there to try and dodge the inevitable round-up by the Free State. After all, why would the Free Staters be any different from the British? They have proven themselves tyrants. De Valera makes a public announcement:

> *Soldiers of the Republic, Legion of the Rearguard: The Republic can no longer be defended successfully by your arms. Further sacrifice of life would now be in vain and the continuance of the struggle in arms unwise in the national interest and prejudicial to the future of our cause. Military victory must be allowed to rest for the moment with those who have destroyed the Republic.*

James knew Liam, even from that first ambush in Fermoy. He is sorry to hear of his death, but he is not surprised. The Free Staters would have cornered him at the edge of the ocean in the farthest reaches of Kerry, and they would have got to it sooner rather than later. Everyone could see it was coming. Everyone except Liam. James reads of his death and feels the weight of the last few years bear down on him. He is alone. If he were known, he would be reviled by the majority of Irish men and women as a member of the Irregulars who plunged their country into an unholy war against each other. His friends are dead or in gaol or in internment camps. Only a lucky few will avoid the long hand of the Free State. The leaders that he once admired, revered, almost venerated, they are all gone. De Valera, of course, has survived, but he is out of politics now, and who knows what will become of him. O'Hegarty is being left in peace, or so it seems, but he too is not involved in politics or the army, no place found for him, no regard allotted, no gratitude shown. James feels the travesty of this injustice in his heart. O'Hegarty, without whom they would all still be wriggling under the unyielding thumb of the cold and cruel English occupiers!

James strides up the gangplank of the massive ship and works his way to the seaward side facing the western sea. He finds a lonely stretch of railing, and stands alone, no one waving goodbye to him. Ever the intelligence man, he and his friend Mick feign ignorance of one another, lest he is being followed. He watches the horizon as the ship makes its way from Liverpool, into the Irish Sea well and proper, past the Isle of Man and along the coast of his country, home of his people, a people torn asunder these last years. He ponders these things, a lonely, well-dressed Irishman, off to visit his uncle in Toronto, hoping for a new life as a Canadian. Not likely, he thinks, that was Seán's broken and battered dream. If anybody is looking for me, they will find me in New York City.

James thinks on Seán's words. Make a new life.

Make a new life indeed.

Short Biographies of Some Historical Figures

Ashe, Thomas (1885 – 1917)

Ashe was born near Dingle, County Kerry, one of ten children in an Irish-speaking family. He won many scholarships at school, became a teacher and then a school principal. Ashe was a playwright, an actor, and a member of a piping band, the Black Ravens. He became president of the Gaelic Athletic Association, and joined the IRB early, rising to become Supreme Commander. Ashe was good-looking, built like the athlete he was, and had a commanding presence. In 1914 he travelled to America to raise money for the Gaelic League and secretly for the IRB. During the Easter Rising Ashe commanded a Dublin battalion that ambushed a local RIC Barracks, killing eleven police officers and acquiring a large number of guns. He narrowly avoided execution and was interned in Wales where he was a popular leader and influence on the men. In 1917 he was arrested for giving a seditious speech and sentenced to two years in prison. He joined forty other prisoners in Mountjoy, making demands for political status. When demands were not met by prison authorities, he began a hunger strike. He was force-fed and died within hours. Ashe was seen as a martyr to the Irish cause for freedom and massive protests were held at the time of his funeral.

Busteed, Frank (1898 – 1974)

Busteed grew up in the village of Blarney just outside Cork City. His father was Protestant, his mother Catholic. Busteed's father died when he was young and two of his brothers were subsequently raised by their Protestant grandparents. One of those brothers was the British soldier who identified the killers of their mother. Busteed joined the IRA in 1917. He quickly became Vice Officer Commanding of the 6th Battalion, which included Blarney and the Battalion Flying Column. He was known as a tough, fearless officer, and was anti-treaty. He left Ireland for Boston and settled in New York City in 1924 where he started his own business with two Irish colleagues. He married an English woman and had seven children. Later he returned to Ireland and became a reputable businessman in the Cork area. Before he died in 1974, he told his story of the Dripsey ambush and kidnapping of the informer, Mrs Lindsay, and her chauffeur. The book telling this almost unimaginable tale, entitled *Execution*, was published shortly after his death.

Collins, Michael (1890 – 1922)

Collins was born in a remote area of West Cork. As a student he took the civil service exam and landed a coveted job in the post office. He worked in London, and it was there that he first joined the Gaelic Athletic Association and the IRB among Irish expatriates. He returned to Ireland before the Easter Rising to help plan and participate. When the main leaders were executed, Collins rose in prominence. He was an exuberant personality, well known for enjoying the *craic* with friends and acquaintances. Collins was good friends with the leading Republicans, even if he virulently disagreed with some of them over the treaty. He was a master of disguise, acting as a quiet middle-class businessman in Dublin throughout the war and had a massive web of intelligence information coming to him regularly. Well-respected in Dublin society, he also had many close calls: the RIC and later the Black and Tans had him at the top of their most wanted list and searched for him daily. Collins's intelligence techniques and what came to be known as guerrilla warfare tactics were subsequently studied by many insurrectionists throughout the twentieth century.

Connelly, James (1868 – 1916)

Born of Irish parents in Edinburgh, Connelly began working at the age of eleven. Poverty drove him to enlist in the British Army at age fourteen, when he was sent to Ireland. Connelly subsequently became a socialist and trade unionist. He founded the Irish Citizen Army, which opposed joining the first world war. A member of the Irish Republican Brotherhood, he was a signatory of the Irish Declaration of Independence. Connelly was executed for his part in the Easter Rising.

Corry, Martin (1890 – 1979)

Martin Corry was born in County Clare and moved to Cork at a young age. One of sixteen children, his father was an RIC sergeant. Corry was Captain of E Company, 4th Battalion outside Cork City. His family farm was used as an interrogation centre for informers and others. Corry was anti-treaty; however, in 1927 he was elected as a member of Fianna Fáil, an opposing party to Sinn Féin. During the War of Independence Corry spent time in jail in Cork, Belfast, and London. Corry remained a politician until his death in 1979, winning every election in fifty-two years. He was an outspoken politician and was vocal throughout his life about the damage he did to the British establishment in Ireland, proclaiming that he wished he had killed more.

Crofts, Tom (1892 – 1971)

Crofts was a well-respected, high-profile member of the Brigade, and was Officer Commanding of the Active Service Unit in Cork City. Crofts was one of the seven escapees from Spike Island in November 1921, during the Truce. He was anti-treaty and was party to organising the ambush where Michael Collins was killed. Later he worked to bring an end to the civil war, and in his later years he helped organise the Old IRA organisation to support elderly veterans of the War of Independence as they aged.

Culhane, Seán (1900 – ?)

Culhane joined the Volunteers in 1917 after moving from the Limerick area to Cork as an apprentice in the drapery trade. In 1918 he became an intelligence officer for the Brigade. In 1920 he joined the IRB. He participated in the shooting of an officer at the Cork Country Club, and also in the shooting of District Inspector Swanzy, perpetrator of Tomás MacCurtain's murder, in Lisburn. He was arrested in May 1921 but escaped three months later.

De Valera, Éamonn (1882 – 1975)

De Valera was an American by birth. His father was a Spanish immigrant, a sculptor, and his mother was a maid from Bruree, County Limerick, a remote, rural area. De Valera was sent there at the age of two when his father left alone for the American west and his mother had to return to work. De Valera won a scholarship to Blackrock College, a prestigious boarding school in Dublin. He was overjoyed to attend this place, staying through holidays, and showing bewilderment at children who wanted to return home. De Valera continued his education into advanced university degrees. He became a teacher and married an Irish teacher, Sinéad, learned Irish, and joined the Gaelic League. At the first meeting of the Volunteers, he joined up and bought himself a gun. He joined the Irish Republican Brotherhood, and participated in the Easter Rising, commanding at one of the posts. After his arrest and before he was due to be shot, his wife pleaded for his life, showing his baptismal certificate as an American citizen. This, combined with the fact that the British authorities saw him only as a schoolteacher, saved his life. His sentence was commuted to life imprisonment. When sent to internment camps he demonstrated great leadership as an older, respected teacher. He quickly rose to the top of the Volunteer Organisation and worked incessantly with Michael Collins, Arthur Griffith, and others to create the Dáil. He was elected president of Sinn Féin and president of the IRA. Later he travelled to America, raising large sums of money for the fight against the British. He was tall, well-spoken, and politically astute. In 1926 he started a new political party to rival Sinn Féin, Fianna Fáil. He was elected prime minister of Ireland, or *Taoiseach* from 1937 to 1948, again from 1951 to 1954, from 1957 to1959, and was the longest serving President in Irish history, from 1959 to 1973. He was president of Fianna Fáil for thirty-three years.

Grey, Jeremiah & Jim (c1898 – ?)

The Grey brothers owned a small garage not far from Victoria Barracks. Tomás MacCurtain took an interest in the brothers and their work as mechanics, and after his death they worked for O'Hegarty and Cork No. 1 Brigade. Jim, the elder of the two, was appointed Transportation Officer to the Brigade. Both brothers were considered the best drivers to be found, both daring and careful of the cars that they used. The cars always belonged to their customers, who had no idea how they were being used.

Griffith, Arthur (1871 – 1922)

Born into a working-class family in Dublin, Griffith's formal education ended at age thirteen, but he was an insatiable reader, often spending long hours at the National Library of Ireland. He apprenticed as a printer. He was involved in the inaugural meeting of the Gaelic League. Later he travelled to South Africa as a journalist. He returned to Ireland to begin publishing *The United Irishmen*, a nationalist magazine. He ran and won a seat in the election, standing in as acting President of the first Dáil. Griffith was quiet and unassuming, but had a temper: he once was jailed for horsewhipping an editor whose views he disagreed with. Griffith was a leading member of the Dáil and part of the group sent to London to negotiate the treaty. During that process he became increasingly ill and died of heart failure shortly after.

Lynch, Liam (1893 – 1923)

Lynch joined the Gaelic League at the age of seventeen, becoming a fluent Irish speaker. He was working as a hardware store clerk in 1916 when he watched Thomas Kent being dragged away by the RIC, barefoot and bleeding, his mother weeping after him. Kent's execution drove Lynch straight into the IRA. He became a fervent leader in the organisation and planned several ambushes in the early days after the Rising. Lynch became the Commanding Officer of Cork No. 2 Brigade, covering the area of Cork County north of the city. Later in the war he went to Dublin to work for Collins while Seán Moylan took over the Brigade. Lynch was anti-treaty from the start but believed that the two sides could work out a solution. He felt very strongly that submitting to the terms of the treaty was a dishonour to those who had died fighting for a republic; however, as hostilities rose and the Free State became more militant, Lynch resolved to continue to fight for a republic. He was twenty-nine years old when he died. A monument in the form of an ancient Irish round tower was erected by his followers on the place in the Knockmealdown Mountains where he was shot.

MacCurtain, Tomás (1884 – 1920)

One of the founding members of the Gaelic League in Cork, Thomas was a teacher and proponent of all things Irish. Together with Terrence MacSwiney and Seán O'Hegarty he planned out and put into action the Irish Volunteers in the Cork area. MacCurtain was Commanding Officer of Cork No. 1 Brigade of the Irish Volunteers and the first Republican mayor of Cork. He was murdered by a British hit team who stormed his home late at night in March 1920. James was the last person to see him alive. Tomás's murder made international headlines around the world. He remains a beloved historical figure in Cork to this day.

MacNeilus, Donnchadha (c. 1892 – 1954)

MacNeilus, originally from Donegal, was a key figure in the Cork No. 1 Brigade. He famously broke out of Cork Gaol in a shockingly bold and intricate plan overseen by Seán O'Hegarty on Armistice Day. Due to his extreme notoriety he went into hiding for an extended period in the Gaeltacht, but managed to work surreptitiously for the IRA throughout the war as well as travelling to the United States to raise money. A memorial was erected to him in Sligo after his death in 1954.

MacSwiney, Mary (1872 – 1942)

Born to an Irish father and English mother, Mary MacSwiney was sickly as a child and at some point had a foot amputated. She became highly educated for her day and earned a degree from University College Cork in 1912. She was a founding member of the Munster Women's Franchise League, a suffragist group. In 1914 she founded a Cumann na mBan chapter in Cork. In 1916 she was fired from her teaching post after she was arrested while teaching her class, just after the Easter Rising. Mary and her sister Annie then opened their own Irish school in Cork, which became very well-regarded. After Terrence's death she became involved in politics in an aggressive way, commanding attention with hunger strikes and speeches. She was anti-treaty. She suffered a debilitating heart attack in 1936, and eventually died in 1942, the same year as her younger brother, Seán.

MacSwiney née Murphy, Muriel (1892 – 1982)

Murphy was born into the Jameson Whiskey family. She led a privileged life, educated in boarding schools in England. From an early age she was against imperialism and colonialism. She was an active member of the Gaelic League and later Cumann na mBan. As such, she worked as a courier and was involved in several escapades, notably the rescue of another Cumann na mBan member from prison, where several women dressed as Red Cross workers to gain access. Murphy married Terrence MacSwiney against her mother's wishes the day after she turned twenty-five and came into her inheritance. She left Ireland in 1923 never to return, and had two children, Mhaire, Terrence's daughter, and in 1926 another daughter, Alix, to Pierre Kaan, who would become a leading member of the French Resistance in World War II and die at the hands of the Gestapo.

MacSwiney, Seán (1896 – 1942)

Youngest brother of Terrence MacSwiney, Seán was James's friend, close in age and living in the same sector of the city. Because of his close connection to Terrence, Seán was privy to much secret information. He moved to Kitchener, Ontario, and was incarcerated in Kingston Penitentiary for refusing the draft in 1918. Seán was planning on marrying in Canada but never returned; he never left Ireland again after returning home just before his brother Terrence's death. His escape from Spike Island became a legendary feat. He was anti-treaty, and remained an officer of the 1st Cork Brigade, but was determined to find a path forward to reunite both sides. After the civil war he was reduced to working as a common labourer, the only work he could procure because of his status as an Irregular.

MacSwiney, Terrence (1879 – 1920)

Eldest member of the MacSwiney family, second Republican mayor of Cork, Commanding Officer of Cork No. 1 Brigade. Terrence played a pivotal role in developing many organisations related to the Gaelic revival through the first decade of the century. He was a member of the Irish Republican Brotherhood, a founding member of the Cork No. 1 Brigade of the Irish Volunteers, as well as a Third Order Franciscan. He was university educated and closely connected to all the senior men in the Nationalist movement across Ireland. His hunger strike was international news. Terrence believed the sacrifice of his life would help lead to Ireland's victory.

Murphy, Mick (1894 – 1968)

Murphy was a very well-known hurling athlete before the War of Independence and after, leading his teams to various championships. He was a carpenter by trade. He was Commandant of Cork No. 1, 2nd Battalion, B and C company. This was James's group that oversaw the core of Cork City. Murphy was known as a fierce member of the Brigade, participant or leader in many of the well-known engagements with the Black and Tans. He was staunchly anti-treaty. Wanted by the authorities, he fled to New York City after the Civil War, but eventually returned to Cork.

Murray, Patrick (1895 – 1967)

Pa Murray was a committed Volunteer from 1915 onwards. He became Officer Commanding of First Battalion C Company and participated in many hair-raising activities throughout the war and beyond, including a trip to New York City to hunt down an informer. He was staunchly anti-treaty. In 1926 he participated in a trip to Russia in a failed attempt to gain support for further IRA activity against the Free State.

O'Connor, Dominic (1883 – 1935)

Born in Cork City to a large, religious family, Father Dominic was educated in Belgium and ordained in Kilkenny in 1906. He volunteered as a chaplain in the war serving with an Irish division in Macedonia. He resigned in 1917, and in 1918 began to organise opposition to conscription in Ireland. He ministered to IRA Volunteers and was appointed Chaplain to Cork No. 1 Brigade by Tomás MacCurtain. He was arrested and convicted of creating written material likely to disaffect the crown and sentenced to three years hard labour. During the Civil War he ministered to both sides, but was banished to the state of Oregon, where the Capuchins had a chapter house for his vocal support of Irregulars. He suffered a bad car accident in 1935 and died of his injuries. He was buried in Oregon, but his remains were repatriated in 1958 thanks to lobbying by his nephew, Joe O'Connor, an officer in the IRA, and O'Hegarty. His popularity among members of the IRA was demonstrated at his massive funeral in Dublin, with over five hundred former IRA members marching alongside the coffin.

O'Donovan, Dan (Sandow) (1895 – 1975)

Dan was referred to as Sandow because of his uncanny resemblance to a famous American circus bodybuilder of the day, Eugene Sandow. He was a well-known player of Gaelic football, a game like hurling that gained prominence following the Gaelic Revival. O'Donovan was a carpenter by trade and a prominent member of the Cork No. 1 Brigade, a member of the IRB, and was against the treaty. O'Donovan participated in many actions. After he was named in the

Cork newspapers as most wanted for a drive-by shooting, he left for New York City and met up with James. He opened his own speakeasy, but wanted only to return to Ireland.

O'Hegarty, Seán (1881 – 1963)

Born in Cork City, O'Hegarty embraced the Gaelic revival at a young age, becoming a distinguished hurling player. Prior to the Easter Rising, O'Hegarty worked for the post office in Dublin. He married Magdalen O'Leary, an enthusiastic proponent of the Irish language, in 1912. O'Hegarty joined the IRB, and in Cork worked with Terrence MacSwiney and Tomás MacCurtain to create the Irish Volunteers in Cork. Throughout the War of Independence and beyond O'Hegarty was the storekeeper at the Cork Workhouse. As his friends died, O'Hegarty moved up the chain of command and quickly became the aggressive face of the Cork Brigade, unfaltering in his determination to fight.

Pearse, Pádraig (1879 – 1916)

Pádraig's father was English, a stonemason and sculptor, and his mother was from a native Irish speaking family. Pearse grew up in Dublin in a prosperous middle-class environment. He joined the Gaelic League at sixteen and became editor of its newspaper. He studied law, his first case in support of a man charged with labelling his cart in the Irish language, which was lost. Believing that the English school system was destroying Irish culture, Pearse opened his own school with some family members, offering an Irish-English curriculum. He is reputed to have taught James Joyce. A devoted member of the secret Irish Republican Brotherhood, he impressed Tom Clarke, convicted felon and leader of the IRB, as well as covert leader of the Easter Rising, and so was drawn in to become the educated, blameless face of Irish Nationalism. Pearse was famously the leader of the Easter Rising to surrender to the British and the first to be executed.

Abbreviations

ASU [Active Service Unit] This is the group composed at the insistence of Michael Collins. The men are paid 4l a week and are always ready to take on both planned ambushes and other activities as well as spontaneous responses to British treachery.

DSO [Distinguished Service Order] This is a United Kingdom military medal reserved for officers above the rank of Corporal who demonstrated bravery under fire.

GHQ [General Headquarters] This refers to the leadership of the IRA in Dublin headed up by Michael Collins.

IO [Intelligence officer] Every brigade needed to have several intelligence officers who collected information and passed it on to the Intelligence squad of Cork No. 1 Brigade. This squad of 6 men were paid 4l a week to work full time intelligence, all of which was passed on to the head of the group. O'Hegarty was in charge of this until he moved up the chain of command. At that point Florrie O'Donoghue took over his role.

IRA [Irish Republican Army] This is the group of Irish Volunteers who are proclaimed to be the National Army at the Dáil in April 1920.

IRB [Irish Republican Brotherhood] This is the secret brotherhood of ardent nationalists who have worked to contrive the Easter Rising. It is composed of men who are invited in personally by others who already sit in the group. The criteria for inclusion includes the strong belief that only acts of war will be sufficient to drive the British out of Ireland.

RIC [Royal Irish Constabulary] This is the national police service in place to 1922, controlled by the British but for the most part made up of Irish constables.

www.ingramcontent.com/pod-product-compliance
Lightning Source LLC
Chambersburg PA
CBHW071807230426
43670CB00013B/2383